# Undoing Aloneness
# & the Transformation of Suffering
# Into Flourishing

# Undoing Aloneness
# & the Transformation of Suffering
# Into Flourishing

---

## AEDP 2.0

Edited by
Diana Fosha, PhD

 **AMERICAN PSYCHOLOGICAL ASSOCIATION**

Published by
American Psychological Association
750 First Street, NE
Washington, DC 20002
https://www.apa.org

Order Department
https://www.apa.org/pubs/books
order@apa.org

In the U.K., Europe, Africa, and the Middle East, copies may be ordered from Eurospan
https://www.eurospanbookstore.com/apa
info@eurospangroup.com

Typeset in Meridien and Ortodoxa by Circle Graphics, Inc., Reisterstown, MD

Printer: Sheridan Books, Chelsea, MI
Cover Designer: Blake Logan, New York, NY

**Library of Congress Cataloging-in-Publication Data**

Names: Fosha, Diana, editor. | American Psychological Association.
Title: Undoing aloneness and the transformation of suffering into flourishing :
  AEDP 2.0 / edited by Diana Fosha.
Description: Washington, DC : American Psychological Association, [2021] |
  Includes bibliographical references and index.
Identifiers: LCCN 2020029386 (print) | LCCN 2020029387 (ebook) |
  ISBN 9781433833960 (paperback) | ISBN 9781433834622 (ebook)
Subjects: LCSH: Loneliness. | Emotions. | Adjustment (Psychology) | Psychotherapy.
Classification: LCC BF575.L7 U56 2021 (print) | LCC BF575.L7 (ebook) |
  DDC 616.89/14—dc23
LC record available at https://lccn.loc.gov/2020029386
LC ebook record available at https://lccn.loc.gov/2020029387

https://doi.org/10.1037/0000232-000

*Printed in the United States of America*

10 9 8 7 6 5 4 3 2

*To the AEDP worldwide community, past, present, and future*
—DIANA FOSHA

# CONTENTS

# CONTRIBUTORS

**Diana Fosha, PhD,** Director and Founder, AEDP Institute, New York, NY, United States

**Ronald J. Frederick, PhD,** Sr. Faculty, AEDP Institute, Los Angeles, CA; Cofounder, Center for Courageous Living, Los Angeles, CA, United States

**Kari A. Gleiser, PhD,** Sr. Faculty, AEDP Institute; Cofounder and Codirector, Center for Integrative Health, Hanover, NH, United States

**Yuko Hanakawa, PhD,** Sr. Faculty, AEDP Institute, New York, NY, United States; Director, AEDP Japan

**Karen Kranz, PhD,** Sr. Faculty, AEDP Institute, Vancouver, BC, Canada

**Jerry Lamagna, LCSW,** Sr. Faculty, AEDP Institute, New York, NY, United States

**Benjamin Lipton, LCSW,** Sr. Faculty, AEDP Institute, New York, NY; Consultant, Crime Victims Treatment Center, New York, NY, United States

**Ben Medley, LCSW,** Faculty, AEDP Institute, New York, NY, United States

**Jenna Osiason, PhD,** Sr. Faculty, AEDP Institute, New York, NY; Consultant, Crime Victims Treatment Center, New York, NY, United States

**Karen Pando-Mars, MFT,** Sr. Faculty, AEDP Institute, San Rafael, CA, United States

**SueAnne Piliero, PhD,** Sr. Faculty, AEDP Institute, New York, NY, United States

**Eileen M. Russell, PhD,** Sr. Faculty, AEDP Institute, New York, NY, United States

**Gil Tunnell, PhD,** Sr. Faculty, AEDP Institute, New York, NY; Adjunct Faculty, Teachers College, Columbia University, New York, NY, United States; Editor, *Transformance: The AEDP Journal*

**Danny Yeung, MD, MDPAC(C), FCFP,** AEDP Institute, Toronto, ON; Faculty of Medicine, University of Toronto, Toronto, ON, Canada

# Undoing Aloneness
# & the Transformation of Suffering
# Into Flourishing

———————

# Introduction

## *AEDP After 20 Years*

Diana Fosha

Two decades ago, I published *The Transforming Power of Affect* (Fosha, 2000b) and introduced accelerated experiential dynamic psychotherapy (AEDP), a new clinical model. I would sometimes say that, at that time, there was only one AEDP practitioner in the world—namely, me. Now, 2 decades later, I am no longer alone. Far from it!

In the 20 years since the publication of *The Transforming of Affect*, the number of AEDP practitioners worldwide has grown into the thousands. There is an AEDP Institute with a faculty of more than 20 members and growing; many certified supervisors; scores of certified therapists; and a passionate, engaged, and lively worldwide community. There is a thriving AEDP Practice Research Network (Edlin, Fosha, & Iwakabe, 2020), where private practice therapists and psychotherapy researchers collaborate to make possible clinically relevant AEDP process-outcome research (Iwakabe, Edlin, Fosha, Gretton, Joseph, et al., 2020; Iwakabe, Fosha, Edlin, Nakamura, et al., 2020). There is an active online community. There are practitioners on six continents, and communities are growing in many countries of the world: AEDP is practiced by therapeutic dyads speaking Arabic, Cantonese, Danish, English, Farsi, French, German, Greek, Hebrew, Italian, Japanese, Korean, Mandarin, Norwegian, Portuguese (as spoken in both Portugal and Brazil), Romanian, Spanish, Swedish, Turkish, and I am sure languages I have left out.

Reflecting on the explosive growth of AEDP in these past 2 decades, I have been asked on numerous occasions if this is "a dream come true." Invariably,

https://doi.org/10.1037/0000232-001
*Undoing Aloneness and the Transformation of Suffering Into Flourishing: AEDP 2.0*, D. Fosha (Editor)

my answer is "no," because I never dreamed it. In 2000, when I wrote my first book, my hope was that it would be read. *That* was the dream. I neither aimed for nor imagined such expansion. Then what explains it? What chord does AEDP strike in people? What is it that therapists worldwide resonate with?

I believe the answer lies not just in AEDP's theory and specific modes of intervention but fundamentally with AEDP's ethos and values, or its spirit: the quest that animates each session to bring forth the healing within, undo aloneness, transform emotional suffering, and sow the seeds of flourishing.

To expand on that a bit: AEDP is a healing-oriented, attachment-based, experiential mind–body therapy that works with trauma and attachment trauma. It eschews psychopathology as a central explanatory construct of therapy, instead using healing as a point of departure. Its *healing orientation* means that we firmly believe all persons carry within them the power to heal and grow, in other words, that the potential for healing is wired in and thus there from the get-go. As AEDP therapists, it is both our mission and our job to help find and unlock this potential. AEDP is also *attachment-based*, in that the processing of all experiences we work with in therapy—emotional, relational, self, and transformational—necessarily occurs in the context of relational safety. The safer the patient feels with the therapist, the greater will be that patient's capacity to explore the inner worlds of disturbing, frightening, and painful emotional experiences. Furthermore, the *experience* of attachment in the here-and-now of the patient–therapist relationship is an important locus of therapeutic engagement. Which brings us to *experiential*: by experiential, we mean that we privilege bottom-up experience and its felt sense, particularly that of adaptive core affective experiences rooted in the body, over top-down narrative and cognition; it also means that we believe that insight follows from transformation, and not the other way around. Through the moment-to-moment in-depth *experiential processing* to completion[1] of difficult emotional, relational and intra-relational experiences, and then also through the *metatherapeutic processing* (discussed later in this Introduction) of the transformational experiences that emerge, patients recover their sense of core self; they also contact increased resilience and renewed zest for life and meaningful connection.

With roots in developmentally informed psychoanalysis and the short-term psychodynamic psychotherapies, from which the approach originated, AEDP is an integrative model of psychotherapy that brings together relational work, experiential techniques, and a focus on the process of change and healing itself, with the aim of not only alleviating negative suffering but also bringing about positive flourishing. Drawing from research on moment-to-moment caregiver–infant interaction, attachment, affective neuroscience, Darwinian emotion theory, existential and somatic approaches to treating trauma, and, last but not least, transformational studies, AEDP navigates the complex interactions between positive and negative emotions toward psychological growth

---

[1]The notion of completion is discussed in detail in Medley's chapter on emotional processing (Chapter 8, this volume). It refers to a process that involves an affective shift from a negative valence to a positive valence.

and adaptation. Its change-based metapsychology and experiential methods reflect an organic integration of these many sources, as well as experience with 2 decades of AEDP practice by a growing number of practitioners worldwide.

Trauma is healed by championing the innate healing capacity of neuroplasticity in a safe, attached therapeutic relationship. Nonpathologizing and patient-affirmative in its ethos, AEDP features an affect-facilitating, emotionally engaged, validating and explicitly affirming therapeutic stance. Psychopathology is understood as fundamentally resulting from the individual's unwilled and unwanted aloneness in the face of overwhelming emotions. And this makes the therapeutic mission clear: undo patient aloneness and use dyadic affect regulation to, together, experientially process the formerly feared-to-be-unbearable experiences.

Highly collaborative, AEDP is a therapeutic model that, through its experiential processing of previously overwhelming experiences, seeks to engender new experiences of feeling understood, of recognizing and expressing emotional truths that previously have gone unacknowledged and of integrating positive affective experiences linked to healthy action tendencies and resources. From the get-go and always informed by an orientation toward healing, the AEDP therapist seeks to facilitate corrective emotional and relational experiences in which the patient feels safe enough to allow core aspects of the self—previously either shielded by defenses or else neglected, and thus unformed (Fosha, 2013a)—to come to the fore, to be processed through to completion and to be reintegrated into the patient's full emotional repertoire.

In AEDP, a patient's transformation is not only a desired goal and a process to be entrained, it is also an experience to be harnessed and mined. *Metatherapeutic processing*, or *metaprocessing* for short, is AEDP's contribution to a systematic methodology for working with transformational experiences and the transformational affects, that is, the innate, invariably positive affects of healing associated with them (Fosha, 2000a, 2009a, 2013b; Fosha & Thoma, 2020; Iwakabe & Conceição, 2016; Russell, 2015; Yeung et al., 2019). We experientially process transformational experiences as assiduously traumatizing experiences. And, countering the bias toward negative emotions both in our brains (Hanson, 2017) and in our field (Fredrickson, 2013), the positive affects that accompany transformational experiences are attended to as carefully as the negative affects and effects of trauma (Fosha, Thoma, & Yeung, 2019).

Its elaborated and detailed phenomenology of the four-state transformational process reveals an arc that organically links suffering with flourishing, trauma with transcendence, stuckness with flow (Fosha, 2005, 2009a, 2009c, 2013b, 2017a). It starts in State 1 with the stress, distress, despair, and symptoms people bring to treatment, as well as with the glimmers of the innate drive to heal, and culminates in State 4 in transformative, fundamentally integrative experiences of wholeness, calm, connection, and resilience, which become the constituents of in-session flourishing (see Figure 1.1 in Chapter 1; also Figure 1 in the Appendix[2]).

---

[2]This figure, and diagrams for all of the representational schemas in AEDP 2.0, may be downloaded for free (http://pubs.apa.org/books/supp/fosha/).

While ever-emergent and created anew by each dyad moment to moment, nevertheless our work is guided by AEDP's precisely articulated transformational phenomenology. It allows its supervision and teaching, which are always from videotapes of actual therapy sessions, to be characterized by "rigor without shame" (Fosha, 2015, quoted in Prenn & Fosha, 2017, p. 71), in a fashion that qualifies AEDP as a model with a strong intrinsic deliberate practice (A. Vaz, January 15, 2020, personal communication).

## AEDP AS DELIBERATE PRACTICE

Deliberate practice has been demonstrated to reliably predict the development of professional expertise in many professions (Ericsson et al., 2018) and is now being applied to psychotherapy (Rousmaniere et al., 2017; Vaz et al., 2018). Deliberate practice aims to move learning from declarative, top-down, left-brain knowledge to supporting an experiential, and more procedural competence. Its core principles are (a) the ongoing observation of one's performance, (b) getting expert moment-by-moment feedback on that observed performance, (c) establishing small learning goals that are just at the edge of one's current capacity, (d) repeated rehearsal of key skills, and (e) assessing one's performance and ongoing development. These principles form a "cycle of excellence" to be repeated throughout one's career (Vaz et al., 2018).

AEDP training, involving repeated cycles of excellence, has been de facto engaging in deliberate practice from its inception (Prenn & Fosha, 2017). Since moment-by-moment tracking is a sine qua non of AEDP, the videotaping of sessions is nondiscretionary, as videotaping becomes a best friend to those wishing to master and grow within this model. Moreover, all AEDP supervision is based around the trainee getting concrete expert feedback from the supervisor based on the trainee's observed performance (Prenn & Fosha, 2017): AEDP therapists are asked to videotape sessions for supervision, and self-supervision, as well as for certification. Furthermore, in AEDP courses and workshops, participants have ample opportunities to watch master therapists at work through videotapes. Finally, AEDP training has always stayed true to its experiential roots by facilitating many hours of group experiential skill-building exercises, always in the presence of an expert trainer, the experiential assistant, giving continuous feedback. These activities are in line with the research on professional expertise and how to achieve it (Ericsson et al., 2018; Rousmaniere et al., 2017).

Having reviewed some key aspects of AEDP, in the next section, I trace the journey from 2000 and AEDP 1.0 to the present and AEDP 2.0, which includes the current status of AEDP research. Following that, I outline the trajectory of this volume, describing the contributions of each author. The 15 chapters in this volume not only document the evolution of AEDP 2.0, they de facto constitute it: Each author offers further elaboration of the AEDP model. This chapter concludes with how you, dear reader, are participating in the spiraling change processes that keep AEDP, like the transformational process it entrains, ever emergent.

## THE JOURNEY FROM AEDP 1.0 TO AEDP 2.0

From its inception, AEDP has been a healing-oriented, attachment and emotion model. However, somewhere in the transition between AEDP 1.0 and AEDP 2.0, it became a healing-oriented, attachment and emotion *and* transformation model. In what follows, I track that metamorphosis and related developments.

AEDP 1.0 de facto started with the publication of *The Transforming Power of Affect* (Fosha, 2000b), and papers on dyadic affect regulation (Fosha, 2001), affective change processes (Fosha, 2002), and metatherapeutic processing (Fosha, 2000a); it culminated with a 2003 paper on AEDP as an attachment and emotion model to treat trauma and disorganized attachment (Fosha, 2003)—that is, with emotion, attachment, and attachment trauma (and the theory and research behind them) as major explanatory constructs. Metatherapeutic processing, the positive affects that accompanied it, and the phenomenon of the upward spiral were all there from the get-go (Fosha, 2000a, 2000b). Yet the transformational theory of AEDP 1.0 primarily emphasized the transforming power of core affect in the context of secure relational connection.

The decade preceding AEDP's arrival on the scene saw the publication of several important works: Allan Schore's (1994) *Affect Regulation and the Origins of the Self: The Neurobiology of Emotional Development*, Dan Siegel's (1999) *The Developing Mind: How Relationships and the Brain Intersect to Shape Who We Are*, Jaak Panksepp's (1998) *Affective Neuroscience: The Foundations of Human and Animal Emotion*, and Antonio Damasio's (1994) *Descartes' Error: Emotion, Reason and the Human Brain*—each the first book of its respective author. It is remarkable that all these threads of new understanding arose independently. They only became interconnected in the next decade.

It is not that AEDP evolved as a translational model. AEDP theory and clinical practice evolved largely independently of those bodies of knowledge yet over time became enriched and entered into an evolving dialogue with those works. AEDP 1.0 had a strong clinical theory and practice based on the transforming power of affect in connection. The dialogue with the work put forth during 1990–1999—"the decade of the brain"[3]—as well as with the work on attachment, intersubjectivity and developmental dyadic interaction, constituted the solid platform from which subsequent explorations in AEDP were launched.

### AEDP's Emergent Transformational Theory

Somewhere between 2004 and 2009, AEDP changed from being a healing-oriented, two-factor attachment-and-emotion model, to being a healing-oriented, three-factor attachment-and-emotion-*and*-transformation model.

---

[3]So designated by the George H. W. Bush administration (https://www.loc.gov/loc/brain/).

Constituting this shift, the concept of transformance was introduced (Fosha, 2008), and the study of positive emotion, transformational affects and core state moved front and center (Fosha, 2004, 2005, 2006, 2009c; Fosha & Yeung, 2006; Russell & Fosha, 2008). A little later, the phenomenology of the transformational process, AEDP's guiding representation, moved from being a three-state to a four-state model (Fosha, 2009a, 2009c; see also Fosha, 2018a, for a description of this change to a four-state transformational phenomenology). With that, its transformational theory was launched full throttle. Subsequently, AEDP's mechanisms of transformational change were further explored and elaborated (Fosha, 2013b, 2017a, 2017b, 2018a; Russell, 2015; Yeung & Fosha, 2015; see also Ecker et al., 2012, and Welling, 2012), as were the transformational affects and the upward spiraling processes undergirding flourishing (discussed in more detail later).

The evolving AEDP 2.0 also took on the *self* (Fosha, 2013a; Russell, 2015) and the phenomenon of recognition (Fosha, 2009a, 2013a; Gleiser, 2013). Solidly rooted in the "this is me" phenomena of core state, the development of theorizing on the "core self" and its felt sense was spurred by the challenge of clinical work with dissociation plus the advent of groundbreaking neurobiological work on the self (Damasio, 2010; Northoff & Panksepp, 2008; Panksepp & Northoff, 2009).

Another important aspect of the evolution to AEDP 2.0 was the contribution made by Lamagna and Gleiser (2007) who developed *intra-relational AEDP*. Integrating AEDP with ego state methodology and developments in internal family systems (Schwartz, 1995) and guided by the aim of fostering internal secure attachment, intra-relational methods seek to facilitate authentic, open dialogue between self-states and foster greater capacities for self-regulation through shared states of affective resonance between therapist, patient, and dissociated self-states. This methodology offered another set of techniques applicable to all patients. Additionally, intra-relational work is particularly helpful with patients on the dissociative disorder spectrum and with those for whom the relational work of AEDP can be disorganizing or even triggering (see Lamagna, this volume).

The years from 2004 to the present have seen the following explorations and applications of AEDP: attachment as a transformative core affective experience and how to best work with it interrelationally (Fosha, 2009b, 2017b; Lipton & Fosha, 2011; Prenn, 2011; Tunnell, 2011) and intra-relationally (Lamagna, 2011); the importance of judicious self-disclosure as a means of promoting relational closeness (Prenn, 2009); the importance of gratitude (Hanakawa, 2011); the importance of experience-near embodied language for experiential work (Fosha & Gleiser, in press); termination in AEDP (Harrison, 2020); and the application of AEDP to the treatment of complex trauma (Fosha et al., 2009; Gleiser et al., 2008), eating disorders (Prenn & Slatus, 2018; Williams & Files, 2018), and teletherapy in the time of the COVID-19 pandemic (McBride et al., 2020; Ronen-Setter & Cohen, 2020).

In 2015, Eileen Russell published her book *Restoring Resilience: Discovering Your Clients' Capacity for Healing* and offered an original conceptualization of *resilience*, which encompassed psychopathology, conceptualized as the individual's best efforts at adaptation in maladaptive environments. She expanded AEDP theory by articulating the transitional space between transformance and resistance: her articulation of the *self-in-transition*, marked by the *yellow signal affects* and signifying mixed feelings about the forward pulse of transformance joined the *self-at-worst* marked by the red signal affects of resistance and the self-at-best marked by the green signal affects of transformance. Similarly, Russell's *transformational other*, a construct very much inspired by Bollas, joined Fosha's *true other* (Fosha, 2000b, 2005), a construct considered the relational counterpart of Winnicott's *true self* (Winnicott, 1960/1965).

A year later, a major article by Karen Pando-Mars (2016) on how to tailor AEDP interventions to the different attachment styles applied AEDP's representational schemas to unpack the characteristic phenomenology and dynamics of each of the four attachment styles, using the four-state transformational process to detail interventions for each. The same year saw the first empirical study of metatherapeutic processing: Iwakabe and Conceição's (2016) task analytic deconstruction of it. A year later, Prenn and Fosha (2017) published *Supervision Essentials for Accelerated Experiential Dynamic Psychotherapy*, introducing "rigor without shame" to describe the application of AEDP to phenomenologically guided, transformative supervision. Although not intended as such, their book became a primer on the ABCs of AEDP's deliberate practice.

Other noteworthy developments were the publication of a series of articles on multicultural aspects of AEDP (Fosha, 2018b; Simpson, 2016; Urquiza Mendoza, 2018; Vigoda Gonzales, 2018; Ye-Perman, 2018); the publication of several case studies (Medley, 2018; Pass, 2012; Simpson, 2016; Vigoda Gonzales, 2018), including a systematic case study (Markin et al., 2018); and two empirical investigations into metatherapeutic processing (Iwakabe & Conceição, 2016; Lee, 2015). We also saw the publication of three books on AEDP for the public, making AEDP ideas more accessible and also constituting a resource for patients: Ron Frederick's *Living Like You Mean It* (2009) and *Loving Like You Mean It* (2019), as well as Hilary Hendel's (2018) *It's Not Always Depression*.

## Empirical Research in AEDP

Most of the work in the first 20 years of AEDP has been dedicated to theory-building and the development of AEDP's descriptive phenomenology; indeed, most of the chapters in the book continue that effort and focus. The past decade, however, has also seen the launching of empirical research in AEDP.

### Effectiveness of AEDP Training

Faerstein et al. (2016) developed and studied the psychometric properties of the AEDP Fidelity Scale, a scale with 22 items describing therapist behaviors considered essential to AEDP, and concluded that "AEDP-FS has promising indications of being a valid self-report measure of AEDP proficiency" (p. 172). Faerstein and colleagues administered the AEDP Fidelity Scale to 249 therapists before and after their AEDP training. Their findings support the effectiveness of AEDP training, showing that it leads to both enhancement of clinicians' knowledge base and their sense of competence in AEDP.

## Healing From the Get-Go

Preliminary results documenting the discontinuous change process character-istic of AEDP in the first three sessions, taken as empirical support for the notion of healing from the get-go, have been presented (Iwakabe et al., 2018) and are being prepared for publication (Iwakabe & Fosha, 2020).

## Effectiveness of AEDP

The year 2015 marked the formation of AEDP's Practice Research Network and the launching of AEDP's process–outcome research program (Edlin, Iwakabe, & Fosha, 2020). We adopted a 16-session AEDP format and treatment occurred in naturalistic private practice outpatient settings in the United States, Canada, Israel, Japan, and Sweden. Patients complete questionnaires pre–post therapy, as well as 6 months and 12 months after the completion of the 16-session AEDP treatment. They, as well as the therapists, also fill out measures and complete questionnaires after each therapy session. All therapy sessions for the research project are videotaped. To date, more than 80 therapies have been completed, and we have 12-month outcome data on more than 62 dyads.

We have just published the first AEDP effectiveness study, which examined outcomes for 62 self-referred adults treated using a 16-AEDP-session format (Iwakabe et al., 2020). Participants completed self-report measures before and after treatment, assessing a variety of psychological problems, and subjective distress, as well as aspects of positive psychological functioning. Our results provide empirical support for the effectiveness of AEDP to provide meaningful and significant improvements across a range of psychological symptoms, including depression, experiential avoidance, general symptom distress, diffi-culties in emotion regulation, and patients' main target problems. We also found a significant decrease in negative automatic thoughts, even though automatic thoughts specifically, and cognitions in general, are not targeted for restructuring in AEDP. There were also significant changes and improvement in nonpathological measures that centered on positive capacities, such as self-compassion and self-esteem. These findings show initial support for the AEDP aim of facilitating not only therapeutic changes from the negative range to the normal range (i.e., the reduction of emotional suffering) but also improve-ment from the normal range to stronger functioning (i.e., the promotion of flourishing). A follow-up paper reporting results for those first 62 dyads at 6 and 12 months (Iwakabe, Fosha, Edlin, Nakamura, et al., 2020) is in the works. Process–outcome investigations will soon follow. (For a more extensive discussion of AEDP research, see Fosha, Chapter 15, this volume.)

## Neuroplasticity, Metaprocessing, and Flourishing

At the same time that AEDP's transformational theory was growing, neuro-plasticity arrived on the scene to stay (e.g., Davidson et al., 2003; Doidge, 2007; Lazar et al., 2005). Notions that neuroplasticity was limited only to early parts of the life cycle became obsolete as the field awoke to the fact that neuroplasticity operates from cradle to grave, just as attachment does. A few years earlier, Barbara Fredrickson (2001) had published her broaden-and-build theory of positive emotion. On the basis of work in her psychology lab, she described the same upward spiraling phenomena engendered by the application of metaprocessing as Fosha (2000a, 2000b)[4] described, based on work in the clinical consultation room. Just as developments in the neuroscience of attachment and emotion were wonderful for dialogue as AEDP 1.0 progressed, the evolution of AEDP 2.0 flourished in the company of such advances.

In the past few years, the field of psychotherapy has become openly interested in questions that have always animated AEDP: how to accelerate transformation (Loizzo et al., 2017), how to promote moments of healing (Siegel & Solomon, 2013) and moments of meeting (Lord, 2017) in therapy sessions, how to use positive emotion in psychotherapy (see the special issue on second-wave positive psychology, *Quarterly of Counseling Psychology*; Wong, 2020) and how to promote in-session flourishing in psychotherapy (see the special issue of *Psychotherapy* on flourishing; Owen & Sandage, in press). The AEDP articles written for these special publications, as well as other works, advanced AEDP thinking on the use of experiential relational work to transform the internal working model (Fosha, 2017b; Frederick, 2019), on how to accelerate transformational work (Fosha, 2013b, 2017a), on the importance of work with both negative and positive emotions to generate positive emotion in psychotherapy (Fosha et al., 2019), on metatherapeutic processing as a methodology to promote in-session flourishing (Fosha & Thoma, 2020), and on the role of intuition in core state phenomena (Yeung et al., 2019).

AEDP is an upward-spiraling cumulative model, folding into it all that has been developed thus far. This volume, with its 15 chapters, describes the culmination of AEDP 2.0 as it currently stands.

## TRAJECTORY OF THIS BOOK

In the chapters that follow, informed by AEDP's quest to set healing in motion, undo aloneness, and transform emotional suffering into flourishing, the authors engage different aspects of AEDP 2.0, elaborating, deepening, and extending the model, as well as introducing new work. Through this broadening and building, AEDP 2.0's theory flourishes.

It is noteworthy that transformation happens in each and every one of the illustrative therapy sessions in the chapters that follow, including those devoted to work with complex trauma, dissociation, or maladaptive affective experiences. In all of these AEDP sessions featuring work guided by the four-state transformational process, aloneness is undone, emotional suffering is transformed, and then metatherapeutic processing is used to further process and reap the benefits of the transformational experiences patients have just had, which in turn often leads to more transformation and connection.

---

[4] I thank Michael Bridges (2005) for bringing the broaden-and-build theory of positive emotion to my attention in the context of the publication of one of his papers.

We begin the book much as we begin our experiential AEDP courses: In our AEDP training sequence, the first course is an immersion in which we first give a brief orientation to the ethos and fundamentals of AEDP, and then set about to have an experience together. And so with this book, Chapter 1 sets the stage, and with Chapter 2, we dive right into clinical work in the first session of therapy: We thus get to have an experience of healing from the get-go, and we are launched. And then, the rest of the AEDP 2.0 model unfolds.

In Chapter 1, I offer an overview of AEDP: AEDP's top ten foundational principles and the affective change processes that they inform, how psychopathology and its relationship to healing is understood in AEDP, and a detailed description of phenomenology of the four-state transformational process.

In Chapter 2, Karen Kranz shows us what *healing from the get-go* means clinically. In a first session with a patient with a significant trauma history, using a stance of relational connection, we witness the unfolding of the patient's process as he goes through all four states of the transformational process in a 50-minute session. Asking what allows AEDP to be transformative, Kranz answers it experientially, through actual clinical work and the articulation of the principles that inform the clinical interventions we witness.

Chapters 3 through 6 are devoted to *context* and *scaffolding*. It is refreshing to switch lenses from the zoom of Chapter 2 to the wide-angle lens of Chapter 3. Coauthored by Gil Tunnell and Jenna Osiason, Chapter 3 addresses AEDP's place in the history of psychotherapy, parsing the history into three waves of psychotherapeutic movements. Tunnell and Osiason address dimensions such as the psychopathology- versus problem- versus solution-focused orientation of different therapy models; notions of linear versus circular versus dynamic causality; and therapist as expert versus patient as expert stances. Discussing AEDP's stance of nonhierarchical, non-expert connection, its theory of psychopathology as rooted in aloneness, and its focus on transformation and emergence, the authors propose that AEDP 2.0 might represent a fourth wave in the history of psychotherapy.

Next is AEDP's phenomenological focus and experiential methodology. In Chapter 4, Yuko Hanakawa addresses moment-to-moment tracking of felt sense experience as a foundational principle of AEDP. She unpacks moment-to-moment tracking, explores the neuroscience that informs it, and shows how it guides interventions. She develops a taxonomy of different types of tracking and details fascinating science behind each, including the insula-based science of the felt sense. It is worth noting Hanakawa's clinical examples are 15 to 45 seconds in duration! Reading her account of the subtle changes she is tracking in response to interventions is like watching a videotape frame by frame.

While Hanakawa's tracking focuses on the patient, in Chapter 5, Benjamin Lipton addresses himself to the self of the therapist. He makes a powerful case that the therapist's therapeutic presence is itself a powerful affective change process in the patient's therapy. He focuses on the moment-to-moment tracking of the *therapist's* experience and explores the nature of therapeutic presence in an attachment-based model. He shows how for AEDP therapists, the moment-to-moment tracking of our own experiences can also be leveraged effectively in the service of the patient's therapy, as his case examples vividly illustrate. Lipton applies the four-state transformational model to the therapist's experience, showing how it may also complement, rather than only directly parallel, that of the patient.

Chapters 6 and 7 by Karen Pando-Mars and Ronald Frederick, respectively, use developmental research, research into positive neuroplasticity, and AEDP's three representational schemas—the Triangle of Experience, the Self–Other–Emotion configuration, and the Triangle of Relational Comparisons[5]—to show both how our early experiences shape our patterns and also how therapeutic work can rewire, restructure, and thus transform emotional (Chapter 6) and relational (Chapter 7) experiences. However, the nonshaded part of the Venn diagram of these two chapters is considerable: Pando-Mars focuses on the processing of emotional experience, especially the unprocessed emotional experiences of the past, whereas Frederick focuses on restructuring the patient's internal working model by relationally processing the patient's here-and-now corrective relational experience with the therapist. Thus, their respective chapters appear in different sections.

In Chapter 6, the last chapter in the Context and Scaffolding section, Pando-Mars elaborates the psychodynamic scaffolding of AEDP's experiential practice. She takes on AEDP's three representational schema triangles and shows how they allow us to orient and track the therapeutic process. It is a masterful unpacking and updating of the AEDP 2.0 understanding of these schemas. In the clinical example, using the categories of the representational schemas to track the therapeutic process move by move allows Pando-Mars to break through the rigid avoidant defenses that had kept her patient frozen for 15 years, undergirding current experiences now threatening to ruin her marriage. The clinical work powerfully illustrates how the updated representational schemas help guide the moment-to-moment tracking of the clinical material as it unfolds and also help the selection of interventions. Here, we also have a clear example of how insight follows transformation, as opposed to preceding it.

With context and scaffolding now in place, the next two sections take on the *how-to* of the transformation of emotional suffering, with chapters about how to bring forth and then harness the transformational power of adaptive core affective experiences (Chapters 7–9), and then chapters on how to transform the pathogenic maladaptive affective experiences to make the most of the information residing in them (Chapters 10–12).

We begin Part III, How to Work With Core Affective Experience, with the processing and metaprocessing of core affective relational experience. While the internal working model reflects how children's experiences with their attachment figures become internalized in psychic structure, new positive relational experiences, including new experiences in adulthood, can transform the internal model. In Chapter 7, Ron Frederick discusses how AEDP's three representational schemas help guide the sometimes quite painstaking

---

[5]Diagrams for all of the representational schemas mentioned here may be downloaded for free (http://pubs.apa.org/books/supp/fosha).

yet profound here-and-now relational processing work by which the internal model can be rewired. Frederick focuses on interventions to both "melt" and restructure defenses to help his patient expand his initially limited receptive affective capacity and thus be able to take in and make the most of the corrective relational experiences his therapist is offering.

In Chapter 8, Ben Medley's focus is on State 2 emotion processing. In a thorough review of emotion and the all-important construct of the adaptive action tendencies wired into each emotion, Medley explores what processing emotional experience entails and what bringing emotion processing work to completion is all about. He focuses on the technique of *portrayals*, an imaginal technique, and describes different types of portrayals and their uses. In one of Medley's clinical examples, he helps his patient ride the wave of emotion from the first inklings of something stirring, through fully accessing, processing, and working through the emotion and its meaning to the end, and then to the release of the emotion's adaptive action tendencies and the changes that follow.

In Chapter 9, Eileen Russell advocates for expanding the State 2 categories of core affective experience to include experiences of agency, will and desire, and expands AEDP theory into the realms of autonomy, separation and differentiation. She explores what's needed in therapeutic work with those individuals whose sense of "I" was thwarted by abuse and neglect or never fostered or sufficiently encouraged to bring online their agentic selves (or both). Russell introduces a technique she calls *attuned disruption*, with the distinct purpose of challenging and disrupting these patients' comfort zone, letting them tolerate some anxiety without rushing to immediately regulate it to stimulate the emergence of at least glimmers, and eventually fuller experiences, of agency, will, and desire.

The clinical work of the authors in the chapters to this point (i.e., Chapters 2–9) has relied mostly on the four-state transformational model, a summary visual of which can be found in Figure 1.1 in Chapter 1 (also Figure 1 in the Appendix). When we move to Part IV, How to Work With Maladaptive Affective Experience and Complex Trauma, a more complex representation of the transformational process becomes necessary. The authors of Chapters 10 to 12, especially, though, 10 and 11, write about the impact of trauma, both abuse and neglect, manifesting in phenomena we call *maladaptive affective experiences*, a category of State 2 experiences constituted of the *pathogenic affects* and the *unbearable states of traumatic aloneness*. These phenomena require a more elaborate diagram to show how they are located in the transformational process, which is schematically represented in Figure 2 in the Appendix (see also Figure 9.1). One of the main differences between the two types of State 2 experiences, the adaptive core affective experiences and the maladaptive affective experiences, is that whereas the adaptive core affective experiences *are* transforming, the maladaptive affective experiences *need* transforming. Unlike adaptive core affective experiences, when it comes to the maladaptive affects, it is not possible just to track them, help the person bear them, and help the patient process them to an adaptive completion. The maladaptive affective experiences do not complete; they are not finite and, left to their own devices, do not have adaptive completion. Merely helping patients experience them is contraindicated and can be downright traumatizing or patho-genic (i.e., creating suffering). Yet, as Lamagna (Chapter 11, this volume) writes, "maladaptive affective states carry meaningful information about the truth of a client's lived experience" and as such are deeply valuable. In Chapters 10 and 11, first Piliero and then Lamagna put forth deep wisdom about how to work with these challenging experiences, and in the process, each of them extends AEDP theory and practice with respect to work to transform these otherwise maladaptive and pathogenic experiences. Then in Chapter 12, Kari Gleiser reprises the theme of rewiring the internal working model, this time in the context of working with complex trauma and dissociation.

In Chapter 10, SueAnne Piliero puts forth her notion of the therapist's "fierce love" as a powerful stance and set of interventions that seek to transform patients' pathogenic affects of toxic shame and the entrenched pathogenic self-states to which the pathogenic affects give rise, defensive states in which patients' sense of or beliefs in their own badness or unworthiness has infected the self. These pathogenic beliefs function as entrenched defenses against both (a) "taking in" the care of the therapist and also (b) seeing one's own fundamental self-worth. Self-loathing arises to stave off unbearable pain and also as a manifestation of the vain hope that something of the bond with the attachment figure can be salvaged. Piliero expands the AEDP relational repertoire, using fierce love and fierce advocacy on behalf of the patient's self to seek to penetrate these entrenched defenses and transform the underlying unbearable maladaptive affective experiences to reveal the core authentic self.

If Piliero takes on how to work with the entrenched defenses that arise out of maladaptive affective experience against the self, Jerry Lamagna describes how to work when defenses have collapsed and maladaptive affective experiences show up in raw form. In Chapter 11, he takes on the transformational challenge of another aspect of State 2 work: when patients are in the throes of reliving the traumatic aloneness they once experienced and the pathogenic affects flood them with felt memories of abuse and emotional abandonment. What ups the ante here is that when in the midst of these experiences, patients can neither self-regulate nor accept dyadic affect regulation from the other. In Lamagna's intra-relational interventions, the experiential work takes place in the "relational space between therapist, client and self-states containing felt memories of abuse and emotional abandonment" to facilitate the emergence of patients' compassionate response to their own suffering, what Lamagna calls "tending and befriending" these "forsaken self-states." Lamagna uses updated versions of the *triangle of experience* and the *self–other–emotion triangle* to navigate these challenging waters, exploring the use of the latter to select entry points for optimally effective experiential work.

The next theme of this section is complex trauma and multiplicity. In Chapter 12, Kari Gleiser explores the application of AEDP's experiential attachment work to patients with complex trauma and dissociation. Relational work, particularly in the here-and-now of the patient–therapist dyad, has often been discouraged in the past, even contraindicated with these patients. Gleiser disagrees. Introducing a new representational schema, Gleiser uses the *relational prism* to help her choose whether to use (a) relational work, (b) intra-relational work, or (c) transitional work involving the therapist and a dissociated part. Her clinical work shows how secure attachment can be aimed for, and achieved, in all three realms. The relational prism can help therapists treating patients with severe fragmentation and patients on the dissociative identity disorder spectrum choose optimal strategies to foster secure attachment in whichever relational realm they need to engage.

The last section of the book—Part V, Integration, Flourishing, Core State, and the Core Self—is devoted to articulating the transformational theory of AEDP 2.0 and looking toward the future. Chapters 13 and 14 explore how AEDP 2.0 conceptualizes integration, flourishing, core state, and the core self, contributing to articulating AEDP's transformational theory, including the hypothesized neurobiological mechanisms underlying the affective changes mechanisms that transform suffering and bring flourishing about in AEDP.

In Chapter 13, Danny Yeung seeks to answer the question "What went right?" by zeroing in on metatherapeutic processing and the profound integration that characterizes core state, and bringing in concepts from neurobiology to shed light on them. His chapter explores the neurobiological underpinnings of what we believe goes on in the brain and nervous system when transformational experiences are being processed in AEDP. In a dialectic that goes back and forth between AEDP's transformational phenomenology and research findings on subcortical brain structures and the autonomic nervous system that have been shown to mediate attachment and integration experiences, Yeung attempts to understand the neurobiology of sacred experiences while simultaneously demonstrating how readily they emerge in State 3 and State 4 work in AEDP. Whether we are dealing with the extraordinary phenomena of core state in AEDP, as illustrated in Yeung's two clinical examples, or the phenomena of sacredness and transcendence shared by so many of the world's contemplative traditions, both those sets of experiences help undo our sense of existential aloneness and connect us with one another. The more we understand the neurobiology of such experiences, the more adept we can become at facilitating them, whether through the clinical practices of transformational therapies such as AEDP, or through the transformational practices of the contemplative traditions worldwide.

The theme of Chapter 14 is the evolutionary mandate to flourish, captured in a powerful phrase from Antonio Damasio: "We are organized to be better than fine." In this chapter, I seek to broaden the transformational theory of AEDP 2.0, folding into it the resonant and congruent insights from positive neuroplasticity, the broaden-and-build theory of positive emotion, energy-based understanding of our evolutionary mandate, and neurobiological theories of the core self, and build on them. Given that positive affects are the phenomenological expression of processes that underlie optimal adaptation, resilience, plasticity, and subjective well-being, I begin with articulating a taxonomy of positive affects that arise in the context of AEDP's experiential work with healing and transformation, an impressive lexicon of positive phenomenologically distinct affects associated with distinct psychological and therapeutic situations, ripe for being put to therapeutic uses given their energy-rich properties. This chapter focuses on the importance of the energetic affective dimension of work with transformational experiences and the innately integrative power of the neurobiologically based core self to link the transformance glimmers of State 1 to the integrative unitive phenomena of State 4 (i.e., core state). The chapter also explores how AEDP's methodology is quintessentially well suited to entrain that evolutionary mandate to flourish in our day-to-day clinical practice. It ends with AEDP 2.0's connotation of the word "core" as fundamentally healthy and healing. Health and healing emanate from the core.

Finally, Chapter 15 is an epilogue devoted to exploring directions that AEDP might take in the future. Having only just finalized the platform of AEDP 2.0, I already look toward the possibilities that AEDP 3.0 might hold. Applying AEDP to the treatment of people whose traumatic suffering is either caused and/or amplified by systemic racism and different forms of discrimination, injustice, and oppression; exploring what understanding of AEDP's mechanisms of change might be yielded by the process–outcome research that is yet to come, and research on the neurobiology of AEDP's mechanisms of change are all emergent areas that promise to change AEDP as it expands to support their emergence.

As noted earlier, the Appendix of this volume contains a summary figure that schematically represents the phenomenology of the four states of the transformational process, figures representing the schematic representations, and a summary figure of the phenomenology of the four states of the transformational process which also includes the maladaptive affective experiences. The figures also appear in the chapters where they are mentioned and all are available for download (http://pubs.apa.org/books/supp/fosha).

## CONCLUSION

This book is the outcome of a deep collaboration, or rather a "multillaboration" (i.e., the labor of many), and the labor in the multillaboration is a labor of love. This book is about AEDP 2.0, a transformational model of clinical work that substantially revises previous theories of psychotherapy: It eschews psychopathology as a central explanatory construct of therapy, instead using healing as a point of departure. It is also about AEDP as a living emergent model, one that is discovered anew by each therapist, by each therapeutic dyad, by each community. This book puts forth a theory and a practice that have been coconstructed, copracticed, and coembodied over 2 decades by the authors represented here, by our faculty colleagues, and also by our colleagues in the expanding community of AEDP practitioners worldwide.

The work represented here, in the chapters of this book, constitutes a platform for launching the next rung of the transformational spiral. Recursively, the transformational theory informs clinical practice such that new phenomena emerge, which in turn stimulate further developments to account for them and how to work with them clinically, which in turn lead to new phenomena, necessitating further developments. And so on. This upward spiraling transformational process mirrors the historical evolution of AEDP as a model: cocreated, phenomenological, relational, emergent, and grounded in nonlinear dynamic systems. And, as we, the contributors, offer it to you, dear reader and practitioner, we hope to further facilitate its intergenerational transmission in how our model will be embodied through you.

We now invite you into this whirling dervish of an ever-emergent, relentlessly relational, relentlessly transformational model. Let us undo your aloneness. Whether you are encountering AEDP for the first time or you are an experienced AEDP practitioner, we hope this book might inspire and accompany you, and maybe, just maybe, change something, even if just a little bit, either with newness, or maybe with a revelation about something you thought you already knew. Maybe, as a result of immersing yourself in this book, your clinical work might change in a way that would give rise to new transformational phenomena, which in turn might inspire you to work a bit differently. And maybe, in the process, you too might change a little bit, growing, transforming, feeling seen and recognized.

Welcome to the dynamic transformational spiral that is AEDP. Welcome to AEDP 2.0.

## REFERENCES

Bridges, M. R. (2005). The bruised heart: Musings on optimal emotional arousal and the importance of positive affects in emotion-focused therapy and STDP. *Ad Hoc Bulletin of Short-Term Dynamic Psychotherapy: Practice and Theory, 9*(1), 35–52.

Damasio, A. (1994). *Descartes' error: Emotion, reason and the human brain.* Grosset Putnam.

Damasio, A. (2010). *Self comes to mind: Constructing the conscious brain.* Pantheon Books.

Davidson, R. J., Kabat-Zinn, J., Schumacher, J., Rosenkranz, M., Muller, D., Santorelli, S. F., Urbanowski, F., Harrington, A., Bonus, K., & Sheridan, J. F. (2003). Alterations in brain and immune function produced by mindfulness meditation. *Psychosomatic Medicine, 65*(4), 564–570. https://doi.org/10.1097/01.PSY.0000077505.67574.E3

Doidge, N. (2007). *The brain that changes itself: Stories of personal triumph from the frontiers of brain science.* Penguin Books.

Ecker, B., Ticic, R., & Hulley, L. (2012). *Unlocking the emotional brain: Eliminating symptoms at their roots using memory reconsolidation.* Routledge. https://doi.org/10.4324/9780203804377

Edlin, J., Fosha, D., & Iwakabe, S. (2020). *A practitioner–research collaborative network in AEDP: Building on AEDP's worldview and capitalizing on the change mechanisms* [Manuscript in preparation]. The AEDP Institute, New York, NY.

Edlin, J., Iwakabe, S., & Fosha, D. (2020). The AEDP Process/Outcome research initiative: A description of the program and its scope [Manuscript in preparation]. Ochanomizu University, Japan.

Ericsson, K. A., Hoffman, R. R., Kozbelt, A., & Williams, A. M. (Eds.). (2018). *The Cambridge handbook of expertise and expert performance.* Cambridge University Press. https://doi.org/10.1017/9781316480748

Faerstein, I., Levenson, H., & Lee, A. C. (2016). Validation of a fidelity scale for accelerated-experiential dynamic psychotherapy. *Journal of Psychotherapy Integration, 26*(2), 172–185. https://doi.org/10.1037/int0000020

Fosha, D. (2000a). Meta-therapeutic processes and the affects of transformation: Affirmation and the healing affects. *Journal of Psychotherapy Integration, 10*(1), 71–97.

Fosha, D. (2000b). *The transforming power of affect: A model for accelerated change*. Basic Books.

Fosha, D. (2001). The dyadic regulation of affect. *Journal of Clinical Psychology, 57*(2), 227–242. https://doi.org/10.1002/1097-4679(200102)57:2<227::AID-JCLP8>3.0.CO;2-1

Fosha, D. (2002). The activation of affective change processes in AEDP (accelerated experiential-dynamic psychotherapy). In J. J. Magnavita (Ed.), *Comprehensive handbook of psychotherapy: Vol. 1. Psychodynamic and object relations psychotherapies* (pp. 309–344). John Wiley & Sons.

Fosha, D. (2003). Dyadic regulation and experiential work with emotion and relatedness in trauma and disordered attachment. In M. F. Solomon & D. J. Siegel (Eds.), *Healing trauma: Attachment, trauma, the brain and the mind* (pp. 221–281). Norton.

Fosha, D. (2004). "Nothing that feels bad is ever the last step": The role of positive emotions in experiential work with difficult emotional experiences. *Clinical Psychology and Psychotherapy, 11*(1), 30–43.

Fosha, D. (2005). Emotion, true self, true other, core state: Toward a clinical theory of affective change process. *Psychoanalytic Review, 92*(4), 513–551. https://doi.org/10.1521/prev.2005.92.4.513

Fosha, D. (2006). Quantum transformation in trauma and treatment: Traversing the crisis of healing change. *Journal of Clinical Psychology, 62*(5), 569–583. https://doi.org/10.1002/jclp.20249

Fosha, D. (2008). Transformance, recognition of self by self, and effective action. In K. J. Schneider (Ed.), *Existential-integrative psychotherapy: Guideposts to the core of practice* (pp. 290–320). Routledge.

Fosha, D. (2009a). Emotion and recognition at work: Energy, vitality, pleasure, truth, desire & the emergent phenomenology of transformational experience. In D. Fosha, D. J. Siegel, & M. F. Solomon (Eds.), *The healing power of emotion: Affective neuroscience, development, clinical practice* (pp. 172–203). Norton. [Reprinted in *Neuropsychotherapist* (2013), Vol. 2.]

Fosha, D. (2009b). Healing attachment trauma with attachment (. . . and then some!). In M. Kerman (Ed.), *Clinical pearls of wisdom: 21 leading therapists offer their key insights* (pp. 43–56). Norton.

Fosha, D. (2009c). Positive affects and the transformation of suffering into flourishing. In W. C. Bushell, E. L. Olivo, & N. D. Theise (Eds.), *Longevity, regeneration, and optimal health: Integrating Eastern and Western perspectives* (pp. 252–261). The New York Academy of Sciences.

Fosha, D. (2013a). A heaven in a wild flower: Self, dissociation, and treatment in the context of the neurobiological core self. *Psychoanalytic Inquiry, 33*(5), 496–523. https://doi.org/10.1080/07351690.2013.815067

Fosha, D. (2013b). Turbocharging the affects of healing and redressing the evolutionary tilt. In D. J. Siegel & Marion F. Solomon (Eds.), *Healing moments in psychotherapy* (pp. 129–168). Norton.

Fosha, D. (2017a). How to be a transformational therapist: AEDP harnesses innate healing affects to re-wire experience and accelerate transformation. In J. Loizzo, M. Neale, & E. Wolf (Eds.), *Advances in contemplative psychotherapy: Accelerating transformation* (pp. 204–219). Norton. https://doi.org/10.4324/9781315630045-18

Fosha, D. (2017b). Something more than "something more than interpretation": AEDP works the experiential edge of transformational experience to transform the internal working model. In S. Lord (Ed.), *Moments of meeting in psychoanalysis: Interaction and change in the therapeutic encounter* (pp. 267–292). Routledge.

Fosha, D. (2018a). Introduction to commentaries on sociocultural identity, trauma treatment, and AEDP through the lens of bilingualism in the case of "Rosa." *Pragmatic Case Studies in Psychotherapy, 14*(2), 115–130. https://doi.org/10.14713/pcsp.v14i2.2039

Fosha, D. (2018b). Moment-to-moment guidance of clinical interventions by AEDP's healing-oriented transformational phenomenology: Commentary on Vigoda Gonzalez's (2018) case of "Rosa." *Pragmatic Case Studies in Psychotherapy, 14*(2), 87–114. https://doi.org/10.14713/pcsp.v14i2.2038

Fosha, D., & Gleiser, K. (in press). The embodied language of integrative states: Unmaligning much maligned language in experiential therapy. In G. L. Schiewer, J. Altarriba, & B. Chin Ng (Eds.), *Handbook on language and emotion.* De Gruyter Mouton.

Fosha, D., Paivio, S. C., Gleiser, K., & Ford, J. (2009). Experiential and emotion-focused therapy. In C. Courtois & J. D. Ford (Eds.), *Complex traumatic stress disorders: An evidence-based clinician's guide* (pp. 286–311). The Guilford Press.

Fosha, D., & Thoma, N. (2020). Metatherapeutic processing supports the emergence of flourishing in psychotherapy. *Psychotherapy, 57*(3), 323–339. https://doi.org/10.1037/pst0000289

Fosha, D., Thoma, N., & Yeung, D. (2019). Transforming emotional suffering into flourishing: Metatherapeutic processing of positive affect as a trans-theoretical vehicle for change. *Counselling Psychology Quarterly, 32*(3–4), 563–593. https://doi.org/10.1080/09515070.2019.1642852

Fosha, D., & Yeung, D. (2006). AEDP exemplifies the seamless integration of emotional transformation and dyadic relatedness at work. In G. Stricker & J. Gold (Eds.), *A casebook of integrative psychotherapy* (pp. 165–184). American Psychological Association. https://doi.org/10.1037/11436-013

Frederick, R. (2009). *Living like you mean it: Use the wisdom and power of your emotions to get the life you really want.* Jossey-Bass.

Frederick, R. (2019). *Loving like you mean it: Use the power of emotional mindfulness to transform your relationships.* Central Recovery Press.

Fredrickson, B. L. (2001). The role of positive emotions in positive psychology. The broaden-and-build theory of positive emotions. *American Psychologist, 56*(3), 218–226. https://doi.org/10.1037/0003-066X.56.3.218

Fredrickson, B. L. (2013). Positive emotions broaden and build. In E. Ashby Plant & P. G. Devine (Eds.), *Advances in experimental social psychology* (Vol. 47, pp. 1–53). Academic Press.

Gleiser, K. (2013, May 30). Seeing the invisible: The role of recognition in healing from neglect and deprivation. *Transformance: The AEDP Journal, 3.* https://aedpinstitute.org/wp-content/uploads/page_Seeing-the-Invisible.pdf

Gleiser, K., Ford, J. D., & Fosha, D. (2008). Contrasting exposure and experiential therapies for complex posttraumatic stress disorder. *Psychotherapy, 45*(3), 340–360. https://doi.org/10.1037/a0013323

Hanakawa, Y. (2011, May 9). Receiving loving gratitude: How a therapist's mindful embrace of a patient's gratitude facilitates transformance. *Transformance: The AEDP Journal, 2*(1). https://aedpinstitute.org/wp-content/uploads/page_Receiving-Loving-Gratitude.pdf

Hanson, R. (2017). Positive neuroplasticity: The neuroscience of mindfulness. In J. Loizzo, M. Neale, & E. Wolf (Eds.), *Advances in contemplative psychotherapy: Accelerating transformation* (pp. 48–60). Norton. https://doi.org/10.4324/9781315630045-5

Harrison, R. L. (2020). Termination in 16-session accelerated experiential dynamic psychotherapy (AEDP): Together in how we say goodbye. *Psychotherapy, 57*(4), 531–547. https://doi.org/10.1037/pst0000343

Hendel, H. J. (2018). *It's not always depression: Working the change triangle to listen to the body, discover core emotions, and connect with your authentic self.* Penguin Random House.

Iwakabe, S., & Conceição, N. (2016). Metatherapeutic processing as a change-based therapeutic immediacy task: Building an initial process model using a task-analytic research strategy. *Journal of Psychotherapy Integration, 26*(3), 230–247. https://doi.org/10.1037/int0000016

Iwakabe, S., Edlin, E., Fosha, D., Gretton, H., Joseph, A. J., Nunnink, S. E., Nakamura, K., & Thoma, N. C. (2020). The effectiveness of accelerated experiential dynamic psychotherapy (AEDP) in private practice settings: A transdiagnostic study conducted within the context of a practice-research network. *Psychotherapy*. Advance online publication. https://doi.org/10.1037/pst0000344

Iwakabe, S., Edlin, J., Fosha, D., & Nakamura, K. (2018, June). *The preliminary results on AEDP outcome research* [Paper presentation]. Society for the Exploration of Psychotherapy Integration 34th Annual Meeting, New York, NY, United States.

Iwakabe, S., & Fosha, D. (2020). Healing from the get-go: Discontinuous change in the first three sessions of *accelerated experiential dynamic psychotherapy (AEDP)* [Manuscript in preparation].

Iwakabe, S., Fosha, D., Edlin, J., Nakamura, K., Gretton, H., Nunnink, S., Joseph, A., & Thoma, N. (2020). *Maintenance of change following accelerated experiential dynamic psychotherapy: 6- and 12-month follow-ups* [Manuscript in preparation].

Lamagna, J. (2011). Of the self, by the self, and for the self: An intra-relational perspective on intra-psychic attunement and psychological change. *Journal of Psychotherapy Integration, 21*(3), 280–307. https://doi.org/10.1037/a0025493

Lamagna, J., & Gleiser, K. A. (2007). Building a secure internal attachment: An intra-relational approach to ego strengthening and emotional processing with chronically traumatized clients. *Journal of Trauma & Dissociation, 8*(1), 25–52. https://doi.org/10.1300/J229v08n01_03

Lazar, S. W., Kerr, C. E., Wasserman, R. H., Gray, J. R., Greve, D. N., Treadway, M. T., McGarvey, M., Quinn, B. T., Dusek, J. A., Benson, H., Rauch, S. L., Moore, C. I., & Fischl, B. (2005). Meditation experience is associated with increased cortical thickness. *Neuroreport, 16*(17), 1893–1897. https://doi.org/10.1097/01.wnr.0000186598.66243.19

Lee, A. (2015). *Building a model for metaprocessing: Exploration of a key change event in accelerated experiential dynamic psychotherapy (AEDP)* [Unpublished doctoral dissertation]. Wright Institute, Berkeley, CA.

Lipton, B., & Fosha, D. (2011). Attachment as a transformative process in AEDP: Operationalizing the intersection of attachment theory and affective neuroscience. *Journal of Psychotherapy Integration, 21*(3), 253–279. https://doi.org/10.1037/a0025421

Loizzo, J., Neale, M., & Wolf, E. (Eds.). (2017). *Advances in contemplative psychotherapy: Accelerating transformation*. Norton. https://doi.org/10.4324/9781315630045

Lord, S. (Ed.). (2017). *Moments of meeting in psychoanalysis: Interaction and change in the therapeutic encounter*. Routledge. https://doi.org/10.4324/9781315389967

Markin, R. D., McCarthy, K. S., Fuhrman, A., Yeung, D., & Gleiser, K. A. (2018). The process of change in accelerated experiential dynamic psychotherapy (AEDP): A case study analysis. *Journal of Psychotherapy Integration, 28*(2), 213–232. https://doi.org/10.1037/int0000084

McBride, H. L., Joseph, A. J., Schmitt, P. G., & Holtz, B. M. (2020). Clinical recommendations for psychotherapists working during the coronavirus (COVID-19) pandemic through the lens of AEDP (accelerated experiential dynamic psychotherapy). *Counselling Psychology Quarterly*. Advance online publication. https://doi.org/10.1080/09515070.2020.1771283

Medley, B. (2018). Recovering the true self: Affirmative therapy, attachment, and AEDP in psychotherapy with gay men. *Journal of Psychotherapy Integration*. Advance online publication. https://doi.org/10.1037/int0000132

Northoff, G., & Panksepp, J. (2008). The trans-species concept of self and the subcortical-cortical midline system. *Trends in Cognitive Sciences, 12*(7), 259–264. https://doi.org/10.1016/j.tics.2008.04.007

Owen, J., & Sandage, S. J. (Eds.). (in press). Flourishing [Special issue]. *Psychotherapy.*

Pando-Mars, K. (2016). Tailoring AEDP interventions to attachment style. *Transformance: The AEDP Journal, 4*(2), 1–91. https://aedpinstitute.org/transformance-journal-2/

Panksepp, J. (1998). *Affective neuroscience: The foundations of human and animal emotions.* Oxford University Press.

Panksepp, J., & Northoff, G. (2009). The trans-species core SELF: The emergence of active cultural and neuro-ecological agents through self-related processing within subcortical-cortical midline networks. *Consciousness and Cognition, 18*(1), 193–215. https://doi.org/10.1016/j.concog.2008.03.002

Pass, E. R. (2012). Combining expressive writing with an affect- and attachment-focused psychotherapeutic approach in the treatment of a single-incident trauma survivor: The case of "Grace." *Pragmatic Case Studies in Psychotherapy, 8*(2), 60–112. https://doi.org/10.14713/pcsp.v8i2.1492

Prenn, N. (2009). I second that emotion! On self-disclosure and its metaprocessing. In A. Bloomgarden & R. B. Menutti (Eds.), *Psychotherapist revealed: Therapists speak about self-disclosure in psychotherapy* (pp. 85–99). Routledge.

Prenn, N. (2011). Mind the gap: AEDP interventions translating attachment theory into clinical practice. *Journal of Psychotherapy Integration, 21*(3), 308–329. https://doi.org/10.1037/a0025491

Prenn, N., & Fosha, D. (2017). *Supervision essentials for accelerated experiential dynamic psychotherapy.* American Psychological Association. https://doi.org/10.1037/0000016-000

Prenn, N., & Slatus, J. (2018). Second helpings: AEDP (accelerated experiential dynamic psychotherapy) in the treatment of trauma and eating disorders. In A. Seubert & P. Virdi (Eds.), *Trauma-informed approaches to eating disorders* (pp. 235–248). Springer Publishing. https://doi.org/10.1891/9780826172655.0018

Ronen-Setter, I., & Cohen, E. (2020). *On becoming teletherapeutic: Harnessing accelerated experiential dynamic psychotherapy for the challenges of the COVID-19 era* [Manuscript submitted for publication].

Rousmaniere, T., Goodyear, R. K., Miller, S. D., & Wampold, B. E. (Eds.). (2017). *The cycle of excellence: Using deliberate practice to improve supervision and training.* John Wiley & Sons. https://doi.org/10.1002/9781119165590

Russell, E., & Fosha, D. (2008). Transformational affects and core state in AEDP: The emergence and consolidation of joy, hope, gratitude and confidence in the (solid goodness of the) self. *Journal of Psychotherapy Integration, 18*(2), 167–190. https://doi.org/10.1037/1053-0479.18.2.167

Russell, E. M. (2015). *Restoring resilience: Discovering your clients' capacity for healing.* Norton.

Schore, A. N. (1994). *Affect regulation and the origin of the self: The neurobiology of emotional development.* Erlbaum.

Schwartz, R. (1995). *Internal family systems therapy.* The Guilford Press.

Siegel, D. J. (1999). *The developing mind: How relationships and the brain interact to shape who we are.* The Guilford Press.

Siegel, D. J., & Solomon, M. F. (Eds.). (2013). *Healing moments in psychotherapy.* Norton.

Simpson, M. L. (2016). Feeling seen: A pathway to transformation. *International Journal of Transpersonal Studies, 35*(1), 78–91. https://doi.org/10.24972/ijts.2016.35.1.78

Tunnell, G. (2011). An attachment perspective on the first interview. In C. Silverstein (Ed.), *The initial psychotherapy interview: A gay man seeks treatment* (pp. 137–155). Elsevier Insight Books. https://doi.org/10.1016/B978-0-12-385146-8.00007-9

Urquiza Mendoza, Y. (2018). The case of "Rosa": The importance of specificity in our quest to integrate cultural competence in practice. *Pragmatic Case Studies in Psychotherapy, 14*(2), 138–146. https://doi.org/10.14713/pcsp.v14i2.2041

Vaz, A., Rousmaniere, T., Wampold, B., & Caspar, F. (2018). *Deliberate practice and psychotherapy expertise: a discussion and live demonstration.* Workshop presented at the 49th Annual Conference of the Society for Psychotherapy Research, Amsterdam.

Vigoda Gonzales, N. V. (2018). The merits of integrating accelerated experiential dynamic psychotherapy and cultural competence strategies in the treatment of relational trauma: The case of "Rosa." *Pragmatic Case Studies in Psychotherapy, 14*(1), 1–57. https://doi.org/10.14713/pcsp.v14i1.2032

Welling, H. (2012). Transformative emotional sequence: Towards a common principle of change. *Journal of Psychotherapy Integration, 22*(2), 109–136. https://doi.org/10.1037/a0027786

Williams, M., & Files, N. (2018). Emotion-based psychotherapies in the treatment of eating disorders. In H. L. McBride & J. L. Kwee (Eds.), *Embodiment and eating disorders: Theory, research, prevention and treatment* (pp. 265–299). Routledge. https://doi.org/10.4324/9781315159645-21

Winnicott, D. W. (1965). Ego distortion in terms of true and false self. In *The maturational processes and the facilitating environment* (pp. 140–152). International Universities Press. (Original work published 1960)

Wong, P. T. P. (Ed.). (2020). Second wave positive psychology [Special issue]. *Quarterly of Counseling Psychology, 32*(3–4).

Ye-Perman, H. J. (2018). The case of "Rosa": AEDP in the realm of cultural diversity—One's new language as a vehicle for exploring new aspects of identity. *Pragmatic Case Studies in Psychotherapy, 14*(2), 147–157. https://doi.org/10.14713/pcsp.v14i2.2042

Yeung, D., & Fosha, D. (2015). Accelerated experiential dynamic psychotherapy. In E. S. Neukrug (Ed.), *The Sage encyclopedia of theory in counseling and psychotherapy* (Vol. 1, pp. 1–5). Sage Publications.

Yeung, D., Fosha, D., Ye Perman, J., & Xu, Y. (2019). After Freud meets Zhuangzi: Stance and the dance of the self-in-transformation with the other-in-contemplative presence. *Psychological Communications, 2*(3), 179–185.

# HEALING FROM
# THE GET-GO

# 1

# How AEDP Works

Diana Fosha

What is it about AEDP that allows it to do what it does? What change mechanisms does it recruit to undo aloneness and transform emotional suffering into flourishing? In this chapter, I provide a synopsis of accelerated experiential dynamic psychotherapy (AEDP) and its defining characteristics.

First, I consider fundamental orientation, ethos, and values and the affective change mechanisms quintessential to AEDP 2.0's operation: (a) healing and theory of change, (b) undoing aloneness, (c) experiential processing of the negative emotions associated with trauma and emotional suffering, and (d) metatherapeutic processing of the positive emotions associated with transformation and change for the better. Next, the chapter explores how AEDP conceptualizes psychopathology and its relationship to healing. Then I describe the phenomenology of AEDP's four-state transformational process. The chapter concludes with a section on flourishing, the neurobiology of the core self, and intactness of the core.

## FUNDAMENTAL ORIENTATION, ETHOS, AND VALUES: AEDP'S TOP 10

An orientation toward healing is AEDP's "North Star." Both its theory and moment-to-moment experiential practice are guided by the foundational principle that healing is an innate, wired-in, biological process, ever present in all of us. This drive to heal resides within everyone, no matter what. No matter

https://doi.org/10.1037/0000232-002
*Undoing Aloneness and the Transformation of Suffering Into Flourishing: AEDP 2.0*, D. Fosha (Editor)

how traumatic our histories, we are not just bundles of pathology, doomed to repeat the past in endless, repetition compulsion. Lodged deeply in our brains and bodies lie dispositions for healing and self-righting that surface under conditions of safety; they are there for the awakening from the first moments of the first session onward, for the duration of the treatment. Below are AEDP's Top 10, i.e., 10 fundamental aspects of AEDP theory and clinical practice.

## 1. We Begin: Healing From the Get-Go

Because the seeds for healing and self-righting are innate and ever present, AEDP practitioners believe in *healing from the get-go*, that is, in the very first session and then in every session thereafter. Given our wired-in dispositions for healing and self-righting, our aim is to entrain them and harness their healing potential for the therapy. We nurture these seeds by providing a safe and facilitating environment.

Not believing that repetition compulsion is inevitable or that the corrective emotional experience can only be a different ending to the same old, same old (Alexander & French, 1946), in AEDP, we strive to *lead with* the corrective emotional experience (Fosha, 2000b). From the beginning, the patient needs to have an experience, a new experience, and that experience should be good— that is, it should feel right and true. From the first moment of the first contact, and throughout treatment thereafter, the aim and method of AEDP is the provision, facilitation, and then experiential processing of such experiences.

*Transformance* is AEDP's term for the innate motivational drive to heal, self-right, and flourish (Fosha, 2008, 2017a). Transformance reflects positive neuro-plasticity (Hanson, 2017, 2018) in action, that is, the brain's capacity to change for the better. This drive and potential, which requires safety to come to the fore, is marked moment-to-moment by positive somatic and affective markers of vitality and energy. Defined as "spontaneous physiological rhythms that are manifest in arousal fluctuations" (Schore, 2001, p. 21), we call these positive somatic/affective markers *vitality affects* (Stern, 1985/2000). By "positive" we do not necessarily mean happy (though of course happy is included): instead, positive refers to a quality of experience that has the subjective felt sense of feeling "right" and "true" the way being able to straighten a crooked picture on the wall feels right once it is properly aligned. This applies even in the midst of painful experiences, the way being able to grieve a loss feels right, even if wrenching.

When moments marked by genuine vitality and energy occur, particularly in the midst of defensiveness or demoralization, it is important for the therapist to take them out of the background and bring them experientially into the foreground. We call this *transformance detection*. At every moment of every session, we are on the lookout for evidence of this wired-in drive to heal and then foster it for the individual's well-being. Thus, a central focus of clinical work in AEDP is finding and then amplifying these glimmers of transformance by noticing them, focusing on them and then experientially working with them.

## 2. A Change-Based Theory of Therapeutic Action

A model of therapy needs in its essence to be a model of change. The meta-psychology of the therapeutic process (i.e., how to bring about change for the better in therapy) should not be derived from a theory of psychopathology (i.e., a theory of how things go wrong). Rather, a theory of therapy should function as a strong explanatory framework in its own right, rooted in a theory of how things go right.

The orientation toward healing translates directly into a change-based, rather than pathology-oriented, theory of therapeutic action. AEDP's theory of how therapy works is not rooted in psychopathology; in other words, it is not based on understanding the mechanisms of psychopathology and then seeking to reverse or counteract them. Instead, AEDP's theory of therapeutic action is rooted in *transformational studies*, fields of endeavor devoted to investigating positive, fundamentally adaptive, naturally occurring, affective change processes that operate powerfully, often rapidly and dramatically—transformationally—yielding substantive changes that are often lasting. The evidence from transformational studies points to affective processes experienced within the context of an affirming relationship as being central in such quantum transformations.

AEDP is particularly interested in naturally occurring, adaptive affective mechanisms of quantum change, that is, discontinuous processes (Adler et al., 2013; Hansen et al., 2015; Hayes et al., 2007; Miller & C'deBaca, 2001), and developing therapeutic methods for recruiting them in the service of the therapeutic work.

### Transformational Studies and Naturally Occurring Adaptive Affective Change Processes

Several transformational affective change processes inform the practice of AEDP 2.0.

1. *Emotion theory and affective neuroscience* (Damasio, 1999; Darwin, 1872/1965; Davidson et al., 2000; Panksepp, 1998) offer an account of change intrinsic to the experience of the categorical emotions, universal phenomena initiating in the subcortical regions of the human brain characterized by specific neurophysiological, facial and body signatures, and by the state transformations and adaptive action tendencies released upon their full, complete, somatically based experience and expression.

2. *Attachment theory* (Bowlby, 1988, 1991; Fonagy et al., 1994, 1995; Hesse & Main, 1999; Main, 1999) and the work of clinical developmentalists on moment-to-moment caregiver–infant interaction (Beebe & Lachmann, 1994; Emde, 1988; Sander, 2002; Stern, 1985/2000; Trevarthen, 2001; Tronick, 1989, 2009) document how optimal development and lifelong resilient functioning have their roots in child–caregiver dyadic processes. Their work highlights the moment-to-moment processes by which infants and caregivers mutually regulate affective states and achieve safety and resonance despite vicissitudes of attachment, self-states, and relatedness.

3. *Somatically rooted experiential and humanistic traditions* (Gendlin, 1981, 1996; Levine, 2010; Perls, 1969; Schneider, 2008) have documented how the psyche is transformed through the simple shifting of focus away from in-the-head cognition and toward in-the-body sensing and feeling ("lose your head and come to your senses"), a process that restores access to the wisdom of the body and releases natural healing processes rooted in the body's basic adaptive strivings and self-righting tendencies. (see also Emde, 1988, on wired-in self-righting tendencies).

4. Finally, there are the explorations of the natural history of *transformational change experiences in adults around experiences of heightened affect* (Beebe & Lachmann, 1994), in the contexts of romantic love (Person, 1988), spirituality and religious conversion (James, 1902; Miller & C'deBaca, 2001), quintessentially relational moments of meeting when self meets self and both are transformed (Buber, 1955), emotional surrender (Ghent, 1990), and spontaneous shared experiences of repairing disruptions in development and therapy. These are processes by which intense, novel, sudden, undefended, and surprising emotional experiences can lead to lasting and even lifelong transformations (Stern et al., 1998; Tronick, 2009).

To illustrate transformational (in contradistinction to slow and gradual) change, I share a favorite quote from William James (1902):

> Emotional occasions . . . are extremely potent in precipitating mental rearrangements. The sudden and explosive ways in which love, jealousy, guilt, fear, remorse, or anger can seize upon one are known to everybody. Hope, happiness, security, resolve . . . can be equally explosive. And emotions that come in this explosive way seldom leave things as they found them. (p. 198)

Adopting James's language, we can say that AEDP is about "precipitating [embodied] mental rearrangements."

Affective change processes have potentially transformational powers that can be harnessed to actively foster therapeutic change for the better. It is precisely this rootedness in transformational studies, rather than in pathology-based theories of therapy, that distinguishes AEDP and has led to the development of AEDP as fundamentally healing-oriented in its theory, metatherapeutics, and clinical practice.

### 3. Experiential and Phenomenological

In addition to its orientation toward healing, equally fundamental is AEDP's experiential focus. The "E" in AEDP occupies a lot of real estate because this mind–body therapy is relentlessly experiential in both ethos and technique. Working experientially refers to an intensive focus on present-tense, internal experience, especially the felt sense of an affective experience as it arises in the body in the here-and-now of the therapeutic encounter; it involves encouraging patients' attention to it and then proceeding to actively work with that experience. Working experientially also involves grounding the work in the moment-to-moment tracking of fluctuations in the experience of patient, dyad, therapist, and process (see Hanakawa, Chapter 4, this volume) and using those fluctuations to guide choice of intervention.

The relentlessly experiential focus of AEDP is key and inextricably intertwined with its change-forward theory. This experiential focus is supported by a paradigm shift in our field, informed by the neuroscientific revolution of the past 2 decades: from a privileging of top-down cognitive attention to thoughts and behaviors, we are witnessing "the shift to a bodily based [i.e., bottom-up] emotional psychotherapy that integrates psychology and biology" (Schore, 2016, p. xii; see also Panksepp, 2009). AEDP's innovations are rooted in privileging bottom-up processing of bodily based experience and seeing that as fundamental to change. Thus, and especially important, healing, safety, attachment, relatedness, and transformation are not only processes to be activated and engaged; in AEDP, they are also crucial bodily based *experiences* to be explored.

### A Phenomenological Sensibility: A Humility Before Phenomena

The moment-to-moment practice of AEDP is phenomenology-driven. This phenomenological sensibility together with AEDP's focus on discontinuous processes of change has led to the precise articulation of the state-specific phenomenology of the transformational process, where each of the four states is characterized by a particular organization (discussed in detail later in the chapter). This phenomenology allows therapists to orient themselves within the transformational process and navigate the terrain of change. As such, it supports "rigor without shame" in both practice and training (Prenn & Fosha, 2017). Phenomena, rather than pet theories, gives us the thumbs up or thumbs down as to whether we are on the right track with any given intervention. Phenomena keeps us humble and always learning.

Yet adaptive affective phenomena, like transformance, require safety to come to the fore. Undoing aloneness is one of the AEDP's main contribution to the coconstruction of safety.

### 4. A Deliberately Positive, Emotionally Engaged Therapist Stance

Aloneness in the face of overwhelming emotion is the epicenter of psychological suffering. AEDP proposes that psychopathology results from "the individual's unwilled and unwanted aloneness" (Fosha, 2009a, p. 182) in the face of emotions too overwhelming to feel, much less regulate and process to completion. This formulation leads to a simple understanding of what needs to happen in therapy. First and foremost is undoing the aloneness of the patient. Then, once patients feel accompanied, the therapeutic dyad can work to help patients experientially access and then dyadically regulate and process experiences that were previously too difficult to contend with alone.

The AEDP therapist is actively and explicitly affirming, validating, empathic. AEDP's transformational practices blossom because they are rooted in an intentionally positive (Lipton & Fosha, 2011), embodied, attachment-informed, intersubjectively and emotionally engaged therapeutic relationship that seeks to replicate "the sociobiology of kin-recognition, secure attachment, limbic resonance, mammalian caregiving, and early development" (Loizzo, 2017, p. 188). "Dyadic mindfulness" (Fosha, 2013b, 2017b), a strong "being with" (Pando-Mars, 2016), the active use of affirmation (Tunnell, 2006, 2011), "fierce love" (Piliero, Chapter 10, this volume), and explicit affirmative advocacy on behalf of patients' fundamental worthiness are other important aspects of the stance.

### Attachment, Sprinkled With Intersubjective Delight

AEDP's therapist stance is based on attachment, sprinkled liberally with inter-subjective delight in and with the patient. Following Lyons-Ruth (2007), Trevarthen (2001), and Tronick (2003), who regard attachment motives for care and protection as different from intersubjective motives for pleasurable companionship, AEDP's stance is conceived as having two strands. In the *attachment-informed strand*, we meet pain, suffering, and fear with empathy and dyadic affect regulation, broadcasting our willingness to both help and be there. Going beyond mirroring, we seek to undo aloneness by demonstrating our willingness not only to accompany that patient but also to bear and share the patient's emotional pain. In the *intersubjective strand*, we focus on, and delight in, the quintessential qualities of the self of the patient. The therapist's delighting in and with the patient is one of the most powerful antidotes to the patient's shame (Hughes, 2017; Kaufman, 1996; Trevarthen, 2001).

### Genuine Emotional Engagement

The AEDP therapist's genuine affective engagement and responsiveness is crucial. AEDP's emphasis on establishing a genuine relationship with the patient, based in the neuroscience of right-brain-to-right-brain communication, fosters moment-to-moment psychobiological state attunement between the members of the dyad (Schore, 2019). Neither undoing aloneness nor dyadic affect regulation nor expressing intersubjective delight can be done with a neutral face or gaze. Neutrality is actually contraindicated.

Therapists are not only attuned to their patient's moment-to-moment state; they are also attuned to their own experience (Lipton, Chapter 5, this volume). And they are also "experientially involved in the relational matrix by reciprocating self-disclosing of [their] own immediate experiences, especially affective experiences in response to the client and/or process" (Iwakabe & Conceição, 2016, pp. 232–233; see also Prenn, 2009).

### Applying Attachment to Therapy

It is essential to establish a patient–therapist relationship in which the patient feels safe. From within an attachment perspective, emotional safety is defined as not being alone with frightening experiences. The safer the patient feels with the therapist, the greater will be that patient's capacity to explore the inner worlds of disturbing, frightening, and painful emotional experiences. In AEDP, we want to proceed from a position of safety to be able to explore what is frightening, shameful, painful, and problematic, as well as what is vulnerable, tender, highly personal. In both development and therapy, in a safe, affect-facilitating environment, affective change processes can be harnessed for the optimal adaptation of the individual.

### The Therapist's Expression of Intersubjective Delight and the "We" Relational Affects

AEDP therapists recognize the importance of spontaneously expressing positive responses to the patient as a highly effective way to both counter and combat shame (Kaufman, 1996); we also know that positively valenced states of psychobiological state attunement are vital to the development of secure attachment (Schore, 2019). We do not hesitate to express our delight in our patients. When moments of connection or resonance occur, we also explore the patient's experience of these new relational experiences. This often leads to experiences of dyadically expanded resonant states of connection and being in sync (Tronick, 2009), accompanied by what we call the relational affects (Fosha, 2000b, 2017b) expressed in "we" language (Emde, 1988).

### 5. Experiential Work With Here-and-Now Relational Experience

*Relational processing* in AEDP refers to working experientially with the patient's experience of the therapeutic relationship in the here-and-now of the therapeutic dyad. In AEDP, attachment and intersubjectivity are not just processes humming in the background, silently working their potent magic; they are also important, and most often new, relational experiences, which, if worked with explicitly and experientially, can be further transformative. There is an AEDP saying: "Make the implicit explicit and the explicit experiential."

By engaging in relational processing and working directly with felt experiences of attachment and intersubjectivity, AEDP therapists foster new experiences of the emotion-in-connection that facilitate earned attachment security in the therapy (Harrison, 2020). It is that which transforms patients' internal working models (Fosha, 2017b; Frederick, 2019; and Pando-Mars, Chapter 6, this volume).

For relational work to be effective, it is not sufficient for the therapist to be caring, empathic, affirming, or validating. Those ways of being are effective if and only if the patient is able to receive that which the therapist is offering. To ascertain this, we use the technique of relational processing—that is, we explore the patient's receptive affective experience, or lack thereof, of the therapist's care, empathy, or validation: Does the patient feel cared about, empathized with, or validated? And if so, what's that experience like? We want to make the implicit explicit through focused inquiry, and then make the explicit experiential by exploring the experience of receiving the stuff of which attachment is made. We are as interested in what patients can take in from us as in what they cannot take in and have blocks against.

Receptive affective experiences are often described in terms of bodily sensations of warmth, melting, or tingling. One patient said that her therapist's empathy felt like "warm liquid honey down her esophagus" (J. Osiason, personal communication, July 13, 2005). Receptive affective experiences of feeling cared for, loved, seen, and delighted in are transformative: They solidify the patient's experience of feeling felt (Siegel, 2012) and understood. For "[t]he biological need to feel understood . . . takes precedence over almost all other goals" (Fonagy et al., 1995, pp. 268–269).

The goal is for patients to viscerally know that they exist in our hearts and minds (Fosha, 2000b, 2003). The phrase "existing in the heart and mind of the other" is an extension of Fonagy's (1997) "existing in the mind of the other." I added "heart" to that phrase to make the implicit explicit. Knowing that one exists in the mind and heart of the other, as oneself, is the essence of being and feeling understood, which is in turn at the heart of attachment security and resilience in the face of trauma:

> The roots of resilience and the capacity to withstand emotionally aversive situations without resorting to defensive exclusion are to be found in the sense of being understood by and existing in the mind and heart of a loving, attuned, and self-possessed other. (Fosha, 2000b, p. 60)

## 6. "Stay With It and Stay With Me": Dyadic Affect Regulation

Dyadic affect regulation organically and inextricably links undoing aloneness and the experiential processing of affective experiences. Dyadic affect regulation refers to the therapist's help in regulating emotional experiences that felt, and still feel, too overwhelming to the individual to process alone. In such moments, the affect-laden experiences exceed the regulatory capacities of the individual.

Dyadic affect regulation is achieved moment-to-moment through right-brain-to-right brain attunement to the patient's psychobiological state (Schore, 2019) and also entraining the process of attunement, disruption, and repair (Tronick, 2009), for rarely is attunement uninterruptedly flawless. When there are misses, disruptions, and ruptures, dyadic affect regulation involves the repair of the disruption to achieve recoordination. In keeping with developmental theory, when the goal is always to enhance the individual's own affect regulatory capacities, when emotional experience is overwhelming, then the dyad can do what the individual can't do alone. Over time, we work to ensure that the affect regulatory strategies of the dyad become internalized in the individual's psychic structure. This is how children develop their affect regulation. Given that we know that attachment is a process that operates from cradle to grave (Bowlby, 1982), the internalization of effective dyadic strategies is also a lifelong process. This has been extensively written about in the AEDP literature (Fosha, 2001, 2003, 2009b, 2017b; Lamagna, 2011; Lipton & Fosha, 2011; Prenn, 2011; Tunnell, 2011) and figures prominently in the clinical work that is presented in many of the chapters of this volume.

When the dyad is effective in processing what the individual could not process alone, not only is there learning by internalizing the regulatory strategies of the dyad, there is also very important relational learning. Individuals learn that when things are too much for the self alone, it is possible to reach out to others. The capacity to trust and ask for help is as crucial to our well-being in our community of humans as is high affect regulatory capacity (Cassidy, 2001).

## 7. The Experiential Processing of the Deep Negative Affects Associated With Trauma and Emotional Suffering

Because evolution has wired emotion and other affective change processes into our brains, bodies, and nervous systems, adaptive core affective phenomena, when regulated and processed, naturally lead to transformation. In addition to emotion, other adaptive affective change processes include (a) the reprocessing of interpersonal relational experience (discussed later in this chapter; see also Frederick, Chapter 7, this volume); (b) working with intrarelational aspects of emotional experience (see Lamagna, 2011; Lamagna & Gleiser, 2007; see also Gleiser, Chapter 12; Lamagna, Chapter 11, this volume); (c) the processing of new experiences of self (see Fosha, 2013a; also Piliero, Chapter 10, this volume); and (d) working with experiences of agency, will, and desire (Russell, Chapter 9, this volume).

Motivation is intrinsic to emotion. Each emotion contains within it the pulse toward its own completion: Emotions evoke bodily changes to support specific action programs, called adaptive action tendencies (Frijda, 1986). Each emotion's adaptive action tendency "offers a distinctive readiness to act; each points us in a direction that has worked well to handle the recurrent challenges of human life" (Goleman, 1995, p. 4). The release of the adaptive action tendencies wired into each emotion is invariably accompanied by positive affect. Their release orients and empowers people to act on their needs, accessing deep emotional resources, renewed energy, and an expanded repertoire of adaptive behaviors (Medley, Chapter 8, this volume).

Trauma and insufficient support for dyadic affect regulation interfere with that process. The methodology of AEDP has patient and therapist emotionally engaged as they together track moment-to-moment fluctuations in affective experience, energy, somatic contact, and connection to be able to dyadically regulate affective experiences. Within the field of safety coconstructed by the dyad, the focus of the work is on helping the patient access, process, and work through previously overwhelming emotional experiences, through a variety of experiential emotion-processing techniques (Fosha, 2000b, 2003) until there is a shift from a negative affective valence ("something doesn't feel good") to a positive affective valence ("something feels good"). The emergence of positive affect signals the release of the adaptive action tendencies and the positive post-breakthrough affects that are the hallmark of successfully processed adaptive emotions (Russell & Fosha, 2008) and other affective change processes. However, what is often an endpoint in other treatment modalities is the starting point of a new round of exploration in AEDP, which is now focused on the experiential processing of these emergent positive affects as systematically as the processing of the negative affects that began the round (Fosha et al., 2020). Enter metatherapeutic processing.

## 8. Metatherapeutic Processing: Processing the Positive Affects Associated With Transformational Experience to Support the Emergence of In-Session Flourishing

With accumulating clinical experience informing the development of the model, we have come to increasingly appreciate how much the processing of positive affective experience has to contribute—not only to healing trauma and emotional suffering but also to bringing about enhanced resilience, well-being, and flourishing.

AEDP has developed a transformational methodology for facilitating the systematic emergence of in-session flourishing (Fosha & Thoma, 2020) through progressive rounds of experiential work with positive emotions: *metatherapeutic processing*, or metaprocessing, a unique and central element of AEDP, describes a way of working with transformational experiences and the transformational affects, the innate healing affects associated with them. It involves experientially investigating what is healing about healing, in the context of a healing relationship. Extensively written about (Fosha, 2000a, 2000b, 2009a, 2009b, 2013b, 2018; Fosha et al., 2020; Fosha & Yeung, 2006; Russell, 2015; Russell & Fosha, 2008; Yeung et al., 2019), metaprocessing has also been the subject of empirical interest and investigation (Iwakabe & Conceição, 2016; Lee, 2015).

In AEDP, transformation is not only a desired goal or process to be entrained; it is also an experience to be harnessed and amplified. We have discovered that experientially processing the experience of transformation is itself transformational, giving rise to yet another round of transformational affects, to be further processed experientially, which gives rise to new and different transformational affects, and so on. Each new experience, once explored in the context of safe attachment, becomes the platform for the next round of exploration. Each new reaching becomes a platform for the next reaching. The essence of metatherapeutic processing is the exploration of an experience of change for the better, which is invariably accompanied by positive affect, followed by reflection on that experience, which in turn gives rise to more positive affect and more change.

AEDP not only precipitates the embodied mental rearrangements that transform trauma, but through metaprocessing, it precipitates more and more embodied "mental rearrangements" and these eventuate in flourishing.

## 9. Flourishing and the Upward Spiral

As noted earlier, we have discovered over countless clinical encounters that focusing on the experience of transformation itself unleashes further rounds of transformation, through which positive changes can be powerfully consolidated, deepened, and expanded in a momentum-generating spiral of healing. Progressive rounds of metatherapeutic processing lead to a nonlinear, nonfinite, transformational spiral, an ever-emergent upward movement (Fredrickson, 2009, 2013) that fuels the system with more and more energy

and vitality (Fosha, 2009a, 2009b). and eventuates in flourishing (Fosha &
Thoma, 2020).

When new pursuits and experiences are accompanied by positive affect,
they bring more energy into the system and recharge the spiral yet again. As
we exercise our new capacities, they become part and parcel of who we are,
new platforms on which to stand and reach for the next level. As I have
written before,

> These positive emotion transformational processes are by their very nature
> recursive processes, where more begets more. This is not a satiation model or a
> tension reduction model, but rather an appetitive model. Desire comes in the
> doing. The more we do something that feels good, the more we want to do more
> of it. (Fosha, 2009a, p. 202)

Likewise, Ghent (2002) wrote that

> just as motivational systems lead to the emergence of new capacities and func-
> tions, so too do new capacities beget new motivational derivatives in an ever
> more complex developmental spiral. (p. 763) . . .
>
>    The acquisition of a new capability is itself a perturbation that destabilizes the
> existing state of motivational organization. To the extent that the use of the new
> capacity provides pleasure and satisfaction, diminishes pain or distress, and, in
> some way, enhances survival, there will, barring inhibitory circumstances, emerge
> a new need to execute and develop the capacity. Functional capacities acquire a
> new feature—the need to exercise that capacity and expand its range. (p. 782)

Thus, "recursive cycles of healing transformation and emergent phenomena
give rise to new transformational cycles and new phenomena, and those give
rise to new capacities that translate into broadened thought-action repertoires" (Fosha, 2009a, pp. 202–203).

AEDP both seeks to make happen and is organized around *moments of
change*. These moments of change for the better, healing moments, or transformational moments—all terms I use interchangeably—are manifestations
of positive neuroplasticity (Hanson, 2017) in clinical action.

At any given moment, the clinician faces a multitude of possible entry
points for intervention. The principles guiding that choice is a defining aspect
of any clinical model. In AEDP, given a choice between focusing on the "same
old, same old" (the result of grooved rigid maladaptive patterns) or a new and
emergent positive experience, we choose the latter (Prenn & Fosha, 2017).
By focusing both on what is positive and also new and emergent, and doing
so recursively, AEDP's methodology gives positive neuroplasticity a hand. To
make something new stick in such a way that it can become integrated and
made more permanent, repetition and sustained practice are required, along
with the conditions of curiosity, motivation, energy, and pleasure (Doidge,
2007). These elements are key for new procedural knowledge to stand a
chance against old procedural knowledge (Hanson, 2017). What strengthens
neuroplasticity and the new synaptic connections to which it gives rise are
"repetition, emotional arousal, novelty, and careful focus of attention" (Siegel,
2010, p. 40). Privileging the new and emergent experiences and then metaprocessing them fulfill those conditions.

## 10. The Transformational Process

AEDP's transformational process organically links emotional suffering with flourishing. It connects a biopsychoevolutionary perspective at one end with acceptance, wisdom, aesthetics, spirituality, and the quest for personal truth at the other. These are seamlessly interlinked through AEDP's four-state model, which guides our therapeutic practice.

The phenomenology of the four states of the transformational process is described later, in the last third of this chapter. However it seemed fitting to end this major section on AEDP's Top 10 with an account of the transformational process that ties it all together.

AEDP's four-state phenomenology of the transformational process (see Figure 1.1 later in the chapter) differentiates between (a) defense-dominated states in which transformational work cannot happen and (b) states where there is embodied somatic access to deep affective change processes. What is involved from the beginning and throughout all four states of the transformational process is the simultaneous cocreation of safety and undoing aloneness. With that foundation and with our moment-to-moment using AEDP's North Star—that is, transformance—to orient ourselves, the remaining sequence through the states is as follows: minimizing the impact of defenses and regulating anxiety to "drop down" to embodied experience; then processing bodily rooted adaptive core affective experience to completion, then metatherapeutically processing the transformational experiences that thus emerge, to then finally reap the fruits of integration in core state. Through such a process, the negative emotions associated with trauma and emotional suffering become transformed into the positive emotions that accompany the emergent transformation and support the emergence of in-session flourishing.

Having elaborated the fundamentals that constitute AEDP's healing-oriented ethos, the next section explores how AEDP, in light of its healing orientation, conceptualizes psychopathology and its development.

## HOW AEDP CONCEPTUALIZES PSYCHOPATHOLOGY AND ITS RELATIONSHIP TO HEALING

As I described earlier, AEDP understands psychopathology as being rooted in the individual's unwilled and unwanted aloneness in the face of emotional experiences that are too painful or overwhelming to bear. Defense mechanisms arise to ensure the individual's survival in adverse conditions. Because defenses so restrict the movement through adaptive affective change processes, when reliance on them becomes chronic, the result is the development of psychopathology. Let's explore how psychopathology unfolds developmentally from within the vantage point of an attachment and emotion and transformation model.

## Resilience

What is important to aver before I unfold the aforementioned development is that in AEDP, we also view psychopathology as evidence of *resilience*, defined by Russell (2015) as reflecting the individual's best adaptive efforts in the face of impossibly adverse circumstances. Much as over time, there is increasing emotional suffering, the very application of defense mechanisms or protective mechanisms is evidence of the individual's capacities exercised on behalf of the self's survival. This understanding is also resonant with Porges's polyvagal theory and the understanding that even the most primitive (evolutionarily speaking) autonomic nervous system responses to threat or life endangerment (i.e., the shutdown mediated by the dorsal vagal branch of the parasympathetic nervous system) still reflect the fundamentally adaptive strivings of the organism.

## The Development of Psychopathology

The child's emotions, be they painful or intense, or joyful for that matter, require support, holding, and dyadic regulation to be able to be handled by the child, so that their adaptive benefits can be reaped. In pathogenic environments (i.e., relational environments that give rise to psychopathology) the child's intense emotions, instead of evoking caregiver care, evoke profound discomfort (i.e., dis-ease) in the caregiver. Caregivers' own unresolved losses, trauma, or attachment traumas are activated. Their own "stuff" thus online, caregivers respond either with errors of omission (e.g., withdrawal, distancing, neglect, denial), or with errors of commission (e.g., blaming, shaming, punishing, attacking). These relational lapses are profoundly disturbing to the child because they disrupt or perhaps even rupture the attachment bond. That's how psychopathology begins.

## Defensive Exclusion

In the absence of relational support and dyadic affect regulation, the individual's aloneness in the face of overwhelming emotions sows the seeds for reliance on defensive strategies instituted to ensure short-term survival. The survival of the attachment relationship becomes possible only through the defensive exclusion (Bowlby, 1988) of the very affective processes that constitute optimal psychic health because those are intolerable to the attachment figure. Core affective experiences and their adaptive consequences are thus preempted, leaving the individual with terribly reduced resources to face the challenges of the world.

## Pathogenic Affects

However, the rupture of the attachment relationship elicits yet another wave of overwhelming emotional reactions, amplifying the initial stress, emotional pain, and emotional overwhelm: the experience of "fear without solution" (Hesse & Main, 1999; i.e., children's being afraid of the very caregiver who is supposed to protect them), toxic shame drenching the child's whole self as a result of the caregiver's attacks or neglect (Piliero, Chapter 10, this volume); or underregulated affective experiences (Lamagna, Chapter 11, this volume). These are the pathogenic affects, the term *pathogenic* indicating that not only are these emotions not transformative, the experience of them can actually be pathology-producing. Pathogenic affects are highly aversive to the person experiencing them, and their hallmark is that they are experienced by an individual who feels alone and overwhelmed because the holding and affect-regulatory function of the attachment relationship has collapsed.

### Unbearable States of Traumatic Aloneness

The combination of overwhelming emotions, disrupted attachment ties, and the resultant pathogenic affects in the context of unwilled and unwanted aloneness leads to unbearable states of traumatic aloneness: brokenness, help-lessness, hopelessness, loneliness, confusion, fragmentation, the fear of falling apart, emptiness, and despair, the "black hole of trauma" (van der Kolk, 2014). Here individuals are at their most depleted, with no safety, no accompani-ment, and no access to emotional resources. The self feels broken and alone, with no help, no hope, or both.

### Maladaptive Affective Experiences

Both the pathogenic affects and the unbearable states of traumatic aloneness are types of maladaptive affective experiences. They are maladaptive because they compromise the individual's capacity to function and relate. Yet these do reflect deep emotional responses, rooted in the body, responses that occur in direct reaction to experience, such as neglect, abandonment, and abuse. Excruciating and overwhelming to the self, the maladaptive affective experi-ences, like the adaptive core affective experiences, also become the objects of defense and eventuate in more psychopathology or languishing.

Given our belief in the presence of the potential for healing being there no matter what our histories, how does AEDP reconcile its healing-oriented focus with psychopathology?

## IMPORTANCE OF SAFETY

The key is safety or lack thereof. Wired-in dispositions for healing and self-righting are always there as dispositional tendencies, but they come to the fore only in conditions of safety. When safety isn't to be had, something else happens: the development of psychopathology.

**Transformance and Resistance**

Let us put this in the context of understanding basic motivational forces in the psyche. We have already discussed *transformance*, which is a motivational force moving toward growth, healing, and self-repair. In AEDP, we recognize another motivational force, however. Side by side with transformance, is a force we call *resistance*, and it is the motivational force to survive (Fosha, 2008, 2013a). Whereas transformance is expansive, risk-taking, and growth-oriented, resistance is constrictive, conservative, and survival-oriented. It is crucial to remember that transformance and resistance are both forces reflecting adaptation but adaptation to fundamentally different emotional environments. Because we recognize that defenses were developed to ensure survival, we respect defenses and our patients' resistance, all while working to minimize their impact.

Transformance requires safety to come online. In safe and affect-facilitating environments, the expansive forces of transformance come to the fore. However, when there is no safety and the individual is alone in affect-thwarting environments inimical to the self, the conservative forces of resistance come online. Absent the attachment relationship, with the integrity of their self threatened, individuals need protective mechanisms to ensure survival.

**Self-at-Best and Self-at-Worst**

Transformance and resistance respectively give rise to two different psychic organizations: The expansive progressive forces of transformance, manifesting in conditions of safety and fueled by hope, organize *self-at-best* experiences in the individual's psyche. The constrictive, conservative forces of resistance, manifesting in environments where the individual does not feel safe and fueled by dread, organize *self-at-worst* experiences in the individual's psyche. Self-at-best and self-at-worst each have a characteristic organization, in other words, different ways in which affect regulation, memory, perception, self, other, and self–other interactions are organized. The ratio of safety to threat in the patient's environment determines which motivational force and respective self-organization is dominant at a given moment.

It is important to underscore that both self-at-worst and self-at-best reflect the individual's best efforts at adaptation. For even the forces of resistance, in the institution of defenses, reflect the self's fundamentally adaptive strivings—its resilience, defined by Russell (2015) as "the self's differentiation from that which is aversive to it" (p. 29).

Nevertheless, the conservative motivational strivings of resistance consume and drain psychic energy and result in languishing, stuckness, and stagnation. Moment to moment, they are marked by negative somatic affect markers, such as tension, depletion, or agitation. In contradistinction, a felt sense of vitality and energy characterizes transformance-based emergent phenomena and the positive somatic–affective markers that accompany them.

Being on the lookout for glimmers of transformance, marked by vitality and energy, to recruit their energetic resources for therapeutic work is a core principle of AEDP work. We seek to work with the self-at-worst under the aegis of self-at best.

Transformance and resistance, self-at-best and self-at worst, healing and psychopathology all coexist. AEDP therapists thus seek to entrain the transformational process to be able to join with the patient, undo aloneness, and together—therapist and the patient's self-at-best—we can work with the patient's self-at-worst, now under conditions of safety, thereby seeking to transform processes that got stuck or became misshaped in conditions of threat or life danger. Enter a clinical practice guided by the transformational process.

Russell (2015) provided us with a good bridge:

> Healing is not simply the receipt and integration of some exogenous corrective experience but, rather, or also, the realignment of one's mode of being from resistance to transformation, from conservation and safety to expansion and freedom. It is a signal switch and a track change. One starts to use something that has been there but has been dormant or distorted and therefore unable to serve one's needs for expansion, exploration, and the elaboration of one's true self. (p. 252)

## MOMENT-TO-MOMENT GUIDANCE OF CLINICAL WORK BY TRANSFORMATIONAL PHENOMENOLOGY

The moment-to-moment guidance of clinical practice by the ethos of a healing orientation and the phenomenology of the transformational process is foundational to AEDP's systematic clinical work. It allows therapists to orient themselves within the transformational process.

Moment-to-moment clinical practice is guided by the phenomenology of four states of the transformational process. Paying attention to the distinctive phenomenology of each state and then working with it systematically allows therapists to orient themselves in any given session and informs our points of entry, our choice of intervention and then of the next intervention based on what the response the current intervention was. Figure 1.1 summarizes the phenomena that characterize each of the four states.

### State 1: Transformance Detection, Undoing Aloneness, and Inviting Felt Experience

We begin with how our patients are when they arrive, with emotional suffering and demoralization. There are two aspects of State 1. On one hand, we have stress, distress, symptoms, and stuckness (the State 1 rectangle on the left in Figure 1.1), resulting from both the success (hyperregulation) and failure (dysregulation) of defenses. The therapist's aim is to reduce the impact of defenses and alleviate the alternately inhibitory or dysregulating impact of affects such as shame and anxiety to help the individual gain access to somatically rooted

**FIGURE 1.1. The Phenomenology of the Four-State Transformational Process in AEDP**

**STATE 1: Stress, Distress, & Symptoms**
Defenses; inhibiting affects (e.g., anxiety, shame, guilt); stress; demoralization; entrenched defenses and pathogenic self states

**STATE 1: Transformance**
Glimmers of resilience, health, strength; manifestations of the drive to heal

**1st STATE TRANSFORMATION**
Cocreating safety; detecting transformance; promoting bodily-based affective experience

**Transitional Affects:** Intrapsychic crisis; heralding affects, i.e., glimmers of core affective experience
**GREEN Signal Affects:** Announcing openness to experience, signaling safety, readiness to shift

**STATE 2: Adaptive Core Affective Experiences**
**"The Wave"**
Categorical emotions; relational experiences, asymmetric (attachment) or symmetric (intersubjective); coordinated relational experiences; receptive affective experiences; somatic "drop-down" states; intrarelational experiences; authentic self-experiences; experiences of agency, will and desire; attachment strivings; the expression of core needs

**2nd STATE TRANSFORMATION**
The emergence of resilience

**Post-Breakthrough Affects:** Relief, hope, feeling stronger, lighter, etc.
**Adaptive Action Tendencies**

**STATE 3: Transformational Experiences**
**"The Spiral"**
*The mastery affects* (e.g., pride, joy); *the mourning-the-self affects* (emotional pain); *the healing affects* associated with recognition and affirmation of the transformation of the self (gratitude, tenderness, feeling moved); *the tremulous affects* associated with the intense, new experiences; *the enlivening affects* (exuberance, enthusiasm, exploratory zest) associated with delighting in the surprise at the unbrokenness of the self; *the realization affects* (e.g., the "yes!" and "wow" affects, the "click" of recognition) associated with new understanding

**3rd STATE TRANSFORMATION**
The coengendering of secure attachment and the positive valuation of the self

**Energy, Vitality, Openness, Aliveness**

**STATE 4: CORE STATE and The Truth Sense**
**"The Broad Path"**
Calm, flow, ease; I/Thou relating; openness; compassion and self-compassion; sense of clarity; wisdom, generosity, kindness; the sense of things feeling "right;" the experience of "this is me;" new truth, new meaning; the emergence of a coherent and cohesive autobiographical narrative

*Note.* Copyright 2020 by Diana Fosha. Reprinted with permission.

core affective experiences. However there is the other aspect of State 1; side by side with the sequelae of trauma and defense-dominated functioning, the realm of psychopathology, marked by negative somatic affective markers, we also see transformance phenomena, marked by positive somatic affective markers (the State 1 rectangle on the right in Figure 1.1). A key part of AEDP's healing orientation is to know that transformance is present even when psychopathology is rampant, and to be on the lookout for it and recognize the glimmers of it, even when small.

The goals of State 1 work are to coconstruct safety, privilege transformance phenomena that are present or emergent, and minimize the impact of defenses and inhibiting affects. This sets the stage for our patients "drop down" into embodied, somatically based affect states, where they can be in contact with emotions that previously were too overwhelming to be dealt with alone and hence needed to be defensively excluded. With aloneness undone and active dyadic affect regulation, what could not previously be processed alone can begin to be dyadically held, shared, and processed in the here and now.

## State 2: The Experiential Processing of Core Affective Experiences

State 2 is the state in which trauma processing and emotional processing take place. It involves accessing, regulating, working through, and processing to completion some of the patient's deep somatically based, wired-in core affective experiences.

In this discussion of State 2, I focus on the adaptive core affective experiences. Work with the maladaptive affective experiences, which constitutes the other aspect of State 2 work, is discussed in later chapters (Lamagna, Chapter 11; Piliero, Chapter 10; Russell, Chapter 9, this volume).

The adaptive core affective experiences include but are not limited to the categorical emotions of sadness, anger, fear, joy, and disgust; coordinated relational experiences; receptive affective experiences; intrarelational experiences and their associated emotions; attachment strivings; somatic "drop-down" states; and experiences of agency, will and desire; and authentic self-states. State 2 experiential work involves first facilitating access to the negative affects associated with trauma and emotional suffering. Here, dyadic affect regulation is achieved through right-brain-to-right-brain communication, back and forth from the therapist's right brain and body to the patient's right brain and body. Through eye contact, tone of voice, gaze, tone, and rhythm, for example, as well as the use of simple, evocative, sensory-laden, imagistic language, we seek to entrain (and facilitate nontraumatic access to) right-brain-mediated, somatically rooted emotional experiences, which can then be experientially processed and gradually worked through to completion. When a whole wave of emotional processing is completed, it is as if an alchemical change has taken place: The pain of suffering has been transformed into something that feels good. The completion of a round of processing of core affective experience is marked by the release of the adaptive action tendencies wired into each affective change process, as well as the post–affective breakthrough affects—feeling relief, hope, lighter, and so forth. The resilience and motivation to act on behalf of the self, which had been defensively split off along with the core affects, is now active.

State 2 work to process to completion adaptive affective experiences exemplifies the experiential processing that is the mainstay of all experiential therapies. As you will see in the chapters that follow, it is equally crucial in AEDP. However, it does not constitute the entirety of AEDP's transformational process. Having processed core affective experiences to completion, we now go on to experientially process the ensuing newly emergent transformational experiences, the second half of experiential work in AEDP. This is meta-therapeutic processing, and the work of State 3.

## State 3: The Experiential Processing of Transformational Experiences

State 3 is characterized by the emergence of the affects of innate healing, the invariably positive transformational affects associated with experiences of healing, transformation and/or change for the better.

Six metatherapeutic processes, each with its characteristic transformational affect, have been identified to date:

1. The metatherapeutic process of mastery, evokes the mastery affects, the "I did it!" feelings of joy, pride, and confidence that emerge when fear and shame are undone.

2. The metatherapeutic process of mourning the self, accompanied by the transformational affect of emotional pain, involves painful but liberating grief and empathy for oneself and one's losses.

3. The metatherapeutic process of traversing the crisis of healing change evokes the tremulous affects operating at the edge between fear and excitement, startle and surprise, curiosity and interest, even positive vulnerability. Regulation here is maintained with the support of the therapeutic relationship because attachment mediates whether what is novel is experienced as exciting or as frightening.

4. The metatherapeutic process of the affirming recognition of the self and of its transformation evokes the healing affects: gratitude and tenderness toward the other, as well as feeling moved, touched, or emotional within oneself.

5. The metatherapeutic process of delighting in the (surprising) recognition of the unbrokenness of the self evokes the enlivening affects: zest, enthusiasm, and delight.

6. Finally, the metatherapeutic process of taking in the new understanding evokes the realization affects, the "yes!" and "wow" of wonder, amazement, and awe when grasping of the magnitude of transformational changes taking place.

Over myriad clinical encounters, we have discovered that focusing on the experience of transformation itself unleashes further rounds of transformation, through which positive changes can be powerfully consolidated, deepened, and expanded in a momentum-generating spiral of healing. As discussed earlier, progressive rounds of metatherapeutic processing engender an ever-emergent, nonlinear, nonfinite transformational spiral of upward movement (Fredrickson, 2009, 2013) that infuses the system (i.e., the patient, therapist, and dyad) with more and more energy and vitality (Fosha, 2009a, 2009b). Each new experience, once explored in the context of safe attachment, becomes a platform and a springboard for the next round of exploration.

The steady oscillation between experience and reflection, between right brain and left brain, between insula and anterior cingulate, between limbic system and prefrontal cortex that is involved in metaprocessing the high arousal positive transformational affects of State 3 leads to recursive cycles of transformation, culminating in State 4.

The state-shift markers that signal the completion of State 3 and the emergence of core state are calm, clarity, and relaxed openness. The stress of State 1 and the emotional tumult of States 2 and 3 are over. The storm has passed. The wind has died down. The sky is clear and the air is fresh. Breathing is deep and slow. Life is good. The metatherapeutic transformational spiraling leads to a profoundly satisfying, deeply felt state of ease, flow, and relaxation. These affects herald the availability of core state, the fourth state of the transformational process as viewed through the lens of AEDP.

### State 4, aka Core State: "This Is Me," Integration, the 'Truth Sense' and the Construction of New Meaning

Also known as core state, State 4, a state of calm and neural integration, is characterized by the natural emergence of the same qualities of mind—well-being, compassion, self-compassion, wisdom, generosity, flow, clarity, joy—that mindfulness and contemplative practices seek to bring forth (Fosha & Yeung, 2006; Yeung, Chapter 13, this volume). Core state is an altered state of openness and contact in which individuals are in touch with essential aspects of their experience. Experience is intense, deeply felt, unequivocal, and declarative; sensation is heightened, imagery vivid, focus and concentration effortless. Anxiety, shame, guilt, or defensiveness are absent. Self-attunement and other-receptivity easily coexist. Mindfulness prevails. In this "state of assurance"(James, 1902), the patient contacts a confidence that naturally translates into effective action. The affective marker for core state is the *truth sense* (Fosha, 2005). The truth sense is a vitality affect whose felt sense is an aesthetic experience of rightness and subjective truth, the rightness of one's experience. This is not about being right, but about things that feel right, like the calm that one obtains when a picture that has been crooked comes into alignment. There is an internal experience of coherence, cohesion, completion, and essence. There is a sense, shared by patient and therapist, that the truth is being spoken.

We also see here the further cultivation of exceptional mind–body traits such as spontaneous altruism (Loizzo, 2017). Guided by the truth sense (Fosha, 2005), the parasympathetically mediated low arousal core state is where the fruits of the transformational process are reaped and folded into the self. Core truths about the self emerge: "This is me" revelations are a common feature of core state. A new, coherent autobiographical narrative, a correlate of resilience and secure attachment (Main, 1999), naturally comes forth as well.

Often, the most powerful work can be done when both patient and therapist are in core state, for it is not unusual for the therapist to join the patient and share in this state, and therefore be fully able to move back and forth between compassion and self-compassion, wisdom and generosity, and I–Thou or True-Self/True-Other relating.

## CONCLUSION

As an AEDP therapist, there is a continual recalibration toward the approach's fundamental guiding principles, a return again and again to its "North Star." These principles include (a) a healing orientation, privileging transformance over a focus on psychopathology; (b) the importance of an intentionally positive, empathic, validating, affect-facilitating, and judiciously self-disclosing therapeutic stance, which includes everything that the therapist does and is intended to make the patient feel seen, respected, accompanied and cared about; (c) the centrality of undoing the patient's aloneness, along with the moment-to-moment coconstruction of safety; (d) a relentlessly experiential focus, guided moment-to-moment by somatic–affective markers that mark attachment experiences, relational experiences, and receptive affective experience emotional experiences, intrarelational experiences, transformational experiences—to process to an affective shift the negative affects associated with trauma and emotional suffering; (e) the importance of metaprocessing the positive affects associated with experiences of change for the better, to engender appetitive and motivational spirals of vitality and energy; and finally (f) to integrate the emergent changes into self and to consolidate and deepen therapeutic changes and new autobiographical narratives, informed by the positive valuation of the self and compassion for self and others.

## REFERENCES

Adler, J. M., Harmeling, L. H., & Walder-Biesanz, I. (2013). Narrative meaning making is associated with sudden gains in psychotherapy clients' mental health under routine clinical conditions. *Journal of Consulting and Clinical Psychology, 81*(5), 839–845. https://doi.org/10.1037/a0033774

Alexander, F., & French, T. M. (1946). *Psychoanalytic therapy: Principles and application.* University of Nebraska Press.

Beebe, B., & Lachmann, F. M. (1994). Representation and internalization in infancy: Three principles of salience. *Psychoanalytic Psychology, 11*(2), 127–165. https://doi.org/10.1037/h0079530

Bowlby, J. (1982). *Attachment and loss: Vol. 1. Attachment* (2nd ed.). Basic Books.

Bowlby, J. (1988). *A secure base: Parent–child attachment and healthy human development.* Basic Books.

Bowlby, J. (1991). Post-script. In C. M. Parkes, J. Stevenson-Hinde, & P. Marris (Eds.), *Attachment across the life cycle* (pp. 293–297). Routledge.

Buber, M. (1955). The life of dialogue. In M. S. Friedman (Ed.), *Martin Buber: The life of dialogue* (pp. 86–91). The University of Chicago Press.

Cassidy, J. (2001). Truth, lies, and intimacy: An attachment perspective. *Attachment & Human Development, 3*(2), 121–155. https://doi.org/10.1080/14616730110058999

Damasio, A. (1999). *The feeling of what happens: Body and emotion in the making of consciousness.* Harcourt, Brace.

Darwin, C. (1965). *The expression of emotion in man and animals.* University of Chicago Press. (Original work published 1872) https://doi.org/10.7208/chicago/9780226220802. 001.0001

Davidson, R. J., Jackson, D. C., & Kalin, N. H. (2000). Emotion, plasticity, context, and regulation: Perspectives from affective neuroscience. *Psychological Bulletin, 126*(6), 890–909. https://doi.org/10.1037/0033-2909.126.6.890

Doidge, N. (2007). *The brain that changes itself: Stories of personal triumph from the frontiers of brain science.* Penguin Books.

Emde, R. N. (1988). Development terminable and interminable. I. Innate and motivational factors from infancy. *The International Journal of Psycho-Analysis, 69*(Pt. 1), 23–42.

Fonagy, P. (1997). Multiple voices vs. meta-cognition: An attachment theory perspective. *Journal of Psychotherapy Integration, 7*(3), 181–194. https://doi.org/10.1037/h0101122

Fonagy, P., Steele, M., Steele, H., Higgitt, A., & Target, M. (1994). The Emanuel Miller Memorial Lecture 1992. The theory and practice of resilience. *Journal of Child Psychology and Psychiatry, and Allied Disciplines, 35*(2), 231–257. https://doi.org/10.1111/j.1469-7610.1994.tb01160.x

Fonagy, P., Steele, M., Steele, H., Leigh, T., Kennedy, R., Matoon, G., & Target, M. (1995). Attachment, the reflective self and borderline states. In S. Goldberg, R. Muir, & J. Kerr (Eds.), *Attachment theory: Social, developmental and clinical perspectives* (pp. 233–278). Analytic Press.

Fosha, D. (2000a). Meta-therapeutic processes and the affects of transformation: Affirmation and the healing affects. *Journal of Psychotherapy Integration, 10*, 71–97.

Fosha, D. (2000b). *The transforming power of affect: A model for accelerated change.* Basic Books.

Fosha, D. (2001). The dyadic regulation of affect. *Journal of Clinical Psychology, 57*(2), 227–242. https://doi.org/10.1002/1097-4679(200102)57:2<227::AID-JCLP8>3.0. CO;2-1

Fosha, D. (2003). Dyadic regulation and experiential work with emotion and relatedness in trauma and disordered attachment. In M. F. Solomon & D. J. Siegel (Eds.), *Healing trauma: Attachment, trauma, the brain and the mind* (pp. 221–281). Norton.

Fosha, D. (2005). Emotion, true self, true other, core state: toward a clinical theory of affective change process. *Psychoanalytic Review, 92*(4), 513–552.

Fosha, D. (2008). Transformance, recognition of self by self, and effective action. In K. J. Schneider (Ed.), *Existential-integrative psychotherapy: Guideposts to the core of practice* (pp. 290–320). Routledge.

Fosha, D. (2009a). Emotion and recognition at work: Energy, vitality, pleasure, truth, desire & the emergent phenomenology of transformational experience. In D. Fosha, D. J. Siegel, & M. F. Solomon (Eds.), *The healing power of emotion: Affective neuroscience, development, clinical practice* (pp. 172–203). Norton.

Fosha, D. (2009b). Positive affects and the transformation of suffering into flourishing. In W. C. Bushell, E. L. Olivo, & N. D. Theise (Eds.), *Longevity, regeneration, and optimal health: Integrating Eastern and Western perspectives* (pp. 252–261). Annals of the New York Academy of Sciences.

Fosha, D. (2013a). A heaven in a wild flower: Self, dissociation, and treatment in the context of the neurobiological core self. *Psychoanalytic Inquiry, 33*(5), 496–523. https://doi.org/10.1080/07351690.2013.815067

Fosha, D. (2013b). Turbocharging the affects of healing and redressing the evolutionary tilt. In D. J. Siegel & Marion F. Solomon (Eds.), *Healing moments in psychotherapy* (pp. 129–168). Norton.

Fosha, D. (2017a). How to be a transformational therapist: AEDP harnesses innate healing affects to re-wire experience and accelerate transformation. In J. Loizzo, M. Neale, & E. Wolf (Eds.), *Advances in contemplative psychotherapy: Accelerating transformation* (pp. 204–219). Norton. https://doi.org/10.4324/9781315630045-18

Fosha, D. (2017b). Something more than "something more than interpretation": AEDP works the experiential edge of transformational experience to transform the internal working model. In S. Lord (Ed.), *Moments of meeting in psychoanalysis: Interaction and change in the therapeutic encounter* (pp. 267–292). Routledge.

Fosha, D. (2018). Moment-to-moment guidance of clinical interventions by AEDP's healing-oriented transformational phenomenology: Commentary on Vigoda Gonzalez's (2018) Case of "Rosa." *Pragmatic Case Studies in Psychotherapy, 14*(2), 87–114. https://doi.org/10.14713/pcsp.v14i2.2038

Fosha, D., & Thoma, N. (2020). Metatherapeutic processing supports the emergence of flourishing in psychotherapy. *Psychotherapy.* Advance online publication. https://doi.org/10.1037/pst0000289

Fosha, D., Thoma, N., & Yeung, D. (2020). Metatherapeutic processing supports the emergence of flourishing in psychotherapy. *Counselling Psychology Quarterly, 32*(3–4), 563–593. https://doi.org/10.1080/09515070.2019.1642852

Fosha, D., & Yeung, D. (2006). AEDP exemplifies the seamless integration of emotional transformation and dyadic relatedness at work. In G. Stricker & J. Gold (Eds.), *A casebook of integrative psychotherapy* (pp. 165–184). American Psychological Association. https://doi.org/10.1037/11436-013

Frederick, R. (2019). *Loving like you mean it: Use the power of emotional mindfulness to transform your relationships.* Central Recovery Press.

Fredrickson, B. L. (2009). *Positivity: Groundbreaking research reveals how to embrace the hidden strength of positive emotions, overcome negativity, and thrive.* Random House.

Fredrickson, B. L. (2013). Positive emotions broaden and build. *Advances in Experimental Social Psychology, 47,* 1–53.

Frijda, N. (1986). *The emotions.* Cambridge University Press.

Gendlin, E. (1981). *Focusing.* Bantam.

Gendlin, E. T. (1996). *Focusing-oriented psychotherapy: A manual of the experiential method.* Guilford Press.

Ghent, E. (1990). Masochism, submission, surrender: Masochism as a perversion of surrender. *Contemporary Psychoanalysis, 26*(1), 108–136. https://doi.org/10.1080/00107530.1990.10746643

Ghent, E. (2002). Wish, need, drive: Motive in light of dynamic systems theory and Edelman's selectionist theory. *Psychoanalytic Dialogues, 12*(5), 763–808. https://doi.org/10.1080/10481881209348705

Goleman, D. (1995). *Emotional intelligence: Why it can matter more than IQ.* Bantam Books.

Hansen, B. P., Lambert, M. J., & Vlass, E. N. (2015). Sudden gains and sudden losses in the clients of a "supershrink": 10 case studies. *Pragmatic Case Studies in Psychotherapy, 11*(3), pp. 154–201. http://pcsp.libraries.rutgers.edu

Hanson, R. (2017). Positive neuroplasticity: The neuroscience of mindfulness. In J. Loizzo, M. Neale, & E. Wolf (Eds.), *Advances in contemplative psychotherapy: Accelerating transformation* (pp. 48–60). Norton. https://doi.org/10.4324/9781315630045-5

Hanson, R. (2018). *Resilient: How to grow an unshakable core of calm, strength, and happiness.* Harmony.

Harrison, R. L. (2020). Termination in 16-session accelerated experiential dynamic psychotherapy (AEDP): Together in how we say goodbye. *Psychotherapy, 57*(4), 531–547. https://doi.org/10.1037/pst0000343

Hayes, A. M., Laurenceau, J.-P., Feldman, G., Strauss, J. L., & Cardaciotto, L. (2007). Change is not always linear: The study of nonlinear and discontinuous patterns of change in psychotherapy. *Clinical Psychology Review, 27*(6), 715–723. https://doi.org/10.1016/j.cpr.2007.01.008

Hesse, E., & Main, M. (1999). Second-generation effects of unresolved trauma in non-maltreating parents: Dissociated, frightened, and threatening parental behavior. *Psychoanalytic Inquiry, 19*(4), 481–540. https://doi.org/10.1080/07351699909534265

Hughes, D. (2017). *Building the bonds of attachment: Awakening love in deeply traumatized children* (6th ed.). Rowman and Littlefield.

Iwakabe, S., & Conceição, N. (2016). Metatherapeutic processing as a change-based therapeutic immediacy task: Building an initial process model using a task-analytic research strategy. *Journal of Psychotherapy Integration, 26*(3), 230–247. https://doi.org/10.1037/int0000016

James, W. (1902). *The varieties of religious experience: A study in human nature.* Penguin Books. https://doi.org/10.1037/10004-000

Kaufman, G. (1996). *The psychology of shame: Theory and treatment of shame-based syndromes.* Springer Publishing Company.

Lamagna, J. (2011). Of the self, by the self, and for the self: An intra-relational perspective on intra-psychic attunement and psychological change. *Journal of Psychotherapy Integration, 21*(3), 280–307. https://doi.org/10.1037/a0025493

Lamagna, J., & Gleiser, K. A. (2007). Building a secure internal attachment: An intra-relational approach to ego strengthening and emotional processing with chronically traumatized clients. *Journal of Trauma & Dissociation, 8*(1), 25–52. https://doi.org/10.1300/J229v08n01_03

Lee, A. (2015). *Building a model for metaprocessing: Exploration of a key change event in accelerated experiential dynamic psychotherapy (AEDP)* [Unpublished doctoral dissertation]. Wright Institute, Berkeley, CA.

Levine, P. (2010). *In an unspoken voice: How the body releases trauma and restores goodness.* North Atlantic Books.

Lipton, B., & Fosha, D. (2011). Attachment as a transformative process in AEDP: Operationalizing the intersection of attachment theory and affective neuroscience. *Journal of Psychotherapy Integration, 21*(3), 253–279. https://doi.org/10.1037/a0025421

Loizzo, J. (2017). Embodied practice, the smart vagus, and mind–body–brain integration. In J. Loizzo, M. Neale, & E. Wolf (Eds.), *Advances in contemplative psychotherapy: Accelerating transformation* (pp. 185–203). Norton. https://doi.org/10.4324/9781315630045-17

Lyons-Ruth, K. (2007). The interface between attachment and intersubjectivity: Perspective from the longitudinal study of disorganized attachment. *Psychoanalytic Inquiry, 26*(4), 595–616. https://doi.org/10.1080/07351690701310656

Main, M. (1999). Epilogue: Attachment theory: Eighteen points with suggestions for future studies. In J. Cassidy & P. R. Shaver (Eds.), *Handbook of attachment: Theory, research and clinical applications* (pp. 845–888). Guilford Press.

Miller, W. R., & C'deBaca, J. (2001). *Quantum change: When epiphanies and sudden insights transform ordinary lives.* Guilford Press.

Pando-Mars, K. (2016). Tailoring AEDP interventions to attachment style. *Transformance: The AEDP Journal, 4*(2). https://aedpinstitute.org/wp-content/uploads/2016/11/tailoring-aedp-interventions-to-attachment-style.pdf

Panksepp, J. (1998). *Affective neuroscience: The foundations of human and animal emotions.* Oxford University Press.

Panksepp, J. (2009). Brain emotional systems and qualities of mental life: From animal models of affect to implications for psychotherapeutics. In D. Fosha, D. J. Siegel, & M. F. Solomon, (Eds.), *The healing power of emotion: Affective neuroscience, development & clinical practice* (pp. 1–26). Norton.

Perls, F. S. (1969). *Gestalt therapy verbatim*. Real People Press.

Person, E. S. (1988). *Dreams of love and fateful encounters: The power of romantic passion*. Norton.

Prenn, N. (2009). I second that emotion! On self-disclosure and its metaprocessing. In A. Bloomgarden & R. B. Menutti (Eds.), *Psychotherapist revealed: Therapists speak about self-disclosure in psychotherapy* (pp. 85–99). Routledge.

Prenn, N. (2011). Mind the gap: AEDP interventions translating attachment theory into clinical practice. *Journal of Psychotherapy Integration*, *21*(3), 308–329. https://doi.org/10.1037/a0025491

Prenn, N., & Fosha, D. (2017). *Supervision essentials for accelerated experiential dynamic psychotherapy*. American Psychological Association. https://doi.org/10.1037/0000016-000

Russell, E., & Fosha, D. (2008). Transformational affects and core state in AEDP: The emergence and consolidation of joy, hope, gratitude and confidence in the (solid goodness of the) self. *Journal of Psychotherapy Integration*, *18*(2), 167–190. https://doi.org/10.1037/1053-0479.18.2.167

Russell, E. M. (2015). *Restoring resilience: Discovering your clients' capacity for healing*. Norton.

Sander, L. (2002). Thinking differently: Principles of process in living systems and the specificity of being known. *Psychoanalytic Dialogues*, *12*(1), 11–42. https://doi.org/10.1080/10481881209348652

Schneider, K. J. (Ed.). (2008). *Existential-integrative psychotherapy: Guideposts to the core of practice*. Routledge. https://doi.org/10.4324/9780203941119

Schore, A. N. (2001). Effects of a secure attachment relationship on right brain development, affect regulation and infant mental health. *Infant Mental Health Journal*, *22*(1–2), 7–66. https://doi.org/10.1002/1097-0355(200101/04)22:1<7::AID-IMHJ2>3.0.CO;2-N

Schore, A. N. (2016). Foreword. In A. Katehakis (Ed.), *Sex addiction as affect dysregulation: A neurobiologically informed holistic treatment* (pp. xi–xxi). Norton.

Schore, A. N. (2019). *Right brain psychotherapy*. Norton.

Siegel, D. J. (2010). *Mindsight: The new science of personal transformation*. Random House.

Siegel, D. J. (2012). *The developing mind: How relationships and the brain interact to shape who we are* (2nd ed.). Guilford Press.

Stern, D. N. (2000). *The interpersonal world of the infant: A view from psychoanalysis and development psychology* (2nd ed.). Basic Books. (Original work published 1985)

Stern, D. N., Sander, L. W., Nahum, J. P., Harrison, A. M., Lyons-Ruth, K., Morgan, A. C., Bruschweiler-Stern, N., Tronick, E. Z., & The Process of Change Study Group. (1998). Non-interpretive mechanisms in psychoanalytic therapy. The "something more" than interpretation. *The International Journal of Psycho-Analysis*, *79*(Pt 5), 903–921.

Trevarthen, C. (2001). Intrinsic motives for companionship in understanding: Their origin, development, and significance for infant mental health. *Infant Mental Health Journal*, *22*(1–2), 95–131. https://doi.org/10.1002/1097-0355(200101/04)22:1<95::AID-IMHJ4>3.0.CO;2-6

Tronick, E. Z. (1989). Emotions and emotional communication in infants. *American Psychologist*, *44*(2), 112–119. https://doi.org/10.1037/0003-066X.44.2.112

Tronick, E. Z. (2003). "Of course all relationships are unique": How co-creative processes generate unique mother–infant and client–therapist relationships and change other relationships. *Psychoanalytic Inquiry*, *23*(3), 473–491. https://doi.org/10.1080/07351692309349044

Tronick, E. Z. (2009). Multilevel meaning making and dyadic expansion of consciousness theory: The polymorphic polysemic flow of meaning. In D. Fosha, D. J. Siegel, & M. F. Solomon (Eds.), *The healing power of emotion: Affective neuroscience, development, & clinical practice* (pp. 86–111). Norton.

Tunnell, G. (2006). An affirmational approach to treating gay male couples. *Group*, *30*(2), 133–151.

Tunnell, G. (2011). An attachment perspective on the first interview. In C. Silverstein (Ed.), *The initial psychotherapy interview: A gay man seeks treatment* (pp. 137–155). Elsevier. https://doi.org/10.1016/B978-0-12-385146-8.00007-9

van der Kolk, B. A. (2014). *The body keeps the score: Brain, mind, and the body in the healing of trauma*. Penguin.

Yeung, D., Fosha, D., Ye Perman, J., & Xu, Y. (2019). *After Freud meets Zhuangzi: Stance and the dance of the self-in-transformation with the other-in-contemplative presence*. *Psychological Communications, 2*(3), 179–185.

# 2

# The First Session in AEDP

## Harnessing Transformance and Cocreating a Secure Attachment

Karen Kranz

What makes accelerated experiential dynamic psychotherapy (AEDP) theory and therapeutic process unique is that from the get-go, it is healing-oriented versus pathology-oriented (Fosha, 2000). AEDP's healing-oriented theory and method of therapy is exemplified by the AEDP therapist stance, transformance, the neurobiological core self, and the four-state transformational process. In this chapter, I illustrate how the four-state transformational process can unfold in a first session, even a first session with a client processing trauma. I present the first session with Sam, a young man whose current difficulties were revealed to go back to a trauma he suffered in adolescence. I use transcribed excerpts from the session to demonstrate how all of AEDP, as I just described briefly and as Fosha discusses in more detail in Chapter 1 (this volume), is at play.

## THE AEDP THERAPIST STANCE: HEALING ORIENTED AND TRANSFORMANCE BASED

The AEDP therapist enters the first session, and every session thereafter, with the intention of cocreating the conditions that foster transformational, or healing, change. To do this, she embodies the knowledge that the naturally occurring, wired-in, growth-promoting motivation for healing and self-righting that in AEDP we call *transformance* (Fosha, 2008) lives and resides in all humans.

https://doi.org/10.1037/0000232-003
*Undoing Aloneness and the Transformation of Suffering Into Flourishing: AEDP 2.0*, D. Fosha (Editor)

Manifestations of this innate motivation—glimmers of vitality, energy, resilience, hope, longings for change, or flexibility—are accompanied by positive somatic affective markers. More often than not, clients enter therapy connected with their pain, shame, stuckness, and suffering, yet the AEDP therapist knows that right alongside the suffering, transformance is also always present. The AEDP therapist draws it out and is explicit about even the smallest glimmers so that clients, from the get-go, start to feel the vitality rising up within them. This focus on transformance also helps to counter the client's shame associated with being broken.

AEDP's healing orientation is contrast with a focus on psychopathology associated with traditional psychoanalytic and psychodynamic treatments, whether long or short term. Rather than point out and confront the client's defenses and resistance to treatment, AEDP therapists point out existing strengths within the client beginning in the first session. AEDP therapists believe such a healing stance reduces resistance, helps clients relinquish their defenses more quickly, and accelerates treatment.

AEDP therapists also know that humans are innately programmed to attach to and care for one another, which allows exploration and growth to occur (Bowlby, 1988; Panksepp & Biven, 2012). Thus, from the first moments of the first session, the AEDP therapist engages the client's attachment system and the therapist's own caregiving system with the aim of cocreating a secure attachment. As is true for many models of therapy, the AEDP therapist is welcoming, empathic, and validating. However, there is more. The AEDP therapist explicitly affirms and explicitly expresses care and appreciation by asking clients how they are being perceived and whether what she is offering is felt by clients (receptive affective capacity) and, if so, whether it helps them embody that the AEDP therapist is making the *implicit explicit* and then is making the *explicit experiential*. This is one example of how using the self of the therapist enhances client safety and helps undo aloneness.

Further, using the self of the therapist, the AEDP therapist goes beyond mirroring to help (Fosha, 2000) and is not hidden from the client. Using judicious self-disclosure (Prenn, 2009), the therapist seeks to be emotionally present, emotionally engaged, emotionally connected, and emotionally competent as she actively feels and deals, while staying in connection (Fosha, 2000). The AEDP therapist stance is central to the client having a corrective relational experience, which is foundational to healing relational trauma. The AEDP therapist stance is also central to facilitating a corrective emotional experience where previously unbearable core emotions can be processed to completion. These corrective emotional experiences can occur when clients feel safe and can risk to feel deeply and therapists are brave—themselves taking chances by putting their own self on the line, in addition to encouraging and accompanying clients into painful emotional experiences.

The AEDP therapist works experientially, which means working in the moment, privileging bodily based affective experiences over story. The AEDP therapist works experientially both with negative (i.e., painful) affective experiences associated with trauma and the positive affective experiences associated with healing (Fosha et al., 2019). Positive affective experiences are important because they are related to transformance, healing, health, safety, secure attachment, change for the better, and transformation. Positive affective phenomena, with their motivational (Doidge, 2016) and broaden-and-build characteristics (Fredrickson & Joiner, 2018), have been deemed crucial to putting positive neuroplasticity into action (Fosha, 2017; Hanson, 2018). The AEDP therapist tracks, works experientially, and makes the most of the therapeutic opportunities these positive somatic affective markers offer. This is foundational to AEDP's capacity to activate healing from the get-go (i.e., from the first session of therapy and then throughout treatment).

## THE NEUROBIOLOGICAL CORE SELF

The AEDP therapist embodies the knowledge that there exists in all humans a fundamentally integrative *neurobiological core self* (Fosha, 2013). It is from the *neurobiological core self* that actions possessed by agency, ownership of experience, behavioral coherence, and identity arise (Fosha, 2013). When brought to the experiential fore, these ways of engaging the world are felt as being reflections of an individual's felt sense of "this is me," unencumbered by the effects of defenses and unprocessed trauma.

## THE FOUR-STATE TRANSFORMATIONAL PROCESS

The process of healing change occurs through four states, each of which has a distinct phenomenology which is captured by and tracked through AEDP's primary representational schema (see Appendix Figure 1),[1] the phenomenology of the *four-state transformational process* (Fosha, 2009). In so doing, the therapist is able to gather substantive psychodynamic and historical information. However, this information is organized in accordance with AEDP's particular emphasis on detecting glimmers of the client's *transformance* drive for self-righting and healing, instead of delineating the client's psychopathology.

The process of transformational change is nonlinear, and the AEDP therapist uses the four-state transformation process as a map, not a manual. The map of the four-state transformational process orients the AEDP therapist and guides her interventions. Through moment-to-moment tracking and close-range affective attunement, the therapist helps the client-therapist dyad move through the four-state transformational process, experientially processing relational, affective and healing phenomena along the way. This dyadic process often leads to the cocreation of emergent states from which new, nascent, and previously unknown phenomena can arise. When that happens, working with the new emergent phenomena takes precedence in the therapeutic work, sometimes causing the therapeutic dyad to detour from the usual map (again, AEDP is not a manualized treatment).

---

[1]This figure, and diagrams for all of the representational schemas in AEDP 2.0, may be downloaded for free (http://pubs.apa.org/books/supp/fosha/).

The phenomena of the four-states arise naturally when the AEDP therapist cocreates the conditions for the four-state transformational process to emerge. The broad brushstrokes of the phenomena of the four-state transformational process and of the therapeutic aims and interventions of the four-state transformational process are as follows.

The phenomena of State 1 include the client's symptoms (as a result of defenses and their sequelae), anxiety, stress, and distress as well as glimmers of transformance, health, and resilience. As previously described, the AEDP therapist focuses on cocreating safety and privileges the client's transformance strivings and their associated *positive affective somatic experiences* of energy and vitality which fuel healing change. On the stress, distress, and symptom side, we have the clinical phenomena, such as anxiety, overwhelm, toxic shame, and fear without solution, that are also represented at the top of the Triangle of Experience. The Triangle of Experience is a representation of internal dynamics in which core affect is inhibited by these top of the triangle clinical phenomena (see Pando-Mars, Chapter 6, this volume; Frederick, Chapter 7; see also Hanakawa, Figure 4.1, in Chapter 4).

Tracking phenomena moment by moment, the AEDP therapist is on the lookout for the phenomena of the *first-state transformations*, which indicate the client is shifting from State 1 to State 2. When clients are safe (sometimes as a result of therapists being brave), they naturally begin to experience State 2 *core affective experiences*, including, but not limited to, embodied experiences of core emotions.

As central State 2 core affective experiences, emotions are important sources of information and are bodily rooted powerful forces (Darwin, 1872/1965; James, 1902; Damasio, 2018), which, when regulated, are highly adaptive (Fosha, 2009). Each emotion's adaptive action tendencies (Frijda, 1986) are activated when emotions are dyadically regulated, processed, and then fully experienced. However, the adaptive capacity residing in each emotion is thwarted when one is alone with intensely difficult emotions that overwhelm one's resources and that cannot be processed to completion. Emotions not regulated overwhelm, disorganize, and become unbearable, which threatens either the integrity of the self or that of the attachment relationship (or both; Fosha, 2000, 2003, 2009); this results in the creation of defense mechanisms, as well as anxiety, survival mechanisms instituted to safeguard as best possible the integrity of the self or of the attachment bond (or both) and to keep the dangerous emotions at bay.

In AEDP, trauma processing occurs in State 2 by working with the different core affective experiences. The AEDP therapist rides the State 2 emotional waves with clients, dyadically regulating affect such that clients are able to process their emotions to completion. Riding the waves of previously overwhelming emotions is new and good. However, good does not refer just to affect that is pleasant. In AEDP, *good* also means right, and what is right does not always feel pleasant or happy. For example, in the therapy case that follows, the client and I return to a serious car accident that is not associated with feeling good in any ordinary sense of the word. However, finally addressing what were previously unprocessed difficult emotions associated with the accident, together with an other who has earned his trust as a competent guide and facilitator, felt good for the client: He is relieved that he can finally deal with what he subconsciously knew he needed to deal with. Thus, it is the subjective felt sense of what is right and true that is encompassed within the word *good* (Prenn & Fosha, 2016).

As the waves of core affective experience complete, we witness the phenomena of the *second-state transformation*, the *postbreakthrough affects* of relief, hope, and feeling stronger arise indicating a shift from State 2 to State 3. The phenomena of State 3 are the six *transformational affects* (Fosha, 2017; see the summary in Fosha, Chapter 1, this volume). The AEDP therapist invites experience and reflection on whatever transformational affect emerges and through experiencing and reflecting on these phenomena, the transformational spiral develops. That is, each round of experience and reflection leads to another experience of healing, another experience of something new and good. The transformational spiral is upward, growth promoting, and associated with positive affective experiences. With this upward spiral, energy, vitality, openness, and aliveness emerge, all of which are positive affective experiences associated with positive neuroplasticity, with the *third-state transformation*, and with the emergence of State 4.

State 4, *core state*, is a highly integrative state in which the neurobiological core self, unencumbered by unprocessed trauma and protective defenses, and is liberated. State 4 phenomena include experiences of openness, compassion for self and other, wisdom, clarity, a sense of truth, and a sense of what is right. When experiencing core state, one has the capacity to integrate one's life experiences into a cohesive and coherent autobiographical narrative that is associated with strength, resilience, well-being, and happiness (Main, 1996; Siegel, 2012). State 4 is also associated with positive affective experiences that broaden the scope of one's attention and cognition, providing greater coping repertoires that, in turn, create upward spirals of increased emotional well-being linked to underlying neuroplasticity as described by Fredrickson and Joiner's (2018) broaden-and-build theory.

## THE FIRST THERAPY SESSION WITH SAM: HEALING FROM THE GET-GO.

Sam, a 24-year-old White man, enters therapy[2] to work on his anger and his abuse of marijuana and alcohol, both of which are negatively impacting his relationship with his female partner. The first task of every session is to cocreate safety. Working experientially, relationally, and somatically with Sam's moment-to-moment affective experience, we *slow down* and discover

---

[2]I have complied with the American Psychological Association's ethical standards in describing the details of treatment; aspects of the client's identity and background have been disguised to protect confidentiality.

what in the past may be fueling his current-day angry outbursts. Our experiential investigation leads us back to a traumatic car accident when he was 15. Together, current-day 24-year-old Sam and I revisit the 15-year-old Sam, who is in the car, uncertain about the outcome of the accident, and so uncertain about his future. The portrayal of an intrarelational dialogue (Lamagna & Gleiser, 2007) in this first session between Sam and his 15-year-old self plays a major role in the healing and state of calm that Sam embodies by the end of this 60-minute session.

## Cocreating Safety

As an AEDP therapist, I take the lead as an attachment figure, engaging with Sam as a "stronger and/or wise other" (Bowlby, 1977, p. 203) to create a secure base. It is this secure base that fosters the client's "willingness to experientially immerse [him]self in the core affective phenomena so crucial to deep therapeutic change" (Fosha, 2000, p. 34).

As the session opens, I welcome Sam warmly and invite him to make himself comfortable. I share with Sam several important aspects about my practice that I want him to know before we begin the clinical work (e.g., confidentiality, the purpose of video recording our sessions). I then lay the foundation of how I work, letting Sam know what he can expect, which helps build our collaborative alliance. This is a form of self-disclosure, transparency, and therapeutic immediacy (Hill, 2008).

THERAPIST:   Come on in and have a seat . . . yeah . . . perfect. And you can make yourself comfortable . . . you can get rid of the pillow . . . do you want some water?

CLIENT:   Yeah . . . please that would be great. (*Client sits in chair*)

THERAPIST:   So a little bit about me . . . is I have a PhD in counseling psychology . . . I'm a registered psychologist . . . on the faculty at the AEDP Institute . . . I do teaching and supervision.

CLIENT:   OK.

THERAPIST:   How I see this work is that I bring me into our relationship, as well as my training and experience in counseling and in therapy and in psychology . . . and you bring you . . . and we work like this (*fingers of both hands interweave*) . . . we come together to work on the things that you've told me about in emails and whatever else that arises for you. I will lead sometimes, and I will be following you sometimes (*client nods*) . . . and we kinda dance a little bit (*hands sway in tandem*) . . . and we find our way. Sometimes we step on each other's toes and hopefully we can always repair anything that doesn't feel right or good for you.

CLIENT:   Right . . . one of the things that I found hasn't worked with counselors in the past is that they've let me lead too much and I haven't felt like there was too much of an engagement . . .

I do like to be cut off . . . I tend to talk a lot. . . . So if you see something that you'd like to bring up, that's a good way of working for me . . .

THERAPIST: You know what? I'm so glad that you invited me into that because I will stop you because the way I work is experientially . . . which means, yeah, you might be telling me about something that happened outside of this room . . . but I'm gonna want to stop you and say, "Sam, what's going on right now (*client nods*) . . . as you're telling me about this what's coming up?" Then I work very emotionally: "So what feelings are coming up? and then let's understand what those emotions are about and what they're telling us."

CLIENT: Mmm-hmm . . .

THERAPIST: I also work very relationally so I'm going to be checking in with you. . . . "How are you feeling? Do you feel like I'm getting you?" or "Am I missing the boat here?" or "Do you feel confident and comfortable with me?" and those kinds of things . . . so . . . and I just also want to say that at any time if I ask you something and you want to put it aside, that's fine . . . you can say, "ahhhh . . . not ready . . . can we set that aside?" Of course, we can set that aside . . . or you can ask me what I'm thinking because I'm happy to be as transparent as I can be about the process that we're engaging in.

CLIENT: (*nods*) Cool . . .

Throughout my description of how we will work, Sam nods, and I ask him explicitly how he feels about what I am saying. Sam enthusiastically welcomes my direction and even my interruptions. I explicitly appreciate what Sam shares with me. As is evident from the video of the session, we are already creating safety through communicating "right-brain to right-brain" (Schore, 2019), activating the social engagement system (Porges, 2017) through voice tone, rhythm of speech, gaze, warm facial expressions, relaxed posture, and prosody. This helps foster emotional resonance and intersubjectivity between us such that our minds can be connected in a shared affective state of consciousness (Tronick et al., 1998). Sam and I are already mutually engaged in creating our own unique way of being together (Tronick, 2003). In my wish to promote an optimal dyadic relationship, I also introduce the possibility of disruptions and disagreements. I make it clear that the goal, then, is to repair these disruptions of attunement. Attunement is the root of establishing states of mutual affective coordination, which in turn is the foundation of securely attached relationships (Fosha, 2000).

Sam's responses to me both verbally and nonverbally indicate that even this early in the session, he is beginning to feel safe with me as we cocreate a "we are in this experience together" stance. In a therapeutic environment in which clients are safe enough to feel, affect-laden experiences are less frightening to experience (Fosha, 2017). Sam and I are starting to feel connected and in affective resonance: There is warmth and openness in the room. Tracking the client–therapist relationship moment by moment continues throughout the first and every session. This early relational work with Sam is occurring in State 1 of the four-state transformational process.

THERAPIST:    Okay . . . any other questions for me?

CLIENT:    No, I think that's pretty good. . . . I'm sure they'll come up.

## Working Experientially in the Here and Now

With safety and emotional resonance growing between us, I next lead with an experiential question to focus our work in the present moment. I ask Sam how he feels about starting this work with me, emphasizing that *we are in this experience together*. Approaching our work together from the stance of *we*, I seek to set the foundation for being able to dyadically regulate Sam's affect if necessary and hopefully to begin to undo Sam's aloneness (Fosha, 2000) with whatever events and emotions he has not been able to process to date.

THERAPIST:    I'm sure . . . anytime . . . so just take a moment and just check in with how you feel even being here, which being anxious wouldn't be a surprise but just . . . how are you doing . . . starting with me.

CLIENT:    I'm . . . there's a mix of anxiety . . . just about sort of putting things out on the table, which I don't with a lot of people (*fingertips touch, glancing at hands*) . . . but then there's also like a huge amount of excitement . . . as well because . . . I don't know, like this is the first time starting therapy where it's really something I want to follow through with. I feel like I'm at the age and point in my life where it's gonna like effect good change and I'm ready for that change so that's where the excitement's coming from . . .

THERAPIST:    Absolutely . . . absolutely . . .

## Moment-by-Moment Tracking Glimmers of Transformance

Sam expresses both his anxiety and his excitement. Sam's excitement to be in therapy, connection to his motivation to make positive changes in his life, his confidence that he can do so, and his readiness to change are all examples of *transformance*. While clearly registering his anxiety as well as the problems that have brought him to treatment, as an AEDP therapist, I *privilege the positive affect* and first meet him in his excitement. I match his enthusiasm by expressing my own delight both nonverbally and verbally. My AEDP *healing-oriented* approach is in direct contrast to the approach therapists working from a pathology-oriented therapy may take if they were to first focus on Sam's anxiety, bypassing his enthusiasm and excitement. This work with transformance is also occurring in State 1.

**CLIENT:** And then I'm also like nervous . . . cause no one wants to believe there's like things with wrong with them and things that they have to change, but there's like two specific outcomes that I want to change . . .

### The Neurobiological Core Self Is Always Present

**THERAPIST:** Yeah, yeah . . . and you know you said nobody likes to see that there are things wrong with them . . . my experience, how I understand things, even how I understand myself . . . because we're both humans trying to figure life out . . . there are things that get in the way of us being fully ourselves . . . (*client nods*)

You being Sam, your best-self Sam, and me being my best-self Karen . . . so when you say there's things to change, I see it as we don't want to change Sam . . . we actually want to kind of bring Sam to life . . .

**CLIENT:** (*nods*) Mmm-hmmm . . .

**THERAPIST:** . . . in the fullness, the sense of him. So it's not like a new improved Sam, but it's Sam that's already there, but all of these other things get in the way of you being fully able to be the person that is compelling you to want to shift some of these behaviors that are getting in the way of you being you . . . does that makes sense?

**CLIENT:** (*nods*) That makes a lot of sense . . . yeah . . .

**THERAPIST:** Yeah . . . how do you feel about what I'm saying?

**CLIENT:** Yeah . . . good . . .

Sam expresses anxiety about seeing things "wrong with him." As an AEDP healing-oriented therapist, I dyadically regulate his anxiety by undoing his aloneness, self-disclosing, and providing psychoeducation. It is the concept of the neurobiological core self to which I was referring when I said to Sam "we don't want to change Sam . . . we actually want to kind of bring Sam to life. . . . In the fullness, the sense of him and so it's not like a new improved Sam, but it's Sam that's already there." This is an example of how the construct of the neurobiological core self (Fosha, 2013) translates into everyday clinical work.

### Unit of Intervention in AEDP: What the Therapist Does, and How the Client Receives It

I ask Sam explicitly how he feels about what I have said because I want to know how my comment or intervention lands inside him, how he receives it (receptive affective capacity). Not assuming, and *making the implicit explicit,* are foundational values in AEDP. Further, by explicitly separating the behaviors Sam has identified as problematic from his core self, I am laying the foundation to bypass or melt defenses that maintain the concerning behaviors by joining with him on the side of his core self.

THERAPIST:   Good . . . ok . . . so . . . so . . . the excitement to change some of the things that get in the way.

CLIENT:   Mmm-hmmm . . .

THERAPIST:   Marijuana, alcohol and anger . . .

CLIENT:   Mmm-hmmm (*hand in front of mouth, index finger strokes lip*)

THERAPIST:   So, tell me about the stirring that's inside you that says it's time.

### Tracking Transformance

With safety continuing to deepen between us and anxiety not overwhelming, again, I focus on Sam's *transformance* strivings: What is alive in him that is motivating him to reach out for change?

CLIENT:   Um . . . well part of it is . . . the girl that I'm dating . . . I really feel like she's the one . . . and I wanna change for us . . . because she's like really level-headed and down to earth. . . . And a lot of the behavior that I've shown in like my worst times . . . really scares her . . . and it's things like I don't know—I couldn't find my gym shorts one morning, and I was like "oh fuck" (*body moves in agitation*) . . . and like I threw the basket and I was like "this is ridiculous . . . our house is so fucking dirty" and like . . . [I want to make] our relationship better by being happy-go-lucky (*hands move a ball of air to the side*) . . . "let's go skiing, let's go for a bike ride . . . let's go for a walk" . . . and not the like "oh fuck, everything's wrong."

Sam being in a good committed relationship and demonstrating that he is motivated to change because of his care for his girlfriend are manifestations of *transformance*. Transformance is also evident in Sam's awareness that the intensity of his response to not finding his gym shorts was excessive. Yet at the same time, we are also getting to see in greater depth the nature of the difficulties that bring him to treatment. The intensity of his response and agitation to a seemingly small frustration lead me to wonder about trauma. Trauma is less about an event and more about the imprint it leaves on the mind, body, brain, and nervous system. Trauma reorganizes one's nervous system, leading one to feel helpless and to believe the world is a dangerous place (van der Kolk, 2014). As Fisher (2017) noted, a body, brain, or nervous system expecting annihilation and abandonment will respond in an exaggerated way to anything perceived as threatening to the self or relationships. I am suspecting that trauma-related perceptions and impulses driven by "situationally activated implicit memories" (p. 219) overtake Sam's here-and-now assessments, leading him to sense danger even in relatively benign situations.

## Working With Embodied Experience

Sam's openness and vulnerability in disclosing behavior that horrifies him indicates that safety is growing between us. However, State 1 phenomena, especially anxiety and panic, are clinical phenomena that need regulation before Sam can drop down and access the bodily rooted core affective experiences of State 2 work.

**THERAPIST:** I love this . . . okay, let's slow it down . . . what comes before the anger . . .

**CLIENT:** Uncertainty . . .

**THERAPIST:** Can we work with a real example . . . either a really significant one or a recent one or . . .

The experience of uncertainty, and the anxiety that goes with it, is identified as a trigger. I ask Sam to walk me through a specific example as I want us to work with specificity and detail (Fosha, 2000; see also Medley, Chapter 8, this volume). Sam shares with me an example of waking up and not having any pot to smoke. He says, "My relationship with pot is so bad . . . and it is something I hide from Beth [his girlfriend]." I internally note this and hypothesize that the substance use can be understood as an attempt to regulate a traumatized nervous system (Fisher, 2017).

**CLIENT:** Yeah . . . and then I was trying to get my stuff ready to go to the gym, which I usually do in the morning and um . . . I was just like looking for stuff and then . . . I don't know what I was uncertain about but it's this feeling of like (*clawed hand makes circular motion near face*) . . . "what am I doing? . . . Where am I going? . . . What do I have to do next?" . . . and then if I'm . . .

**THERAPIST:** Okay, so wait . . . tell me more . . . cause you're telling me what you *think* is happening but I'm wondering what's happening in your body . . . that uncertainty . . . how it sits with you . . .

I interrupt Sam because I want to know how he is experiencing the present moment. It is in the present moment that sensations, feelings, and images arise that lead to associative pathways, and it is the present moment experiencing that can alter past experiences (Stern, 2004). To stay in the present moment, I want to distinguish between Sam's conceptual self-awareness (i.e., what he *thinks* about what he is experiencing) from his embodied self-awareness (i.e., what he is *actually* experiencing in his body; Fogel, 2013). In so doing, I am helping Sam regulate emotional experience of State 1 anxiety by having him focus on his somatic experience. As I remain calm, centered, and empathic, I also hope to help him regulate his anxiety through his being in dyadic relationship with me. In the next passage, we explore his anxiety.

**CLIENT:**   Sort of like butterflies. . . . Like a nervous angst . . . that I don't really know where it's coming from to be honest . . .

**THERAPIST:**   Can you feel it right now?

**CLIENT:**   Yeah . . .

**THERAPIST:**   Okay . . . I know it's uncomfortable, but can we just stay with it . . . this nervous angst, butterfly, edgy . . .

**CLIENT:**   Yeah . . .

**THERAPIST:**   Is it chest or stomach or . . .

**CLIENT:**   (*hand in front of chest*) It's in the chest . . .

**THERAPIST:**   Ok so it's . . . just let's stay with it . . . and let's just imagine that it's actually talking to you . . . and letting you know something about what's happening either in your thoughts or happening in your circumstances . . . (*client's eyes closed, hand remain in front of chest*) . . . mmm-hmmmm . . . just notice when you don't try and shove it away and you don't try and react to it . . . just observe it with really gentle, compassionate eyes . . . mmmm . . .

**CLIENT:**   It's almost like . . . and it is linked with the caffeine as well . . . but the feeling is like if you've had too much caffeine . . .

**THERAPIST:**   Yeah. . .

**CLIENT:**   Like a little jittery . . . a little bit sort of like ready to (*fingers of both hands spread wide and gesture tension*) . . .

**THERAPIST:**   Yeah . . . and this is kind of a familiar feeling, experience for you . . .

**CLIENT:**   Mmm-hmmm . . .

**THERAPIST:**   This arises quite frequently . . .

**CLIENT:**   Yeah . . . yeah . . .

**THERAPIST:**   And . . . then you shift it either. . . .you have a little bit of explosion and that kind of shifts it or you smoke a joint or something and that shifts it . . .

**CLIENT:**   Mmm-hmmm. . . .

**THERAPIST:**   Or maybe do a big workout and maybe that shifts it . . .

**CLIENT:**   Yeah . . .

**THERAPIST:**   But you kinda don't really know . . . 'What is that agitation that I live with?' . . . Does that feel true?

**CLIENT:**   It's somewhat, yeah . . .

THERAPIST: Somewhat? . . . tell me more . . .

CLIENT: Um . . . I think that. . . . .there's this also some shortness of breath that happens . . . as well . . .

### Dyadic Affect Regulation to Promote Safety for Processing State 2 Affect

I am tracking Sam and our relationship moment by moment. To keep this State 1 work in the present moment and to also move it toward the State 2 affective experiences that I am assuming are underneath this anxiety and jitteriness, I am encouraging Sam to stay with his somatic and affective experience, all the while suggesting through my presence and calm that we will do this together and he will be okay. I am dyadically regulating Sam and undoing his aloneness by asking if *we* can stay with this. I am helping when I notice Sam struggle. For example, I offer "Is it [affect, sensation] in the chest or stomach?" I am also helping organize Sam's experience by narrating what I think is happening for Sam. I am tracking him closely to ensure that my narrative is true to Sam's experience. Feeling in emotional resonance with him and with gentle curiosity, I offer the word *panicky*.

THERAPIST: Feels a little bit panicky . . .

CLIENT: Panic is exactly it . . . yeah . . . like I've got something to do or something to get to or something to complete like immediately but. . . . and there's this urgency to it . . . that um . . . is . . . um . . . unsettling because I'm not entirely sure of what the urgency's for . . .

Being in emotional resonance with Sam, I am able to express just the right word to describe his experience. The word "panicky" resonates for Sam and evokes a *click of recognition* (Fosha, 2013), a moment between us when the word I use matches Sam's internal experience. Even though the experience itself is scary, the feeling of being seen and understood leads Sam to experience a positive affective experience in the midst of the anxiety.

CLIENT: You know like it's . . . like I tend to rush things . . . even in social situations . . . um . . . like if a friend texts me and they're like "hey, meet me here." . . . I'll like try and get ready to go there in like half an hour but the next text is like oh no, in like two and half hours and I've been like (*hands show flurry of activity*) . . . "Oh they're not gonna be my friend if I don't get there" (*frenetic*) . . . and it's a little silly . . .

### The "D" in AEDP: Current-Day Struggles Rooted in Past Unprocessed Experience

A theme emerges as Sam describes another situation in which his response is out of proportion to the current circumstance. I ask Sam about his history with feeling "panicky."

**THERAPIST:** Can I ask you something, Sam? (*Client nods*) Do you have a memory or memories of this kind of feeling that you're describing, this urgency, panicky . . . that takes you back in time? Like do you remember it as a child?

**CLIENT:** Um . . . I don't know . . . my whole childhood is such a . . . such a blur . . .

I note internally that Sam does not have a cohesive autobiographical narrative of his life. Having a cohesive autobiographical narrative of one's life is a reflection of one's capacity for an integrated sense of self. Without an integrated sense of self across past, present, and future, one may experience chaos, rigidity, or both, as opposed to emotional well-being (Siegel, 2012).

**THERAPIST:** This feeling . . . do you remember it from teen years . . . like when, if you were to just do a little review of your life . . . do you remember when you first started noticing this feeling . . . being aware and conscious of it?

**CLIENT:** I don't know if this is the first time cause I've always had a little bit of a short temper but the real like . . . one that sticks out as being the first instance of this sort of panic attacks I've had . . . was after I got out of hospital . . .

Sam describes the following experience: It is soon after a car accident that occurred when he was 15 years old. Sam is in his bedroom in his parents' house. He hears a song.

**CLIENT:** It [the song] sent me into this like panic state where I ended up like in the fetal position by the front door like of my bedroom . . . just like screaming "Aaaaahhh . . . make it stop!" . . . and my parents had no idea what was going on . . . they really like didn't understand . . . they were like . . . they were saying like "calm down" and . . . the usual reaction . . .

Sam's description of this experience suggests that the song was a trigger: When Sam heard the song, his physiology reacted, and he became flooded with intense emotions and terror. Sam was in need, and his parents could not help him. Their response, "Calm down," which Sam acknowledges is a familiar response, did not help. As a result, Sam is left alone with what in AEDP we refer to as the root of psychopathology: "aloneness in the face of overwhelming affective experience" (Fosha, 2000, p. 5). Therefore, doing what his parents could not do at that time becomes the here-and-now experiential focus of the therapy. Sam instituted defenses and when those defenses don't totally work, there is anxiety, "jitteriness," and the "panicky feeling." By linking his current symptoms of panic (State 1) to an earlier traumatic event allows us to move toward the core affective experiences underlying those symptoms, which will constitute the work of State 2. I want to provide Sam with a corrective relational experience by being responsive, deeply emotional, affect regulating, and affect facilitating. I wish to undo his aloneness and help him both feel and cope effectively by helping him share and bear this pain. As Fosha (2000) stated, "When previously disallowed experiences can be explored, the client becomes better able to deal with them within himself, and life-shrinking anxiety dissolves" (p. 37).

THERAPIST: Sam, as you're telling me about this, in this moment, do you feel more connected to the space that you were in when you were in the fetal position by the door, or do you feel like you're here with me looking at that younger you?

CLIENT: It feels like I'm kinda there . . .

## Unblending: "Now" From "Then" and Adult Sam From 15-Year-Old Sam

We have now dropped down into State 2. With anxiety and panic lessened, and with my solid support, connection and moment-to-moment attunement, Sam is able to access the feelings associated with his trauma, overwhelming experiences that defenses protected him from. Sam indicates that he experientially is more back in the "there-and-then" of the time of the trauma (i.e., "kinda there"), at the time of the car accident, than he is present in the "here-and-now" with me. In trauma language, his current-day self is *blended* (Schwartz & Sweezy, 2019) with his 15-year-old self. As an attachment figure, I take the lead and focus on *unblending* (Fisher, 2017; Schwartz & Sweezy, 2019) the 15-year-old Sam from adult Sam. What follows is an example of State 2 work with intrarelational experience.

I invite Sam into a *portrayal*, a technique used to process previously unprocessed State 2 emotional experiences (Davanloo, 1990; Fosha, 2000; see Medley, Chapter 8, this volume). A portrayal is also an opportunity to undo the aloneness and helplessness—and in this case, the uncertainty—of 15-year-old Sam with the help of adult Sam, with me supporting and guiding him through this work. The type of portrayal Sam and I work with is an intrarelational portrayal (Lamagna, 2015; Lamagna & Gleiser, 2007) in which we encourage the capacity for self-regulation through shared affective states of resonance between adult Sam, 15-year-old Sam, and me (see Gleiser, Chapter 12; Lamagna, Chapter 11, this volume). We foster attunement and recognition between 15-year-old Sam and adult Sam, as well as facilitating the development of a secure internal attachment between them. By doing so, we are working toward lessening the internal chasm between young and adult Sam.

## Cocreating the Portrayal: Leading and Following

THERAPIST: 'Cause what I'm wondering . . . if we could . . . so it's 10 years ago, the car accident? I'm wondering if there's a way . . . 24-year-old Sam and I can very gently . . . watch but be with that 15-year-old self who was really, really scared . . . I'm assuming scared and panicky and . . . "make it stop" and out of

CONTROL . . . I don't want you to go there . . . I want us to be able to hang in together but be as close to him as we can. . . . Do you think that is possible?

CLIENT:    I'll try, yeah . . .

THERAPIST:    Okay, so, so you and I are here, and there's the younger you against the door in the fetal position saying "make it stop, make it stop." . . . You and I are going, "oh my goodness . . . what does he want to stop? What is it that's happening inside him that's so scaring him in this moment?"

CLIENT:    Um . . . you know . . . you mentioned like going back to the . . . the point where I felt the feeling for the first time . . . like a real like (*hand in front of gut, fingers spread wide*) . . . I don't know what's about to happen and it was . . . like I . . . I remember play-for-play the accident . . .

I guide and accompany Sam into the experience in his bedroom, and then Sam takes the lead and redirects us to the actual car accident. So much safety has been created and his aloneness so undone, that Sam starts to describe the experience of the trauma, except that this time he is not alone with it as he was in the accident or emotionally alone with it as he was with his parents who, sadly, were not able to help him. Sam's capacity to redirect us to the precise moment of the reactivation of the trauma also speaks to the security of our attachment as security allows for a broader range of exploration. Sam describes the accident in detail. I work to dyadically regulate Sam to ensure that he stays within his window of tolerance and thus does not have an experience of emotionally reexperiencing the car accident, which could be retraumatizing. Rather, I want to ensure adult Sam stays present with me (i.e., in my office, in the present moment), so that he is able to give 15-year-old Sam a corrective experience of not being alone, helpless, and filled with uncertainty. The goal is to acknowledge, experientially process, and help the young and adult Sams to connect (Lamagna & Gleiser, 2007). We are continuing State 2 work.

THERAPIST:    So . . . so . . . right now, it feels like you're here with me . . . you're not in that car right now . . . does that feel true?

CLIENT:    Yeah . . .

THERAPIST:    And there is the 15-year-old you saying, "make it stop, make it stop, slow down, stop"

CLIENT:    Mmm-hmm

THERAPIST:    And he's scared . . .

CLIENT:    Mmm-hmm . . .

THERAPIST:    And he sees what's gonna happen . . . (*Sam nodding*) . . . and he can't do anything about it . . . yeah?

CLIENT:     Mmm-hmm (*nodding*) . . . it's a very . . . yeah, accurate portrayal . . .

THERAPIST:  Uh-huh . . . (*exhales*) . . . and as you and I together sit here and we're looking at that moment in time that the younger you was sitting in, what's happening inside you?

CLIENT:     I feel quite calm . . .

Adult Sam is feeling "quite calm" in the present moment, which indicates to me that he is unblended from 15-year-old Sam in the car accident and that the dyadic affect regulation is effective.

THERAPIST:  Okay . . . so what do we want to give him? Because right now he's in the crux of that experience where he wants it to stop, he's not in control, he can't do anything . . . he sees it coming, his life is flashing before his eyes . . . now, on the other side of that experience, the you here today . . . what do we want to be able to say to him?

CLIENT:     Um . . . I mean at first, like the obvious thing I would say is that it sort of turns out okay . . .

THERAPIST:  Yeah . . .

CLIENT:     I'm still here (*chuckles*) . . . I didn't die (*voice trembles*) . . .

THERAPIST:  If we imagine he's frozen in space, he doesn't know that so he actually needs to know that . . .

CLIENT:     Yeah . . .

THERAPIST:  That panicked 15-year-old in that freeze-frame moment needs to know that . . . (*Sam nodding*) . . . and what happens inside when I say that?

CLIENT:     It kind of makes me want to cry (*emotion rising*) . . .

THERAPIST:  Yeah . . . could you just feel that please? Could you please let those tears come? (*Client softly crying*) Yeah . . . yeah Sam, just be with that . . . mmm-hmmm . . . yeah . . . just let them come . . . let yourself feel . . .

I encourage Sam to experience the emotion that arises, accompanying him with my presence and right-brain-to-right-brain paraverbal utterings (e.g., "mmm-hmmm . . . yeah"). We are in deep affect, State 2 experiencing, expressing, and processing emotion that was too unbearable and overwhelming to feel alone at the time of the accident or in subsequent flashbacks.

CLIENT:     It's just (*sighs*) . . . like that point, it was just such a . . . like I look back and try and remember my childhood and I can't really remember because I can only remember up until that point . . . and like I know I've said it before that I feel like there was this pre-accident Sam where there was like . . . and there was two years of me trying to learn who I was again . . . um . . .

Sam is reminding me that his autobiographical narrative is fragmented, mirroring others who have experienced trauma. Sam not remembering his childhood also suggests to me that there may have been trauma that precedes the car accident when he was 15 years old.

### Staying Focused and on Target

THERAPIST:    So I want you to just stay with me . . . and I want you to go back to that Sam . . . and let's give him a little bit of attention . . . and I get, and I want to go back to, the preaccident Sam . . . the two years of Sam trying to come back, and then the Sam now and the last number of years, but let's go back to that Sam who, in that moment, is feeling like "holy fuck" . . . cause we need to let him know that he comes out . . . (*Sam is nodding*) . . . yeah . . . what's happening inside as I say that?

Sam is letting me know that there are many unprocessed painful experiences associated with the car accident. I explicitly acknowledge this to Sam and gently ask to set those aside so that we can continue to process *this* piece of work. Sam returns to a play-by-play of the accident. The word "uncertainty" is sprinkled throughout.

THERAPIST:    So you just backed us up and now we're with the 15-year-old . . . yup . . . go ahead . . .

CLIENT:    And . . . the last stretch was the real piece of uncertainty . . . and when the first of moment of seeing the tires go out, that's when I was first like "ok, we're fucked" . . . (*Therapist: Mm-hmm . . .*) But obviously we're both okay . . .

THERAPIST:    Tell that to that 15-year-old . . .

CLIENT:    Like out loud?

THERAPIST:    Yeah . . .

CLIENT:    "We're okay." . . .

THERAPIST:    Reach a hand out to him . . . and say, "I see we're gonna be ok . . . it's fucked up but we're gonna be ok" . . .

CLIENT:    Yeah . . .

THERAPIST:    And I want him to look at you. . . . I want you to just take a moment out of the time space continuum . . . just look at him and tell him again . . .

CLIENT:    (*softly, eyes open, looking ahead*) "We're gonna be OK."

**THERAPIST:** Let him really breathe that in . . . yes . . . feel that . . . feel that. Sam . . . tell me what's happening inside?

## Integrating the Healing Experience Through Embodiment

I encourage Sam to breathe in this new experience of "We're going to be okay" to help him embody this truth. For integration to occur, it must be embodied because the "brain learns from each experience of embodied self-awareness . . . neural learning is reflected in physiological changes in the nerve cells and their connections" (Fogel, 2013, p. 60).

**CLIENT:** (*voice is trembling*) Well I'm trying to . . . I'm trying to like imagine myself in the moment before impact with the first car . . .

**THERAPIST:** Yeah . . .

**CLIENT:** And . . . and I'm sorting of trying to imagine myself . . . like I'm sitting as the 15-year-old but I'm also trying to imagine myself and how . . . like what I've done in the last few years. . . . Looking and trying to say, like through the windshield almost . . . as the car's coming that we're gonna be okay. . . . And that makes me feel horrible because not everyone was okay . . .

**THERAPIST:** Okay . . . you know what, Sam? We can spend some time with how not everybody was okay . . . but can we just stay with 15-year-old Sam right now?

Again, I acknowledge other aspects of the car accident and ask Sam if we can set those aside for a later time. We want to be where we are and not lose this healing opportunity.

**THERAPIST:** And just let him know . . . and make sure he can feel it so that he can also come into the future . . . into today with you and he doesn't get left in that car at that moment.

**CLIENT:** Right . . . (*sniffs*) . . .

**THERAPIST:** Frozen in time . . .

**CLIENT:** I think one of the things that's really useful to imagine is when I'm like imagining myself in that seat . . . (*voice cracking*) . . . it's also easy to imagine myself in like a university . . . you know that's when we . . . you know . . .

By tracking Sam and our relationship moment by moment, we are in affective resonance in which we lead and follow each other seamlessly. Sam now takes the lead and wants to let younger Sam know that he attends university after the accident.

**THERAPIST:** Yes, it's like saying to the 15-year-old . . . "yes, you're in this seat right now and you're gonna be in a seat in university" . . .

> so feel that, Sam . . . feel the truth of that . . . this seat in the car
> and then you're gonna be in the seat in university . . . yeah . . .
> (*Client: crying, tears*) . . . just let yourself feel . . . so important . . .
> from this seat in the car, which is holy fuck and so scary, to this
> seat in university.

Adult Sam wants to connect the scared, uncertain 15-year-old Sam to his life after the accident, to his life in university. Another wave of State 2 emotion moves through Sam. Tracking moment by moment, I attend to the phenomena associated with each wave of emotion. I notice Sam's tears lessening, and he sighs, indicating both that *this* wave of emotion is passing and that *this* round of processing is completing. Now I can ask him about his experience without interrupting the wave of emotion.

THERAPIST:   Yeah . . . yeah . . . can you tell me what's happening inside?

CLIENT:   Um . . . I feel quite calm . . .

THERAPIST:   Wow . . .

For Sam, emotion previously unbearable, now expressed and experienced, results in calm. The "calm" Sam is experiencing appears to be is deeply embodied and suggests the phenomena of State 4. What is important to note is that the process in which client–therapist dyads are engaged does not always follow the four-state transformational process linearly: Sam and I just moved from State 2 emotional processing to an experience of State 4 core state.

CLIENT:   But then also quite like I don't feel very (*shoulders raise*) . . .
          tense . . . I think a lot of the tension that I had this morning,
          I can already feel that kind of leaving . . .

## State 3 Phenomena Emerge, Which, When Metaprocessed, Foster Integration

As Sam notices the tension leaving his body, I lean into the post-breakthrough affects associated with completing a wave of emotion and urge him to experience the feelings that mark *change for the better* that is taking place as a result of our work. Sam is present, in-the-moment experiencing an ease inside himself. From State 4, we now proceed to State 3, metaprocessing, the positive affective experiences that emerge after the completion of the emotional State 2 work.

THERAPIST:   Yup . . . so just feel that . . . your body's relaxing . . .

CLIENT:   And I think I feel. . . . like okay. . . .I just um . . .

THERAPIST:   Tell me about feeling okay . . .

In *metaprocessing*, I invite Sam to reflect on and embody the experience of feeling calm, which leads to the experience of being aware of tension releasing that, when reflected upon, leads to his feeling "okay." This is the transformational spiral that metaprocessing often brings about (Fosha, 2009; Fosha et al., 2019). Each new experience reflected upon leads to yet another new healing experience. We are in State 3.

**CLIENT:**  I feel like it's . . . I haven't ever really cried about the accident after . . . I think it's good to go back.

**THERAPIST:**  Yeah . . . yes . . . it really feels good to back to that 15-year-old who was so scared and let him know he's gonna be sitting in a university seat . . .

As painful as it is to feel his emotions, to cry about the accident, Sam reports it is "good." It is good because it is true, real, and needed.

**CLIENT:**  Yeah . . . it's almost like resolve . . . if you will . . . the unfinished story . . .

## State 4: The Creation of a New Autobiographical Narrative

Sam articulates that a shift has occurred, from something being unfinished to something being finished. Sam is creating a new autobiographical narrative. Sam intuits that healing also involves resolving the "unfinished story." He is creating a cohesive and coherent narrative in which the car accident is not the end but just a point in the timeline of his life. The time after the accident and the clarity of being okay, manifested through, among many other things, Sam going to university. The explicit autobiographical narrative of Sam's life is evolving through connecting the 15-year-old Sam who is scared, alone, and filled with uncertainty with the adult Sam who is okay and goes to university. By providing continuity between those two points in time, the previously unfinished story moves through to resolution.

**THERAPIST:**  Exactly . . . so really let yourself feel that because you've been holding . . . he has been holding that uncertainty right back to where we started this session for a long time.

**CLIENT:**  (*nodding*) Yeah . . .

**THERAPIST:**  He needs to know that you are the man that you are today . . . (*Sam now crying*)

**THERAPIST:**  Mmm what happens when I say those words "he needs to know the man that you are today?"

**CLIENT:**  It feels good (*both chuckle*) . . . I mean I've done a lot of things that I'm really proud of . . .

Another wave of State 2 emotion arises and is followed by his sense of pride in the self who has come so far since the accident. Pride is often a phenomenon associated with State 3 *mastery affects* emerging from the therapeutic work just experienced.

**THERAPIST:** You have . . . tell him . . . I've done . . . "you, buddy" . . . (*Sam nodding and smiling*) . . . "buddy, we do good."

**CLIENT:** Yeah . . .

**THERAPIST:** Mm-hmm . . . let yourself release any emotions there Sam . . . yeah . . . for him, for you . . . and let the two of you come together in the reality of today and all you've been through and all that is good in your life . . . like Beth [girlfriend] . . .

**CLIENT:** Yeah . . . (*emotion rising*) . . . yeah . . . [Therapist: Yeah . . . yeah. . . (*nodding*)] It feels quite good actually . . .

**THERAPIST:** Tell me more about it feels quite good . . .

**CLIENT:** I just . . . it feels like a relief . . . like it feels um . . .

**THERAPIST:** Tell me about *you* feeling relief . . . "I" feel relief . . .

I encourage a verbal shift from "*it* feels like a relief" to "I feel relief" to help Sam personalize, embody, and own the experience of relief resulting from our work together. I invite Sam to go back to where we started, with uncertainty, from the vantage point of where we have arrived.

**CLIENT:** I feel that . . . I can sort of like go back to that moment now . . . like or the subsequent moment that followed . . . (*Sam lists a number of memories associated with the car accident filled with uncertainty*) . . . the uncertainty of like I can sort of go back there now . . . and I know how to . . .

**THERAPIST:** Go back there and . . . fill in the uncertainty . . .

**CLIENT:** Exactly . . .

**THERAPIST:** Cause now you know . . .

**CLIENT:** Yeah . . . and be able to . . . at least now in this moment I'm going back and looking at those situations rather than feeling the uncertainty that I used to feel . . .

Sam clearly and spontaneously articulated the nature of the healing that he is experiencing from the vantage point of how he feels now. He can go back to uncertainty-filled situations of the past feeling okay, rather than "feeling the uncertainty I used to feel."

**THERAPIST:** That you felt then . . . yes . . .

**CLIENT:** I'm going back and sort of approaching it with the lens of "it's ok, but this did happen."

Sam describes feeling resourced in a way he did not previously. More evidence of State 4 experiencing is indicated by Sam's broadening repertoire of responses and his building capacity to access resources (Fredrickson & Joiner, 2018).

THERAPIST: Yes . . . how does that feel?

CLIENT: That feels really good.

THERAPIST: OK feel that . . . feel that feeling of this feels really good . . . yeah . . .

CLIENT: It's almost like empowering . . .

By asking metaprocessing questions, I help Sam deepen into feeling "really good" and another transformational spiral emerges as he moves from feeling "pride" to "really good" to feeling "empowered." *Empowering* is a State 3 mastery affect. This is a great outcome for Sam, who felt overwhelmed with uncertainty at the beginning of the session.

THERAPIST: Yes . . . tell me about empowering . . .

CLIENT: Um (*voice trembles*) . . . it . . . (*sighs*) . . . sort of feels like I have a strategy to work with . . .

THERAPIST: You do have a strategy to work with . . . and tell me how younger Sam feels . . .

CLIENT: Younger Sam still feels a little uncertain . . .

Metaprocessing queries sometimes bring up the next round of unfinished work. As Sam feels empowered, another round of State 2 affect also appears to be emerging as indicated by the tremble in Sam's voice and that young Sam still feels "a little uncertain."

THERAPIST: Uh-huh . . . like he hasn't quite heard you?

CLIENT: No, I don't . . . I don't know . . . um . . . I feel like there's still that feeling of panic and not being able to go back to the healthiest I will ever be because of all the surgeries and stuff . . . that was a result of that and that makes me feel a little anxious . . .

THERAPIST: So that feels like, and correct me, but that feels like another piece for us to work on . . . (*Sam nods*) . . . is the losses that did come out of that accident. . . . Yeah . . . so . . . we can bring some certainty to that 15-year-old you in terms of all that does happen for you and there's some things that that 15-year-old is still holding that don't turn out okay and we need to do some work around that . . .

CLIENT: Yeah. . .

THERAPIST: Does that feel right?

CLIENT: It does, yeah . . . yeah . . .

THERAPIST: How do you feel about this piece that we did today?

I validate for Sam the work that remains and that will need to be pursued in future sessions. While acknowledging the need for further work, I also want to help him solidify the work we did together in this first session. I use a *metaprocessing* question to encourage Sam to verbalize his experience of our work together with the aim of fostering further integration of this affect laden session.

CLIENT:     Really good . . . I mean I've never worked with a counselor who was like able to get me into that sort of . . . scenario . . . I think that worked really well . . .

THERAPIST:  Yeah . . . it feels right . . . it feels good . . . like it felt like *we* were in it and *we're* doing this, right? . . . And then you can really distinguish between the you you are today and the 15-year-old that was in that situation. And that you're not there anymore . . .

CLIENT:     Mmm-hmmm (*nods*) . . .

THERAPIST:  Yeah . . . well it's delightful working with you (*both smile*) . . . it was very fun . . . it is very fun for me . . . (*fingers interweave*) when this kind of stuff happens . . .

CLIENT:     That's good . . . that's good . . .

As this session closes, Sam and I share a moment of intersubjective delight for what we just experienced together. In this intersubjective state, not only is Sam changed by the experience, but I am as well. Although the therapeutic relationship is asymmetrical, it is also mutually, although differentially, growthful (Fosha, 2000). Sam feels empowered by his experience with me. And I too felt empowered as an AEDP therapist by this experience with Sam. I feel grateful Sam was able to accept what I offered and that he benefited from the experience. It helps me feel more confident in myself and in AEDP.

## CONCLUSION

From the get-go, as an AEDP therapist, I approach the work from a healing-oriented versus pathology-oriented stance. I embody the knowledge that transformance is always present, that a neurobiological core self is always ripe for liberation, and that new experiences and positive affective experiences create new neural pathways. With this knowledge on board, I work to create the conditions for the four-state transformational process to emerge and unfold. Knowing the phenomenology of the four-state transformational process allows me to track the material moment by moment and choose my interventions, aiming to foster the unfolding of the transformational process in the context of a safe and secure therapeutic relationship.

In State 1, Sam and I cocreated a secure attachment that allowed Sam to feel *safe* and me to feel *brave*. With Sam feeling safe, and through the dyadic affect regulation of his anxiety, Sam is able both to access an affect-laden traumatic experience and to remain within his window of tolerance. We engage State 2 work where we were able to process to completion core affective experiences associated with trauma that were previously too unbearable and overwhelming to experience, much less process, alone. With Sam feeling safe, I became brave, which manifested in taking the risks an AEDP therapist takes on behalf of her client's healing: I self-disclosed, joined in emotional resonance with Sam (as opposed to hiding my emotions), dyadically regulated Sam's emotional experience, did not leave him alone with overwhelming emotions, engaged with him in an emotionally responsive manner, trusted the four-state transformational process, encouraged deep emotional processing of a traumatic event in a first session, invited emergent experiences within Sam and between Sam and me, and explicitly asked Sam how he experienced our work together. Working intrarelationally with Sam's present-day adult self and his 15-year-old self enabled the adult Sam to begin to integrate into a new emergent autobiographical narrative the fact that he survived the accident, that he subsequently reengaged his life as manifested by his having gone to university, and that he has a lot of resources and an increased repertoire of behaviors from which to draw upon. What also emerged were several more places that require healing that Sam and I need to attend to in subsequent sessions. Nevertheless, healing happened in this first session, and this allowed Sam to have a *new* experience, and a *good* one at that.

## REFERENCES

Bowlby, J. (1977). The making and breaking of affectional bonds: Aetiology and psychopathology in the light of attachment theory. *The British Journal of Psychiatry*, *130*(3), 201–210. https://doi.org/10.1192/bjp.130.3.201

Bowlby, J. (1988). *A secure base: Parent–child attachment and healthy human development*. Basic Books.

Damasio, A. (2018). *The strange order of things: Life, feeling, and the making of cultures*. Pantheon Books.

Darwin, C. (1965). *The expression of emotion in man and animals*. University of Chicago Press. (Original work published 1872) https://doi.org/10.7208/chicago/9780226220802.001.0001

Davanloo, H. (1990). *Unlocking the unconscious: Selected papers of Habib Davanloo*. Wiley.

Doidge, N. (2016). *The brain's way of healing: Remarkable discoveries and recoveries from the frontiers of neuroplasticity*. Penguin.

Fisher, J. (2017). *Healing the fragmented selves of trauma survivors: Overcoming internal self-alienation*. Routledge. https://doi.org/10.4324/9781315886169

Fogel, A. (2013). *Body sense: The science and practice of embodied self-awareness*. Norton.

Fosha, D. (2000). *The transforming power of affect: A model for accelerated change*. Basic Books.

Fosha, D. (2003). Dyadic regulation and experiential work with emotion and relatedness in trauma and disordered attachment. In M. F. Solomon & D. J. Siegel (Eds.), *Healing trauma: Attachment, trauma, the brain and the mind* (pp. 221–281). Norton.

Fosha, D. (2008). Recognition, vitality, passion. And love. *Constructivism in the Human Sciences, 12*, 57–77.

Fosha, D. (2009). Emotion and recognition at work: Energy, vitality, pleasure, truth, desire, and the emergent phenomenology of transformational experience. In D. Fosha, D. J. Siegel, & M. F. Solomon (Eds.), *The healing power of emotion: Affective neuroscience, development, clinical practice* (pp. 172–201). Norton.

Fosha, D. (2013). A heaven in a wildflower: Self, dissociation, and treatment in the context of the neurobiological core self. *Psychoanalytic Inquiry, 33*(5), 496–523. https://doi.org/10.1080/07351690.2013.815067

Fosha, D. (2017). How to be a transformational therapist: AEDP harnesses innate healing affects to re-wire experience and accelerate transformation. In J. Loizzo, M. Neale, & E. J. Wolf, (Eds.), *Advances in contemplative psychotherapy: Accelerating transformation* (pp. 204–219). Routledge.

Fosha, D., Thoma, N., & Yeung, D. (2019). Transforming emotional suffering into flourishing: Metatherapeutic processing of positive affect as a trans-theoretical vehicle for change. *Counselling Psychology Quarterly, 32*(3–4), 563–593. https://doi.org/10.1080/09515070.2019.1642852

Fredrickson, B. L., & Joiner, T. (2018). Reflections on positive emotions and upward spirals. *Perspectives on Psychological Science, 13*(2), 194–199. https://doi.org/10.1177/1745691617692106

Frijda, N. (1986). *The emotions.* Cambridge University Press.

Hanson, R. (2018). *Resilient: How to grow an unshakable core of calm, strength, and happiness.* Harmony.

Hill, C. E. (2008). Rejoinder: The what, when, and how of immediacy. *Psychotherapy, 45*(3), 324–328. https://doi.org/10.1037/a0013308

James, W. (1902). *The varieties of religious experience: A study in human nature.* Penguin Books. https://doi.org/10.1037/10004-000

Lamagna, J. (2015). Making good use of suffering: Intra-relational work with pathogenic affects. *Transformance, 6*(1). https://aedpinstitute.org/transformance-journal-2/

Lamagna, J., & Gleiser, K. A. (2007). Building a secure internal attachment: An intra-relational approach to ego strengthening and emotional processing with chronically traumatized clients. *Journal of Trauma & Dissociation, 8*(1), 25–52. https://doi.org/10.1300/J229v08n01_03

Main, M. (1996). Introduction to the special section on attachment and psychopathology: 2. Overview of the field of attachment. *Journal of Consulting and Clinical Psychology, 64*(2), 237–243. https://doi.org/10.1037/0022-006X.64.2.237

Panksepp, J., & Biven, L. (2012). *The archaeology of mind: Neuroevolutionary origins of human emotions.* Norton.

Porges, S. W. (2017). *The pocket guide to the polyvagal theory: The transformative power of feeling safe.* Norton.

Prenn, N. (2009). I second that emotion! On self-disclosure and its metaprocessing. In A. Bloomgarden & R. B. Menutti (Eds.), *Psychotherapist revealed: Therapists speak about self-disclosure in psychotherapy* (pp. 85–99). Routledge.

Prenn, N., & Fosha, D. (2016). *Essentials of accelerated experiential dynamic psychotherapy supervision.* American Psychological Association.

Schore, A. N. (2019). *Right brain psychotherapy.* Norton.

Schwartz, R. C., & Sweezy, M. (2019). *Internal family systems therapy* (2nd ed.). Guilford Press.

Siegel, D. J. (2012). *The developing mind: How relationships and the brain interact to shape who we are* (2nd ed.). Guilford Press.

Stern, D. N. (2004). *The present moment in psychotherapy and everyday life.* Norton.

Tronick, E. Z. (2003). "Of course all relationships are unique": How co-creative processes generate unique mother–infant and client–therapist relationships and change other relationships. *Psychoanalytic Inquiry, 23*(3), 473–491. https://doi.org/10.1080/ 07351692309349044

Tronick, E. Z., Bruschweiler-Stern, N., Harrison, A. M., Lyons-Ruth, K., Morgan, A. C., Nahum, J. P., Sander, L., & Stern, D. N. (1998). Dyadically expanded states of consciousness and the process of therapeutic change. *Infant Mental Health Journal, 19*(3), 290–299. https://doi.org/10.1002/(SICI)1097-0355(199823)19:3<290::AID-IMHJ4>3.0.CO;2-Q

van der Kolk, B. A. (2014). *The body keeps the score: Brain, mind, and the body in the healing of trauma*. Penguin.

# II

# CONTEXT AND SCAFFOLDING

# 3

# Historical Context

## AEDP's Place in the World of Psychotherapy

Gil Tunnell and Jenna Osiason

Beginning with the establishment of psychotherapy in the late 19th century by Freud and others, the field evolved in three distinct movements, or "waves" as Bill O'Hanlon (1994) called them. The *psychopathology-based* First Wave focused exclusively on individuals and their memories of past childhood experiences, without considering their current interpersonal contexts or their contemporaneous environments. The *problem-focused* Second Wave in the middle 20th century focused more narrowly on the specific problem and the microenvironmental and immediate familial contexts that maintained the problem. The *solution-focused* Third Wave began in the late 20th century and was based on postmodern, constructivist thinking. Contrasted with the first two waves that emphasized past and present factors, the Third Wave helped patients imagine and experience a different future and "reinvent" themselves. Postmodernism allowed for alternative views of the same phenomena and, in particular, examined the wider role of culture and society in defining "normal" and who decides what normal is.

Each wave of psychotherapy posed a distinct challenge to previous waves, and in addressing that challenge often produced a paradigm shift (Kuhn, 1970). In this chapter, we explicate each wave to discuss how psychotherapeutic models have evolved and continue to this day, discuss where AEDP fits

We thank our mentor and director of the AEDP Institute, Diana Fosha, for her astute and careful reading of our work. We also thank Martha Edwards of the Ackerman Institute in New York City, who painstakingly edited our manuscript with helpful edits and clarifications.

https://doi.org/10.1037/0000232-004
*Undoing Aloneness and the Transformation of Suffering Into Flourishing: AEDP 2.0*, D. Fosha (Editor)

in the three waves, and end with a Coda that recognizes other theorists who have contributed to AEDP's development.

## THE FIRST WAVE OF PSYCHOTHERAPY

Freud's psychoanalysis best exemplifies the First Wave. The analyst was the expert who treated the patient's psychopathology by analyzing the transference and challenging the patient's defenses and resistance to treatment. Focusing on the patient's past, psychoanalysis had as its goal to understand how the patient's symptoms had developed historically and intrapsychically. Freud's paradigm was based on linear causality: Unconscious conflict between the id and superego caused symptoms but not the other way around as in circular causality. Once the intrapsychic conflict was understood and the patient gained insight, the symptoms would presumably dissipate.

Freud's theory was based on drives, and these drives were what propelled behavior. The therapeutic stance was one of neutrality, abstinence (denying gratifying the patient verbally), and passivity as a therapeutic stance with little to no attention to the real relationship between patient and analyst. The patient's history was reflected in his or her mental representations, and the patient's reports of childhood sexual trauma were understood to be imagined and not based on actual experience. Analysts sat mostly in silence but in clinical judgment of the patient's psychopathology as it was exposed and became projected onto them throughout treatment. Through their interpretations, analysts aimed to help the patient develop insight, held to be the principal mechanism of change. The analyst was the all-knowing expert/authority. Once the transference was resolved, the patient's functioning was expected to improve.

It is worth noting that Freudian psychoanalysis was itself a major advance in how mental illness had been conceptualized. Theretofore, the mentally ill were viewed as morally deficient or in demonic possession, and more or less untreatable (Foucault, 2009). The First Wave led to a more systematic understanding of types of psychopathology and produced the first *Diagnostic and Statistical Manual of Mental Disorders* in 1952.

## THE SECOND WAVE OF PSYCHOTHERAPY

In a radical departure from the First Wave of psychotherapy, the Second Wave focused on the "here and now" of the patient's behavior patterns, not the "there and then" of the past. Second Wave therapies applied a laser-sharp lens on the patient's specific problem, not overall intrapsychic psychopathology per se. Initiating the problem-focused Second Wave, behaviorism (Skinner, 1953) posed a serious and direct challenge to Freud: It was not the individual's past that determined behavior but rather current environmental stimuli and reinforcement contingencies. Skinner put forth a conditioning paradigm whereby new, more adaptive behaviors were reinforced, and maladaptive stimulus–response connections were extinguished. Later, cognitive behavioral therapy (CBT;

Beck, 1964) brought the brain, albeit in a top-down fashion, into behaviorism's Black Box: The patients' thoughts controlled their feelings and behaviors; CBT sought to change the behaviors by changing the patient's cognitions. Like psychoanalysis, both behavior therapy and CBT followed a linear causality paradigm: Environmental stimuli and cognitions determine behavior, but not, as in circular causality, the other way around. Again, the therapist was the expert in treating the maladaptive behavior.

Behaviorism sparked the Second Wave in that it ushered in, for the first time in the history of psychotherapy, a focus on specific problematic behavior, not on overall psychopathology as First Wave Freudians did, nor on moral deficiency before Freud.

In the second part of the Second Wave, family therapy in the 1980s introduced "systems thinking" and, from cybernetics, the idea of circular causality, where A affects B, and in turn B affects A (Bateson, 1972; Von Foester, 1952). All three major models of family therapy—structural (Minuchin, 1974), three generational (Bowen, 1985), and strategic (Haley, 1976)—posited that the "identified patient" is reacting to family dynamics and vice versa. The entire family was the patient, not the individual. These models zeroed in on the current interpersonal context that contained and maintained the problem, with the Bowenians emphasizing the influence of past generational patterns on the present ones.

As O'Hanlon (1994) noted, the Second Wave "attempted to remedy the over-focus on pathology and the past" (p. 21) that the First Wave had emphasized. Moreover, Second Wave models of systems thinking and behaviorism held that the individual functioned in a "closed" system that would continue to sustain the specific problem unless there was outside intervention by a family therapist or a behaviorist. Whereas First Wave Freudian psychoanalysis was primarily a mental or reflective endeavor to help the patient gain insight, the Second Wave therapies of behaviorism and family systems devalued insight and sought to change the patient's actual behavior. Finally, Second Wave therapies offered significantly shorter treatments than psychoanalysis did, again, by focusing on the specific behavioral problem, not on overall psychopathology.

Like First Wave psychoanalysts, Second Wave therapists believed they were the experts who treated symptoms and problems. Moreover, unlike postmodern thinking yet to come, "modern" Second Wave thinking held that objective Truth exists in reality and can be discovered. These master therapists argued they had discovered the Truth, even though psychoanalysis, behaviorism, and family systems offer quite different conceptualizations of psychopathology and its treatment. Because in "modern" thinking there can be only one Truth,[1] the theories competed against each other, and each lay claim to having

---

[1] Minuchin did not actually believe there is only one Truth, but rather multiple truths as in Nagy's concept of "multidimensional partiality" (Boszormenyi-Nagy & Sparks, 1984). Minuchin offered the family an alternative "construction" of the family dynamics they were showing him, one which he believed would lead to rapid behavioral change. Tunnell wishes to thank his colleagues Gail Woods, Martha Edwards, David Greenan and Anne Rivers for pointing this out.

proposed the most accurate and most definitive description of human behavior and its determinants yet to date.

## THE THIRD WAVE OF PSYCHOTHERAPY

The Third Wave of psychotherapy—dominated by postmodern constructivist thinking—went well beyond both the First Wave's focus on the individual and the past, as well as the Second Wave's emphasis on the individual's current interpersonal or environmental context. Instead, the Third Wave focused on the future and finding solutions. Postmodernism demanded that traditional psychotherapeutic models consider the effects of the broader culture and society in determining what is a problem, and once defined, developing novel and faster ways to solve it. The Third Wave vigorously challenged both systems thinking and behaviorism, which had assumed that family life and the surrounding environment "tell us how to think and who to be" (O'Hanlon, 1994, p. 23). O'Hanlon (1994) wrote:

> Third Wave approaches take very seriously philosopher Martin Heidegger's concept of 'throwness.' Like clay thrown on a potter's wheel, we are shaped from the moment of our birth, not only by our family legacy, but by the culture that creates the way we see and talk about ourselves and the world. (p. 23)

Tunnell (2019) argued that the shift from modern to postmodern therapeutic models was facilitated by three transitional movements or bridges: (a) feminism, (b) multiculturalism, and (c) seminal concepts introduced by the Italian systemic family therapist Mara Selvini Palazzoli and her Milan Group (Palazzoli et al., 1978).

As part of constructivist thinking, feminist theory challenged the dominance of male hierarchy—not only in society but in family life as well (Walters et al., 1988). Feminism argued that women had been neglected in both theory and clinical practice and that a feminist point of view (i.e., the advocacy of women's rights on the basis of the equality of the two genders) is an equally valid perspective on the same phenomena and must be taken into account (Chodorow, 1989; Gilligan, 1982).

The second bridge to postmodern psychotherapy was multiculturalism (Sue & Sue, 2015), which challenged the way therapists had defined "normal." Multiculturalism insisted that each particular culture determined what is "normal," and culture most certainly went beyond Western European, White, heterosexual male views and values (Miller, 1976).

The third forerunner to postmodernism was Palazzoli and her Milan Group (Palazzoli et al., 1978) who introduced the concept of "positive connotation" and clinically explored the power of paradox. These "reframes" presented the family with an alternative view of the problem that paradoxically put a positive spin on it while pointing out the negative consequences, placing the patient in a "therapeutic double bind." The Milan Group also developed an innovative technique called *circular questioning* (asking each member of the family to comment on the relationship between two other members), which uncovered multiple subjective views of how the family functioned.

Both positive connotation and circular questioning imply that there are almost always multiple, "small-t" truths. Who is to say which reality is Truth? Here specifically we begin to see the shift from the stance of one Truth to multiple truths.

Perhaps more important than anything else, the postmodern constructivist models of the Third Wave fundamentally defied both First Wave and Second Wave models by challenging their twin ideas that (a) therapists were experts who treated serious psychopathology or solved specific problems and (b) there is only one big-T Truth, be it Freud's psychoanalysis, Skinner's behaviorism, or family systems therapy. Postmodernism questioned the essence of reality (Held, 1995).[2]

What, then, did the Third Wave of psychotherapy offer as alternative treatments? The Third Wave comprises competency-based models (O'Hanlon, 1994). A radical shift occurred in the move from treating the patient's overall psychopathology or specific problems, to uncovering underutilized competencies (and capacities) patients already possessed. Third Wave therapists believed the Second Wave's "focus on problems often obscures the resources and solutions residing within the person" (O'Hanlon, 1994, p. 23). Moreover, Third Wave therapists no longer considered themselves the only experts in the consultation room but instead shared their expertise by working collaboratively with patients to identify and reap the benefit of their existing internal resources. A shift in language in the Third Wave reflected a less demeaning, more collaborative view of persons in psychotherapy: "Patients" were now "clients" or even "customers" (deShazer, 1985).

In O'Hanlon's (1994) analysis, the Third Wave consisted of only two models: narrative therapy (White & Epston, 1990) and solution-focused therapy (deShazer, 1985). Both models (a) developed faster ways of helping patients get symptom relief, (b) explored solutions rather than problems from the very beginning of therapy, (c) emphasized what was positive in the patient's life *now* and built on that, and (d) optimistically forecasted how the patient would be in the future, rather than dwelling on the past or the present.

While narrative therapy helped patients reinvent themselves and write new narratives, solution-focused therapists adopted an attitude of curiosity and "not knowing" (Anderson & Goolishian, 1992) by asking questions where the answer might appear to be patently obvious. Upon hearing the complaint in the first session, the solution-focused therapist always asks the "miracle question":

> Do you believe in miracles? Suppose in the middle of the night while you are sleeping, a miracle occurs that entirely eliminates your problem. When you wake up, what is the very first thing you notice that is different from yesterday? (deShazer, 1985)

---

[2]Barbara Held (1995) challenged Third-Wave therapists in their subjective interpretation of reality. She asked: Surely there must be a reality somewhere.

When Insoo Kim Berg (1994) asked a couple this question in the middle of their first session, the wife, who had felt estranged and unattractive to her husband, answered, "Well, the very first thing I would notice that a miracle had occurred is that my husband is kissing me as I wake up." Adopting an attitude of "not knowing," Kim Berg continued, "And how does that early morning kiss from your husband affect you? How does his kiss change anything? What does his early morning kiss mean to you?"[3]

Like narrative therapy, solution-focused therapy was an extremely brief yet efficient treatment (insurance companies loved it!) that took the patient's presenting complaint at face value and did not look for deeper problems to solve. As deShazer (1985) quoted from the saying, "If it ain't broke, don't fix it."

When O'Hanlon published his article in 1994, he presented narrative and solution-focused therapy as the entire Third Wave of psychotherapy. However, competency-based models have existed before and after those models. Earlier, the humanistic patient-centered therapy of Carl Rogers (1951) focused on uncovering, shifting attention to, and highlighting the individual's competencies, if we define "competencies" also to include the capacities for healing and self-righting.

In fact, the Third Wave of psychotherapy continued beyond narrative and solution-focused therapies to include a range of shorter term, competency-based, collaborative talk-based therapies that emphasized strengths and positives. More contemporaneously, Seligman (2011) introduced positive psychology as a major competency-based model. Here the emphasis was on strengths and privileging the positive. Positive psychology (Seligman, 2002) accentuated both the patient's resources and encouraged the experience of having *and enjoying* the positive emotions (gratitude, pride, joy, and genuine happiness in creating a meaningful life). Seligman completely upended the focus on psychopathology! Moreover, unlike Palazzoli's positive connotation and reframes that were paradoxical, provocative, and premeditated, positive psychology held that there are *real* positives and competences within the individual that can be brought to the fore and expanded or that are skills that can be taught.

Finally, going significantly beyond O'Hanlon's conceptualization of the Third Wave are the experiential, emotion-based therapies (Elliott et al., 2003, 2004) that emphasized how the full expression of underlying core emotions can provide symptom relief, accelerate treatment, and bring about healing. Although Ferenczi and Rank (1924/1986) and Alexander and French (1946/1980) in the First Wave recognized the value of the patient having a "corrective emotional experience" within a psychoanalytic treatment, the Third Wave

---

[3]The husband responded to the Miracle Question: "She is smiling at me first thing in the morning!" and the therapist continued to microanalyze the meaning of that to him. In a way, Kim Berg's having clients go into specific and explicit detail about what the imagined kiss or smile signified is similar to AEDP's metatherapeutic processing, which also delves much deeper into specifics what may seem so obvious on the surface. However, the former is a fantasy and the latter, an elaboration of the real experience between client and therapist.

went much further to develop entire models of emotion-based psychotherapy that can be conceived of being corrective emotional experiences for patients and couples (Goldman, 2018; Greenberg & Goldman, 2019; Johnson, 2004).[4]

## AEDP'S PLACE IN THE "WAVES" OF PSYCHOTHERAPY

Where does AEDP fit in O'Hanlon's schema of three waves of psychotherapy? AEDP is clearly a capacity- and competency-based treatment that rests on the foundation provided by the Third Wave. AEDP privileges the positives and affirms patients from the first session on. In early sessions with patients, the AEDP therapist becomes a detective maven looking for "glimmers of transformance strivings."

*Transformance* is the term Fosha (2008, 2010) coined to identify the innate drive that all human beings have for healing, growth, and transformation. Although Carl Rogers (1951) assumed something similar,[5] he did not name it. Transformance is a new term Fosha introduced and has expanded exponentially. Moreover, along with uncovering capacities, competencies and resources patients already have, AEDP actively exploits this transformance drive clinically, helping patients potentiate their innate capacities to become their self-at-best (Fosha, 2000), rather than targeting their psychopathologies, resistance, and defenses (their self-at-worst) as psychoanalysis did. Russell (2015) has also expounded on the individual's innate resilience that exists despite all odds. She contends that it is this innate resilience that needs to be harnessed in the work of psychotherapy.

Fosha (2000) has made a particularly compelling assertion about the origins of all environmentally caused mental suffering—*unbearable aloneness in the face of emotionally overwhelming experience.* This bold statement redefines and integrates more simply and more precisely most previous understandings of how individual psychopathology develops. Embedded in this statement are the conditions under which healing can happen: With the therapist actively working to undo the patient's aloneness, the patient faces, experiences, and processes the previously overwhelming affects together with a trusted, supportive, and explicitly empathic therapist.

Elaborating on the Second Wave's emphasis that interpersonal relationships are encased in circular causality, this concept is implicit in AEDP and is ultimately made explicit in our clinical practice (Fosha, 2009a, 2009b; Russell &

---

[4]In our review of the history of psychotherapy, we have struggled with where to place the emotion-based therapies. We are rather arbitrarily putting them in the Third Wave because they are more collaborative, offer immediate symptom relief, and speed up treatment, but another argument is that they are a class unto themselves.

[5]In the preface to his ground-breaking book, Rogers (1951) wrote "a client in my office who sits there by the corner of the desk, struggling to be himself, yet deathly afraid of being himself—striving to see his experience as it is, wanting to *be* that experience, and yet deeply fearful of the prospect" (p. 4)

Fosha, 2008). In the dyadic regulation of affect (Fosha, 2000, 2017), the thera-pist's interventions affect the patient, whose reactions influence what the therapist does next, to which the patient then responds, and so on. AEDP therapists continuously go around this dyadic spiral using attunement and "moment-to-moment tracking" (Fosha, 2000, 2017; see also Hanakawa, Chapter 4, this volume) to closely observe the patient's verbal and nonverbal somatic responses to our interventions, keeping them within an emotional range the patient can manage, within a window of tolerance (not too much, not too little) (Frewen & Lanius, 2015; Levine, 2010; Siegel, 1999), changing course when necessary during this rapidly moving dynamic helix.

Instead of challenging defenses,[6] we meet patients where they are when they first show up, expressing respect for, and even empathizing with, their defenses (AEDP State 1) that helped them survive difficult circumstances. From the start of treatment, AEDP takes a "healing orientation" (Fosha, 2008; see also Fosha, Chapter 1; Kranz, Chapter 2, this volume) rather than a pathologizing one. This healing orientation that begins in the first session in which we affirm the patient, leads to less patient resistance, enhances the relational experience, and speeds up symptom relief, and also kick-starts the AEDP transformational processes.

Unlike First and Second Wave therapists who viewed themselves as experts with the answers, the AEDP therapist does not wear a hierarchical mantle. At the start of therapy, the role of an AEDP therapist is to join more collabora-tively with the patient to begin the process of growth, healing, and transfor-mation. As an attachment figure, the therapist meets patients where they are and then guides them through a series of four states and three state transfor-mations (Fosha, 2017; see Appendix Figure 1, this volume),[7] ultimately leading to patients' own clarity, wisdom, and their own Truth Sense (i.e., an integrated understanding of what feels right and true to them).

Although the original Third Wave models of narrative and solution-focused therapies did punctuate the positive and emphasized uncovering existing competencies, both have been accused of "manipulating" patients and ignoring their problems (Held, 1995). AEDP neither manipulates nor ignores the patient's problems, but instead is more respectful in understanding the patient's struggles while simultaneously finding and privileging the strengths within the patient (Seligman, 2011). Unlike Seligman's positive psychology, AEDP is attachment-based (Frederick, 2009; Pando-Mars, Chapter 6, this volume). Instead of coercing patients or minimizing their distress, the AEDP thera-pist engages in right-brain-to-right-brain attunement and provides a True Other experience (Fosha, 2005) through real therapeutic presence (Geller,

---

[6]In intensive short-term dynamic psychotherapy (ISTDP; Davanloo, 1978, 1990), the therapist immediately in the first session starts aggressively confronting the patient's defenses and resistance, rather than recognizing them with empathy. Steve Shapiro, senior faculty at the AEDP Institute, has developed a milder version of ISTDP (Shapiro, 2019).

[7]This figure, and diagrams for all of the representational schemas in AEDP 2.0, may be downloaded for free (http://pubs.apa.org/books/supp/fosha/).

2017; Lipton, Chapter 5, this volume). We coconstruct (Tronick, 2005) with the patient "from the bottom up" an emotional, empathic, right-brain experiential understanding (rather than a top-down, left-brain cognitive one) of what has been underneath the patient's anxiety and defenses before treatment.

Like the patient-centered therapy of Carl Rogers, by cultivating the patient's transformance drive, AEDP nurtures that lone blade of grass (or a daisy in Fosha's PowerPoint presentations, an even more colorful symbol) poking up between the concrete slabs in a sidewalk. Yet AEDP goes well beyond Rogers's nurturing: Patients experience in the here-and-now of the session—through our active engagement, explicit empathy, emotional support, dyadic resonance, and active emotion-processing interventions—the long-warded-off emotions that could be neither experienced nor expressed to their original attachment figures in childhood (Bowlby, 1969; Fosha, 2000; Greenan & Tunnell, 2003; Tunnell, 2012).

One way AEDP brings about this Core Affective Experience (State 2) is through the therapeutic device of portrayals[8] (Medley, Chapter 8, this volume). We borrow, and elaborate on, "portrayals" from gestalt therapies (Perls, 1969), emotion-focused therapies (Greenberg & Goldman, 2019) and intensive short-term dynamic psychotherapy (ISTDP, Davanloo, 1978, 1990). However, AEDP therapists markedly expand the technique of portrayal by using our own empathic resonance of anger, rage, or grief (therapist's use of self: Lipton, Chapter 5; Piliero, Chapter 10, this volume), as well as judicious self-disclosure (Prenn, 2009; Prenn & Fosha, 2017) toward this person to encourage patients to have an utterly complete processing of the core emotion—be it anger, rage, sadness, or grief.

We know a major breakthrough has occurred and the processing of core affective experience has ended when the patient breathes deeply, sighs, relaxes, and looks up, as they enter the transformational affects of State 3 and the calm of State 4 with its cascading multiple positive affects of mastery, relief, and tranquility. As Fosha writes (Chapter 1, this volume),

> the patient needs to have an experience, a new experience, and that experience should be good. . . . From the first moment of the first contact, and throughout treatment thereafter, the aim and method of AEDP is the provision, facilitation, and then experiential processing of such experiences. (p. 28)

Hence, we start treatment by affirming the patient and aiming to provide the patient with a new and good experience in the first session (Fosha, 2004). When AEDP treatment culminates successfully, a transformation occurs that is better than good: The patient starts to flourish. The patient begins to live more fully in healthy and vigorous ways.

---

[8]In brief, in a portrayal the therapist asks the client to imagine the attachment figure here in the room, the person who betrayed, abused or neglected them (there is often more than one attachment figure who has betrayed the client, but only one person at a time is focused on). Once the client has "dropped down" and is activated somatically (e.g., anger rising up in the chest, shedding a tear), the client is asked to say or do anything he wants to say or do in the portrayal. Clients are often hesitant to do a full-blown portrayal that might end up, even in fantasy, hurting, beheading, or otherwise killing the failed attachment figure.

Diana Fosha is a student of phenomenology and has also studied transformational processes that occur outside the realm of psychotherapy, for example, moments of genuine meeting, being with nature, listening to music, having intense religious experiences, and falling in love (Fosha, 2000, 2009b, 2013). She believes transformation need not be a lengthy process, particularly when the therapist is on the lookout for transformational strivings from the beginning. In fact, major transformation can sometimes occur "in a heartbeat" in a single session.

Transformation is deepened by an innovative technique that Fosha discovered and named *metatherapeutic processing*, or *metaprocessing* for short (Fosha, 2000; Fosha et al., 2019; Russell, 2015; Yeung, Chapter 13, this volume). Metaprocessing is a major and unique contribution that AEDP has made to the world of psychotherapy and is now quintessential to it (Welling, 2019).

Although we may think patients have had a corrective emotional experience in State 2, we want to hear explicitly from them about their here-and-now experience while it is still alive in the room. In metaprocessing, once the corrective emotional experience is over, we ask the patient to focus on what just happened, with the goal to deepen, elaborate, and expand a therapeutic event that has just taken place. So we inquire, "What was this experience like for you just now?" This simple question kicks off the upward spiraling phenomenon that Fosha has described, a new therapeutic mechanism that facilitates substantially deeper healing. Additional rounds of *relational* metaprocessing—"What is it like to have this new emotional experience *with me?*"—help further undo the patient's aloneness and solidify the attachment bond. Previously unbearable to face alone in isolation, childhood trauma is processed and metabolized within a new, far more supportive (and indeed loving) relationship with the therapist. Not only is the trauma processed, the patient's "competencies" greatly expand.

One mantra of AEDP is "make the implicit explicit, and the explicit experiential" (Fosha, 2000)[9] and then, "make the explicit relational" (Pando-Mars, Chapter 6, this volume). Thus, patients' version of their corrective emotional experience must be investigated, made explicit, and worked with experientially. Given the brain's neuroplasticity and its responsiveness to new conditions and positive affect (Doidge, 2007; Hanson, 2017), the very process of metaprocessing—the deepening and expansion of the transformational experience—leads to a cascade of further transformational experiences. The entire sequence helps to rewire the brain.

Metaprocessing reflects the position of "not knowing" as solution-focused therapists do (Anderson & Goolishian, 1992) by closely examining the impact of a positive in-session change experience (State 2 emotions processed to completion). AEDP actually adopts a position of "not knowing" throughout

---

[9]Interestingly, Peggy Papp (1994), a family systems therapist, also said it was important in therapy to "make the covert overt" (p. 60).

the entire treatment, not just toward the end of the therapeutic journey. We have a curious and open mind toward the patient and do not have a set agenda in any given session. We can never precisely predict which core emotion is going to come up. In that regard, we either follow or lead by attuning to the patient. Attunement and moment-to-moment tracking (Hanakawa, Chapter 4, this volume) are acquired skills taught in our trainings. These skills inform us when to follow and when to lead.

Particularly in AEDP State 4, patients become the experts in their own experiences *and* gain clarity in understanding their own psychological development. Here they begin to rewrite the narrative of their lives. Thus, patients determine their own Truths (AEDP's *Truth Sense*), not the therapist. The Truth Sense is what "feels right" to the patient. Again, AEDP therapists are not experts in defining the truth but have expertise in helping patients find their own Truths.

## SUMMARY: SEVEN SIGNIFICANT CONTRIBUTIONS OF AEDP TO PSYCHOTHERAPY

When we step back and look at the entire model, AEDP's contribution to the world of psychotherapy is compelling and astonishingly vast. The highly original, if not unique, concepts introduced by Fosha and elaborated by our colleagues are as follows:

(a) recognizing, naming, and then capitalizing on the innate *transformance drive* that every person has the capacity to heal, change, and grow;

(b) emphasizing phenomenology and believing that transformation can occur rapidly within a single session as well as incrementally during treatment;

(c) essentially redefining the origins of most environmentally caused psychopathology to be *aloneness in the face of overwhelming emotional experience*;

(d) forming and actively using *an attachment bond* between therapist and patient as a scaffolding to subsequently undo aloneness and to face and successfully process difficult, long-warded-off feelings;

(e) *dyadically regulating affect and using moment-to-moment tracking* to uncover the patient's deeper core emotions;

(f) significantly *expanding the use of portrayals* to help produce the core affective experience in State 2; and

(g) *metaprocessing* the transformational affective experience, with an emphasis on the relational component, as a mechanism that leads to deeper healing by restructuring and rewiring the brain.

With these seven elements, it is our thesis that AEDP goes significantly beyond the Third Wave.

## A FOURTH WAVE OF PSYCHOTHERAPY

Our mission in this chapter has been to situate AEDP in the history of psycho-therapy from past to present. AEDP has stood on the shoulders of a number of masterful and brilliant theorists, many not mentioned here (see this chapter's Coda), to provide a more integrated view of psychopathology and its treatment. We propose that AEDP—with its emphasis on the transformation of the individual from suffering to flourishing—has initiated a Fourth Wave of psychotherapy, a model that both accomplishes the primary goals of the three previous waves and goes beyond them by achieving its own goal of trans-forming the patient.

That is to say: The First Wave of psychoanalysis was primarily a *cognitive–intellectual–reflective* paradigm with the goal of helping the patient gain insight, which might or might not lead to change, much less transformation.[10] Behav-ioral therapy and family therapy in the Second Wave focused entirely on *behavioral* change with emotion absent, the therapeutic relationship mostly ignored, and insight unnecessary. Third-Wave postmodernism, including positive psychology, was based on collaborating with patients to *creatively imagine* alternative futures in which they will behave differently for the better, as they utilize existing and new-found capacities and competencies. Transformation either happened or didn't, but it was not the deliberate aim of the therapy, nor something that was the object of systematic clinical work with specific techniques to achieve it.

Transformation in the AEDP sense leads to long-term thriving of the patient after treatment ends. Not only does AEDP help the patient gain symptom relief in the short run, it may foster more lasting change than other therapies in that patients end up *transformed*, that is, open to exploring new experiences, expanding their interests, and taking more interpersonal risks. Patients tell us near the end of treatment that they are thriving and "flourishing" (Fosha et al., 2019; Fosha, Chapter 1, this volume;). We believe such flourishing comes about by dealing not only with the difficult negative emotions in State 2, but *processing to completion the new positive emotions* that occur in States 3 and 4 (Fosha et al., 2019; Yeung, Chapter 13, this volume). As Fosha (2000) has written and Russell (2018) has stated, we "hang out" with these positive emotions a long while to help the transformation graft so that a rewiring of the brain can occur via positive neuroplasticity (Hanson, 2017).

The proposed Fourth Wave, with AEDP at the vanguard, prioritizes and expands the role of *emotional processing of both negative and positive emotions* to bring about more expansive, if not more enduring healing (Fosha & Thoma, 2020; Fosha et al., 2019; Yeung, Chapter 13, this volume). In other words, culminating in Core State (State 4), the patient achieves an *emotional and*

---

[10]As discussed in the chapter Coda, even in the insight-driven psychoanalytic First Wave, Ferenczi, Alexander, and French planted the seeds to recognize the importance of having an in-session emotional experience. However, Freud and others disavowed their ideas.

*intellectual integration* that goes beyond emotional processing, cognitive insight, and first-level behavioral change. AEDP is fundamentally and thoroughly integrative—not so much left brained based but rather prefrontal cortex based, a deep integration of bottom-up experiencing of right-brain emotion to its completion (State 1), then metaprocessing that (State 3), which leads to both bottom-up and top-down insight (State 4): an integration of left brain and right brain, Self and Other, past and present.

It bears repeating: A major tenet of AEDP is that to create change that lasts, it is not sufficient for the patient to have a corrective emotional experience in session with the therapist and facilitated by the therapist. That experience must be further processed through metatherapeutic processing to explore the experience of the new relational connection and the experience of the new transformation, and it is that which brings about cognitive and emotional integration, deeper healing, and flourishing, all of which, by the way, results in quantifiable behavioral change.[11]

The proposed Fourth Wave rests on recent research demonstrating that the ultimate "competency" is the brain's capacity for lifelong "positive" neuroplasticity (Doidge, 2007; Hanson, 2017), which can be tapped into by using specific and systematic techniques to provide both symptom relief and a general neural reorganization, even for patients who have experienced significant big-T trauma.[12] Extending beyond the previous three waves of psychotherapy and introducing a major paradigm shift in how psychopathology can be treated, the Fourth Wave might include other therapies that have mechanisms to alleviate suffering by "rewiring the brain." Ecker et al. (2012) suggested that AEDP does so, as do other therapies: (a) coherence therapy (Ecker et al., 2012) with its focus on memory reconsolidation (Fredrick & Goldman, 2019), (b) eye movement desensitization and reprocessing (EMDR; Shapiro & Forrest, 1997), (c) emotion-focused therapy (EFT; Greenberg & Goldman, 2019), and (d) interpersonal neurobiology (IPNB; Siegel, 1999, 2017). Indeed, our proposed Fourth Wave is congruent with what Ecker et al. (2012) presented as a "framework for psychotherapy integration" (pp. 149–152).

However, unlike coherence therapy, EMDR, EFT, and IPNB, AEDP works *much more relationally* to ground the experientially based transformation in an I–Thou context. It is the relational component that becomes the operative element of change. It is through the *therapeutic relationship* that the emotional and relational experiences are metaprocessed, and, rather momentously, *the unbearable aloneness is undone.* AEDP seeks not only to rewire the brain to

---

[11]Some early results from our follow-up research indicate that clients make behavioral changes during and after treatment and often report examples of "flourishing."

[12]A big-T trauma is distinguished as an extraordinary and significant event that leaves the individual feeling powerless and possessing little control in their environment. Such events could take the form of a natural disaster, terrorist attack, sexual assault, combat, or a car or plane accident, for example (from PsychologyToday.com). To this, we add: Little-t trauma can also be as devastating to the individual (e.g., countless repetitions of microaggressions or microshaming comments or actions). Little-t trauma is more subjective and more personal. Both types are traumatic, but big-T trauma is more environmentally explicit and therefore can be objectively agreed on.

reduce suffering but to further rewire the brain by rewiring attachment experience and processing the new good emotional experiences, both of which systematically put flourishing into action.

It is an exciting time to be in a new world of psychotherapy.

## CODA: SOURCES, THREADS, AND TRACES OF INFLUENCE

We want to cite specific theorists who cannot be neatly classified in any one of O'Hanlon's three waves but who nevertheless have either had a strong impact on the development of AEDP and its evolution to the present, or whose work resonates with particular aspects of AEDP and with whom AEDP has been in conversation. Many of these seminal theorists and paradigms overlap in time and development and contain elements of the different waves. However, apart from the waves, they are worthy of mention separately because their threads have contributed to the tapestry of AEDP theory.

Although this list is by no means complete, it gives a sense of the panoply of theories that have contributed to AEDP's multiplicity, nonlinear, affective model of change. As Fosha (2003) wrote,

> In its ethos, theory, stance, and technique, AEDP lives and breathes multiplicity: there is no one path, there is no one core affect, there is no one core dynamic in psychogenesis that can account for the phenomena encountered in the treatment of a wide range of patients by a wide range of therapists. There are different paths to different cores and different mechanisms of change are responsible for healing. (pp. 335–336)

### Early Psychoanalysts Apart From Freud

Ferenczi and Rank (a) emphasized the authenticity of the relationship between patient and analyst, rather than the transference; (b) valued emotional experience over intellectual insight; (c) preferred the analyst to use the *active technique* instead of taking a passive neutral stance; and (d) accepted the patient's subjective experience as truth rather than fantasy (1924/1986). They began to question the neutral posture of the analyst. They wrote about the value of emotional experience over intellectual insight and came to emphasize the value of the *real* relationship of therapist and patient. Ferenczi and Rank also began to explore techniques that opened the door to what is now called a two-person psychology. Treatment was based on authenticity, with the therapist sincerely and humanly involved and actively participating in the therapeutic relationship. They understood that the subjective experience was the objective "truth" of the patient. Ferenczi and Rank explored being active, providing verbal gratification through explicit empathy, even the self-disclosure of feelings towards the patient as a means of facilitating the work. They explored working in the here and now and proposed that the analyst was not all-knowing but fallible and human, and that this was part of the therapeutic dialogue. Emotion was becoming central to the discourse.

Two decades later, Alexander and French (1946/1980) gave a name to what Ferenczi and Rank were doing, advocating for the necessity of providing the patient with a "corrective emotional experience" to deepen the therapy and to shorten the length of treatment: "It is in this therapeutic experience that repair of the traumatic influences of previous experiences can take place" (Alexander & French, 1946/1980, p. 66). AEDP strongly values and incorporates all these tenets.

### Attachment Theory and Attachment Styles

Initially working together with Robertson (Robertson & Bowlby, 1952) on showing how devastating separations from parents were for children, Bowlby (1969) went on to develop attachment theory. Bowlby recognized the need for social interactions for the infant to have a secure relationship with adult caregivers, without which normal social and emotional development does not occur. If attachment is interfered with—through separation, or insensitive, unresponsive or inconsistent caregivers—the seeds are sown for maladaptive and poor social interactions later in life. Ainsworth (Ainsworth & Bell, 1970; Ainsworth et al., 1978) and Main (1990, 1999) based their research on Bowlby's theory, developing attachment classifications. Different styles of attachment help us understand the person's defenses against closeness and emotion and guide our clinical interventions in AEDP (Fosha, 2000; Pando-Mars, 2016; Pando-Mars, Chapter 6, this volume).

### Emotion Theory, Experiential Therapies, and Emotion-Focused Therapies

Early on, Charles Darwin (1872/1965) stressed the importance of emotions as survival mechanisms and as "guides to living" (Frederick, 2009), while William James (1988) wrote how emotions reflect our bodies' assessment of the environment, rather than our brains. Later, Damasio (1999, 2010) and Panksepp (1998) introduced contemporary neurobiologically based understandings of how emotional experiences are encoded in the brain. Gendlin (1996) and Greenberg and Goldman (2019), among others, developed specific techniques to work with bodily experience and emotions, rather than thoughts, tracking the "felt sense" of emotional experience to guide interventions. Emotion theories and emotion research have profoundly influenced the development of AEDP. AEDP has deep resonances, as well as some differences, with other experiential, emotion-focused therapies (see Fosha et al., 2009).

### Infant/Early Childhood Research and Developmental Theorists

The infant/early childhood caregiver–infant interaction research of Beebe and Lachman (2002, 2014), Stern (1985), and Tronick (2007, 2009; Tronick & Reck, 2009) provided a lens for understanding the significance of early attachment and attunement (or lack thereof), which we constantly and actively monitor in the moment-to-moment tracking in AEDP sessions. It also alerted us to the profound importance of repair to developing resilience and secure attachment. AEDP most definitely creates and provides a holding environment with its emphasis on the attachment between patient and therapist. The AEDP therapist's attunement to the patient is the sine qua non for constructing safety and risk taking.

### Relational Theorists

From the early writings of Ferenczi and others, contemporary relational analysts brought about a more complete shift from a one-person to a two-person psychology. Winnicott (1965/1974) gave special importance to the *holding environment*[13] provided by the therapist as key in facilitating growth and exploration and to promote a sense of emotional security of self. In addition to Ferenczi and Winnicott, other current theorists in the relational tradition with whom AEDP has been in ongoing conversation, so to speak, include Bromberg (1998), Eigen (1980), Ghent (1990), and Grotstein (2004).

### Interpersonal Neurobiology, Affective Neuroscience, and Trauma

In the 2 decades during which AEDP has evolved, there has been a concomitant wealth of research on the brain, understanding the role of emotion and development, and the impact of developmental trauma upon the personality and behavior on the growth of the individual. AEDP incorporates many of these findings to better understand the nature of the phenomena that constitute AEDP's clinical work. Just to mention a few of those whose work has been influential for us:

1. Damasio (1999, 2010), one of the main contributors to our understanding of how the brain processes emotion, developed a subcortically rooted theory of emotion and consciousness. He used the term *autobiographical self* and proposed that it was the result of understanding core self and core consciousness. These are phenomena we identify as States 3 and 4 in AEDP where there is movement towards transformation, personal truth and a coherent, cohesive autobiographical narrative.

2. Panksepp's (1998; Panksepp & Biven, 2012) research on emotions and neurobiology has helped expand emotion theory based on his articulation of affective neuroscience. According to Panksepp, emotions are what sustains survival: both the positive affects that support survival, and the negative affects that might impair survival. He articulated seven basic emotional systems, all of which we work with in AEDP State 2.

---

[13]The holding environment refers to the relational capacity of the other (the caregiver) to provide safety and attunement and to hold the good, bad, and ambivalent feelings of the infant or child.

3. Bessel van der Kolk (2014) understood trauma within the context of neuro-science, developmental trauma, and the importance of working with the body in trauma work. Indeed, a focus on the somatic affects of experience informs all AEDP clinical work. The emphasis van der Kolk places on the central importance of developmental trauma is reflected in AEDP's relational focus as an invariant in trauma work, along with trauma processing.

4. Schore (2003, 2019) has made huge contributions to AEDP, drawing from affective neuroscience, trauma theory, developmental psychology and attachment theory. He emphasizes how crucial right-brain to right-brain communication is to the development of secure attachment: His work informs the AEDP therapist's reliance on right-brain to right-brain communication in both the coconstruction of safety and in dyadic affect regulation of the "vehement" emotions of trauma.

5. Siegel (1999, 2017) developed interpersonal neurobiology (IPNB), which is an interdisciplinary view that draws on many branches of science to create a framework for understanding our subjective and interpersonal lives. His emphasis on human relationships, emotions, and empathy is a principal guidepost of clinical work in AEDP.

6. Porges (2011) developed his polyvagal theory: What happens physiologically when the person experiences a traumatic event? In his work on the autonomic nervous system, Porges (2017) makes us look beyond the effects of fight or flight, and puts social relationships, that is, the social engagement system, front and center in our understanding of what heals trauma (van der Kolk, 2014).

7. Levine (2010, 2015), a psychotherapist and trauma expert, has had a major impact on linking trauma states within the body. In his somatic experiencing (SE) model, he uses the technique of pendulation to work within the "window of tolerance," the working edges AEDP also uses to monitor if and how interventions are heard and accepted, or not. Levine's use of understanding how the neural-energy pathways of fight, flight, freeze and collapse get activated is core to helping regulate emotions and social functioning. Levine's conceptualizations and techniques inform AEDP work as we monitor somatic markers of change.

8. Lanius (2019) and Frewen and Lanius (2015) have done research on the neurobiology of posttraumatic stress disorder and dissociation, identifying the five dimensions of consciousness, including intersubjectivity and emotion, that are compromised in trauma and thus need to be addressed in therapeutic work. AEDP uses the relationship and the experience of the relationship as a compass to navigate uncovering the trauma events and to coconstruct safety so as to help patients with trauma histories process the emotions associated with those events. Lanius's own clinical work utilizes the "window of tolerance" to gauge interventions.

9. Doidge (2007) is a psychoanalyst. He has examined neuroplasticity, and how the brain can be adaptable and modifiable, which is a tenet inherent in AEDP.

## Transformational Studies

William James (1988) studied transformational experiences through the lens of subjective religious experiences. More recently, the Boston Change Process Study Group (2010), created in 1995, has been examining developmental studies as well as dynamic systems theory to better understand and model change processes in therapeutic interactions. Buber (1970) wrote about the transformational power of genuine contact and moments of meeting. *I–Thou* describes the meaning of the intersubjective space: We exist in relation to the other; it is a shared psychological space for developing reciprocal meaning. This has been a major contribution to the development of the relational meta-processing in AEDP: "How do you feel about *my* feelings of care and compassion *for* you?" This is a major and most significant undoing of the classical psychoanalytic "blank screen." AEDP has continued to study the phenomenology of change and transformation and to document specifically how major transformation can be fostered in psychotherapy. This is reflected in the development of AEDP's four-state transformational model.

## Short-Term, Time-Limited, Psychodynamic Therapies

Our coda would not be complete without discussing the influence on AEDP of the short-term, time-limited psychodynamic therapies. Short term dynamic therapy, especially that of Malan (1979) and his use of the paradigm of the triangle of conflict (Ezriel, 1952), contributed to Fosha's expanding it into the Triangle of Experience. Davanloo (1978) stressed the importance of rapid access to the visceral experience of the affective phenomena worked with in therapy. Mann (1973) advocated time-limited psychotherapy of only 12 treatment sessions. Davanloo (1978, 1990), Vaillant (1997) and Abbass (2007) emphasized the importance of getting past defenses to help the patient access and viscerally feel the core affects at the bottom of Malan's triangle, underneath the anxiety and defenses. AEDP aims not only to reach the bottom of the triangle with its core affects and their visceral correlates, but, through metatherapeutic processing to explore the after-effects of doing so. This is where AEDP's transformational theory comes in. AEDP's States 3 and 4 represent a substantial expansion beyond the reaches of the Triangle of Experience.

As important as these short-term dynamic therapies are in the heritage of AEDP, these therapies were neither relational nor attachment based. More-over, they remained psychopathology oriented; they did not recognize and value the patient's existing capacities or competencies; and, following First-Wave thinking, they were committed to the view that the therapist held all the expertise, not the patient.

AEDP is in deep gratitude to all the above theorists and therapists, and others not mentioned here, from whom we have drawn, to develop what we believe is a more comprehensive theory and therapy. AEDP has long been, and will continue to be, in dialogue with the many theorists who introduce important nascent concepts that play a role in shaping AEDP as an ever emergent nonstatic living model.

## REFERENCES

Abbass, A. (2007). Bringing character changes with Davanloo's intensive short-term dynamic psychotherapy. *Ad Hoc Bulletin of Short-Term Dynamic Psychotherapy, 11*(2), 26–40.

Ainsworth, M. D., & Bell, S. M. (1970). Attachment, exploration, and separation: Illustrated by the behavior of one-year-olds in a strange situation. *Child Development, 41*(1), 49–67. https://doi.org/10.2307/1127388

Ainsworth, M. D., Blehar, M. C., Waters, E., & Walls, S. (1978). *Patterns of attachment: A psychological study of the strange situation.* Lawrence Erlbaum Associates.

Alexander, F., & French, T. M. (1980). *Psychoanalytic therapy: principles and application.* University of Nebraska Press. (Original work published 1946)

American Psychiatric Association. (1952). *Diagnostic and statistical manual of mental disorders.*

Anderson, H., & Goolishian, H. (1992). The patient is the expert: A not-knowing approach to therapy. In S. McNamee & K. J. Gergen (Eds.), *Inquiries in social construction: Therapy as social construction* (pp. 25–39). Sage Publications.

Bateson, G. (1972). *Steps to an ecology of mind.* University of Chicago Press.

Beck, J. S. (1964). *Cognitive therapy: Basics and beyond.* Guilford Press.

Beebe, B., & Lachman, F. M. (2002). *Infant research and adult treatment: co-constructing interactions.* The Analytic Press.

Beebe, B., & Lachman, F. M. (2014). *The origins of attachment: infant research and adult treatment.* Routledge.

Boston Change Process Study Group. (2010). *Change in psychotherapy: A unifying paradigm.* Norton.

Boszormenyi-Nagy, I., & Sparks, G. (1984). *Invisible loyalties: Reciprocity in intergenerational family therapy.* Brunner/Mazel.

Bowen, M. (1985). *Family therapy in clinical practice.* Jason Aronson.

Bowlby, J. (1969). *Attachment. Attachment and loss: Vol. 1. Loss.* Basic Books.

Bromberg, P. M. (1998). *Standing in the spaces: Essays on clinical process, trauma, and dissociation.* The Analytic Press.

Buber, M. (1970). *I and thou.* Charles Scribner's Sons.

Chodorow, N. J. (1989). *Feminism and psychoanalytic theory.* Yale University Press.

Damasio, A. (1999). *The feeling of what happens: Body and emotion in the making of consciousness.* Harcourt, Brace.

Damasio, A. (2010). *Self comes to mind: Constructing the conscious brain.* Pantheon Books.

Darwin, C. (1965). *The expression of emotion in man and animals.* University of Chicago Press. (Original work published 1872) https://doi.org/10.7208/chicago/9780226220802.001.0001

Davanloo, H. (Ed.). (1978). *Basic principles and techniques in short-term dynamic psychotherapy.* Spectrum.

Davanloo, H. (1990). *Unlocking the unconscious: Selected papers of Habib Davanloo.* Wiley.

deShazer, S. (1985). *Keys to solution in brief therapy.* Norton.

Doidge, N. (2007). *The brain that changes itself: Stories of personal triumph from the frontiers of brain science.* Penguin Books.

Ecker, B., Tucic, R., & Hulley, L. (2012). *Unlocking the emotional brain: Eliminating symptoms at their roots using memory reconsolidation.* Routledge. https://doi.org/10.4324/9780203804377

Eigen, M. (1980). On the significance of the face. *Psychoanalytic Review, 67*(4), 427–441.

Elliott, R., Greenberg, L., & Lietaer, G. (2003). Research on experiential psychotherapy. In M. Lambert (Ed.), *Bergin & Garfield's handbook of psychotherapy and behavioral change* (pp. 493–539). John Wiley & Sons.

Elliott, R., Watson, J. C., Goldman, R. N., & Greenberg, L. S. (2004). *Learning emotion-focused therapy: The process-experiential approach to change.* American Psychological Association. https://doi.org/10.1037/10725-000

Ezriel, H. (1952). Notes on psychoanalytic group therapy. II. Interpretation and research. *Psychiatry, 15*(2), 119–126. https://doi.org/10.1080/00332747.1952.11022866

Ferenczi, S., & Rank, O. (1986). *The development of psychoanalysis.* International Universities Press. (Original work published 1924)

Fosha, D. (2000). *The transforming power of affect: A model for accelerated change.* Basic Books.

Fosha, D. (2003). Dyadic regulation and experiential work with emotion and relatedness in trauma and disordered attachment. In M. F. Solomon & D. J. Siegel (Eds.), *Healing trauma: Attachment, trauma, the brain and the mind* (pp. 221–281). Norton.

Fosha, D. (2004). "Nothing that feels bad is ever the last step": The role of positive emotions in experiential work with difficult emotional experiences. *Clinical Psychology and Psychotherapy, 11*(1), 30–43.

Fosha, D. (2005). Emotion, true self, true other, core state: Toward a clinical theory of affective change process. *Psychoanalytic Review, 92,* 513–552.

Fosha, D. (2008). Transformance, recognition of self by self, and effective action. In K. J. Schneider (Ed.), *Existential-integrative psychotherapy: Guideposts to the core of practice* (pp. 290–330). Routledge.

Fosha, D. (2009a). Emotion and recognition at work: Energy, vitality, pleasure, truth, desire & the emergent phenomenology of transformational experience. In D. Fosha, D. J. Siegel, & M. F. Solomon (Eds.), *The healing power of emotion: Affective neuroscience, development and clinical practice* (pp. 172–203). Norton.

Fosha, D. (2009b). Healing attachment trauma with attachment (and then some!). In M. Kerman (Ed.), *Clinical pearls of wisdom: 21 leading therapists offer their key insights.* Norton.

Fosha, D. (2010, February 6). *Transformance, transformational theory and healing-based practice* [Keynote address]. "The Heart of Healing: Understanding the Principles of Deep Emotional Change," New York, NY.

Fosha, D. (2013). "Turbocharging" the affects of innate healing and redressing the evolutionary tilt. In D. J. Siegel & M. F. Solomon (Eds.), *Healing moments in psychotherapy* (pp. 129–168). Norton.

Fosha, D. (2017). How to be a transformational therapist: AEDP harnesses innate healing affects to rewire experience and accelerate transformation. In J. Liozzo, M. Neale, & E. Wolf (Eds.), *Advances in contemplative psychotherapy: Accelerating transformation* (pp. 204–219). Norton.

Fosha, D., Paivio, S. C., Gleiser, K., & Ford, J. (2009). Experiential and emotion-focused therapy. In C. Courtois & J. D. Ford (Eds.), *Complex traumatic stress disorders: An evidence-based clinician's guide* (pp. 286–311). Guilford Press.

Fosha, D., & Thoma, N. (2020). Metatherapeutic processing supports the emergence of flourishing in psychotherapy. *Psychotherapy.* Advance online publication. https://doi.org/10.1037/pst0000289

Fosha, D., Thoma, N., & Yeung, D. (2019). Transforming emotional suffering into flourishing: Metatherapeutic processing of positive affect as a trans-theoretical vehicle for change. *Counselling Psychology Quarterly, 32*(3–4), 563–593. https://doi.org/10.1080/09515070.2019.1642852

Foucault, M. (2009). *History of madness.* Routledge.

Frederick, R. (2009). *Living like you mean it: Use the wisdom and power of your emotions to get the life you really want*. Jossey-Bass.

Fredrick, A., & Goldman, R. (2019, June). *Memory reconsolidation and emotional arousal: An explorative study of psychotherapy models*. Society for the Exploration of Psychotherapy Integration (SEPI).

Frewen, P., & Lanius, R. (2015). *Healing the traumatized self: consciousness, neuroscience, treatment*. Norton.

Geller, S. M. (2017). *A practical guide to cultivating therapeutic presence*. American Psychological Association. https://doi.org/10.1037/0000025-000

Gendlin, E. T. (1996). *Focusing-oriented psychotherapy: A manual of the experiential method*. Guilford Press.

Ghent, E. (1990). Masochism, submission, surrender: Masochism as a perversion of surrender. *Contemporary Psychoanalysis, 26*(1), 108–136. https://doi.org/10.1080/00107530.1990.10746643

Gilligan, C. (1982). *In a different voice psychological theory and woman's development*. Harvard University Press.

Goldman, R. N. (2018). *Emotion-focused couple therapy* [DVD]. American Psychological Association.

Greenan, D., & Tunnell, G. (2003). *Couple therapy with gay men*. Guilford Press.

Greenberg, L., & Goldman, R. N. (Eds.). (2019). *Clinical handbook of emotion-focused therapy*. American Psychological Association. https://doi.org/10.1037/0000112-000

Grotstein, J. S. (2004). Notes on the superego. *Psychoanalytic Inquiry, 24*(2), 257–270. https://doi.org/10.1080/07351692409349082

Haley, J. (1976). *Problem-solving therapy: New strategies for effective family therapy*. Jossey-Bass.

Hanson, R. (2017). Positive neuroplasticity: The neuroscience of mindfulness. In J. Loizzo, M. Neale, & E. Wolf (Eds.), *Advances in contemplative psychotherapy: Accelerating transformation* (pp. 48–60). Norton. https://doi.org/10.4324/9781315630045-5

Held, B. S. (1995). *Back to reality: A critique of postmodern theory in psychotherapy*. Norton.

James, W. (1988). *William James: Writings 1902–1910: The varieties of religious experience, pragmatism, a pluralistic universe, the meaning of truth, some problems of philosophy, essays*. Library of America.

Johnson, S. M. (2004). *The practice of emotionally focused couple therapy: Creating connection* (2nd ed.). Routledge.

Kim Berg, I. (1994). *Irreconcilable differences: A solution-focused approach to marital therapy* (Videotape). Brief Family Therapy Center.

Kuhn, T. (1970). *The structure of scientific revolutions* (2nd ed.). University of Chicago Press.

Lanius, R. (2019, October). *The neuroscience of trauma and its healing: The road back to the neurobiological core self* [AEDP seminar]. Mount Sinai West Medical Center, New York, NY.

Levine, P. (2010). *In an unspoken voice: How the body releases trauma and restores goodness*. North Atlantic Books.

Levine, P. (2015). *Trauma and memory: Brain and body in search for the living past: A practical guide for understanding and working with traumatic memory*. North Atlantic Books.

Main, M. (1990). Cross-cultural studies of attachment organization: Recent studies, changing methodologies, and the concept of conditional strategies. *Human Development, 33*(1), 48–61. https://doi.org/10.1159/000276502

Main, M. (1999). Attachment theory: Eighteen points with suggestions for future studies. In J. Cassidy & P. R. Shaver (Eds.), *Handbook of attachment: Theory, research, and clinical applications* (pp. 845–887). Guilford Press.

Malan, D. M. (1979). *Individual psychotherapy and the science of psychodynamics*. Butterworth.

Mann, J. (1973). *Time-limited psychotherapy*. Harvard University Press.

Miller, J. B. (1976). *Toward a new psychology of women*. Beacon Press.

Minuchin, S. (1974). *Families and family therapy*. Harvard University Press.

O'Hanlon, B. (1994, November/December). The Third Wave: Can a brief therapy open doors for transformation? *The Family Therapy Networker*, 19–29.

Palazzoli, M. S., Boscolo, L., Cecchin, G., & Prata, G. (1978). *Paradox and counterparadox*. Jason Aronson.

Pando-Mars, K. (2016). Tailoring AEDP interventions to attachment style. *Transformance: The AEDP Journal, 6*(2).

Panksepp, J. (1998). *Affective neuroscience: The foundations of human and animal emotions*. Oxford University Press.

Panksepp, J., & Biven, L. (2012). *The archaeology of mind: Neuroevolutionary origins of human emotions*. Norton.

Papp, P. (1994). *The process of change*. Guilford Press.

Perls, F. S. (1969). *Gestalt therapy verbatim*. Real Peoples Press.

Porges, S. W. (2011). *The polyvagal theory: Neurophysiological foundations of emotions, attachment, communication, and self-regulation*. Norton.

Porges, S. W. (2017). *The pocket guide to the polyvagal theory: The transformative power of feeling safe*. Norton.

Prenn, N. (2009). I second that emotion! On self-disclosure and its metaprocessing. In A. Bloomgarden & R. B. Mennuti (Eds.), *Psychotherapist revealed: Therapists speak about self-disclosure in psychotherapy* (pp. 85–95). Routledge.

Prenn, N., & Fosha, D. (2017). *Supervision essentials for accelerated experiential dynamic psychotherapy*. American Psychological Association. https://doi.org/10.1037/0000016-000

Robertson, J., & Bowlby, J. (1952). Responses of young children to separation from their mothers. *Courrier of the International Children's Center, Paris, 2*, 131–140.

Rogers, C. R. (1951). *Patient-centered therapy*. Houghton Mifflin.

Russell, E. M. (2015). *Restoring resilience: Discovering your clients' capacity for healing*. Norton.

Russell, E. M. (2018, January). *Agency, will and desire as core affective experiences in AEDP* [Seminar]. Mount Sinai West Medical Center, New York, NY.

Russell, E. M., & Fosha, D. (2008). Transformational affects and core state in AEDP: The emergence and consolidation of joy, hope, gratitude and confidence in the (solid goodness of the) self. *Journal of Psychotherapy Integration, 18*, 167–190.

Schore, A. N. (2003). *Affect regulation and the origin of the self: Neurobiology of emotional development*. Lawrence Erlbaum Associates.

Schore, A. N. (2019). *Right brain psychotherapy*. Norton.

Seligman, M. E. P. (2002). *Authentic happiness: Using the new positive psychology to realize your potential for lasting fulfillment*. Simon & Schuster.

Seligman, M. E. P. (2011). *Flourish: A visionary new understanding of happiness and well-being*. The Free Press.

Shapiro, E., & Forrest, M. S. (1997). *EMDR: The breakthrough therapy for overcoming anxiety, stress and trauma*. Basic Books.

Shapiro, S. S. (2019, November). *Working with the challenges of defense and anxiety to promote rapid therapeutic change* [Training retreat]. Philadelphia, PA.

Siegel, D. J. (1999). *The developing mind*. Guilford Press.

Siegel, D. J. (2017). *The pocket guide to the polyvagal theory: The transformative power of feeling safe*. Norton.

Skinner, B. F. (1953). *Science and human behavior*. The Free Press.

Stern, D. N. (1985). *The interpersonal world of the infant: A view from psychoanalysis and development psychology*. Basic Books.

Sue, D. W., & Sue, D. (2015). *Counseling the culturally diverse: Theory and practice* (4th ed.). John Wiley & Sons.

Tronick, E. Z. (2005). Why is connection with others so critical? The formation of dyadic states of consciousness: Coherence-governed selection and the cocreation of meaning out of messy meaning making. In J. Nadel & D. Muir (Eds.), *Emotional development: Recent research advances* (pp. 293–315). Oxford University Press.

Tronick, E. Z. (2007). *The neurobehavioral and social-emotional development of infants and children*. Norton.

Tronick, E. Z. (2009). Of course all relationships are unique: How co-creative processes generate unique mother-infant and patient–therapist relationships and change other relationships. *Psychological Inquiry, 23*, 473–491.

Tronick, E. Z., & Reck, C. (2009). Infants of depressed mothers. *Harvard Review of Psychiatry, 17*(2), 147–156. https://doi.org/10.1080/10673220902899714

Tunnell, G. (2012). Gay male couple therapy: An attachment-based model. In J. J. Bigner & J. L. Wetcher (Eds.), *Handbook of LGBT-affirmative couple and family therapy* (pp. 25–42). Routledge.

Tunnell, G. (2019). *Lectures on family and couple therapy*. Teachers College, Columbia University.

Vaillant, L. M. (1997). *Changing character: Short-term anxiety-regulating psychotherapy for restructuring defenses, affects and attachment*. Basic Books.

van der Kolk, B. (2014). *The body keeps the score: Brain, mind, and body in the healing of trauma*. Viking Penguin.

Von Foester, H. (1952). *Circular causal and feedback mechanisms in biological and social systems*. Josiah Macy Foundation.

Walters, M., Carter, B., Papp, P., & Silverstein, O. (1988). *The invisible web: Gender patterns in family relationships* (pp. 15–30). Guilford Press.

Welling, H. (2019). Is this AEDP? Six unique characteristics of AEDP. *Transformance: The AEDP Journal, 9*.

White, M., & Epston, D. (1990). *Narrative means to therapeutic ends*. Norton.

Winnicott, D. W. (1974). *The maturational process and the facilitating environment*. International University Press. (Original work published 1965)

# 4

# What Just Happened? and What Is Happening Now?

## The Art and Science of Moment-to-Moment Tracking in AEDP

Yuko Hanakawa

Moment-to-moment tracking is a foundational practice in accelerated experiential dynamic psychotherapy (AEDP). It refers to the moment-to-moment mindful recognition of emotional states in the client as well as in the therapist and the dyad based on observed or felt changes in facial expression, body movements, posture, tone of voice, gaze direction, and rhythm of breathing. Additionally, the context and words that indicate affective reactions are considered. Moment-to-moment tracking is actually what allows attunement and is indispensable to AEDP clinical work that depends on identifying subtle and not so subtle nonverbal cues of affective shifts in the emotional, relational, and transformational experience of the client, therapist, and dyad.

Although we, as AEDP therapists, literally use moment-to-moment tracking every moment, moment-to-moment tracking itself—how it operates, what it is—has not been the focus of investigation, nor has a detailed inventory of tracking been articulated. AEDP supervisors often lament the difficulties that their beginner AEDP supervisees encounter because they lack basic tracking skills, which would enable them to register, and thus respond to, important and subtle nonverbal cues from their clients. This chapter addresses moment-to-moment tracking at all phases of the transformational process, as it applies

https://doi.org/10.1037/0000232-005
*Undoing Aloneness and the Transformation of Suffering Into Flourishing: AEDP 2.0*, D. Fosha (Editor)

to all types of affective experience that AEDP works with—emotional, relational, and transformational—and marks shifts in each member of the therapeutic dyad, as well as their interaction. To reference the categories of the Triangle of Experience, moment-to-moment tracking helps us swiftly spot core affects, anxiety, and defenses and find an entry point from which to deepen affect. This chapter also articulates the mechanisms of moment-to-moment tracking using data from current neuroscientific thinking and research on emotion, attachment, and somatic experience.

## FUNDAMENTAL STANCE BEHIND TRACKING IN AEDP: DYADIC MINDFULNESS

Tracking in AEDP is characterized by the stance of *dyadic mindfulness* (Fosha, 2013a), which "involves both members of the therapeutic dyad in the moment-to-moment tracking of fluctuations in internal states *from a position of compassion, curiosity, acceptance, and kindness toward whatever emerges*" (italics added; p. 134). AEDP therapists track their clients from a *caring, affirmative, and safety-conscious dyadic stance* that simultaneously facilitates secure attachment experiences for clients and allows therapists to note the fluctuations in a client's affective experience and in the relationship and use those to guide their choice of intervention.

## FOUR TYPES OF MOMENT-TO-MOMENT TRACKING FROM A DYADIC MINDFULNESS PERSPECTIVE

Moment-to-moment tracking is informed by the research into developmental dyadic interaction of the "baby watchers" (e.g., Beebe, Stern, Trevarthen, Tronick). These researchers microanalyzed moment-to-moment nonverbal interactions between babies and mothers on videotapes and proposed a mutual bidirectional regulation model of communication. Mutual regulation is based on each person's perception of micromomentary shifts and assessment of these shifts produce corresponded reactions (Beebe & Lachmann, 2013). The perception of micromomentary shifts is what we call moment-to-moment tracking in AEDP.

We moment-to-moment track different channels of experience, such as sensations, emotion, energy, movement, and auditory, visual, and imaginal channels (Mars, 2011; Mindell, 1996). We, as AEDP therapists, attune to the whole body experience of a client by tracking these channels; we find out the channels where the client experientially "lives," and we meet them through these channels so that the client can build a greater affective tolerance and develop the capacity to drop into a core affect in that channel (Mars, 2011).

In what follows, I discuss four categories of what we are tracking. Note that the assumption here is that it is the therapist who is doing the tracking to support the therapeutic work. Note also that this chapter primarily focuses on

State 1 and 2, in which moment-to-moment tracking most effectively helps the therapist work through defenses and inhibitory affects and facilitate emotion processing to completion; in reality, therapists continuously use tracking in all four states, and thus in States 3 and 4 as well.

*1. Client-focused tracking* is informed by Paul Ekman's extensive research on emotion recognition (Ekman & Friesen, 1982; Ekman et al., 2002). Ekman developed the FACS (Facial Affect Coding Scheme), which uses the 33 sets of muscles of the face, called action units, to identify emotions and offers training in the FACS to those whose profession depends on the recognition of subtle changes in expression. Research suggests that the fundamental capacities for tracking subtle shifts in affective experience are innate and ecologically essential for survival in social environments (Dzafic et al., 2019). Several research findings also suggest that the processes of tracking affective changes are linked to different cortical areas, such as anterior cingulate cortex and insula for pain (Botvinick et al., 2005), the anterior insula for disgust (Wicker et al., 2003), the amygdala network for anger (Dzafic et al., 2019), and the frontotemporal-subcortical functional network for happiness (Dzafic et al., 2019). It assumes that we are wired to recognize others' emotional states based on their expressive behaviors, such as facial expression, body posture, the blush, pupil activation, voice quality, gaze direction, movements of hands and arms, gestures, head movements, respiration, and full-body actions, including fleeting signs of microexpressions.[1]

Everything just expressed about the recognition of facial microexpressions also applies to tracking shifts in the other six channels of experience. For example, the auditory channel provides important affective data; we closely track the tone of voice—for instance, if someone has a gentle, fluid way of speaking and then, in response to an empathic comment from the therapist, her voice suddenly strains. Or the volume of the voice rises (or falls), or the mellifluousness of the voice becomes flat, for example, when the client starts to talk about her mother. The speed of speech and volume of voice also give the therapist a critical piece of information about the client's internal affective experience.

The attuned therapist registers fluctuations in energy, for example, shifts from liveliness to flatness or vice versa. Shifts in the continuum of brightness and dullness of gaze, color, or flushing of the skin are also important indicators of the client's affective shifts.

The attuned therapist integrates the aforementioned multimodal channels of experience to track the most accurate affective state of the client. Sometimes, one channel of experience does not match up with information from other channels. For example, the client is smiling and says that she is feeling calm and appreciative. Her facial expression shows a perfect smile with beaming eyes. However, the therapist may notice the client's leg nervously moving

---

[1]The research on face recognition and how it is mediated in the brain is extensive and beyond the scope of this chapter.

back and forth. This tells the therapist that the client's words and facial expressions alone do not represent the whole picture of her affective state; her leg is saying something different. The therapist needs to track shifts in all channels of experience holistically to utilize pieces of affective information for attuned interventions.

In AEDP, tracking aims to understand the client in the therapeutic context, in terms of AEDP fundamental representational schemas. More specifically, it involves an assessment of the client's location in the four states and three-state transformation of the transformational process (Fosha, 2009) or the Triangle of Experience; examples of this include a client who appears anxious as she encounters a new and good feeling about herself (tremulous affect in State 3) or recognizing a trace of anxiety as an inhibitory affect in State 1 (see also Pando-Mars, Chapter 6; Frederick, Chapter 7, this volume).

*2. Therapist-focused tracking*, or how we track ourselves, is based on "simulation theory" that suggests that we recognize others' feelings through empathy (vicarious experience of others' emotions) via the amygdala, insula, and the mirror neuron systems (Suzuki, 2014, 2016; Winkielman et al., 2009; see also Yeung, Chapter 13, this volume). In other words, the therapist's own interoception, that is, "the sense of the physiological condition of the entire body" (Craig, 2018, p. 215), also informs her sense of the client's emotional state via "embodied simulation" (Suzuki, 2014). Neuropsychological research to date suggests that vicarious activations of interoceptive and somatosensory cortices, at least in some forms and in some instances, facilitate facial emotion recognition of the other, for example, seeing client's angry face activates the therapist's interoceptive and somatosensory areas in the brain; as a result, the therapist experiences anger-related visceral sensations, such as heat in the hands or in the belly, which leads the therapist to feel the anger and helps her recognize the client's anger (Suzuki, 2014).[2]

*3. Relational tracking of the dyad*, or the moment-to-moment tracking of "we," is a way to assess the relational closeness and distance, safety and lack of safety, trust and lack of trust between therapist and client in the dyad. If, for example, a client's body backs off as the therapist affirms him, it may suggest the client's need for distance or an aversive reaction to affirmative recognition. Alternatively, a therapist notices her own tension and discomfort and gaze aversion as the client is speaking in a particular tone of voice. Flow, in synch, deepening, and so on are positive relational states, whereas awkwardness, tension, and a superficial atmosphere are negative relational states.

*4. Integrative moment-to-moment tracking* refers to how we weigh and integrate multimodal cues such as emotional expression of the client, the therapist's subjective emotional reactions, relational and process-related, as well as linguistic/contextual cues in making inferences of the client's emotional states

---

[2]Interestingly, the embodied simulation of perceived emotions tends to occur more strongly between people who are relationally close or perceived to be an in-group member (Lanzetta & Englis, 1989; Xu et al., 2009).

and make a goal-oriented decision about choice of intervention (Barrett et al., 2018; Suzuki, 2014, 2016; Zaki, 2013). This is a meta-level of tracking that weighs, prioritizes, and integrates observed or experienced emotion-related cues from both the client and therapist, and allows the therapist to decide on a next intervention.

We, as AEDP therapists, use all of these kinds of tracking simultaneously and aim to make informed decisions in assessing the other person's emotional state at the moment and make the most beneficial next move.

## USING THE DYADIC TRACKING FEEDBACK LOOP TO DETERMINE THE UNIT OF INTERVENTION

In AEDP, a unit of intervention is what a therapist says and a client's response to it (Fosha, 2000). It is ultimately clients who decide the effectiveness of the intervention, so to speak, by how they respond to it. Does an intervention lead to deepening and greater contact, or does it evoke defensiveness and greater distance? (see also Malan, 1976). It is through tracking that we can answer that question.

Even when the therapist offers a most empathic comment, if the client is not receptive to it and remains unaffected in their emotional state, the intervention did not yield the fruit that was intended. Then something has to shift in the next intervention. The unit of intervention in AEDP depends on close moment-to-moment tracking in assessing the client's affective state in response to the therapist's therapeutic comment, including but not limited to clients' nonverbal facial and bodily moves, as well as what they say and how they say it.

After each intervention, the therapist closely tracks the client's response. We not only pay attention to words but also carefully listen to what the client's face and body say. Does he lean forward? Does she smile brightly? Does she have a flash of wrinkles around the nose, showing disgust? Then the therapist makes a decision, both consciously and intuitively, about the next intervention: Lean forward? Smile back? Say something or opt not to about the flash of disgust on the client's face? If the therapist decides to comment on the disgust that flitted across the client's face, then how does the client's body respond to *that*? The therapist continues to watch the impact (or lack thereof) of what she just did and how the client responds. This moment-to-moment dyadic feedback loop is the primary tool that maximally keeps the AEDP therapist's interventions on target according to the client's emotional and relational states.

Additionally, tracking the nonimpactful interventions is as important as tracking the impactful ones; a nonimpactful intervention contains rich information, perhaps indicating the therapist's misattunement or the client's defense response. Carefully tracking the impact of interventions, and lack of impact, gives therapists a way to assess whether their interventions are on course.

## NEUROSCIENCE, THE FELT SENSE, AND MOMENT-TO-MOMENT TRACKING

Recent neuroscience findings suggest that we, as mammals, seem to have a neurobiological capacity for and a predisposition to track and attune to someone else's internal world. Specifically, *mirror neurons* are said to be specialized in tracking the actions and some emotions of others (Iacoboni et al., 2005; Lamm & Majdandžić, 2015; Suzuki, 2014, 2016; Wicker et al., 2003) as well as our own actions, such as the gestures, facial expressions, and body postures. They also get us ready for action by subconsciously mimicking someone else's actions (Iacoboni, 2008/2009). It has been suggested that the mirror neurons are important for attuning to others' internal states (Siegel, 2010), which in turn has great survival value in navigating the complex interpersonal world. Mirror neurons are also hypothesized to be the major constituents of the resonance circuits that underlie experiences of contact and connection (Fosha, 2013b; Siegel, 2010).

Research findings suggest that as we track social signals in others via mirror neurons, shifts are created first in the anterior insula, then in our subcortical limbic, brain stem, and body proper (Siegel, 2010). The insula is a tiny part of the brain that creates awareness of the internal state of our body, activates the resonance circuits, and does the energy management of emotional regulation (Craig, 2002, 2010, 2015). The awareness of one's internal bodily state is called *interoceptive awareness* by Craig (2015), and the *felt-sense*—"the wholistic, implicit bodily sense" (Gendlin, 2012, p. 58)—by Gendlin. Interoceptive awareness and the felt sense, concepts often used in the clinical field, are particularly important notions in the areas of tracking and attunement, for that is how we notice and experience the other person's internal state shifts.

A recent theory in neuroscience suggests the neurological underpinnings of the *felt sense*. Bud Craig, a neuroanatomist who, in his research, has focused on the insula and anterior cingulate, created a term, "GEM" (*global emotional moment*), that "*incorporate[s] feelings representing neural activity . . . in a 'map' of all current feelings*" (2015, p. 49, italics added). The insula is the crucial integrative center in the brain associated with the GEM experience, in which the *felt sense* is formed and experienced. Based on Craig's acronym, Fosha (2013a, 2013b) proposed that we call moment-to-moment tracking "GEM-to-GEM tracking," which in AEDP involves tracking fluctuations in the felt sense between therapist and client enables intersubjective attunement, dyadic mindfulness, and experiential work. This mutual, moment-to-moment, GEM-to-GEM tracking is critical both for the emotional processing of the energy-draining emotions of trauma, mediated by the right insula and for the emotional processing of the expanding energy-enriching positive emotions associated with healing and transformational affects in a coherent and integrative way, processed by the left insula (Craig, 2015; Fosha, 2013b).

Although both the therapist and the client's brains are tracking each other all the time, this chapter focuses on intentional *therapist-focused* tracking of the *felt sense*, which informs our awareness about the client's inner state.

## EMOTION THEORY AND MOMENT-TO-MOMENT TRACKING

As neuroscience and emotion theory suggest, emotions are rooted in the body (e.g., Craig, 2002, 2010, 2015; Damasio, 2003, 2018). Documented clinical evidence suggests that when adaptive, bodily rooted emotions—called *core affects* in AEDP—are processed to completion, the subsequent processing of this completion experience becomes a vehicle for affective, physical, cognitive, and psychological transformation (Fosha, 2000, 2002, 2003, 2008, 2009, 2013a, 2013b; Jacobs-Hendel, 2018; Prenn & Fosha, 2016; Russell, 2015). The expression of core affect is manifested somatically via visible and audible nonverbal cues, such as shifts in facial expressions; tone, intensity, and speed of the voice; arm muscles; eye movements; posture; and movements of hands and legs. Thus, it is crucial to accurately recognize core affects as they emerge as well as the presence of defenses and anxiety, which can interfere with the expression and processing of core affective experience. It is vital for therapists to have the ability to track these subtle body-based, implicit, often fleeting signs of core affect, including microexpressions (Ekman, 2007), to offer effective, immediate, and attuned interventions. It is equally important to accurately recognize the subtle and not so subtle markers of the transformational phenomena that follow the successful resolution of a piece of emotional processing.

As mentioned earlier, microexpressions are flashes of affective expression lasting less than 0.5 seconds, visible "leakages" of genuine internally experienced emotion—in the language of AEDP, core affect—which are quickly concealed from others by utilizing defenses (Ekman, 2007). In AEDP, we proactively use moment-to-moment tracking to catch these fleeting yet vital expressions as entry points and make use of such information for a next intervention. "What just happened?" "What is happening right now?" "While you are saying 'fine,' I just saw a flash of sadness on your face. Am I right?" are some examples of interventions to catch and zoom in on microexpressions. When done sensitively, the client may feel recognized by the therapist in a new way, that is, recognized for witnessing a part of them that is often unseen, neglected, or forbidden; such an experience of recognition may allow the client to feel safe, easing access to the experience of core affect, the vehicle of transformations.

## ATTACHMENT THEORY AND MOMENT-TO-MOMENT TRACKING

Attachment theory and research have demonstrated that babies need to feel safe for them to be able to explore their environment with curiosity. AEDP, an attachment-based therapy model, postulates that creating a sense of safety is a primary therapeutic task. The establishment of safety must precede and accompany all experiential work with affective experiences and blocks, that is, defenses, against it. One aspect of attachment-based therapy is that it serves as a present-time reparenting-type process through which the client experiences a corrective, secure attachment experience; the therapist can serve as a secure base and thus be a potential agent of change (Beebe & Lachmann, 2013; Fosha, 2000, 2009; Holmes & Slade, 2019; Lipton & Fosha, 2011; Prenn, 2011). Just as babies need attuned caretakers to establish a consistently secure base before exploring the world around them, our clients need a *secure therapy base* (i.e., their therapists) to risk exploring their inner emotional and relational fields. To provide this necessary sense of safety, we need to provide clients with consistently appropriate, good enough, and reliable attunement.

Neuroscience research suggests that a higher level of oxytocin is released in the neuroendocrine system when parent–infant dyads are positively interacting with each other (Feldman et al., 2010). Neuroimaging studies show when a positive emotional experience is shared, there is neural synchrony within dyads and groups (Hasson et al., 2004; Lamm & Majdandžić, 2015; Stephens et al., 2010), suggesting that synchronized gestures, biochemistry, and neural patterns occur during a positive emotional state.

We can use moment-to-moment tracking to capitalize on a moment of positive emotional experience, creating and enhancing the sense of safety and security within the therapeutic dyad. When our bodies, biochemistry, and neural patterns in the brains are synchronized with our clients, they feel less alone, more secure, and more safe with us.

## TRACKING AND ATTUNEMENT: THE INPUT AND OUTPUT OF DYADIC COMMUNICATION

In psychotherapy, our tool in trade is attunement. The question is: How can we be reasonably consistent and accurate in providing attunement to our clients? The key seems to be moment-to-moment tracking. Studies on interactions between babies and their mothers suggest that when baby and mother are in sync in their nonverbal communication—in other words, attuned— they are also affectively in sync and emotionally regulated, and the interaction is suffused with positive affect (Beebe & Lachmann, 2013). Moment-to-moment tracking refers to the requisite skill set for the therapist's ongoing attunement. It allows the therapist to accurately recognize emotional states in our clients, variations in closeness and distance in the therapeutic dyad, and how and when to make necessary adjustments, which, in turn, are followed up by continued tracking to see if, and precisely how, the therapist's adjustment (i.e., intervention) is being received by the client.

Moment-to-moment tracking and attunement can be considered "input" and "output" aspects of dyadic communication, respectively. Tracking is the therapist's ongoing, versatile multichannel input capacity to mindfully observe, recognize, and recall body-based signs of clients' affective experience and expressions, however fleeting or subtle they may be. Attunement, the main ingredient of secure attachment experience, on the other hand, is the therapist's ongoing output ability. It uses the tracked input information to respond (output) mindfully, sensitively, and meaningfully to the client.

Moment-to-moment tracking enables the therapist to synch with the client's dynamically changing internal states, engendering a shared inter-subjective experience of connection and resonance, which is said to be cor-related with activation in the insula. When done well, tracking and attunement can work harmoniously in creating the maximally secure attachment experi-ences in clients.

## MOMENT-TO-MOMENT TRACKING OF TRANSFORMANCE AND REPRESENTATIONAL SCHEMAS

Up to the present time, no systematic literature has been written about the how-to of moment-to-moment tracking in AEDP. This section aims to articulate targets and techniques of tracking within the AEDP theoretical framework.

Tracking in AEDP has a wide range of targets. It can be used for spotting core affects, defenses, and anxiety and for catching a core affect in a microexpression, when concealed by a defensive affect or otherwise unremarkable verbal expression. Tracking carefully, therapists can find entry points, identify glimmers of resilience and transformance, notice somatic shifts in the client and in themselves, assess the relational environment and check the impact of an intervention, and evaluate the moment-to-moment impact of the therapist on a client.

### Tracking Transformance

Before describing how to recognize the categories of the Triangle of Experi-ence, it is important to discuss how to identify signs of *transformance* (Fosha, 2008), as these signs can be present throughout all states. Transformance phenomena are identified by somatic/affective markers which AEDP denotes as the *vitality affects*. They include exhaling sighs, fleeting smiles, head nods, sideways head tilts (Fosha, 2009); brightening of the eyes, slight flushing of the cheeks, and vitality in the voice. In general, the dynamic fluctuations in affective intensity (Stern, 2010) reflect manifestations of energy and vitality (e.g., the feeling of being alive).

The Triangle of Experience is a central representational schema in AEDP (see Figures 4.1 and 4.2). This section highlights some of the signs by which clinicians can recognize the categories of the Triangle of Experience.

### Tracking the Triangle of Experience (Defense, Signal Affects, Core Affects)

The signs described here may mean different things to different people depending on their particular social, interpersonal, historical, and cultural

**FIGURE 4.1.  The Triangle of Experience**

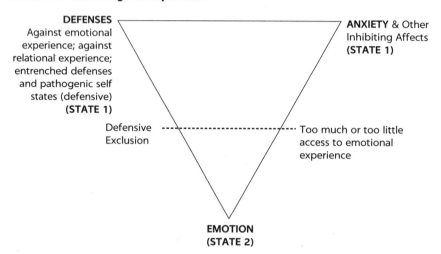

**DEFENSES**
Against emotional
experience; against
relational experience;
entrenched defenses
and pathogenic self
states (defensive)
**(STATE 1)**

**ANXIETY** & Other
Inhibiting Affects
**(STATE 1)**

Defensive
Exclusion

Too much or too little
access to emotional
experience

**EMOTION**
**(STATE 2)**

**MALADAPTIVE AFFECTIVE**
**EXPERIENCES**
**(need transforming)**

**ADAPTIVE CORE AFFECTIVE**
**EXPERIENCES**
**(are transforming)**

**Legend: Affective Experiences**

**Maladaptive Affective Experiences**
The Pathogenic Affects (e.g., Overwhelm, Toxic Shame, Fear
Without Solution); Unbearable States of Traumatic Aloneness
(e.g., Helplessness, Fragmentation, Brokenness; Despair, "The
Black Hole Of Trauma")

**Adaptive Core Affective Experiences**
Categorical Emotions; Relational Experiences, Asymmetric
(Attachment) or Symmetric (Intersubjective); Coordinated
Relational Experiences; Receptive Affective Experiences; Somatic
"Drop-Down" States; Intrarelational Experiences; Authentic
Self-Experiences; Experiences of Agency, Will Desire; Attachment
Strivings; The Expression of Core Needs

*Note.* Copyright © 2020 by Diana Fosha. Reprinted with permission.

**FIGURE 4.2. The Triangle of Experience: Two Versions of the Triangle of Experience—The Self-at-Worst and the Self-at-Best**

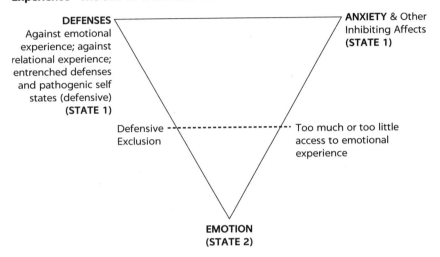

**DEFENSES**
Against emotional experience; against relational experience; entrenched defenses and pathogenic self states (defensive)
**(STATE 1)**

**ANXIETY** & Other Inhibiting Affects **(STATE 1)**

Defensive Exclusion

Too much or too little access to emotional experience

**EMOTION (STATE 2)**

**MALADAPTIVE AFFECTIVE EXPERIENCES (need transforming)**

**ADAPTIVE CORE AFFECTIVE EXPERIENCES (are transforming)**

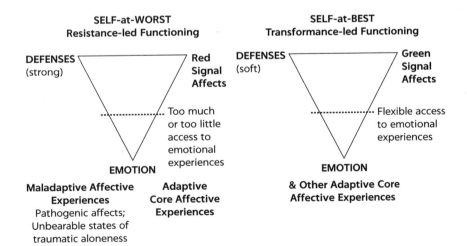

**SELF-at-WORST**
**Resistance-led Functioning**

**SELF-at-BEST**
**Transformance-led Functioning**

**DEFENSES** (strong)

**Red Signal Affects**

**DEFENSES** (soft)

**Green Signal Affects**

Too much or too little access to emotional experiences

Flexible access to emotional experiences

**EMOTION**

**EMOTION**

**Maladaptive Affective Experiences**
Pathogenic affects; Unbearable states of traumatic aloneness

**Adaptive Core Affective Experiences**

**& Other Adaptive Core Affective Experiences**

*Note.* Copyright © 2020 by Diana Fosha. Reprinted with permission.

contexts. It is important for the therapist to assess the baseline patterns of each client and her or his unique context, which may affect emotional expression.

- *Signs of defense*: avoiding eye contact restlessness, moving the body away from therapist, a stone-faced expression, crossed arms, tension in the shoulders, speaking rapidly, loudly, very softly, being excessively wordy, changing topics, crossing legs, crossing and uncrossing legs; discrepancies between emotion-related words and facial and bodily expressions, including microexpressions (e.g., clients say "I'm fine" while showing sadness on their face).

- *Signs of red signal (inhibitory) affects*:
  - Anxiety—muscle tension in the chest, shallow breathing, trembling hands or legs, frequent blinking, averting of the eyes, self-touching, rapid speech, high-pitched speech, wordiness, use of words that indicate anxiety (e.g., worry, fearfulness)
  - Trace amounts of fear—raised upper eyelids, tense lower eyelids, eyebrows drawn together, lips stretched back (Ekman, 2013)
  - Trace amounts of shame/guilt—gaze aversion, head turned sideways or tilted, disrupted ongoing behavior, confusion in thoughts, inability to speak, shrinking of the body, collapse of shoulders, and lowering of head (Ekman, 2013; Lewis, 2018; Tracy et al., 2009) (Note: The somatic phenomenological distinction between shame and guilt is difficult to make because both are the kind of feelings the client does not want others to register, and, additionally, they are often intertwined; Ekman, 2013.)

- *Signs of green signal affects*: a deep exhale, a head nod (Fosha, 2009), direct eye contact, leaning forward, sitting up straight, a slight smile, use of words that indicate curiosity and openness (e.g., "I'm interested . . .")

- *Signs of core affects: the categorical emotions*:
  - Anger—lowered and drawn-together brows, tightness in the jaw, lips open in a rectangle-like shape, showing clenched teeth, or if lips are closed, lip pressed against lip, frown, nostrils dilated, the wings of the nose flared out, red flushes (Harmon-Jones & Harmon-Jones, 2018), the experience of heat in the body, often rising; activation of the muscles of the limbs
  - Sadness and grief—tears, rhythmic sobbing, downcast eyes, arched eyebrows, downturned mouth, physical pain, experienced often in the heart or behind the eyes (Ekman, 2013; Tomkins, 1963)
  - Disgust—the raised upper lip, the slightly protruded lower lip, the raised nostril wings, and wrinkling on the sides and bridge of the nose (Ekman, 2013); the gape, tongue extension, retraction of the upper lip (Rozin et al., 2018)
  - Happiness—eyes sparkle, the skin under eyes winkled, mouth drawn back at corners (Keltner et al., 2018), Duchenne smile (Ekman et al., 1990)

    – Joy—muscle tremors, purposeless movements, laughter, clapping hands, jumping, dancing about, stamping feet, chuckling or giggling, smiling, the muscles around the eyes are contracted, raised upper lip (Keltner et al., 2018; Stephens et al., 2010); Duchenne smile (Ekman et al., 1990)

- *Signs of core affects: the relational affects*:
  - Love—beaming eyes, "smiling cheeks" (Fosha, 2000), urges to touch and move toward the other, gentle smile, protruding lips, tender eyes (Keltner et al., 2018), head nods and head movements up (Sauter, 2017), open-mouthed Duchenne smile with head tilts, closed eyes (Campos et al., 2013)
  - Admiration—eyes opened, eyebrows raised, eyes bright, smile; conventionalized exclamations (Sauter, 2017)
  - Compassion—smile, tender or beaming eyes; oblique eyebrows, fixed gaze; head movement forward, forward leans, patting and stroking the other (Sauter, 2017) or "warm sadness with a comforting intention" (D. Fosha, personal communication, September 29, 2019)
  - Resonance—mutually coordinated facial expression, rhythm, timing, and tone of speech, body movements (Baylin & Hughes, 2016; Beebe & Lachmann, 2013; Siegel, 2010); "social synchrony," such as mirrored hand gestures (Dumas et al., 2010)
  - Feeling close, feeling the "we"—compassion, genuine interest, engagement, coordinated breathing rhythm, mirrored facial expressions, matching voice tones, experiencing the other's internal affective state (e.g., a therapist spontaneously tears up as a client talks about a deeply sad story; Siegel, 2010); leaning forward toward each other[3]

- *Signs of core affects: the self-related affects*:
  - Pride—facial expression of joy, chest expansion, arms raised or out (Ekman, 2013)
  - Self-respect, self-compassion, self-love—smile, tender eyes, hugging oneself, putting a hand over the heart
  - Feeling moved, touched, emotional—soft tears of joy, uplifted gaze, internal surges of energy (Fosha, 2000)

## CLINICAL VIGNETTES

The short vignettes[4] of clinical interactions that follow illustrate the use of moment-to-moment tracking in clinical action in AEDP. These small vignettes from video-recorded sessions demonstrate the power and versatility

---

[3]It is of interest that gratitude "was associated with a distinct core relational theme but not an expressive display" (Campos et al., 2013, p. 27). Also Ekman (2007) said, "I doubt that there is a universal gratitude signal" (p. 198).

[4]I have complied with the American Psychological Association ethical standards in describing the details of treatment; aspects of the clients' identities and backgrounds have been disguised to protect confidentiality.

of moment-to-moment tracking. Note that *italics* indicates description of non-verbal expressions or movements, and **bold** indicates theoretical comments.

**Vignette 1: "I Can't Say 'Very Good.'"**

We are in the opening moments of an initial session with a young woman, Susan.

CLIENT:     (*nervously laughs, making eye contact with the therapist as her upper body withdraws*) **[showing tension, defensive laughter, and relational distancing, State 1]**

THERAPIST:  (*laughs along with the client*) So . . .

CLIENT:     (*looks up to the ceiling and then to the side*) I don't know where to start . . .

THERAPIST:  First of all, I want to check in with you how you're feeling right now . . . (*gentle tone of voice*) **[tight focus on here-and-now affective experience from the get-go]**

CLIENT:     (*immediately leans backward, distancing herself from the therapist for a few seconds, then comes back to the erect position. She looks around the room, away from the therapist*) I can't say "very good." (*her hands between the knees, her legs move slightly up and down, showing tension. As she speaks, she laughs*)

THERAPIST:  Yeah? (*laughs along with the client*) **[attunement to the client's defensive affect]** And you're laughing. (*said quickly but in a warm and playful tone of voice*) **[integrative tracking]**

CLIENT:     (*smiles*) I know . . . (*her legs move up and down slightly; more tension in the legs*) So that I won't cry right now. (*smiles as she points at her eyes; nods and scratches her ear*) **[deepening; the client reveals that there is crying, i.e., deeper affect that she is trying to contain]**

THERAPIST:  There is a LOT (*gentle tone of voice with an emphasis on "a LOT"*). **[validating the underlying affect and estimating its magnitude and depth]**

We can see that the client is showing a high level of defense and anxiety at the beginning of the initial session. The therapist quickly decides to make the first intervention, focusing on the client's affect instead of the content of the primary reason for a consultation. She (the therapist) quickly assesses and makes an in-the-moment clinical judgment that the emotional aspect, primarily high anxiety, calls for immediate attention.

The next exchange is characterized by the client's mixed signals: laughter and verbal statement, "I can't say 'very good,'" that is, she does not feel well. Integrative tracking signals to the therapist the discrepancy between the verbal utterance and the nonverbal cues. The therapist decides to focus on one of the nonverbal cues (i.e., the laughter). Notice the therapist's tone is warm and playful, not judgmental, as she attempts to engage the client at the affective level. The therapist communicates to the client that she is curious about her client's inner experiences from the get-go. The client understands the message right away, and her communication deepens and becomes more authentic; Susan says, "I know . . . so that I won't cry right now." She is aware of the tears behind the laughter and communicates clearly to the therapist what is motivating her distance, anxiety, and defenses. We don't know why she feels it is necessary to suppress her tears. That is for later therapeutic work to reveal.

Integrative tracking allows the therapist to swiftly catch a glimmer of defense and cut to the chase, acknowledging an underlying core affect. To be precise, this exchange started at 11 seconds after the start of the session and ended at 39 seconds, lasting only 28 seconds. Moment-to-moment tracking enables the therapist to make a quick assessment of the client's state from the very beginning of an initial session.

### Vignette 2: Catching the Vulnerability—Emerging Core Affective Experience

The following section is a session with a different client, Yoko, and is also at the beginning of an initial session. This client came in concerned about her new job situation. She did not know why she sometimes found herself tearing up in the morning as she got ready to go to work. This was a mystery to her, given that her coworkers were "nice" and there were no obvious troubles at work.

CLIENT:  I've been thinking a lot about getting out of the current work situation (looking down), but things aren't moving forward (*looks up and makes eye contact with the therapist*). I recently had a chance to (*looking down*) find a way to get out of it (*looking at the therapist fleetingly as she pushes her left hand outward*) (*the therapist mirrors the same hand gesture*) **[client-focused tracking; mirroring]**, but that didn't work out either. (*the client slows down in her speech and the tone of voice gets deeper*) Yeah . . . (*nods a few times*). People say, "Everything happens for a reason." I started to wonder why these things keep happening to me (*when she says, "why these things," her voice slightly trembles; her heads tilts sideways and nods slowly; a vulnerable facial expression that signals an emotion is rising*) . . . (*silence*) (*The client's gaze goes up, then nods as she makes eye contact with the therapist*) (*Therapist nods along with the client at the same pace*) **[client-focused tracking; attunement]**

The client is struggling with the emerging vulnerable core affective experience and expression. We can see her struggle in her slightly shaky voice, but although she is not letting the core affect fully express itself, neither is she going to great lengths to hide it. Evidence of transformance is in the client's openness, a green signal affect, which the therapist registers. As the therapist closely tracks the client's facial and vocal expressions, notes her transformance glimmers, and senses her struggle, she decides to focus on the vulnerable core affect instead of the defense. We will see how that intervention works for the client in the next vignette.

### Vignette 3: "A Little Bit of Emotion Coming Up"—The Emergence of Core Affect

THERAPIST: What's coming up right now as you talk about this? **[zooms in on the subtle emotional cues that indicate the emergence of core affect]**

CLIENT: I feel a little bit of emotion coming up . . . (*When she says "emotion," her voice trembles again and a flash of sadness emerges, then a quick smile takes over her face as she nods a few times*) **[a defensive smile quickly kicks in to conceal the vulnerable core affect of sadness]**

A lot is going on here. Having registered the green signal affect of the client's relative openness, the therapist makes an intervention to focus on the client's emerging core affect suggested by the slightly trembling voice and invites that she focus on her inner affective experience. The client understands the therapist and confirms the therapist's experience of her emerging emotion; she says, "I feel a little bit of emotion coming up. . . ." However, her face is not congruent with her words: A smile quickly takes over and conceals the close-to-unfolding sadness. There is a conflict between expression and defense. However, there are also signs that this is a soft defense (i.e., not very entrenched). Let's see what the therapist does at this moment.

### Vignette 4: Would You Allow That Emotion to Come? Explicit Invitation to Experience of Core Affect

THERAPIST: Right. (*synchronizes the client's nods. The gentle tone of voice*) [client-focused tracking; attunement] Would you allow that emotion to come . . . (*Client looks down as she shows sadness on her face; nods a few times*) . . . without any judgment? (*gentle tone of voice*) **[integrative tracking]**

CLIENT: Yeah . . . (*shows a sad facial expression more clearly and holds it longer; her voice trembles. She then tries to hold back tears. The eyebrows move inward, the eyes look downward, both corners of the lips go down, suggesting sadness. As she stays with the sadness longer, the defensive smile disappears*) **[dropping down to State 2]**

THERAPIST:   Yeah . . . ummmm (*gentle tone of voice*) **[use of paraverbal sounds to let the client know the therapist's supportive presence with her]**

Here, the therapist decides to explicitly invite the client to focus on the core affect (sadness), instead of defense (smile), using integrative tracking. She does so in a gentle and inviting tone of voice, matching her pace and pitch. The verbal and nonverbal aspects of the intervention are congruent. There are not many words exchanged in this section, but a good deal of non-verbal activity is occurring in the client's facial and vocal expressions. The client's nonverbal expression—maintaining the sad facial expression without interruptions of defense—indicates her engagement in experiencing the sadness. Her defensive smile gradually disappears and the client drops down, at least momentarily, toward State 2 experiencing.

### Vignette 5: The Return of Defense

CLIENT:   (*16 seconds of silence*) (*fast blinking; rubbing fingers; slight head tilt*) Can I use the tissue? (*nervous laughter*)

THERAPIST:   Yes, it's there. (*pointing at the tissue box near the client*)

CLIENT:   And, then . . . (*as she wipes her nose. She makes a gesture, using both hands pushing out something to the side*) What's making it hard for me is . . . (*tries to explain the context of the matters and to ignore the tears in a matter of fact way; smiling*) **[avoidance of core affect, State 1, process and integrative tracking]**

THERAPIST:   Oh, can I stop you for a second? (*The client is still smiling*) Before we get to the story, I am wondering what's coming up right now . . .? (*slow pace, gentle tone of voice*)

We can see a lot of somatic activation at the beginning of this section. The fast blinking of eyes and rubbing fingers suggest the clear emergence of core affect. Then something happens. The client suddenly laughs as she asks for the tissue. A quick drop from the defense to the core affective experience of sadness seems to trigger another round of defensive reactions, leading to nervous laughter and her attempt to move past her tears. The client is back in State 1 again.

The therapist identifies the sudden shift in the client and immediately stops her from going into the verbal content. Here, integrative tracking is used as a decision-making tool, as the therapist identifies the gap between the verbal ("What's making it hard for me is . . .") and the nonverbal (tears in the eyes). The AEDP training gives special weight to affective phenomena and helps the therapist choose the nonverbal cue over the verbal, supporting the client in quickly getting back to the emotional exploration.

Let's see what follows after this intervention, keeping in mind that the unit of intervention in AEDP is what the therapist says *and* what the client does with it.

### Vignette 6: The Emergence of Core Emotions Again

CLIENT:    Oh . . . (*looks downward as if she is checking in with herself inside*) Hmmm. I thought I was even-keeled a few minutes ago. (*sliding a hand horizontally before her chest as she says, "even-keeled." When she says, "I thought I was," her voice trembles. Her eyes quickly go up to the upper left side*) . . . (*looks as if she is about to cry. She looks down with both of lips going down, showing sadness*) I don't know why . . . (*hides her mouth with her left hand, shakes her head a few times, her voice trembling more as she makes good eye contact with the therapist*) **[dropping down from State 1 to State 2 again; relational tracking]**

THERAPIST:    (*attuned to the client's tone, pitch, and speed of speech*) It looks like you, Yoko, have a lot of feelings inside your heart . . . (*raises her right hand and makes a gesture pointing at her own heart*) **[attunement; deep empathy; validation of the client's inner experience, and offering to locate the part of the body that may be holding the feeling]**

CLIENT:    (*nods. Listening intently as she wipes her nose with tissue*) **[green signal]**

What we see here is the client's discomfort with her sadness, yet without hard defenses. Her comment suggests that she is accustomed to being "even-keeled" and struggles as she encounters the undeniable emergence of sadness as suggested by her trembling voice. While the client makes eye contact with the therapist as if she is seeking support, the therapist who is relationally tracking the client takes some therapeutic actions: She provides nonverbal relational support (engages the client through the eye contact) and verbally offers deep empathy (i.e., the mention of the heart) and validates Yoko's inner affective experience that is yet unknown but felt. The client takes in the therapist's relational support and sends a green signal (nods) that she is taking in her therapist's care.

### Vignette 7: Let Tears Come

THERAPIST:    It looks as if they are just about to come out . . . (*right hand, facing up, makes movements of opening up*) **[client-focused tracking; attunement; amplifying the client's inner affective state]**

CLIENT:    Yes, that's right. (*Big nod. Making good direct eye contact with the therapist. Tears are coming out*) **[clear green signal affect, indicating readiness to shift; the verbal and nonverbal are congruent]**

THERAPIST:    Yes, hmm hmmm (*gentle tone of voice*) . . . let these tears come . . . this is a place to do this. (*gentle voice, slow pace*) **[encouragement, inviting her to welcome the emerging**

**affect].** Client: (*big nod as tears do come out freely. The client cries for about 2 minutes*) **[clear drop down to State 2, processing the core affect]**

The process is deepening. The client is receptive to the therapist's verbal and nonverbal encouragement to experience sadness. As we relationally track the exchanges between the two, we can see that the client's need for relational support from the therapist, expressed by a quick glance, was immediately met with the therapist's attuned eye contact, leading to the client's substantial dropping down to her sadness (State 2) and deep crying, with no words, for 2 minutes. We can see the interplay between tracking and attunement that results in deepening the affect processing and the drop-down to State 2.

### Vignette 8: The End of Processing Core Affective Experience and Metaprocessing

**CLIENT:** (*cries as she looks down and wipes the nose frequently with the tissue. After a while, she touches the edge of the paper on her lap, then quickly glances at the therapist*) **[end of affect processing; client-focused and relational tracking]**

**THERAPIST:** Having shed some tears, what's that like right now? **[metaprocessing]**

**CLIENT:** (*nods as she wipes the nose*) I feel a little bit of relief. (*nods*) **[post-breakthrough affect]** (*Therapist nods at the same pace as the client*) **[client-focused tracking; attunement]**

Here, the client is deeply processing her sadness. Meanwhile, the therapist quietly holds the space for her and actively continues moment-to-moment tracking, waiting for a sign indicating the completion of affective processing.

As she comes to the end of processing her sadness, the client signals the therapist by making eye contact again and nods to her, suggesting her readiness to shift. The therapist understands the signals from the client and then asks a metaprocessing question: "What's that like right now?" The client reports a sense of relief and confirms that this wave of affective processing has come to completion, resulting in a postbreakthrough affect (relief).

The client-focused tracking and relational tracking work harmoniously in accurately assessing the client's affective and relational needs and her readiness to shift from one state to the next.

### Vignette 9: Catching the Glimmers of Transformance

Another client, Clare, has been working with this therapist for some time. Clare reports work-related anxiety (what she calls the "anxiety vortex") and tells the therapist that she wants to work on it without getting overwhelmed by it; she has to go back to work after the session and cannot afford to be taken over by her anxiety.

Clare is in State 1. She holds anxiety while wanting her strength to contain it. In this case, the therapist took the "strength" as a glimmer of transformance. The inner resources needed to work on her anxiety are already present and ready to be drawn on.

CLIENT:    I have to access that part of myself that is strong. (*firmness in her tone of voice, fast pace in her speech*) **[a glimmer of transformance and a glimmer of anxiety; client-focused tracking]**

THERAPIST:  I really appreciate you bringing in that strength of yours. I agree with that strategy (*smile, slower speech*). **[focus on her transformance striving]** Can you locate the strength in you? In your body or around you? **[somatic focus]**

CLIENT:    When I think about it . . . I think it's in my arms (*makes a spontaneous forward-movement in her right arm; her tone of voice is strong*) **[vitality affect]**

THERAPIST:  Arms! **[catching the vitality affect]** What would be the gesture (of strength)?

CLIENT:    (*silently extends her right arm forward and smiles proudly*) Marching ahead. **[sign of pleasure]**

THERAPIST:  Do that a couple more times. (*therapist does the gesture together with the client a few times*) **[amplification of the vitality affect; mirroring]**.

CLIENT:    Feels like swimming—at least for me. (*smile; does the gesture several times*) **[personal, action metaphor]**.

THERAPIST:  (*smiles back, nods, continues the arm gesture*) **[mirroring]** (*both repeat the same arm movements several times for a few minutes*) **[mirroring; relational tracking]**

THERAPIST:  Let's pause and see.

CLIENT:    It feels hot—good, energized, good to move. (*sits up straight and spontaneously does the same arm gesture using both arms*) . . . Feels fun! (*smiles as she does the arm gesture several more times with the downcast eyes*) **[vitality affect, playfulness, ease, lightness, increased energy; shared positive emotional experience; secure attachment experience; State 2]**

THERAPIST:  (*does the gesture together along with the client; smile; feeling the playfulness, ease, excitement*) **[mirroring; relational tracking]**

CLIENT:    (*looks at the therapist*)

THERAPIST:  How does that feel? **[client-focused and relational tracking]**

CLIENT:    That really woke me up! (*smile, excitement*) **[increased energy, upward spiral of vitality affect]**

In this vignette, the therapist closely tracks the traces of vitality affect in the client. In the beginning, her (client's) energy is firm yet tense with anxious energy; she says that she wants to have the "strength" to contain her anxiety vortex. One may see it as a form of defense against anxiety. However, the therapist, knowing the client, sees it differently: the therapist considers the traces of vitality in it as an energy-building transformance striving, an attempt to counter the energy-draining anxiety; the therapist strategically focuses on amplifying the client's emergent vitality affect by inviting a body movement of "strength" to come forward. The client spontaneously responds with an arm movement, "marching ahead" with pleasure, another sign of vitality affect. As the client and therapist engage in the mirrored, resonant, and matching arm movements together, the vitality affect (the strength, playfulness, lightness, increased energy) becomes increasingly more powerful, activating the client's resources in the body and mind.

With this new vitality, the original glimmer of anxiety transformed into an experience of mastery and pleasure, coconstructed nonverbally with the therapist's attunement, mirroring, and encouraging, the client becomes more able to look at her anxiety vortex without getting overwhelmed by it.

## HOW TO LEARN MOMENT-TO-MOMENT TRACKING: VIDEO-RECORDING AS AN IMPORTANT TOOL

Readers may wonder how AEDP therapists acquire the moment-to-moment tracking ability that allows the therapist to swiftly catch fleeting affective expressions, assess relatedness, weigh conflicting verbal versus nonverbal cues, and finally make therapeutic decisions. The answer is threefold: studying video recordings, clinical experiences in supervision, and some suggestions from neuroscience.

First and foremost, video recording sessions in AEDP training is critically important (discussed in depth in Prenn & Fosha, 2016). The development of AEDP therapists' competencies, particularly sharp sensitivity to nonverbal cues, relies heavily on the use of video-recorded sessions in supervision. Video-based supervision allows the supervisee to show the actual reality of the therapy session to her supervisor, instead of unreliable self-reporting from memory. Video-recorded sessions also make it possible for the therapist to have immediate feedback from the recordings during self-supervision, thus facilitating precise deliberate practice (Prenn & Fosha, 2016).

Our clinical experience in supervision tells us that beginner AEDP therapists learn moment-to-moment tracking by watching numerous clinical recordings with the help of their supervisors to train their eyes and ears to catch subtle affective expressions (Prenn & Fosha, 2016). AEDP supervision requires supervisees to video-record sessions, watch the recording, stop it for a moment, go back a few seconds, and watch the same section again to catch fleeting affective expressions and understand what they signify. This painstaking process, a clear instance of deliberate practice, sharpens supervisees' tracking sensitivity to big and small affective expressions.

Additionally, some research in neuroscience (Behrens et al., 2007; Rushworth et al., 2007; Zaki et al., 2010) suggests that we can acquire cognitive biases—clinically informed priorities in tracking—that would allow us to choose which cues to focus on when faced with conflicting verbal and nonverbal information, based on our learning history. "Relying on nonverbal cues tended to produce adaptive decisions about a given target's affective states, perceivers may learn over time to weigh nonverbal cues more strongly when subsequently encountering that target" (Zaki et al., 2010, p. 8487).

As we watch our own and other advanced AEDP therapists' sessions on recordings and identify meaningful moments of affective change process, we internalize the feedback loop: Choosing nonverbal cues gives us access to more accurate, vital, and raw affective data that are therapeutically beneficial for the clients, and we feel the difference when we practice moment-to-moment tracking in actual sessions with our clients.

The process of learning moment-to-moment tracking may feel like learning freestyle dance without a protocol at first, and yet when practiced numerous times, one can dance to the natural flow of healing and flourishing processes with ease as if it were second nature. The flow that we dance to is the affect.

## SUMMARY

This chapter identified four types of moment-to-moment tracking seen in AEDP theory and practice. Moment-to-moment tracking is essential in (a) rapidly and accurately identifying core affects, defenses, and anxiety; (b) providing relational attunement and secure attachment experiences; and (c) identifying the vitality affects, the positive somatic affective markers of transformational states and transformance phenomena. Nine short vignettes demonstrated the ways in which different types of tracking are used in actual sessions, leading to different types of affective, relational, and transformational phenomenology. Ways to hone moment-to-moment tracking skills were suggested at the end, emphasizing the central importance of video-recorded sessions used in AEDP training.

The reader may wonder about the ultimate goal of using moment-to-moment tracking. Combined with the Triangle of Experience and the four-state transformational process (see Figure 1 in the Appendix),[5] moment-to-moment tracking helps us make informed-judgment calls as we find a path—sometimes straight forward, other times long and winding—to the pearl of transformance inside each person, to access the vitality and energy for healing, flourishing, and transformation. Moment-to-moment tracking gives us the accuracy and speed to get to that living pearl.

## REFERENCES

Barrett, L. F., Lewis, M., & Haviland-Jones, J. (Eds.). (2018). *Handbook of emotions*. Guilford Press.

Baylin, J., & Hughes, D. A. (2016). *The neurobiology of attachment-focused therapy: Enhancing connection & trust in the treatment of children & adolescents*. Norton.

---

[5]This figure, and diagrams for all of the representational schemas in AEDP 2.0, may be downloaded for free (http://pubs.apa.org/books/supp/fosha/).

Beebe, B., & Lachmann, F. (2013). *The origins of attachment: Infant research and adult treatment*. Routledge. https://doi.org/10.4324/9781315858067

Behrens, T. E., Woolrich, M. W., Walton, M. E., & Rushworth, M. F. (2007). Learning the value of information in an uncertain world. *Nature Neuroscience, 10*(9), 1214–1221. https://doi.org/10.1038/nn1954

Botvinick, M., Jha, A. P., Bylsma, L. M., Fabian, S. A., Solomon, P. E., & Prkachin, K. M. (2005). Viewing facial expressions of pain engages cortical areas involved in the direct experience of pain. *NeuroImage, 25*(1), 312–319. https://doi.org/10.1016/j.neuroimage.2004.11.043

Campos, B., Shiota, M. N., Keltner, D., Gonzaga, G. C., & Goetz, J. L. (2013). What is shared, what is different? Core relational themes and expressive displays of eight positive emotions. *Cognition and Emotion, 27*(1), 37–52. https://doi.org/10.1080/02699931.2012.683852

Craig, A. D. (2002). How do you feel? Interoception: The sense of the physiological condition of the body. *Nature Reviews Neuroscience, 3*(8), 655–666. https://doi.org/10.1038/nrn894

Craig, A. D. (2010). The sentient self. *Brain Structure & Function, 214*(5–6), 563–577. https://doi.org/10.1007/s00429-010-0248-y

Craig, A. D. (2015). *How do you feel? An interoceptive moment with your neurobiological self*. Princeton University Press. https://doi.org/10.1515/9781400852727

Craig, A. D. (2018). Interoception and emotion: A neuroanatomical perspective. In L. F. Barrett, M. Lewis, & J. M. Haviland-Jones (Eds.), *Handbook of emotions* (pp. 272–288). Guilford.

Damasio, A. (2003). *Looking for Spinoza: Joy, sorrow, and the feeling brain*. Harcourt Books.

Damasio, A. (2018). *The strange order of things: Life, feeling, and the making of cultures*. Pantheon Books.

Dumas, G., Nadel, J., Soussignan, R., Martinerie, J., & Garnero, L. (2010). Inter-brain synchronization during social interaction. *PLOS ONE, 5*(8), e12166. https://doi.org/10.1371/journal.pone.0012166

Dzafic, I., Oestreich, L., Martin, A. K., Mowry, B., & Burianová, H. (2019). Stria terminalis, amygdala, and temporoparietal junction networks facilitate efficient emotion processing under expectations. *Human Brain Mapping, 40*(18), 5382–5396. https://doi.org/10.1002/hbm.24779

Ekman, P. (2007). *Emotions revealed: Recognizing faces and feelings to improve communication and emotional life*. St. Martin's Press.

Ekman, P. (2013). *Emotion in the human face*. Malor Books.

Ekman, P., Davidson, R. J., & Friesen, W. V. (1990). The Duchenne smile: Emotional expression and brain physiology II. *Journal of Personality and Social Psychology, 58*(2), 342–353. https://doi.org/10.1037/0022-3514.58.2.342

Ekman, P., & Friesen, W. V. (1982). Felt, false, and miserable smiles. *Journal of Nonverbal Behavior, 6*(4), 238–252. https://doi.org/10.1007/BF00987191

Ekman, P., Friesen, W. V., & Hager, J. C. (2002). *Facial action coding system* [ebook]. Research Nexus.

Feldman, R., Gordon, I., & Zagoory-Sharon, O. (2010). The cross-generation transmission of oxytocin in humans. *Hormones and Behavior, 58*(4), 669–676. https://doi.org/10.1016/j.yhbeh.2010.06.005

Fosha, D. (2000). *The transforming power of affect: A model for accelerated change*. Basic Books.

Fosha, D. (2002). The activation of affective change processes in AEDP. In J. J. Magnavita (Ed.), *Comprehensive handbook of psychotherapy: Vol. 1. Psychodynamic and object relations psychotherapies* (pp. 309–344). John Wiley & Sons.

Fosha, D. (2003). Dyadic regulation and experiential work with emotion and relatedness in trauma and disorganized attachment. In D. J. Siegel & M. F. Solomon (Eds.), *Healing trauma: Attachment, trauma, the brain, and the mind* (pp. 221–281). Norton.

Fosha, D. (2008). Transformance, recognition of self by self, and effective action. In K. J. Schneider (Ed.), *Existential-integrative psychotherapy: Guideposts to the core of practice* (pp. 290–320). Routledge.

Fosha, D. (2009). Emotion and recognition at work: Energy, vitality, pleasure, truth, desire, and the emergent phenomenology of transformational experience. In D. Fosha, D. J. Siegel, & M. F. Solomon (Eds.), *The healing power of emotion: Affective neuroscience, development and clinical practice* (pp. 172–203). Norton.

Fosha, D. (2013a). A heaven in a wild flower: Self, dissociation, and treatment in the context of the neurobiological core self. *Psychoanalytic Inquiry, 33*(5), 496–523. https://doi.org/10.1080/07351690.2013.815067

Fosha, D. (2013b). Turbocharging the affects of healing and redressing the evolutionary tilt. In D. Siegel & M. Solomon (Eds.), *Healing moments in psychotherapy* (pp. 129–168). Norton.

Gendlin, E. T. (2012). *Focusing-oriented psychotherapy: A manual of the experiential method.* Guilford Press.

Harmon-Jones, E., & Harmon-Jones, C. (2018). Anger. In L. F. Barrett, M. Lewis, & J. Haviland-Jones (Eds.), *Handbook of emotions* (pp. 774–791). Guilford Press.

Hasson, U., Nir, Y., Levy, I., Fuhrmann, G., & Malach, R. (2004). Intersubject synchronization of cortical activity during natural vision. *Science, 303*(5664), 1634–1640. https://doi.org/10.1126/science.1089506

Holmes, J., & Slade, A. (2019). The neuroscience of attachment: Implications for psychological therapies. *The British Journal of Psychiatry, 214*(6), 318–319. https://doi.org/10.1192/bjp.2019.7

Iacoboni, M. (2008/2009). *Mirroring people.* Pan Books.

Iacoboni, M., Molnar-Szakacs, I., Gallese, V., Buccino, G., Mazziotta, J. C., & Rizzolatti, G. (2005). Grasping the intentions of others with one's own mirror neuron system. *PLOS Biology, 3*(3), e79. https://doi.org/10.1371/journal.pbio.0030079

Jacobs-Hendel, H. (2018). *It's not always depression: Working the change triangle to listen to the body, discover core emotions, and connect to your authentic self.* Spiegel & Grau.

Keltner, D., Tracy, J., Sauter, D. A., McNeil, G., & Cordaro, D. (2018). Expression of emotion. In L. F. Barrett, M. Lewis, & J. Haviland-Jones (Eds.), *Handbook of emotions* (pp. 467–482). Guilford Press.

Lamm, C., & Majdandžić, J. (2015). The role of shared neural activations, mirror neurons, and morality in empathy—A critical comment. *Neuroscience Research, 90,* 15–24. https://doi.org/10.1016/j.neures.2014.10.008

Lanzetta, J. T., & Englis, B. G. (1989). Expectations of cooperation and competition and their effects on observers' vicarious emotional responses. *Journal of Personality and Social Psychology, 56*(4), 543–554. https://doi.org/10.1037/0022-3514.56.4.543

Lewis, M. (2018). Self-conscious emotions: Embarrassment, pride, shame, guilt, and hubris. In L. F. Barrett, M. Lewis, & J. Haviland-Jones (Eds.), *Handbook of emotion* (pp. 792–814). Guilford Press.

Lipton, B., & Fosha, D. (2011). Attachment as a transformative process in AEDP: Operationalizing the intersection of attachment theory and affective neuroscience. *Journal of Psychotherapy Integration, 21*(3), 253–279. https://doi.org/10.1037/a0025421

Malan, D. H. (1976). *The frontier of brief psychotherapy: An example of the convergence of research and clinical practice.* Plenum Medical Book.

Mars, D. (2011). From stuckness and reactivity to the felt experience of love. *Transformance: AEDP Journal, 2*(1). https://aedpinstitute.org/transformance/aedp-for-couples/

Mindell, A. (1996). Discovering the world in the individual: The world channel in psychotherapy. *Journal of Humanistic Psychology, 36*(3), 67–84. https://doi.org/10.1177/00221678960363005

Prenn, N. (2011). Mind the gap: AEDP interventions translating attachment theory into clinical practice. *Journal of Psychotherapy Integration, 21*(3), 308–329. https://doi.org/10.1037/a0025491

Prenn, N., & Fosha, D. (2016). *Supervision essentials for accelerated experiential dynamic psychotherapy.* American Psychological Association.

Rozin, P., Haidt, J., & McCauley, C. (2018). Disgust. In L. F. Barrett, M. Lewis, & J. Haviland-Jones (Eds.), *Handbook of emotions* (pp. 815–834). Guilford Press.

Rushworth, M. F., Buckley, M. J., Behrens, T. E., Walton, M. E., & Bannerman, D. M. (2007). Functional organization of the medial frontal cortex. *Current Opinion in Neurobiology, 17*(2), 220–227. https://doi.org/10.1016/j.conb.2007.03.001

Russell, E. (2015). *Restoring resilience: Discovering your clients' capacity for healing.* Norton.

Sauter, D. A. (2017). The nonverbal communication of positive emotions: An emotion family approach. *Emotion Review, 9*(3), 222–234. https://doi.org/10.1177/1754073916667236

Siegel, D. J. (2010). *The mindful therapist: A clinician's guide to mindsight and neural integration.* Norton.

Stephens, G. J., Silbert, L. J., & Hasson, U. (2010). Speaker–listener neural coupling underlies successful communication. *Proceedings of the National Academy of Sciences of the United States of America, 107*(32), 14425–14430. https://doi.org/10.1073/pnas.1008662107

Stern, D. N. (2010). *Forms of vitality: Exploring dynamic experience in psychology, the arts, psychotherapy, and development.* Oxford University Press. https://doi.org/10.1093/med:psych/9780199586066.001.0001

Suzuki, A. (2014). Facial expression recognition and embodied simulation. *Japanese Psychological Review, 57*(1), 5–23.

Suzuki, A. (2016). Psychological and neural bases of emotion recognition: Current theories and their clinical implications. *Studies of Higher Brain Functioning, 36*(2), 271–275. https://doi.org/10.2496/hbfr.36.271

Tomkins, S. (1963). *Affect, imagery, and consciousness: Vol. 2. The positive affects.* Springer.

Tracy, J. L., Robins, R. W., & Schriber, R. A. (2009). Development of a FACS-verified set of basic and self-conscious emotion expressions. *Emotion, 9*(4), 554–559. https://doi.org/10.1037/a0015766

Wicker, B., Keysers, C., Plailly, J., Royet, J.-P., Gallese, V., & Rizzolatti, G. (2003). Both of us disgusted in my insula: The common neural basis of seeing and feeling disgust. *Neuron, 40*(3), 655–664. https://doi.org/10.1016/S0896-6273(03)00679-2

Winkielman, P., McIntosh, D. N., & Oberman, L. (2009). Embodied and disembodied emotion processing: Learning from and about typical and autistic individuals. *Emotion Review, 1*(2), 178–190. https://doi.org/10.1177/1754073908100442

Xu, X., Zuo, X., Wang, X., & Han, S. (2009). Do you feel my pain? Racial group membership modulates empathic neural responses. *The Journal of Neuroscience, 29*(26), 8525–8529. https://doi.org/10.1523/JNEUROSCI.2418-09.2009

Zaki, J. (2013). Cue integration: A common framework for social cognition and physical perception. *Perspectives on Psychological Science, 8*(3), 296–312. https://doi.org/10.1177/1745691613475454

Zaki, J., Hennigan, K., Weber, J., & Ochsner, K. N. (2010). Social cognitive conflict resolution: Contributions of domain-general and domain-specific neural systems. *The Journal of Neuroscience, 30*(25), 8481–8488. https://doi.org/10.1523/JNEUROSCI.0382-10.2010

# 5

# A Shift in Focus

## Making Use of Therapist Experience in AEDP

Benjamin Lipton

A foundational tenet of accelerated experiential dynamic psychotherapy (AEDP), *making the implicit explicit*, describes a central clinical technique of bringing into dyadic awareness the moment-to-moment phenomena of the therapy process to use that information to activate positive psychological change within our clients. Although this concept is thoroughly addressed in the AEDP literature with regard to unpacking *client* experience (see Hanakawa, Chapter 4, this volume), discussion has been lacking when it comes to describing how AEDP *therapists* use their own moment-to-moment experience to guide the clinical process. Referenced in just a few articles and two dissertations (Prenn, 2009, 2010; Schoettle, 2009; Tavormina, 2017), the exploration of therapist experience remains underrepresented in the AEDP literature. This chapter aims to focus squarely on the therapist side of the AEDP dyad to (a) elaborate on the ways in which the therapist experience parallels that of a patient through the four-state process of psychological healing; (b) examine the relevance of tracking therapist experience in the context of an attachment based model of therapy; (c) focus on the seminal role of therapeutic presence in AEDP; (d) explore when and why the therapist experience may complement, rather than parallel, patient experience; and (e) discuss how all of this information can be leveraged effectively in the service of AEDP psychotherapy.

https://doi.org/10.1037/0000232-006
*Undoing Aloneness and the Transformation of Suffering Into Flourishing: AEDP 2.0*, D. Fosha (Editor)

## THE EXPERIENTIAL VERSUS INTERPRETIVE FOCUS IN AEDP

The phenomenological focus of AEDP (Fosha, 2017a, 2018) challenges the historical "expert" stance in many models of psychotherapy that privileges therapist interpretation over emergent patient experience with regard to what it means to be psychologically healthy (Summers & Barber, 2012; Norcross & Goldfried, 2019; see also Tunnell & Osiason, Chapter 3, this volume). For example, an AEDP therapist spends less time working "top-down" to create intellectual meaning of verbal narratives and more time helping clients notice and elaborate on the moment-to-moment specifics of their somatosensory and affective experiences from which subjectively accurate meaning—an organized, experientially true and nuanced narrative of the self's experience—may then organically emerge from the "bottom-up" (Lipton & Fosha, 2011). An in-depth understanding of the role of dyadic attunement in the cocreation of secure attachment informs this client-centered strategy in AEDP (Fosha, 2003, 2017b; Hughes, 2017; Lipton & Fosha, 2011; Pando-Mars, 2011, 2016; Schore, 2019).

Furthermore, if attunement is a central goal in an attachment-based model of therapy—and it very much is in AEDP—then it follows that a "top-down" intellectual approach can actually interfere with attunement: It can function as a therapist's own avoidant defense against feeling deeply and dealing directly with what emerges in both the client and the therapist. In AEDP, as we do with all impinging defenses, we work to move the intellectual defenses of the therapist, however cloaked in certainty or necessity, to the side. In their absence, the AEDP therapist strives first to open their heart and mind and then to resonate with what is emerging right here and right now, in body and mind, for the client—and for the therapist. The therapist then uses this information to deeply attune to the client's in-the-moment experience. This client-centered and also therapist-centered focus in the context of a dyadic, attachment-based process of attunement, disruption, repair and re-coordination allows for tracking and making explicit the cocreation and recognition of emergent, healing phenomena in the psychotherapy process (Fosha, 2017b).

## THERAPIST EXPERIENCE ACROSS THE FOUR-STATE MODEL OF TRANSFORMATIONAL CHANGE IN AEDP

Among many important contributions that AEDP has made to psychotherapy, careful attention to the phenomenology of affective change processes has yielded an exquisitely robust transformational model (see Appendix Figure 1, this volume)[1] that describes processing emotions through to completion in service of releasing their adaptive potential on behalf of the self (Fosha, 2017a; Russell, 2015). By alternately (a) processing the *experience* of what it feels like to embody and express new, adaptive ways of relating to oneself and others

---

[1]This figure, and diagrams for all of the representational schemas in AEDP 2.0, may be downloaded for free (http://pubs.apa.org/books/supp/fosha/).

and then (b) reflecting together on these new experiences—what in AEDP we call *metatherapeutic processing* or *metaprocessing*, for short—therapists and clients can collaboratively deepen, expand, organize, and encode therapeutic gains in explicit memory (Fosha et al., 2019). This two-phase project of processing core emotions to completion and then metaprocessing the experience of doing so, in the presence of an available and attuned therapist, is the central agent of change in AEDP (Fosha, 2017b; Fosha et al., 2019). Since the inception of AEDP, a core commitment of AEDP clinicians to phenomenological accuracy in describing the process of therapeutic change and providing a refined road map for attuned intervention along that path has led to the current version of the four-state model of transformational change (see Appendix Figure 1, this volume). For a detailed exploration of the four states, see Fosha (2009a).

## WHY ATTUNE TO THERAPIST EXPERIENCE?

Although the AEDP four-state model and its accompanying experiential methodology has focused squarely on the client, AEDP implicitly recognizes the importance of therapists also tracking their own internal experience (see also Hanakawa, Chapter 4, this volume). Efforts toward attunement, as well as attuned sharing of therapist experience, convey to clients that they exist "in the heart and mind of the other" (Fosha, 2000, p. 57) and often open the door to deeper, more intimate, and more emotionally engaged connection. In the context of creating safety in the relationship, for example, Prenn (2009) explained that therapists attune to their own affective experience and may judiciously share it with clients as a means of deepening authentic, positive connection. References such as this to the dyadic focus of AEDP, along with the recognition of the essential place of intersubjectivity in the cocreation of both safety and self, are valuable reminders to attend to and leverage the therapist's experience in the clinical process (Fosha, 2009b). Nonetheless, this area of exploration remains largely untouched. There is much more to discover and unpack as we consider the function of therapist experience in AEDP.

First and foremost, the therapist experience serves right alongside the client experience as a way to locate a therapy process within the four-state model. Based on her dissertation research on the experiences of AEDP therapists, Schoettle (2009) wrote,

> Across clients, therapists and dyadic pairs, therapists appeared to have consistently similar experiences within states. . . . These experiences remained consistent whether clinicians discussed specific individual clients or their general experiences working with clients in the [four] states. The research findings provide evidence for an intersubjective process in which AEDP therapists' experiences parallel the experiences of their clients. (p. 97)

This parallel process of therapist and client continues state by state and offers the therapist a catalogue of predictable, contingent responses to a client's experience in each state. Of course, given what we know about the relationship between dyadic attunement and cocreated states of affective coordination and disruption, this is not surprising. Schore (2005) explained: "The critical elements of implicit unconscious intersubjective communications are more than mental contents, rather they are interactively communicated, regulated and dysregulated psychobiological somatic processes that mediate shared conscious and unconscious emotional states" (pp. 843–844). In this way, individual states of consciousness become shared states and open the door to empathy and attuned therapeutic intervention.

In State 1, for example, when a patient is stuck in defense or consumed with anxiety, a parallel sense of disconnection and distress may prevail for the therapist. He may feel rejected or kept out. As a result, he may experience tension, anxiety, pressure, caution, frustration, or a sense of inadequacy. He may feel activated, overtaken by thinking, or drawn toward problem solving on the one hand, or disengaged, distracted or disinterested in the client's experience on the other. In this context, the therapist may spend considerable time internally with his own self-regulation and efforts at defense softening in the service of refocusing on bottom-up, experiential strategies for softening a client's defenses, or similarly, regulating his own anxiety in the service of affective repair and dyadic re-coordination.

Alternatively, because bidirectional affect sharing is indeed bidirectional, a therapist who is able to track and contextualize his own process within the four-state model may more readily be able to disidentify with a client's State 1 distress. On the basis of what we know about the relationships among defense, anxiety, and adaptive core emotion, a therapist who is able to remain in or return to a relatively undefended, regulated internal state would be able to draw on the present moment, affectively informed experience as an empathic complement, rather than parallel, to a client's experience (Hendel, 2018). With firm footing in the role of a security-engendering attachment figure— remaining kind, calm, curious, and caring—they may implicitly leverage their embodied state of regulation to lend a neurobiological hand to a client mired in defense or anxiety. Russell (2015) described this attachment-informed process as "pressuring with empathy": leading by implicit example and patiently inviting a client to recognize that it is safe enough to drop down into less defensive or anxious states of being. Moreover, from this place of grounded awareness and a disposition to support resilience, a therapist may be more likely to notice and attend to glimmers of transformance—markers of emergent capacity, health and vitality—when a client remains in State 1.

### Clinical Vignette 1

The following vignette[2] introduces us to "Kevin," a queer man in his 40s with a history of severe emotional neglect, both within his family of origin and his early social communities, that has led to many symptoms of relational trauma including chronic depression, paralyzing social anxiety and isolation,

---

[2]I have complied with American Psychological ethical standards in describing the details of treatment; aspects of the clients' identities and backgrounds have been disguised to protect confidentiality.

unstable relationships, substance misuse, states of toxic shame, and recurring suicidal ideation. While he has frequently fantasized about suicide over the course of his life as a maladaptive—but understandable—strategy for managing chronic shame and despair, he fortunately has no history of any actual attempts. Kevin's chronic suicidal ideation seems to be a complex communication of the anguish that conveys the unbearable burden of a predominantly disorganized attachment style. He is simultaneously yearning to be cared for and terrified of being rejected if he allows himself to receive that care; he suffers under the heavy, seemingly irreconcilable burden of carrying both hope and hopelessness side by side.

Just before the start of this vignette, Kevin shared about a suicidal fantasy he had on his recent birthday. With his habitual defenses of sarcasm and self-contempt that work all too well to stave off both access to his core emotions and healthy dependence on his therapist for help with his distress, Kevin rolls his eyes and states, in response to choosing *not* to harm himself, "Score one for me. Yippee. I guess I'm even weaker than I thought."

Note that *italics* indicates description of nonverbal expressions or movements, and **bold** indicates theoretical comments.

THERAPIST: **[Tentative effort to bypass defense and use parts language to make space for different self-states]** So, if we look beneath the sarcasm, I guess this also means that there's at least a part of you that holds onto just a bit of hope. I wonder what that part of you might know . . .

CLIENT: **[Defense of contempt toward hopeful part]** No, it's stupid.

THERAPIST: **[Therapist notices his own internal tightening in response to client's contemptuous part. Therapist's internal voice: "Oh no, here we go again . . . deep breaths . . . feel your feet on the ground . . ."]** I know that's what other parts say *and* it seems like the hope is also pretty tenacious.

CLIENT: No, it's stupid . . . it's blind.

THERAPIST: **[Therapist backs off, validates defense once again]** You *really* don't like it.

CLIENT: (*anger rising*) I don't. It's caused me more pain than anything else. Because it's what feeds you . . . to the people who are then willing to fuck you over **[articulation of internal working model of dangerous early attachment]**.

THERAPIST: Mmm **[resonance]**. It's like having any hope is hopeless **[attempt at organizing and empathizing with client's experience]**.

CLIENT: (*ignores therapist's comment*) It's the . . . It's why I'm still in therapy! (*sarcastically*) "Eventually, it'll get better . . . eventually, it'll work." (*Makes dramatic, hostile physical gesture of false enthusiasm.*)

THERAPIST:   [Therapist works to regulate spike in his own anger at client. Also recognizes client's anger conveys how devastating and terrifying hope has been for client.] Right. . . . Of course. . . . You're just *so* enraged.

CLIENT:   (*sarcastically*) It's the part that was lied to, it's the part that believes in Santa Claus, it's the part that, it's very Sesame Street. It's, you know, "Cops are your friends!" Um, "Everything's fine with the world!" Um, "No problem is too big that it's insurmountable!" Such bullshit!

THERAPIST:   [deep, explicit exhale and sigh in service of mutual regulation allows therapist to resonate with client's underlying pain] So much pain . . . [making implicit explicit, pressuring with empathy]

CLIENT:   (*shakes head, sighs, closes eyes*)

THERAPIST:   What just happened? [Moment-to-moment tracking, making implicit explicit] You kind of shook your head, and now you're closing your eyes . . .

CLIENT:   (*soft, mournful voice*) I do . . . I hate that part of me. [A glimmer of genuine sadness for the truth of his self-hatred indicates defense of contempt is softening]

THERAPIST:   [Therapist is able to deepen access to genuine empathy in response to client's softening and simply resonates with client's pain.] Mm-hmm.

CLIENT:   [glimmer of self-compassion] And I don't want to. I want to respect it and like it. (*Drops head and covers eyes with hands as grief emerges*)

THERAPIST:   (*kindly, soothingly*) I know you do . . . I know.

CLIENT:   (*genuinely*) Because I want it to be true. I want people to be nice to each other. I want to be able to trust people [important glimmer of transformance].

At the start of the preceding vignette, the therapist is led by his own intellectual defenses and mounting anxiety as he strives to maintain an apparent disposition of care and concern in the face of the client's hostile and dismissive defenses. As a result, the therapist actually—and unintentionally—strengthens these defenses as he tries to convince the client to hold on to hope. Only after the therapist turns inward and attends to his own anxiety and distress is he able to shift from recreating the client's familiar model of being alone with others who do not understand his experience to then providing a new and different model of genuine empathy. The therapist conveys a willingness to *be with* the pain beneath the client's defenses and invites the client to join him there. In turn, the client then softens just a little as glimmers of authentic sadness, self-compassion, hope, and a yearning for safety in relationships emerge from behind the barricades of contempt and dismissiveness.

In State 2, when a client is able to access core affects and a disposition toward authentic relating, the ever-present challenges and frustrations of State 1 give way for the therapist, as well. The dyad experiences feelings of coordination, resonance, and collaboration. Increased eye contact and gaze sharing, synchronized head nodding, postural alignment, striated muscle activation, a narrowing of focus to the task at hand, and the disposition to literally lean in all signal to the therapist that transformance is online and positive change is at hand. Additionally, a distorted sense of time, either condensed or elongated or both, often accompanies experiences of deep affective engagement (Schoettle, 2009). As the client comes to the end of a wave of core affect in State 2 and postbreakthrough affects emerge, the therapist also likely feels an emergent sense of settling and calm accompanied by corresponding physiological markers such as a sigh, a postural shift, slowing of breath, and gaze re-coordination, each of which herald the dyad's shift into State 3.

Now, in State 3, the therapist helps his client to reflect on and metatherapeutically process the preceding core affective experiences of State 2. As different categories of transformational affects emerge within a client (Fosha, 2017a), the therapist is likely to resonate with these affects as his own feelings of pride, awe, gratitude, surprise, feeling moved, and tremulous, among others, come online. The dyadic processing of transformational affects by alternately facilitating somatosensory experiencing and then cognitively reflecting on those experiences catalyzes an ever-deepening spiral of transformation and ever stronger encoding of the experiences of change for the better in explicit memory (Fosha, 2009a, 2009b).

## Clinical Vignette 2

In this vignette, we return to the same session, just moments later, with Kevin. Having now established a degree of dyadic coordination, the therapist works to further soften the client's defenses, deepen relational connection, and gain access to core experiences of State 2.

CLIENT: Imagine a day, any day. Pick a day . . . in your life, waking up to going to sleep—

THERAPIST: Mm-hmm.

CLIENT: And now imagine that day with 100 pounds strapped to your back, and try to present normally. (*points fingers at me and gives an order*) Like right now. You're interacting with me, and you have to ignore the fact that you have 100 pounds strapped to your back . . .

THERAPIST: **[Excited by engagement and imaginative play coming online: marker of increasing safety]** What comes to mind is—

CLIENT:    And you can't let it show on your face, and you can't let any-one know how much weight you're carrying.

THERAPIST:    I couldn't do it. **[Paradoxical affirmation of client's strength]**

CLIENT:    You want to go to the bathroom? (*pointing finger at* therapist) You're taking that 100-pound weight with you.

THERAPIST:    I mean . . . **[Therapist fully surrenders to embodying the experience client describes.]** What it feels like to me is just . . . like . . . I would just . . . (*therapist intentionally collapses onto the floor in a heap at client's feet*)

CLIENT:    (*eyes widen with surprise*) That's is how I feel all the time! (*sobs and covers eyes*) **[core sadness flows]**

THERAPIST:    **[Accompanying client and affirming core grief]** Yeah . . . Yeah . . . Yeah . . . Yeah.

CLIENT:    (*sighs*). **[Marker of completing wave of emotional experi-ence]** (*eyes still covered with hands*) Oh god.

THERAPIST:    Mmm **[resonating with client's pain]**. Kevin . . . can you see me here?

CLIENT:    (*peeks out from behind hands, nods*) Yes.

THERAPIST:    **[Still on ground, now making implicit explicit]** Can I ask you what it is like to see me here, just down on the ground, collapsed?

CLIENT:    (*another big wave of sobs*) **[Therapist offers client embodied empathy with his internal experience—a True Other moment.]** That's what it feels like.

THERAPIST:    **[paraverbal holding]** I know . . . I know . . . I know. I don't know how you do it, Kevin. I don't know how you do it . . . Mmm (*tenderly*) Can you, can you let yourself open your eyes?

CLIENT:    (*shyly, whispering*) Yes **[green light—safety and authentic connection coming online]**.

THERAPIST:    **[Assessing for adaptive directionality and making implicit explicit, metaprocessing.]** When you see, when you open your eyes and see me, does that, does that feel helpful, like good to know that I'm here?

CLIENT:    It feels a little embarrassing.

THERAPIST:    **[Assessing for maladaptive shame vs. tremulous transformational affect of something new emerging.]** Embarrassing?

CLIENT: Not in a bad way. **[Important: This is a State 3 tremulous affect of positive vulnerability and a big green light.]** I don't think you're actually judging me because of that . . . but my instinct is to be embarrassed **[Client's established internal working model and new, better, current experience are now side by side]**.

THERAPIST: So you feel both? You kind of feel both . . . the immediate reaction is "Oh, this is embarrassing," and then you also have an awareness that, um—

CLIENT: That it's Ben. (*making eye contact*) That it's safe. **[new, better working model encoded]**

THERAPIST: Yeah . . . (*kind smile*) I'm so glad **[metaprocessing the new experience of safety]**. What's that like?

CLIENT: Surprising . . . in a good way **[another State 3 transformational affect]**. It's like you really get me. It's just really hard to let myself believe it **[State 4: core state articulation of truth]**.

If, through the collaborative metatherapeutic processing of State 3, the dyad arrives in Core State, the fourth state of the AEDP model, then both client and therapist are likely to feel a robust sense of embodied expansiveness and deep connection to themselves, as well as to the world at large—the hallmarks of core state. Schoettle (2009) wrote about the phenomenology of State 4:

> Clinicians had the dichotomous experiences of feeling peaceful and calm along with excited and enlivened. Additionally, they felt present and engaged with their clients while at the same time being able to think toward the future. Thinking, feeling and imaginal experiences were integrated for therapists, and they experienced a sense of greater meaning . . . and had positive feelings of gratitude, pride, happiness, love and being moved. Finally, clinicians experienced awe, wonder and sacredness and felt connected to a process bigger than themselves. (p. 99)

### Clinical Vignette 3

We meet a different client now, "Helena," on the "other side" of a deep, transformational process of working through waves of fear and sadness embedded in early trauma of unbearable aloneness. In this vignette, Helena finds her footing in a new way of being—authentic, spontaneous, undefended—in the context of the safe and secure connection with her therapist. In core state, Helena finds the words to describe her emergent experience. She speaks in metaphor about the earned secure attachment she and her therapist are cocreating and references the caregiver–infant experience of deep, dyadic connection that she did not have in her early development. In this context, there is nothing for the therapist to "do." In fact, "doing" would likely initiate an empathic rupture. This is now about *being* deeply present and available in heart and mind as the dyad plays at the edges of tolerance for relational contact—for both members. Notice the pride of place of gazing—the importance of Helena seeing herself being seen and delighted in by her therapist in this process.

CLIENT:   (*making sustained eye contact*) I think I'm ready to be held right up close . . . in your arms and just . . . and then just get lost in your eyes or just . . . completely merge . . . into that ocean . . . the ocean of your chest (*hands lift, palms face in, smiling*) . . . and your eyes and just um . . . (*hands make undulating gestures*) . . . and like merge . . . feel that oneness . . . in that kind of sea of oneness and kind of a bliss . . .

THERAPIST:   (*smiling*) Mmm . . . **[paraverbal resonance, nothing more to "do"]**

CLIENT:   I mean as it is, there's the sense of separateness of course right here . . . **[a clear indication of self-awareness and client's attunement to therapist's potential anxiety in this new terrain of deep openness and closeness]**. But I could just see (*smiles, hands lifted, eyes glance around*) . . . that's the original state, you see, if things go well . . . there's the . . . there's the embodied oneness . . . the oneness, but in the *body*, cause I'm being completely held in my body **[Client gives voice to here and now corrective emotional *embodied* experience missing from her early life.]**

THERAPIST:   What do you notice? **[Keeping it experiential and present-focused.]**

CLIENT:   Um . . . I feel clear . . . and . . . present **[markers of core state]**.

THERAPIST:   Mm-hmmm . . . **[Therapist resonates with this deep state of presence and affirms client.]**

CLIENT:   And . . . and separate but connected **[eloquent, precise descriptors of secure attachment]**.

Through all four states, therapists' ability to attune inwardly to their own somatosensory and affective processes and stay regulated, state by state, dramatically augments their toolkit for tracking where a client may be on the AEDP road map. While AEDP therapists' experience likely parallels that of the clients from one state to the next, they simultaneously hold an additional layer of meta-awareness throughout, informed by their knowledge of the phenomenology of the four-state model of emotional processing and transformational change. Resources for moment-to-moment tracking literally double as the AEDP therapists begin to look *inwardly* toward themselves as well as outwardly to the client for information about where the dyad may be located within the four states. Moreover, the therapist's awareness of the potential for embodied resonance with the felt sense of a client's experience enhances the likelihood for a client's receptivity to any intervention. In other words, a therapist's interoceptive capacities help to ensure that the corresponding emotional scaffolding—the interpersonal delivery system—of any intervention is more likely to convey resonant attunement and therefore be effective (Damasio, 2010; Siegel, 2010). In this way, a therapist can employ interoceptive and affective awareness in the service of locating the therapeutic dyad within the four-state model and orienting the dyad toward positive transformational work.

Learning to recognize and work with the phenomenological markers of a client's process is often consuming for beginning students of AEDP. Initially, developing intervention skills that are rooted in moment-to-moment tracking often requires full, focused attention on the client at the temporary expense of a therapist's own interoceptive awareness. For example, as anxiety likely rises in a therapist in State 1, rather than using that information to help guide an intervention, a novice AEDP therapist may instead suppress or bypass these feelings to keep focused on trying to track the phenomenology of the client's process. Moreover, because the therapeutic task of State 1 is to lessen a client's anxiety and soften defenses, therapists may unconsciously suppress or disavow their own anxiety, as illustrated in the first clinical vignette, rather than use it as valuable information, in an effort to inhibit any emergent feelings of shame or inadequacy they may feel as a result of the client being in an anxious state.

As a therapist becomes more familiar with and adept at moment-to-moment tracking, psychic space becomes available for tracking the somatosensory and emotional process of both the client *and* therapist. In my experience as a clinical supervisor, this expanded capacity usually emerges organically and offers a sense of relief and satisfaction for clinicians. Dual attention to interoception on the one hand, and external tracking of the client's process on the other, heralds real possibility for in vivo attachment repair. As the previous clinical vignettes illustrate, when resonance, attunement, and careful tracking are online, the dyad discovers, privileges, and elaborates on a new, more attuned, and vital way of authentic relating that offers a corrective to previous, compromised internal working models of relational capacity (Lipton, 2020; Lipton & Fosha, 2011).

## ATTACHMENT, THERAPIST SELF-DISCLOSURE, AND THE FOUR STATES

As important as the therapist's stance of authenticity, kindness, caring, and deep engagement is for the therapy process, for new, more adaptive ways of relating to emerge, clients need to feel more than cared for and respected: They must also experience their capacity to successfully make a perceptible—and welcomed—impact on their therapist. The glue of attachment relationships, after all, is their bidirectionality (Wallin, 2017). When all is going well, each member of the dyad contingently responds to the moment-to-moment impact of the other, thus shaping each successive moment in the unfolding history of the relationship (Schore, 2019). To this end, therapists must first know what they are experiencing and then be willing to comfortably and mindfully self-disclose aspects of their own experience in service of enhancing a client's sense of self-efficacy and relational competence, undoing aloneness and building trust (Prenn, 2009).

For many clients, experiencing and then reflecting on the experience of earned secure attachment in therapy with the very person with whom they have cocreated it may spontaneously catalyze healing experiences of adaptive grief for the past. Recognizing and integrating a new, positive relationship in the here-and-now organically evokes its historical contrast—the painful experiences of earlier relational deficits. The new, safer relationship with a therapist then provides the base from which earlier attachment traumas can be mourned and worked through to completion so that energy in the system is freed up for current adaptive usage (Lipton & Fosha, 2011).

### Clinical Vignette 4

In the following vignette, we shift to an early session with a different client, James. James gives voice to an internal working model of unbearable aloneness in the face of emotional distress that represents his early attachment history with a mother whose own extreme anxiety would amplify, rather than regulate, his difficulty. Feeling alone in the presence of the very person he was wired to turn to for help, he was left feeling hopeless and angry.

CLIENT:       This part of me is like, "How can you . . ." (*blinking*) . . . yeah . . . "Like how the fuck can you help me, you know?"

THERAPIST:    Uh-huh **[Feeling deep empathy, the therapist simultaneously holds on to the knowledge that he *can* help and that the client's protest is actually a marker of positive change: transformance in action.]**

CLIENT:       Like I'm gonna be just as alone whether you help me with it or not . . . **[clearly articulates working model of early attachment]**.

THERAPIST:    Is that part interested in hearing how I could help or it doesn't even want to hear? **[Asking permission and leading with empathy—planting seeds for a new model of attachment. Use of "parts" language implicitly acknowledges client's own awareness of his multiple, simultaneous experiences of himself, as well as the positive differences present in the current dyad compared with his early attachment relationships.]**

CLIENT:       I think it's kind of interested, yeah . . . (*head tilted*) . . . you could probably tell it (*chuckles*). **[Transformance glimmer— a green light]**

THERAPIST: **[Tender, rhythmic, soothing paraverbal intention scaffolds explanation of client's early attachment experience.]** Okay . . . I'm happy to do that. Y'know . . . I think that part doesn't know what it's like to have somebody really want to be . . . and also be able . . . to be *present* (*client nods*) . . . with really big, dark difficult feelings . . . because that part is from a much younger time in your life when people, even who were very well-meaning and who loved you very much, couldn't tolerate it . . . and couldn't be with you in it . . . and so you felt just as alone, even though you were in the presence of other people (*client nodding*) . . . and a lot of times you were also just alone, too. (*client nodding*) **[Therapist confidently embodies his own strength and capacity to organize client's experience.]** . . . So I think, I believe that I could help because . . . I would really want to be with you . . . through whatever you are feeling . . . and I know that I could bear and be with you in the depth of your sadness and your loneliness . . . so that you don't have to be alone anymore **[defenses soften]** (*client's eyes close tightly; sniffs, tilts head, and one finger strokes eyelid, begins to cry*) . . . yeah . . . (*client crying silently*) . . . yeah . . . (*client begins to sob openly*) yeah . . . yeah . . . yeah . . . so much held inside . . . just let it come, it's alright . . . it's okay (*continues to sob*) **[Therapist provides paraverbal affirmation and accompaniment.]**

CLIENT: (*wave of grief organically completes*) I think I need you to hug me (*therapist follows client's lead as client rises from his chair and extends arms for an embrace*). **[The adaptive result of feeling through core affect is a poignant attachment repair—the disposition to reach out for comfort *and* to be met with an attuned, welcoming response.]** (*therapist and client hug and then sit back down; client sighs, wipes face with hands, smiles*) I guess that's what I needed to hear. . . . It's like I just felt like I had to be . . . alone with it all. **[State 3 Realization affect: Client spontaneously makes sense of his experience.]**

THERAPIST: Yeah . . . because you were alone back then, right? **[affirmation, organizing]**

CLIENT: Yeah . . . yeah. In fact, I . . . I feel like that's what . . . so much of the anxiety was about I guess . . . at least that felt like 90% of it (*smiles*) . . .

THERAPIST: Yeah . . .

CLIENT: And this sure is different (*shy smile and then a long pause as client tracks his internal experience; eyes open with wonder*) Wow. **[State 3 realization affects registering the magnitude of the change taking place.]**

The relational catalyst for the transformational process illustrated in this vignette is the therapist's readiness to embody an attachment engendering stance and to disclose aspects of his experience in the service of explicitly offering a new and better experience of care for his client. Self-disclosure of the therapist's experience is a key technique in AEDP for challenging expectations of negative relational receptivity (Prenn, 2010). Heartfelt, judicious, and authentic self-disclosure—that is, the therapist's sharing of his positive feelings about a client—beckons the softening of defenses, lessens shame, and regulates anxiety in State 1; invites curiosity about new and better relational experiences emerging in therapy and thus deepens access to State 2; scaffolds the elaboration and flourishing of receptive affective capacities in State 3; and allows for a shared elaboration of compassion for self and others, for human triumph as well as tragedy, and a profound undoing of aloneness in State 4. Processing the affective and somatosensory experience of feeling deeply seen, valued and cared for opens the door for the client to revise and update internal working models of relating. These new intersubjective experiences can now accommodate greater resilience and potentiate flourishing in the context of an earned secure attachment relationship that offers bidirectional authenticity, safety in connection, and value in regulated emotional expression.

Alternatively, working to make the implicit explicit through self-disclosure when the therapy dyad gets stuck in negative cycles of maladaptive, non-progressing ways of relating provides opportunities to the therapist and client alike for course correction and repair (Wallin, 2017). As a security engendering attachment figure embodying strength, stability, and curiosity, AEDP therapists make explicit the specifics of a rupture, their experience of it, as well as a wish for repair and re-coordination. The disposition toward repair and re-coordination works to catalyze transformance strivings rather than reactivating defensive behaviors or reinforcing pathogenic states of aloneness and distress. This process draws from Tronick's (2007) dyadic expansion of consciousness hypothesis: Infants and parents engage in a mutual regulatory system through which emotional connectedness and intersubjective states are constantly sought out. Coordinated communication in this way leads to expanded states of consciousness for both parent and child. AEDP applies this knowledge to the therapy process with the goal of catalyzing positive changes for the client that is inevitably accompanied by positive changes in the self of the therapist as well.

We now return to our earlier session with Helena to illustrate these concepts in action. Just before this next vignette begins, Helena is deeply immersed in exploring her new, unfamiliar sense of embodied aliveness. In that context, she asks the question "Who am I?" The therapist, brimming with excitement about what is unfolding and wanting to avoid any detours into intellectualizing in the midst of Helena's experiential exploration, blurts out his response. In so doing, he unintentionally disrupts the process. But rather than being a danger to the safety of the dyad, this disruption offers the opportunity for repair and re-coordination that further solidifies relational safety between therapist and client.

**Clinical Vignette 5**

CLIENT:        So who *am* I? [**Client is working to integrate her new, un-familiar state of greater openness and safe vulnerability.**]

THERAPIST:    You are this (*gestures toward client*) . . . [**Therapist feels desire to say something but doesn't know what to say. Anxiety leads him blurt out words that don't really make sense.**]

CLIENT:        Then it stops . . . [**Therapist's misattunement literally stops the process.**]

THERAPIST:    Yeah, I think what I just said wasn't so helpful . . . [**Recognizing the misattunement and rupture, the therapist immediately owns it and shares with the client.**]

CLIENT:        No, all you said is, "You are this . . ." [**Client overrides rupture and becomes caretaking**]

THERAPIST:    I know. But somehow . . . I think that was just such a big moment . . . that we just had together . . . and that you had in yourself . . . and I think I got like . . . a little dysregulated . . . [**Client chuckles with recognition as therapist acknowledges his misattunement.**] . . . so I just said something . . .

CLIENT:        Oh *no* . . . (*smiles*) [**We are playing now—an important marker that even in the rupture, we are creating a new working model of safer relating—now even ruptures can be playfully acknowledged and collaboratively repaired.**]

THERAPIST:    (*playfully imitating his earlier excitement*) Just to say *something* (*client chuckles*) . . . cause it felt so big and so important . . . huge . . .

CLIENT:        Well it's . . . it's here again . . . I feel back in my body . . . there's something weighted . . . [**The rupture is repaired and the dyad is back on track as the client refocuses on her somatic experience and the session continues.**]

## ATTACHMENT AND THERAPEUTIC PRESENCE IN AEDP

Attachment research is foundational to the theory and practice of AEDP. While many other models of psychotherapy also reference attachment in their theory base, AEDP has sought to precisely translate the knowledge emerging at the intersection of attachment (Bowlby, 1991; Cassidy & Shaver, 1999; Wallin, 2017) and affective neuroscience (Panksepp, 2009; Schore, 2019) into powerful innovations to its clinical practice (Fosha, 2000, 2003, 2008, 2009a, 2009b, 2017a; Fosha & Yeung, 2006; Fosha et al., 2009; Lamagna & Gleiser, 2007; Lipton & Fosha, 2011; Pando-Mars, 2016; Prenn, 2009, 2010;

Russell, 2015). Recognizing that the emergence of earned secure attachment is a potentially transformative experience in and of itself, we aim to work with it both explicitly and experientially in the clinical process. Seeking to deliver a safe, secure, authentic, and new context for welcoming and exploring previously inaccessible aspects of a client's Self, the AEDP therapist, from the get-go, privileges mutual authenticity and radical empathy over potentially retraumatizing transference enactments or neutrality (Lipton & Fosha, 2011).

Beginning at birth, right-brain-to-right-brain, contingent processes such as holding, touch, gaze sharing, face-to-face contact, entrained vocal rhythms, and spontaneous moments of play and delight are crucial for (a) the regulation of the autonomic nervous system, (b) optimal brain development, (c) the emergence of stress and affect regulation, and (d) the creation of secure attachment (Porges, 2018; Schore, 2019). Our earliest perceptions of both safety and danger are prelinguistic and somatosensory. Because the hippocampus, a region of the brain responsible for organizing our memories in an "autobiography" of time and space, is not fully functioning until 1.5 to 3 years of age (Siegel, 2010), early organization of emotional experience literally remains a felt experience that emerges untethered by chronology or geography. We then implicitly carry these embodied, affectively imprinted early self-states with us throughout our lives. Thus, when working to repair problematic patterns of early attachment in psychotherapy, how we are actually *being* in ourselves as therapists is the foundational clinical intervention of AEDP's attachment-based, neurobiologically informed, transformationally driven model.

Everything we "do" in AEDP begins with the therapist's ability to be present in body and mind while being oriented to what is happening in the client and staying both open to being explicitly impacted by the intersubjective results and retaining the capacity to respond adaptively (or contingently) to the other's state. This is what Fosha (2000, 2003) has named "feeling and dealing while relating," the AEDP therapist's relational North Star. It references the foundational role of attachment theory in AEDP (Fosha, 2000; Lipton & Fosha, 2011; Pando-Mars, 2016). It also corresponds to what is now known more broadly in the field of psychotherapy as therapeutic presence (Geller, 2017; Geller & Greenberg, 2012). More recently, conversations about therapeutic presence are broadening from the realms of theory and clinical technique to include emerging empirical research on its transtheoretical nature and therapeutic effectiveness (Geller, 2017; Geller & Greenberg, 2012). Geller (2017) described therapeutic presence as multifaceted: a method of therapist preparation, a subjective experience, and a relational process in therapy. Rooted in a phenomenological approach, AEDP complements this conceptualization with the assertion that therapeutic presence is not only a precondition for transformative therapy and a method for attuning in the therapeutic process but also a powerful affective change process in itself (Lipton, 2020; Lipton & Fosha, 2011) that can be made explicit and metatherapeutically processed in the service of deepening and broadening relational and intrapsychic capacities in both client and therapist.

The concept of *affective competence* (Fosha, 2000) is useful to further elaborate the functional requirements for an optimal dyadic relationship to take root (Lipton & Fosha, 2011). For caregivers to respond helpfully to a child's verbal or nonverbal cries for help, they must be able to regulate their own emotional experience simultaneously with that of the child's. A crucial aspect of that capacity for emotional self-regulation is what Fonagy used to label the "reflective self-function" and now calls "mentalization" (Fonagy & Campbell, 2016; Fonagy et al., 2002) and what in the current zeitgeist is termed "mindfulness" (Siegel, 2010; Wallin, 2017). This reflective capacity needs to be online and in action (Hendel, 2018). Caregivers' ability to experience their child as a separate individual with a resonant but distinct subjective experience is essential for affect regulation and self-development (Fonagy & Campbell, 2016). Fosha (2000, 2006) emphasized the relational thrust of these intrapsychic processes and described the fundamental importance of "going beyond mirroring" and actively helping to facilitate the recovery from a rupture and the return to dyadic attunement and coordination. She wrote, "The roots of security and resilience are to be found in the sense of being understood by and having the sense of existing in the heart and mind of a loving, caring, attuned and self-possessed other, an other with a heart and mind of her own" (Fosha, 2000, p. 228).

In AEDP, therapeutic presence describes processes that are both vertical (i.e., intrapsychic processes within the therapist's own body and mind) and horizontal (i.e., relational processes conveyed through a therapist's energetic disposition, therapeutic stance, and relational availability to being impacted in both heart and mind by a client). Some key attachment-based AEDP components that inform this concept are promoting an embodied sense of safety, privileging affirmation and intersubjective delight, leading with authenticity; moment-to-moment tracking of the therapeutic process (both verbal and nonverbal, in patient and in therapist), a focus on affect regulation, "going beyond mirroring" and actively helping, self-disclosure in the service of undoing aloneness and decreasing shame, and receptivity to being impacted by our clients. Together, these ideas inform a therapeutic stance that is welcoming, grounded, embodied, affirming, encouraging, delighting, explicitly emotionally engaged, and regulating.

In summary, therapeutic presence is the embodied, heart-centered, mindfully informed clinical manifestation of the knowledge that right-brain-to-right brain, affect-regulating processes are crucial for brain growth and creating secure attachment (Schore, 2019). It is this empirical truth that speaks to the essential place of therapeutic presence in AEDP. Unless our "left-brain," intellectual knowledge, and theoretical understanding gives way, in the moment, to privileging right-brain, intuitive experience and attuned relating, our knowledge is of little therapeutic value—and potentially counterproductive. The tension between knowing and not knowing, tracking self and other, but not coercing or predicting, is essential to the success of therapy and all deep interpersonal connections.

## ACTIVE EMPATHY: A MODEL FOR CULTIVATING THERAPEUTIC PRESENCE IN AEDP

After reviewing the literature on therapeutic presence, relational processes in therapy, neurobiology of attachment, somatosensory processes, and mindfulness, I synthesized five key concepts that together comprise the construct of *PAIRR* (Lipton, 2020; see also Exhibit 5.1). Accompanying each concept in PAIRR—presence, attunement, intention, resonance, reflection—is a key question for therapists to ask themselves as they are working to be deeply present with clients. The term "active empathy" in the title of this section emphasizes the active, relational thrust of these processes in PAIRR and the stance of deep engagement that both informs them and is central to AEDP. This *active* approach to empathy operates in contrast to the more widely held stance of implicit, measured engagement or neutrality that informs many therapy models. Although the component concepts of PAIRR extend beyond some academic definitions of empathy, the label is valuable for its evocative potency and experiential accuracy. What follows is a description of the component concepts that together comprise this idea.

### Presence

We need to be attuned to ourselves in order to attune to others (Geller, 2017; Geller & Greenberg, 2012; Lipton & Geller, 2018). *Presence* (as distinct from therapeutic presence, which is a more comprehensive concept) describes our capacity to be grounded and mindful *in ourselves* in the present moment.

---

**EXHIBIT 5.1**

**PAIRR (Presence, Attunement, Intention, Resonance, Reflection), a Construct for Therapeutic Presence**

*Active Empathy* is the fuel for change

**Presence:** grounded and mindful in the present moment
  "Am I aware of what is happening in my body and open to my own physical and emotional experience?"

**Attunement:** tracking right and left brain processes moment-to-moment
  "Am I tracking my own and my patient's verbal and nonverbal, moment-to-moment communications?"

**Intention:** actively caring and wanting to help: positive vulnerability
  "Am I explicitly conveying my care, concern and openness to deep engagement?"

**Resonance:** moments of meeting
  "Am I slowing down and allowing myself to be impacted by my client and to explicitly communicate this when helpful?"

**Reflection:** metaprocessing
  "Am I actively and explicitly reflecting with my client on their experience with and of me?"

---

Interoception, the ability to sense what is happening inside of us, in our bodies, is a fundamental skill for cultivating and deepening our awareness of the present moment (Craig, 2014). The therapeutic question that orients us to embodied presence is: "Am I aware of what is happening in my body and open to my own physical and emotional experience?"

### Attunement

Presence within ourselves allows us to attune to others. *Attunement* describes a subjective sense of authentic connection, of sensing someone deeply. It refers to how we focus on the other and take their experience into our own inner world and then allow it to shape who we are at that moment (Schore, 2019; Siegel, 2010). To accurately attune to another, we must strive to be open to the bottom-up flow of intersubjective phenomena rather than aligned with any top-down expectations or requirements of how the other could or should be feeling or acting. We must have a willingness to *not* know and a readiness to say, "Tell me more." Moment-to-moment tracking of both right and left brain processes in the client and therapist is fundamental to attunement. It is what Fosha (2013) called "dyadic mindfulness" (see also Hanakawa, Chapter 5; Yeung, Chapter 13, this volume). The therapeutic question that orients us to attunement is: "Am I tracking my own and my patient's verbal and nonverbal, moment-to-moment communications?" In other words, "Am I tracking the emergent "we"-ness of our therapeutic dyad?"

### Intention

*Intention* refers to the directionality and energetic disposition of many of the qualities that make up the therapeutic stance in AEDP. As AEDP therapists, our intention is to lead with authenticity, delight, affirmation, and privileging of our client's transformance strivings. We hold a healing orientation (rather than a pathologizing one) of actively caring and wanting to help in addition to a willingness to be open and impacted. The therapeutic question that grounds us in our intention is: "Am I explicitly conveying my care, concern and openness to deep engagement?" This is where AEDP is different from mindfulness: we are open to experience and emergence; however, our "being with" is informed by an explicit intention.

### Resonance

*Resonance* refers to the physiological and emotional markers of coordination such as heart rate, breathing, physical behaviors and gestures, posture, gaze alignment, and emotional experience. These are the constituents of moments of meeting, of becoming a "we" (Geller, 2017; Schore, 2012; Siegel, 2010). As we orient ourselves to resonate with our clients, once again we are not focused on *knowing* but rather on being open to, accepting, and connecting with whatever is coming our way from our client. The therapeutic question that facilitates resonance is: "Am I slowing down and allowing myself to be impacted by my client and to explicitly communicate this when helpful?"

## Reflection

*Reflection* refers to AEDP's unique contribution to understanding how new experience is encoded and integrated into explicit memory by reflecting on it in the context of metatherapeutic processing. Metatherapeutic processing, reflecting explicitly on the experience of change in therapy as it is unfolding moment-to-moment, is the vehicle for engaging with our clients in the integration of sensory experience with meaning making activities. By metaprocessing the client's experience of our presence, attunement, intention, and resonance, we make the impact of these implicit experiences explicit and relationally experiential. Mediated by the prefrontal cortex, left-brain learning joins right-brain experience in the service of creating explicit knowledge of what is transpiring in the therapy process both intrapsychically and relationally (Siegel, 2010). The therapeutic question that facilitates the therapist's metaprocessing his own impact on the client is: "Am I actively and explicitly reflecting with my client on their experience with and of me?"

The fortuitous acronym PAIRR, which incorporates the first letter of each of its contributing concepts, evocatively conveys the construct's embeddedness in a relational context. Moreover, the consecutive *Rs* in the acronym reference the iterative nature of the AEDP concept of metatherapeutic processing—alternating between rounds of experience and reflection. PAIRR provides an organized, user-friendly methodology to assist the AEDP therapist in cultivating mindful awareness of his own embodied experience and leveraging that information to help a client to access and work through affective and relational processes in need of either transformation or reinforcement.

## THE PERSONAL CHALLENGES OF PRACTICING AEDP

While the experience-near, radically relational focus of AEDP is the very catalyst for positive change for clients, working from this stance also can present personal challenges for the therapist. As the previous vignettes illustrate, AEDP requires the therapist truly to "show up"—and to do so with a demanding combination of embodied presence, radical empathy, and courageous authenticity. In this model, bravery is a central part of the therapist's job description. Working from this perspective is no small task, especially when one is engaging in work with an explicit mission of healing trauma and transforming emotional distress into psychological flourishing.

Therapists are not immune from the activation of their own attachment history in the context of a therapy dyad. At the dynamic level, it is not unusual for countertransference processes to activate a therapist's own attachment wounds and unresolved pockets of trauma. This may manifest in the activation of powerful defenses or anxiety on the one hand, or more overwhelmingly as a descent into pathogenic affects on the other (Prenn & Fosha, 2017). When this happens, finding one's bearings and reorienting toward greater regulation may present temporary, but significant, challenges. Seeking out consultation in these moments to navigate the clinical process responsibly and effectively is essential for the integrity of the therapy. Moreover, exploring necessary aspects of one's own dynamic material in consultation with a supervisor often leads to a parallel process of healing and transformation *for the therapist*, the experience of which then can be leveraged once again in the service of helping the client. Thus, what may begin as an unsettling and disorienting rupture may become a multidimensional portal to healing and positive transformation for both therapist and client.

Lastly, as the preceding discussion implies, it must be acknowledged that working from an experiential, authentic, and emotion-focused approach is, at times, an energetically expensive way to provide psychotherapy. This is both the blessing and the challenge of AEDP. For the most part, the absorbing and intensive nature of the work actually energizes the therapist (Fosha, 2009a; Schoettle, 2009). In accordance with the predictable, positive outcomes of processing emotion to completion, the clinical process of AEDP, when going well enough, leads both therapist and client through a reciprocal cascade of appetitive transformational affects—excitement, exuberance, pride, and tremulousness. The payoff for stepping forward with both heart and mind is well worth the emotional and physiological investment of intense engagement for both client and therapist. However, as with all worthwhile yet demanding challenges, developing the skills of appropriate pacing and strategically managing the expenditure of energy are necessary tasks for an AEDP therapist. Successfully bringing to bear the principle of "feeling and dealing while relating" (Fosha, 2000, 2003) requires the therapist to navigate the balance between separateness and connection, intrapsychic wellness, and interpersonal contact, in the service of maintaining the integrity of the self of the therapist as a prerequisite to successfully nurturing the self of the client.

## CONCLUSION

As AEDP therapists—and human beings—we need to open our hearts and minds and allow our true selves to reach out and touch the souls of our clients who are bravely coming forward to share of themselves in ways that past injuries have taught them not to do. This intentional mutuality is the foundation of relational healing. If we are asking our clients to access vulnerable places within themselves and to commit to authenticity, then we must demonstrate a willingness to lead the way ourselves. We do this by cultivating therapeutic presence and mindfully tracking our own moment-to-moment process right alongside that of our clients. In this endeavor, our awareness of our embodied affective experience, not just our intellectual insight, is a necessary and primary tool.

Current demands for empiricism notwithstanding, therapy is, among other things, a form of improvisational art. Deep, embodied technical knowing supports in-the-moment spontaneity and creativity. Like all well-trained, skillful artists, the AEDP therapist must be immersed in the theory and technique of a robust and effective model: in the case of AEDP, this includes the phenomenology of the four states of the transformational process, the therapeutic stance of affirmation and delight, techniques for softening defenses, regulating anxiety, deepening affect, undoing aloneness, and metaprocessing transformational affects and the experience of change for the better. Knowledge and technique are, of course, essential for any psychotherapy model. But we must be steeped in them only to be able to trust that they will be there for us as we surrender to the improvisational, emergent truth of the therapeutic moment. We must recognize the ways in which a reliance on explicit knowledge can disrupt the fundamental, deeper (both literally and metaphorically) healing power of mindfully *being*, in heart and mind, that we are aiming for. We must trust that what needs to happen can and will if we hold to the core AEDP principle of feeling and dealing while relating. Geller (2017) wrote,

> My use of the word *sensing* rather than *knowing* or *thinking* was purposeful—in this state of flow, overthinking actually interferes with the implicit knowing that rises inside. This reflects the paradigm shift from thinking (knowing through cognition and analysis) to knowing from the inside out of embodiment (knowing through sensing and being in relational connection). (italics in original; p. 100)

Attachment research with parents and children—just regular parents and children, not psychotherapists with postgraduate degrees—demonstrates that healthy relationships emerge from contexts of implicit, compassionate presence and sufficient relational capacity (Cassidy & Shaver, 1999; Tronick, 2007). This suggests that we must hold our techniques lightly, tune inward to attune outward, and "simply" *be*—be aware of our own moment-to-moment experience, be available to the same in our clients, be authentic, be kind, be helpful, be mindful. Some of us may have to unlearn aspects of previous ways of "doing" therapy from a certain distance so that we really can *be* with our clients up close: heart to heart, body to body, mind to mind, in the service of tracking what is emergent right in front of our eyes. For if we are grounded in our ourselves, regulated, open-hearted, appropriately boundaried but in no way constrained, then we are optimally positioned to be the relational conduit to psychological healing that our clients are asking for and need.

## REFERENCES

Bowlby, J. (1991). Post-script. In C. M. Parkes, J. Stevenson-Hinde, & P. Marris (Eds.), *Attachment across the life cycle* (pp. 293–297). Routledge.

Cassidy, J., & Shaver, P. R. (Eds.). (1999). *Handbook of attachment: Theory, research and clinical applications.* Guilford Press.

Craig, A. D. (2014). *How do you feel? An interoceptive moment with your neurobiological self.* Princeton University Press. https://doi.org/10.23943/princeton/9780691156767.001.0001

Damasio, A. R. (2010). *Self comes to mind: Constructing the conscious brain*. Pantheon.

Fonagy, P., & Campbell, C. (2016). Attachment theory and mentalization. In A. Elliott & J. Prager (Eds.), *The Routledge handbook of psychoanalysis in the social sciences and humanities* (pp. 115–131). Routledge.

Fonagy, P., Gergely, G., Jurist, E., & Target, M. (2002). *Affect regulation, mentalization, and the development of the self*. Other Press.

Fosha, D. (2000). *The transforming power of affect: A model for accelerated change*. Basic Books.

Fosha, D. (2003). Dyadic regulation and experiential work with emotion and relatedness in trauma and disordered attachment. In M. F. Solomon & D. J. Siegel (Eds.), *Healing trauma: Attachment, trauma, the brain and the mind* (pp. 221–281). Norton.

Fosha, D. (2006). Quantum transformation in trauma and treatment: Traversing the crisis of healing change. *Journal of Clinical Psychology, 62*(5), 569–583. https://doi.org/10.1002/jclp.20249

Fosha, D. (2008). Transformance, recognition of self by self, and effective action. In K. J. Schneider (Ed.), *Existential-integrative psychotherapy: Guideposts to the core of practice* (pp. 290–320). Routledge.

Fosha, D. (2009a). Emotion and recognition at work: Energy, vitality, pleasure, truth, desire & the emergent phenomenology of transformational experience. In D. Fosha, D. J. Siegel, & M. F. Solomon (Eds.), *The healing power of emotion: Affective neuroscience, development, clinical practice* (pp. 172–203). Norton.

Fosha, D. (2009b). Healing attachment trauma with attachment (and then some!). In M. Kerman (Ed.), *Clinical pearls of wisdom: 21 leading therapists offer their key insights* (pp. 43–56). Norton.

Fosha, D. (2013). Turbocharging the affects of healing and redressing the evolutionary tilt. In D. J. Siegel & M. F. Solomon (Eds.), *Healing moments in psychotherapy* (pp. 129–168). Norton.

Fosha, D. (2017a). How to be a transformational therapist: AEDP harnesses innate healing affects to re-wire experience and accelerate transformation. In J. Loizzo, M. Neale, & E. Wolf (Eds.), *Advances in contemplative psychotherapy: Accelerating transformation* (pp. 204–219). Norton. https://doi.org/10.4324/9781315630045-18

Fosha, D. (2017b). Something more than "something more than interpretation": AEDP works the experiential edge of transformational experience to transform the internal working model. In S. Lord (Ed.), *Moments of meeting in psychoanalysis: Interaction and change in the therapeutic encounter* (pp. 267–292). Routledge.

Fosha, D. (2018). Introduction to commentaries on sociocultural identity, trauma treatment, and AEDP through the lens of bilingualism in the case of "Rosa." *Pragmatic Case Studies in Psychotherapy, 14*(2), 115–132. http://pcsp.libraries.rutgers.edu

Fosha, D., Paivio, S. C., Gleiser, K., & Ford, J. (2009). Experiential and emotion-focused therapy. In C. Courtois & J. D. Ford (Eds.), *Complex traumatic stress disorders: An evidence-based clinician's guide* (pp. 286–311). Guilford Press.

Fosha, D., Thoma, N., & Yeung, D. (2019). Transforming emotional suffering into flourishing: Metatherapeutic processing of positive affect as a trans-theoretical vehicle for change. *Counselling Psychology Quarterly, 32*(3–4), 563–593. https://doi.org/10.1080/09515070.2019.1642852

Fosha, D., & Yeung, D. (2006). AEDP exemplifies the seamless integration of emotional transformation and dyadic relatedness at work. In G. Stricker & J. Gold (Eds.), *A casebook of integrative psychotherapy* (pp. 165–184). American Psychological Association. https://doi.org/10.1037/11436-013

Geller, S. (2017). *A practical guide to cultivating therapeutic presence*. American Psychological Association. https://doi.org/10.1037/0000025-000

Geller, S., & Greenberg, L. (2012). *Therapeutic presence: a mindful approach to effective therapy*. American Psychological Association. https://doi.org/10.1037/13485-000

Hendel, H. J. (2018). *It's not always depression: Working the change triangle to listen to the body, discover core emotions, and connect to your authentic self.* Random House.

Hughes, D. (2017). *Building the bonds of attachment: Awakening love in deeply traumatized children* (6th ed.). Rowman and Littlefield.

Lamagna, J., & Gleiser, K. A. (2007). Building a secure internal attachment: An intra-relational approach to ego strengthening and emotional processing with chronically traumatized clients. *Journal of Trauma & Dissociation, 8*(1), 25–52. https://doi.org/10.1300/J229v08n01_03

Lipton, B. (2020). The being is the doing: The foundational place of therapeutic presence in AEDP. *The AEDP Journal: Transformance,* 10. https://aedpinstitute.org/transformance-journal-2/

Lipton, B., & Fosha, D. (2011). Attachment as a transformative process in AEDP: Operationalizing the intersection of attachment theory and affective neuroscience. *Journal of Psychotherapy Integration, 21*(3), 253–279. https://doi.org/10.1037/a0025421

Lipton, B., & Geller, S. (2018, November 11). *Strengthening your clinical heart, mind and practice by cultivating therapeutic presence.* AEDP Institute Seminar, New York, NY.

Norcross, J., & Goldfried, M. (Eds.). (2019). *Handbook of psychotherapy integration* (3rd ed.). Oxford University Press. https://doi.org/10.1093/med-psych/9780190690465.001.0001

Pando-Mars, K. (2011). Building attachment bonds in the wake of neglect and abandonment through the lens and practice of AEDP, attachment and polyvagal theory. *The AEDP Journal: Transformance,* 10. https://aedpinstitute.org/transformance-journal-2/

Pando-Mars, K. (2016). Tailoring AEDP interventions to attachment styles. *The AEDP Journal: Transformance, 6*(2). https://aedpinstitute.org/transformance-journal/transformance-volume-6-issue-2/

Panksepp, J. (2009). Brain emotional systems and qualities of mental life: From animal models of affect to implications for psychotherapeutics. In D. Fosha, D. J. Siegel, & M. F. Solomon (Eds.), *The healing power of emotion: Affective neuroscience, development, clinical practice* (pp. 1–26). Norton.

Porges, S. W. (2018). *Clinical applications of the polyvagal theory: The emergence of polyvagal-informed therapies.* Norton.

Prenn, N. (2009). I second that emotion! On self-disclosure and its metaprocessing. In A. Bloomgarden & R. B. Mennuti (Eds.), *Psychotherapist revealed: Therapists speak about self-disclosure in psychotherapy* (pp. 85–95). Routledge.

Prenn, N. (2010). How to set transformance into action. In *The AEDP Journal: Transformance, 1*(1). https://aedpinstitute.org/transformance/how-to-set-transformance-into-action/

Prenn, N. C. N., & Fosha, D. (2017). *Supervision essentials for accelerated experiential dynamic psychotherapy.* American Psychological Association. https://doi.org/10.1037/0000016-000

Russell, E. (2015). *Restoring resilience: Discovering your client's capacity for healing.* Norton.

Schoettle, E. (2009). *A qualitative study of the therapist's experience practicing accelerated experiential dynamic psychotherapy (AEDP): An exploration of the dyadic processes from the clinician's perspective* [Unpublished doctoral dissertation]. The Wright Institute, Berkeley, CA.

Schore, A. (2005). A neuropsychoanalytic viewpoint: Commentary on paper by Steven H. Knoblauch. *Psychoanalytic Dialogues, 15*(6), 829–854. https://doi.org/10.2513/s10481885pd1506_3

Schore, A. (2012). *The science of the art of psychotherapy.* Norton.

Schore, A. (2019). *Right brain psychotherapy.* Norton.

Siegel, D. (2010). *The mindful therapist.* Norton.

Summers, R., & Barber, J. (2012). *Psychodynamic therapy: A guide to evidence-based practice.* Guilford Press.

Tavormina, E. M. P. (2017). *How is attunement, disruption, and repair experienced by the therapist in an attachment approach to psychotherapy* [Unpublished doctoral dissertation]. University of British Columbia, Vancouver, Canada.

Tronick, E. (2007). *The neurobehavioral and social-emotional development of infants and children.* Norton.

Wallin, D. (2017). *Attachment in psychotherapy.* Guilford Press.

# 6

# Using AEDP's Representational Schemas to Orient the Therapist's Attunement and Engagement

Karen Pando-Mars

Accelerated experiential dynamic psychotherapy (AEDP) is a complex, and yet instinctive, experiential model that aims for our patients to transform their suffering into healing and has developed a method for doing so by helping patients progress through four states of the transformational change process. As has been demonstrated in previous chapters, this four-state model functions as a map and a guide for the clinical application of AEDP. In addition, AEDP's three representational schemas—the Triangle of Experience, the Self–Other–Emotion (S-O-E) Triangle, and the Triangle of Relational Comparisons—are used to organize vast amounts of information in highly schematic patterns that help the therapist orient and choose how to intervene. With the four-state transformational process map in the background (Figure 1, Appendix, this volume),[1] this chapter illustrates the use of these three representational schemas, using clinical examples to show how they provide underlying structure for the therapist's purposeful moment-to-moment clinical activities—in this case, helping a patient work through unresolved emotion.

To foster meaningful change, AEDP psychotherapists are trained both to be *transformance detectives* (i.e., seek and elaborate signs of health and motivational strivings to heal; Fosha, 2017; see also Kranz, Chapter 2, this volume), while simultaneously also seeking to discover the roots of a patient's suffering and the dynamics that underlie their functioning. AEDP's understanding of the human psyche is to a large degree informed by attachment theory, interpersonal

---

[1]This figure, and diagrams for all of the representational schemas in AEDP 2.0, may be downloaded for free (http://pubs.apa.org/books/supp/fosha/).

https://doi.org/10.1037/0000232-007
*Undoing Aloneness and the Transformation of Suffering Into Flourishing: AEDP 2.0*, D. Fosha (Editor)

neurobiology, emotion theory, and transformational studies. What happens to people early in life—whether it is how they are treated by caregivers or whether they suffered loss, deprivations, or traumatic events—is wired into their nervous systems. Each of the representational schemas guide the translation of fundamental understanding into concrete and specific interventions. They are designed to help psychotherapists focus treatment by transposing the nitty gritty of experiential process onto these structural schemas and then back again. This offers precision as AEDP integrates foundational theory with practical interventions in an experiential treatment that maximizes the potential of positive neuroplasticity (Fosha, 2017).

## HOW EXPERIENCE SETS NEUROPLASTICITY IN MOTION

Neuroplasticity is the brain's innate capacity to grow and to heal itself (Doidge, 2007). Our brains form with experience; and, in turn, how our brains perceive experience is based on how the brain has developed. The brain can be altered in an instant by a trauma or by injuries repeated over time. The brain of a child developing in conditions of extreme stress of abuse or neglect may miss the right kind of stimulation it needs to develop in healthy ways. And yet, the brain is not a fully formed structure, rather it is a dynamic process undergoing constant development across the life span (Cozolino, 2006), continuing to develop into adulthood in fundamental ways:

> . . . the brain takes in experience with the activation of neural firing. . . . These changes can involve 1) the growth of new neurons from neural stem cells, at least now documented in one area the hippocampus; 2) the growth and modulation of synaptic connections among neurons, changing their ways of communicating with each other; [and] 3) the laying down of myelin by the supportive glial cells, enabling action potentials of ions flowing in and out of the neuron's membranes to stream . . . [leading to] more coordinat[ion] in timing and distribution. (Siegel, 2017, p. 177)

These discoveries of how the brain changes in response to experience are a hopeful gift from neuroscience researchers to psychotherapy clinicians. Having new experiences actually impacts the brain itself; this is true in how both trauma as well as psychotherapy and change for the better affect the brain (Solomon & Siegel, 2017). This validates the aim and target of AEDP: Having a new experience—a *good* experience, a corrective emotional or relational experience—mobilizes changes in the brain; this mobilization has an effect on memory and also promotes the capacity to reflect on experience. All of these changes enhance healing and transformation.

To engage the healing drive of positive neuroplasticity, AEDP psychotherapists set the focus for the therapeutic process on facilitating new healing experiences and on the direct experience of what is happening somatically in the body. It is not enough to merely think and talk about their problems; patients need to experience how they have been impacted viscerally by both past trauma and therapeutic healing in the here and now. They need to be able to tune in to their "felt sense" of what is happening and then, moment to moment, notice what opens from there.

"A 'felt sense' is a special kind of internal bodily awareness . . . it must form . . . it may feel vague and murky. It feels meaningful, but not known" (Gendlin, 1981, p. 10). With attention and presence, what first appears as a stirring becomes something more: a tightening in the belly, then a pang in the heart, then tears in the eyes. Piece by piece, by going further, meaning comes into awareness. When our patients tune into a felt sense, they focus on affective experience that unfolds in each moment. This is what is meant by proceeding in a bottom-up fashion: attending to experience and paying attention, moment-to-moment, to what emerges (see also Hanakawa, Chapter 4, this volume). This allows implicit memory, emotion, and significant realizations to surface. When our patients have new and good experiences (Fosha, 2002), these experiences have the power to rewire the brain. Furthermore, the process of having new experiences, juxtaposing them with the old experiences, and heightening the contrast is what contributes to memory reconsolidation (Ecker et al., 2012). In other words, when an old experience is challenged by a new experience, conscious reflection on and experience of that contrast brings a new order of what can be expected—and with it, the potential for change that can last.

## BEING WITH NEW EXPERIENCES CREATES NEW NEURAL PATHWAYS

Having new experiences stimulates neural firing, which generates new neural pathways (Cozolino, 2006; Siegel, 2017). When psychotherapists and patients engage in dyadic processes in which the therapist is helping the patient to face what they have avoided and to regulate what they feared to be overwhelming, the therapist is helping the patient to be with what was previously considered unmanageable. Thus, the patient's reliance on their old reactive patterns is reduced. Instead, by having new experiences of being met responsively, new neural pathways are being encoded. Cozolino (2006) said it well: "In relationships, like mother and child, we are constructing neural networks in the brain, transposing maternal behavior into biological structure" (p. 87). This is one aspect of how having these new therapeutic relational experiences can harness neuroplasticity. Instead of getting caught up in the "same old, same old," our patients have a *new experience* of being with their emotions in the presence of a caring other who reflects them, and validates and affirms their self-awareness and core knowing. These new, corrective experiences enable patients to become capable of perceiving what they feel and then how to be with what they feel; thus, they are key to the development of new neural circuitry. The new neural circuitry in turn further supports patients' capacities of being with, feeling into and attuning to their relationships and world around them.

## METAPROCESSING PROVIDES OPPORTUNITIES FOR NEURAL INTEGRATION

Another feature of neuroplasticity is neural integration. Dan Siegel (2017) referred to an integrated brain as one in which the flow of information is happening between parts of the brain that allow it to reflect on experience while being in connection to the experience. In AEDP, as important as having a new—and good—experience, is patients' knowing that they have had the experience (Fosha, 2002). To help patients achieve this embodied knowing, the AEDP therapist makes sure to initiate a period of reflecting on the new experience, called *metatherapeutic processing,* or *metaprocessing* for short. This provides an opportunity for the patient both to feel into the impact and also to realize the significance of what is shifting. AEDP's metaprocessing provides an opportunity for distinct neural networks in the brain that were previously dissociated and deficient of necessary stimulation, to connect, and for new neural pathways to grow, thus increasing the patient's capacity for sustaining connection and integration.

Hebb's (1949) pioneering contribution has become one of the central laws of neuroplasticity: "Neurons that fire together wire together." In terms of trauma, our patients are often suffering from activation that rises when reminders of traumatic memory hijack the nervous system. For example, in the case illustration later in the chapter, G is triggered whenever her husband leaves to go out of town. She has the same overwhelming reaction each time. "Trauma time" (van der Hart et al., 2010) describes the out-of-sync experience that happens when a person cannot distinguish between what happened "then" and what is happening "now"; thus, in trauma time, what happened then is being experienced as though it is happening now. Through the psychotherapeutic exploration of moment-to-moment experience, we discover that G's loving husband's planned departure, even for a few days, links directly, although unconsciously, into the memory of her father's abrupt and permanent departure from her life when she was 12 years old. For G, the neural networks that fire together in response to the stimulus of a significant other's leaving need to be untangled and differentiated from the neural networks of abandonment; the different tendrils of each distinct life experience need to be tended with care to what each aspect truly needs.

On the positive side, "neurons that fire together wire together" might be a way to conceive of what happens as the brain distinguishes these two experiences and becomes more flexible to function specifically to each one. Healing might now be described as the firing and wiring together of new experiences that strengthen and build alternate neuronal connections—distinct, differentiated neural connections. Having an experience with a trusted other who is present, attuned, and responsive to the patient's uncomfortable feelings and distress is a new experience of accompaniment: It reduces the need for defenses, and, if repeated, it can be internalized. It can be held next to, but in contrast with, the old experience of an attachment figure who abandoned. The healing mechanism is one that helps the patient process her emotions about the old trauma to completion, which then evokes greater self-reflection and self-knowing. From these depths of an interconnecting brain, patients grow more able to welcome all aspects of their emerging self, and their capacity to reflect on experience also grows.

## THE ART OF ATTUNEMENT

The AEDP therapist stance draws from both attachment theory and mother–infant interaction studies (Bowlby, 1982, 1988; Beebe & Lachman, 1998; Tronick, 2009). The AEDP therapist aims to be attuned, coordinated, and capable of noticing disruptions and making repairs (Fosha, 2003, 2017; Lipton & Fosha, 2011; Pando-Mars, 2011, 2016). Developmentally, from the earliest weeks of life, the interactions between a child and caregiver are mutual and synchronous, even if asymmetric (Fosha, 2000). In therapy, therapist and patient are engaging, both verbally and nonverbally, resonating, being in sync, falling out of sync and seeking to rapidly repair and thus get back in (a new) synch. The way the therapist helps the dyad navigate this dance reflects the art of attunement. And the patient's *experience* of this attunement and of the repair that restores it when it is disrupted is what is most essential.

To fully engage the process of building attunement, resonance and helping patients to feel felt and known, I keep the research of Mary Ainsworth and her collaborators in mind. Sensitivity and responsiveness are central qualities of caregivers that build security. Ainsworth's Strange Situation research focused on what occurs between children and caregivers during separation and reunion (Ainsworth et al., 1978; Main et al., 2005). Four decades later, Beatrice Beebe and her collaborators corroborated this research with studies of face to face mother–infant interactions at 4 months of age (Beebe & Lachman, 2014). Beebe videotapes these mother–infant interactions and through a second-by-second microanalysis shows what is imperceptible to the naked eye. This allows the intricate details of engagement and disengagement, self-regulation and coregulation to be studied for how each partner of the dyad changes and synchronizes in coordination with the other. Infants form expectancies and anticipations about how the interactive patterns will proceed, which are early formations of internal working models (Beebe & Lachman, 2014). Films of disruption and repair depict how a mother's responsiveness, or lack thereof, to her infant's emotional distress has a significant impact on whether the baby feels safe and understood. Each dyad reveals its characteristic self–other representation "on their way" to secure and insecure attachment, which can be assessed once the child is mobile and able to move toward and away from the mother, usually between 12 and 18 months old.

In dyads, when the infant becomes distressed, and the mother joins the infant's distress, displaying matching behaviors, the baby calms and reconnects with the mother, showing markers of security. When the mother mismatches her infant, ignoring or even overriding her infant's distress, the baby become confused, not understanding the mother nor feeling understood by her, showing markers of disorganization/insecurity (Beebe & Lachman, 2014). As Cozolino (2006) said, the characteristic relational patterns of the dyad are what become internalized in psychic structure. When our patients show up for treatment, these early relational patterns appear implicitly, and sometimes explicitly, making this research all the more relevant in the implication that healing must include the realization and rewiring of expectancies of self and other to lead to earned secure attachment.

## THE UNIT OF INTERVENTION: REWIRING IMPLICIT EXPECTANCIES

One of AEDP's most salient guides to clinical work is that the unit of intervention is the therapist's intervention *and* the patient's response to it (Fosha, 2000). Beebe's research illustrates how the moment-to-moment intersubjective processes of relatedness have their attachment origins at 4 months and also show up in adult-to-adult face-to-face communications. They show up when therapists inquire about their patient's felt experience. They show up in how patients are able to regulate or become dysregulated by their emotions and in how they are able to make use of the therapist's presence and care.

Babies who have missed being adequately mirrored and responded to by their mother or caregiver often end up disconnected from the emotional signals of their body. Instead, they rely on defenses to shut down awareness of feelings that were previously untended, or they become anxious and escalate distress in a reflexive cry for help. These are the kinds of communications we are exploring when we intervene, *and then notice what happens next*. How patients relate to their own experience and to the therapist manifests on a moment-to-moment basis. In tracing these interactive sequences along the lines of AEDP's three representational schemas, therapists have a way to organize experience and follow specific guidelines and interventions to make an experiential impact, "precipitate mental rearrangements" (James, 1902, quoted in Fosha, Chapter 1, this volume) and set in motion a trajectory of healing and repair.

## AEDP'S THREE REPRESENTATIONAL SCHEMAS

While the detailed phenomenology of the four-state transformational process (described in Fosha, Chapter 1, this volume) provides markers of change and transformation that orient the therapist to where the patient is at any moment in the overall transformational process, the Triangle of Experience, the S-O-E Triangle, and the Triangle of Relational Comparisons are representational schemas that assist psychotherapists to address the moment-by-moment emergence, heightening or waning of defense, anxiety, and glimmers of affective experience and the significant past, current, and present relational influences.

Each of the three schemas has two versions: *self-at-best* and *self-at-worst*. Fosha (2000) described how different developmental and relational experiences during affectively charged moments give rise to a sequential development of affective experience that map onto the two different configurations. The self-at-worst configuration is stress-based and driven by the dread. The self-at-best version of the schemas comes to the fore when safety prevails and thus, transformance (Fosha, 2009) is in ascendance and reflects an openness to emotional experience: it is a hope-driven configuration. The knowledge that the potential for both modes of functioning is present in all individuals at all times but that an individual's functioning at a given moment is best captured by one or the other of these two schemas helps the therapist have a sense of whether, at that given moment, patients are more motivated by dread and moving away from connection and experience (self-at-worst) or more motivated by hope and moving toward connection and experience (self-at-best). All three schemas help therapists orient and inform therapists' choice of interventions.

In what follows, I describe each of the triangles and how they represent significant aspects of the patient's experience. The Triangle of Experience represents the internalized emotional regulation strategies that appear in the moment-to-moment unfolding of the therapeutic exploration (see Figure 6.1). The S-O-E triangle, which depicts the patient's internal working model, represents the patient's experiences of self, other, and emotion and shows their intrinsic interrelatedness (see Figure 6.3). The Triangle of Relational Comparisons (see Figure 6.4) represents relationships across time, both those that are repetitive and those that are corrective, new, and healing. Links among the patient's historical relationship(s), current relationships, and the therapeutic relationship surface during the course of treatment and become the focal point of our psychotherapeutic interactions.

## THE TRIANGLE OF EXPERIENCE

In her chapter on structuring tools, Fosha (2000) said that "to facilitate affective experience, the therapist must be quick to recognize defenses, anxiety and repeating patterns. She must also be quick to recognize genuine emotions" (p. 103). That's precisely what the Triangle of Experience helps us do. It also provides a way to see the dynamic structure of internal experience and allows us to map out the patient's emotion regulation strategies (see also Frederick, Chapter 7, this volume).

When functioning is best represented by the self-at-worst version of the Triangle of Experience (Figure 6.2), we can identify that some patients are overregulated and protect themselves by blocking emotion (defense), inhibiting emotion with fear, shame, or guilt (anxiety); at the same time, it helps us to see that other patients are underregulated and challenged by affective regulatory difficulties (see Lamagna, Chapter 11, this volume). The AEDP therapist aspires to help each patient work through defenses, inhibiting affects or dysregulated emotions so as to gain regulated access to their experience. The aim is building an alliance and fostering experiences that can help patients shift from a self-at-worst configuration to a self-at-best configuration, prompting patients to access hope, curiosity, and openness to experience. This potentiates

**FIGURE 6.1. The Triangle of Experience**

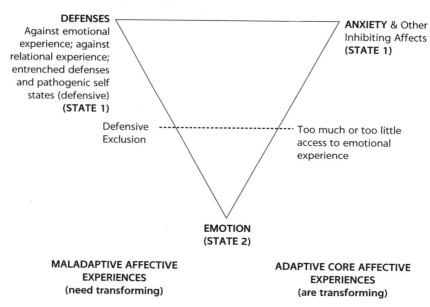

**DEFENSES**
Against emotional
experience; against
relational experience;
entrenched defenses
and pathogenic self
states (defensive)
**(STATE 1)**

**ANXIETY** & Other
Inhibiting Affects
**(STATE 1)**

Defensive
Exclusion

Too much or too little
access to emotional
experience

**EMOTION**
**(STATE 2)**

**MALADAPTIVE AFFECTIVE**
**EXPERIENCES**
**(need transforming)**

**ADAPTIVE CORE AFFECTIVE**
**EXPERIENCES**
**(are transforming)**

**Legend: Affective Experiences**

**Maladaptive Affective Experiences**
The Pathogenic Affects (e.g., Overwhelm, Toxic Shame, Fear
Without Solution); Unbearable States of Traumatic Aloneness
(e.g., Helplessness, Fragmentation, Brokenness; Despair, "The
Black Hole Of Trauma")

**Adaptive Core Affective Experiences**
Categorical Emotions; Relational Experiences, Asymmetric
(Attachment) or Symmetric (Intersubjective); Coordinated
Relational Experiences; Receptive Affective Experiences; Somatic
"Drop-Down" States; Intrarelational Experiences; Authentic
Self-Experiences; Experiences of Agency, Will Desire; Attachment
Strivings; The Expression of Core Needs

*Note.* Copyright © 2020 by Diana Fosha. Reprinted with permission.

having new, reparative experiences that will turn on neural firing to initiate
positive neuroplasticity.

*Defenses*, represented at the top of the Triangle of Experience, are self-
protective strategies that function to manage the overwhelm of unbearable
emotional experiences that threatens either the integrity of the self or the integrity of the relational–attachment bond. When patients are relying on defenses,
therapists may notice a lack of flow. Defenses distract and avert attention. They

**FIGURE 6.2. The Triangle of Experience: Two Versions of the Triangle of Experience—The Self-at-Worst and the Self-at-Best**

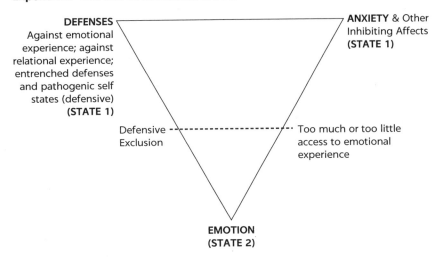

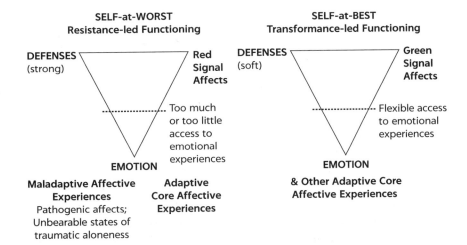

*Note.* Copyright © 2020 by Diana Fosha. Reprinted with permission.

disrupt, avoid, or shut down awareness in order to manage anxiety and conceal their vulnerability. Defenses can be classic, like intellectualization, dismissiveness, or withdrawal; or they can be tactical, like vagueness, generalization, or indirect ways of speaking. Even emotions can be defensive, for example, when emotions are used for protective purposes, such as tears instead of anger, anger instead of sadness, or contempt instead of vulnerability.

When patients use defenses, they may not initially realize that what they are doing is defensive. AEDP therapists engage defenses with the same acceptance and interest with which they respond to core emotional experiences. Inviting patients to explore what is happening and acknowledging the adaptive nature of defenses can often melt the need for self-protection and avoidance. Sometimes bypassing the defense, undeterred, with a gentle request to set the defense aside is compelling, touching some long-buried yearning in the patient to be seen and known. Ultimately, helping patients to recognize their defenses as adaptive, being open and willing to become curious about their function and how they originated, can open pathways to self-discovery. With this collaborative alliance, patients learn to understand how defenses block emotional experience and start to realize how incompletely processed emotions are often a culprit in the problematic disturbances in their lives (Levine, 1997). This often generates willingness to move beyond defenses. In AEDP, working through defenses to access emotion and process it to completion is central to transformational process. This generates the release of adaptive action tendencies particular to each emotion (Darwin, 1872; Fosha, 2000, 2007, 2009; Frijda, 1986).

*Anxiety and signal affects* are also represented at the top of the Triangle of Experience (Figures 6.1 and 6.2). Defenses shut down experience for protection, attempting to ensure that what happened in the "there and then" will never happen again. Anxiety and signal affects arise when what is happening in the "here and now" triggers implicit or explicit memories of what did happen then. Something went wrong, and the nervous system coded this memory. It becomes charged in reaction to a reminding stimulus. This stimulus may activate negative expectancies that infants developed early on, which were corrosive to their growing trust and ease in the process of feeling core affective experience in relationship (McCullough Vaillant, 1997). Sometimes a signal affect triggers protective strategies.

When defenses break down, anxiety appears in the mind as preoccupation, rumination, obsession, distraction, cognitive distortion, and vacillation in self-image and self-worth. Anxiety shows up in the body as shallow breathing, agitation, fidgeting hands and legs, gaze aversion, postural shifts, exaggerated or constricted movement, and somatization. The combination of anxiety and defense shows up in the emotional field as dysregulation, mood fluctuations, and emotionality (emotion mixed with anxiety) that is not core emotion. Anxiety and defense are located at the top of the Triangle of Experience (Figure 6.1) and represent State 1 phenomena in the four-state transformational process (Figure 1, Appendix, this volume).

The AEDP therapist aims to be present and responsive with a patient who is feeling anxiety, offering dyadic regulation in the form of slow and low voice tone and prosody, a leaning-in posture, audible breathing, intending toward entraining right-brain-to-right brain experience toward settling and soothing. One of the favored early interventions is to be explicit about going through what is arising together and checking for the patient's receptivity. "Can we do this together? "Can you feel me with you?" "Can we both breathe and s-l-o-w down?"

Depending on the patient's attachment style, the degree to which the patient can make use of this intervention will vary. More avoidant patients may benefit from the more general "we" of the question "Can *we* do this together?" as well as, at first, a focus on "doing" (Pando-Mars, 2016). Sometimes psychoeducation about using breathing practices and increasing somatic awareness to reduce anxiety can boost collaboration with someone bent toward self-reliance. The ambivalent patient might appreciate how the therapist explicitly offers accompaniment to counter the fear of being alone. Directive interventions such as "Slow down here and take a breath, exhale slowly through pursed lips" or "Let's slow down and breathe together" can be perceived by the ambivalent patient as the longed for help at last being given (Pando-Mars, 2016).

Exploring anxiety and the other inhibiting affects (e.g., fear, shame, or guilt) is important and useful because it often brings patients from what initially feels like a vague upwelling of overwhelm into awareness of something significant yet upsetting that needs attention. Exploring anxiety can lead to accessing the underlying emotion represented at the bottom of the Triangle of Experience, which then allows the processing of that emotion.

Please note that the following discussion on emotion is a brief one. Because emotion is also at the bottom of the next representational schema, the S-O-E Triangle, I discuss them more fully after the S-O-E is presented.

*Emotions*, and other adaptive core affective experiences that when processed are transformative, are represented at the bottom of the Triangle of Experience (Figure 6.1); these are State 2 phenomena in the four-state transformational process (Figure 1, Appendix, this volume). When patients face their emotion with a present and caring other who helps dyadically regulate and process that emotion to completion, this can release the adaptive action tendency of that emotion (see also Medley, Chapter 8, this volume). The markers of a completed wave of affective experience are often feelings of relief and lightness, and it is so important that psychotherapists help patients tune into these shifts that occur in the wake of their previously warded-off emotional experience.

Metaprocessing such relief and lightness can initiate patients' recognition that they *can* navigate and survive their emotions. This energizes their hope and trust in the process and motivates their courage to be able to do it again and risk feeling what needs to be felt in their emotional life.

Just as important as the therapist's being able to detect where on the Triangle of Experience a patient is at a given moment, just as important, if not more important, is the way in which the therapist meets the patient. The relational context in which the patient's original wounds arose, and for some, the current relationship in which the patient is dwelling, set a precedent for the patient's expectations of the therapeutic encounter. In the next representational schema, the S-O-E Triangle, Fosha has set a template for understanding these relational dynamics that operate from the get-go, and then throughout the session and the course of the therapy. This triangle elaborates the relational matrix in which our patients develop their relationship to emotion, and in which they develop emotion regulation strategies in relationship.

For this purpose, I now introduce the S-O-E Triangle before further discussing the emotion at the bottom of the Triangle of Experience.

## THE SELF–OTHER–EMOTION TRIANGLE

Shown in Figure 6.3, the S-O-E Triangle depicts how the Self's experience of the Other's response to the Self's Emotion becomes internalized as the Self's own reaction to that emotion, as well as representations of Self and Other (see also Lamagna, Chapter 11, this volume). This original patterning between a caregiver and child, and its impact on the nature of emotion regulation that tends to characterize that constellation, form the patient's internal working model(s), which is what the S-O-E represents, with the emotion regulation explicitly and schematically represented (see also Frederick, Chapter 7, this volume). This relational response to emotion affects the individual's own representation of Self and Other, as well as the individual's Emotion-regulation strategies, which are represented at the bottom of the S-O-E Triangle, as a Triangle of Experience embedded within the S-O-E.

### Self-at-Best Configuration of the S-O-E Triangle

As shown in Figure 6.3 (bottom right), when an Other's response to the Self or Emotion (or both) is experienced as welcoming and interested and the Other is experienced as available to help regulate emotion, the child develops trust in both Self and Other (secure functioning), and develops the capacity to engage emotional and relational experiences. The Other is perceived realistically. Even if an Other in a particular moment in the individual's current life is actuality in some way problematic, the individual's Self sustains being fundamentally okay and effective and can maintain its own integrity as well as optimal Emotion regulation, even in the face of current challenges (as long as the self's resources have not been exceeded). By accompanying patients with attunement and dyadic regulation as needed, we aim to be with them in such a way that can facilitate self-at-best.

### Self-at-Worst Configuration of the S-O-E Triangle

As shown in Figure 6.3 (bottom left), when an Other ignores, intrudes upon, or disdains the Self or the child's Emotional experience, the child comes to have complicated (insecure) reactions to experiencing and expressing this particular emotion (Triangle of Experience). This is what is represented on the self-at-worst constellation of the S-O-E Triangle, which develops in conditions of stress. In this configuration, the Self is perceived or represented and is experienced as compromised and not okay. The Other is perceived or represented and is experienced as triggering, and the individual's way of dealing with core Emotions reflects these problematic early attachment experiences. In what follows, we can further map out experiences that give rise to the

**FIGURE 6.3. The Self–Other–Emotion Triangle: Two Versions of the Self–Other–Emotion Triangle—The Self-at-Worst and the Self-at-Best**

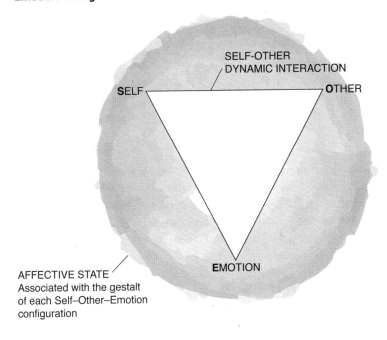

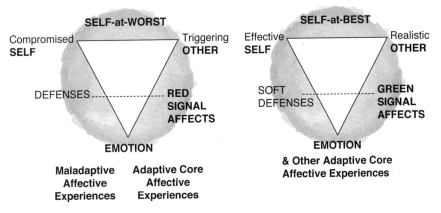

*Note.* Copyright © 2020 by Diana Fosha. Reprinted with permission.

specific internal working models of insecure attachment that characterize the different attachment styles.

### Avoidant

On the S-O-E triangle, dismissive, rejecting, intrusive, or humiliating responses to the individual's emotions are the classic hallmarks of the triggering Other (caregiver) for people who display avoidant patterns with respect to attachment and emotion. The individual develops an internal working model of avoidance of both emotion and counting on others, the compromised Self (child) becoming defensively self-reliant, avoiding attachment figures and attachment needs. On the Triangle of Experience, perceived or experienced vulnerability in oneself can activate the avoidant self-at-worst constellation. In the avoidant attachment style, arousal of the attachment system evokes deactivating strategies (Cassidy & Kobak, 1988). There is a tendency toward autoregulation and defenses against emotion are overly detached. We witness shutting down, minimization, and a wall of silence (Pando-Mars, 2016; Pando-Mars & Fosha, 2020).

### Ambivalent

On the S-O-E triangle, preoccupation is the classic hallmark of the triggering Other (caregiver) of people who display ambivalent attachment patterns: The Other's response to the Self's emotions are characterized by inconsistency, self-centeredness, or unreliability (or a combination of these). The compromised Self (child) develops the ambivalent internal working model, becoming Other-focused and overly immersed in the Other's experience at the expense of attending to their own Self's experience and needs. On the Triangle of Experience, fear of abandonment can activate this self-at-worst constellation. In the ambivalent attachment style, anxiety drives hyperactivating strategies (Cassidy & Kobak, 1988) which center on seeking external regulation. Defenses against emotion characteristic of ambivalent patterns include clinging, protest, emotionality, and a wall of words (Pando-Mars, 2016; Pando-Mars & Fosha, 2020).

### Emotion

Being alone in the face of overwhelming emotion is a most significant genesis for psychopathology (Fosha, 2000). The crushing weight of disappointment and the immensity of sorrow can be devastating, and to be alone with such emotion is unbearable. Dyadic failures and stress bring about the dread that triggers self-at-worst configurations. Subsequent emotion regulatory difficulties are often what drive patients to seek psychotherapy. Therefore, exploring experiences of emotion in the context of a relationship with a safe and trusted Other becomes the healing mechanism most central to helping our patients deal with the trauma, loss, and emotional difficulties that have plagued them.

Internal working models of attachment change across relationships and emotions. Both self-at-worst and self-at-best exist side by side, ready for activating. Thus, AEDP therapists invite our patients to experience their emotion in an attuning and regulating relational context, aiming to provide them with experiences of being seen and feeling felt, to set the conditions for dyadic safety to help them access self-at-best from the start and then facilitate their access to core emotion, which can then be processed.

AEDP therapists tend explicitly and experientially to the attachment and intersubjective happenings in the therapist-patient dyad. (see also Frederick, Chapter 7, this volume). We want to help patients have a relational experience that can offset the dread of disappointment and shows them that we *want* to be with them and with what is stirred within them. In the clinical vignette that follows, the therapist is primarily focused on helping the patient be in touch with the emotion she has been avoiding. Picking up her cues, bringing explicit focus to her implicit patterning, being a sensitive and responsive Other (Ainsworth et al., 1978), the therapist offers accompaniment in the forms of affect regulation and empathy. Instead of ignoring the patient's suffering, the therapist helps the patient learn how to be with her feelings and tend to the root of her emotional experience. This dyadic coordination and attuned engagement fosters the patient's self-at-best: the sense of being an effective Self, capable of feeling emotion and worthy of compassionate response.

*Emotion* is located at the bottom of both the S-O-E triangle and of the Triangle of Experience embedded in it (Figure 6.3, bottom half). To facilitate the processing of unresolved emotions, we focus our patients on what happens somatically. We help them notice signals of defense and anxiety and identify them, so that we can use our dyadic relationship to regulate whatever underlying conflicts may arise about feeling emotion. As they surface, we invite emotions by suggesting to the patient, "Let's slow down here." "Can we make space for this?" "Breathe into this." Making room for the felt sense of emotion allows it to emerge and come into expression. It is so important for patients to experience the felt sense of their emotion before trying to give it words. So often words and meaning come *after* emotion has run its course. We need to help patients let go of the strategy of "figuring out" emotions and encourage "feeling into" emotions instead. Sometimes emotion brings contact with younger parts of self that housed forgotten affective memories, which creates the possibility for intrarelational connection and meaningful contact (see also Medley, Chapter 8 this volume). Processing emotion to completion gives rise to the release of their specific adaptive action tendencies, new tendrils of self-knowledge, and motivational value-laden direction; it can bring forgotten memories to mind, linking to significant early life events (Darwin, 1872; Fosha, 2003; Frijda, 1986). This processing of categorical emotion is a significant catalyst of transformation and is one of the key phenomena located in State 2 of the four-state map.

## THE TRIANGLE OF RELATIONAL COMPARISONS

The third representational schema, the Triangle of Relational Comparisons (Figure 6.4), allows us to look at significant relationships over time and compare them with each other. This representational schema helps us see both the dynamic roots of the patient's suffering and early signs of the patient's resilience and transformance manifestations and how they operate in past relationships, current relationships, and the therapeutic relationship.

The Triangle of Relational Comparisons elegantly depicts the patient's experience of Past, Current, and Therapeutic relationships (the nature of the T-C-P links) to each other (see also Frederick, Chapter 7, this volume). It embeds the first two triangles we discussed, the Triangle of Experience and

**FIGURE 6.4. The Triangle of Relational Comparisons**

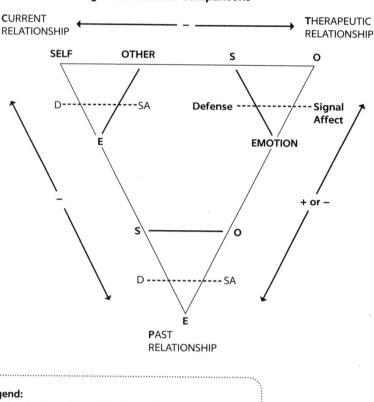

Legend:
**− (Minus) = Repetition** (Old, Same, Same Old Same Old)
**+ (Plus) = Corrective Experience** (New, Different)

| Triangle of Relational Comparisons | | Self-Other Emotion Triangle (Self-at-Worst or Self-at-Best) | | Triangle of Experience (Self-at-Worst or Self-at-Best) | |
|---|---|---|---|---|---|
| C | Current Relationship | S | Self | D | Defense |
| T | Therapeutic Relationship | O | Other | SA | Signal Affects (Red or Green) |
| P | Past Relationship | E | Emotion | E | Emotion |

*Note.* Copyright © 2020 by Diana Fosha. Reprinted with permission.

the S-O-E Triangle, at each corner. The top right corner holds how the patient experiences how the Therapist engages with the patient. The top left corner shows the patient's experience of Current relationship(s). The bottom of the triangle is the place for Past relationship(s), usually family of origin.

In AEDP, the Therapeutic relationship corner is seen as the fulcrum that can initiate the process of transformation and can be corrective and security inducing from the get-go. In AEDP's transformation-based psychodynamics, we do not believe that the maladaptive past must repeated before it can be corrected. Deep believers in healing from the get-go, we notice how the

Therapeutic relationship often inspires connection from the start (Fosha, 2000). The Current relationship corner depicts the current problematic relationship(s) that drive patients to seek therapy. The bottom Past relationship corner houses past suffering with historical figures. Although patients are often cognitively aware of the suffering endured from relationships with past historical figures, they are usually disconnected from how this affects their current experience and the toll of this implicit influence on day-to-day encounters in their lives.

Curiously, something that we often see is this: Having come into therapy feeling and believing that no one was ever there for them, following a new and positive experience with a therapist, patients often remember the presence of a supportive caring figure who was there for them at an earlier significant moment in their life. Or they recall a time when they found a determination to rise above hardships. Therefore, while we can locate a repetition of the historical relationships that set existing current problematic dynamic patterns into play, we may simultaneously encounter an existing adaptive figure or healing pattern that departs from the maladaptive patterns (transformance in action) that may be the patient's presenting complaint.

The Triangle of Relational Comparisons offers a kind of x-ray with which we can see what happened in the past that needs healing (repetition) and what patients were already able to achieve on their own (transformance: healing or corrective relationships, e.g., earned secure attachment). By helping our patients to connect the dots, they can discover and link where and how their unresolved issues are being played out in their current life situations. The AEDP therapist, unlike therapists of other orientations, helps the patient to identify places and relationships where their adaptive, healing-oriented strivings are already manifesting as significantly different patterns, that is, corrective, reparative patterns in contrast to the trouble-engendering ones in their early life. This tends to be a helpful reminder and evidence of a patient's resilience and provides a meaningful way to consciously call upon resources during sessions.

Thus, using the Triangle of Relational Comparisons, we focus on both repetitions and exceptions, on detecting both retraumatizing patterns and healing-oriented, transformance-reflecting ones. For this purpose, "relational comparisons" is the name of this representational schema. From a place of relational support and connection to self, the therapist helps the patient do the precise work needed to bring corrective emotional and relational experiences to wounded places, as well as illuminate, affirm, and celebrate the manifestations of resilience. The combination of exploring and reexperiencing early painful experiences by attending to what needs help and building on positive experiences is a powerful catalyst for integration and wholeness which gives rise to transformation. The Triangle of Relational Comparisons organizes the patient's new meaning-making, when guided by the truth of State 4 core state. It grounds the emerging newly cohesive and coherent autobiographical narrative associated with secure attachment. It sets in motion new self-realizations such as, "This is me." "I am worthy." "I see you for who you are." "I can be understood."

## CLINICAL VIGNETTE

Following is a clinical example[2] illustrating use of the three representational schemas. We begin with how, by having these three schemas, therapists use them to help conceptualize the simultaneous multiple layering of what's happening with patients and guide a clear course of clinical action. The therapist uses the Triangle of Experience to identify when the patient is moving away from emotion (defense) or feeling anxious, and she shares this with the patient. This helps the patient learn how to recognize for herself when she is avoiding feelings by going into her thoughts or when she is feeling anxious and may need to attend to what is stirred.

   This following transcript is taken from the seventh psychotherapy session of G, a woman in her early 40s, married, and mother of three. She initially came to treatment with an awareness of her avoidant patterns of relating to her husband, of her discomfort with affection and her heightened sensitivity at times of his planned departures. In the preceding six sessions, I noticed how, in keeping with the avoidant tendency to remain overly detached, G ignores signals of emotion that appear in the moment, her tendency being to talk through tears that appear in the corners of her eyes. While I am present with her words, I also am present with the signals which reveal underlying affective experience (transformance glimmers) and call her attention to them. Not only do I want to help my patient identify and pause to feel her emotional experience, I want to help her to identify her defenses so that she can register just how *she moves away from knowing* her own experience more fully. With this awareness, she can choose to move toward her emotional life and thus benefit with new gains in self-knowledge.

   G has come to treatment to explore this pattern that seems to contradict the love she has for her husband. I believe her wish to address these conflicts is demonstrative of her care. This session begins with G talking about her reaction to her husband going out of town, claiming "I really don't care." Engaging her with a kind and receptive presence, I intervene right away: I want to counter her relational defense with what I sense is her transformance striving, and so I say that I believe she does care.

   Please note that experiences represented at the top of the Triangle of Experience (i.e., defenses and anxiety) are State 1 phenomena in the four-state transformational process, and experiences represented at the bottom of the Triangle of Experience (i.e., emotions and other core affective phenomena) are State 2 phenomena. State 3 and State 4 phenomena are only represented in the four-state transformational model and thus were not part of the three representational schemas discussed earlier. (Note that italic text indicates description of nonverbal expressions or movements, and bold indicates theoretical comments.)

---

[2]I have complied with APA ethical standards in describing the details of treatment; aspects of the patient's identity and background have been disguised to protect confidentiality.

### State 1: Stress, Distress, Symptoms, and Looking for Transformance— Using the Triangle of Experience and the S-O-E Triangle

PATIENT: I really don't care—but implicit in your partner going out of town . . . if he's just going to have fun . . . I don't really care . . . **[State 1: defenses in operation]**

THERAPIST: But you do care. **[Pressuring with empathy and with what's really at the bottom of the Triangle of Experience. The S-O-E Triangle: a welcoming Other inviting genuine feeling.]**

PATIENT: I shell up. I get really defensive, I suppose. **[Self-reflection: patient identifies her own defense.]** I don't think intellectually that he's abandoning me, but I have this whole process that I go through intellectually where I get mad at him.

THERAPIST: Okay. (*hand on heart*) Well let's just slow down. **[Slowing down is critical to experiential work and identifying patterns of response.]**

PATIENT: (*tears appear*) . . . Every time he leaves (*She speaks through tears appearing in her eyes.*)

THERAPIST: I see emotion coming. **[Making the implicit explicit, resonating with bottom of the Triangle of Experience as an attuned other: S-O-E Triangle]**

PATIENT: (*smiles*) Okay. **[In response to my comment, she slows down.]**

THERAPIST: Do you notice that? **[Bringing her attention to her own self-at-worst defensive response]**

PATIENT: (*Shakes her head side to side*) I didn't even notice it, no. **[Evoking self-at-best awareness]**

THERAPIST: (*Smiles warmly*) As I say it, do you notice?

This is an important intervention. Not only do I want to help G realize she is tearing up, I want to her notice that she can feel her tears. I reflect what I see to orient her to what is happening in her body, in the present moment, as a way to strengthen her own awareness of affective experience and ultimately to build her self-agency. Now, the impact of the therapist's comment is that the patient becomes aware, growing her self-at-best.

PATIENT: Yes. (*Nodding*).

THERAPIST: Good for you. **[Affirmation of her shift]** Let's just take a minute and be . . . and feel into what you're saying . . . **[Asking her to "feel into" her words is a powerful intervention for someone who uses avoidant strategies and is starting to relinquish them.]**

PATIENT:     (*Nods*)

THERAPIST:   "Every time he leaves, I get mad" **[I repeat her key words.]** (*my hand moves from sternum to solar plexus*) and I see . . . sadness. **[I reflect her emotion.]**

PATIENT:     I want to be able to say to him, I could, but I can't, that I'm not mad. I just feel like he's abandoning me, but that sounds so ridiculous.

THERAPIST:   Can we slow down . . . when you say, "I feel like he's abandoning me" . . . what's the feeling?" **[The patient reverted to self-at-worst by projecting her feeling as what *he* is doing, and she leaves the present moment with me. I ask her what she is feeling.]**

Many patients aren't aware that their ideas are not feelings, that just saying "I feel" doesn't indicate a genuine feeling. It is important for therapists to help patients discern the difference between thoughts and feelings. When patients shift into thoughts, therapists recognize this defensive response, and reattune to the glimmer of emotion. In this way, we invite the patient to be aware and present to explore their own *felt sense*.

PATIENT:     I feel tight, hot. I get short with my kids. **[She responds with sensation at first, then generalizes, goes away from this moment to her kids, and she reports a pattern.]**

THERAPIST:   Slow down. Feeling tight and hot right now? **[I repeat her words, to redirect her attention to what is happening in her body right now.]**

Here, I hold the Triangle of Experience, noticing that as affect emerges, anxiety appears in the form of sensations of tightness and heat. She goes to defense by thinking about her kids. I redirect her to the first part of her comment to bypass the defense.

PATIENT:     (*Nodding*)

THERAPIST:   Sounds like anxiety. **[Identify what is happening on the Triangle of Experience]** [Patient: Um hmm] Sounds like a reaction to the feeling. . . . So, could you just see if you could let yourself be with the tightness, be with the heat . . . **[I want her to tune into the anxiety. . .—not to change it, but for both of us to be with it, which is a new Self–Other–Emotion configuration.]**

It is new for G to have an attuned and accompanying other. My slow, engaged voice tone conveys my regulating presence and my willingness to meet each experience with her. In the next few minutes she moves back and forth between a glimmer of emotion and trying to figure it out. I reflect how when she starts to notice emotion, she feels some anxiety and then pops back into her head. Being explicit about how she shifts between corners on the Triangle of Experience is organizing for her, as she sits at the edge of what is unknown. This helps her understand the meaning in her behavior, and that we are privileging approaching genuine emotional experience.

Patients need a lot of encouragement to allow themselves to enter uncharted territory. There is risk in moving towards what they have been avoiding due to unconscious expectancies: in this case the implicit memory of being alone with devastating emotions. On the one hand, G is quite open and receptive to my guidance, yet looking closely, each step requires my steady hand, pointing in the direction of affective unfolding, insisting with a gentle voice and affirming each approach. I am attuned, and also persistent, staying focused on deepening into her experience. On the Triangle of Comparisons Therapist corner, I nudge her, without pushing. I lead her, without pulling. I affirm her each step she takes, which allows her to find ground to support her next step, each new experience strengthening new neuronal pathways.

### First-State Transformation: Transitional Affects Signaling Openness to Shift With a Mixture of Anxiety—Using the T Corner on the Triangle of Relational Comparisons

**THERAPIST:** (*Her tears appear*) There you go, I see that . . . **[Affirming the emergence of more tears]**

**PATIENT:** (*Wipes tears from the corners of her eyes*)

**THERAPIST:** Is that okay? **[Asking permission respects her choice to sign on as she opens to her feelings.]**

**PATIENT:** Yeah, yeah . . . I just don't understand though. **[First-state transformation: transitional affects signaling openness to shift with a mixture of anxiety.]**

**THERAPIST:** I know, that's part of feeling . . . is the desire to make sense of it. . . . (*soothing voice tone*) And sometimes that comes after the feeling. **[Triangle of Relational Comparisons: Therapist as "older, wiser" attachment figure. "T" corner offers guidance to steady her and regulate her anxiety.]**

During the next few minutes, we continue to explore how G moves toward and away from core affect by naming the Triangle of Experience and feeling into the affect-laden words that herald the core emotion nearby. Now slowing down, G shows more openness to explore her experience. She recognizes that her feelings are not entirely about the current situation with her husband. She names that her feelings toward him are complicated (activation from an unresolved trauma from her past history). I resist interpreting but instead have her repeat certain loaded phrases or affect-laden words, to help her deepen into her unfolding experience. We reenter the session as she describes the effort she puts into *not* feeling vulnerable.

## State 2 Phenomena: Emergence of Core Affective Experience and Linking C–P Corners on the Triangle of Relational Comparisons

THERAPIST:   What kind of vulnerability do you feel when he goes out of town? **[We explore her anxiety to regulate it, which reemerges as we get closer to historical material.]**

PATIENT:   I don't know . . . I know I would be devastated **[powerful affect-laden word]** if he didn't come back. And maybe . . . clearly, it's some subconscious level. **[Emergent realization]** I don't actually think he's not going to come back . . . but on some level, I think while he's gone, I'm vulnerable. What if he didn't come back? **[New felt sense]** I've never thought about this, but he is the only man, after my dad, that I've ever loved this much. And my dad left . . . and if my husband leaves too, that would be . . . (*wiping eyes*) **[Click of recognition]**

THERAPIST:   Ooh . . . just let yourself . . . **[Empathic resonance with her tears]**

PATIENT:   I don't think he's going to, though . . . **[Bargaining: transitional affect]**

THERAPIST:   Right . . . just to feel . . .

PATIENT:   But that's the fear **[Realization of the old; patient herself identifies the Anxiety corner of the Triangle of Experience]**

THERAPIST:   That's the fear (*G is nodding*) **[Validation]**

THERAPIST:   What if he leaves like Dad left . . . so this fear sounds like it's like Dad leaving . . . **[Triangle of Relational Comparisons: linking the Current and Past affective experience]**

I am aware that she is in the intersection of Current and Past historical trauma. I make the link explicit, following her affective connection, trusting that the neuronal wires crossed between her husband's leaving and her father's early abandoning departure are surfacing. Here, we are mapping out the Triangle of Relational Comparisons, and my steady presence with G helps her untangle the past experience with her father from her current experience of her husband.

PATIENT:   I think it is . . . (*wiping tears–head tilting*)

THERAPIST:   Okay . . . oh, (*gentle soothing tone of voice*) so important we let yourself really feel this . . . [Patient: (*G breathes*)] That would account for some really old feeling that didn't get comforted . . . so courageous. **[Affirming: Triangle of Relational Comparisons: P-C link, i.e., linking a Current experience with a Past fear]**

PATIENT: Thank you. (*blows nose*)

THERAPIST: What vulnerability. **[Affirming that she is allowing herself to experience her emotion and the truth of her experience]** [Patient: (*G nodding*)] And that really happened.

PATIENT: That did happen.

THERAPIST: So, what you are afraid of with your husband did happen when your dad left . . . **[Triangle of Relational Comparisons: P–C link. Names the overlay of historical material on current life experience.]**

This is huge. We are carefully and painstakingly attending to each emergent point of moving toward and away from emotion. When she says she would be devastated if her husband didn't return, the power of this affective memory opened. Having her repeat this affect-laden word slowly, with awareness, G becomes more receptive to the emergent realization that her Current affective response with her husband fits what she feared, which actually did occur with her father in her past. We can also view this as memory reconsolidation; here is an opportunity to see these two experiences in high relief: What she is afraid of with her husband actually did happen with her father. This contrast puts both experiences in their respective places and differentiates her past and present experiences.

### Metaprocessing New Awareness Leads to State 3 Transformational Affects

PATIENT: Ooh . . . (*takes a deep breath*)

THERAPIST: Take your time, let yourself be with yourself here . . . **[Following her breath, her lead]**

PATIENT: Thank you. **[State 3 expression of feeling moved and expressing gratitude for the realization]**

THERAPIST: What do you feel as you say this . . . what's happening? **[Metaprocessing the shift]**

PATIENT: That's an epiphany for me . . . it's probably so obvious . . . but I just never felt it . . . I never believed it. **[She had disconnected from being alone with unbearable experience. Now that she can put the past in perspective, she is experiencing deep realization: State 3 mastery, feeling moved, realization affects.]**

THERAPIST: It's the feeling it that makes all the difference . . .

In the next segment of the session, G realizes what she would want to hear from her husband if she were to share this with him, which is: "I have compassion for you and I'm so sorry that this happened to you . . ." I acknowl-edge that, and I suggest that she try to offer to her younger self that which she wants from her husband.

### State 2 Transformational Work: Connecting Self-to-Self Changes Her S-O-E Configuration From Self-at-Worst to Self-at-Best

THERAPIST:   Can you picture that? Letting someone say that to her. Can you see if she can receive that? "I have compassion for you and I'm so sorry that this happened to you . . ." Give her a minute with this and take your time . . . **[State 2: intrarelational work to bring a corrective experience to the younger self with the vehicle of a miniportrayal]** What's that like?

PATIENT:   I haven't done that before . . . say something to her and she acknowledges that she hears me. Before it's just me telling her things, but that's really nice . . . **[From self-at-worst being talked at, to self-at-best being seen and heard: correc-tive emotional and relational experience]**

THERAPIST:   What's nice? **[Metaprocess the new experience]**

PATIENT:   To connect . . . to have her . . . she just looked up at me and smiled . . . **[Self-to-self connection; emotional trans-formation]**

THERAPIST:   Ooh . . . can you just drink in that looking up at you and smile? **[Deepen what is revealed through the metaprocessing.]**

Here she opens further on the self-at-best Triangle of Experience, as she connects with her younger self and her underlying attachment needs. In the self-at-best configurations of the S-O-E triangle, she *sees* her younger self and her younger self responds *as seen*. This moment of meeting marks the moment of transformation: What was disconnected and "left behind" is now realized and brought into connection, further transforming the P–C link on the Triangle of Relational Comparisons.

### State 3: Transformational Affects

PATIENT:   yeah . . .

THERAPIST:   That contact feels *sooo* necessary . . . **[More affirmative reflection—stay with, deepen, and honor this new corrective experience]**

PATIENT:   It does . . .

THERAPIST:   Just feels precious to me . . . **[State 3 healing affects: feeling moved]**

PATIENT:   It does . . . thank you very much . . . **[State 3: gratitude]**

THERAPIST: You're welcome. . . . What are you feeling thankful for right now? **[Deepen and elaborate]**

PATIENT: I feel tremendous gratitude that you're helping to guide me through this stuff. **[Elaborating State 3—feeling moved, gratitude]** This is a tremendous piece of it . . . I think that if I have any issues in my marriage this is the root of it . . . **[Now, realization affects emerge: State 4: core state declarative truth sense]**

Once G and her younger self make actual contact, gratitude emerges spontaneously; knowing that what she missed and sorely needed has now been given and received. The gratitude she expresses is a State 3 transformational healing affect that arises organically when she realizes what is actually the true origin of her fear of devastation, and she knows that my guidance has been instrumental. Recognizing where her deep feelings originate, she links the Past and Current corners of the Triangle of Relational Comparisons. This insight helps her make meaning of her experience into a more coherent and cohesive narrative.

### State 4: Core State Reflections, New Narrative, and Core Knowing Emerge

THERAPIST: Yup. I love that you can know and say that, think of how far that's come in today's session. **[Making explicit and celebrating the bigness of the change]**

PATIENT: I know, it has

THERAPIST: There's avoiding the vulnerability and now being able to acknowledge the connection between the fear of him going away . . .

PATIENT: Or even just being intimate and letting my guard down **[More self-understanding: State 4: core state and more openness to seeing the Other realistically and understanding herself better.]** [Therapist: Umm, yeah . . .] I am prepared for him to leave, and I have done all the things for myself to prepare for when it happens. Like I believe it's a given that he is going to leave . . . **[State 4: declarative knowing; the truth sense]**

THERAPIST: What do you think about that now when you see what you've done? **[Metaprocessing in State 4: compare before with after the session]**

PATIENT: I don't need to be that way . . . I just don't know how to not . . . **[There is no need to be self at worst; can be self at best. She is in a state of transition, realizing that she has choice**

**and what she once perceived is much more related to her past wounding than her current relationship.]**

THERAPIST:   I think this is the first step . . . **[Reassurance during transitional state]** [Patient: okay] So, let me just ask you this. What do you want to say to your husband right now? **[I return to a concern she had raised earlier, to revisit this from the platform of the new place.]**

PATIENT:   That I'm sorry. I feel like I do this to him, and then he leaves in a bad place feeling guilty upset—like I'm taking something from him? **[Core state: she reflects on her patterns. She shifts from S-O-E self-at-worst (self is compromised) and now perceives her husband from S-O-E self-at-best (other is seen realistically)].**

THERAPIST:   Do want to tell him what you're sorry for? **[Going for the specific learning]**

PATIENT:   Not being able to articulate my feelings. **[The stage is set for effective action on behalf of herself—corrective relational experience.]**

Here we see how G has shifted in relationship to her husband. Now that she understands herself, she wants to share from a place of true intimacy with him what she has learned in therapy and apologize—express sorrow—for what is truly at the root of the challenges they have had as a result of her difficulties: her not having been in touch with her feelings because of her fear and unprocessed early experience of abandonment by an attachment figure.

## CONCLUSION

This clinical example illustrates how the therapist's moment-to-moment clinical decision-making is guided by the three representational schemas discussed in this chapter, along with the four-state transformational model. Working with the patient's movement toward and away from emotional experience (Triangle of Experience; State 1), the therapist helps G regulate and explore emergent signals that lead her to encounter unresolved historical material that is triggered by her current life experience. The therapist's attunement and tracking of the patient on the Triangle of Experience helps the therapist know whether defense work or anxiety regulation is needed to continue the unfolding of a bodily rooted experience: emotion. By offering the mirroring and understanding that was sorely lacking when she was as a child, the therapist entrains a new Self–Other–Emotion configuration of self-at-best for the patient, which stabilizes the patient's working through what was blocked by her self-at-worst. By affirming each opening to her inner world, noting how she receives my attunement and encouragement (S-O-E Triangle), we are able to foster a new connection between her present self and younger self, linking what is triggered by her current relationship with her husband to the historical wounding by her father. (Triangle of Relational Comparisons; State 2). With deep facilitation by the Therapeutic connection, as the wires from the neural circuitry of her Past history are differentiated from her Current relationship, she not only brings soothing to the aspect of herself that has been so alone in devastating loss, she is also able to reflect on (four-state transformational model: State 3) and understand her current reactivity with her husband (four-state transformational model: State 4). Operating from a now-integrated brain and supported by an attuned and responsive therapeutic relationship, she "knows" what she needs and what she wants to share with him.

When therapists can truly be present with the experience of what emerges, noticing and mapping out how patient's process unfolds on our representational schemas, we can intervene precisely and deliberately, attuned and in sync. Keeping AEDP's representational schemas in mind allows therapists to stay close to and in service of patients. Adjusting interventions to match patients' responses each step of the way helps them repair lost connections with their emotional experience and then process it to completion. Therapists' participation thus builds new possibilities and expectancies of Self and Other. This sensitive and deliberate engagement excites the very neural pathways that need stimulation to evoke the positive neuroplasticity most fitting for each patient to achieve transformational outcomes in AEDP.

## REFERENCES

Ainsworth, M., Blehar, M., Waters, E., & Wall, S. (1978). *Patterns of attachment: A psychological study of the strange situation*. Lawrence Erlbaum Associates.

Beebe, B., & Lachman, F. M. (1998). Co-constructing inner and relational processes: Self and mutual regulation in infant research and adult treatment. *Psychoanalytic Psychology, 15*(4), 480–516. https://doi.org/10.1037/0736-9735.15.4.480

Beebe, B., & Lachman, F. M. (2014). *Origins of attachment: Infant research and adult treatment*. Routledge.

Bowlby, J. (1982). *Attachment and loss: Vol. 1. Attachment*. Basic Books. (Original work published 1969)

Bowlby, J. (1988). *A secure base*. Basic Books.

Cassidy, J., & Kobak, R. R. (1988). Avoidance and its relationship with other defensive processes. In J. Belsky & T. Nezworski (Eds.), *Clinical implications of attachment* (pp. 300–323). Lawrence Erlbaum Associates.

Cozolino, L. (2006). *The neuroscience of human relationships: Attachment and the developing social brain*. Norton.

Darwin, C. R. (1872). *The expression of the emotions in man and animals*. John Murray. https://doi.org/10.1037/10001-000

Doidge, N. (2007). *The brain that changes itself*. Penguin Books.

Ecker, B., Ticic, R., & Hulley, L. (2012). *Unlocking the emotional brain: Eliminating symptoms at their roots using memory reconsolidation*. Routledge. https://doi.org/10.4324/9780203804377

Fosha, D. (2000). *The transformational power of affect*. Basic Books.

Fosha, D. (2002). The activation of affective change processes in AEDP. In J. J. Magnavita (Ed.), *Comprehensive handbook of psychotherapy: Vol. 1. Psychodynamic and object relations psychotherapies* (pp. 309–344). John Wiley & Sons.

Fosha, D. (2003). Dyadic regulation and experiential work with emotion and related-ness in trauma and disordered attachment. In M. F. Solomon & D. J. Siegel (Eds.), *Healing trauma: Attachment, mind, body, and brain* (pp. 221–281). Norton.

Fosha, D. (2007). Transformance, recognition of self by self, and effective action. In K. J. Schneider (Ed.), *Existential-integrative psychotherapy: Guideposts to the core of practice* (pp. 290–320). Routledge.

Fosha, D. (2009). Emotion and recognition at work: Energy, vitality, pleasure, truth, desire & the emergent phenomenology of transformational experience. In D. Fosha, D. J. Siegel, & M. F. Solomon (Eds.), *The healing power of emotion: Affective neuroscience, development, clinical practice* (pp. 172–203). Norton.

Fosha, D. (2017). How to be a transformational therapist: AEDP harnesses innate healing affects to re-wire experience and accelerate transformation. In J. Loizzo, M. Neale, & E. Wolf (Eds.), *Advances in contemplative psychotherapy: Accelerating transformation* (pp. 204–219). Norton. https://doi.org/10.4324/9781315630045-18

Frijda, N. H. (1986). *The emotions*. Cambridge University Press.

Gendlin, E. (1981). *Focusing*. Random House. (Original work published 1978)

Hebb, D. O. (1949). *The organization of behavior*. John Wiley & Sons.

James, W. (1902). *The varieties of religious experience: A study in human nature*. Penguin Books. https://doi.org/10.1037/10004-000

Levine, P. (1997). *Waking the tiger: Healing trauma*. North Atlantic Books.

Lipton, B., & Fosha, D. (2011). Attachment as a transformative process in AEDP: Operationalizing the intersection of attachment theory and affective neuroscience. *Journal of Psychotherapy Integration, 21*(3), 253–279. https://doi.org/10.1037/a0025421

Main, M., Hesse, E., & Kaplan, N. (2005). Predictability of attachment behavior and representational processes at 1, 6, and 19 years of age: The Berkeley Longitudinal Study. In K. E. Grossmann, K. Grossmann, & E. Waters (Eds.), *Attachment from infancy to adulthood: The major longitudinal studies* (pp. 245–304). Guilford Press.

McCullough Vaillant, L. (1997). *Changing character*. Basic Books.

Pando-Mars, K. (2011). Building attachment bonds in AEDP in the wake of neglect and abandonment: Through the lens and practice of AEDP, attachment and polyvagal theory. *Transformance: The AEDP Journal, 1*(2). https://aedpinstitute.org/wp-content/uploads/page_Building-Attachment-Bonds-in-the-Wake-of-Neglect-and-Abandonment.pdf

Pando-Mars, K. (2016). Tailoring treatment interventions to attachment style. *Transformance: The AEDP Journal, 6*(2). https://aedpinstitute.org/wp-content/uploads/2016/11/tailoring-aedp-interventions-to-attachment-style.pdf

Pando-Mars, K., & Fosha, D. (2020). *Tailoring psychotherapy interventions to attachment style: Healing relational trauma with an experiential approach* [Manuscript in preparation]. Norton.

Siegel, D. (2017). *Mind: A journey to the heart of being human*. Norton.

Solomon, M., & Siegel, D. J. (2017). *How people change: Relationships and neuroplasticity in psychotherapy*. Norton.

Tronick, E. Z. (2009). Multilevel meaning making and dyadic expansion of consciousness theory: The polymorphic polysemic flow of meaning. In D. Fosha, D. J. Siegel, & M. F. Solomon (Eds.), *The healing power of emotion: Affective neuroscience, development, clinical practice* (pp. 86–111). Norton.

van der Hart, O., Nijenhuis, E. R. S., & Solomon, R. (2010). Dissociation of the Personality in Complex Trauma-Related Disorders and EMDR: Theoretical Considerations. *Journal of EMDR Practice and Research, 4*(2), 76. https://doi.org/10.1891/1933-3196.4.2.76

# III

# HOW TO WORK WITH CORE AFFECTIVE EXPERIENCE: ATTACHMENT, EMOTION, SELF

# 7

# Neuroplasticity in Action

## Rewiring Internal Working Models of Attachment

Ronald J. Frederick

Early attachment experiences between caregiver and child shape emotional development and leave lasting imprints on the neural circuitry of the brain (Costello, 2013; Cozolino, 2014; Fosha, 2003; Frederick, 2019; Schore, 2019; Siegel, 2015). Potent lessons about emotion and connection—about who we are, how relationships work, and what we can expect from others—become represented and internalized, forming what Bowlby (1969) referred to as internal working models of self and other in relationship. Left unchallenged, these implicit lessons persist into adulthood where, for better or worse (relative to the quality of one's early attachment experience), they continue to color perception and guide behavior.

Accelerated experiential dynamic psychotherapy (AEDP) understands psychopathology as a by-product of internal working models, borne out of internalized insecure attachment experiences, that now thwart adaptive functioning in adulthood. Motivated by the biological imperative to preserve the attachment bond and avoid unbearable aloneness in the face of intense affect, individuals learn to adjust their emotional repertoire by *defensively excluding*[1] those aspects of one's emotional experience that seem to negatively impact the caregiver and, thus, threaten relational security (Bowlby, 1979; Costello, 2013; Fosha, 2000). Although adaptive at the time of their development,

---

[1]Bowlby (1980) originally defined defensive exclusion as an adaptive coping strategy that enables one to process information (e.g., emotional, cognitive, perceptual) in a manner that prevents the conscious awareness, and, thus, the associated pain, of unmet attachment needs.

https://doi.org/10.1037/0000232-008

*Undoing Aloneness and the Transformation of Suffering Into Flourishing: AEDP 2.0*, D. Fosha (Editor)

these survival strategies come at a high cost because they compromise one's inborn ability to feel, communicate, and connect.

But internal working models are not immutable and can be rewired in response to new relational experiences—those in which adaptive emotional expression is welcomed and will not have untoward effects on relationship security. Along with how it understands the formation of psychopathology, there is a recognition of what in AEDP is called *transformance*—the "overarching motivational force, operating both in development and therapy, that strives toward maximal vitality, authenticity, and genuine contact" (Fosha, 2008, p. 292). We are wired to self-right, connect, and grow and the capacity to do so is ever present. Therefore, side by side with working models of insecure attachment based on past experiences is the innate potential to develop a secure attachment based on corrective here-and-now experiences.

Grounded in this understanding and with an awareness of the capacity for positive neuroplasticity, the AEDP therapist aims to facilitate a corrective attachment experience from the get-go in which it is clear that the patient will not be alone with overwhelming emotions (see also Kranz, Chapter 2, this volume). Through explicit empathy, affirmation, and emotional engagement and an embodied willingness to help (i.e., dyadic affect regulation), the therapist facilitates a relational experience in which the motivational vector can decisively tilt toward self-righting, and transformation can occur. In other words, the patient can feel safe enough to shed the constraints of the past and allow defensively excluded, core aspects of the self to come to the fore and be reintegrated into one's emotional repertoire, thus disconfirming and rewiring one's early relational programming in support of adaptive emotional functioning. To that end, *relational processing*, in which relational experiences between the patient and therapist are made explicit, experientially explored, and processed in the service of healing and transformation, takes center stage in AEDP.

Yet the therapist's provision of empathic attunement, responsivity, and care is often not sufficient for deep transformation to occur (Ecker et al., 2012; Fosha, 2009b), particularly when the history of relational trauma is prominent. In many cases, defenses against fully receiving what was once longed for can be formidable and obstructive to the process. For treatment to be effective, the new relational experience offered by the therapist needs to be fully registered, received, and experienced by the patient (Fosha, 2017). In other words, that which is offered needs to be received. The patient needs to be willing to open up to and lean into a new and different experience. Only then can internal working models based on what once was (i.e., the there-and-then) be disconfirmed, reworked, and updated to reflect what is now possible (i.e., the here-and-now). Therefore, increasing the patient's *receptive affective capacity* is a primary focus of the treatment (Fosha, 2009a; McCullough Vaillant, 1997).

This chapter examines the various methods by which the AEDP therapist helps to diminish the need for defenses against yearned for attachment experiences so that patients can take in what is being offered to them, new learning can take place, attachment schemas can be reworked, and healthy functioning can be restored. The chapter begins with a discussion of AEDP's understanding of how defenses develop and are maintained over time, highlighting the central role of implicitly stored, internal working models of attachment and their impact on one's nervous system.

I then explore how the AEDP therapist helps to grow the patient's awareness of and presence with his or her emotional process by *making the implicit explicit and the explicit experiential*. Key here is the patient's capacity to "take in and experience" the therapist's care, empathy, and so forth. Interventions aimed at "melting," bypassing, and restructuring defenses erected specifically against relational experience (being affected by and having an effect on a significant other) with an eye toward tracking and focusing on right brain processes, working within and yet also expanding the patient's window of tolerance, and expanding his or her receptive affective capacity over time are discussed.

We also look at how three representational schemas—the Triangle of Experience, the Self–Other–Emotion Triangle, and the Triangle of Relational Comparisons—help the therapist to make sense of the patient's behavior, structure listening, and serve as guides that inform how best to intervene at any given moment in the therapeutic process to promote change and more specifically a transformational change in the patient's internal working model of self and other in relationship.

Lastly, to illustrate relational processing, I describe clinical material from two separate psychotherapy sessions that proved pivotal in fostering a major transformation in the relational capacity—both expressive and receptive—of the featured patient. Detailed transcript material is microanalyzed to illustrate AEDP interventions involved in restructuring defenses and reworking internal working models of self and other.

## WHERE TROUBLE STARTS

Attachment theory, one of the most empirically supported perspectives on human development and relationships, explains how our early emotional experiences with our caregivers shape who we are, how we see the world, and how we behave in relationships. Initially proposed by British psychiatrist John Bowlby, it is based on the assertion that, as human beings, our need to be in a close relationship with an other *"perceived* as older and wiser" (i.e., an attachment figure) is fundamental to our existence, starting from the time we're born and continuing throughout our lives (Bowlby, 1979). Our primary instinct, wired in by evolution, is to seek contact, comfort, and connection and to form a safe and secure bond.

At no point in our lives is this more apparent than when we are just born. As infants, we come into the world completely helpless, entirely reliant on our caregivers to take care of, bathe, clothe, and feed us; to soothe our fear and distress; and to protect us from harm. In addition, our social and emotional development is dependent on our parents being attuned, responsive, and engaged with us as the brain grows through stimulating interaction. Thus, our caregivers are our lifeline, and we are biologically programmed to develop and build a connection with them. If we didn't, we wouldn't survive.

It then follows that maintaining a secure attachment with one's caregivers is a high-stakes matter, and the drive to do so overrides all other primary needs. Therefore, children do whatever it takes to stay connected to their caregivers to prevent the possibility of loss or abandonment, which, to an infant or child, is the equivalent of death. As humans, we are motivated to maintain a secure connection with our primary caregivers at all costs. That motivation operates, as Bowlby also said, "from the cradle to the grave," activated, in particular, during times of fear, distress, or illness.

While physical closeness provides an important source of connection, the main way in which infants experience a connection with their caregivers and how it gets encoded in the brain is through emotion (Fosha, 2000; Schore, 1994). They sense and experience connection and disconnection through their emotions and the emotional responses they engender in their caregivers as well as through the emotional state and expression of others (Beebe, 2000; Schore, 1994; Trevarthen & Aitken, 1994; Tronick, 1989). Without words to express themselves, everything is communicated in the nonverbal, emotional realm—through the right brain "language" of the face, the eyes, and the body, and through touch, sounds, vocal tones, and rhythms. Infants let others know about their experience through emotional expression and, in return, they learn about others, themselves, and the world by sensing and reading their caregiver's emotional reactions. Attachment security is borne out of a synchronized dance of attuned and responsive right-brain-to-right-brain emotional communication between infant and caregiver.

As such, infants are extremely sensitive to the emotional cues they receive. When their caregivers are emotionally open and reliably responsive, children feel securely attached and, in turn, safe to explore their affective being, their relationships, and their ever-widening world. In addition, they develop the ability to balance and make good use of their emotions, calm and soothe themselves, and emotionally relate to and connect with others. Thus, they develop a capacity to "feel and deal, while relating"—to regulate their affective experience and be emotionally present and engaged with another—essential components of healthy functioning (Fosha, 2000, p. 42).

However, when caregivers react negatively to a child's emotional needs—for instance, become frustrated when the child feels afraid and needs their reassurance, withdraw when the child is hurt and needs to be soothed, or are admonishing when the child expresses anger or is assertive—it signals a threat to one's survival, and over time, through associative learning, the child comes to fear emotional experience and expression. Instead of feeling emotionally safe to explore relationships and the world in a way that fosters learning and growth, the child becomes anxious and holds back certain feelings, needs, and desires, adjusting behavior to avoid the danger of disconnection from the primary attachment figures. In short, children adapt by suppressing emotions that threaten a sense of safety and security and amplifying those that seem to allow for some degree of connection.

These potent lessons about emotion and connection—about how relationships work and what we can anticipate—form instructional blueprints, or what Bowlby (1980) referred to as "internal working models." Attachment experiences with one's caregivers become represented and internalized as schemas, templates, or maps that are stored in implicit memory, the only form of memory available to us early in life. They contain a set of beliefs and expectations about the self, one's own and other people's behavior, one's self-worth, whether one is lovable, and whether individuals can depend on others to be there for them. Encoded in the brain and expressed through the neurophysiology of the body, internal working models influence and shape one's affective experience, exploratory behavior, and relationship to the attachment figure. Constructed in and based on the past, they persist into and throughout one's adult life and color the individual's perceptions of self and other, govern the nervous system, and guide one's behavior. In short, they develop into the unconscious programming that dictates how one does relationships and are reflected in the attachment style the individual develops.

Defensively excluding core affective experience from one's emotional repertoire is adaptive for children because it maximizes the caretaking and connection they receive. But these survival strategies come at a high cost, as they compromise individuals' inborn ability to feel, communicate, and share their core affective experience. Vital aspects of the self, essential to healthy functioning, are dissociated, and the individual is deprived of the resources one's emotions would afford. Over time, constrained by less-than-optimal early programming, psychological development is thwarted, and emotional and interpersonal functioning is impaired. It is the continued effect of these early learnings and the subsequent "misshaping" of the self that underly the conditions for which people seek treatment (Costello, 2013). And it is the undoing of these learnings and the restoration of adaptive functioning that inform and guide an AEDP treatment.

## UPDATING THE WIRING

By definition, internal working models are not immutable and can be updated. As is now well known, the brain remains malleable over a lifetime and reorganizes or "rewires" itself in response to new experiences—a capacity known as *neuroplasticity*. When implicit memories and their associated emotions are activated, they become amenable to change, and adaptive information can then be incorporated (Lane et al., 2015). In fact, evidence suggests that when implicit learnings are activated or "unlocked" and come into direct contact with what researchers term a "mismatch experience"—one that disconfirms learned expectations—prior learning may be dissolved or erased (Ecker, 2015). Thus, old wiring is reworked, and new wiring is forged through emotional experiences that diverge from usual stimulus-response patterns and, as such, lead to different outcomes.

Through the experience of a different, more optimal attachment relationship, neural structure can be changed. As Bowlby (1988) suggested, therapy for attachment trauma requires that the patient have new learning experiences of what was originally missing. Thus, internal working models of insecure attachment are updated through new, positive relational experiences—those in which adaptive emotional experience and expression are welcomed and will not have untoward effects on attachment security. However, for new relational learning to take place, patients need to feel safe enough to venture outside of the dictates of their early wiring and have the kinds of dyadic experiences that will foster secure attachment and healthy affective functioning. AEDP provides, entrains, and facilitates such experiences.

While brain change is experience dependent, several factors have been shown to foster and enhance positive neuroplasticity (Hanson, 2017; Schwartz & Gladding, 2012; Siegel, 2012). They include (a) *novelty*—experiences that diverge from the usual and expected stimulate neuronal firing; (b) *attention*—neurons fire and wire together in regard to what is in one's field of focused awareness; (c) *emotional arousal and intensity*—the more intense and embodied the experience, yet still within the window of tolerance, the stronger the subsequent neuronal connections; (d) *duration*—the longer one intentionally engages in a particular experience, the more firing and wiring occurs; (e) *repetition*—the more often one engages in a particular action or behavior, the stronger neuronal patterns become; and (f) *relationships*—attuned, resonant, and dyadic relational experience fosters brain growth and neural integration. As we will see, all of these factors are put to maximal use in an AEDP treatment.

The work of AEDP consists of three central processes: (a) the formation of a progressively more secure and open relationship between therapist and patient; (b) the processing and transformation of the old experiences in which once defended against core affective experiences are processed to completion, true self states are fostered and integrated, and adaptive functioning is restored; and (c) the metaprocessing of the new experiences that emerge from the work. As Fosha (2005) stated, "The therapeutic process aims towards a transformation that will produce a state where the misshaping effects of procedural knowledge will be transcended, and the self will emerge from the shadow cast by its history" (p. 543). The transformational process that AEDP has described, with its four states and three state transformations, both traces and, when fostered and worked through to completion, enables such transformations to occur.

From the get-go, the AEDP therapist seeks to create a safe and affect-facilitating environment in which the patient's defenses against authentic relating are no longer deemed necessary and innate capacities for self-righting, growth, and healing can come to the fore (see also Kranz, Chapter 2, this volume). Drawing on the characteristics of an emotionally competent or "good-enough" caregiver and by responding in a manner that is attuned to the particular needs of the individual, the AEDP therapist aims to be dyadic—explicitly empathic, affirming, emotionally engaged, and affect-regulating—thus cocreating the "secure base" from which constructive risk taking and emotional exploration can proceed and positive neuroplasticity is enabled and potentiated (Lipton & Fosha, 2011).

However, it is not sufficient for an emotionally engaged other to be on the scene; he or she needs to be present and accounted for. The therapist's empathic engagement needs to be made explicit and not only register for the patient but also be taken in and experienced for it to have impact. A way of being for the therapist that might be relegated to the background in another model of therapy becomes foreground in AEDP. Throughout treatment, the therapist's emotional offering and the patient's dyadic experience of it is made explicit, attended to, and experientially explored. In addition, for deep change to occur, the patient needs to be able to receive, be affected by, and make good use of the therapist's empathy, love, and care. Right brain processes need to be engaged to activate and rework implicitly stored, right-brain-mediated, internal working models. For, as Schore (2003, 2012) has explained, right-hemisphere-to-right-hemisphere contingent contact is the "golden road" to neural change and healing (Badenoch, 2008). Therefore, the work of therapy needs to be infused with emotion, and the patient's experience needs to be embodied and felt.

Given that attachment strivings are innate and that we are wired to connect, engaging with a good-enough other is often sufficient to tip the motivational vector toward adaptive emotional expression and relating. As the therapist undoes the patient's aloneness and empathizes with that individual's emotional truth, the forces of transformance—wired-in dispositions for self-healing, self-righting, and resuming impeded growth—galvanize the therapeutic process and lead the way toward actualization (Fosha, 2009a). The path toward healing is illuminated and, although there may be bumps to navigate along the way, the therapeutic dyad is in working order, and the way forward naturally unfolds.

## Relational Processing and Metaprocessing

However, treatment often requires a more concerted and sustained effort on the part of the therapist to loosen the patient's defenses to allow for a new way of engaging to emerge and take hold. Although some attachment schemas are more amenable to updating, others can remain insulated in implicit memory and impervious to the therapist's efforts (Ecker et al., 2012). Memories created in the presence of strong affect—as is the case in attachment schemas—are stored in specialized subcortical structures that are extremely durable (Roozendaal et al., 2009), especially when not countered by corrective relational experiences that are accompanied by equally strong affect.

Working relationally, in and of itself, tends to reactivate insecure attachment learnings that, for some people, can prompt formidable barriers to emotional connection. In such cases, while patients may consciously know they are safe with their therapist, their nervous system tells them otherwise, and procedural learning prevails. In addition, emotionally opening up to another person not only goes against the dictates of one's neural programming but can also give rise to the dreaded pain of unmet attachment needs, disavowed feelings, and unprocessed memories. Thus, the AEDP therapist needs to be skilled at helping the patient relinquish long-held defenses against relational affective experience and expression and to do so in a way that allows for a positive, transformative experience. Only then can old internal working models be reworked and updated to fully reflect what is now possible.

## Defense Work

Defense work requires a close tracking and rapid analysis of the unfolding moment-to-moment process to enable the disruption of deeply entrenched patterns of responding, undo defensive exclusion, and allow patients' innate emotional and relational strivings to be felt and reintegrated into their affective repertoire. Defensive strategies that are more activating in nature, as in the "feeling, and reeling, but not dealing" (Fosha, 2000, p. 43) of patients who exhibit resistant or preoccupied attachment, will need to be regulated to reveal what aspect of the patient's core affective experience is getting lost in the swirl of distress (Fosha, 2000; Pando-Mars, 2016). In contrast, deactivating strategies, as in the "dealing but not feeling" (Fosha, 2000, p. 43) of patients exhibiting an avoidant attachment, will need to be softened to allow underlying affective experience to be felt (Fosha, 2000; Pando-Mars, 2016). In all cases, the therapist is working to expand the patient's capacity to "feel, and deal, while relating" (Fosha, 2000, p. 42) with another—a capacity indicative of an internal working model of secure attachment (Fosha, 2000).

Working collaboratively with the patient, from an "engaged, empathic, side-by-side stance" (Fosha, 2000, p. 247), the AEDP therapist uses a variety of clinical strategies to restructure the patient's emotional dynamics and enable adaptive affective processing of both emotional and relational experience (Fosha, 2000). As the patients' defenses and associated distress are often outside of their awareness, the therapist may draw their attention to what is happening for them in the present moment. The objective here is multi-faceted: To grow patients' mindful awareness of their behavior as well as what is emotionally happening for them and for them to begin to put words to their experience, to connect right and left brain, and to create space for alternative, more adaptive ways of responding. What was heretofore implicit becomes explicit and then, in turn, is made an *experiential* focus of the work (Lipton & Fosha, 2011). In addition, by cultivating an observational stance on the part of the patient, their underlying distress (that which is prompting defensive responding in the first place) gets regulated and renders defenses less necessary (Frederick, 2009, 2019). The patient can then enter a window of affective tolerance more conducive to exploration, discovery, and transformation.

Part and parcel of the intensely experiential relational work, AEDP therapists judiciously disclose their emotional experience in response to the patient. Such a disclosure can not only disarm patients' defenses but also stimulate the emergence of their core affective experience (Prenn, 2009, 2011). In particular, "pressuring with empathy"—the therapist's explicit self-disclosure of feeling compassion, warmth, and appreciation for the patient—can be a powerful intervention to bypass defenses (Russell & Fosha, 2008, p. 181). In addition, as internal working models of self and other are created by affectively charged dyadic experience, the therapist's emotional disclosure and presence also allow the relationship, and associated affects, to come alive. Patients feel "felt" (Siegel, 2010) and experience their impact on another, and vice versa. In this way, AEDP can be considered an exposure therapy of sorts where "the therapist is the intervention" (S. Piliero, personal communication, October, 2012) and expanding the patient's receptive affective capacity is paramount.

The therapist might also highlight the cost of patients' defenses by making explicit how, while momentarily providing a sense of safety, contribute to their suffering and keep them from having what they truly desire. Such an intervention can soften the patient's defenses by evoking an emotional response on behalf of the self and catalyze a desire to respond. The patient then feels emboldened to risk moving in a different, more constructive direction, one more aligned with the individual's core emotional truth.

Oftentimes, the work proceeds slowly, with successive approximations toward a greater capacity for openness. At other times, the work's cumulative effect will lead to quantum shifts in experiencing, as we see in the case that follows. Prolonged and repeated exposure to the here-and-now corrective and affirming relational experience within a session and over the course of treatment, while fostering positive neuroplasticity, may be necessary to disconfirm one's unconscious expectations, disarm defenses, and break through to adaptive affective states and communications. Throughout, the therapist titrates exposure to the new, allowing the patient to experientially adapt to each step taken, before moving forward. Over time, the patient's affective capacity and ability to stay connected while relating is expanded, deepened, and strengthened.

As patients' behavior begins to shift, as they take risks and open up to new emotional and relational experiences, the AEDP therapist invites them to reflect on what has occurred and accomplished and on new ways of being both within the self and with another. Through such "metatherapeutic processing" of one's experience, each moment is then symbolized and woven into patients' narratives (Fosha, 2000; Lipton & Fosha, 2011; Prenn, 2011). Left and right brain come together, and new ways of being are integrated and downloaded into a new more comprehensive, flexible, and adaptive internal working model.

## WORKING ON THE CUSP OF CHANGE

Change for the better, however longed for, is often a daunting process. Patient and therapist come face-to-face with the terror of abandonment and rejection that, despite being encoded long ago, feels present and real to the patient. In addition, navigating the new tremulous emotional waters involved in closeness, care, connection, and receptivity, can feel overwhelming. At each turn, the potential to default to the safe and known—the procedural—can be tempting. To catalyze healing and transformation, therapists need to be able to recognize and work with defenses, anxiety, and repeated relational patterns when they arise, as well as the emergence, however small, of core affective experience and their associated attachment strivings (Fosha, 2000). To that end, the AEDP therapist uses three representational schemas to make sense of the patient's moment-to-moment behavior, structure listening, and guide one's interventions. These schemas, noted earlier, are the *Triangle of Experience*, the *Self–Other–Emotion Triangle*, and the *Triangle of Relational Comparisons* (see also Pando-Mars, Chapter 6, this volume).

## TOOLS OF THE TRADE

Starting up close and personal, we have the Triangle of Experience (Figure 7.1). Derived from a long history of short-term psychodynamic therapy models, it graphically depicts what happens when anxiety-provoking core affective phenomena get activated in the patient. As such, it lays bare the coding of one's internal working models by illuminating learned patterns of responding that were developed early in life in an environment that was inimical to genuine relating and to the experiencing or expression of genuine emotion and that continue to govern the patient's nervous system and subsequent behavior.

By identifying and graphically separating out the main aspects of one's emotional experience (defenses, inhibitory affects, and core affective phenomena) and then illustrating how they relate to one another (how the emergence of core affect gives rise to inhibitory affects that now prompt defensive responding), the triangle enables the therapist to understand what is happening for the patient in any given moment. Once the in-session locale on the Triangle of Experience is determined, the therapist can then assess how best to respond. For instance, if we are in the land of relational defenses (the "D" corner of the triangle), we can ask ourselves what needs to happen to render them unnecessary so that the patient can safely open up to the new experience with the therapist and the associated affective phenomena. If we're in the realm of red-signal, inhibitory affects (the "A" corner), what do we need to do to help regulate and calm the patient so that receptive affective capacity can be increased and emotional experiencing can be allowed to come to the fore? And if we are in the presence of adaptive attachment strivings and associated core affective experiences (the "E" corner), what do we need to do to foster, regulate, and process them through to completion?

On the basis of the patient's in session presentation (as well as through self-report), the therapist can step back a bit and begin to put the pieces together about the patient's early experiences in life. The Self–Other–Emotion Triangle (Figure 7.2) captures the relational matrix within which emotional experience occurs and highlights the role that the "Other," be that other a caregiver (there-and-then) or therapist (here-and-now) plays in just how that experience will or will not unfold. As a direct translation of the internal

**FIGURE 7.1. The Triangle of Experience**

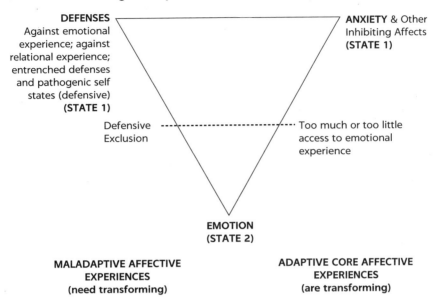

**DEFENSES**
Against emotional
experience; against
relational experience;
entrenched defenses
and pathogenic self
states (defensive)
**(STATE 1)**

**ANXIETY** & Other
Inhibiting Affects
**(STATE 1)**

Defensive
Exclusion

Too much or too little
access to emotional
experience

**EMOTION
(STATE 2)**

**MALADAPTIVE AFFECTIVE
EXPERIENCES
(need transforming)**

**ADAPTIVE CORE AFFECTIVE
EXPERIENCES
(are transforming)**

**Legend: Affective Experiences**

**Maladaptive Affective Experiences**
The Pathogenic Affects (e.g., Overwhelm, Toxic Shame, Fear
Without Solution); Unbearable States of Traumatic Aloneness
(e.g., Helplessness, Fragmentation, Brokenness; Despair, "The
Black Hole Of Trauma")

**Adaptive Core Affective Experiences**
Categorical Emotions; Relational Experiences, Asymmetric
(Attachment) or Symmetric (Intersubjective); Coordinated
Relational Experiences; Receptive Affective Experiences; Somatic
"Drop-Down" States; Intrarelational Experiences; Authentic
Self-Experiences; Experiences of Agency, Will Desire; Attachment
Strivings; The Expression of Core Needs

*Note.* Copyright © 2020 by Diana Fosha. Reprinted with permission.

working model, the Self–Other–Emotion Triangle depicts how patients' relationships with their primary caregivers influenced their experience and shaped their emotional programming. From patients' here and now experience, whether what occurs in session or in other contexts in their present-day life, we can trace a line back in time to a relational context that bore fruit, that either supported or hindered authentic self-expression. Moreover, although the Self–Other–Emotion Triangle can provide us with a window into the past, it can also serve as a guide for healing. Just as patients' primary caregivers had

**FIGURE 7.2. The Self–Other–Emotion Triangle: Two Versions of the Self–Other–Emotion Triangle—The Self-at-Worst and the Self-at-Best**

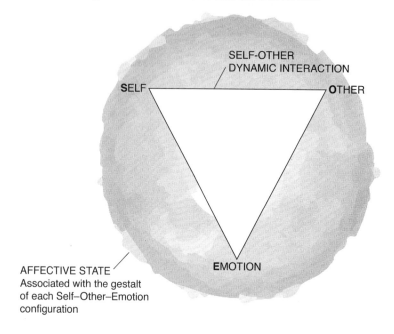

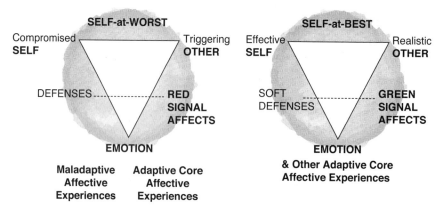

*Note.* Copyright © 2020 by Diana Fosha. Reprinted with permission.

bearing on their emotional experiences, so now does the therapist. As we contemplate how to help our patients heal, we can ask ourselves, what would a corrective Self–Other–Emotion Triangle look like? How are we helping or hindering the patient's emotional experience? How and in what ways do we need to emotionally show up to facilitate a new, growth enhancing experience?

Lastly, stepping back to take in the whole picture, the Triangle of Relational Comparisons (Figure 7.3) illustrates how one's internal working models of self and other and their concomitant patterns of responding are carried forward

**FIGURE 7.3. The Triangle of Relational Comparisons**

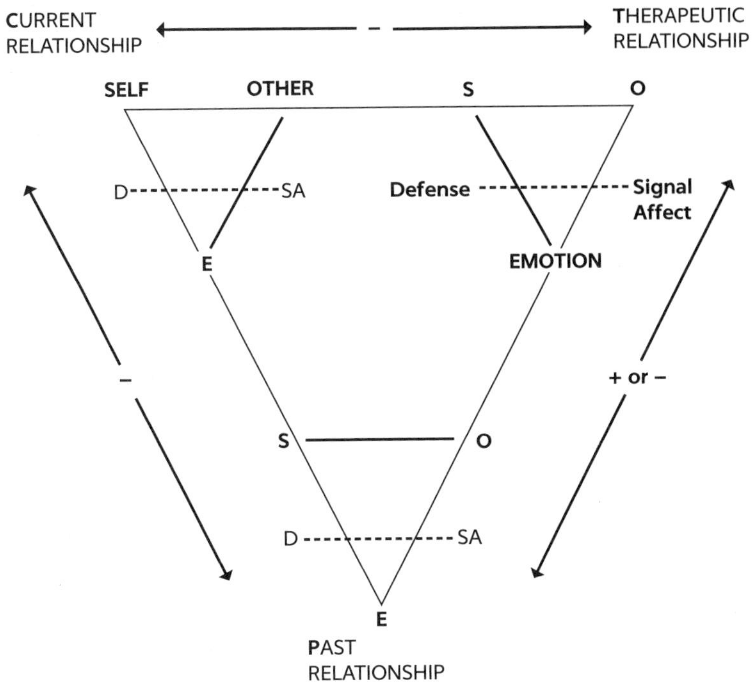

Legend:
– **(Minus)** = **Repetition** (Old, Same, Same Old Same Old)
+ **(Plus)** = **Corrective Experience** (New, Different)

| **Triangle of Relational Comparisons** | **Self-Other Emotion Triangle (Self-at-Worst or Self-at-Best)** | **Triangle of Experience (Self-at-Worst or Self-at-Best)** |
|---|---|---|
| C   Current Relationship | S   Self | D   Defense |
| T   Therapeutic Relationship | O   Other | SA   Signal Affects (Red or Green) |
| P   Past Relationship | E   Emotion | E   Emotion |

*Note.* Copyright © 2020 by Diana Fosha. Reprinted with permission.

across time. We see what they were like in the *past* relationships in which they originated (the "P" corner) and how they may be showing up (or not) in both the patient's *current* relationships (the "C" corner), as well as in the moment-to-moment *therapeutic* relationship (the "T" corner). The AEDP therapist is always on the lookout for either repetitions or healing exceptions—hence the name the Triangle of Relational Comparisons. How are the old and the current related? Are they the same or different? Are the relational patterns under examination in the therapy (i.e., a current relationship or the therapeutic relationship itself) a repetition of the old pathology-engendering early patterns, or do they reflect a new corrective experience? A line can be traced from the past to the present, as well as from the present to the past, that links together all three corners of the triangle. As such, the triangle of comparisons provides a lens through which the therapist can make historical sense of various aspects of the patient's emotional and relational experience. In addition, we can see how present relationships that provide a corrective experience, stand in contrast to what came before. Although the past often casts a long shadow, the AEDP therapist is on the lookout for glimmers of adaptive strivings, however inchoate or masked, that, with proper intervention and care, can be fostered and harnessed in the service of transformation. Thus, ties to the past can be broken, and the patient's core self can come more fully into the present. A new, more coherent and cohesive autobiographical narrative—a marker of secure attachment—then emerges in which patients can see how their past influenced their experience and how new ways of being stand in contrast to what came before.

With these tools, the aforementioned interventions, and the six factors that promote positive neuroplasticity in mind, let us turn our attention to the clinical work.

## CLINICAL ILLUSTRATION

The patient is a partnered gay man in his early 30s who sought treatment for a chronic, underlying depression.[2] Although having achieved some success in his career, he reported feeling uninspired and empty, without any sense of what might bring him pleasure. While intrigued by his partner, he described him as stubborn and controlling, and, overall, felt dissatisfied with their relationship. Finding people irritating and unlikeable, he had few, if any, close friends. Of historical note, the patient's parents divorced when he was a child. His father moved out and became distant; his mother, consumed with work and the demands of attending to their children on her own, was less present. Here we see where the seeds of an avoidant attachment style were sown, leaving the patient self-sufficient but disconnected from others and estranged from his emotional self.

Early therapeutic work, which sought to foster relational safety and "emotional mindfulness" (i.e., awareness of and presence with emotional experience), was slow going (Frederick, 2009, 2019). The patient was often at a loss when asked to attune to and elaborate on his inner experience. The session material that follows is from two separate sessions that occurred about midway into a 2-year treatment. The italicized comments in parentheses

---

[2]I have complied with American Psychological Association ethical standards in describing the details of treatment; aspects of the patient's identity and background have been disguised to protect confidentiality.

describe the nonverbal aspects of the interaction, and bolded comments in brackets are about the process.

### Vignette 1

The session starts with the patient sharing thoughts and realizations he has been having about his relationship with his partner. He states that he is not sure that what they have is enough to sustain a healthy relationship. The therapist stops the process to share his appreciation of the patient's growing clarity. The patient seems slightly taken aback, looks puzzled, and responds, "I guess I am too." His answer seeming more like a coping than an embodied expression of agreement. The patient then proceeds to recount a story in which an older friend recently disclosed to him that she never really loved her partner of many years. The patient shares being astonished by this disclosure because he had assumed otherwise and states, with some agency, "I don't want to wake up in 10 or 20 years and still be frustrated with my relationship and have it be 10 times as hard to cut ties." It is here that we enter the scene.

THERAPIST:   So Russell, I'm just really moved by what you said. You want something different for yourself. **[emotional disclosure]**

PATIENT:   Umm (*crossing his arms and holding himself, uncomfortable*). **[Patient is in the "D" corner of the triangle of experience.]**

THERAPIST:   **[Priming positive neuroplasticity by focusing patient's attention on new (novel) relational experience and making implicit emotional process explicit]** Can I just ask you something? What happens? A moment ago, I said that I'm really appreciating your clarity. You said, "I am too" and then got into a story. And, right now, I tell you I'm really moved by what you're saying, and you go like this (*mirrors patient's puzzled expression*). I'm not sure what happens. Whether what I say lands somewhere for you or . . .? **[Initially, the patient's innate receptivity appears to come on line as he seems open and curious. But by the time the therapist is finished speaking, he is back to seeming anxious and puzzled, his hands crossed in front of his mouth. We are in the top of the triangle of experience. In an attempt to bypass defenses against receiving, the therapist shifts focus to the present moment experience.]** What happens inside?

PATIENT:   It lands. It doesn't . . . I don't mean to dismiss it but that's probably the way it looks and I probably don't give it the time it deserves. **[Patient appears anxious and mannered, yet he identifies his own defenses against connection (i.e., dismissiveness).]**

THERAPIST: **[dyadic regulation, maintaining internal focus, attempting to drop below defenses and stay with the new]** So, if we slow down, I'm really curious about what's happening inside of you (*patient's head tilts to the side*) **[marker of receptivity]** that would cause you to do that.

PATIENT: Um. (*long pause*) It's almost like I'm hardwired to only listen for the negative things. Like if you were to say, "That sounds really bad. I don't think you should do that. Or, you're wrong . . .," that would make me perk up and want to assess. But, because it's positive reinforcement . . . uh . . . **[Patient is at a loss for language, this is the new relational experience not yet represented.]** I guess I'm feeling like . . . "okay, that's good. Moving on . . ." **[Patient is articulating the old internal working model: He's put on alert as he expects the other will reprimand him. Although stressful and negative, it is what he knows and, in that way, comfortable. What is positive and longed for (e.g., affirmation and recognition) does not register; or, if it briefly does, he needs to move past it, leave it behind.]**

THERAPIST: So then I sort of have a pained feeling in my chest. **[emotional disclosure, pressuring with empathy, reexposing patient to disconfirming relational experience]** It's like, "Okay, I'm just going to move on," (*patient grimaces, seems to have an empathic reaction*). **[Empathy from another is foreign and does not fit. He has no internal working model to accommodate it.]** Mmm. (*more empathy*)

PATIENT: It's harder to swallow. **[Patient articulates trouble with receptivity: It is hard to take in.]**

THERAPIST: Well, I'm curious. Given what we now know about the brain, that we can rewire things, is that what you want for yourself? **[pressuring to inspire will and agency and bypass defenses]**

PATIENT: (*long pause, initially more vulnerable, open, then shifts, crosses his arms*) Not at this time. **[defenses back in ascendance, we're in the "D" corner]**

THERAPIST: Wow.

PATIENT: I would like to . . . (*slight softening*)

THERAPIST: **[maintaining pressure and focus on emotional experience, highlighting contradiction]** It's interesting because one of the things you said you liked about Kevin (*former partner*) is that he's tender and caring. **[Patient seems puzzled; the language of attachment needs is foreign to him.]**

PATIENT: Probably also why I . . . (*hand gesture, shooing the other away*). **[patient acknowledging and recognizing role of defenses]**

THERAPIST: **[reexposure to the recent, affectively charged, relational moment]** Okay, I wonder if we could just do a little experiment? Let's come back to what just happened and try to make a little more room. **[more puzzlement, more physical barriers from patient]** You were saying in this definitive way, "I don't want to get 10 years down the line and be as frustrated." (*patient softens slightly*) And, I said, "Wow. I'm really moved by that." **[repeats emotional disclosure] [Patient shifts; his body has a big reaction whenever therapist discloses feelings.]** So, in this moment, if you're not just skating by, how does that feel? **[Therapist invites patient to relinquish defenses and feel into his experience and receive.]**

PATIENT: (*long pause*) I don't feel anything. **[Consciously he doesn't, but his body is saying otherwise as he continues to keep his legs and arms crossed in front of him, scrunches his face, and nervously moves his tongue and fingers.]**

THERAPIST: Mmm. Okay. **[Therapist is accepting where patient is at—taking the pressure off which, paradoxically, can soften defenses.]**

PATIENT: Yet. **[significant statement, heralding what's to come]**

THERAPIST: Well, I appreciate your honesty (*patient looks pained*). Mmm. **[more empathy, dyadic regulation, relational support]**

PATIENT: (*voice softening*) This is starting to sadden me that . . . um . . . I'm . . . I guess **[heralding affects, core emotion arising]** not more vulnerable in this part of my life, my personality.

THERAPIST: You're feeling sad? **[tight focus on felt experience, privileging emerging affect—seeking to foster neuroplasticity]**

PATIENT: Yeah, because I think that I'm supposed to and I think that there's a . . . connection you were hoping to make with it . . .

THERAPIST: **[continued pressure]** Mmm. Well, I hear a "supposed to" in there. But, I'm more interested in what *you* want rather than what you're supposed to do.

PATIENT: **[Ground is shifting, and the old template is no longer true. Language is not readily available.]** I guess I'm not entirely convinced that I do . . . that I should want it . . . (*pause*). No, that's not right (*struggling*). I feel like . . . I'm fine (*pause*). Whatever I have going on is working (*discordance evident on his face*). **[It's as though the tectonic plates are shifting: As hard as he tries, patient can't quite endorse the old** relational schema. Although terrified of the new, his defenses are crumbling.]

THERAPIST: Hmm [**pointing out the dissonance**] . . . you look like you're not so sure about that.

PATIENT: Yeah. Well, I'm just telling you what's coming up [**Defenses are procedural, but the surface is cracking.**]. It's almost like I don't understand how these things relate. I mean I do but . . . (*gestures hands coming together but not meshing*). [**physically illustrating discordance, being between two models**]

THERAPIST: [**maintaining pressure, further highlighting the cost of his defenses**] Look, you tell me that you don't feel close to anyone.

PATIENT: Yeah. I know it. (*eyes wide, nodding in agreement*)

THERAPIST: That you don't have any close relationships. You often feel empty and depressed.

PATIENT: (*long pause, direct eye contact, looks sad then smiles*) So just by . . .

THERAPIST: (*interrupting*) What? There's a smile but you look sad.

PATIENT: (*cringes, looks down*). Well . . . yeah . . . that . . . (*looking back at therapist*) It's almost like I want that stuff to go away, but I don't want to take a compliment. I want to be able to do both. [**He wants to not have the consequences of old internal working model, but does not want to deal with anxiety caused by relinquishing his defenses and opening up to the new.**]

THERAPIST: [**platforming, giving him ground to stand on**] So there's this way that you have this wall up (*patient nodding in agreement*). And, while I get that it's reflexive, I'm also aware of the cost (*long pause*). You built this wall to keep out the pain but now it keeps out everything. [**applying pressure to relinquish defenses by pointing out their cost**]

PATIENT: (*cringing*) Yeah (*soft voice*) . . . for sure (*pause, then thinking face*).

THERAPIST: [**focusing back on affective experience**] So, where are you going inside?

PATIENT: I'm just thinking (*long pause*). Yeah, it's definitely a fear because . . . [**huge declaration: names and acknowledges feeling afraid ("A" corner)**]

PATIENT: Uh . . . I'm afraid of what's on the other side. I'm afraid that I'm going to kill someone or something. If my emotions . . . maybe they're not as intense as I'm afraid that they could be. You know, to . . . **[old internal working model and Self–Other–Emotional Triangle in which his feelings will have untoward effects on the other, that, if they were to be expressed, he will be abandoned and alone; echoes from the "P" corner of the triangle of comparisons]**

THERAPIST:   Well, instead of talking about things in general, let's talk about us. **[shifting focus to the here and now, disconfirming relational experience]**

PATIENT:   Okay. (*anxious mouth movement but amenable*)

THERAPIST:   We've known each other for a while now. So, if you let me in, what's going to happen? **[Therapist ups the ante and exposes patient to new internal working model.]**

PATIENT:   (*sighs, long pause, inward gaze, eyes closed; looks at therapist for a bit, then looks down*)

THERAPIST:   (*empathizing*) Mmm. **[regulating, maintaining focus on here and now affective experience]** What are you noticing inside, physically?

PATIENT:   Umm . . . (*knitting his brow, thinking*) **[shift to the "D" corner]**

THERAPIST:   Not in your head. **[bypass intellectual defense]**

PATIENT:   (*opens eyes, looks around; then, in a soft voice, appearing vulnerable*) This makes me kind of nervous . . . talking about this. **[good sign: shift back to the "A" corner]**

THERAPIST:   (*tenderly*) Yeah, I sense that. How do you experience the nervousness? **[describing is regulating and also keeps an attentional spotlight on embodied experience]**

PATIENT:   Um . . . (*long pause*) Shallow breathing. My heart's beating a little faster (*sighs*).

THERAPIST:   Well, actually, that feels encouraging to me (*patient smiles*) because it means that we're leaning into something. From not feeling anything 10 minutes ago to now feeling anxious.

PATIENT:   (*sits up, direct eye contact*) Mm hm.

THERAPIST:   So, what's so scary about my care for you? (*patient's head tilts to the side*) About you having an impact on me? That I'm moved by you? **[Therapist names the new internal working model, a different Self–Other–Emotional Triangle. Therapist is also explicit in declaring his care for the patient.]** Consult the anxiety. Not your head. **[encouraging bottom-up processing and taking in the new]**

PATIENT:   (*quiet voice*) I don't know. I don't know. (*sighs*)

THERAPIST:   Mmm. **[dyadic regulation; sensing patient's sadness]** What're you feeling?

PATIENT:   Um . . . (*long pause, trouble finding words*) a lot of sadness. **[As the affect begins to be experienced, patient's body is quieter. He is now in "E" corner.]** I don't know how to let anyone in. **[big acknowledgment, brings sadness for the self]**

THERAPIST:   (*with much empathy*) Mm. Wow, that's quite a statement, huh?

PATIENT:   (*soft voice*) I mean I can be vulnerable with certain people, but that fear of someone leaving me is very big. I haven't really allowed anyone to do that, in a way.

THERAPIST:   Get close?

PATIENT:   Yeah. And there's some security in knowing that no matter how fucked up or complicated the relationship may be, Steve (*current partner*) would never leave me.

THERAPIST:   (*gentle empathic tone; pained on patient's behalf*) That seems like it comes at such a cost. You have the safety of never being left but you don't feel close or satisfied (*rubs his forehead*). In fact, you feel over it. (*head tilts to the side, direct eye contact*) And I really can appreciate why that is, knowing how far back this fear goes **[connecting the dots between present and past; triangle of relational comparisons]**—your experience with your father. (*patient nods*) And really feeling the effects of that in this moment as we try to be close and come up against the fear (*more nodding, looking sad*) . . . that keeps me out, keeps others out, and keeps you alone. **[empathic highlighting of the cost of the relational defense]** You just looked sad. What's there? **[focusing on emotional experience]**

PATIENT:   (*long pause, vulnerable*) I'm sad for my father as well. **[a lot less anxiety, speech less halting; patient in a deeper emotional state; the "E" corner]**

Russell comes to the realization that his father's tendency to be distant must also be due to a fear of closeness. He feels pained that his father must not know that he is loved "no matter what." Recognizing the cost of avoidance, he says, "It just seems like such a waste."

THERAPIST:   **[focusing patient back on himself]** And coming back to you?

PATIENT:   I can't um . . . I can't . . . **[heralding affects, more emotion arising]**, I can't behave the way . . . he . . . is. Because I know what it's going to look like. **[motivation to change, breaking identification with his father, wanting more for himself]** It's such a waste of a life.

THERAPIST: Mmm. (*tenderly*) You don't want that. (*pause, long, deeply held gaze*) So, I'm going to give you a preemptive warning that I'm going to say something about my feelings and you. **[readying the patient's nervous system, rendering procedural defenses unnecessary]**

PATIENT: (*smiles*) Okay.

THERAPIST: I was just really moved by what you said. (*patient smiles, is open, staying present*) I can't do that. **[affective self-disclosure; reexposure to new relational experience]**

The therapist's heralding, as well as all the work that went before it, has helped the patient to be less defensive and tolerate being more open to relational experience. He maintains direct eye contact throughout.

THERAPIST: (*continuing*) Because there's two sides. One that says, I can't let anyone in (*patient's eyes fill with tears*). And then this. Mmm. (*empathizing; patient reaches for tissue and wipes his eyes, sighs, is pensive, then looks at therapist and smiles*) What? Tell me what's inside. **[dyadic regulation]** I know it's stretching . . . **[dyadic support]**

PATIENT: (*puts hand on heart, pushes himself to speak*) I felt differently . . . when you said that (*very emotional, healing affects; tears of being moved*). It made me feel good.

A huge statement. The patient had a new relational experience *and* it is positive. To his surprise, as he opens up and allows himself to experience core emotions with another—a relational and emotional breakthrough—it feels good, not bad. He is so moved, happy, and open.

THERAPIST: (*moved, with much feeling*) Mmm. I'm so grateful for that. (*patient smiles, gently nods; long pause with deep gaze*) Mmm. (*gently*) Wow.

PATIENT: I can feel it (*moved, eyes moist with tears*). **[asserts and owns the new; capacity to feel and deal while relating with another is getting reintegrated]**

THERAPIST: Yeah. Wow. I feel it too. Mmm. (*long pause, patient and therapist wipe tears from their eyes; patient is pensive, then looks at therapist*) What's that like? **[encouraging metaprocessing]**

PATIENT: (*pause, and then, in a soft voice*) It felt new . . . **[the essence of tremulousness: "it felt new"]** (*shy, slightly puzzled*) . . . and I like it. **[quintessential AEDP with the experience of change for the better, and working with the new experience]**

THERAPIST: And what's your sense of me here with you? I've been having a lot of feeling. **[highlighting self-other relational aspect of his experience; maintaining focus on the new]**

PATIENT: Touching that I had that effect on you. And surprising that . . . I could . . . move someone like that. **[expectations of old internal working model disconfirmed]**

Patient and therapist continue to process the new relational experience before having to stop. The therapist shares how moved and grateful he is to be received and have the patient be so open and connected. (Here the Triangle of Relational Comparisons helped to guide the work.) The patient begins to flesh out his autobiographical narrative, noting how, for much of his life, judgment was a defense against emotional connection. He ends by acknowledging that the fear he has had of being overwhelmed or out of control should he share feelings with another has dissipated and says, with evidence to the contrary, "It's not like that."

This session marked a pivotal moment in the treatment. The patient's relational defenses softened, and he began to open up to his affective experience and attachment strivings. In a subsequent session, the patient talks about a new, evolving friendship. He describes feeling compassion for his new friend as he sees "the little boy inside him" and wants to care for him. Moreover, opening up to his feelings highlights just how lonely he's been, a significant admission from someone who learned to deactivate his attachment needs. Moved, the therapist affirms how the patient is honoring his feelings and desire for connection and sharing them openly with him—in effect, providing what was missing in the patient's early life (an attuned, responsive, and caring other). The patient appears unsettled, unsure of what to do with these feelings. We enter here.

## Vignette 2

THERAPIST: Let's try to be with this together. **[dyadic regulation]** This feels like a deeper opening up to me, and it moves me. **[emotional disclosure, further expose to the new]** I'm just wanting to be with you with that (*patient smiles slightly, eyes brighten*) and make as much room as possible. **[making relational support explicit]** So you say that you're not sure what to do but I feel like you're doing a lot. You seemed to smile a bit when I said I'm wanting to be here with you with this? (*patient nods*) **[focusing attention on affectively charged relational experience; fostering neuroplasticity]** What are you in touch with?

PATIENT: (*pause, maintains a long gaze*) Um. (*soft voice*) That, I am happy that you want to be there with me. [huge declarative statement: acceptance of attachment needs and appreciating the care and support; able to stay present with experience and remain connected]

THERAPIST: (*moved*) Mmm. I'm glad for that (*patient smiles, another long gaze*). Mmm. I think it takes a lot of courage; I don't think this comes easy at all. **[dyadic regulation]** You know, in the same way that you say you see this little boy in your friend, I see this little boy in *you* and I want to take care of him. **[therapist self-disclosure, focus on relational experience, pressuring with empathy; further exposure to new relational experience]** Mmm. (*patient nodding, eyes teary*) That touches something in you?

PATIENT: Yeah.

THERAPIST: What's there? Tell me. **[dyadic regulation]**

PATIENT: Well, I wish someone had (*pause*). **["E" corner]** But I also feel like it's too late. **[soft defense; shift to "D" corner]**

THERAPIST: Stop. **[by-passing defense and redirecting patient back to his feelings]** You wish someone had. And what about that I feel that way? **[reexposure to therapist's care; repetition fosters neuroplasticity]**

PATIENT: But at this point, does it matter? **[soft defense; shift to "D" corner]**

THERAPIST: **[making defense explicit]** Just notice what you're doing. (*sadness registers on patient's face, his lips quiver*) I think it matters immensely (*patient nods in agreement, his eyes filling with tears*). Yeah. Don't push it away. Because you know it matters. And you can take it in, it's okay. It brings up a lot of feelings, and we don't want to deny that and leave you feeling lonely. (*patient sighs, tears now flowing*) **[We're in the "E" corner, dealing with core relational experience.]**

PATIENT: (*soft, vulnerable voice*) This is really hard.

THERAPIST: **[dyadic regulation throughout, regulating intensity and stretching duration]** Yeah, but you're staying with me, which I'm really appreciating, and not pushing it away. (*patient looks pained*) And, I know it brings up a lot of pain around not having and that's what you fight, but that's what we want to take care of. You don't have to leave the wall up and feel lonely (*upwelling of sadness*). Just let it out (*patient opens mouth, audible grief, cries more deeply*). I'm right here with you. **[making relationship explicit, he's not alone]** It's okay (*patient wiping away tears, sniffling*). Yeah. It goes really deep.

PATIENT: Yeah (*sighs deeply, followed by brief gentle smile*). **[positive marker of relief, affective wave has come to completion]** (*long pause, then patient sits up*) Um, that was really amazing cause as hard as that was, I felt things begin to soften (*gestures heart opening*) **[patient naturally starts to make sense of his** experience, and spontaneously articulates the surprising experience of change for the better.]

THERAPIST:    Mmm. That's huge! (*patient making direct eye contact throughout, face soft and open*) I'm so appreciating you hanging in, not pushing it away, I know that there's all this feeling inside—the pain of not having, being lonely—that you fight off. But it also keeps you alone. And in this moment, you let me in, a little more (*patient nods*). And I'm really glad. It's really hard (*patient nods*). It takes a lot of energy, a lot of strength (*patient sighs, dries his eyes*). Tell me a bit about the softening before we have to stop? **[staying with and deepening the new; enhancing neuroplasticity through duration and intensity]**

PATIENT:    Um . . . (*pause*) . . . it . . . you know, you called me on it, but the minute you said it, I knew that I was pushing you back. **[patient mindful of internal process]** But then, I just allowed that question to not be there. **[doing his own defense work]** And then just sit with the . . . wish that I had had someone. **[allowing for his attachment needs and the pain of them not being met in the past]** It . . . almost felt like you were getting through to something. **[he is allowing someone to have an impact on him *and* he is also letting himself be mindful of that]**

THERAPIST:    And how was that? [staying with the felt sense of the novel experience; enhancing neuroplasticity and integration]

PATIENT:    (*long pause*) Um . . . new. **[hearing the shift of the internal working model; having had an experience, patient now trying to put it into words]**. It felt, like, why would I let him here? It doesn't feel like anyone else should be here. It wasn't necessarily scary.

THERAPIST:    Uh huh. So, it felt different?

PATIENT:    Yeah, it felt different to have someone else in that space . . . with me (*pain registers on patient's face, he cries deeply while maintaining eye contact*) **[the old internal working model is being updated in real time]**

THERAPIST:    Mmm. Mmm. **[dyadic regulation throughout]** Mmm hmm (*patient crying*). Wow. It's a lot of feeling. It's really powerful. And I'm right here with you. I'm right there in that space with you. I'm really appreciating you letting me in. It's too long . . . to be alone there. It's not okay **[therapist undoing patient's aloneness, helping to traverse deep pain and grief; rewiring internal working model, a new self-other emotion triangle]**

PATIENT:   (*deep sighs, another affective wave completed*) Um, can I ask you a question?

THERAPIST:   Yes.

PATIENT:   So . . . if people had, you know, great fathers, or whatever, *which is all that this is about*, it's not that . . . it's not like my intimate relationships . . . that I would feel this way with them all the time. It's just that this pain wouldn't have built up this blockage? **[succinct connecting of the dots between then and now, recognition of origin and effects of attachment schema]**

THERAPIST:   Yes. You got it. You're putting it together. That's important.

Having had a new experience, the patient, with an unknowing nod to the Triangle of Comparisons, makes sense of it in light of his history. His autobiographical narrative is unfolding and becoming more coherent and cohesive. Later, the therapist revisits the patient's experience and asks him how he feels to have let the therapist in more deeply.

PATIENT:   I feel good about it. That *was* hard. It was very uncomfortable. Because . . . I also . . . I had felt like I had never even . . . I guess . . . been there with anybody or something, so . . . that was profound (*big smile*). **[recognition of the new, and its magnitude]**

## CONCLUSION

The therapeutic encounter provides fertile relational ground in which the patient's internal working models of self and other can be reworked and updated to support adaptive functioning and new ways of relating. Although seemingly not always apparent, the patient's innate desire to emotionally connect is ever present, just waiting for the right conditions to emerge. Using the Triangles of Experience, Relational Comparisons, and the Self-Other-Emotion Triangle to track, analyze, and guide the process, the AEDP therapist slowly and steadily works to increase the patient's receptive affective capacity by gradually and repeatedly exposing the patient to a new, positive relational experience. Concomitantly, the therapist helps to regulate anxiety and provide increased levels of safety and security so that defenses ultimately give way to adaptive strivings and the processing of core affective experiences can ensue. Thus, all of the factors that potentiate neuroplasticity—novelty, attention, emotional arousal, duration, repetition, and dyadic relational experience—are harnessed and put to effective use.

The clinical material shared here illustrates such a process. It allows us to see, on a moment-to-moment basis, how the psyche copes with the formidable challenge involved in embracing the good, but new and scary, and in venturing outside of the confines of an old internal working model that, although the source of the patient's pain and depression, is known and feels safe. However, when a tight focus on his present moment affective and relational experience is held, dyadically regulated, and experienced through to completion, the patient goes from being defensively closed off from genuine contact to shedding his defenses against closeness and allowing himself to be open and vulnerable and receive the therapist's real care and compassion. In addition, the patient not only understands where his fear came from and why he had kept himself so closed off for most of his life but (both markers of a more coherent autobiographical narrative), in the ultimate validation of this new and different way of being, he experiences relational connection as "good" and preferable. He says simply, "I like it." Thus, the patient's attachment programming is updated so that "feeling and dealing while relating" is not only possible but also experienced as positive and motivating.

To traverse such an experience, both patient and therapist must tolerate a considerable amount of anxiety, which is intrinsic to the process of deep and transformative change, as well as considerable emotion that emerges in association with the patient's trauma. Although clinical skill and tools can help manage this emotional terrain, equally important to this whole endeavor is the therapist's own affective capacity (see also Lipton, Chapter 5, this volume). In addition, an essential ingredient in the work of healing attachment trauma and creating new internal working models of self and other is the therapist's willingness to provide what was missing—to be an emotionally present, caring, and resonant other to patients. Or, to paraphrase van der Kolk (2014), to be there for the patient in the here-and-now in the ways the patient needed in the there-and-then. To do so, therapists may be called upon to show up in ways that stretch beyond the confines of their own internal working models. In this way, AEDP and the work of transforming one's attachment wiring asks as much from the therapist as is does from the patient (Fosha, 2000). Only through such emotionally engaged collaboration can treatment be truly transformative.

## REFERENCES

Badenoch, B. (2008). *Being a brain-wise therapist: A practical guide to interpersonal neurobiology.* Norton.

Beebe, B. (2000). Coconstructing mother–infant distress: The microsynchrony of maternal impingement and infant avoidance in the face-to-face encounter. *Psychoanalytic Inquiry, 20*(3), 421–440. https://doi.org/10.1080/07351692009348898

Bowlby, J. (1969). *Attachment: Attachment and loss* (Vol. 1). Basic Books.

Bowlby, J. (1979). *The making and breaking of affectional bonds.* Tavistock.

Bowlby, J. (1980). *Loss: Sadness and depression* (Vol. 3). Basic Books.

Bowlby, J. (1988). *A secure base: Clinical applications of attachment theory.* Routledge.

Costello, P. (2013). *Attachment-based psychotherapy: Helping patients develop adaptive capacities.* American Psychological Association. https://doi.org/10.1037/14185-000

Cozolino, L. (2014). *The neuroscience of human relationships: Attachment and the developing social brain* (2nd ed.). Norton.

Ecker, B. (2015). Memory reconsolidation understood and misunderstood. *International Journal of Neuropsychotherapy, 3*(1), 2–46. https://10.12744/ijnpt.2015.0002-0046

Ecker, B., Ticic, R., & Hulley, L. (2012). *Unlocking the emotional brain: Eliminating symptoms at their roots using memory reconsolidation.* Routledge. https://doi.org/10.4324/9780203804377

Fosha, D. (2000). *The transforming power of affect: A model for accelerated change.* Basic Books.

Fosha, D. (2003). Dyadic regulation and experiential work with emotion and relatedness in trauma and disordered attachment. In M. F. Solomon & D. J. Siegel (Eds.), *Healing trauma: Attachment, trauma, the brain and the mind* (pp. 221–281). Norton.

Fosha, D. (2005). Emotion, true self, true other, core state: Toward a clinical theory of affective change process. *Psychoanalytic Review, 92*(4), 513–551. https://doi.org/10.1521/prev.2005.92.4.513

Fosha, D. (2008). Transformance, recognition of self by self, and effective action. In K. J. Schneider (Ed.), *Existential–integrative psychotherapy: Guideposts to the core of practice* (pp. 290–320). Routledge.

Fosha, D. (2009a). Emotion and recognition at work: Energy, vitality, pleasure, truth, desire and the emergent phenomenology of transformational experience. In D. Fosha, D. J. Siegel, & M. F. Solomon (Eds.), *The healing power of emotion: Affective neuroscience, development, clinical practice* (pp. 172–203). Norton.

Fosha, D. (2009b). Healing attachment trauma with attachment (and then some!). In M. Kerman (Ed.), *Clinical pearls of wisdom: 21 leading therapists offer their key insights* (pp. 43–56). Norton.

Fosha, D. (2017). Something more than "something more than interpretation": AEDP works the experiential edge of transformational experience to transform the internal working model. In S. Lord (Ed.), *Moments of meeting in psychoanalysis: Interaction and change in the therapeutic encounter* (pp. 267–292). Routledge.

Frederick, R. (2009). *Living like you mean it: Use the wisdom and power of your emotions to get the life you really want.* Jossey-Bass.

Frederick, R. (2019). *Loving like you mean it: Use the power of emotional mindfulness to transform your relationships.* Central Recovery Press.

Hanson, R. (2017). Positive neuroplasticity: The neuroscience of mindfulness. In J. Loizzo, M. Neale, & E. J. Wolf (Eds.), *Advances in contemplative psychotherapy: Accelerating healing and transformation* (pp. 48–60). Routledge. https://doi.org/10.4324/9781315630045-5

Lane, R. D., Ryan, L., Nadel, L., & Greenberg, L. (2015). Memory reconsolidation, emotional arousal, and the process of change in psychotherapy: New insights from brain science. *Behavioral and Brain Sciences, 38,* e1. https://doi.org/10.1017/S0140525X14000041

Lipton, B., & Fosha, D. (2011). Attachment as a transformative process in AEDP: Operationalizing the intersection of attachment theory and affective neuroscience. *Journal of Psychotherapy Integration, 21*(3), 253–279. https://doi.org/10.1037/a0025421

McCullough Vaillant, L. (1997). *Changing character: Short-term anxiety-regulating psychotherapy for restructuring defenses, affects, and attachment.* Basic Books.

Pando-Mars, K. (2016). Tailoring AEDP interventions to attachment style. *Transformance: The AEDP Journal, 6*(2). https://aedpinstitute.org/wp-content/uploads/2016/11/tailoring-aedp-interventions-to-attachment-style.pdf

Prenn, N. (2009). I second that emotion! On self-disclosure and its metaprocessing. In A. Bloomgarden & R. B. Mennuti (Eds.), *Psychotherapist revealed: Therapists speak about self-disclosure in psychotherapy* (pp. 85–99). Routledge.

Prenn, N. (2011). Mind the gap: AEDP interventions translating attachment theory into clinical practice. *Journal of Psychotherapy Integration, 21*(3), 308–329. https://doi.org/10.1037/a0025491

Roozendaal, B., McEwen, B. S., & Chattarji, S. (2009). Stress, memory and the amygdala. *Nature Reviews Neuroscience, 10*(6), 423–433. https://doi.org/10.1038/nrn2651

Russell, E., & Fosha, D. (2008). Transformational affects and core state in AEDP: The emergence and consolidation of joy, hope, gratitude and confidence in the (solid goodness of the) self. *Journal of Psychotherapy Integration, 18*(2), 167–190. https://doi.org/10.1037/1053-0479.18.2.167

Schore, A. N. (1994). *Affect regulation and the origin of the self: The neurobiology of emotional development.* Erlbaum.

Schore, A. N. (2003). *Affect regulation and the repair of the self.* Norton.

Schore, A. N. (2012). *The science of the art of psychotherapy.* Norton.

Schore, A. N. (2019). *The development of the unconscious mind.* Norton.

Schwartz, J. M., & Gladding, R. (2012). *You are not your brain.* Penguin Books.

Siegel, D. (2010). *Mindsight: The new science of personal transformation.* Bantam Books.

Siegel, D. (2012). *Pocket guide to interpersonal neurobiology.* Norton.

Siegel, D. (2015). *The developing mind: How relationships and the brain interact to shape who we are* (2nd ed.). Guilford Press.

Trevarthen, C., & Aitken, K. J. (1994). Brain development, infant communication, and empathy disorders: Intrinsic factors in child mental health. *Development and Psychopathology, 6*(4), 597–633. https://doi.org/10.1017/S0954579400004703

Tronick, E. Z. (1989). Emotions and emotional communication in infants. *American Psychologist, 44*(2), 112–119. https://doi.org/10.1037/0003-066X.44.2.112

van der Kolk, B. (2014). *The body keeps the score: Brain, mind, and body in the healing of trauma.* Viking.

# 8

# Portrayals in Work With Emotion in AEDP

*Processing Core Affective Experience and Bringing It to Completion*

Ben Medley

**M**y client Jeff sat across from me, having just completed an emotional portrayal in which he interacted with his younger self in his imagination after recounting a painful experience with his father. True to accelerated experiential dynamic psychotherapy (AEDP) methods, I began to metaprocess with him asking, "What is this like to do with me?" A Duchenne smile (Damasio, 1999; Harker & Keltner, 2001) spread across his face, genuine and deeply felt. He answered, "It's very beautiful. We took a very dark moment that was very defining and traumatic and brought it back to life and threw new energy into it . . . and we're now allowing it to exist on a different plane." In the portrayal, Jeff had been able to viscerally experience his feelings of sadness and grief associated with this memory in the safety of the therapeutic relationship. In this new, imagined experience, my client was then able to do something that had not occurred in real life: to experientially access his grief because he was no longer alone with it, and then to comfort, soothe, and encourage his younger self. He imagined his younger self receiving his care and reacting with joy and pride. What was once a "dark" and painful memory now felt lighter to my client. This is one example of the effectiveness of portrayals in accessing and processing emotion to completion.

A portrayal is an experiential technique in AEDP that is used to help clients access, heighten, and deepen the visceral experience of core affect and then process it to a satisfying completion (Fosha, 2000). This technique originated with Davanloo (1990) in intensive short-term dynamic psychotherapy and then was expanded and refined by Fosha (2000) in AEDP (Welling, 2019).

https://doi.org/10.1037/0000232-009
*Undoing Aloneness and the Transformation of Suffering Into Flourishing: AEDP 2.0*, D. Fosha (Editor)

Portrayals are similar to other experiential techniques that use the imagination—for example, chair work in emotionally focused therapy (Greenberg et al., 1997) and gestalt therapy (Perls et al., 1951), imagery rescripting (Smucker, Dancu, Foa, & Niederee, 1995), and parts work in internal family systems (Schwartz, 1995) and other parts work or ego state models (e.g., Watkins & Watkins, 1997). Portrayals are real or imagined scenes from the past, present, or even future in which the client is invited to have a reparative, feared, or wished-for experience through the boundless world of the imagination (Fosha, 2000; Fosha & Prenn, 2017). Simply put, portrayals can help clients get "unstuck" and can be used to multiple effect in sessions. They help build emotional and expressive capacities to move a client from being passive to active, build self-compassion, expand one's ability to be assertive, create different possibilities that can be used in the future, and help with integration or bring a sense of justice, rightness, and repair (Fosha, 2000; Fosha & Prenn, 2017). Above all, however, portrayals can help clients deeply experience affect that has been defensively excluded, release it through the body, process it through to completion, and then access, and perhaps play out in fantasy, the adaptive action tendencies that had previously been thwarted (Fosha, 2000; Fosha et al., 2019; Russell, 2015). They are one of AEDP's leading techniques for processing the emotions associated with trauma and emotional suffering.

By helping my client open what he referred to as the "dark box" of childhood trauma and experience feelings of grief and anger within the safety of a trusted, responsive, and empathic relationship with the therapist, he arrived at a new place of feeling relief, pride, and even joy. What was once traumatic and unbearable is now transformed. As Hendel (2018) wrote, "We cannot change the past, but we can change how we feel about the past" (p. 53). My client added his own version of this concept, stating, "I'll always have that [experience] and live with that, but I also have this [experience] now." To understand this process more and how to use portrayals effectively, this chapter first explores the role of emotional processing in AEDP. After this investigation, I return to discussing the use of portrayals and how to utilize them in therapy with clients.

## EMOTIONS AS TRANSFORMATIONAL AGENTS

Emotion theory posits that emotions, wired into us by thousands of years of evolution, are adaptive and necessary for our survival (Fosha, 2004, 2009a), what Panksepp (2009) referred to as "ancestral tools for living" (p. 1). Experientially, an emotion often makes a quick, unexpected appearance and, as Damasio (1999) quipped, "we are about as effective at stopping an emotion as we are at preventing a sneeze" (p. 49). However, emotions also make us feel alive and authentic and give meaning to our lives (Fosha, 2009a). In essence, they come online to let us know that something has changed for good or for bad and that we must respond in some way to adapt and survive (Fosha, 2009a). Darwin (1872/1965) first described the categorical emotions and the distinct phenomenology and dynamics of each. These are the categorical emotions of anger, sadness, fear, disgust, surprise, and joy.

Ekman (2007) and others (Nummenmaa et al., 2014; Volynets et al., 2019) have also discovered that these emotions physiologically follow certain characteristics across cultures, although different cultures may have different societal rules and expectations about how they are expressed. Alongside these physiological experiences, each bodily rooted emotion contains within it a "pulse toward completion" (Fosha, 2009a, p. 177) and has a correlating adaptive action tendency that give one the resources needed to respond to the situation evoking the feeling (Frijda, 1986, as cited in Fosha, 2009a). In short, emotions give us the impulse to act. Fosha (2009a) wrote,

> Emotion is the experiential arc between the problem and the solution: Between danger and escape lies fear. Between novelty and its exploration lies joyful curiosity. Between the loss and its eventual acceptance lies the grief and its completion. (p. 32)

Needless to say, not having access to these emotions means operating at a disadvantage. If defenses and inhibitory affects block one's access to emotion, then the adaptive action tendencies linked to each are also out of reach. Grief cannot give way to acceptance, sadness cannot lead to comfort, anger cannot lead to assertion on behalf of the self, and on and on. Instead, one can become stuck in experiences of overwhelm, avoidance, and suffering.

Emotions not only work as a motivational force toward action but also evoke responses in the other (Fosha, 2004). As both Darwin (1872/1965) and Bowlby (1977, 1991) have emphasized, the most important function of emotional expression is communication. It is through emotion that we are able to communicate to ourselves and others that which is most important (Bowlby, 1991; Ekman, 2007). As Fosha (2000) asserted, "Without deep affect, there can be no deep relating" (p. 4). Emotions are essential for establishing open, trusting relationships (Fosha, 2004).

Like other experiential dynamic therapies, AEDP holds the fundamental belief that psychiatric conditions such as depression and anxiety occur as a result of trying to regulate strong emotions associated with adverse experiences in important attachment relationships during childhood (Lilliengren et al., 2016). What was once adaptive becomes maladaptive, in that individuals cannot feel what they feel and know what they know.

## TRANSFORMATION: A MAP FOR PROCESSING EMOTIONS

AEDP provides an elaborate four-state phenomenological map of the transformational process (Fosha, 2009a, 2009b, 2018, 2019). The goal of AEDP is to help a client move through a healing process and access the core self. The four-state map (see Figure 1, Appendix, this volume)[1] serves as a guide moving

---

[1]This figure, and diagrams for all of the representational schemas in AEDP 2.0, may be downloaded for free (http://pubs.apa.org/books/supp/fosha/).

from negative to positive, stuck to unstuck, from bad to good, and from the self-at-worst to the self-at-best. A client may begin therapy in State 1 with distress and defense, move into State 2 core affective experiences, reach State 3 transformational affects, and then arrive in Core State, or State 4, an integrative state of calm, "feelingful" truth and authenticity. In addition, in recognizing where one is on the map, the AEDP model helps therapists know what to do at any given point in the process to help facilitate this change. Here, I focus on the processing of emotions to completion: moving out of State 1 inhibiting affects and defenses, through the first state transformation; into State 2 core affective experience, reaching the postbreakthrough affects in the second-state transformation; and then arriving in the State 3 transformational experiences.

## Core Affective Experiences

Although in this chapter I am mostly focusing on emotions as vehicles for transformation, it is important to state that there are a number of experiences that are considered core affective experience in AEDP. Beyond the categorical emotions of sadness, joy, fear, anger, and disgust, Fosha (2000) also recognized other types of core affective experience. As such, AEDP identifies types of *core relational experiences*, which include dyadic attunement, resonance, and rupture and repair, as well as *receptive affective experiences*, which include a sense of feeling seen, known, and understood (Fosha, 2000; Lamagna, 2011). Furthermore, AEDP core affect may also include, but is not limited to, authentic self-states, intersubjective experiences of pleasure, embodied ego states and their associated emotions and somatic "drop-down" states (Russell, 2015; Fosha et al., 2019). All of these experiences can effectively move a client into State 3 and State 4 processes. As Fosha (2000) simply stated, core affect "refers to our emotional responses when we do not try to mask, block, distort, or severely mute them" (p. 15).

## The Processing of Core Affective Experience, With a Focus on Emotion

Many clients, although certainly not all, enter the therapeutic relationship with difficulties accessing their emotions. Armed with the knowledge that safety heals, the AEDP therapist aims to create secure attachment beginning with the very first session (Fosha, 2000, 2006; Lipton & Fosha, 2011; Prenn, 2011; Markin et al., 2018; Tunnell, 2012) and bring transformance strivings to the fore (see Kranz, Chapter 2, this volume). Lipton (2019) offered a somatic device to remember some of these skills, instructing practitioners to use "the S.A.N.E.R. way" to help clients navigate this transition from defense and anxiety to affective experience. Functioning as an acronym, this device reminds the therapist to Slow down, Affirm, Notice, Explore, and Reflect. With a trusted other by their side, the client can then begin to relinquish State 1 defenses used to manage emotions and the fear, anxiety, and shame associated with them to become curious and emboldened to venture forward into new territory with the therapist (Fosha, 2006). As a result, previously overwhelming emotions can be explored, somatically experienced, dyadically regulated, and then mined for all of their healing potential (see Frederick, Chapter 7; and Pando-Mars, Chapter 6, this volume).

In taking the AEDP stance, the therapist lets the client know experientially that all of the client's feelings, both positive and negative, are welcome in the therapeutic relationship, including those that had to be disavowed, defended against, and excluded from experience or expression (Lipton & Fosha, 2011; Fosha et al., 2019). As the client enters State 2 and begins to access an emotional experience that is rooted in the body, what could not be handled alone can now be handled dyadically with therapist empathy, attunement, and responsiveness (Fosha, 2001, 2009b). This is how secure attachment in the relationship with the therapist is formed. As with the caregiver–child relationship, security is not achieved through perfect attunement by the therapist in every moment, but rather through a preparedness to go through many cycles of attunement, disruption, and repair with and be there for the client (Beebe & Lachmann, 2002; Fosha, 2009a; Tronick, 1989; Tronick et al., 1998). In support of this concept, Lilliengren et al. (2016) concluded in their analysis of experiential dynamic therapies that the more therapists facilitated affective experience, the more clients improved. Likewise, research has also demonstrated that exposure to intense emotions is the strongest predictor of positive outcome in many models of treatment (Iwakabe et al., 2000; Greenberg & Pascual-Leone, 2006; Lilliengren et al., 2016; Pascual-Leone, 2018).

## State 2 Core Affective Experience: Riding "the Wave"

State 2 adaptive core emotions have a sense of movement and can be thought of—and experienced—as a wave. Like a wave in the ocean, core emotion ideally rises, reaches a peak, and then dissipates. Often, if allowed to follow its natural course, a wave of emotion might last no longer than 90 seconds (Taylor, 2006), although a client may experience more than one wave of emotion in secession. However, not all emotions feel positive when processing them (Fosha, 2008). As a wave begins to build, clients may exit a "window of tolerance" (Siegel, 1999) and need assistance from the therapist. As Lamagna (2011) wrote, "facing one's emotional truths is an ordeal that is both painful and feared to be overwhelming" (p. 293). When this optimal window of arousal is exited, the therapist needs to move "beyond mirroring" to actively help regulate arousal back within a window of tolerance (Fosha, 2000, p. 272). If emotions become overwhelming or dysregulated (hyperarousal), the therapist actively helps to downregulate affective experience. For instance, a client flooded with grief may need help breathing or making eye contact to reenter the window. Likewise, a client may need help upregulating experiences that have been held at bay or when a client begins to shut down emotional expression (hypoarousal). One example of upregulation is to have a client pay attention to a clenched fist or to increase one's volume or pace of speech when helping a client access anger, affirming and encouraging the client with each step.

To help effectively, the therapist must also be emotionally engaged, feeling along with and for the client (Fosha, 2009b). Through affective self-disclosure, therapists may verbally share the impact a client is having on them (e.g., "I feel sad too") or display what they are feeling through the face and body (e.g., tears in the eyes). If clients are able to receive this help, via the receptive affective capacities, and register that they had an impact on the therapist, healing, positive affects can be released. This produces a felt sense of safety and a greater ability for the client to authentically explore feelings and experiences. With each round of affective work, what is initially handled interrelationally, can increasingly be handled intrarelationally (Prenn, 2011; Schore, 2003).

## Second State Transformation: The Emergence of Resilience

Once the wave of emotion begins to come to a completion, the client experiences a state shift and begins to enter the second-state transformation. The markers of this transformation are the *postbreakthrough affects* and the release of the *adaptive action tendencies* wired into each emotion (Fosha et al., 2019). Here resiliency and the motivation to act, previously warded off along with the core emotion, are now free to move forward. When this occurs, a client may experience a feeling of release and relief, hope, a sense of being lighter, a relaxation of the body and a feeling of being stronger or more assertive. In addition, a client may also express feelings of tiredness. However, this tiredness may be imbued with a sense of relief, much like the tiredness of completing a challenging task or activity, such as running a marathon. Some fatigue after doing an intensive piece of emotional processing work is reasonable. Carefully tracking for these experiences, the AEDP therapist again makes the implicit explicit and the explicit experiential (Fosha & Prenn, 2017) by calling attention to these experiences and exploring them with the client. As Gendlin (1981) stated, "the process of actually changing feels good" (p. 8). Fosha (2004) expanded on this concept, adding,

> By good, I do not mean happy; [the person] may or may not. What I do mean is (i) that the process of therapeutic transformation is accompanied by a feeling of relief and a relaxation of tension; (ii) that the felt sense of what is happening has to do with things feeling "right" and "true"; and (iii) that something inside the person says "yes." (p. 38)

Once the emotional wave is complete, the client also has access to new information about the self, the other, and the situation that was not previously available (Fosha, 2000, 2004, 2009b). The client is then able to act in ways that achieve mutually regulated states with the other or propels the client to act to fulfill the newly identified needs with the adaptive action tendencies (Fosha, 2000). Goleman (2006) remarked,

> All emotions are, in essence, impulses to act, the instant plans that evolution has instilled in us. . . . That emotions lead to actions is most obvious when watching animals or children: it is only with "civilized" adults we so often find the great anomaly in the animal kingdom, emotions—root impulses to act—divorced from obvious reaction. (p. 6)

As Fosha (2004) noted, the combination of the felt experience of the post-breakthrough affects with the increased energy and motivation to act can be a powerful antidote to the previously debilitating experiences motivating clients to seek help.

Immediately following the postbreakthrough affects, the client enters State 3. At this point in AEDP therapy, the next therapeutic activity is metatherapeutic processing (metaprocessing) and the processing of the emotions associated with transformation. (Although this is illustrated in the case example that follows, for a description of metatherapeutic processing, see Fosha, 2017; Russell, 2015; Yeung, Chapter 13, this volume).

In the next section of this chapter, I illustrate the accessing and processing of emotion in therapy with a case example. With respect to what has been discussed, the case example shows the initiation of a portrayal, the movement into State 2 categorical emotion, the dyadic regulation of emotion, and the emergence of postbreakthrough affects after riding the wave of emotion together. Later in this chapter, I exemplify with a case example from the next session how this experience led to a more complete intrarelational portrayal.

## HEALING THE WOUNDS YOU CAN'T SEE: A CASE EXAMPLE

Daniel[2] is a Hispanic, gay, cisgender, male-identified client in his early 20s who engaged in AEDP therapy to address feeling stuck in his career and relationships, as well as an overall feeling of unhappiness. Combining gay affirmative therapy with AEDP (see Medley, 2018), we began to explore the effects of heterosexism on his development and early relationships with caregivers (other aspects of marginalized identity were explored in other sessions). In this exploration, Daniel recalled a specific memory in which, at age 7, he performed a dance for his father in the backyard of his home. Daniel's father responded with a still face that clearly communicated disapproval, and my client recalled becoming flooded with feelings of shame and embarrassment. During our sessions, he was able to see how his father's models of masculinity were a probable influence on his reaction. However, he also internalized the emotional learning that he himself was not acceptable to his father and that it was unacceptable to express exuberance and joy. As a result of this experience and others like it, he defended against his emotional experience and erected a false self to hide core aspects of his identity. Over the course of therapy, he returned to this memory several times. In one session, 7 months into his therapy, my client brought a picture of himself as a child into the session and expressed feelings of sadness about his experiences growing up. Daniel added that he felt very alone in the session with me and that he had felt alone "for a very long time." Seeing this as opportunity to process emotion and perhaps initiate a portrayal, we began to explore his experience.

[2]I have complied with American Psychological Association ethical standards in describing the details of treatment; aspects of the patient's identity and background have been disguised to protect confidentiality.

Because he shared that he felt disconnected from me, I began by making explicit that I wanted to be more connected to him. Daniel's eyes reddened. When I asked about these tears, he said, "Just to be explicit, I'm feeling both defensive . . . my shoulders up . . . and on the verge of sobbing." I invited him to tell me more about the part of him that wanted to sob and he spoke again of feeling alone and added that he had reached out to a friend who hadn't responded to him. Aware that he was having difficulty relinquishing his defenses, I then tried slowing us down and returned to what was happening in the here-and-now. (Note that italic text indicates description of nonverbal expressions or movements, and bold indicates theoretical comments.)

THERAPIST:    If we just go slow with us. Just to tune into how I'm responding to you . . . and make lots of space, because you're saying, "I need space to sort this through." **[slowing down and staying with, pressuring with empathy to stay with the feeling]**

CLIENT:    Sure. **[green signal to keep moving forward]**

THERAPIST:    Yeah . . . and just notice what is happening in your body. **[somatic intervention to deepen experience]**

CLIENT:    I felt kind of tired and sad last night and this morning and this is sort of opening up the faucet . . . which is good, I think.

THERAPIST:    What's letting you know this is good? **[noticing and seizing glimmer of transformance]**

CLIENT:    I just feel a little bit of relief . . . in terms of congestion.

THERAPIST:    Okay, yeah, yeah. How do you notice "relief" inside? **[somatic intervention to expand positive affect and further lower anxiety and tension]**

CLIENT:    A little less tense, a little less tight.

THERAPIST:    And shoulders? **[using moment-to-moment tracking to bring more attention to his experience]**

CLIENT:    Shoulders are down . . . there's an openness in the back of my throat. **[green signal to move forward]**

THERAPIST:    Great. Good. And just noticing in terms of our connection . . . more, less, or the same? **[tracking receptive affective capacities]**

CLIENT:    Same.

THERAPIST:    Okay . . . and this last wave of tears came when I said that my goal was to get closer to you. What about that brings tears?

CLIENT:    *(tearing again)* I'm not sure.

THERAPIST:    Yeah, let's take our time. **[slowing down and staying with and using "we" language]** Even when I said it again, a little . . . (*I motion to my eyes. He exhales and his eyes redden again.*) Yeah . . . lots of feeling. **[moment-to-moment tracking]**

CLIENT: I brought in the photo because I think that a lot of this just has to do with that kid . . . I just wanted to make that explicit. (*His voice becomes shaky and quieter as his eyes fill with tears.*) Something about that kid being alone is really affecting me 15 to 20 years later.

THERAPIST: Right . . . yeah. That makes a lot of sense. (*exhales again*) Good . . . yeah . . . lots of room. How do you feel for that kid?

CLIENT: (*barely audible*) I feel really sad.

THERAPIST: Yeah. Me too. **[self-disclosure]** I see that picture, and I see such a sweet, young, innocent kid.

The slowing down and focusing on the somatic correlates of his experience, while simultaneously making explicit and focusing on my being there with him, succeeded in loosening his defenses and Daniel began to cry as he named his feeling. After a moment, he told me that his younger self was once happy and carefree only to then become guarded. As he said this, the wave of sadness began to grow. I affirmed him by telling him that he was doing a great job and encouraged him to simply let the emotion flow. He began to cry more intensely.

THERAPIST: You're doing great. Just let it come. **[affirming, encouraging feeling the emotion]**

CLIENT: I'm just going to cry.

THERAPIST: That's great. That's great. **[affirming]** I'm right here with you. **[being with to help dyadically regulate]** (*The wave of emotion begins to grow even more. I move my chair closer to him to dyadically regulate.*) Is this okay? **[asking permission]**

CLIENT: (*He nods yes and begins to laugh through his tears.*) I just feel really flushed and self-conscious.

THERAPIST: It's okay. You are flushed, and it makes sense.

CLIENT: I'm crying and giggling at same time because I'm so self-aware.

THERAPIST: You're doing great. **[support and encouragement]**

CLIENT: I just don't know what I'm supposed to do with all of that.

THERAPIST: Let's just take it one step at a time. **[using collaborative "we" language]**

CLIENT: Okay, what's the first step then?

THERAPIST: Right now, just letting you do this. **[guiding and encouraging, staying with his experience]**

CLIENT:      Okay. (*another wave of sadness as he cries*)

THERAPIST:   And letting me be with you . . . with this. (*He exhales. Sensing the end of a wave, I speak.*) That was a big wave so first we just had to ride it. **[organizing experience]**

CLIENT:      It just feels so dramatic . . . like wounds you can't see.

THERAPIST:   That's exactly what it is. Wounds that have been there a long time.

CLIENT:      And I was papering over them by working all the time and focusing on image. **[Client identifies his own defense.]**

THERAPIST:   Yeah . . . how is it to ride that together? **[metaprocessing]**

CLIENT:      It's still uncomfortable but it helps. I was just catching myself shielding myself and trying not to do that (*He motions, covering his face.*) Not because that reaction is bad, but because it's okay to feel this way.

THERAPIST:   That's right. As far as I'm concerned there's nothing to be ashamed of about feeling sad for that kid. **[affirming and supporting new experience through self-disclosure]**

CLIENT:      I feel sad for me too, because of that kid. **[self-compassion is emerging]**

THERAPIST:   Yeah to have to carry that for so long. **[empathy]**

CLIENT:      Yeah, I did, and I did it alone. And I don't want to be proud of that anymore.

THERAPIST:   You're not doing it alone right now. (*He nods and exhales.*) **[making the implicit explicit]** Do you have a sense of that? **[checking receptive affective capacities]**

CLIENT:      (*nodding*) Yeah.

THERAPIST:   Good. How's that to know?

CLIENT:      I see it right now.

THERAPIST:   Good. And how's that to see?

CLIENT:      I don't know . . . maybe it's contributing to my discomfort . . . just because it's foreign.

THERAPIST:   Sure. And just to check: I moved closer to you. For the part of you that's uncomfortable, does that part of you need me closer or further way? **[Making the implicit explicit to make certain I wasn't contributing to discomfort.]**

CLIENT:      I think you're fine because I think if you didn't come closer, it would reinforce that I'm over here doing this thing. "Look at me being histrionic." So, coming closer makes me feel uncomfortable, but it feels like pushing into a stretch that's uncomfortable but feels good.

THERAPIST:   Ah, okay, good to know (*He exhales again.*) I'm not sure if you saw, but I want to point out that as I was getting closer to you I was also tearing up. Did you see that?

CLIENT:   No, but I can believe it.

THERAPIST:   That's why I'm letting you know because I want to make sure you know that. And how is that to believe and to know? That actually I'm tearing up too? **[stretching receptive affective capacities]**

CLIENT:   It makes me think of a couple of weeks ago when you told me you were reading my favorite book because of me and there was just something fundamentally charged about that in the sense that I had a lot of disbelief. . . . It's easy to believe that I can inspire someone based on it being identified that I'm smart or talented or dress well or that I'm a good cook, but not something like that, and I think it relates to—I don't have a strong sense of value of myself when it comes to the intangible. When it comes to the special and unique things that makes me me and the things that I can give to someone that no one else can give . . . that's just a symbol of my reluctance . . . to accept that those parts of me that don't obtain things that mainstream society hold up as the most valuable that those parts of me that are silly frivolous or fun could be special and that someone could be really moved by that part of me.

Daniel started to cry again. Another big wave of feeling began, and he started to uncomfortably laugh through his tears again and had difficulty breathing. Observing that he was out of his window of tolerance through moment-to-moment tracking, I leaned forward and gently but firmly placed my hand on his knee to help him regulate his strong emotions.

THERAPIST:   I'm right here. Is this okay? **[asking permission]** (*He nods "yes"*) **[green signal]** To be clear, this isn't to stop you. **[making the implicit explicit]**

CLIENT:   I know.

THERAPIST:   Yeah . . . whatever else needs to happen.

CLIENT:   (*He catches his breath, and I remove my hand.*) It's just very strong, it just felt very passionate and authentic and forceful while connecting those dots, and it just seems to have a lot to do with what that kid was taught.

THERAPIST:   It's like a direct line.

CLIENT:    (*after another wave of feeling*) It just feels so uncomfortable.

THERAPIST:    You're doing great. **[affirming]** (*He cries and again begins to laugh through tears. I put my hand on his knee again.*)

CLIENT:    It feels weird.

THERAPIST:    It's not weird, it's just new. **[helping to organize experience]**

CLIENT:    (*Looking into my eyes, beginning to breathe more regularly*) That's true.

THERAPIST:    It's just new. (*I point to my eyes, full of tears, to make sure that he sees my affect this time. The wave surges again, followed by a big exhale.*) It's a lot.

CLIENT:    Yes.

THERAPIST:    You're doing great. **[support and encouragement]**

CLIENT:    (*taking a big breath*) I think so too. **[postbreakthrough affects]**

THERAPIST:    This just feels really needed.

CLIENT:    Yes. (*He exhales, followed by a deeper more resonate, "yes" With his exhale he settles into the chair and his body visibly relaxes.*) **[postbreakthrough affects]**

Indeed, "new" and "needed" things are happening for Daniel in this session. We rode a wave of core emotion, and the postbreakthrough affects began to appear. Knowing that something new had occurred, we began metaprocessing the experience. He told me that the experience was uncomfortable but needed. When I asked him to tune into his here-and-now experience, he noticed that he was actually feeling the opposite in the wake of the experience: He felt comfortable, calm, and relaxed. As we processed these feelings, the healing affects of gratitude (see Yeung, Chapter 13, this volume) began to emerge, and he thanked me. Asking him to expand on what he was thanking me for, he replied with tears in his eyes, "The paradox is that I crave being seen, but it feels so deeply uncomfortable to tread that path . . . but you're seeing me and letting me process and feel the things that I'm feeling however large or small they are, wherever it goes . . . I just feel very grateful for your empathy and compassion." His response illustrates the powerful subjective experience of undoing aloneness through dyadic affect regulation in emotion processing. The session ended with him feeling connected to me and we took a moment to anchor this new feeling in his body. As we will see in the next session described later in this chapter, he was able to internalize his experience with me, and we were then able to build on the interrelational work of this session to continue our work with a reunion portrayal. Before continuing with the next session, however, I first discuss the technique of portrayals to better understand the goal of portrayals, some of the types of portrayals that are used in AEDP, and how to use them to process emotion.

## USING PORTRAYALS TO PROCESS EMOTION TO COMPLETION

A portrayal, "the pinnacle of experiential-dynamic affect work," is an AEDP technique that builds on the work so far described, aiding the client in accessing core affect and processing it to completion through use of the imagination (Fosha, 2000, p. 284). Central to this process is the use of image. As Fosha (2000) asserted, image-based information processing is more tightly wound with emotion than word-based strategies, and a fuller affective experience can be achieved if the actions associated with the emotions are lived rather than described. "Lived" seems to be an accurate description for portrayals, given that neuroimaging studies have shown that mental imagery is, in fact, encoded similarly to actual perception (Blackwell, 2019). Portrayals can bring many channels of experience into play (Pally, 2000) to help heighten our client's experience: sight, smell, taste, sound, and so on, often described as "seeing with the mind's eye" or "hearing with the mind's ear" (Blackwell, 2019). In fact, Blackwell (2019) noted that experimental studies have shown that "processing emotionally valanced information via mental imagery has a greater impact on subjective emotion than verbal processing" (p. 236). For example, one study demonstrates that participants who were instructed to imagine themselves in particular situations experienced a greater change in state mood than participants who were asked to "think about them verbally" (Blackwell, p. 236). The more specific and vivid the imagery, the more dynamic and alive the experience may become. Thus, portrayals may increase the capacity for a fuller emotional experience (Fosha, 2000; Fosha & Prenn, 2017).

Once a specific scenario is identified by the client and therapist, the client is invited to find the moment of strongest affect within the scene and then allow the scenario and the characters involved to interact and come to life (Fosha, 2000). These scenarios can be from the *perspective of the client as an observer*, such as seeing a younger self in relationship with another, or through direct involvement from *a field perspective*, such as being oneself and then imagining interacting with and speaking directly to the other who evoked the emotion in the client (Blackwell, 2019). Often a portrayal can use both perspectives, such as recalling a specific memory and observing the scene and then entering the memory from a field perspective to do something corrective or assertive. Portrayals can be imagined as interrelational scenes (between two people), or intrarelational (between parts of self; Lamagna & Gleiser, 2007; see also Lamagna, Chapter 11; Gleiser, Chapter 12, this volume). The aim is to take these imagined scenarios to their natural conclusion to reap the full benefits of the adaptive action tendencies of the emotion being "portrayed" (Fosha, 2000). For example, with Daniel, in the preceding session excerpt, the client was able to viscerally experience feelings of grief and sadness through the initiation of a portrayal ("How do you feel for that kid?") and process the emergent feeling to completion in the safety of the therapeutic relationship. In the next session, described later in the chapter, he then was able to follow the portrayal to its completion by giving comfort to his younger self.

Ecker et al. (2012) advanced the idea that experientially reactivating the emotional experiences associated with painful and traumatic memories, when paired with a powerful, new contrasting emotional experience, can erase and revise the traumatic memories. "Erased" signifies not that the memory is necessarily forgotten or replaced but that the emotional learning (and thus the behavioral, cognitive, somatic, and emotional manifestations) associated with the memory changes and is transformed (Ecker, 2015). Although this can occur by having a new experience—processing emotion through to completion relationally with the therapist as outlined previously— portrayals also offer the client a powerful, emotional opportunity to have a contrasting, new experience by creating new, healing experiences and memories imaginatively. Indeed, in writing about mental imagery, Blackwell (2019) noted that some studies have shown that imagined events often can be remembered as having actually occurred. What is lived in the imagination can be just as real as what the client has actually experienced. Portrayals offer the client new positive (i.e., right and true) experiences that can have a lasting healing effect.

## Types of Portrayals

There are many kinds of portrayals that therapists can use to help clients viscerally experience their emotions, and the "right" portrayal always depends on the client and the clinical moment. However, AEDP emphasizes a few specific scenarios that are often discussed and utilized in AEDP. These include emotion to completion portrayals, reparative portrayals, reunion portrayals, and rescue portrayals.

*Emotion to completion portrayals* involve imagining expressing or acting on emotions in relationship to an imagined other or part. Anger portrayals are one kind of emotion to completion portrayals: They help clients access, express, and process anger toward another person who has hurt or wronged them in some way. Feelings of anger and murderous rage can often be difficult to express and manage, and a portrayal can help desensitize clients and thus have greater access to their feelings (Fosha, 2000). As a result of this type of work, and with practice over time, the client becomes more familiar and at ease with experiences of anger (Fosha, 2000) and gains greater ability to have access to its adaptive potential, manifested as being able to be more assertive and stand up for oneself. Similarly, portrayals can be used to process fear, sadness, disgust, or even joy to completion. The preceding case example uses an emotion to completion portrayal to process grief and sadness.

*Reparative portrayals* are used to complete a longed-for experience that was thwarted in some fashion or remains incomplete. This type of portrayal can be particularly effective in helping to process grief work that is stalled. Asking a client to imagine a lost other (which may not always mean deceased), the client could be invited to say goodbye in words (which can be directly vocalized) and in action (which can be imagined and described). Clients could also express to another how they may have been affected or hurt by the other person, something that was not said or vocalized at the time. Additionally, clients can imagine receiving a longed-for response that was needed or absent in a past situation. For instance, in the preceding case example, Daniel might imagine telling his father how much he was hurt by his father's reaction to his dancing and then, in turn, imagine his father apologizing for his hurtful reaction. This imagined response is similar to the "ideal parent figure" Brown and Elliott (2016) outlined in their protocol for healing childhood attachment trauma. With this work, the client is asked to imagine an "ideal parent figure," or figures, who responds with attunement to the client's experience and emotional needs (Parra et al., 2017). A reparative portrayal also bears similarities to techniques found to be effective in Gestalt therapy in which a client is asked to speak directly to a deceased other and imagine a satisfying resolution to "unfinished business" (Dannenbaum & Kinnier, 2009).

A reparative portrayal is by no means intended to replace or ignore the original lived traumatic experience. Instead, the aim is to help clients viscerally access their feelings connected to the traumatic experience by imagining communicating their internal experience directly with the other person and then processing the associated emotions through to completion with the help of the therapist. In imaging an "ideal other" responding in just the right way, clients may not only experience what needed to happen, and thus gain new insight into the original experience, but also see themselves as capable of taking action and worthy of attunement and repair. Although a client may not have been able to have this corrective experience in real life, the new, imagined experience could help renegotiate the traumatic memory, thus giving it new meaning and changing how the client feels about it (Giacomucci, 2020; Moritz et al., 2018).

*Reunion portrayals* bring help, relief, and acknowledgment intrarelationally to younger parts of the self. A *part* is a term referring to an internal entity thought of as a "discrete and autonomous mental system that has an idiosyncratic range of emotion, style of expression, set of abilities, desires and view of the world" (Schwartz, 1995, p. 34). In AEDP, intrarelational work focuses on direct work with parts of the self to help foster self-compassion and internal integration (Lamagna & Gleiser, 2007). In attachment environments of abuse and neglect, individuals often relate to parts of themselves with punishment, distance, or devaluation, much like the responses of the original attachment figure (Lamagna, 2011; Lamagna & Gleiser, 2007; Pando-Mars, 2016). Building on the security developed interrelationally in the therapeutic dyad, reunion portrayals help the client gain greater understanding of younger parts of the self and to witness the younger self's experience and emotions, allowing feelings that had to be managed and/or excluded to be released and processed. Hendel (2018) asserted,

> Our brains have the ability to visualize traumatized parts of us by imagining them outside of ourselves in order to see them through our present-day adult eyes . . . imagining isolating a part of us is the most efficient way to learn more about and heal from traumatized aspects of ourselves. (p. 118)

Through the imagination, clients can undo the aloneness experienced by a younger version of the self and respond to their unmet needs in both word and action to help soothe, calm, and relieve them. Similarly, with *rescue portrayals*, when recalling a traumatizing event or situation, clients can be asked to enter the scene with their younger selves to remove, protect, or save them in some way from the harm being inflicted. For instance, in a memory of being sexually abused, a client could begin to feel anger toward the perpetrator and enter the scene to assertively defend the self or "rescue" and take the younger self to safety. A client could also be guided to imagine an important other behaving differently from how they did in the past life experience. To illustrate, a client could spontaneously say, "If only my father had stopped her from abusing us" and then be invited by the therapist to experientially imagine this occurring.

As discussed with reparative portrayals, imaging a better conclusion to a traumatic event is not meant to avoid what actually occurred. The therapist and client are not pretending the event did not happen. Quite the contrary, when a client's defenses and inhibitory affect are low, reunion and rescue portrayals can help a client access and process the emotions tied to the traumatic experience and undo traumatic aloneness interrelationally with the therapist and intrarelationally with themselves. As Morina et al. (2017) reported in discussing imagery rescripting, the results of experientially scripting a new, better narrative are often beneficial for clients even though they still hold the memory of the original aversive event. The intent of these imagined, "better" scenarios and interactions is not to change the memory itself but "only its representation in consciousness and its impact on well-being" (Moritz et al., 2018, p. 75).

Even when the client imagines an interrelational scene that involves an interaction with another person, it may be helpful to also consider reparative, reunion, and rescue portrayals as *intrarelational* healing attachment portrayals. For the clinician, this shift in thinking allows one to view each type of portrayal as working with the client's internal attachment models of self and others through imagined representation. For example, in a portrayal involving a perpetrator of verbal abuse, a client may have internalized the abuser and could respond harshly to a younger part of the self. The therapist would then work with the client to deepen understanding of and build compassion for either the abusing or the abused part. Ultimately, we seek to integrate these parts by fostering secure internal attachment experiences between the parts (Lamagna, 2011; Lamagna & Gleiser, 2007). Additionally, working with one part may lead to work with another part. Thus, a rescue portrayal may lead to a reunion portrayal, which could lead to a reparative portrayal. The point is to be flexible and let the unfolding of affect and sequence of action guide where the portrayal and the client might need to go next.

## Portrayals in Motion

To begin a portrayal, the therapist must first find an entry point. Fortunately, opportunities to begin a portrayal can take many forms. In general, these opportunities arise when the client is in the first-state transformation or in

State 2. Through moment-to-moment tracking (see Hanakawa, Chapter 4, this volume), the AEDP therapist might notice somatic activation like the clenching of a fist or a sigh; affective activation, as with the categorical emotions; verbal activation, such as a spontaneous shift to what a client might want to say or do; recalling of a memory that was important and impactful; or the appearance of pathogenic affects and states. When pathogenic affects arise, this could be an opportunity to work with younger aspects of the self to alleviate shame, guilt, and even anxiety (see Gleiser, Chapter 12; Lamagna, Chapter 11; Piliero, Chapter 10, this volume). As Hendel (2018) asserted, being able to externalize a part of oneself and have some distance from the experience can be relieving, lower anxiety, and reduce shame. Often this experience also allows clients to begin to understand more about their experience, how the present connects to the past, and to develop more self-compassion.

Once an opportunity arises, the therapist invites the client to "paint the picture" with as many details as possible. Specificity helps bring the imagined scene alive: "Who are we talking to? Where are we? How old were you then?" Vagueness, in contrast, can be a defense against emotional experience. The client is also asked to use present-tense language with the first-person pronouns of "I" and "you" (Fosha, 2000) and, as mentioned before, to use as many channels of experience as possible: "What do you see, smell, feel, and hear?" Following the sequence of emotional processing, the therapist helps the client to connect with the emotions that arise in the portrayal, viscerally experience them, dyadically regulate them if needed, and notice, stay with, or follow the postbreakthrough and adaptive action tendencies. Depending on what occurs, the therapist may not complete the portrayal for the sake of privileging the processing of a wave of emotion to completion, as with the previous case example.

When a client says or does something in a portrayal, the therapist can also have the client imagine the impact of this on the other. For instance, in an anger portrayal, a therapist may say, "Imagine your fist making impact with his face. Really see that in your mind's eye." In a reunion portrayal, the therapist might say, "Imagine your younger self hearing you say that. What do you see?" or "What's that like for your younger self to be held?" Finally, following a sequence of events to their end, the therapist may also nudge the client toward imagining the adaptive action tendencies realized by asking "What do we do now?" and asking the client to imagine this happening (Fosha & Prenn, 2017).

Once the portrayal is completed, the AEDP therapist then metaprocesses the experience to reflect on it together and to help consolidate the emotional learning: "What is different after the portrayal? How do you see this situation/person/younger self now? What is this like to have done with me?" Metaprocessing not only helps consolidate emotional learning from the new experience but also aids in bringing the transformational affects forward to process.

## Contraindications for Portrayals

There may also be times in which it is necessary to reconsider using a portrayal in sessions. For instance, Russell (2015) asserted that when our clients are operating from their selves-at-worst (stuck in rigid defenses, high inhibitory affect, or maladaptive affective experiences), asking how they feel toward a younger part will most likely be counterproductive. Often, when posed this question, clients—having internalized how they were once treated (Pando-Mars, Chapter 6, this volume)—respond with dismissal or disgust, wanting to behave in rejecting and bullying ways toward this part of themselves. This can be useful information, indicating that the client may need help developing compassion and understanding for themselves before attempting another intrapersonal portrayal. However, continuing with imagined self-abuse may only reinforce an insecure and abusive intrapersonal relationship, often reflective of real-life traumatic experiences that have been internalized. Likewise, with clients experiencing suicidal ideation, it is unlikely to be therapeutic to encourage detailed descriptions of clients inflicting harm on themselves. In fact, some studies have found a direct link between a high prevalence of suicidal and self-harm imagery and an increased desire to enact these images behaviorally (Blackwell, 2019; Hales et al., 2011). Imagining acting in destructive ways toward the self is often unproductive at best and destructive and harmful to the client at worst.

In addition, anger portrayals detailing *intentional* plans to harm another person are not therapeutic. Simply stated, violent portrayals should not be used as a "rehearsal" for action by the client. At times it may be difficult to assess the difference between "I want to harm this person" and "I am going to harm this person." As exemplified here, language certainly can help indicate one's intention. However, it can also be useful to evaluate whether a client struggles with externalizing feelings and acting out these feelings rather than demonstrating an ability to manage them internally. If the therapist is unsure and becomes concerned about homicidal ideation, the portrayal can be halted in favor of assessment.

Lastly, if a client demonstrates impairment in reality testing and has difficulty differentiating between reality and fantasy, as with clients experiencing psychosis, therapeutic work using the imagination to process emotion could cause the client to lose greater contact with reality and may not be appropriate (Dannenbaum & Kinnier, 2009).

In sum, portrayals can and should be used judiciously in practice. These examples are not meant to serve as strict rules but rather as cautionary guidelines. Assessment of client functioning, careful moment-to-moment tracking of client experience, and attention to the client's needs in the moment are not only helpful but necessary.

In the next section, I provide an example of an intrarelational attachment portrayal or reunion portrayal. Working with the same client from the previous case example, having accessed, dyadically regulated, and processed to completion sadness for himself as a child, I then turn to building on our interrelational work to express this newfound compassion for his younger self and build a more secure internal attachment intrarelationally (Lamagna, 2011; Lamagna & Gleiser, 2007).

## MORE LOVE TO MYSELF: A CASE EXAMPLE CONTINUED

Daniel returned the next week feeling "good" about the previous session. As soon as he sat down, Daniel said, "I had a very busy, productive and good week, and I think it had a lot to do with last week's session." As we continued to process, he stated, "To put my finger on it, I just felt less alone this past week, and it feels like it stemmed from last week's session." Soon, through metaprocessing, we were riding the transformational spiral that occurs as one metaprocesses the transformational affects of State 3. Daniel felt a new level of compassion for his younger self and what he experienced in the past, as well as for his present, adult self. This was Daniel operating from an experience of self-at-best. Recognizing an opportunity to continue with a reunion portrayal, I suggested we return to the memory of performing for his father. As we began, I asked him to visualize the scene and describe to me what he remembered, bringing as many senses into the experience as possible. He shared that he was called "Danny" at the time, and we began to refer to his younger self by this nickname. After asking him to "paint me a picture" of where this interaction occurred, I asked, "And if we go to your backyard then . . . me there to support you . . . and we find Danny, what would you say or do?" After a moment of thought, Daniel began to imagine helping his younger self.

CLIENT: We would probably squat because he was short.

THERAPIST: So, we would get down on his level.

CLIENT: Um hmm . . . and we would adopt an exuberance and tell him that that was great and that was so creative, that you came up with that all on your own and I think that's very special and I'm glad that you shared that with me.

THERAPIST: Yeah . . . that sounds just right. **[affirming]** Really let yourself see yourself doing that with him. Down on his level. **[having him imagine the impact on the other]**

CLIENT: (*eyes full of tears*) He would probably grin.

THERAPIST: Yeah. Really see that. This big grin. **[helping him imagine the impact on his younger self]**

CLIENT: Goofy.

THERAPIST: Yeah, goofy. Like that picture you showed me, right?

CLIENT: Yeah.

THERAPIST: A really genuine grin. Yeah. It makes him happy? (*He nods and begins to tear.*) Yeah. What's that like to give to him? I'm seeing lots of emotion. Tears. **[moment-to-moment tracking]**

CLIENT: It's what I know I needed. He wouldn't know how big of a deal it was, but I hope that it would implicitly communicate to him to continue doing it. To continue being who he is.

THERAPIST:   Yeah. Yeah. Imagine saying that: "Keep it up, keep being you. This is great" (*He exhales.*) And I know we're in our imagination, but check in with Danny. Can he hear that? Can he get that? **[checking receptive affective capacities]**

CLIENT:   Yeah, because he wasn't scarred yet.

THERAPIST:   That's right. Just notice that, yeah, he can hear it. Is there anything else we would say or do for him? **[following the adaptive action tendencies to their natural conclusion]**

CLIENT:   A hug sounds nice.

THERAPIST:   Yeah. Nice. And, again, just picture that in your mind's eye, down on his level, giving him a big hug. **[having him imagine the impact on the other]**

He sat silently as he imagined the hug. Checking the receptive affective capacities of this younger part to receive the hug, I asked, "How is it for him to get that hug if you let yourself imagine that?" Daniel responded, "I think he feels good about the dance he came up with . . . and would think about doing something similar again." I then self-disclosed to Daniel that I was moved to hear him say this and imagine him hugging his younger self. With a sense of mastery, he responded, "It's easier than I thought it would be." Following my direction to follow the scene to its conclusion, Daniel imagined his younger self bounding into his childhood home with excitement and joy.

As the portrayal and session came to a close, we began to metaprocess. I asked him what it was like to walk through this with me, and he answered, "I think it helps me give more love to myself now." I responded by affirming that in loving his younger self, he was loving himself. With tears in his eyes and a smile on his face, he looked at me and said, "I'm out of practice, but getting more flexible." I then move to metaprocessing the interrelational aspects of the experience, asking, "And how's this to do with me?"

CLIENT:   Good and easy. There's historically been a resistance in me to acknowledging you're special to me or I'm special to you. And I guess, I'm bringing that up because I feel that and that's what makes this easier.

THERAPIST:   Great, that makes me happy. And you said it right—you are special to me and this is very special to do with you. **[affirming, self-disclosure]**

CLIENT:   Yes.

THERAPIST:   How's that to acknowledge that I'm special to you and you're special to me? **[metaprocessing]**

CLIENT:   Good (*long pause as he takes that in with several breaths, then a smile emerges*) Poco a poco, I'm getting there! **[affirmation of self and therapeutic process]**

In the first case example, one can see how using a portrayal to access deep feelings of grief and sadness, viscerally experience these emotions, and dyadically regulate them together led to feeling less alone, as well as to reaping the benefits of the expression to completion and its adaptive action tendencies. In the session just described, the client was then able to use this new sense of relational connection to be compassionate with himself intra-relationally through a reunion portrayal. Realizing what his younger self needed through the use of imagination led to an expanded sense of self and more positive, transformational, healing affects.

## CONCLUSION

Emotion and the processing of emotion to completion in the context of a secure attachment-based relationship is a central component of AEDP. As a result of accessing previously overwhelming or dysregulated emotion and riding the wave of emotion to completion with the help of the therapist, the adaptive action tendencies can be released. The client then has access to new information and emotional learning, allowing them to "know what they know and feel what they feel" in relationship to others (Fosha, 2000). Portrayals offer the clinician a technique to heighten the experience of the client by engaging as many channels of experience as possible. In doing so, clients may have greater access to their emotions and, through the imagination, be able to follow the adaptive action tendencies released through to their natural conclusion. As seen in the case example, what is handled relationally through dyadic regulation then paves the way for interrelational and intra-relational healing and transformation. Thus, the three main theoretical tenets of AEDP—emotion theory, attachment theory, and transformational studies—weave together to create lasting change and transformation.

## REFERENCES

Beebe, B., & Lachmann, F. M. (2002). *Infant research and adult treatment: Co-constructing interactions*. The Analytic Press.

Blackwell, S. E. (2019). Mental imagery: From basic research to clinical practice. *Journal of Psychotherapy Integration, 29*(3), 235–247. https://doi.org/10.1037/int0000108

Bowlby, J. (1977). The making and breaking of affectional bonds: I. Aetiology and psychopathology in the light of attachment theory. *British Journal of Psychiatry, 130*(3), 201–210. https://doi.org/10.1192/bjp.130.3.201

Bowlby, J. (1991). Post-script. In C. M. Parkes, J. Stevenson-Hinde, & P. Marris (Eds.), *Attachment across the life cycle* (pp. 293–297). Routledge.

Brown, D. P., & Elliott, D. S. (2016). *Attachment disturbances in adults: Treatment for comprehensive repair*. Norton.

Damasio, A. (1999). *The feeling of what happens: Body and emotion in the making of consciousness*. Harcourt, Brace.

Dannenbaum, S. M., & Kinnier, R. T. (2009). Imaginal relationships with the dead: Applications for psychotherapy. *Journal of Humanistic Psychotherapy, 49*(1), 100–113. https://doi.org/10.1177/0022167808323577

Darwin, C. (1965). *The expression of emotion in man and animals.* University of Chicago Press. (Original work published 1872)

Davanloo, H. (1990). *Unlocking the unconscious: Selected papers of Habib Davanloo.* Wiley.

Ecker, B. (2015). Understanding memory reconsolidation. *The Neuropsychotherapist*, 4–22. https://www.researchgate.net/publication/281571640_UNDERSTANDING_MEMORY_RECONSOLIDATION

Ecker, B., Ticic, R., & Hulley, L. (2012). *Unlocking the emotional brain: Eliminating symptoms at their roots using memory reconsolidation.* Routledge. https://doi.org/10.4324/9780203804377

Ekman, P. (2007). *Emotions revealed: Recognizing faces and feelings to improve communication and emotional life* (2nd ed.). Henry Holt.

Fosha, D. (2000). *The transforming power of affect: A model of accelerated change.* Basic Books.

Fosha, D. (2001). The dyadic regulation of affect. *Journal of Clinical Psychology, 57*(2), 227–242. https://doi.org/10.1002/1097-4679(200102)57:2<227::AID-JCLP8>3.0.CO;2-1

Fosha, D. (2004). "Nothing that feels bad is ever the last step:" The role of positive emotions in experiential work with difficult emotional experiences. *Clinical Psychology & Psychotherapy, 11*(1), 30–43. https://doi.org/10.1002/cpp.390

Fosha, D. (2006). Quantum transformation in trauma and treatment: Traversing the crisis of healing change. *Journal of Clinical Psychology, 62*(5), 569–583. https://doi.org/10.1002/jclp.20249

Fosha, D. (2008). Transformance, recognition of self by self, and effective action. In K. J. Schneider (Ed.), *Existential-integrative psychotherapy: Guideposts to the core of practice* (pp. 290–320). Routledge.

Fosha, D. (2009a). Emotion and recognition at work: Energy, vitality, pleasure, truth, desire & the emergent phenomenology of transformational experience. In D. Fosha, J. Siegel, & M. F. Solomon (Eds.), *The healing power of emotion: Affective neuroscience, development, clinical practice* (pp. 172–203). Norton.

Fosha, D. (2009b). Healing attachment trauma with attachment (and then some!). In M. Kerman (Ed.), *Clinical pearls of wisdom: 21 leading therapists offer their key insights* (pp. 43–56). Norton.

Fosha, D. (2017). How to be a transformational therapist: AEDP harnesses innate healing affects to re-wire experience and accelerate transformation. In J. Loizzo, M. Neale, & E. Wolf (Eds.), *Advances in contemplative psychotherapy: Accelerating transformation* (pp. 204–219). Norton. https://doi.org/10.4324/9781315630045-18

Fosha, D. (2018). Moment-to-moment guidance of clinical interventions by AEDP's healing-oriented transformational phenomenology: Commentary on Vigoda Gonzalez's (2018) case of "Rosa." *Pragmatic Case Studies in Psychotherapy, 14*(2), 87–114. https://doi.org/10.14713/pcsp.v14i2.2038

Fosha, D. (2019). *AEDP: The phenomenology of the transformational process* [Handout]. AEDP Institute, New York, NY.

Fosha, D., & Prenn, C. N. (2017). *Supervision essentials for accelerated experiential dynamic psychotherapy.* American Psychological Association.

Fosha, D., Thoma, N., & Yeung, D. (2019). Transforming emotional suffering into flourishing: Metatherapeutic processing of positive affect as a trans-theoretical vehicle for change. *Counselling Psychology Quarterly, 32*(3–4), 563–593. https://doi.org/10.1080/09515070.2019.1642852

Gendlin, E. T. (1981). *Focusing.* Bantam New Age Paperbacks.

Giacomucci, S. (2020). Addiction, traumatic loss, and guilt: A case study resolving grief through psychodrama and sociometric connections. *The Arts in Psychotherapy, 67*, 1–6, 101627. https://doi.org/10.1016/j.aip.2019.101627

Goleman, D. (2006). *Emotional intelligence* (10th anniversary ed.). Bantam Dell.

Greenberg, L. S., & Pascual-Leone, A. (2006). Emotion in psychotherapy: A practice-friendly research review. *Journal of Clinical Psychology, 62*(5), 611–630. https://doi.org/10.1002/jclp.20252

Greenberg, L. S., Rice, L. N., & Elliott, R. (Eds.). (1997). *Facilitating emotional change: The moment-by-moment process.* Guilford Press.

Hales, S. A., Deeprose, C., Goodwin, G. M., & Holmes, E. A. (2011). Cognitions in bipolar affective disorder and unipolar depression: Imagining suicide. *Bipolar Disorders, 13*(7–8), 651–661. https://doi.org/10.1111/j.1399-5618.2011.00954.x

Harker, L., & Keltner, D. (2001). Expressions of positive emotions in women's college yearbook pictures and their relationship to life outcomes across childhood. *Journal of Personality and Social Psychology, 80,* 112–124. https://doi.org/10.1037/0022-3514.80.1.112

Hendel, H. J. (2018). *It's not always depression: Working the change triangle to listen to the body, discover core emotions, and connect to your authentic self.* Spiegel & Grau.

Iwakabe, S., Rogan, K., & Stalikas, A. (2000). The relationship between client emotional expressions, therapist interventions, and the working alliance: An exploration of eight emotional expression events. *Journal of Psychotherapy Integration, 10*(4), 375–401. https://doi.org/10.1023/A:1009479100305

Lamagna, J. (2011). Of the self, by the self, and for the self: An intra-relational perspective on intra-psychic attunement and psychological change. *Journal of Psychotherapy Integration, 21*(3), 280–307. https://doi.org/10.1037/a0025493

Lamagna, J., & Gleiser, K. A. (2007). Building a secure internal attachment: An intra-relational approach to ego strengthening and emotional processing with chronically traumatized clients. *Journal of Trauma & Dissociation, 8*(1), 25–52. https://doi.org/10.1300/J229v08n01_03

Lilliengren, P., Johansson, R., Lindqvist, K., Mechler, J., & Andersson, G. (2016). Efficacy of experiential dynamic therapy for psychiatric conditions: A meta-analysis of randomized controlled trials. *Psychotherapy, 53*(1), 90–104. https://doi.org/10.1037/pst0000024

Lipton, B. (2019). *The S.A.N.E.R. way* [PowerPoint presentation at AEDP Essential Skills]. AEDP Institute, New York, NY.

Lipton, B., & Fosha, D. (2011). Attachment as a transformative process in AEDP: Operationalizing the intersection of attachment theory and affective neuroscience. *Journal of Psychotherapy Integration, 21*(3), 253–279. https://doi.org/10.1037/a0025421

Markin, R. D., McCarthy, K. S., Fuhrmann, A., Yeung, D., & Gleiser, K. A. (2018). The process of change in accelerated experiential dynamic psychotherapy (AEDP): A case study analysis. *Journal of Psychotherapy Integration, 28*(2), 213–232. https://doi.org/10.1037/int0000084

Medley, B. (2018). Recovering the True Self: Affirmative therapy, attachment and AEDP in psychotherapy with gay men. *Journal of Psychotherapy Integration.* Advance online publication. https://doi.org/10.1037/int0000132

Morina, N., Lancee, J., & Arntz, A. (2017). Imagery rescripting as a clinical intervention for aversive memories: A meta-analysis. *Journal of Behavior Therapy and Experimental Psychiatry, 55,* 6–15. https://doi.org/10.1016/j.jbtep.2016.11.003

Moritz, S., Ahlf-Schumacher, J., Hottenrott, B., Peter, U., Franck, S., Schnell, T., Peter, H., Schneider, B. C., & Jelinek, L. (2018). We cannot change the past, but we can change its meaning. A randomized controlled trial on the effects of self-help imagery rescripting on depression. *Behaviour Research and Therapy, 104,* 74–83. https://doi.org/10.1016/j.brat.2018.02.007

Nummenmaa, L., Glerean, E., Hari, R., & Hietanen, J. K. (2014). Bodily maps of emotions. *Proceedings of the National Academy of Sciences of the United States of America, 111*(2), 646–651. https://doi.org/10.1073/pnas.1321664111

Pally, R. (2000). *The mind–brain relationship.* Karnac Books.

Pando-Mars, K. (2016). Tailoring AEDP interventions to attachment style. *Transformance: The AEDP Journal, 6*(2). https://aedpinstitute.org/transformance/tailoring-aedp-interventions-to-attachment-style-pg1/

Panksepp, J. (2009). Brain emotional systems and quality of mental health life: From animal models of affect to implications for psychotherapeutics. In D. Fosha, D. J. Siegel, & M. F. Solomon (Eds.), *The healing power of emotion: Affective neuroscience, development & clinical practice* (pp. 1–26). Norton.

Parra, F., George, C., Kalalou, K., & Januel, D. (2017). Ideal parent figure method in the treatment of complex posttraumatic stress disorder related to childhood trauma: A pilot study. *European Journal of Psychotraumatology, 8*(1), 1400879. https://doi.org/10.1080/20008198.2017.1400879

Pascual-Leone, A. (2018). How clients "change emotion with emotion": A programme of research on emotional processing. *Psychotherapy Research, 28*(2), 165–182. https://doi.org/10.1080/10503307.2017.1349350

Perls, F., Hefferline, G., & Goodman, P. (1951). *Gestalt therapy: Excitement and growth in the human personality*. Dell.

Prenn, N. (2011). Mind the gap: AEDP interventions translating attachment theory into clinical practice. *Journal of Psychotherapy Integration, 21*(3), 308–329. https://doi.org/10.1037/a0025491

Russell, E. (2015). *Restoring resilience: Discovering your clients' capacity for healing*. Norton.

Schore, A. N. (2003). *Affect regulation and the repair of the self*. Norton.

Schwartz, R. (1995). *Internal family systems therapy*. Guilford Press.

Siegel, D. (1999). *The developing mind*. Guilford Press.

Smucker, M. R., Dancu, C., Foa, E. B., & Niederee, J. L. (1995). Imagery rescripting: A new treatment for survivors of childhood sexual abuse suffering from posttraumatic stress. *Journal of Cognitive Psychotherapy, 9*(1), 3–17. http://www.ingentaconnect.com/content/springer/jcogp/1995/00000009/00000007/art00001. https://doi.org/10.1891/0889-8391.9.1.3

Taylor, J. B. (2006). *My stroke of insight: A brain scientist's personal journey*. Penguin.

Tronick, E. Z. (1989). Emotions and emotional communication in infants. *American Psychologist, 44*(2), 112–119. https://doi.org/10.1037/0003-066X.44.2.112

Tronick, E. Z., Bruschweiler-Stern, N., Harrison, A. M., Lyons-Ruth, K., Morgan, A. C., Nahum, J. P., Sander, L., & Stern, D. N. (1998). Dyadically expanded states of consciousness and the process of therapeutic change. *Infant Mental Health Journal, 19*(3), 290–299. https://doi.org/10.1002/(SICI)1097-0355(199823)19:3<290::AID-IMHJ4>3.0.CO;2-Q

Tunnell, G. (2012). Gay male couple therapy: An attachment model. In J. J. Bigner & J. L. Wetchler (Eds.), *Handbook of LGBT-affirmative couple and family therapy* (pp. 25–42). Routledge.

Volynets, S., Glerean, E., Hietanen, J. K., Hari, R., & Nummenmaa, L. (2019). Bodily maps of emotions are culturally universal. *Emotion, 111*(2), 646–651. https://doi.org/10.1037/emo0000624

Watkins, J. G., & Watkins, H. H. (1997). *Ego states: Theory and therapy*. Norton.

Welling, H. (2019). Is this AEDP: 6 characteristics of AEDP. *Transformance: The AEDP Journal, 9.* https://aedpinstitute.org/transformance-volume-9-summer-reading-issue-4/

# 9

# Agency, Will, and Desire as Core Affective Experience

*Undoing Disempowerment to Foster the Emergence of the Agentic Self*

Eileen M. Russell

One young woman reacted with incredible relief when I suggested that there was a way in which she carried herself in the world as if she were vapor rather than something solid. Another woman described feeling like a bag of bones, a lifeless heap collapsed after years of constant criticism and physical abuse with no sense of being able to make a difference and sense of despair about trying. She was neither depressed nor impaired in her functioning, but rather was describing an experience of self. And a man was so riddled with anxiety about not being taken seriously or respected that the only way he could find to have an impact was to become suddenly and inappropriately aggressive, which he would then pay for with a hangover of intense shame. Whatever other emotional issues needed to be dealt with, in all of these cases, something essential was missing from the sense of self that was not simply going to "emerge" fully formed in conditions of even the safest, most secure therapeutic relationship.

Specifically, an embodied sense of personal agency, of mattering and making a difference, and of being able to authentically effect one's life, to know and assert one's will, to declare one's desires, and to have an impact on important relationships and goals are underdeveloped core affective experiences in many people who present with symptoms of languishing, depression, anxiety, defenses, and intrapsychic and interpersonal conflict. Therapeutic work with these issues often requires a slightly different process and focus than accelerated experiential dynamic psychotherapy (AEDP) therapists may be accustomed to when the focus is on reaching repressed or unprocessed emotions. Instead, the

https://doi.org/10.1037/0000232-010
*Undoing Aloneness and the Transformation of Suffering Into Flourishing: AEDP 2.0*, D. Fosha (Editor)

work involves noticing what is missing and actively seeking conditions and circumstances in which *crucial developmental processes* of separation, individuation, and autonomy that were cut short or largely abandoned can be resumed, nurtured, expanded, and delighted in.

In cases like these, as well as myriad others, there is something fundamentally happening *or not happening* in the self (the self being conceived of as "I") that is an affectively mediated, embodied way of relating the self to the world and is fundamental; it cannot be equated to any current State 2 category in AEDP theory and is not something that is simply derived from processing emotions to completion. Rather, the sense of agency, will, and connection to one's desire that are missing are themselves State 2 core affective experiences that deserve to be named because of their centrality to pathology, development, and healing.

This chapter explores the phenomena of agency, will, and desire as State 2 adaptive core affective experiences, thus expanding AEDP's previous conceptualizations of State 2 core affective experiences and will contextualize them in developmental theory and relational psychoanalytic theory. Further, the chapter illustrates how these affective, somatically based experiences are the exact opposite of what we see in State 2 *maladaptive affective experience*—specifically, the experience of helplessness, toxic shame, and even fragmentation. Energetically, posturally, and affectively felt experiences of agency, will, and desire (Porges's *ventral vagal response*) are the opposite of pathogenic shame states (Porges's *dorsal vagal response*). The latter manifest at two corners of the Triangle of Experience (Fosha, 2000). At times, they represent maladaptive affective experiences such as the loss of agency, too much aloneness, or overwhelming shame; at other times, they serve the purpose of defense, keeping the individual small, unnoticeable, and unthreatening to others (Porges, 2011). At still other times, they serve both functions simultaneously. Reinforced and entrained states of helplessness or ineffectuality lead to an embodied experience of being unaware of one's own desires, disconnected from one's own will, and alienated from a sense of agency to act *on behalf of the self* (Russell, 2015) in a transformance-oriented way. It is as if the adaptive action tendency—adaptive there-and-then and grossly maladaptive here-and-now—is to not be, to not matter. The chapter illustrates these theoretical and clinical connections through brief vignettes of work with a particular patient whose hard work and perseverance have done much to inform my understanding of the centrality of these issues for many who present for psychotherapy.

## EXPANDING STATE 2 CORE AFFECTIVE EXPERIENCE

Babies and toddlers need a lot of responsive caregiving to develop a sense of trust and safety in their caregivers and in their worlds more generally. Attachment theory shows how the safety of that caregiving bond allows developing children to explore and engage with their world (Ainsworth et al., 1978; Main et al., 1985). AEDP's model of replicating that early, necessary safety in the therapeutic relationship allows individuals in psychotherapy to explore and engage in their interior world of thoughts, feelings, self-states, and relational experiences to live freer, more integrated, and fulfilling lives (Fosha, 2000; 2003; Lipton & Fosha, 2011; Pando-Mars, 2016; Russell, 2015). Part of how this sense of safety is achieved is through the AEDP stance, which is warm, curious, permission-giving, affectively engaged, and explicitly empathic. It is often marked by a shared sense of closeness and being in something "together."

But, according to Erikson (1968), developing safety and trust is only the very earliest emotional–relational task of development, although like all the tasks, it continues to be relevant through the life span. Later tasks involving differentiation and individuation are not only part of childhood development, they are also necessary core capacities of healthy adulthood and therefore crucial elements of many psychotherapeutic relationships. Interpersonally, the environment required for the development of differentiation may be less characterized by softness, "in sync-ness," or "we-ness," and more by a focus on self–other and the possibility that the self may need to push *against* the other and be recognized for doing so.

For many, however, particularly those who have experienced relational trauma, neglect, abuse, oppression, debilitating depression, or severe illness or disability, their capacity to access these core affective phenomena is compromised. Importantly also, people who have been raised in apparently loving but very enmeshed environments or individuals used as narcissistic extensions of compromised caregivers, rather than recognized as individual persons in their own right, can have great difficulty accessing an agentic self (i.e., agency, will, or desire). In situations when the agency or will of a person is regularly, even systematically, subjugated to that of another or a system that is dominant and likely dominating, there can be an unknowing of one's own desires and a disconnection from a felt sense of one's own will and sense of agency (the capacity to express or assert that will). It is in such cases that therapy must place an explicit focus on facilitating this reconnection to and building up of an individual's personal agency, will, and authentic desires.

Developmental tasks are achieved in contingent relationship. If a baby is not responded to with predictable caregiving, the child will fail to develop the capacity to trust and the experience of safety with another. If a child's own will and sense of autonomy are not met with curiosity and respect, as well as limits, the child does not have the *experience* of being a separate, good-enough self that has the capacity to effect relationships and the environment. The kind of contingent relationship that fosters the development of agency, autonomy, and industry involves responsive caregiving as well as limits, the experience of conflict, and capacity on the part of the caregiver to notice and respect difference, to allow for the expression of the separate will and desires of the child. In the therapeutic relationship, this may require the therapist's offering of oneself as the person to come up *against* to discover and expand the patient's self and its capacities and uniqueness.

## The Transformational Other as Seeder of Potential

This chapter and its musings slowly grew out of working in AEDP for more than 20 years and finding that there were a few patients for whom affective and relational processing was not leading to significant change and vitality in their lives. It became clear that a bottom-up metapsychology that trusts all ingredients are there and ready to flourish if given enough light, warmth, and air (i.e., "making space") may not be sufficient to help restore critical developmental capacities that have been stalled or impaired by circumstance and repeated experiences with being invisible, overlooked, marginalized, disempowered, criticized, shamed, overshadowed, and the like. In these cases, something new had to be identified, nurtured, and grown in the person. In AEDP, we tend to think of State 2 processing as "making space" to feel and process something that has been psychically forbidden for people to gain access to the latent adaptive capacities and power they already have. What I want to address here is the possibility of deficit—that neglect, exploitation, and oppression of any kind leave holes in the development of self. When these holes exist, State 2 processing needs to involve, on the part of the therapist, active and patient calling attention to those places, insistence that some self-capacities must exist within the patient if the person is to become whole, and intrepid faith that the patient can and deserves to develop these capacities.

In earlier writing (Russell, 2015), I introduced the concept of the *transformational other*. This refers to the possible role of the therapist as someone who can "identify and elaborate that which is emerging; to privilege hope, curiosity and openness and the yet to be fully expressed core affective experience over fear, anxiety, shame, and one's characteristic defenses" (p. 120). In the clinical situations discussed later in the chapter, it is clear that a therapist is not in a position to identify and help elaborate something if it is *not emerging* (as in *glimmers* or *heralding affects*) if it is too unconscious or underdeveloped even to make an appearance for the therapist to respond to. Rather, as *transformational others*, we may at times need to identify what is *not there*, what *seems to be* chronically absent, and to be curious about that and to introduce the possibility that an *agentic self* exists or should exist. Not infrequently an AEDP therapist may feel anger or sadness on behalf of patients who may not yet be able to feel this on their own behalf. Similarly, when face-to-face with people who consistently fail to act on their own behalf, whose passivity and lack of reaction is the default drive, AEDP therapists may feel the need to move—to do *something*. Sometimes this translates into our *doing for*, offering advice, or even taking on the collapse as if it is our own. What is needed instead is to create conditions in which such individuals can begin to experience their own desires, will, and sense of agency. Sometimes this may require a push from us. And sometimes it requires us to be willing to be pushed against. It requires us to be willing to allow the "disruption" in the coordination–disruption–repair cycle of a secure relationship.

## Dependency and Togetherness *and* Autonomy and Individuation

The heart and art of AEDP is helping people to feel safe enough to *lean into* the therapeutic relationship to explore their interior worlds and to heal from the inside out. Less developed in our theory and practices is how to use the security of this connection to help people *lean out*. Many patients, in fact, have historically felt too unsafe to lean *away* from relationship to know their own minds and hearts. Fosha (2013; see also Fosha, Chapter 14, this volume) began to explore this separate, differentiated "I" in a paper on the *neurobiological core self*, glimpsed even in people with highly dissociative presentations. Erik Erikson's developmental theory clearly spells out the necessity of the developmental tasks of nurturing and growing this self in early stages of life. In fact, only one of Erikson's early developmental stages is devoted to safety in togetherness as primary: trust versus mistrust (Erikson, 1968). Beyond that, his theory lays out the ways in which the child is tasked with finding, experiencing, and expressing an increasingly differentiated and complex self in the context of ongoing relationships of responsiveness and care. "I" is no longer simply "we." Rather, there is a building up of an "I" and a moving back and forth between "I" and "we." It is not that safety is no longer operative or important; far from it. Rather, it is absolutely necessary, and although still functioning, safety moves more to the background as tasks of developing an "I" increasingly come to the foreground.[1]

In Margaret Mahler's observations of infants-becoming-children, dependent children develop a sense of autonomy and independence as they are increasingly able to recognize themselves and their mothers to be different and separate. This allows for *individuation*, or the birth of the sense of self (Mahler et al., 1975). In Erikson's Stages 2 through 4, the differentiation of the self is primary: Autonomy versus Shame, Initiative versus Doubt, Industry versus Inferiority (Erikson, 1968). So, while being loved, protected and cared for, the child is actively deepening a sense of self and the self's capacities. These are the kind of motivated, energized, and enlivened positive self-states that Fosha (2013) identified with the *core self*. But as with any task of development, if things go awry, the process of differentiation in which one discovers that "I am ok. You are ok" may be sacrificed for togetherness at the expense of self, or self-ness at the expense of relatedness, the latter representing isolation rather than real autonomy.

Jessica Benjamin (1990) wrote about the birth of this self and the paradoxical nature of the child's dependence on an other to become a separate or independent self. She stated that "the need for recognition entails this

---

[1] I am aware of the potential limitations of these developmental theories across cultures, particularly ones that do not prize individuality. For now, I am happy to limit this discussion to Western cultures in which the self is arguably even too prominent.

fundamental paradox: in the very moment of realizing our own independent will, we are dependent on another to recognize it" (p. 39). In other words, in the context of safe dependency, the child learns ideally to become independent, and later to become interdependent. Any attuned parent can attest to the subtle and sometimes tricky territory of threading this needle: of recognizing the child's independent wishes, will, and capacity to act without conferring too much power to a being who may not be ready for such responsibility or extinguishing that independent will by asserting too much parental/adult authority and forcing the child to submit. Rather, what Benjamin was talking about is that just as dependency and care/safety needs require responsiveness and recognition in the infancy years, so too do independence and autonomy strivings need recognition and permission with limits in the childhood years. As I see it, it is in the former that the child infers important information about the reliability, capacity, and benevolence of the world and others. In the latter, the child infers information about the reliability, capacity, and benevolence of the self.

The *agentic self* is the term I use in this chapter to refer to an embodied sense of being able to act in the world, to have an impact on one's surroundings and important relationships, and the felt sense of connection between one's will and desires and one's goals. It is the opposite of the pathogenic self-states marked by terror, toxic shame, helplessness, or hopelessness.

## LIVING IN THE BALANCE BETWEEN CREATING ONE'S OWN DESTINY AND DETERMINISM OR FATE

I do not hope to resolve the age-old dilemma between a view of human beings as largely determined by forces outside of their control (or even awareness) versus being masters of their own destiny. I do believe it is fair to say that healthy psychological development needs to make space for both and that it is reasonable to assume that most people function optimally in subjectively placing themselves somewhere in the middle: having a sense of responsibility, desire, energy, and agency to act in a way that benefits their own lives and the lives of people they care about, while also being humble and accepting of the complexity of the world, their own strengths and limitations, the multiple and complex systems of which they are a part, and the natural world. But many people present to psychotherapy burdened by the rigid demands of one side of this dialectic or the other.

On the one hand, we have a "pull yourself up by the bootstraps" and "create your own destiny" (albeit they are not wholly equivalent) perspective, which suggests that we will our way through overcoming obstacles and have ultimate power over the course of our lives. On the positive side, this is hopeful about our own capacity to affect our lives; it is encouraging of clear thinking and taking action. The shadow side of this perspective is that it ignores the many forces that move against implementing one's will, desires, and goals and can leave a person to internalize shame when they face hardship, experience a loss, fail to achieve a goal, or are suffering in general. This part of the dialectic is reflected in positive psychology, "the Secret," the "prosperity gospel," and our idolization of rich, famous, and successful people. It is also highly individualistic and, at its extremes, does not take into account concern for the common good or the effect of a person's will or willingness on other people or the planet.

On the other hand, we have a view of "experience is fate." This is generously exemplified in many of our psychological theories and currently in the field's emphasis on trauma. Often well-meaning and compassionate (although arguably also condescending and undermining at times), our current manifestations of determinism emphasize the limited capacity of the individual to effect his or her own life and can spell out in remarkable detail the myriad negative consequences of trauma on the autonomy and efficaciousness of the individual. This view marvels at resilient people in part because it cannot make sense of them through its own theories. The shadow side of this perspective is that it may fail to recognize untapped or unexpressed forces of transformance and resilience, and similarly, it may fail to recognize the power of unconscious forces of resistance. People can remain "safe" in very self-limiting patterns of behavior, thoughts, emotions, and relationships.

Bollas's (1989) concept of fatedness—a sense of having very little capacity to affect one's own destiny—is a counterpoint to the sense of agency, will, and desire that is being discussed here. For many who present to psychotherapy, this sense of fatedness is strong. The support, safety, and hope offered by the therapeutic attachment creates a window of opportunity to develop a capacity that may have been derailed or shamed out of being—a chance to invest in an agentic self and risk knowing the desires of one's heart, the will of one's mind, and the sense of being able in one's body.

### Wired to Try but Conditioned to Fail

We know from attachment theory and research that when babies and children feel safe and seen, they are willing and able to explore their environments (Bowlby, 1989). If their caregiving environments are too unstable, unpredictable, neglecting, or cruel, the drive to explore may be shut down in deference to the need to find safety. We seem to be wired to try, to reach, to explore, to push our own boundaries and find what we are capable of and how the world responds. When this drive is unencumbered, the individual can accumulate experiences of trying, of agentic involvement with his world that are positive and self-reinforcing—what Panksepp has called the "seeking system" (Panksepp & Northoff, 2009). But if, for some reason, this drive is blocked or met with repeated experiences of failure to effect or connect, the recursive pattern of self-doubt or despair about the self can lead to an embodied sense of not mattering, not existing, not making a difference in one's world or one's life. The core sense that "I can do" is missing; an essential propulsive force in life is absent. This is particularly true if avoidance, withdrawal, or helplessness have been successfully protective. In the words of the patient in the case study later in the chapter: "It's also a lack of a sense of like . . . that I take up space in the world . . . or have a momentum that touches other things and changes them . . . I have a hard time seeing myself as an actor" and "I don't really believe in my own presence."

*Transformance* is AEDP's term to describe the "overarching motivational force, operating in both development and therapy that strives toward maximal vitality, authenticity, and genuine contact" (Fosha, 2008, p. 292). Others have used different terms to try to capture the energy, action, and sense of self and willingness that are associated with affecting the world and one's life: "destiny drive" (Bollas, 1989), "striving" (Adler, 1964), "self-actualization" (Maslow, 1943), "surrender" (Ghent, 1990), "positive will" (Rank, 1936). Both transformance and resistance operate in all people at all times (Fosha, Chapter 1, this volume). For people who have an underdeveloped sense of agency, resistance (what Rank [1936] termed "negative will") easily takes over, and so do maladaptive affective states of shame, helplessness, hopelessness, apathy, and the like. In earlier work (Russell, 2015), I explored how AEDP conceptualizes resilience as existing on a continuum from being *on behalf of the self* in conservative and resistance-oriented ways to more expansive and transformance-oriented ways.

## To Expand or to Contract on Behalf of the Self

The *New Yorker* magazine had an exposé about children in Sweden facing deportation to their parents' country of origin (Aviv, 2017). Hundreds of these children went into a catatonic collapsed state for weeks to months with no movement and no responsiveness. They neither ate nor moved, even to use the bathroom. The director of a child psychiatry institute there referred to it as a kind of "willed dying," an interesting way of formulating the problem, as it reflects some of the language of the late Otto Rank (1936), who conceptualized much of psychological pathology as an expression of the "negative will."[2] As I understand it, given such limited possibilities for the expression of will or agency, the self has little choice but to *move against the self in an effort to preserve the self.* Children about to be deported will cut themselves off, lose massive amounts of weight, urinate and defecate on themselves, becoming completely dependent, and even require invasive medical care because there is no healthy, adaptive, fruitful expression of their will or sense of agency. They literally become hopeless and helpless (as in maladaptive State 2). This is a brilliant "defense." But it is also an embodied affective experience, and as such, it is a wired way human beings have to adapt to extreme circumstances of fear and chronic disempowerment.

Porges's (2005, 2011) polyvagal theory explains that humans have evolved a functional neural organization that regulates visceral states to support social behavior that Porges called the "social engagement system." It allows people to engage with and use others to regulate internal states and negotiate stress

---

[2]Rank (1936) stated, "The goal of constructive therapy is not the overcoming of resistance, but the transformation of the negative will expression (counter-will) underlying them into positive and eventually creative expression" (p. 19).

and threat. This is human beings' highest level of nervous system response strategy and is also referred to as the ventral vagal system (e.g., head turning, vocalizations, facial expression, gaze). When unable to use the ventral vagal system, humans resort to earlier, more primitive responses to threat and challenge, such as fight-or-flight. These are less social and more survival oriented. The lowest level is the dorsal vagal system or the immobilization system that allows for freezing and even feigning death, as the children described earlier seem to have employed.

To unconsciously or unwittingly regress to less movement and agentic, purposive action for the sake of remaining alive is remarkable. But although it may be "on behalf of the self" (Russell, 2015), it can hardly be said to involve agency or even conscious will. In fact, it is the complete opposite. It is the collapse that is evolutionarily built in for the simple and sole purpose of preserving life. And although not all human experiences of collapse involve feigned or near death, maladaptive affective experiences of collapse due to toxic shaming, terror, chronic experiences of helplessness or hopelessness are devoid of personal agency, will, and desire and the self's dignity. This is precisely because, in many cases, these individuals were not respected, nor was their dignity preserved, by those in the person's environment who were the progenitors of that shame or disempowerment. There is no allowance for these expressions of self, so they are abandoned in preference for a more basic need, which is to survive and to maintain connection with a needed other, no matter how problematic that other may be.

Figure 9.1 (see State 2 of Figure 9.1) illustrates what has been said so far—namely, that agency, will, and desire belong in State 2 as a distinct category of *adaptive core affective experience*. They stand in contradistinction in a particular way to what Fosha earlier highlighted as *maladaptive affective experience* (Fosha, 2002). Naming agency, will, and desire, as a separate category of adaptive core affective experience, having to do with individuals' will (conscious and unconscious) and felt sense of capacity to act constructively on their own behalf in their present lives, should help clinicians look for these clinical phenomena as well as to notice their absence, especially among people with histories of trauma and neglect or being used as a surrogate by a dominant other.

## CASE VIGNETTE 1: DEFINING THE PROBLEM AND IDENTIFYING WHAT IS MISSING

The case I use in this chapter to illustrate these concepts is a young woman with whom I have worked for several years.[3] She is articulate, thoughtful, sensitive, intelligent, and funny. It is partly because of her careful sharing of her experience that I have come to understand the clinical importance of agency, will, and desire for many people.

---

[3]I have complied with American Psychological Association ethical standards in describing the details of treatment; aspects of patients' identities and backgrounds have been disguised to protect their confidentiality.

**FIGURE 9.1. The Phenomenology of the Four-State Transformational Process in AEDP, Including the Maladaptive Affective Experiences (i.e., the Pathogenic Affects and the Unbearable States of Traumatic Aloneness)**

**STATE 1: Stress, Distress, & Symptoms**
Defenses; inhibiting affects (e.g., anxiety, shame, guilt); stress; demoralization; entrenched defenses and pathogenic self states

↔

**STATE 1: Transformance**
Glimmers of resilience, health, strength; manifestations of the drive to heal; glimmers of access to embodied affective experience

**Transitional Affects:** Intrapsychic crisis; heralding affects, i.e., glimmers of maladaptive affective experience; **RED Signal Affects:** Announcing danger of overwhelm, toxic shame etc.

**Transitional Affects:** Intrapsychic crisis; heralding affects, i.e., glimmers of core affective experience
**GREEN Signal Affects:** Announcing openness to experience, signaling safety, readiness to shift

**1ST STATE TRANSFORMATION**
Cocreating safety

**STATE 2: Maladaptive Affective Experiences (need transforming)**
"The Abyss"
The pathogenic affects (e.g., overwhelm, toxic shame, fear without solution); unbearable states of traumatic aloneness (e.g., helplessness, fragmentation, brokenness; despair, "the black hole of trauma")

↔

**STATE 2: Adaptive Core Affective Experiences (are transforming)**
"The Wave"
Categorical emotions; relational experiences, asymmetric (attachment) or symmetric (intersubjective); coordinated relational experiences; receptive affective experiences; somatic "drop-down" states; intra-relational experiences; authentic self-experiences; experiences of agency, will and desire; attachment strivings; the expression of core needs

**2nd STATE TRANSFORMATION**
The emergence of resilience

**Post-Breakthrough Affects:** Relief, hope, feeling stronger, lighter, etc.
**Adaptive Action Tendencies**

**STATE 3: Transformational Experiences**
"The Spiral"
*The mastery affects* (e.g., pride, joy); *the mourning-the-self affects* (emotional pain); *the healing affects* associated with recognition and affirmation of the transformation of the self (gratitude, tenderness, feeling moved); *the tremulous affects* associated with the intense, new experiences; *the enlivening affects* (exuberance, enthusiasm, exploratory zest) associated with delighting in the surprise at the unbrokenness of the self; *the realization affects* (e.g., the "yes!" and "wow" affects, the "click" of recognition) associated with new understanding

**3rd STATE TRANSFORMATION**
The coengendering of secure attachment and the positive valuation of the self

**Energy, Vitality, Openness, Aliveness**

**STATE 4: CORE STATE and The Truth Sense**
"The Broad Path"
Calm, flow, ease; I/Thou relating; openness; compassion and self-compassion; sense of clarity; wisdom, generosity, kindness; the sense of things feeling "right;" the experience of "this is me;" new truth, new meaning; the emergence of a coherent and cohesive autobiographical narrative

*Note.* Copyright © 2020 by Diana Fosha. Reprinted with permission.

Alex is in her mid-30s. She suffers with a relatively hidden disability that has been present all her life but that was not diagnosed until adolescence. It currently prevents her from supporting herself financially and makes many activities of daily living more laborious than for most people. Early in our work, we recognized that she had a tendency to not finish things and to have elaborate fantasies of being the best at something, of being admired by all. She came to call these her "every woman" fantasies. At the time of the following sessions, her life is more stable, she is committing to a man with whom she shares a secure attachment bond, and she is trying to create a life of part-time work that she is physically capable of doing.

Alex's parents were generally loving, although with limited emotional intelligence, and were sometimes critical and shaming, particularly around incapacities that were a product of her disability without their knowing it.

In this first section of transcript, the patient comes in announcing three developments in her own independence and assumption of adult roles and responsibilities. She is evidently happy and excited, although typically muted in her expression, about all of this. The therapist joins her in that for the first few minutes until we hit some inhibitory affect (the "A" corner of the Triangle of Experience) around exposing to others the importance of and commitment to her primary relationship. She begins to say that it is hard and "weird" to see herself doing things in the world, as if there is a disowning of her agentic self, and admits that she is more comfortable being "surreptitious." Noting the presence of the inhibition, the therapist starts with a transformation-oriented observation. (In the dialogue that follows, the italicized comments in parentheses describe the nonverbal aspects of the interaction, and bolded comments in brackets are about the process.)

THERAPIST: I think what I'm struck by right now as we obviously continue to explore the inhibitory feeling . . . is that it's not actually inhibiting your actions . . . **[Transformation focus, inhibition is consciously mediated: Transformation and resilience are embodied, action-oriented but less conscious.]**

PATIENT: Mmm-hmmm . . . (*smiles*) . . . yeah . . .

THERAPIST: That's really huge to me . . .

PATIENT: No, that feels like a really big deal . . . **[accessing more of the self-at-best; the part of the self that does have agency, will, and desire and can act on her own behalf]** It's like it's something that feels a little new for me in a way. . . . But I think that there's also just a sense of, or a lack of the sense that I . . . take up space in the world or have an impact in the world or have a, like a momentum that touches other things and changes them. It's strange, I guess I have sort of a hard time . . . (*one hand lifts near temple*) . . . seeing myself as an actor . . . as somebody who *does* (*hand sweeps forward*) . . . somebody who . . .

THERAPIST: Has agency?

PATIENT:        Has agency, has desire, has will.

THERAPIST:    (*emphatically but gently*) Yes . . . (*patient nodding*) that feels really important to me.

PATIENT:        Yeah.

## EFFECTING ONE'S WORLD: MIRRORING BEING

Here the patient has finally named what is really bothering her, what feels missing, what is related to the inhibitory feeling and to a sense of the lack of reality around doing new things. This is certainly sad, as the patient will say and process. But the expression and processing of the emotion around the lack or loss of something is not the same as, and does not necessarily lead to, the development of that thing. Something new still has to be grown and nurtured. The experiences of agency, will, and desire are not simply byproducts of processing affective experience, although they are present and integrated in core state. Nor are they simply the adaptive action tendencies that come from processing certain states. They are affectively laden self-experiences that if disrupted, get derailed, repressed, denied, and even turned against the self. In State 2 work, they are yet to be felt and experienced in an embodied way; they are emergent and not yet integrated.

Jonathan Slavin's examination of personal agency focuses on the early developmental negotiation of "mutual impact" that a child must experience with caregivers; that is, he must internalize the experience of being recognized and having an impact on others as well as being impacted as a separate self (Pollack & Slavin, 1998; Slavin, 2010). Slavin (2010) also asserted that part of what is healing in psychoanalysis is the patient's experience of being recognized by and having an impact on the self of the therapist. In fact, that is an important piece of what happens experientially and explicitly with this patient using AEDP in the excerpts that follow. We are not simply affectively mirroring. We are also mirroring the *being of the person's self.*

We need to act, to do, and to be real. If that is not recognized, allowed, nor fostered, it will get expressed somehow, but usually to the patient's detriment. Pollock and Slavin (1998) articulated it well: "Through repression, dissociation, and symptom formation, the self can be a motivated, 'agentic' initiator in the dismantling of its own agency" (p. 858). Rank (1936) recognized that it is the will of the patient that manifests as "resistance" and rejected the psychoanalytic notion that "cure" comes through the letting go of resistance. Rather, as he saw it, people got better through the transforming of their negative will ("resistance") into positive will. Rank did not use the term "transformance," but it seems fair to say that he was getting at something quite similar: The success of therapy, he said, depends on "the ability to allow this will-to-health to be preserved and strengthened in the patient himself, instead of permitting it to be projected upon the analyst" (1936, p. 17). This is similar to how I have conceptualized resilience (Russell, 2015) and the function of therapy to be an opportunity to convert the expression of resilience (being on behalf of oneself) from resistance and conservation to transformation and flourishing.

PATIENT:   I think that . . . like this feels like a really key thing (*index finger and thumb press together*) and I want to know it and I want to figure it out and like in a way, I'm frustrated 'cause I just . . . want to be better, you know . . . by that I mean cured of this thing. **[increasing transformation and vitality]** . . . I feel sort of ghostly in a way like I'm sort of moving through life and I don't really believe in my own like presence. . . I mean I guess what it feels like to sort of not matter . . . like the idea that I matter. . . . It's not like I rejected it or . . . it just feels like it was not there to begin with or it has not been there for a really long time and . . . like for me I feel in a way like I . . . like I just sort of don't exist . . . even though that's not true but it . . .

THERAPIST:   (*interrupting to help*) I get you . . . I hear you. . . . What are you feeling? Do you feel anything as you're saying . . . or if you hear what you're saying? **[affective/somatic exploration of core truth]**

PATIENT:   I don't know . . . I feel like I'm supposed to be sad about that, but I don't necessarily feel totally like sad. I mean it sort of sounds devastating . . . it just feels kind of matter of fact to say it . . . it feels like it should be sad.

THERAPIST:   It feels that to me . . . I had a feeling of sadness hearing you say that . . . I'm sure you read that on my face too. **[therapist self-disclosure of impact of patient on therapist; speaking to the bottom of the triangle of experience]**

PATIENT:   Yeah.

THERAPIST:   What's it like for you that I feel sad? **[metaprocessing of patient having an impact on therapist]**

PATIENT:   Well I mean it makes sense . . . like if somebody told me that, I would be sad . . . I would do the same thing. **[somewhat intellectualized response; mostly defense; still no feeling]**

THERAPIST:   And it feels okay in this moment that your kind of speaking your own truth has an impact on me? **[pressuring with empathy;⁴ acknowledging explicitly the patient's impact indicates that she matters and also affects relationships in her life]**

---

⁴"Pressuring with empathy" is a term introduced by Russell (2015), borrowing from concept of "pressuring" from short-term dynamic psychotherapy (Davanloo, 1990) in which the therapist puts pressure on the defenses to get them to relinquish. In AEDP, we do this in a less confrontational style and with empathy, connection, and warmth.

PATIENT:   Yeah . . . but like the *sense* that it would have an impact on you . . . it's just not very close to the surface . . . you know like the sense that I am a person with presence and agency . . . that is buried way down . . .

THERAPIST:   (*nodding with serious face; listening intently*) Mm-hmm.

This is a beautiful example of what Benjamin's (1990) earlier quote referred to about the need for recognition in the process of becoming a self. What is critically important, developmentally and therapeutically, and what the therapist pays explicit attention to and metaprocesses, is the experience of the emergent agentic self being recognized and welcomed by a caring other who is capable of seeing the person as an authentic and autonomous self with a mind and heart of her own.

## CASE VIGNETTE 2: AGENCY AS THE ANTIDOTE TO MALADAPTIVE SHAME

At another time, Alex shares how aware she has become of how she has dissociated from her own experience of shame, which is quite pervasive in her life and manifests in defenses like obsessiveness and escaping into fantasy images of herself as invulnerable that the dyad came to call the "every woman." She realized that the shame was about what she couldn't do (referring to her disability as a child) as well as her parents' reaction to those incapacities and difficulties. We spend some time opening up and witnessing the shame itself (Russell, 2015).

PATIENT:   (*eyes closed*) I feel, like, sad that this feeling (*shame*) is there . . . that it's there and I don't know about it. . . . It feels like this emotion of shame that feels so . . . (*head tilts side to side*) . . . so like integrated into my life . . . to the extent that . . . the every woman thing . . . feels like . . . a reasonable way of responding . . . understandable way of responding (*eyes widen, one hand lifts upward*) . . . to like this feeling of just being so . . . (*hands sweep inward*) . . . I don't know . . . bad or like not capable.

THERAPIST:   Mmm-hmm . . . I'm really . . . struck by and glad to hear that understanding this part . . . helps you understand a little bit more . . . but also to feel more compassionate about that part . . . really understanding if there is this deep pocket of shame that kind of infiltrates a lot in you, then it really makes sense for you to have this kind of compensatory fantasy self that is . . . kind of invulnerable. **[appreciating the need for and function of the defense of the fantasy self]**

PATIENT:   And in a way like I don't want to reject that part of it **[Patient recognizes *resilience potential* (Russell, 2015) in fantasy**

**that is largely counterproductive as not black and white; it, too, holds some truth, some hopefulness about herself.]** . . . I don't know. I want to like (*one hand lifts and flutters to find words*) . . . I guess I want . . . I'm just like hungering for some **[desire, deep yearning on behalf of the self]** like confidence I think . . . like some sense that "oh, I want to do this" **[desire, will]** and . . . I *can* do this thing **[sense of agency]**.

THERAPIST: Wow! . . . I want to invite you . . . see if you feel . . . where and how you feel that in your body . . . just what's it like to say that to yourself? And then maybe what's it like to say that to me, to have me witness you saying that? **[inviting very specific focus on State 2 sense of agency, will, and desire to deepen it and her embodied and relational connection to it; opposite of the shame we were just talking about or the ghostly nonexistence from Vignette 1]**

PATIENT: Yeah . . . I mean I feel like want to cry . . . I feel like it's in my head kind of (*hands briefly cover face*) . . . and I sort of feel myself tearing up a little bit but I also feel it in my heart (*hands touch heart*) . . . and like in this place that I have a lot of feeling a lot of the time.

THERAPIST: It's very powerful what you're saying. (*patient nods*) And it's very important. And it touches me too, which is why I'm asking you to slow down around it and let's just be with the feeling that comes up . . . for you to say that "ok this person (*part*) is, doesn't always serve me . . . has been a distortion, gets in my way and yet there's something about the energy (*patient nodding*) and focus of that part of myself that I don't want to lose . . . I don't want to lose that piece that she holds." **[therapist focus on the transformance drive hidden in the largely self-destructive defense, the resilience potential expressing itself in "negative," conservative ways because it does not yet have another way; encouraging the capacity to hold both; using the language of desire ("want") to mirror patient's will]**

PATIENT: Mmm-hmm. I mean it's like a cradle (*one cupped hand lifts, palm faces up*) . . . of . . . like ability.

THERAPIST: (*nodding, eyes open wide*) Mm-hmm.

PATIENT: Like being able to do something you know (*pause*) . . . which is like blowing my mind right now in a sense like the (*eyes close, sighs, begins to cry*) . . .

THERAPIST: (*pauses during patient tears*) What's blowing your mind?

PATIENT:    I mean it's like . . . like you're always talking about why is this? . . . why do you think this thing is present? . . . this way of working in the world. And it seems to me like this is a very intelligent like . . . like construction for . . . keeping safe like the sense of agency. **[very deep experiential insight into the need to preserve and protect the sense of agency, but in a way that interferes with it being used constructively in her current life]**

THERAPIST:  Wow.

PATIENT:    And I feel like it's a very intelligent response to—

THERAPIST:  Yes, it is. **[validating adaptiveness of defenses]**

PATIENT:    —to feeling as a child like "I can't do this; I can't do this . . . I don't want to do this . . . I feel ashamed because of my parent's reaction or my friend's reaction or my own reaction."

THERAPIST:  Mmm (*nodding; soft tears*)

PATIENT:    . . . and I feel like (*chuckles*) **[postbreakthrough affect]** . . . I feel like (*one hand sweeps in front of body*) . . . my whole . . . that there's like this protection of this like really important part of myself . . .

THERAPIST:  Absolutely . . . I could never have said it so beautifully . . .

PATIENT:    (*smiles, nods*) Thanks.

THERAPIST:  What's it like for you to say it?

PATIENT:    I mean like I said, it's like blowing my mind in a way. **[State 3: realization affects; profound, compassionate insights in the wake of transformation, in the wake of feeling and owning her own agency, will, and desire]**

THERAPIST:  It's blowing your mind. It's blowing my mind! (*chuckles and wipes tears*)

PATIENT:    It has seemed like this thing that is bad . . . **[Patient's relationship to the defense changes from judgment and shame to compassion, understanding, and even admiration and appreciation.]**

THERAPIST:  Yeah. Right.

PATIENT:    And in plenty of ways it has not served me well **[this is not glossing over; it is facing reality squarely]** but . . . (*pause, eyes close, softly weeping*) **[State 3 transformational affects: healing affects—feeling moved within the self]**

THERAPIST:  Wow . . .

PATIENT: It's like . . . (*slightly shaking head no*) . . . I mean it's like a perfect strategy for dealing with this feeling. **[State 4 core state statement—wise, understanding, generous, compassionate]**

THERAPIST: What's it like for both of us to cry about it today? **[therapist metaprocessing the *relational* transformance[5]; the relationship itself fostering the growth, expansion, and connection of the patient but also of the dyad; an example of what Tronick (1998) called the "dyadic expansion of consciousness"]**

PATIENT: (*smiles*) It's good . . . it really is extremely (*hand on heart*) meaningful to me for us both to be crying about it . . . for you to have that response to me is super touching and meaningful. (*deep mutual gaze*) **[State 3 transformational affects: healing affects]**

THERAPIST: I'm glad.

PATIENT: And it makes me feel (*chuckles*) . . . it makes me feel capable of saying something that is so meaningful; that is beautiful. **[experience of agency is expressed interpersonally in that the patient has an effect on therapist, which solidifies and deepens her own sense of being able]**

THERAPIST: Mm-hmm (*nodding*) You are *so* capable of that . . . (*dabs tears from eyes; chuckles*) . . . right, right.

PATIENT: I mean it's a good feeling you know . . . but it's also just like lovely to have like this connection. **[State 2: intersubjective experience of delight; relational state of connection, mixed with State 3 ("it's lovely") healing affects because the patient is simultaneously having the experience and reflecting on it in the moment]**

THERAPIST: It's lovely for me too.

   From the broad and knowing perspective of State 4 (core state), the patient further recognizes and articulates the dynamic between the pervasive shame ("I cannot do"—maladaptive State 2) in constant struggle with the every woman fantasy ("I can do anything and be the best"—State 1 defense) and how this battle waged on at the expense of real action, or of even knowing the desires of her heart and mind and of trusting herself enough to pursue them (State 2 core affect). She realizes that she has settled instead for focusing almost entirely on pleasing others. At the end, therapist and patient have a good laugh at a metaphor she comes up with to describe the divide within herself, and she says that this was one of the most important moments of experiential insights she has had in therapy.

---

[5]Term introduced by Russell (2015).

## THE PLACE OF DISRUPTION IN AEDP

Working to increase agency and access to will and desires is not always so smooth as the preceding transcripts might suggest. Particularly when being passive, meek, demurring and unaware of one's own wants and wishes has served the person well in maintaining certain relationships, patients may be reluctant to give this up, and our inviting it may engender real resistance. This happened in another session with the same patient. Before I present that, I want to clarify some aspects of AEDP work that I think are underappreciated to the point that some may not recognize them as AEDP.

### The Danger of Overregulating: Trusting "Safe Enough" to Allow for Friction

Some people just learning AEDP believe that anxiety or whatever inhibitory affects are in the A corner of the Triangle of Experience is a signal that the therapist should back off or help "regulate" the patient. Although this is sometimes true, anxiety is also an important signal that we are likely in the territory of core affective experience. Many people's defenses work well to decrease their anxiety but also to keep them away from healing, core affective truth. We should expect that if what we are discussing is *core* and important, it will trigger anxiety and possibly well-worn defenses. The question about regulation is a question of degree and tolerance. Many patients actually need to learn to tolerate their anxiety without resorting to defenses to allow themselves to have new experiences both intrapsychically and interpersonally. As long as we are within the window of tolerance, it is okay to also push, encourage, and proceed, instead of feeling the need to back off. People can be too regulated to grow.

In the session that follows, the therapist is being more assertive—"pushy," to use the word of the patient. At first this may not seem like quintessential AEDP because there are moments when the patient feels "overwhelmed." Some might believe that the therapist should back off and do something to regulate, calm, or soothe the patient. AEDP has sometimes become equated with softness and "privileging the positive" with indiscriminate affirmation. And transformance is sometimes confused for what *feels* positive to a patient in a given moment. I want to take this chapter as an opportunity to speak to those issues and to what I believe are misunderstandings of AEDP.

### Privileging the Positive

*Privileging the positive* really means that when a patient presents with some ambivalent experience where one part gravitates toward resistance, pathology, or habit and the other gravitates toward growth, health, and transformation, even if the latter is smaller, this is usually what we privilege *to start*. This is in keeping with our concepts of *self-at-worst* and *self-at-best* (Fosha, 2000) and the idea that we work to connect to and strengthen the self-at-best to use it to work with the self-at-worst to facilitate healing, transformation, and integration, and not simply to leave the self-at-worst to flounder on its own as if it stops existing. I have recommended that as long as the signals are yellow and there are glimmers of transformance strivings, the therapist should go with what is positive and moving toward growth, however tenuous and new (Russell, 2015). In such cases, this necessarily involves some tension or anxiety. So, while *privileging the positive* sometimes does mean privileging positive affect,[6] what it really means is *privileging deep truth*. For, after all, "the positive" in AEDP is specifically defined as not limited to happy, pleasant feelings but includes that which feels "right" and "true," which sometimes can be uncomfortable and even painful.

## Transformance Needs a Counterpart: Resistance

Fosha's (2008) concept of transformance ultimately makes sense only in the holistic view that contains its opposite: resistance. This is important because AEDP is also grounded in psychodynamic thought, and resistance is a central concept and a real phenomenon. Transformance strivings are often underdeveloped in people presenting for therapy. Leaning into resistance and defenses that have worked in the past, therefore, is what people understandably do when challenged or even when presented with a new and unfamiliar opportunity or situation. The problem with this is that those old defenses may no longer work very well for two reasons. First, they do not work in different environments, with different people, or at different stages of life. Second, they may interfere with new goals people have for themselves in the present that they may not have had in the past.

The reality of resistance combined with a psychodynamic appreciation for the unconscious brings about a humility that can buffer what could otherwise be a purely experiential therapy. Not all in-the-moment affective experiences are created equal. Some are, in fact, defensive. Some others are outer layers of the onion. If we take the idea of "creating safety" too far, people will not come upon or stay with more challenging interpersonal or intrapersonal moments that have the seeds of growth planted in them. It is helpful to remember classic concepts such as the "window of tolerance" (Siegel, 1999) or "optimal level of anxiety" (Ogden et al., 2006) and not be afraid to accompany people to places in themselves and interpersonally (including directly with the therapist) where things do not always immediately feel "safe." This is why I have shifted to using the term "safe enough," rather than simply "safe," because the latter sometimes connotes a comfort and calm that *can be* inimical to the hard work and discomfort of making real change.

---

[6]See Chapter 7 of Russell (2015) and Russell and Fosha (2008) for a thorough discussion of the importance of deepening positive affect.

## SECURE THERAPEUTIC ATTACHMENT: THE PLACE OF DISRUPTION IN SECURITY

This brings us to what is meant by *secure therapeutic attachment relationship*. What has happened in our culture appears to have happened in the spread of AEDP. Namely, some are too rigid about the language of security and safety and therefore too limited in relationships. Attachment theory has adherents who have taken core principles to the extreme and in the process distorted attachment theory, which is fundamentally about *safety promoting exploration* and not simply safety for safety's sake. There is a whole movement of parents who never say no to their children or who never risk betraying the slightest amount of anger, for example, based on a deep a misunderstanding of attachment theory. Similarly, there are some who understand "secure therapeutic attachment" in AEDP to mean promoting the feeling of safety all the time for the patient and not risking what is probably most important in a secure relationship next to plenty of affectively in-sync moments, which is disruption, the possibility of repair, and the expansion of capacity through new and challenging experiences. Some children, particularly shyer or less assertive kids, need to be encouraged and even pushed to try new situations to discover they can not only manage them but even derive the pleasure and self-expansion that come from engaging them. Some patients in psychotherapy need the same.

In attachment relationships, it is sometimes the job of the parent to be attuned not so much to the feeling of the moment but to the need or readiness of the child to make a leap forward (i.e., what is at the bottom of the triangle that is not being felt or expressed, that triggers anxiety, and is warded off by defenses). That may be perceived in the parent's own feelings or awareness shifting or in picking up on subtle clues in the child that suggest a readiness for or a resistance to something the child actually needs for his or her growth. Never abandoning empathy, good parenting requires the parent to communicate the message "you can do it!" even when the child does not believe it or is afraid to try. I think of this as *attuned disruption*. The same is necessary in therapy with people who have internalized their own disempowerment, do not have faith in their own capacity to act, or in whom differentiation has historically led to rupture or abandonment of some kind.

That said, it is important to remember that our willingness to push is only one side of the equation. When it comes to engaging agency and inviting will and desire, people often need something or someone solid to push against. That may be us. This involves an energy that may be uncomfortable for the patient, but also, similarly, unfamiliar or uncomfortable for the therapist.

## CASE VIGNETTE 3: ACCESSING AGENCY IN THE THERAPEUTIC ENCOUNTER

The patient presents feeling "kind of down." She has been asked to voluntarily assist in teaching more classes than she would like. It takes a lot of back-and-forth for her to even acknowledge fully that this is not what she wants to do, but she feels "stuck" and afraid of speaking on her own behalf or even asking what the parameters are. Anxiety and the defense of "not knowing" what she wants become evident in this session when she and the therapist role-play constructive ways of speaking up. It emerges that a conversation with her mother reinforced her inclination to be passive and to "go along," and she admits to feeling "deflated" afterward. Some anger arises but quickly turns to "bitterness" toward herself (defense). The therapist begins to ask her not about how she feels that, but where that feeling of bitterness goes.

**THERAPIST:** So if you stay with the resentment . . . this bitterness that you're noticing . . . you start to feel this uprising of some anger about this just being the situation . . . something happens . . . it kinda gets turned on yourself so it's this kind of bitterness towards yourself . . . and I'm just wondering if we just stay with that . . . if you notice that kind of bitter feeling towards yourself . . . what happens? **[This is not an invitation to "deepen" as we do with *adaptive affective experiences,* but rather an invitation to notice the pattern of the squashing of core affect and the defense of self-attack and where that leads. It is important for the patient to be able to feel this pattern and not simply for the therapist to name it.]**

**PATIENT:** Well I think it makes me depressed. (*Therapist:* Yeah, uh-huh) I think that it sort of (*thoughtful pause*) . . . I mean it makes me depressed. I don't like want to do anything. It sort of shuts me down. It feels like it shuts me down a little . . . or a lot. **[Bingo: Patient's own insight into how her own defensive pattern of surrendering her own agency and turning her anger on herself[7] perpetuates her own depression.]**

As the therapist continues to express interest in this pattern, the patient becomes "confused," there is some very passive protest and eventually the tiniest bit of anger at the therapist.

**PATIENT:** It feels like . . . like you haven't pushed me to go this deep before like with the feelings . . . like you're always asking me how does that feel, how does that feel . . . but now you're asking me (*becoming more animated and stronger voice*) how does it feel to feel that way and what happens when you feel that way and where does that bring you and it's like . . . and I'm really like struggling . . . I'm really having a hard time . . . I'm trying to push back (*hands push outward, palms face out*) . . .

---

[7]This is the kind of pattern that Rank (1936) referred to as the "negative will" expression, the energy of which he believed needed to be directed in a more positive direction.

a little bit. **[Lots of resistance in the confusion and over-whelm, and the patient is also in the end starting to stand up for herself with the therapist! Resistance and transformance are co-occurring.]**

THERAPIST:   Push me off a little bit? **[focusing not on the anxiety or over-whelm but on the transformance strivings of actively being on her own behalf; therapist explicitly not wanting to regulate, soothe, or calm the patient]**

PATIENT:   Yeah, a little bit . . .

THERAPIST:   (*mimicking gesture of pushing; eyes wide and curious*) Yeah so what are the feelings toward me . . .? **[inviting agency and anger]**

PATIENT:   Like a little anger (*chuckles*)

The therapist stays with the "little anger" not because she believes there is core rage toward her in the moment but because Alex's agency on behalf of herself is in that, rather than in the collapse of feeling depressed or the bitterness of being angry at herself. Disappointment, frustration, and anger are common reactions to violated boundaries or to unfulfilled strivings, needs, or desire—situations in which one's will is not enacted, one's desires are not fulfilled, or one's agency is not recognized. As we stay with that, Alex is able to say that there is something deep she does not want either herself or the therapist to see. Only after that is she able to be curious about what she is hiding. As we stay with it, there are a lot of *yellow signal affects* (Russell, 2015) of openness to what is emerging followed rapidly by defense. There remains a little bit of anger at the therapist and a desire to push her away. The therapist begins to pursue an anger portrayal at her, but it is off; not really where she is. Finally, in a moment that feels like a big breakthrough for both therapist and patient, even though outwardly it was not terribly dramatic, Alex declares herself.

PATIENT:   But I don't feel like I want to hurt you . . . I just feel like I want to tell you . . . (*raises hands as if preaching*) like "don't keep pushing me to go further" . . . (*energy in room shifts; mutual gaze*) **[recognition by therapist]**. "I don't want you to" (*chuckles*) . . . **[embodied assertion of will and agency, followed by some relief in the chuckle]**

THERAPIST:   Mm-hmm. What's it like to say that? And what's it like to have your body involved in you saying that? **[exploration of core affective–somatic experience of assertion of self]**. "I don't want you to. I have not given you permission."

PATIENT:   It feels freeing . . . yeah. **[postbreakthrough affect]**

THERAPIST:   Mm-hmm . . . what's the freeing like? **[metaprocessing experience of transformation]**

PATIENT: Well like I'm just saying what I want . . . you know . . . of course, I feel very divided about it . . . I feel like I want you to . . . and I feel like I don't want you to . . . **[recognition of expression of desire and owning of ambivalence; no longer acted out as defense]**

THERAPIST: What's it like to say that?

PATIENT: Good . . . that feels correct, yeah . . .

THERAPIST: That feels truthful . . .

PATIENT: Yeah, it feels truthful . . . (*nodding*)

The processing or feeling of one affect does not always "drop the patient down" into postbreakthrough affects and then State 3. Sometimes one core affective experience easily morphs into another, as in grief leading to anger or joy leading to a felt sense of intimacy. We follow, stay with, and deepen each one. In the preceding transcript, although it may appear that agency is the outcome of anger, a more careful read suggests that there is no deep processing of anger; there is only the littlest bit that comes as the vehicle carrying the patient's agentic self and will, much as toddlers learning to assert themselves often appear angry and can be quite forceful. To only focus on the anger and miss the self's assertion and confidence in their own abilities would be an incomplete view and potentially elicit a misattuned response. Secure parents recognize and even celebrate and help elaborate (Russell, 2015) the agency that may come in an angry package. This often softens the anger because children realize that their will has been recognized and respected. Here, too, the larger point, and the affective experience that needed to break through before the sense of relief, freedom, and truth could settle in was that of the patient's will and desire: "Don't keep pushing me to go further. I don't want you to."

## CONCLUSION

The intention of this chapter has been to expand AEDP's understanding and conceptualization of State 2 core affective experience to include the phenomena of agency, will, and desire and to illustrate why these are important. The embodied experience of agency, of being able to act on one's own behalf in a way that is connected with core desires and needs and that is in alignment with one's own will is an essential core affective experience and not simply a consequence of processing emotions to completion. For many, especially those who have been undifferentiated from enmeshed relationships, systematically disempowered in traumatizing environments based more on power than love, or those who have experiences of physical or emotional shutdown, the sense of one's own agentic self can be impaired or even missing. It is not that an agentic self does not exist; it is simply that the psychosocial environment did not sufficiently permit, elicit, or encourage differentiation and autonomy to begin with. Simply making space for an affective self-experience to emerge that was developmentally derailed long ago may fail to recognize the active, repeated, relational, and sometimes disruptive ingredients that go into the development of more autonomous experiences when they grow naturally and optimally in childhood and adolescence. Rather than prioritizing a focus on "safety" and being in sync, these developmental tasks often require some disruption, some pushing against rather than "being with," some recognition that one's will might exist in opposition to another's. These developmental tasks will ultimately lead to the necessary expansion of the relationship to include separation, disruption, and being out-of-sync.

Fortunately, AEDP has all the ingredients it needs to help grow this capacity in the individual and in the therapeutic dyad. This work is done empathically, with the best interest of the patient in mind and with love and trust in the other as a foundation. It leans into the security of the therapeutic attachment to allow for *attuned disruption*, knowing that both partners are desirous of repair should the need arise. It trusts that transformation resides in the individual and that in conditions of safety and encouragement, it can become activated. It allows the therapist to use her own somatic–affective experience to notice what is missing at the bottom of the triangle and perhaps to *feel for* and not simply *with* in order to invite the patient to stretch. It has faith in the truth sense as a positive affective marker of being on the right path even when the path feels bumpy. And it delights in the patient's acquisition of new capacities, especially when they are hard won.

## REFERENCES

Adler, A. (1964). *The individual psychology of Alfred Adler: Systematic presentation in selections from his writing* (H. L. Ansbacher & R. R. Ansbacher, Eds.). Harper Torchbooks.

Ainsworth, M. D. S., Blehar, M. C., Waters, E., & Wall, S. (1978). *Patterns of attachment: Assessed in the strange situation and at home.* Erlbaum.

Aviv, R. (2017, March 27). The trauma of facing deportation. *The New Yorker.* https://www.newyorker.com/magazine/2017/04/03/the-trauma-of-facing-deportation

Benjamin, J. (1990). An outline of intersubjectivity: The development of recognition. *Psychoanalytic Psychology, 7*(Suppl.), 33–46. https://doi.org/10.1037/h0085258

Bollas, C. (1989). *Forces of destiny: Psychoanalysis and human idiom.* Routledge.

Bowlby, J. (1989). *A secure base: Clinical applications of attachment theory.* Routledge.

Davanloo, H. (1990). *Unlocking the unconscious: Selected papers of Habib Davanloo.* John Wiley & Sons.

Erikson, E. H. (1968). *Identity youth and crisis.* Norton.

Fosha, D. (2000). *The transforming power of affect: A model for accelerated change.* Basic Books.

Fosha, D. (2002). The activation of affective change processes in AEDP. In J. J. Magnavita (Ed.), *Comprehensive handbook of psychotherapy: Vol. 1. Psychodynamic and object relations psychotherapies.* John Wiley & Sons.

Fosha, D. (2003). Dyadic regulation and experiential work with emotion and relatedness in trauma and disordered attachment. In M. F. Solomon & D. J. Siegel (Eds.), *Healing trauma: Attachment, mind, body, and brain* (pp. 221–281). Norton.

Fosha, D. (2008). Transformance, recognition of self by self, and effective action. In K. J. Schneider (Ed.), *Existential-integrative psychotherapy: Guideposts to the core of practice* (pp. 290–320). Routledge.

Fosha, D. (2013). A heaven in a wildflower: Self, dissociation, and treatment in the context of the neurobiological core self. *Psychoanalytic Inquiry, 33*(5), 496–523. https://doi.org/10.1080/07351690.2013.815067

Ghent, E. (1990). Masochism, submission, surrender: Masochism as a perversion of surrender. *Contemporary Psychoanalysis, 26*(1), 108–136. https://doi.org/10.1080/00107530.1990.10746643

Lipton, B., & Fosha, D. (2011). Attachment as a transformative process in AEDP: Operationalizing the intersection of attachment theory and affective neuroscience. *Journal of Psychotherapy Integration, 21*(3), 253–279. https://doi.org/10.1037/a0025421

Mahler, M. S., Pine, F., & Bergman, A. (1975). *The psychological birth of the human infant.* Basic Books.

Main, M., Kaplan, N., & Cassidy, J. (1985). Security in infancy, childhood, and adulthood: A move to the level of representation. *Monographs of the Society for Research in Child Development, 50*(1/2), 66–104. https://doi.org/10.2307/3333827

Maslow, A. (1943). Conflict, frustration, and the theory of threat. *Journal of Abnormal Psychology, 38*(1), 81–86. https://doi.org/10.1037/h0054634

Ogden, P., Minton, K., & Pain, C. (2006). *Trauma and the body: A sensorimotor approach to psychotherapy.* Norton.

Pando-Mars, K. (2016). Tailoring AEDP interventions to attachment style. *Transformance: The AEDP Journal, 6*(2). https://aedpinstitute.org/wp-content/uploads/2016/11/tailoring-aedp-interventions-to-attachment-style.pdf

Panksepp, J., & Northoff, G. (2009). The trans-species core SELF: The emergence of active cultural and neuro-ecological agents through self-related processing within subcortical-cortical midline networks. *Consciousness and Cognition, 18*(1), 193–215. https://doi.org/10.1016/j.concog.2008.03.002

Pollack, L., & Slavin, J. (1998). The struggle for recognition: Disruption and reintegration in the experience of agency. *Psychoanalytic Dialogues, 8*(6), 857–873. https://doi.org/10.1080/10481889809539298

Porges, S. W. (2005). The role of social engagement in attachment and bonding: A phylogenetic perspective. In C. S. Carter, L. Ahnert, K. E. Grossmann, S. B. Hrdy, M. E. Lamb, S. W. Porges, & N. Sachser (Eds.), *Attachment and bonding: A new synthesis* (pp. 33–54). MIT Press.

Porges, S. W. (2011). *The polyvagal theory: Neurophysiological foundations of emotions, attachment, communication, and self-regulation.* Norton.

Rank, O. (1936). *Will therapy: The therapeutic applications of will psychology.* Norton.

Russell, E. (2015). *Restoring resilience: Discovering your clients' capacity for healing.* Norton.

Russell, E., & Fosha, D. (2008). Transformational affects and core state in AEDP: The emergence and consolidation of joy, hope, gratitude and confidence in the (solid goodness of the) self. *Journal of Psychotherapy Integration, 18*(2), 167–190.

Siegel, D. (1999). *The developing mind: How relationships and the brain interact to shape who we are.* American Psychological Association.

Slavin, J. H. (2010). Becoming an individual: Technically subversive thoughts on the role of the analyst's influence. *Psychoanalytic Dialogues, 20*(3), 308–324. https://doi.org/10.1080/10481885.2010.483957

Tronick, E. Z. (1998). Dyadically expanded states of consciousness and the process of therapeutic change. *Infant Mental Health Journal, 19*(3), 290–299. https://doi.org/10.1002/(SICI)1097-0355(199823)19:3<290::AID-IMHJ4>3.0.CO;2-Q

# IV

## HOW TO WORK WITH MALADAPTIVE AFFECTIVE EXPERIENCE AND COMPLEX TRAUMA

# 10

# Fierce Love

## Championing the Core Self to Transform Trauma and Pathogenic States

SueAnne Piliero

There is an age-old saying: "We are harmed in relationships and we are healed in relationships." Many psychotherapy models ascribe to this belief, but in accelerated experiential dynamic psychotherapy (AEDP) we *live* this belief. AEDP, a healing-oriented, change-based theory of therapeutic action, places the therapeutic relationship front and center in its mission to heal relational trauma and transform the self. Simply put, in AEDP the therapeutic relationship—attuned, emotionally engaged, authentic, moment-to-moment present—is a sine qua non in healing trauma and the traumatized self.

This chapter focuses on the central place of maladaptive affective experiences, that is, the pathogenic affects (e.g., feelings of worthlessness, toxic shame) and unbearable states of traumatic aloneness and the entrenched relational defenses and pathogenic self states to which these give rise in relational trauma and the integral part that therapeutic presence, active engagement, and active relational interventions play in transforming these entrenched defenses and the pathogenic self states that give rise to them. I discuss experiential relational interventions that in AEDP make active use of therapeutic presence to work with the entrenched defenses that pathogenic affects generate. To be specific, I focus on an approach I developed that I call "Fierce Love," a relationally bold stance that involves psychobiologically attuned leading and assiduously championing the patient's core authentic self in order to break through entrenched defenses and reclaim the self.[1]

---

[1]I wish to acknowledge Ken Benau for coining the term "Fierce Love" to describe my clinical work.

https://doi.org/10.1037/0000232-011
*Undoing Aloneness and the Transformation of Suffering Into Flourishing: AEDP 2.0*, D. Fosha (Editor)

## HOW PATHOGENIC AFFECTS AND PATHOGENIC SELF STATES DEVELOP

In AEDP, psychopathology is understood as the result of unbearable aloneness in the face of intense and overwhelming emotional experiences (Fosha, 2000). To the developing self, the threat of losing attachment ties is nothing short of self-disintegration or psychic annihilation. With this in mind, core affective experiences that threaten to disrupt attachment ties must be avoided at all costs, which is how defense mechanisms come into play. To maintain this life-dependent connection to their caregivers, people resort to defense mechanisms (e.g., denial, repression, self-blame, dissociation) to cope with these overwhelming affective experiences. Adaptive initially, because they serve a survival purpose for the individual,[2] these defense mechanisms become maladaptive later in life as they distance one's self from genuine emotional experience and, as such, one's core authentic self.

Seen through an attachment lens, psychopathology develops when caregivers do not meet a child's core affective experiences with openness, responsiveness, attunement, and willingness to help when the child is in distress. This happens either through what Fosha (2000) referred to as *errors of omission* (e.g., withdrawal, distancing, denial, neglect) or through *errors of commission* (e.g., shaming, blaming, outright abuse). Over time, the inattention, disinterest, and/or blatant abuse on the part of the caregiver "map onto the self as shaming unworthiness" (Fosha, 2013, p. 513).

In AEDP, we refer to toxic shame and toxic fear (i.e., fear without solution) and the feelings of worthlessness and helplessness they engender as *pathogenic affective experience* or *pathogenic affects*. Experiencing these feelings or states without intervention will only cause further suffering that ultimately gives rise to psychopathology, as the name "pathogenic" makes clear (Fosha, 2002). Pathogenic affects develop when the caregivers' response to the person's core affective experience is disturbing and disruptive, threatening the self, the attachment bond, or both: The result is compromised self-integrity and a compromised attachment relationship (Fosha, 2003). If children grow up with pervasive experiences of separation, traumatic aloneness, distress, fear, and rage, they will go down a compromised and compromising psychological and neurological pathway (Schore, 1996, 2003, 2019; Siegel, 1995, 2015). According to Schore (2019), during early critical periods, frequent dysregulated and unrepaired relational experiences are "affectively burnt in" to the infant's early developing right brain.

*Pathogenic self states*, whereby the pathogenic affects turn in on the self, result from traumatic relational experiences that affectively "burn" into the developing brain deep-seated feelings of shame, worthlessness, and despair.

---

[2]Core affective experience includes the categorical emotions as defined by Silvan Tomkins and others (e.g., anger, fear, disgust, joy), as well as authentic self states (e.g., feeling good about one's self, feeling lonely, powerful, proud) and relational experiences (e.g., feeling close to an other, feeling intimate, distant, abandoned, rejected).

Shame is where there is a "breaking of the interpersonal bridge" (Kaufman, 1996) between self and other, which also results in a psychic break from one's own core authentic self. As Fosha (2003) asserted,

> The combination of (1) interrupted core affective experiences, (2) compromised self-integrity and disrupted attachment ties, and (3) the overwhelming experience of the pathogenic affects in the context of unwilled and unwanted traumatic aloneness leads to *unbearable emotional states*: these include experiences of helplessness, hopelessness, confusion, fragmentation, emptiness and despair, the "black hole" (van der Kolk, 2001) of human emotional experience. The attempt to escape the excruciating experience of these unbearable emotional states becomes the seed for defensive strategies, that, when chronically relied on, culminate in the development of psychopathological conditions. (italics in original; p. 242)

To summarize, when children are emotionally neglected or chronically abused by their caregivers, and yet need to maintain connection to their attachment figures for survival, they resort to defenses, that is, protective mechanisms that preserve the attachment bond, though with terrible consequences for the self: Children resort to blaming themselves for not having their needs met and, furthermore, on a deep, visceral, often unconscious level, they come to believe that they *deserved* the maltreatment, which is the deepest intrapsychic wound of all. In short, in order to survive, the child exonerates the caregiver by condemning the self.

As a result of these entrenched defenses, instituted at all costs to protect the attachment ties, core erroneous beliefs about the self develop, such as "I am bad, unworthy, defective, stupid, unlovable, and so on." These core erroneous beliefs about the self, which develop as a result of entrenched defenses, become deeply embedded in the child's psyche. Seen through an attachment lens, these core erroneous beliefs about the self become integrated into the internal working model of the developing self (Bowlby, 1969).

Why would children resort to blaming themselves for the incompetence, neglect, and outright abusive behaviors of their caregivers? Viewing the self as defective instead of viewing the caregiver as defective is a highly adaptive survival strategy because it allows the child to maintain connection with the primary attachment figure, on whom, for better for worse, the child literally depends for psychological, emotional, and physical survival. This defense strategy also gives the child's self some sense of power and control in an otherwise frightening, out-of-control experience. Ultimately, self-blame and self-hate are infinitely more tolerable than feeling the depth of terror and helplessness that one has to feel in order to walk back into that house every day. As DeYoung (2015) stated, "It is so much easier to believe that I am 'bad and disgusting' than it is to understand, 'something happened outside of my control and I feel like I'm falling apart'" (p. 46). Viewed in this way, these pathogenic beliefs about the defectiveness of the self, much like dissociation and denial, serve a defensive function. They have short-term benefits for the emotional survival of the individual in pathogenic relational environments. However, they have long-term devastating consequences when those environmental conditions no longer exist, that is, when the adult's survival no longer depends on the bond with the attachment figure in the same way that the child's survival did. What is particularly insidious about long-term reliance on these pathogenic beliefs, which become internalized in the psychic makeup of the individual as pathogenic self states, is that they prevent the individual from taking in all the good, self-affirming relational experiences that are present in nonpathogenic environments. This failure to take in the good and have it affect personal experience, beliefs about the self, and, thus, psychic structure, serves to further deepen pathogenic self states and experiences of unbearable aloneness.

What distinguishes maladaptive affective experiences from adaptive affective experiences is that, unlike adaptive emotions, which have adaptive action tendencies associated with them (e.g., anger = fight, sadness = mourn, fear/ terror = flight) and are transformative for the person experiencing them (see Medley, Chapter 8, this volume), pathogenic affects,[3] and the entrenched defenses and pathogenic self states to which they give rise, are in need of transforming (Fosha, 2002). A major way in which we do this in AEDP is through the healing power of the patient–therapist relationship.

## THE HEALING POWER OF THE THERAPEUTIC RELATIONSHIP: THE AEDP THERAPIST *IS* THE INTERVENTION

Trauma theorists and researchers alike have discovered that the most salient traumatic experience in childhood trauma tends to be not the trauma memory itself but the felt experience of nobody being there (Fisher, 2017; Fosha, 2000, 2003; Herman, 1992; Stolorow & Atwood, 1992; van der Kolk, 2001). Undoing aloneness in the face of overwhelming affective experience, and undoing the pathogenic defenses that have arisen as a result of needing to survive intolerable situations, are primary ways we work to heal trauma and the traumatized self in AEDP. Through our active emotional engagement, we implicitly and explicitly let our patients know that we really want to "be there," "bear witness," and "stay with" our patients' core affective experiences, whether this involves the release of a heretofore warded-off categorical emotion (e.g., anger, sadness, joy, disgust); the engagement of a relational experience between therapist and patient (e.g., the viscerally felt experience of feeling seen, heard, delighted in); or validating, deepening, and championing authentic self states that arise within the patient (e.g., feeling proud, expressing core desires, exhibiting self-compassion, standing up for one's self).

Our primary therapeutic aim is to become the secure base from which fear, shame, and distress can be dyadically regulated, thus obviating the

---

[3]Please note there are different kinds of pathogenic affects, including stable though toxic pathogenic affects (State 2) and defensive pathogenic self states (State 1) resulting from the internalization of caregiver loathing or neglect, as discussed here (and in Lamagna, Chapter 11, this volume), which manifest as trauma-based overwhelming affective flooding (State 2).

continued need for pathogenic defenses. Once safety and "we-ness" have been established—that is, when patients have a felt sense of the therapist being "with them"—previously forbidden emotional and relational experiences can be accessed and processed to completion with the therapist, thus activating the healing and self-righting tendencies residing within them (Fosha, 2003, 2017; Lipton & Fosha, 2011). This genuine, active emotional engagement with patients plays an integral part in healing the self because it was precisely the caregiver's emotional absence during critical moments in the individual's formative years that made the person feel alone, terrified, and needing to disconnect from their core affective experience in order to psychically survive.

In AEDP, it is our hope that the therapist will be experienced by the patient as what Fosha (2005) referred to as a "true other." The true other, the relational counterpart of Winnicott's (1960/1965) true self, describes an experience-near construct in which one person responds to another person in just the right way; when that happens—for that moment—the other is experienced by the self as a true other (Fosha, 2000). The true other is the "midwife of the true self" (Fosha, 2005). A deep transformation occurs within the self as a result of being with a true other and being seen, loved, understood, empathized with, affirmed; being that which hitherto had been too frightening; being in touch with aspects of emotional experience that previously had feared to be beyond bearing. As a result of this transformation, one is closer to one's true self, the self one has always known oneself to be.

Being engaged in such a way that our patients will experience us as a true other involves being psychobiologically attuned to both their verbal and nonverbal cues moment to moment and responding in such a way that they feel genuinely seen, felt, and understood. This psychobiological attunement between therapist and patient is similar to optimal caregiver–infant dyads in which the caregiver's right brain is synchronized to respond to the ever-oscillating verbal and nonverbal emotional states of the infant. In the context of therapy, psychobiological attunement is demonstrated through our affectively charged responses to what we are hearing, seeing, feeling, and intuiting from our patients. These affectively charged responses are embodied in our tone of voice, our mindfully chosen words, our facial and body gestures, and our paraverbal utterances. Whether it be validation, affirmation, anxiety regulation, affective self-disclosures, or a simple, empathic head nod, all of these powerful verbal and nonverbal communications reveal to our patients how we see and feel them and, equally important, how we feel *for* them. This right brain-to-right brain interplay between therapist and patient enables patients to feel felt on a visceral level, which is the royal road to healing and reclaiming the core authentic self. As Schore (2019) asserted, "It is this two person right brain-to-right brain implicit emotional communication and affect regulation that lies at the core of the right brain change mechanisms of psychotherapy, underscoring their fundamental role in the psychotherapeutic repair of the self" (p. 12).

Pathogenic experiences and pathogenic self states are by their very nature deeply isolating, existential experiences of unbearable aloneness. To that end, undoing these states of bone-crushing aloneness through the use of the patient–therapist relationship is paramount in transforming trauma and reclaiming the self. It is here, in these deep, dark, shame- and terror-filled, warded-off places within the human psyche, where the deepest healing needs to take place. It is here, in these most wounded and disavowed places within the self, where our patients most need us to be with them. This is not an easy task for a therapist. Going to these deeply painful, dark places with our patients requires building the knowledge, awareness, and capacity within our *selves* to be with and stay with the depth of emotional pain, shame, and unbearable traumatic aloneness that lie at the heart of pathogenic affective experiences (a process that I have worked on, both personally and professionally, for many years).

The following session excerpts[4] are an example of a moment when my patient experienced the healing power of a true other. Six months into treatment, my patient, whom I will call Susan, a 32-year-old woman with a significant history of emotional neglect and relational trauma, painfully and fearfully shared with me that a "part of [her]" wanted to die. I wish to put emphasis on "part" because it implicitly communicated that not all of her wanted to die. I was also keenly aware that the part of her who wanted to live was the one who was entrusting me with this information, seeing what I would do with it. This was a huge disclosure for this patient because although there already was a strong connection between us, up to this point in the treatment she had been relatively relationally withdrawn and reticent about sharing the depths of her pain with me.

As Susan struggled to get the words out, sensing that she was going to tell me something deeply raw and anxiety provoking, I moved gently and slightly forward in my chair in an effort to see whether my doing so could contribute to regulating her anxiety and undoing her aloneness in this moment. I was also implicitly inviting her to feel my holding presence in that moment as she shared with me one of the most painful human experiences one can feel. When she finally uttered the words "a part of me wants to die" through muffled sobs, my immediate, heartfelt response was:

> I'm *so* glad you shared that with me, Susan (*said empathically and tenderly*). Ohhhhhh (*said painfully*). . . . That's *so* hard to carry alone . . . **[10-second pregnant pause where I continue to connect with her energetically and take in on a visceral level what she has shared with me]** . . . there's nothing worse than feeling that feeling, and being so alone with it.

My tender, empathic words implicitly and explicitly communicate to Susan that I "get" what she is saying on a personal level and that I am with her in

---

[4]Aspects of patients' identities and backgrounds have been disguised to protect their confidentiality.

this feeling state. Equally important, I am also powerfully communicating to her that I am not afraid of these intense scary feelings and that, in contradistinction, I want to be with her in this dark, bleak hole of utter despair, hopelessness, and aloneness. Upon hearing and feeling my healing presence, Susan immediately looked up from her head-down position, smiled at me intently for a moment, then sat up in her chair and moved closer up in her chair toward me. Her strong nonverbal responses relayed that my relational interventions were well received and that she was in closer connection with me, which was precisely my intention.

In AEDP, every intervention is based on the patient's response to the therapist's prior intervention. Given Susan's strong positive somatic–affective response to my relational interventions, I continued to lend my self relationally for the remainder of the session by explicitly inviting her to feel me with her as she rode the waves of painful affect, reminding her that she was no longer emotionally and physically alone with these feelings and that I was right there with her to help her hold and regulate them.

An important point that I wish to underscore is that I did not react with alarm to her saying that a part of her wanted to die, despite the fact that I took it very seriously. Neither did I just listen passively to what she was experiencing; instead, I bore witness; I sought to dyadically regulate her distress through my steady, psychobiologically attuned presence; and I shared my affective responses selectively and judiciously. All those contributed to undoing her aloneness in the face of heretofore overwhelming and frightening affective experience. In short, Susan's "taking in" of my caring, nonjudgmental, steady, regulating presence, and my active explicit verbal and nonverbal interventions to help her bear this heretofore-unbearable affect, provided the antidote to the implicit memory of "nobody being there" in critical moments of her development and thus provided a *corrective emotional experience* (Alexander & French, 1946) in the here-and-now relationship with the therapist.

In using the patient–therapist relationship to provide the corrective emotional experience, the AEDP therapist focuses not only on giving the patient what they need in any particular moment but also relationally processing and metaprocessing each aspect of the healing experience as a way of further deepening and encoding the corrective emotional experience. Metaprocessing the corrective experience is a hallmark of AEDP treatment and is the vehicle through which change happens on the deepest level.

In the case of Susan, my therapeutic focus was not only helping her to feel and express these painful and shameful feelings but to also have her viscerally take in the healing effects of having me bear witness without judgment or undue concern and of empathically holding these feelings right alongside her. For example, following a wave of deep pain where I am steadfastly present and coregulating her in her experience, I gently asked her, "What's it like sharing . . . coming up for a moment and sharing these feelings with me?" Susan slowly looked up, smiled at me for a moment, and then said, "I'm glad I made myself say it." In AEDP, her warm, grateful smile and budding feelings of pride are phenomenological markers that a corrective emotional experience has occurred, which I further deepened and encoded by continuing to relationally metaprocess her experience of feeling held and felt by me, thus expanding and deepening the corrective experience.

Another integral piece to healing the sequelae of relational trauma is for our patients to internally register that they "matter." As humans, part of knowing that we matter is to really *feel* that we exist in the "heart and mind of the other" (Fosha's, 2000, adaptation of Fonagy's, 1997, phrase "existing in the mind of the other"). In AEDP, we seek to actively promote patients' experience of existing in the heart and mind of the therapist. As Susan left our session that day, I told her that I would continue to think about her and that if she wanted to feel my presence at any point during the week to imagine me sending her "tender lines of light from my heart space to hers" (N. Napier, personal communication, March 6, 2012). A few days after our session I also left her a voicemail reminding her that I was continuing to think about her, that I was "carrying her with me," and that I hoped that she was carrying me with her.

The next week when she came into session Susan was in a completely different self state. She was perky, cheerful, and playful, a state that I had never witnessed before. She was dressed in a brightly colored pink blouse, which was uncharacteristic of her normal monochromatic attire. Also, her posture was quite different: Rather than resorting to her normal, slumped-in-the-chair position, she sat upright in her seat, looking more adultlike. Most significantly, she was much more relationally engaged with me. In metaprocessing her experience of our prior session, Susan told me that what helped her the most was that she really *felt* my healing presence. "It was nice in your [voicemail] message when you said that you hoped that I was carrying you with me," she said, her moist eyes and trembling voice revealing that she was deeply touched. Years later, when Susan came in for a posttreatment check-in session, I asked her if there were any moments that stood out in our work together. She referenced this particular session as being the moment that she knew that I was truly "there" for her, because I did not do what she feared I might do (i.e., hospitalize her for expressing suicidal thoughts) but rather stayed with her in that moment of despair, offering my acceptance, love and, most of all, faith in her ability to heal.

## BUILDING RECEPTIVE AFFECTIVE CAPACITY: AN INTEGRAL COMPONENT OF TRANSFORMATION

The effectiveness of all our interventions is determined by the patient's capacity to take them in and internally receive them. This takes us to the all-important notion of building the patients' *receptive affective capacity.*

*Receptive affective experience* refers to the patients' capacity to accept and viscerally take in that which the therapist has to give, for example, the therapist's love, care, compassion, and unconditional acceptance of them (Fosha, 2000, 2017; McCullough, 1997). As McCullough (1997) observed, "If the patient cannot take in what we/others offer them, no revision of the pathological inner representations is possible and little character change can occur" (p. 315). In short, it is not enough for the therapist to care, be empathic, be compassionate, offer to help regulate patients in times of distress, and so on. For healing and deep characterological change to occur our patients must be able to viscerally experience and internalize that which we are offering them.

Building the client's receptive affective capacity by means of experiential work using the here and now of the patient–therapist relationship is the key agent of change in AEDP (Lipton & Fosha, 2011). The clinical work involved in building a patient's receptive affective capacity involves inquiring and experientially exploring on a visceral level what they are receiving (or not receiving) from us. "What does it feel like inside to hear me say I appreciate you?" "What does it feel like to know that you're not alone anymore?" "What happens inside when you take in this truth about yourself . . . that you're actually a strong, multitalented, resilient person?" These are some examples of questions the therapist might ask to build a patient's receptive affective capacity. Also important to note is that these affectively targeted experiential questions in and of themselves are an invitation for the patient to slow down and viscerally take in that which we are offering them, thus deepening the corrective emotional experience.

## USING FIERCE LOVE TO WORK WITH PATHOGENIC SELF STATES AS ENTRENCHED DEFENSES

Very often, a history of trauma or relational trauma manifests through blocks in the patient's capacity to receive that which they so crave and yearn for, yet are afraid of. Feeling inherently bad, unworthy, and unlovable—that is, being in a pathogenic self state—is so much safer than accepting love and care from an other because the latter, though much desired, puts the self at the risk of being hurt again. This fear of being hurt again results in the development of entrenched defenses against relational experience that give rise to and fuel pathogenic affects and pathogenic self states. Put another way, in order to stay psychically safe in the world, the person develops a protective wall around themselves that fiercely guards all the bad stuff that is inside and wards off all the good stuff from coming in. The psychic survival-driven motivation that fueled these entrenched defenses against relational experience (i.e., the pathogenic self states) is a mighty force to be reckoned with.

In both the cognitive and relational realms, working to transform pathogenic beliefs about the self requires an opposing powerful voice of the therapist that can do battle with the destructive voices of the past. It requires that the therapist powerfully advocate for the patient's disavowed, shame-based parts of the self. It requires the AEDP therapist's persistently and tenaciously championing of the patient's core authentic self, the self that is completely intact, that has been living in the shadows, to finally come out into the light. In short, it requires "Fierce Love."

Fierce Love is an internal stance. Fierce Love is about honoring and upholding our patients' wholeness, no matter how broken, damaged, or unworthy they may feel about themselves. Fierce Love is about advocating for our patients' disavowed parts of self when they themselves aren't able to. Fierce Love is about taking the lead on behalf of our patients' core authentic self when the timing is right while simultaneously being willing to step back and shift gears at any moment. Microattuning and micro moment-to-moment tracking of your patient, your self, and the relationship is the fuel of all your endeavors. Fierce Love is an active, embodied presence. As a therapist, sometimes you are relationally bold; sometimes you are simply there, fully present, holding the space and your patient's whole self.

Fierce Love goes beyond a bold, embodied presence as well as beyond words and actions. It requires a willingness on our part to truly *feel* our patients' emotional states, communicated both verbally and nonverbally. Feeling our patients' emotional states requires not just conceptually under-standing what they are going through but also joining them in their affective experience on a visceral level and then turning that felt experience into an intervention that involves championing the wired-in longing to transform. For example, fiercely defending the disavowed child part (e.g., "That child was innocent and didn't deserve what he got. You will never un-convince me of this!" said to a patient steeped in shame, blame, and self-attack), sharing our moral outrage to attachment failures and abuse (e.g., "That should *not* have been!"), courageously speaking the truth on behalf of the self (e.g., "It was your father who was the monster, not you!" said to a patient whose father emotionally, psychologically, and physically sadistically abused him throughout his childhood, who referred to himself as a "monster" when he couldn't find anything positive to say about his father).

As the above examples illustrates, Fierce Love is about holding the duality of patients' experience of their truth: the traumatized part or parts who believe they are a failure, bad, deserving of the neglect and outright abuse they received, and so on, and the core authentic self who knows that what the therapist is saying is true. The therapist's role is to fiercely advocate on behalf of the core authentic self while showing love and compassion for the part or parts of the patient that cannot believe it—yet, with "yet" being the operative word here. For example, when I express a warded-off truth that cannot be acknowledged and or spoken—yet—by my patients I often say to them, "That's OK. I'll hold that truth about you until you can because it *is* the truth about you." It is the therapist's deep conviction in the client's innate capacity to reclaim, to use the expression of one of my most traumatized clients, their "unshakeable core," that fuels the fierceness in defense of the self.

Simply put, Fierce Love is about is about pressuring our clients with love to see themselves for who they really are in their core. Fierce Love is about letting our patients viscerally feel—from our words, from our actions, from our overall presence—that they are lovable. It is precisely the therapist's implicit and explicit fierceness in defense of the self of the patient that communicates to our patients that they were and still are worthy of love.

My AEDP colleague Matt Fried, who has assisted me in teaching AEDP workshops over the past several years and has viewed many hours of videotape of my clinical work, described my practice of Fierce Love in this way:

> Your notion of "fierce love" directly suggests protection, the protectiveness of a parent for his or her loved young ones. The parent is charged, by evolution, species memory, to guide the young one towards maturity and adulthood, to instill hope, to nurture the uniqueness of the other, the born and as yet unborn aspects of the core self . . . and you, SueAnne, are not just guiding, you are championing, in the most active of ways, the core self as it moves into the light. You are swatting away the shamers of the self, you are proclaiming loudly and clearly the integrity of the core self, you are defending it against detractors and those who would injure it or who have tried to injure it. You are always on the patient's side, not the sidelines. Every utterance you make carries with it a sense of the patient's inherent goodness, resilience, right to be and thrive, etc. You are always saying, "Not on my watch!" (M. Fried, personal communication, November 11, 2017)

In the following clinical example, I demonstrate how my Fierce Love eventually broke through the many thick, protective barriers (i.e., entrenched pathogenic defenses) my patient needed to enclose around himself in order to emotionally survive his childhood and the world at large; this resulted in deep transformation and lasting change.

## TRANSFORMING TRAUMA AND SHAME THROUGH THE THERAPIST'S FIERCE LOVE

My patient, whom I will call Bob, is a 65-year-old man who came to therapy loaded with shame, blame, and disgust toward himself because of the significant relational trauma, severe neglect, and emotional impoverishment he had experienced growing up. Bob was raised in an upper-middle-class household with all the external trappings of a wealthy, prosperous family. Emotionally, however, he grew up in abject poverty. He describes his parents as hardly ever being around, cold, distant, uninterested, rejecting, and even sadistic at times. As a result, Bob grew up feeling unseen, unheard, and ultimately unfelt. As many theorists have stated, it is only when the child feels "felt" that they know they exist (Bowlby, 1988; Stern, 1985; Winnicott, 1960/1965). If these theorists are right, and I believe that they are, my patient grew up feeling nonexistent.

Recognizing this early on in the treatment, my primary goal in working with Bob was to help him transform the shame, blame, and hatred he felt toward himself by providing for him in the here and now what he had needed in the there and then (van der Kolk, 2001). Drawing on what we know about optimal parent–child dyads, my work with Bob in large part involved seeking to right the wrongs of his insecure attachment experiences and to provide for him the mirror in which he could finally see his core authentic self. The primary ways in which I attempted to help Bob reclaim his sense of self was through explicitly showing in my words and in my actions, just like a parent to a child, my keen interest in him. I shared my authentic feelings for him as well as my delight and affection for him. Most important, I persistently worked to break through his thick pathogenic defenses and make sure that he was taking in and viscerally experiencing what I was offering him. In this way, our relationship provided him with a major corrective emotional experience, a healing experience that allowed him to feel self-worth, self-compassion and, ultimately, to feel himself to be someone who is worthy of love.

The following clinical vignettes are from a session 6 months into treatment. In this session I am actively working to help Bob transform his trauma and his pathogenic self states. Building compassion for the self through the Fierce Love of the therapist is an integral component in penetrating entrenched defenses and transforming pathogenic self states. The work features numerous attempts to vigorously counter and thus weaken his defenses in order to facilitate his feeling compassion toward his younger self, a self he had long ago disavowed in order to maintain connection with his indifferent, even hostile, caregivers.

The session begins with Bob handing me a framed 5- × 7-inch childhood photo of himself and his older brother. While his older brother is hamming it up in the photo, Bob, who appears to be around age 2 years, is staring off into the distance with a sad, detached, vacant gaze. Upon his handing me the photograph, I intentionally take a few moments to viscerally feel into and connect to his sad and disconnected toddler self as a way of affectively connecting with him and fueling myself up for the work ahead. After a few moments, I self-disclose my personal reactions, stating how it is heartbreaking seeing this photo of him. I then share my moral outrage that a child this young was exposed to this kind of relational environment. As I speak, Bob is listening to me with rapt attention. As he listens to my fierce defense of his self, his face begins to soften as he experiences my love and compassion, expressed through my words, my facial expressions, and my animated tone of voice. Looking at the photograph intently again for a second time, I spontaneously say, "Oh! I just want to go over and grab that little boy and really hug him." What I am doing here is providing for my patient in the imaginal realm what I know both from his history and from what I intuitively sense that he never got enough of as a child—that is, emotional and physical warmth, holding, and care. This is where the therapist comes in.

THERAPIST (T):   What's your reaction to my reaction? **[Relationally meta-processing his response to me imaginally hugging his younger self as a way of building his receptive affective capacity]**

PATIENT (P):   Oh, well you're always over the top. **[Soft defenses as evidenced by his genuine smile. His lit-up face and huge smile reveal that he appears to be deeply pleased]**

T:   (*Laughs*) OK. But, no, what's your reaction? **[Bypassing the defense directly]**

P:   (*Laughs as if he's been caught trying to sneak away*) You touched me for a minute there when you were first looking at it and you were saying something about the little boy . . . I actually felt pain for a moment . . . I actually got tearful. . . . But, then I just went blank. . . . But there was a moment there. . . . The memory of it and how you saw it . . . reminded me of it. But, yeah. It was a painful thing.

Bob's defenses are beginning to melt as he shares with me the emotional impact my desire to hug and rescue the little boy had on him. This is a big step for him to admit to me that I touched him on a heart level. It signals to me that my relational interventions are having a healing impact, prompting me to continue down this path of using our relationship to provide the corrective emotional experience for him.

From here, Bob tells me some painful stories from his childhood that help explain why his toddler self was so detached and disconnected. Growing up, he remembers feeling "discarded" by his parents, ostracized and rejected by his peers, and psychologically and physically tortured by his older brother. Most of all he remembers no one, "absolutely no one," showing any sign of interest in him. "I grew up feeling worthless," he says. He underscores this statement by telling me how 6 months earlier his uncle told him that his parents had wanted to have an abortion when they found out they were pregnant with him. The next vignette starts here.

P:  I was just gonna say that the decision was made half-heartedly because [my parents] screwed up (i.e., by not having an abortion). . . . You know, obviously, I was not wanted. There's no question in my mind. **[Words infused with pain as evidenced in his eyes, which are welling with tears]**

T:  And, the part of you that is in touch with that still believes that you're not wanted.

Trauma memories and pathogenic affects and the pathogenic beliefs about the self to which they have given rise have the feeling of being in the here and now, even when the context is historic. By pointing out that a part of him still feels unworthy of being born, said with disbelief in a strong declarative tone of voice, I am implicitly enlisting him to feel compassion for his self.

P:  Well, it's not that much of a stretch to the worthlessness, no.

T:  Absolutely . . . Absolutely. **[Validating emphatically as a way of underscoring the truth]**

P:  And that's why unless I have a deal or a job, or something with my hands . . .

T:  . . . to justify your worth . . . **[Relational intervention: sentence bridging]**

P:  . . . I don't get it. I don't have it. That's a terrible thing. **[Beginning to show signs of feeling compassion towards the self]**

T:   That's a terrible thing is right. **[Validating in both my words and bold tone of voice in order to prime the pump of his affective experience]**

P:   But, I don't know how we're going to undo that. **[Defenses rise as he expresses futility around change, which will require him to let down his well-developed protective character armor]**

In the preceding vignette, Bob begins to drop down into affective experience: His voice is much softer and tremulous, his face softens, and the pain around his eyes is palpable. But it's only for a moment, and his defenses rise again. In the next vignette I continue to try to melt these entrenched defenses by bringing him back to the little boy in the photo in yet another attempt to get him to reconnect to his younger self by building compassion for himself at that age.

T:   How do you feel toward that little boy in that photo?

P:   (*Big sigh*) Well, it's hard to separate it because I know who it is. But, I'd say if I was looking at that, I would say that's a very disturbing picture. Very sad example of a child . . .

T:   What do you think that little boy needed?

P:   A reason.

T:   To what? **[Through my methodical Socratic questioning, I am trying to get him to reconnect to his affective experience.]**

P:   (*With conviction*) To enjoy being alive.

T:   Wow. **[Said tenderly, wanting him to know that I really heard the stark words that he just said]**

P:   That's what I see on his face.

T:   And, what's at the core . . . of a reason . . . to enjoy . . . being alive? **[Said very slowly, deliberately pausing between words. This is an intentional right brain vocal intervention used to attempt to get him to drop down and draw him in closer to his affective experience.]**

P:   To be wanted. **[Voice drops, face softens; he's beginning to get in touch with his affective experience again.]**

T:   Yes . . . That's exactly right. . . . **[There is a 3-second pause as I look at Bob intently to communicate my steady, warm, holding presence as he begins to slowly approach his fiercely guarded emotional safe.]** So, there's that little boy inside of you that's still longing to really be wanted by his parents, which will never happen in the way that he needed it to happen, right?

### Speaking Truth on Behalf of the Self

One of the primary Fierce Love interventions is speaking the truth on behalf of the self. Here, I am presenting Bob with the harsh reality of how he will *never* get his needs met by his parents in the way that he needs it to be done. With many of our trauma patients, accepting this painful truth is an integral part of their healing journey. Knowing that our relationship is solid, that he implicitly and explicitly knows that I am truly there for him, in the next vignette I am going to champion him to see his disavowed child self for who he really is—that is, a loveable little boy—and by doing so, reclaim him.

P:  (*Softly, with tinges of pain and sadness reflected both in his voice and face*) No.

T:  So, the *only* person who can do it at this point . . . there's no one else. . . . . there's no [wife's name], there's no me, there's no one else. There's only you. **[Stated slowly, words enunciated, as a way of drawing him in affectively]**

P:  How?

T:  By feeling the feeling that you would feel if you could feel for him? By really feeling compassion, love . . . I'm serious. I know it sounds so hokey, Bob, but it really is the key. . . . That little boy still feels like he shouldn't have been born . . .

Here, I am laying out the deepest intrapsychic work that needs to happen in order for this man to truly heal—that is, to undo the split in his psyche and restore the connection between his present-day adult self and the disavowed parts of himself.

P:  (*Big sigh. Looks visibly upset*)

T:  I can't even say that without . . . **[Winces in pain and lets out a big, heavy sigh]**

I am using my own visceral felt experience of feeling what it must be like for Bob to believe that he should never have been born to prime the pump of his own affective experience that is still in the shadows.

T:  What are you feeling? **[Having now laid out the road we need to traverse together, I check in with him to see his internal reaction.]**

P:  I'm feeling upset. That's a tough one. If that's how I'm gonna get better, I've got a tough road. (*Appears visibly upset*)

T:  Why can't you love that little boy, Bob? What holds you back? He's a precious little boy. **[Fierce Love intervention: Boldly confronting the defense by directly challenging him and showing him his core self]** Why can't you love him?

P:  (*Nods*) I don't know. (*Shakes head with puzzlement and a bit of contempt, as reflected in his harsh face*)

T:   Why can't you really embrace him? It doesn't have to make sense. What holds you back? Ask your body, not your brain. Whatever comes up. **[Experiential bottom-up intervention urging patient to bypass his logical defenses and allow something from his body to come up]**

P:   But, that's the problem. My self-preservation has been logic.

Witnessing Bob's deep internal struggle to connect to his younger self, I switch gears by making it less experience near by replacing himself with another child of the same age.

T:   I know. Let me just ask you: If you saw that little boy sitting on the playground, how would you feel toward him?

P:   (*Tearfully*) Are you kidding? I was that little boy on that playground forever. I was always alone and sitting there. Every dance. Every playground. Every single event. I was alone in the corner. Everyone. Hated it. . . . (*harshly, displaying disgust and scorn in tone and facial expressions*) How am I supposed to feel compassion for that?!

Bob's affective experience comes to the fore in a burst of historical content laced with affect as he underscores the severity and starkness of his unbearable traumatic aloneness. Sad, painful feelings begin to emerge, but he quickly shuts them down by feeling anger, disgust, and contempt toward his self, and perhaps a little toward me for prompting him to feel in the first place. "How am I supposed to feel compassion for that?" he says with disgust and scorn. Schore (2011, cited in DeYoung, 2015) discussed a study that showed that people suffering from severe developmental and relational trauma are especially prone to have disgust-prone implicit concepts. Disgust sensitivity is elevated in trauma-related disorders, and this self-disgust is also likely to be dissociated (DeYoung, 2015).

Over the next few minutes, my primary intervention to melt these entrenched pathogenic defenses is done through cognitive restructuring of the core erroneous beliefs:

T:   It's not his fault. It was *never* his fault. . . . **[Fierce Love intervention: speaking the truth on behalf of the self in a very bold, directive manner]**

P:   (*Shakes head in almost disbelief*). . . . (*tears form*) I just . . .

T:   You've got tears coming. **[Naming the affect that I'm witnessing as a way of embracing and amplifying it]**

P:   Yeah. Of course. Because it's horrible. . . . But, I don't see how . . . (*defenses rising again*)

T:   So, how did you feel when I said that I just want to grab that little boy. I think I said something to that effect. **[I interrupt his defensive response by bringing him back to his remembered experience of me embracing his younger self in an attempt to get him to drop down into that corrective experience once again.]**

P:   Yeah, you did.

T:   That was my impulse.

P:   Yeah, I know. I don't get that. (*Shakes head*)

Bob's defenses are in full force as he remains in shut-down emotional mode. As DeYoung (2015) observed, "Shame persists when self acceptance is out of reach" (p. 47). Bob doesn't yet have access yet to a relational/emotional process that allows him to embrace a whole sense of self.

T:   You're still blaming this child for never being loved by his parents . . . when it had nothing to do with him. And, in fact, just the opposite is needed . . . it's like crying out. It's such an injustice what was done to this child. And you're blaming him . . . **[Fierce Love intervention: boldly defending and advocating on behalf of the disavowed child part when the patient is unable to]**

P:   So, you're . . . let me get this straight. You're saying my lack of self now . . . worthlessness . . . not having anything substantial other than money . . . is because of how I feel about . . .

T:   . . . yourself as a result of what happened to you.

P:   Yeah.

T:   That was *no fault* of yours. **[Trying to get him to cognitively understand and, more important, viscerally experience how the self-hatred came to be as a way of helping him relinquish the defenses that he no longer needs in order to feel safe in the world]**

P:   And that's why I overcompensate with everyone else in business because I don't deal with people other than business.

As Bob receives my efforts to advocate fiercely on behalf of the neglected-child part of him, he also is beginning to weave a coherent narrative about his life. One of the central aims of AEDP's four-state transformational process is to develop a "cohesive and coherent autobiographical narrative" (Fosha, 2000, 2003) deemed crucial to secure attachment (Main, 1999). Bonnie Badenoch (2008) also discussed the importance of helping our patients develop a "coherent story" that is contextualized within both a right brain and left brain understanding. What I am doing here is helping Bob to develop a coherent autobiographical narrative with an emotional layer to the understanding—that is, helping him to make visceral sense of his life in multiple relational contexts.

T:   Yes! When the person who needs more than anyone to be given to in an emotional way is your self. **[Said in a bold, strong voice as a way of underscoring the vital importance in what I am saying]**

P:   And that's why when that sister or somebody touched me like that it was like electricity. **[Referring to a moment in his adult life between his**

**sister-in-law and himself where she softly touched his arm, and in that particular moment he felt pure, unadulterated love]**

T:   Right.

P:   . . . Because it's so rare.

Bob is finally allowing himself to begin to see three important truths about himself: (a) his feelings of worthlessness, although they may have originated from parental errors of omission and commission (Fosha, 2000), are now being sustained by his own feelings of disgust and loathing toward his self; (b) he overcompensates through work and excess generosity to make up for what he perceives and experiences as deficiencies in his self; and (c) most important, the person who needs to be given to more than anyone else in his life is himself, which is why, when it happens, it's like "electricity, because it's so rare."

The seeds of compassion are beginning to take root in my patient. I want to seize the moment by sharing how I feel toward him as a way of turbo-charging the healing that I can palpably feel is already happening.

### Metaprocessing the Corrective Emotional Experience: Explicitly Sharing My Love for Him

T:   Yeah. So, what's it like to be cared for . . . or to see the care . . . the love and caring from me toward you?

P:   It's strange. **[Patients often refer to new, positive, corrective experiences as strange, weird, or foreign. In AEDP we view this as one of the markers of one of the transformational affects, referred to as "tremulous affects."]**

T:   (*Laughs a bit self-consciously as I gear up to tell him that I love him*) I know. You know I show you sometimes to my supervisor (referring to our video-taped sessions that I show my supervisor). . . . I say, "Here's Bob . . . I love Bob . . . Here's Bob. I love Bob." . . . I was just noticing that a couple weeks ago.

Here, I am self-disclosing mindfully and judiciously that I love him: I first say it in an indirect way by telling him that I have told my supervisor that I love him. This is a deliberate titration on my part as I want to see how he receives this bold intervention.

P:   You make me cry. (*Patient is visibly moved. His face is significantly softened, his eyes are welled up with tears.*)

T:   Awww . . . stay with that! **[Said softly but firmly and directly as I want him to viscerally take in this corrective emotional experience]**

Seeing that Bob is visibly moved by my self disclosure—that is, that it has had a corrective impact on him—I immediately direct him to stay with the feelings as a way of building his receptive affective capacity around "taking in" my love for him. What I am doing here is "gluing the glimmer" of the corrective affective experience by inviting him to stay with the visceral experience of the corrective emotional experience.

**P:** Well, obviously that's what I never felt . . .

**T:** Yeah . . . so, stay with that feeling in you . . . and, it really is true. I really do love you. **[Witnessing the strong healing impact my bold self-disclosure had on him, I directly tell him that I love him as a way of deepening and neuronally encoding the corrective emotional experience even more.]**

**P:** Mmmmm.

**T:** I *really* do. **[Again, trying to deepen and encode the corrective experience]**

**P:** (*In a childlike voice brimming with happiness*) That's very sweet . . . (*softly, clearly still moved*) Thank you.

**T:** You're welcome. I can't help it. It's just a feeling . . . (*Long, pregnant pause of 20 seconds where patient and therapist are immersed in this healing moment between them*)

**T:** So, what's happening inside now? . . . What's your reaction to what I just said? **[Soft voice shows that she, too, is clearly moved and affected in the intersubjective realm; moment-to-moment tracking and deepening the healing moment through relationally meta-processing the experience]**

**P:** Oh, it's a very warming quality about it.

**T:** Are you able to take it in?

**P:** Yes.

**T:** You are? **[Asked deliberately in a strong, declarative voice as a way of deepening the healing experience even more by having the patient acknowledge, and therefore reexperience, the corrective experience again]**

**P:** Yes.

**T:** Where do you feel that right now inside? **[Exploring somatic aspects of the experience: taking the experience to the body as a way of enhancing it, deepening it, encoding it]**

**P:** Oh, I felt it everywhere.

**T:** Everywhere. What's it feel like? **[Deepening, encoding the experience through metaprocessing the experience somatically]**

P:    It's actually a very soothing, very warm feeling.

T:    Yeah . . .

P:    But, then, I don't know if I made it worse, or it was good, but I said to myself . . . "That'd be nice to carry to my grave" . . . (*3-second pause as both patient and therapist take in the powerful impact of these words*)

T:    Awwwwww . . . **[Therapist is clearly moved; her eyes become moist and her voice is filled with affect.]**

P:    But that might not be a bad thought.

T:    Noooooo. Not at all. **[Therapist is still deeply touched; speaking in a very soft, loving tone.]**

P:    That's what I said. . . . As I was feeling it, that's what I said to myself . . . (*Patient and therapist spend a few moments in silence as the intersubjective field is charged with love and connection*)

T:    (*Nods*) What are you feeling right now? **[Moment-to-moment tracking of his affective emerging experience]**

P:    (*Scratches head*) I'm not sure.

T:    What do you feel between us right now? What's going on? I think that's the first time I ever told you that I loved you? **[Relational meta-processing: deepening the healing process by reintroducing the phrase that provided the corrective emotional experience as a way of continuing to encode the corrective emotional experience]**

P:    Yeah. (*Big beaming, yet shy smile*)

T:    (*Laughs shyly, tremulously*)

P:    It's actually very believable from you. (*Said tenderly, infused with positive affect*)

T:    (*In bold, declarative voice*) Is it? **[I phrase it as a question intentionally because I want to deepen the corrective experience even more by inviting him to confirm the corrective statement: "It's actually very believable from you."]**

P:    Yeah. It feels very genuine, which is not easy for me to take from anyone.

T:    So, you can take it? Wow! I'm honored. Wow, I've crossed that wall? **[Referring to his metaphor of the "red brick wall" he put up at age 4 to keep everyone outside of his personal sphere]** Have I crossed that wall?

P:    Oh, for sure.

T:    For sure. Wow . . . **[Nonverbally acknowledging the significance of him taking in our deep connection]**

P:   (*With laughter that serves to mask his vulnerability in the moment*) Yeah. I've probably been more intimate with you than most people in my life.

T:   (*Joins him in his laughter, feeling a bit vulnerable herself*) I'm honored . . . (*Therapist and patient smile and gaze at one another for a few moments*)

In this deeply healing session, like a parent to a child, I boldly acknowledged my authentic love and care for my patient. This marked a major turning point for Bob, as well as for myself as a therapist. From this session onward Bob viewed himself and his life story in a much more compassionate light, and he increasingly felt more worthy and deserving of love, as evidenced in his being able to seek out and develop friendships for the first time in his life, as well as in his ability to be emotionally intimate with his wife of 25 years.

As for me, I no longer felt internally blocked around expressing feelings of love and care toward my patients. This experience brought me to a new clinical understanding of the therapeutic power of *mindfully* and *judiciously* explicitly expressing feelings of love for patients when the therapist has a strong sense that it will be a corrective emotional experience for them. Also, as with all AEDP interventions, metaprocessing is key to knowing whether what we are therapeutically giving to our patients is being received and, if it is, whether it is having a positive or negative impact on them. With Bob—and, indeed, with all of patients to whom I have expressed my love and care over the years—the experience, whether it is fraught with insecurity and anxiety to begin with, has invariably proved to be healing and, in the majority of cases, integral (as we see with Bob) in transforming pathogenic self states, developing self-compassion and reclaiming the core authentic self.

## CONCLUSION

In her beautifully titled book *The Leaven of Love*, Izette De Forest (1954) described how one of the important roles of the therapist is to provide their patients with the "gift of love," an experience that every child should have received just by virtue of being born but which, under traumatic circumstances, was withdrawn. She described this loving gift we bestow on our patients as "a replica of the *birthright of love* [emphasis added], which was denied [them], as an infant or growing child, but, which, if granted would have assured him full stature as an individual in his own right" (pp. 16–17).

In AEDP, we seek to restore the birthright of love in all of our patients. However, we do not believe that it is the therapist's love alone that heals; instead, it is the therapist's love *and* the patient's being able to fully *receive* that love and care viscerally that allows the deepest healing to occur, in particular in patients whose entrenched pathogenic self states, resulting from maltreatment and neglect and everything that is the opposite of love that they have suffered, prevent them from seeing the truth about themselves: That they are, and were all along, deserving and worthy of love. The process by which we work with patients includes systematic moment-to-moment work with the entrenched defenses erected against hurt, defenses that prevent positive experiences from being absorbed. These entrenched defenses—thick, protective barriers that patients use to close in on themselves in order to emotionally survive the traumas of their childhood and the world at large—must be restructured and transformed so that the person can take in and benefit from the corrective emotional experience that the therapist is offering.

It is through the therapist's Fierce Love, fueled by a steadfast belief in the transforming power of affect and the self-righting tendencies that live within all of us, that these entrenched defenses and pathogenic self states are finally able to be transformed and, when they are transformed, and self-compassion replaces shame and self-blame, the core authentic self emerges into the light.

## REFERENCES

Alexander, F., & French, T. M. (1946). *Psychoanalytic therapy: Principles and application.* Ronald Press.

Badenoch, B. (2008). *Being a brain-wise therapist: A practical guide to interpersonal neurobiology.* W. W. Norton.

Bowlby, J. (1969). *Attachment: Vol. 1. Attachment and loss.* Basic Books.

Bowlby, J. (1988). *A secure base: Parent–child attachment and healthy human relationships.* Basic Books.

De Forest, I. (1954). *The leaven of love: A development of the psychoanalytic theory and technique of Sándor Ferenczi.* Harper Brothers.

DeYoung, P. (2015). *Understanding and treating chronic shame: A relational/neurobiological approach.* Routledge. https://doi.org/10.4324/9781315734415

Fisher, J. (2017). *Healing the fragmented selves of trauma survivors: Overcoming internal self-alienation.* Routledge. https://doi.org/10.4324/9781315886169

Fonagy, P. (1997). Multiple voices vs. meta-cognition: An attachment theory perspective. *Journal of Psychotherapy Integration, 7*(3), 181–194. https://doi.org/10.1037/h0101122

Fosha, D. (2000). *The transforming power of affect: A model for accelerated change.* Basic Books.

Fosha, D. (2002). The activation of affective change processes in AEDP, (Accelerated Experiential-Dynamic Psychotherapy). In J. J. Magnavita (Ed.), *Comprehensive handbook of psychotherapy: Vol. 1. Psychodynamic and object relations psychotherapies* (pp. 309–334). Wiley.

Fosha, D. (2003). Dyadic regulation and experiential work with emotion and relatedness in trauma and disordered attachment. In M. F. Solomon & D. J. Siegel (Eds.), *Healing trauma: Attachment, mind, body, brain* (pp. 222–281). W. W. Norton.

Fosha, D. (2005). Emotion, true self, true other, core state: Toward a clinical theory of affective change process. *Psychoanalytic Review, 92*(4), 513–552. https://doi.org/10.1521/prev.2005.92.4.513

Fosha, D. (2013). A heaven in a wildflower: Self, dissociation, and treatment in the context of the neurobiological core self. *Psychoanalytic Inquiry, 33*(5), 496–523. https://doi.org/10.1080/07351690.2013.815067

Fosha, D. (2017). How to be a transformational therapist: AEDP harnesses innate healing affects to re-wire experience and accelerate transformation. In J. Loizzo, M. Neale, & E. Wolf (Eds.), *Advances in contemplative psychotherapy: Accelerating transformation* (pp. 204–219). Taylor & Francis. https://doi.org/10.4324/9781315630045-18

Herman, J. (1992). *Trauma and recovery.* Basic Books.

Kaufman, G. (1996). *The psychology of shame: Theory and treatment of shame-based syndromes* (2nd ed.). Springer.

Lipton, B., & Fosha, D. (2011). Attachment as a transformative process in AEDP: Operationalizing the intersection of attachment theory and affective neuroscience. *Journal of Psychotherapy Integration, 21*(3), 253–279. https://doi.org/10.1037/a0025421

Main, M. (1999). Attachment theory: Eighteen points with suggestions for future studies. In J. Cassidy & P. R. Shaver (Eds.), *Handbook of attachment: Theory, research and clinical applications* (pp. 845–888). Guilford Press.

McCullough, L. (1997). *Changing character: Short-term anxiety-regulating psychotherapy for restructuring defenses, affects, and attachment.* Basic Books.

Schore, A. N. (1996). The experience-dependent maturation of a regulatory system in the orbital prefrontal cortex and the origins of the development of psychopathology. *Developmental Psychology, 8*(1), 59–87. https://doi.org/10.1017/S0954579400006970

Schore, A. N. (2003). *Affect regulation and the repair of the self.* W. W. Norton.

Schore, A. N. (2019). *Right brain psychotherapy.* W. W. Norton.

Siegel, D. J. (1995). Memory, trauma, and psychotherapy: A cognitive science view. *Journal of Psychotherapy Practice and Research, 4*(2), 93–122.

Siegel, D. J. (2015). *The developing mind: How relationships and the brain interact to shape who we are.* Guilford Press.

Stern, D. N. (1985). *The interpersonal world of the infant: A view from psychoanalysis and developmental psychology.* Basic Books.

Stolorow, R., & Atwood, G. (1992). *Contexts of being: The intersubjective foundations of psychological life.* Analytic Press.

van der Kolk, B. (2001). Beyond the talking cure: Somatic experience, subcortical imprints and the treatment of trauma. In F. Shapiro (Ed.), *EMDR: Toward a paradigm shift* (pp. 57–83). American Psychological Association. https://doi.org/10.1037/10512-003

Winnicott, D. W. (1965). Ego distortion in terms of true and false self. In *The maturational process and the facilitating environment: Studies in the theory of emotional development* (pp. 140–157). International Universities Press. (Original work published 1960)

# 11

# Finding Healing in the Broken Places

## Intra-Relational AEDP Work With Traumatic Aloneness

Jerry Lamagna

Accelerated experiential dynamic psychotherapy (AEDP) is a treatment approach that brings elements of experiential, relational, and psychodynamic psychotherapies together with ideas drawn from the study of positive emotion and neuroplasticity (Doidge, 2007; Fosha, 2000, 2002, 2009a, 2017a; Fosha et al., 2009; Fredrickson, 2001; Hanson, 2009, 2017; Lipton & Fosha, 2011). At the center of its efforts to promote change is the sustained focus on *felt experience*, a process that occurs within the context of a safe, supportive, and engaged relationship with the therapist (Fosha, 2000, 2017b; Fosha & Yeung, 2006; Lipton & Fosha, 2011). Here *core affective experiences* (Fosha, 2000)—adaptive mind–body phenomena that include categorical emotions (sadness, anger, fear, joy), meaningful interpersonal connection (i.e., recognition, care, appreciation, compassion), and open contact with inner self states (i.e., self-recognition, self-compassion, self-understanding, harmony, wholeness; Lamagna, 2011, 2015; Lamagna & Gleiser, 2007)—provide the experiential fuel for transformation. Expressed more specifically, this experiential fuel propels psychotherapy clients from states of defensive avoidance (State 1); to direct emotional processing of particular events or relationships (State 2); to the somatic exploration of the change experience itself (State 3; Fosha, Thoma, & Yeung, 2019); and finally, to a sense of wisdom, calm, ease and wholeness (State 4; Fosha, 2017a).

This transformational sequence allows for the emergence, reconsolidation, and reintegration of unfinished business from the past and the activation of healthy affects and related impulses that support mental flexibility, personal

https://doi.org/10.1037/0000232-012
*Undoing Aloneness and the Transformation of Suffering Into Flourishing: AEDP 2.0*, D. Fosha (Editor)

authenticity, and well-being. Reclaiming feelings such as anger and assertion (i.e., adaptive core affective experiences) allows clients to set and maintain personal boundaries or fight injustice. Recovering their fear helps guide them to avoid or flee from dangerous situations. Regaining their ability to mourn, clients are able to come to terms with painful and immutable realities of their life. And recouping joy allows them to recover an intrinsic capacity for openness and zest for life (Fredrickson, 2001; McCullough Vaillant, 1997). Even affects associated with States 3 and 4—mastery, mourning, gratitude, hope, wisdom, and ease—bring with them a broadening and building of capacities that support resilience and well-being (Fosha, 2009a, 2009c; Fosha, Thoma, & Yeung, 2019; Fredrickson, 2001; Russell & Fosha, 2008; see also Chapters 13 and 14, this volume).

Although affective processing is seen as the fundamental means for generating momentum through AEDP's four-state model of transformational change (Fosha, 2000, 2002), not all affects function as catalysts for transformation. Some affective responses, in fact, have a defensive function, serving to prevent access to a client's authentic, adaptive responses by masking them with preferred forms of affective self-experience (Fosha, 2000). Intense vulnerability, for example, can be masked by more powerful feelings, such as rage or contempt. Mourning can be derailed by the presence of anxiety, shame, or distress. As experiential markers of affective avoidance, these phenomena indicate the client's presence in State 1 and signal their unconscious trepidation around approaching core affect. Tracking such phenomena informs the therapist of the need to cultivate greater interpersonal safety and trust, dyadically regulate inhibitory anxiety and shame, and, when needed, engage in subsequent work to identify and restructure defenses.

Even more disruptive to the process of transformation is the unbidden upwelling of affective memories associated with unbearable aloneness, despair, terror, desperation, helplessness, and humiliation. Previously described in the AEDP literature as "pathogenic affect" (Fosha, 2002), and now subsumed under "maladaptive core affective experiences" (Chapter 9, this volume), and now "maladaptive affective experience" (Introduction & Chapter 9, this volume), these intensely felt flashbacks, in which *traumatic aloneness* plays a central role, threaten the functional integrity of the self. As such, pathogenic affect poses a very real challenge to an AEDP therapist's invitation to "stay with it and stay with me" because solely deepening a client's felt contact with these pathogenic affective phenomena is much more likely to retraumatize than to heal.

It is important to note that maladaptive affective states, although aversive and overwhelming when triggered, carry meaningful information about the truth of a client's lived experience. Helping our clients face, take in, and integrate this information provides powerful opportunities for growth and transformation through moments of self-compassion, self-understanding, and self-forgiveness (Gleiser & Lamagna, 2004; Lamagna, 2011, 2015; Lamagna & Gleiser, 2007; see also Chapter 12, this volume). As I discuss in this chapter, however, unlike adaptive affective experiences that involve core affect, traumatic aloneness and related pathogenic experiences need to be transformed in order to become an impetus for transformation itself.

In this chapter, I offer a way of transforming pathogenic affect and unbearable states of traumatic aloneness that involves explicit experiential work in the relational space among the client, the therapist, and self states representing felt memories of abuse and emotional abandonment. This *intra-relational* focus (Gleiser & Lamagna, 2004; Lamagna, 2011, 2015; Lamagna & Gleiser, 2007; see also Chapter 12, this volume) extends the active provision of safety, affect regulation, understanding, mutual resonance, and compassion found in AEDP relational work (Fosha, 2000) to the client's internal relationship with their own suffering. Through a process of mutual regulation and differentiation from the aversive feelings, the client is actively supported to "tend and befriend" forsaken self states, foregoing customary tendencies toward either defensive exclusion (fueled by dread of maladaptive affect) or overidentification (fully reliving the dread contained in the self state).

This reparative movement toward felt attunement, recognition, resonance, inclusion, compassion, and understanding between client and self states provides a means for transforming what was previously too much into an impetus for transformational (i.e., State 2) experience (Lamagna, 2011, 2015; Lamagna & Gleiser, 2007). The subsequent expansion and cohering of consciousness brings the past into existence in the heart and mind of the client in ways that generate more positive affect (i.e., State 3 and 4 phenomena, such as pride, gratitude, solidity, truth, spaciousness, and wholeness) fueling additional rounds of transformational work (i.e., an "upward spiral"; Fosha, 2009a, 2009c; Fosha et al., 2019; see also Chapters 13 and 14, this volume). I explore how this way of working with dysregulated experience (i.e., self-at-worst) by forging a partnership with the grounded, clear, well-regulated present-day self (i.e., self-at-best) creates opportunities to revise past learnings and support well-being in the present (Ecker et al., 2012; Welling, 2012). Put more specifically, I explore how to work with dysregulated experience (i.e., self-at-worst) by forging a partnership with the grounded, clear, well-regulated self-at-best.

## PATHOGENIC AFFECT, TRAUMATIC ALONENESS, AND DISCONNECTION

*Traumatic aloneness . . . is what really renders the attack traumatic, that is, causing the psyche to crack. The [person] being left alone like this must help himself, and for this he must split himself.*

—S FERENCZI, 1932, p. 193

AEDP's views on transformation and psychopathology are both very much organized around the polarity of safety/connection–threat/aloneness. In near-optimal attachment environments, children who feel meaningful emotions are able to use their bonds with their caregivers to amplify what is positive and soothe what is negative (Schore, 1994, 2003). Regardless of the valence of the emotional experience, a securely attached child ultimately feels something positive in having their truth (whether pleasant or unpleasant) received and responded to by a receptive, caring other. In environments of maltreatment, however, children's emotional responses are repeatedly responded to inadequately, with errors of omission (i.e., a lack of understanding, withdrawal, distancing, denial) or with errors of commission (i.e., physical or emotional punishment, blame, ridicule; Fosha, 2002). From an AEDP perspective, it is the recurrent pattern of ruptures to the attachment bond—the destabilizing assault on one's sense of security, safety, worth and trust, plus the subsequent lack of repair that together give rise to most forms of environmentally based psychopathology (Fosha, 2000, 2003).

The destructive nature of emotional desertion, betrayal, and personal disregard becomes even more virulent in clients who have experienced severe forms of trauma and neglect. In such cases, disorganizing implicit memories containing the felt sense of threat, violation, abandonment, and fragmentation create emotional vulnerabilities that profoundly disconnect the client from themselves, from others, and from the present moment (Fisher, 2017; Fosha, 2013; Fosha et al., 2009; Maté, 2015; van der Hart et al., 2006). Like other experiential treatment models, AEDP is familiar with helping clients regulate, experientially process, and integrate the rage, fear, hurt, and sadness associated with traumatic experience. However, like Ferenczi (1932), AEDP takes the position that the most profound emotional injuries are not those that occurred during the moment of violation but those that result from the aloneness, desperation, demoralization, helplessness, and intrapersonal/ interpersonal disconnection that followed and is subsequently rekindled by the mind thereafter (Ferenczi, 1932; Fosha, 2002, 2013; Maté, 2015).

A number of clinical challenges are associated with addressing these maladaptive affective states. First, because of the pervasiveness of such abandonment experiences in childhood, they are harder to address therapeutically than those that occur in response to discrete, acute incidents of abuse. Second, although experiential work with anger, fear, hurt, sadness, and so on, gives rise to transformational experiences and adaptive action tendencies, feelings of unbearable aloneness, humiliation, despair, and powerlessness do not; in fact, their activation often results in a compromising of psychological functioning. This leads us to the final challenge, namely, the paradox that although maladaptive affect needs transforming to heal, its qualities are incompatible with the sense of safety, stability, and supportive human connection needed to do so.

Although these difficulties are formidable, AEDP's recognition that unwilled and unwanted aloneness and disaffection lie at the heart of a complex trauma survivor's suffering provides a direction for therapeutic work with maladaptive affective experiences; specifically, it suggests that it is in the relational space—that is, at the point of contact among therapist, client, and their inner world—where unbearable aloneness can give way to regulation and transformation. It is here that states of threat and reactivity linked to emotional memories of aloneness and other negative emotions can give way to mindful states of engagement, strength, and reconnection with others and oneself (Fosha, 2009a).

To more deeply explore AEDP work with traumatic aloneness, it will be useful to better understand two of its representational schemas: the Triangle of Experience (Figures 11.1 and 11.2; see also Ezriel, 1952) and the Self–Other–Emotion (S-O-E) Triangle (Figure 11.3). These can help make sense of a client's responses to feeling and relating and guide the proposed approach to working with the aversive states linked to maladaptive affective experience. (Please see Chapter 6, this volume, for an in-depth account of these representational schemas.)

**FIGURE 11.1. The Triangle of Experience**

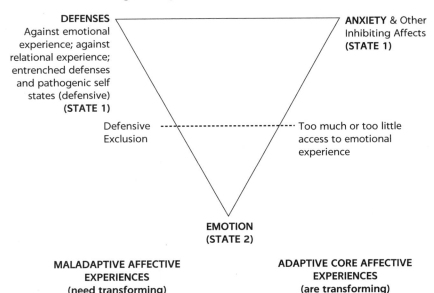

*Note.* Copyright © 2020 by Diana Fosha. Reprinted with permission.

**FIGURE 11.2. The Triangle of Experience: Two Versions of the Triangle of Experience—The Self-at-Worst and the Self-at-Best**

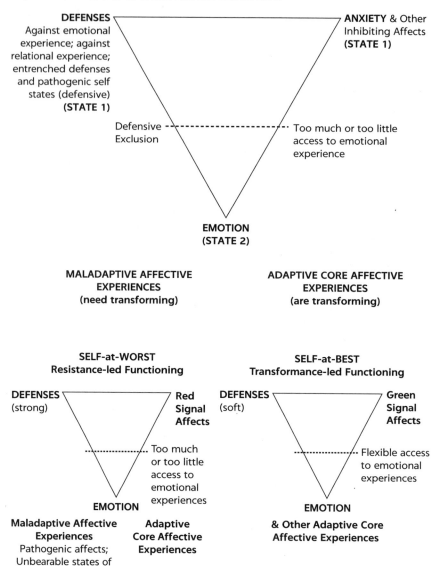

*Note.* Copyright © 2020 by Diana Fosha. Reprinted with permission.

## MAKING USE OF AEDP SCHEMAS IN WORK WITH TRAUMATIC ALONENESS

The Triangle of Experience (see Figures 11.1 and 11.2), and the S-O-E Triangle (see Figure 11.3) offer a comprehensive, three-dimensional map for tracking a person's patterns of relating to their own experience (intrapsychic) and to others (interpersonal). Nestled within each other like Russian dolls, these interdependent schemas highlight the dynamic interplay of internal and external

**FIGURE 11.3. The Self–Other–Emotion Triangle: Two Versions of the Self–Other–Emotion Triangle—The Self-at-Worst and the Self-at-Best**

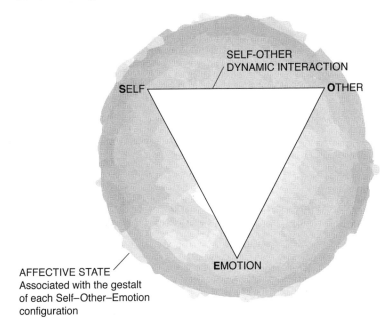

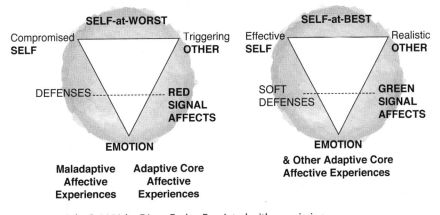

*Note.* Copyright © 2020 by Diana Fosha. Reprinted with permission.

aspects of one's subjective experience and their impact on the individual's ability to either regulate and face what is genuinely felt or instead experience too little (defensive/inhibitory response) or too much of it (primarily pathogenic affect/unbearable states of traumatic aloneness). Whereas the *self-at-best* describes optimally regulated psychobiological states engendering the safety, security, expressiveness, receptivity to connection, and risk taking needed to promote change for the better (i.e., transformation, Fosha, 2008), it is the *self-at-worst* where maladaptive affect abides.

At the intrapsychic level, the Triangle of Experience places self-at-worst experience into two different categories. The first one, located at the upper portion of the triangle in Figure 11.1, represents states of mind organized around defensive responses or inhibitory affect (anxiety/shame) when psychically prohibited, frightening, or destabilizing affects are evoked. The second, located at the bottom of the triangle (to the left of adaptive affective experience, i.e., core affective experiences), represents maladaptive affective experiences (i.e., pathogenic affect, traumatic aloneness) involving aversive, intrusive states of unbearable aloneness, desperation, shame, hopelessness, and so on.

What makes the Triangle of Experience so clinically useful here is its recognition of the existence of two distinct subtypes of self-at-worst presentations: (a) top-of-the-triangle, resistance-based, affect-excluding states requiring bypassing, softening, and/or restructuring, and (b) bottom-of-the-triangle, affect-rich, unbearable/unprocessed trauma-based states requiring regulation, accompaniment, and experiential processing. Although both subtypes of self-at-worst compromise the client's ability to experience their present-day internal and external realities, and therefore their capacity to transform, the location of maladaptive affect alongside transformation-engendering core affects is instructive. It suggests that although such affective states are experienced as highly aversive, they, unlike defenses and inhibitory anxiety and shame, contain vital, valuable, nutritive information, capable of fueling transformational experience. Our work as AEDP therapists, therefore, is to help make these overwhelming states "digestible" for us and our clients in order to make good use of them in transformational work.

Moving out from the Triangle of Experience's rendering of internal conflicts around feeling/connecting, we expand to include the client's experience of self in-relation-to-others (i.e., the interpersonal). The S-O-E Triangle (see Figure 11.3) schema was developed by Diana Fosha (2000) to recognize the ways a client's internal working models shape their explicit patterns of relatedness and emotion processing. The resulting expanded triangular map (with the Triangle of Experience embedded in the bottom corner) plots three, interdependent, co-arising elements representing the client's experience of Self (the "S" corner, occupying the point at the upper left), their experience of the Other (the "O" corner, located at the point at the upper right), and Emotion (the "E" corner, positioned at the point on the bottom).

At this interpersonal level, for example, a self-at-best iteration of the S-O-E Triangle might involve a client manifesting an emotion (E) within their window of tolerance that cocreates a reality-informed sense of the therapist (Other) as safe and supportive of their feelings, which cocreates a Self representation of themselves as safe and worthy. Such a configuration of self experience would be conducive to adaptive change because it creates the conditions for the open expression of affect, the development of interpersonal trust, and access to inner resources that support well-being and healthy action.

Looking at the self-at-worst experience associated with maladaptive affective experience through the interpersonal lens of the S-O-E Triangle yields a very different picture. Here, the client's emotional experience involves a collapse into relived moments of intense aloneness, fear and shame, cognitive disorganization, and felt insecurity with little or no ability to recognize that they are triggered but currently safe in the present (Fisher, 2009; van der Kolk et al., 1996). From the perspective of the S-O-E Triangle this might be depicted as a constellation of subjective experience that includes Self as small and vulnerable; Other as either threatening or absent to the client; and Emotion as overwhelming fear, aloneness, desperation, shame, and so on.

Although the S-O-E Triangle is helpful in making sense of the client's experience of the self in relation to others, its real clinical utility is found in its design. For example, the overall configuration of the schema demonstrates that if we change the client's experience at one corner of the triangle we will also, simultaneously, change the other two corners. In other words, targeting and positively shifting the client's affective experience will positively shift their perception of the therapist and positively shift their perception and experience of self. Targeting and positively shifting the client's perception of the therapist will positively modify the client's affective experience as well as their perception and experience of self at the same time. Also, as I discuss shortly when I examine intra-relational work, the same is true when we shift the client's experience of self.

In effect, each pole of the S-O-E Triangle highlights three major change processes available to the AEDP therapist when working with core affective experience. The Emotion pole represents a focus on processing of categorical emotions such as anger, sadness, fear, and joy (which are simultaneously located at the bottom corner of both the Triangle of Experience and the S-O-E Triangle). The Other pole represents a focus on the client's perception/experience of the therapist along with the processing of the affects that arise between client and therapist (intersubjective resonance, recognition, appreciation, support, compassion, and understanding). Finally, the Self pole represents a focus on processing somatic experience and intra-relational affects that arise when the client's relationship is being adaptively altered to their own inner experience.

The nature of maladaptive affect and self-at-worst experience in general has a limiting effect on these avenues for intervening, however. Although it is common in AEDP to focus on working with core affects generated at the Emotion pole (i.e., processing categorical emotions), attempting to track and deepen pathogenic affect as we would grief and anger is contraindicated because this is likely to kindle a downward spiral of distress and disorganization. Instead, when clients experience a reactivation of traumatic aloneness, desperation, shame, and so on, AEDP therapists typically intervene at the Other corner by focusing experiential work on the relationship between client and therapist and the client's experience of the (one would hope) attuned therapist. Helping the client come out of the vividly relived past to connect with the therapist in the present is done through the process of dyadic regulation to reestablish a state of emotional balance, orientation to the present, interpersonal connection, and openness to experience.

## RELATIONAL WORK

Clinical work focused on the connection between client and therapist is an elemental process in AEDP in general and in specific efforts to address maladaptive affect (Fosha, 2002; Lipton & Fosha, 2011; Chapter 10, this volume). As someone outside of "trauma time" (Steele et al., 2017; van der Hart et al., 2006), the therapist, and their active presence, provides a potent stimulus for enlarging the client's focus of attention beyond the relived past (Fosha, 2009b, 2013; Fosha et al., 2009). Work here centers on helping the client shift out of the old, familiar patterns of procedural reactivity and into a new one, where their aloneness can be undone so that they can sufficiently take in the new corrective experience of the other as safe and supportive. As noted in my earlier discussion of the S-O-E Triangle, a positive shift in registering the Other as present, nonthreatening, attuned, and supportive lawfully involves co-occurring positive shifts in Emotion (relieved, soothed, calm) and Self experience ("now safe and accompanied").

With AEDP's recognition that change begets more change, the therapeutic dyad now experientially tracks and reflects on affects arising from elements of experience that are new and different. Questions such as "What is it like to sense me here with you?" "What is it like to go to that difficult place and see that we can come back together?" and "What is it like to sense my understanding in this moment?" invite additional rounds of processing focused on the felt sense of resilience and of being connected to someone in a way that brings relief and healing rather than trauma and abandonment. I suggest that a rupture in one's sense of safety, followed by its relational repair (i.e., reestablishing psychobiological equilibrium), provides something akin to rupture and repair sequences as studied by Sander (2002) and Tronick (Tronick & Beeghly, 2011; Tronick et al., 1999). With repeated iterations, the sequence of rupture of safety and connection and its relational repair instills an increasing sense of security, personal worth, and resilience (e.g., "I can get flooded, but I can also get through it"; Schore, 1994, 2003).

Thus far I have discussed how working relationally in the space between client and therapist can be instrumental in addressing the challenges associated with maladaptive affective experience. I now turn to the primary focus of this chapter and explore another means for making good use of the suffering associated with traumatic aloneness. The alternative, intra-relational approach offered provides opportunities for reestablishing safety, promoting emotional equilibrium, and engendering transformational experiences by altering the qualitative character of the client's relationship to their own inner pain and aloneness (Lamagna, 2011, 2015; Lamagna & Gleiser, 2007). This is an active process of "tending and befriending" one's self-states—a departure from the complex trauma survivor's tendency to view inner experience as an adversary to be fought, avoided, or surrendered to (Bradshaw, 1990; Forgash, 2005; Paul, 1992; Schmidt, 2004; Schwartz, 1995; Steele, 2007; Whitfield, 1987).

For context, let's return once again to the S-O-E Triangle. Earlier I explained about how the diagram maps a client's momentary subjective experience of emotion in relation to their sense of self and of the other. I also noted that the constellation of emotions and perceptions of self and other that make up each configuration of the triangle consist of mutually co-arising elements, such that a change in one element brings changes in the other two. Finally, I discussed how the overwhelming experience of maladaptive affect can be transformed by shifting the client's distorted experience of the therapist from unsafe or nonexistent to a realistic one that registers the therapist's engagement, presence, and willingness to help.

It is important to note that the S-O-E Triangle shows us that, in addition to transforming pathogenic affect and unbearable states of traumatic aloneness by means of the Other corner (with relational work between client and therapist), we can do this by working at the Self corner, that is, by altering the client's self-identification from vulnerable, lonely child to resourced, compassionate, adult witness to one's inner experience. Helping the client to fully experience themselves as a Self existing in the safety of the present simultaneously induces an awareness of and receptivity to the felt accompaniment of a supportive, actively engaged, therapist (Other) and simultaneously changes the previously overwhelming Emotion (unbearable aloneness, desperation, shame, terror) into an experience that can now be approached and experientially processed. This allows our clients to enter a mode of self-at-best that can be open to State 2 work and a new transformational experience of undoing one's own aloneness with the offer of care and compassion in real time.

As shown in the transcript excerpts presented later in this chapter, the intra-relational approach can provide a helpful way of working with under-regulated maladaptive affect when its intensity compromises the client's felt safety or connection with the therapist. I suggest that it is also useful when working with clients who struggle with dissociation, initiative, autonomy, or excessive reliance on others because it offers another way to help them develop agency, motivation to change, and awareness of internal resources they did not know they had (see also Chapter 9, this volume).

## INTRA-RELATIONAL AEDP

*[The pain of trauma] comes back to that original disconnection and so . . . I am going to make the astonishing statement—that the fundamental problem was not that you were sexually abused, was not that you were beaten, was not that you were abandoned, not that your parents couldn't love you the way you needed to be loved. It's that as a result of all that, you lost your connection to yourself. That is the trauma.*

—G. MATÉ, 2015

Intra-relational AEDP is a variant of AEDP originally developed for clinical work with severely traumatized clients (Gleiser & Lamagna, 2004; Lamagna, 2011; Lamagna & Gleiser, 2007). Its aim is to promote a client's sense of inner safety, security, and harmony through moments of meaningful connection among therapist, client, and heretofore–dis-integrated self states. As in standard AEDP, intra-relational work also looks to make use of core affective experiences that promote transformation, integration, and adaptive psychological functioning.

Working with affective change mechanisms engendered through intra-relational interventions, clinicians and clients experientially process core affects associated with moments of resonance, recognition, warmth, openness, care, compassion, and wholeness occurring between client and different aspects of their own self (Lamagna, 2011; Lamagna & Gleiser, 2007). The juxtaposition of previous memories of aloneness with new memories of care, soothing, and acknowledgment also provides a powerful experiential disconfirmation of past emotional learnings, catalyzing the process of memory reconsolidation and resolution (Ecker et al., 2012; Welling, 2012). Such moments of positive self-state-to-self-state contact can also be particularly helpful when working experientially with clients who have significant difficulty tolerating affects related to painful events from the past.

## THE POWER OF DIFFERENTIATION: FROM ENMESHMENT TO CONTACT

*A sensing and the object sensed, an intention and its realization, one person and another are confluent when there is no appreciation of a boundary between them, when there is no discrimination of the points of difference or otherness that distinguish them.* Without this sense of boundary—this sense of something other to be noticed, approached . . . there can be no emergence and development of the figure/ground, hence no awareness . . . no contact *[emphasis added]*.

—F. PERLS ET AL., 1951, p. 118

*That which we are looking for, is that which is looking.*

—ST. FRANCIS OF ASSISI

*The essence of resilience is the self's differentiation from that which is aversive to it.*

—E. RUSSELL, 2015, p. 5

If the triggering of and identification with implicit memories of traumatic aloneness create the conditions for maladaptive affect to surface, then processes that support differentiation, connection, and the formation of new healing memories should result in both the cessation of pathogenic affect and the emergence of well-being. As mentioned earlier, such interventions in AEDP (and, in fact, in most parts-oriented models, including psychodrama, gestalt therapy, and emotion-focused therapy) begin by fostering differentiation between the client (Self) and those aspects of self that block or hold the emotion that is the focus of therapeutic exploration. Intra-relational work in AEDP (as in standard AEDP) begins by asking clients to pay attention to what is going on in their body. The invitation to attend to their emergent emotions, energy, sensations, and so on, helps them move from just *being in* a particular state to also *being with* the subjective experience contained in the state (Schwartz, 1995; Siegel, 2007). This conscious awareness regulates the affect itself while at the same entraining self-reflective processes that have been described as "mindsight" (Siegel, 2009) and "mentalization" (Fonagy et al., 2002; Fonagy & Target, 1997).

The act of explicitly fostering separation between the client and their pathogenic experience can be achieved through the use of techniques drawn from any number of clinical approaches: AEDP ("portrayals," Fosha [2000], see also Davanloo, 1980), psychodrama ("mirroring" and "role playing," Moreno & Fox, 1997), Jung's active imagination (The Foundation of the Works of C. G. Jung, 2019), gestalt therapy ("empty chair," Perls et al., 1951), psychosynthesis ("dis-identification," Assagioli, 1971), ego state therapy (Watkins & Watkins, 1997), internal family system therapy ("unblending," Schwartz, 1995), and Buddhist psychology (the RAIN [Recognize, Allow, Investigate, Non-identification] technique; Brach, 2013). In all of these models there is an effort to foster an experience of observing, with openness, the afflicted feelings from the outside. This can be done by imagining the afflicted or blocking part in one's mind (seeing them from the outside, so to speak) or locating the part somewhere else in the room (empty chair, drawn image, figurine).

The key point in intra-relational work is that once the technique of choice effectively creates a space for engagement between the present-day client and self state holding the maladaptive affective experience, then tracking, processing, and metaprocessing of core affects associated with self-to-self resonance, recognition, warmth, openness, care, and compassion that follow (Lamagna, 2011; Lamagna & Gleiser, 2007). Embodied tracking of the felt sense of relatedness to self activates intra-relational affective change processes that progress through States 3 and 4 (Lamagna, 2011; Lamagna & Gleiser, 2007).

There will be times when the client is not yet capable of differentiating sufficiently from the part holding the afflicted experience; in such cases it is important that the therapist take the lead in reflecting on and recognizing the experience of the part's felt aloneness. Examples include the therapist explicitly speaking to the part: acknowledging, empathizing, and appreciating the discomfort of the feelings ("I see how upsetting these feelings are for you"), reducing shame and self-recrimination ("It makes so much sense why these feelings would exist given how things were for you at that time. I really get it."), or (with the client's permission) engaging directly with the afflicted part ("I know this is so much for you right now," "Would it be OK if I tried to help you get some relief?" "I am here to help. Can we begin by you sensing me here with you and sensing that you are in my office right now?").

Any shift in the direction of relief, opening, lightening, hopefulness, and clarity is then tracked in the body and metaprocessed. Important in this process is working toward helping the client begin to differentiate and open to joining the therapist in being a sympathetic presence to the afflicted part: "Are you able to see how alone this part has been feeling all this time?" "How is it for you to experience me being compassionate with the pain in you?" then "Where do you notice that inside?" and then, "Can we stay with that for a few moments?" "What feelings do you sense in you as you see that?" or "How are you feeling toward these lonely feelings?" (Schwartz, 1995).

## LINKING AND SYNCING

*When the child splits his personality, then the whole ego doesn't suffer,* but individual components suffer *by themselves [emphasis added].*

—FERENCZI, 1932, p. 170

Diana Fosha (2003) stated that when we as therapists come to exist in the hearts and minds of our clients we can transform the unbearable aloneness that AEDP proposes lies at the roots of our client's psychopathology (Fosha, 2000). Intra-relational work adds that explicitly helping segregated self states to come to exist in the heart and mind of the present-day client provides additional opportunities for inter- and intrapersonal connection; the integration of mind and body; and the effective transformation of the inner aloneness, shame, despair, and distress that characterize maladaptive affect (Lamagna, 2015).

Movement from enmeshment with the psychic pain to differentiation from that pain creates the conditions for the formation of a dyadic field within the individual and a multilayered relational field among the client, the therapist, and the afflicted part of self (Lamagna, 2011; Lamagna & Gleiser, 2007; see also Chapter 12, this volume). Work can now focus on helping the alone part to feel felt, supported, and acknowledged by the self of the client and therapist, generating intra-relational core affects linked to shared resonance, recognition, other prosocial affects between self and part. Such "linking and syncing" (Siegel, 2009) in this way integrate energy and information by creating a more inclusive, coherent, data-rich, *super-state* whose boundary is enlarged to incorporate aspects of the consciousness from the past into a new, coherent form (Tronick et al., 1999). This relational/intra-relational emergence of new forms and the positive affects that foster and mark them underlie intrinsic tendencies toward growth, fueling expansion and transformative psychotherapeutic processes (Fosha, 2003, 2009a, 2009c).

Let's take a look at this process through a clinical illustration.

## CLINICAL ILLUSTRATION: INTRA-RELATIONAL WORK WITH MALADAPTIVE AFFECTIVE EXPERIENCE

Linda is a 60-year-old, White, married, heterosexual woman who presented for treatment 2 months before the session discussed below.[1] She came to therapy depressed, anxious, "fragile," and on the verge of leaving her husband of 20+ years. These feelings had been precipitated by upsetting incidents with her grown stepchildren during the holidays that had left her feeling hurt, dismissed, angry, and unsupported by her husband. The incidents had evoked deeply painful feelings associated with her problematic attachment to her alcoholic, emotionally abusive mother, her abandonment by her father while Linda was a young child, and recurrent relocations during her childhood. As the eldest child, Linda admitted to having a lifelong need to view herself as strong and independent. To do this, she dissociated any and all affects associated with pain, loneliness, and vulnerability.

This transcript of vignettes of a session illustrate intra-relational affective change processes in the context of both AEDP work with pathogenic affect and unbearable states of traumatic aloneness, guided by AEDP's four-state model of change.

We begin 4 minutes into the session as Linda reports a pervasive sense of unease that emerges with no clear trigger. I initially invite Linda to explore her feelings by asking her to note what is going on internally, locating the sensations in her body, verbalizing her visceral experience, and tracking her felt experience moment to moment.

**CLIENT (C):**   (*Voice shaky, agitated*) I don't know why, but I'm terrified.

**THERAPIST (T):**   Yeah.

**C:**   I don't know why. It doesn't make sense . . .

**T:**   Um-hmm. You are feeling terror now?

**C:**   Yes.

**T:**   Where in your body? **[Inviting client to track sensation]**

**C:**   I was thinking about it when I was driving down here. It's like a really, really empty stomach if I had to feel it. It's like a hunger or the opposite . . . like the dry heaves . . . up in here (*gestures to mid-abdomen*).

**T:**   It feels like an empty space?

**C:**   Yes . . . hollow.

**T:**   Uh-huh.

---

[1]Aspects of the client's identity and background have been disguised to protect confidentiality.

C: (*Anxiously*) I don't know why I'm doing this. **[State 1: Defenses come to the fore]**

Linda's agitation and unease with the feeling, combined with mental confusion and descriptors like "empty stomach," "dry heaves," and "hollowness" signal the dysregulation associated with maladaptive affective experience. Her questioning statement "I don't know why I am doing this" is markedly different from her usual openness to the therapeutic process. Taken together, her presentation suggests the need for affect regulation.

T: Is it possible that this is coming from a young place—that this is an old feeling in some ways we are reexperiencing? **[An early attempt on my part to differentiate the old—that is, the there-and-then—distressing feelings from the here-and-now safety in the room with me]**

C: I guess so, but I'm back to the same thing—I'm going through the motions at home . . . doing everything I'm supposed to to keep going. (*Pause*) I'm very surprised by this. **[She does not respond to my question and again expresses surprise at the vehemence of her state.]**

T: The depth?

C: After everything happened (the precipitating incidents during the holidays), I anticipated the mourning of something; the death of something. Someone. Me. (*With increasing agitation*) I just can't understand why I'm feeling this so deeply.

T: Can we just accept for the moment that we are and that we can bring everything to bear to heal this today? Together . . .

I invite Linda to stay with her experience rather than question or fight it. My use of "we" and "together" emphasizes for her my presence, support, and willingness to help regulate her experience. Safety and affect regulation are needed in order for us to return to a state of self-at-best and process the experience of aloneness then and connection now in State 2.

C: (*Getting more distressed*) It just hurts so much. (*Tears up*) It's still so close—that feeling . . . (*pauses*) and I feel afraid of it. **[Clear statement of fear of being overwhelmed]**

T: Yes. Let me help you with that feeling. **[Acknowledging her struggle, I again emphasize my readiness to help: explicit relational offer for dyadic affect regulation]**

C: (*Increasingly agitated, gasping, with tears in her eyes*) I don't know what I'm feeling. It's too hard for me.

T: Linda . . . can you just check in with me for a second? Can you feel me here with you? **[Inviting her to take in my presence so as to initiate dyadic regulation]**

C: It all hurts too much. I miss my mother (*breaks into sobs*). **[She's not registering me]**

T: (*Softly*) Yes.

C: (*Sobbing*) I missed so much.

T: (*Slowly and with softness*) Yeah, you did. Keep breathing. **[Empathy; dyadic affect regulation]**

C: I keep telling myself I'm doing well. I have this wonderful world around me . . . (*sobs*)

T: Can we work on this together? I really want to help you today. **[For a third time, I try to make her conscious of me attending to her distress.]**

C: (*Sobs*)

T: First, can you check in and see that I'm here with you? **[Seeing that the relational option isn't working, I shift to intra-relational work.]** See if we can ask this distressed part of you if she would be willing to separate out—just a little bit. And if she won't, it's OK. We'll figure out other ways of helping.

Linda is struggling with the vehemence of her distressed state and is not able to get grounded or make meaningful contact with me. Shifting to an intra-relational approach, I seek to help her establish herself in the here and now and differentiate from her overwhelming emotions. Here I use Internal Family System's *unblending* technique (Schwartz, 1995; sometimes I use an empty chair, or work symbolically using figurines, etc.), using differentiation in space ("See if you can put the feelings over there") and time ("Those are feelings from when you were 6 years old") to undo her identification with and lack of differentiation from the overwhelmed, abandoned self.

C: I'm just surprised it's so deep. **[First sign of being able to reflect on state]**

T: OK. **[I check her response to the intervention to assess its effectiveness in helping her down regulate.]** Do you have a sense whether there is a willingness for the distress to step back? Did you feel any shifting in your body?

C: I'm just able to breathe (*seems slightly calmer*). **[A glimmer of shifting toward a regulated self-at-best state]**

T: Just notice that you can breathe now. **[Inviting her to experientially track the felt sense of this small positive shift]** (*Long pause*) What are you noticing now?

C: I just want to know why. (*Calmer but still employing intellectualizing defense*)

T: The "why" question isn't going to get us out of this.

**C:**    (*Laughs nervously*) I know.

**T:**    So ask the why question if it would be willing to move to the side. **[Looking to bring focus back to body]** Check in with your body.

**C:**    (*Long pause. Sighs*)

**T:**    Is the distress up, down, or about the same?

**C:**    I can breathe. That's the best way I can say it. **[This is a small but positive shift that would be helpful to seize upon.]**

**T:**    (*Jokingly*) Well, we *did* ask for breathing room . . .

**C:**    (*Laughs*)

**T:**    Right?

**C:**    Yes.

**T:**    That's what we got. (*Long pause*)

**C:**    (*Tears up*)

**T:**    Some feelings coming?

**C:**    (*First with derision, then softening*) This sounds so *soppy*! (*Tearing up*) It means I have to trust you. **[Here the client provides a possible clue as to why efforts at dyadic regulation failed and differentiation has worked only marginally to this point.]**

**T:**    Yes, a little bit.

**C:**    And I have to trust that I'll be OK.

**T:**    Is there in willingness to try trusting me for a few minutes?

**C:**    Yes.

As a result of our prior work together in the treatment, my unflagging accompaniment through afflicted affects here, and the nascent lucidity manifesting from the breathing room that was recently negotiated, Linda is now able to register me as a supportive other. Once a sufficient degree of differentiation and regulation is achieved, I look to foster meaningful, contact among me, the client, and the state holding the traumatic aloneness. Affects associated with curiosity, interest, appreciation, sympathetic sadness, warmth, tenderness, concern, or compassion—whether relational or intra-relational—become the focus of moment-to-moment experiential tracking. Together, we follow the associative flow of emotions, images, thoughts, and recollections that arise emergently. These intra-relational affects that manifest through self-to-self contact (Lamagna, 2011, 2015; Lamagna & Gleiser, 2007) become the fuel that propels the client beyond grounding and to further rounds of transformational work in States 2, 3, and 4.

T:   Can we bear witness to these old feelings with one foot in 2013 (the present, that is, the year when the work was taking place)? That requires some space here.

C:   Um-hmm. **[Assent given; green light]**

T:   Notice how you feel toward her. Someone who wanted love more than anything. See her with your mom over there (*gesturing to the chair in the corner of the room to reinforce differentiation/space*).

T:   (*Pause*) If it feels like it's too much, you let me know. **[Ongoing dyadic affect regulation while doing intra-relational work]**

C:   (*Pause*) It's sad.

T:   Are you feeling *her* sad or sad *for her*?

C:   Feeling sad for her.

This is a good sign because it indicates current feelings about the past experience rather than a triggering of feelings from the past experience.

T:   **[Sensing differentiation, I encourage empathic contact.]** Sad for her? Let her know that, and let her know why.

C:   (*Tearing up*) I'm telling her I want to hold her and rock her.

T:   (*Softly and slowly*) Hold her. Rock her. (*Pause*) We are so sorry it was like this for you. (*Long pause*)

C:   I'm feeling . . . (*becoming agitated again*)

T:   *Your* feelings or *hers*?

C:   *Her* feelings.

Linda initially differentiates from the pathogenic affect held in the young part and spontaneously engages the part's aloneness with some care and tenderness (as evidenced by her wish to soothe). In fostering some processing of this movement from threat and vulnerability to caring engagement, she is invited to track the felt sense of this change for the better; however, after a brief time staying with this positive affect the differentiation between present-day client and the pathogenic experience collapses, as she notes the return of her prior state of agitation. I work to reestablish the differentiation to keep the process moving forward.

T:   See if she would be willing to step back just a little bit.

C:   (*Cries*) This is *so hard*.

T:   I know it's hard. I am going to help you through this. See if she is willing to trust you. **[Empathy and reinforcement of my presence and readiness to help with affect regulation]** All I need is 15 minutes. Are you willing to give me 15 minutes? I guarantee that if you give me

15 minutes, you're going to be in a different space when you leave here. **[I offer this "guarantee" with confidence only because I have seen differentiation work successfully for this client in a previous session.]**

C:   Umm. (*Smiles*)

T:   Is there a willingness to try?

C:   (*Nods*) **[Assent given; green light]**

To reduce any additional retriggering of pathogenic affect, I educate Linda about the goal of differentiation and invite shared reflection on what triggered her shift back to the maladaptive affective experience.

T:   About 10 minutes ago or so you told me you were feeling sad for her. And it was your feelings in 2013 (here and now) about what she experienced back then.

C:   Um-hmm.

T:   And you felt compelled to hold her and rock her.

C:   Um-hmm.

T:   And as you started to rock her, what was it that happened?

C:   It was just me wanting it for myself. It was me wanting to be held. It was me wanting to say "Mommy." **[This indicates a return of her identification with the pathogenic state.]**

T:   Was it you saying, "I'm here"? **[Assessing where her identification is here—present-day self or younger, afflicted one]**

C:   It started out with me saying "I'm here" *to her* and ended up with me saying "I'm here" to the world. (*Cries*)

T:   I see. So when you hugged her, you *became* her?

C:   Yes. **[The client explicitly confirms that she had slipped back into identifying with her younger self.]**

T:   OK. Can she see that when that happened the hug went away?

C:   Um-hmm.

T:   Is she willing to stay separate enough to experience that? She needs to keep all of the pain in her body and allow you to be with her rather than you becoming her. Is she willing to try it as an experiment?

C:   Um-hmm.

T:   Keep seeing her through your eyes. (*Long pause*) How you are feeling toward her?[2]

---

[2]See Schwartz (1995).

In intra-relational work, the emergence of this shift into an open-hearted state prompts experiential tracking of State 2 (direct emotional processing of particular events or relationships) affects associated with care, compassion, and understanding and following the associative flow that results. Tracking and metaprocessing this change for the better reinforces, deepens, and broadens the movement of the experiential work in the direction of positive affect and additional rounds of transformational work (Hanson, 2017).

C: (*Softly*) It's too bad. **[Empathy arises. The affects linked to this empathic contact constitutes core affect just as it would if being offered by the therapist in relational change processes.]**

T: Yeah. So sorry it was that way for you then. We are here now. We are here now. (*Long pause*) **[Explicitly emphasizing the differentiation of there and then from here and now]**

After a relatively short time processing feelings of empathy, Linda suddenly moves from State 2 to State 3 (somatic exploration of the change experience itself).

C: It's out of nowhere. **[Suddenly struck by the emergence of positive feelings of pride and self-appreciation]**

T: Is your heart open or closed?

C: Open—because I admire her.

With the differentiation solidly in place, Linda suddenly experiences a discontinuous expansion in her positive feelings toward her afflicted self state, moving into a sense of admiration and mastery for having survived the difficult challenges of her childhood. This feeling of admiration and mastery are evidence of the transformational affects characteristic of State 3 work (Fosha et al., 2019). She and I continue the process of tracking and metaprocessing each additional moment of change for the better.

T: What do you admire about her?

C: To keep on going.

T: Tell her that.

C: To have a normal life. To try and separate all that neurotic, sick stuff.

T: Do you get that she wanted her mother's love more than anything? **[Facilitating compassionate awareness]**

C: (*Slowly*) Yeah. Yeah.

T: Let her know we understand that. It's normal.

C: Yeah. It's not selfish. (*Long pause*) I'm OK now. I can see it. I can breathe. It's not taking my life away. It sounds so dramatic but these are the *only* words that make sense. **[Core state: The client is now fully centered in her current-day adult self experience and is reflecting on the markers of that centered state.]**

T:   OK. Let's go with them.

C:   It may sound corny, but I like who I am. I like how I made it in spite of this. **[Core state: "This is me" and positive valuation of the self]**

Linda has segued from overwhelming distress, desperation, and aloneness to tentative connection, to admiration of herself. A previously terrifying memory is now being reconsolidated with the juxtaposition of an avoided, overwhelming, symptom-generating memory of traumatic aloneness with this new emergent experience of facing, acknowledging, reclaiming, and reconciling with the past (Ecker et al., 2012; Welling, 2012). She is in core state, a state of deep integration, calm, and capacity to reflect with compassion and self compassion (Fosha, 2017a).

T:   Just notice. Feel that admiration. **[Somatic tracking]**

C:   It's funny. I've never been able to think about my childhood without being very dismissive, or I guess feeling it so much that I couldn't breathe. **[State 4, accurate autobiographical narrative]**

T:   Right. So what's this like? **[Metaprocessing of emergent, new experience]**

C:   It feels "handle-able." (*Both laugh at her new word.*)

T:   And when it feels "handle-able," how do you feel toward her?

C:   I feel sorry, but not overwhelmed. I feel admiration, I have to tell you.

T:   Yes.

C:   I don't know how I did it.

T:   You feel respect, admiration, appreciation, gratitude?

C:   (*Nods*) Um-hmm.

T:   What do you feel drawn to do?

C:   Acknowledge it. All of it. Me. What it really was.

T:   Let's make room for that.

C:   (*Pause*) I think there is a moment of clarity coming. (*Giggles*) I always found myself worrying about what others felt—how others suffered—how it was worse for someone else.

T:   And now? **[Inviting attention to the *new* experience of the moment]**

C:   And now . . . it's not that I don't care. It's just that it doesn't matter for me. There is nothing I could do about it. And I shouldn't have that burden.

T: Can we ask her (the part) what it is like for her to have you and I bear witness to her in this way today? **[Metaprocessing]**

C: That makes it mean something. That it is not imagined. And it's not self-pity and it's not . . . it is . . . it *was.* **[Client sees her pain placed appropriately in the past and as it really was—not through the lens of dismissive defenses and not consumed by the feelings themselves.]**

T: I like your correction. (*Both laugh.*) It *was,* yes. It really was. See how it sits with you to allow that . . . **[Inviting attention to the new experience of distinguishing was from is]**

C: I don't have to fix it. I didn't know I thought that, but I guess I did somehow.

T: What's it like to know you don't have to fix it? **[Metaprocessing]**

C: It's *so* freeing. For this moment, I can think about it without getting sucked into a hole. **[The afflicted sense of self and associated pathogenic affect now appear to be integrated, neutralizing its negative impact on her; furthermore, she is experiencing a transformational affect: "freeing."]**

T: What does that say?

C: It takes away some fear that I've always lived with. **[With the pain neutralized/integrated, the fear and perceived fragility dissipate.]**

T: What's that like? (*Pause*) What do you get to feel more when there is less fear? **[Metaprocessing—attending to the new and good]**

C: Stronger. **[Mastery affect]**

T: And in this moment how are you feeling toward her (the afflicted part of herself) and her empty stomach and all that?

C: I see it in perspective. It was sad. It was hard. Sometimes it was terrible. Sometimes it was OK. (*Smiles*) **[Core state: constructing a new narrative]**

T: Right.

C: I still had fun. I still found meaning. **[Again client indicates a integrative transformation of her pathogenic experience. Good and bad are both there and available as part of her true experience.]**

T: This is big. This is big. **[Affirming the magnitude of the transformation]**

Several days after this session, Linda sent the following email message, which indicated that the shift observed in session had held:

> This may sound corny, but as I sit here listening to the rain and enjoying it, I want to let you know I'm doing well. Churchill said, "If you're going through hell, keep going." Thanks for helping me through.

## CONCLUSION

AEDP is a clinical approach whose primary focus is on creating the conditions that facilitate change for the better in our clients. Although at first glance maladaptive affective experiences may be seen as a formidable challenge to this goal, the reactivation of unbearable aloneness that they signal can also provide an opportunity to jump-start transformational processes that bring healing, acceptance, and integration. In intra-relational work this is done by first regulating affect through the differentiation of past experiences of aloneness from their here-and-now experience and then facilitating corrective moments of connection between the client and inner self states. This regulation and reintegration of previously warded-off experience, when unfettered by defenses, shame, and anxiety, evoke affective change processes (i.e., core affects) linked to moments of self to self-resonance, appreciation, compassion, warmth, joy, and understanding (Lamagna, 2011). Further tracking of this process of linking and syncing yields the feelings of mastery, mourning, gratitude, realization, wisdom, ease, and wholeness that signal the completion of the client's movement through AEDP's four-state model of transformational change (Fosha, 2017a; Fosha, Thoma, & Yeung, 2019).

## REFERENCES

Assagioli, R. (1971). *Psychosynthesis: A collection of basic writings.* Penguin Group.

Brach, T. (2013). *True refuge: Finding peace and freedom in your own awakened heart.* Random House.

Bradshaw, J. (1990). *Homecoming: Reclaiming and championing your inner child.* Bantam Books.

Davanloo, H. (1980). *Basic principles and technique in short-term dynamic psychotherapy.* Jason Aronson.

Doidge, N. (2007). *The brain that changes itself: Stories of personal triumph from the frontiers of brain science.* Penguin Books.

Ecker, B., Ticic, R., & Hulley, L. (2012). *Unlocking the emotional brain: Eliminating symptoms at their roots using memory reconsolidation.* Routledge. https://doi.org/10.4324/9780203804377

Ezriel, H. (1952). Notes on psychoanalytic group therapy: II. Interpretation and research. *Psychiatry, 15,* 119–126. https://doi.org/10.1080/00332747.1952.11022866

Ferenczi, S. (1932). *The clinical diary of Sándor Ferenczi* (J. Dupont, Ed.; M. Balint & N. Z. Jackson, Trans.). Harvard University Press.

Fisher, J. (2009). Sensorimotor psychotherapy. In C. Courtois & J. Ford (Eds.), *Treating complex trauma disorders (adults): Scientific foundations and therapeutic models* (pp. 312–328). Guilford Press.

Fisher, J. (2017). *Healing the fragmented selves of trauma survivors.* Routledge. https://doi.org/10.4324/9781315886169

Fonagy, P., Gergely, G., Jurist, E., & Target, M. (2002). *Affect regulation, mentalization and the development of the self.* Other Press.

Fonagy, P., & Target, M. (1997). Attachment and reflective function: Their role in self-organization. *Development and Psychopathology, 9*(4), 679–700. https://doi.org/10.1017/S0954579497001399

Forgash, C. (2005). The therapeutic triad: Applying EMDR and ego state therapy in collaborative treatment. In C. Forgash & M. Copeley (Eds.), *Healing the heart of trauma: Integrating EMDR and ego state therapy* (pp. 313–342). Springer.

Fosha, D. (2000). *The transforming power of affect: A model for accelerated change.* Basic Books.

Fosha, D. (2002). The activation of affective change processes in AEDP (Accelerated Experiential-Dynamic Psychotherapy). In J. J. Magnavita (Ed.), *Comprehensive handbook of psychotherapy: Vol. 1. Psychodynamic and object relations psychotherapies* (pp. 309–344). Wiley.

Fosha, D. (2003). Dyadic regulation and experiential work with emotion and relatedness in trauma and disordered attachment. In M. F. Solomon & D. J. Siegel (Eds.), *Healing trauma: Attachment, trauma, the brain and the mind* (pp. 221–281). W. W. Norton.

Fosha, D. (2008). Transformance, recognition of self by self, and effective action. In K. J. Schneider (Ed.), *Existential–integrative psychotherapy: Guideposts to the core of practice* (pp. 290–320). Routledge.

Fosha, D. (2009a). Emotion and recognition at work: Energy, vitality, pleasure, truth, desire and the emergent phenomenology of transformational experience. In D. Fosha, D. J. Siegel, & M. F. Solomon (Eds.), *The healing power of emotion: Affective neuroscience, development, and clinical practice* (pp. 172–203). W. W. Norton.

Fosha, D. (2009b). Healing attachment trauma with attachment (and then some!). In M. Kerman (Ed.), *Clinical pearls of wisdom: 21 leading therapists offer their key insights* (pp. 43–56). W. W. Norton.

Fosha, D. (2009c). Positive affects and the transformation of suffering into flourishing. In W. C. Bushell, E. L. Olivo, & N. D. Theise (Eds.), *Annals of the New York Academy of Sciences: Vol. 1172. Longevity, regeneration, and optimal health: Integrating Eastern and Western perspectives* (pp. 252–261). New York Academy of Sciences. https://doi.org/10.1111/j.1749-6632.2009.04501.x

Fosha, D. (2013). A heaven in a wild flower: Self, dissociation, and treatment in the context of the neurobiological core self. *Psychoanalytic Inquiry, 33*(5), 496–523. https://doi.org/10.1080/07351690.2013.815067

Fosha, D. (2017a). How to be a transformational therapist: AEDP harnesses innate healing affects to re-wire experience and accelerate transformation. In J. Loizzo, M. Neale, & E. Wolf (Eds.), *Advances in contemplative psychotherapy: Accelerating transformation* (pp. 204–219). W. W. Norton. https://doi.org/10.4324/9781315630045-18

Fosha, D. (2017b). Something more than "something more than interpretation": AEDP works the experiential edge of transformational experience to transform the internal working model. In S. Lord (Ed.), *Moments of meeting in psychoanalysis: Interaction and change in the therapeutic encounter* (pp. 267–292). Routledge.

Fosha, D., Paivio, S. C., Gleiser, K., & Ford, J. (2009). Experiential and emotion-focused therapy. In C. Courtois & J. D. Ford (Eds.), *Complex traumatic stress disorders: An evidence-based clinician's guide* (pp. 286–311). Guilford Press.

Fosha, D., Thoma, N., & Yeung, D. (2019). Transforming emotional suffering into flourishing: Metatherapeutic processing of positive affect as a trans-theoretical vehicle for change. *Counselling Psychology Quarterly, 32*(3–4), 563–593. https://doi.org/10.1080/09515070.2019.1642852

Fosha, D., & Yeung, D. (2006). AEDP exemplifies the seamless integration of emotional transformation and dyadic relatedness at work. In G. Stricker & J. Gold (Eds.), *A casebook of integrative psychotherapy* (pp. 165–184). American Psychological Association. https://doi.org/10.1037/11436-013

The Foundation of the Works of C. G. Jung. (2019). *The art of C. G. Jung.* W. W. Norton.

Fredrickson, B. L. (2001). The role of positive emotions in positive psychology: The broaden-and-build theory of positive emotions. *American Psychologist, 56*(3), 218–226. https://doi.org/10.1037/0003-066X.56.3.218

Gleiser, K., & Lamagna, J. (2004, November 18–20). *Reaching through the walls: Diana Fosha's Accelerated Experiential Dynamic psychotherapy (AEDP) as an attachment based model for treating dissociation and complex trauma* [Conference presentation]. International Society for the Study of Dissociation Conference, New Orleans, LA.

Hanson, R. (2009). *Buddha's brain: The practical neuroscience of happiness, love, and wisdom.* New Harbinger.

Hanson, R. (2017). Positive neuroplasticity: The neuroscience of mindfulness. In J. Loizzo, M. Neale, & E. Wolf (Eds.), *Advances in contemplative psychotherapy: Accelerating transformation* (pp. 48–60). W. W. Norton. https://doi.org/10.4324/9781315630045-5

Lamagna, J. (2011). Of the self, by the self, and for the self: An intra-relational perspective on intra-psychic attunement and psychological change. *Journal of Psychotherapy Integration, 21*(3), 280–307. https://doi.org/10.1037/a0025493

Lamagna, J. (2015). Making good use of suffering: Intra-relational work with pathogenic affect. *Transformance, 6*(1). https://aedpinstitute.org/wp-content/uploads/page_Making-Good-Use-of-Suffering:-Intra-relational-Work-with-Pathogenic-Affects.pdf

Lamagna, J., & Gleiser, K. A. (2007). Building a secure internal attachment: An intra-relational approach to ego strengthening and emotional processing with chronically traumatized clients. *Journal of Trauma & Dissociation, 8*(1), 25–52. https://doi.org/10.1300/J229v08n01_03

Lipton, B., & Fosha, D. (2011). Attachment as a transformative process in AEDC: Operationalizing the intersection of attachment theory and affective neuroscience. *Journal of Psychotherapy Integration, 21*(3), 253–279. https://doi.org/10.1037/a0025421

Maté, G. (2015, October 24). *Manifesting the mind: Inside the psychedelic experience* [Video]. YouTube. https://www.youtube.com/watch?v=ZdO-Nyk4-jU&list=LLGL2JwotiBamTwlQQ9rYmlg

McCullough Vaillant, L. (1997). *Changing character: Short-term anxiety regulating psychotherapy for restructuring defenses, affects and attachment.* Basic Books.

Moreno, J. L., & Fox, J. (1997). *The essential Moreno: Writings in psychodrama group method and spontaneity.* Springer.

Paul, M. (1992). *Inner bonding: Becoming a loving adult to your inner child.* HarperCollins.

Perls, F. S., Hefferline, R., & Goodman, P. (1951). *Gestalt therapy.* Dell.

Russell, E. (2015). *Restoring resilience: Discovering you client's capacity to heal.* W. W. Norton.

Russell, E., & Fosha, D. (2008). Transformational affects and core state in AEDC: The emergence and consolidation of joy, hope, gratitude and confidence in the (solid goodness of the) self. *Journal of Psychotherapy Integration, 18*(2), 167–190. https://doi.org/10.1037/1053-0479.18.2.167

Sander, L. (2002). Thinking differently: Principles of process in living systems and the specificity of being known. *Psychoanalytic Dialogues, 12*(1), 11–42. https://doi.org/10.1080/10481881209348652

Schmidt, S. J. (2004). Developmental needs meeting strategy: A new treatment approach applied to dissociative identity disorder. *Journal of Trauma & Dissociation, 5*(4), 55–78. https://doi.org/10.1300/J229v05n04_04

Schore, A. N. (1994). *Affect regulation and the origin of self: The neurobiology of emotional development.* Erlbaum.

Schore, A. N. (2003). *Affect regulation and the repair of the self.* W. W. Norton.

Schwartz, R. (1995). *Internal family systems therapy.* Guilford Press.

Siegel, D. (2007). *The mindful brain.* W. W. Norton.

Siegel, D. (2009). Mindfulness, mindsight and neural integration. *The Humanistic Psychologist, 37*(2), 137–158. https://doi.org/10.1080/08873260902892220

Steele, A. (2007). *Developing a secure self: An attachment-based approach to adult psychotherapy.* Author.

Steele, K., Boon, S., & van der Hart, O. (2017). *Treating trauma-related dissociation: A practical, integrative approach.* W. W. Norton.

Tronick, E., & Beeghly, M. (2011). Infants' meaning-making and the development of mental health problems. *American Psychologist, 66*(2), 107–119. https://doi.org/10.1037/a0021631

Tronick, E. Z., Bruschweiler-Stern, N., Harrison, A. M., Lyons-Ruth, K., Morgan, A. C., Nahum, J. P., Sander, L., & Stern, D. N. (1999). Dyadically expanded states of consciousness and the process of therapeutic change. *Infant Mental Health Journal, 19*(3), 290–299. https://doi.org/10.1002/(SICI)1097-0355(199823)19:3<290::AID-IMHJ4>3.0.CO;2-Q

van der Hart, O., Steele, K., & Nijenhuis, E. S. (2006). *The haunted self: Structural dissociation and the treatment of chronic traumatization.* W. W. Norton.

van der Kolk, B. A., McFarlane, A. C., & Weisaeth, L. (Eds.). (1996). *Traumatic stress: The effects of overwhelming experience on mind, body and society.* Guilford Press.

Watkins, J. G., & Watkins, H. H. (1997). *Ego states: Theory and therapy.* W. W. Norton.

Welling, H. (2012). Transformative emotional sequence: Towards a common principle of change. *Journal of Psychotherapy Integration, 22*(2), 109–136. https://doi.org/10.1037/a0027786

Whitfield, C. (1987). *Healing the child within.* Health Communications.

# 12

# Relational Prisms

*Navigating Experiential Attachment Work With Dissociation and Multiplicity in AEDP*

Kari A. Gleiser

When light passes through the multifaceted triangular surfaces of a glass prism, it is transformed from an invisible stream to a rainbow palette of rich colors. A prism defies the illusion of the unitary to reveal the richness of multiplicity and thus is an ideal metaphor for the matrix of relationships present in a therapeutic dyad: the many selves of the patient and the therapist and the interrelatedness of these many parts. The invisible rendered visible. The many within the whole. The beauty in diversity.

The multiplicity of the self is a widely accepted paradigm in psychology (Bromberg, 1998). The mind's ability to manage diverse roles efficiently and to compartmentalize and selectively access knowledge, memories, and emotions is highly adaptive. Most of the time this system serves us nobly. In the case of life-threatening trauma, abuse, neglect, or deprivation, this adaptive capacity protects the psyche from overwhelming fear, horror, and helplessness. Dissociation is one of the mind's inborn protections against trauma, especially ongoing developmental trauma (Fisher, 2017; Steele et al., 2016; van der Kolk, 2015). Dissociation creates internal splits, or disconnects, in the psyche, sequestering overwhelming emotions, memories, and disowned parts of the self to contain the life-threatening "mess" of trauma and traumatic neglect (van der Hart et al., 2006). An unfortunate consequence of this life-saving defense is the fragmentation and subsequent hiding away of many aspects of self and experience, which creates special challenges for the experiential treatment of complex trauma

https://doi.org/10.1037/0000232-013
*Undoing Aloneness and the Transformation of Suffering Into Flourishing: AEDP 2.0*, D. Fosha (Editor)

and dissociation. Fragmentation of the self can compromise many basic elements of effective relating, including trust, continuity, ability to tolerate conflict (Fisher, 2017; Steele et al., 2016), diminished reflective capacity, and impaired theory of mind (Fonagy & Target, 1997). These splintered elements pose prodigious obstacles in trauma therapy.

The *intra-relational* interventions (Lamagna & Gleiser, 2007) of accelerated experiential dynamic psychotherapy (AEDP) address this fractured inner landscape, creating an attachment map to navigate segregated attachment needs embodied in dissociated parts of the self. AEDP's relational, experiential, and transformational interventions are imported into a patient's internal system of dissociated parts of self to foster relational safety between the therapist and all parts of a patient's internal system of parts, as well as between parts of the self that may harbor conflicting impulses, needs, and protective strategies. This lattice of relational and intra-relational security is an essential healing element in restructuring disorganized attachment, emotional processing, and transformation of traumatic experiences.

This chapter is designed to help AEDP therapists work effectively with patients with complex trauma and dissociative disorders. First, I explore the unique challenges dissociation poses to attachment and emotional processing in AEDP. I then present an overview of AEDP's intra-relational interventions, that is, how AEDP's relational, experiential, and transformational interventions are imported into a patient's internal system of dissociated parts of self to foster healing. Finally, I consider how imbalances in interventions geared toward different aspects of the relational matrix can create or exacerbate attachment dilemmas, therapeutic ruptures, and intrapsychic crises in patients. AEDP therapists strive for dynamic equilibrium across the entire relational matrix of parts of the self.

## DISSOCIATION AND ATTACHMENT: THE INTERNAL FRAGMENTATION OF SELF

Often, the greater the traumatic history, the greater the fragmentation and related habitual impulse to push away dissociated pockets of unmetabolized terror, shame, loss, and betrayal. These forbidden, trauma-tinged, and feared-to-be-unbearable emotions are "safely" sequestered in split-off parts of the self through dissociation. In a severely traumatized individual this creates an internal system of parts of the self, separated by barriers of varying degrees of "not knowing" or disowning. Vitality, valuable internal resources, and cohesion are also tragically disintegrated (Fosha, 2013a). A prodigious challenge in treating dissociative disorders is building enough relational and emotional safety across the client's entire fragmented internal system to ultimately reclaim what has been banished from awareness.

To understand the impact of dissociation on attachment behaviors we must first review the function of attachment and the genesis of different attachment styles in childhood.[1] Infants and young children are vulnerable in the world and dependent on the protection of older, strong, wiser adults for survival (Bowlby, 1969/1982) or, as Bowlby (1969/1982) wisely observed, those *"perceived* to be older and wiser."

From birth, humans face a prolonged physical and mental developmental trajectory before they are equipped to function and survive independently of caregivers. Babies and young children have limited abilities to regulate their own distress, read their internal cues and needs, and protect themselves from the dangers of the world. They are dependent on caregivers to perceive their biological and emotional needs (i.e., hunger, fatigue, fear, distress, protection) and to meet them adequately (with nourishment, comfort, soothing). Affectively charged interactions with caregivers over the course of childhood shape the child's emerging sense of self and forge neural pathways that govern affect regulatory capacities, that is, the ability to manage strong emotion and stress (Schore, 2009; Siegel, 1999). Over time, the caregiver's affective and relational stance toward the child becomes an internal working model (Bowlby, 1988) that governs the child's operative schemas about the self and relationships.

If the primary caregiver's stance toward the child is characterized by detachment, rejection, or neglect, the child learns that needing others is futile and that the self is inherently unworthy of care and love. Attachment needs remain painfully unmet, and a child in this scenario often copes by developing an *avoidant* attachment style: precocious self-reliance, banishing relationship needs, and dissociating unmanageable feelings (Main, 2000). In contrast, if caregivers are inconsistent, unpredictable, or intrusive, the child can develop a *preoccupied* attachment style: overly focused on getting needs met by others, engaging in exaggerated displays of affect, and frequently flooded by dysregulated emotions (Main, 2000).

Most survivors of chronic developmental trauma present with a *disorganized* attachment style (Main & Solomon, 1990) because of experiences with primary caregivers that are characterized by an ongoing clash of contradictory signals. With caregivers either chronically scary (i.e., abusive or neglectful) scared (i.e., themselves, traumatized), or both, the child is faced with an inescapable dilemma: If the child is hurt or scared, attachment needs pull toward the caregiver, but if the hurt or fear is also created by the caregiver, survival needs pull the child away from the source of danger, in this case, also the caregiver. The child cannot move toward and pull away from the caregiver at the same time, so the child freezes, locked in an unbearable state of "fear without solution" (Main & Solomon, 1990).

The best solution to this dilemma is *dissociation*, which gives the child, and later the adult, distance from the acute terror and helplessness of irreconcilable conflict, segregating the conflicting survival mandates into separate parts of

---

[1] I review here only the basic tenets of attachment theory that are relevant to the current discussion. For a more thorough discussion of attachment styles in AEDP, see Pando-Mars (2016).

the self. When working with highly dissociative clients, a therapist must be cognizant that dissociated parts of the self likely encapsulate different attachment styles. This is a shift from traditional attachment categorizations, which identify a predominant style by the time the individual reaches adulthood (see Main's, 2000, Adult Attachment Inventory). In fact, in disorganized attachment what may look like chaos and contradiction on the surface may be illuminated in the course of therapy as possessing a deeper logic and organization.

Even in the absence of fully articulated dissociative parts, a therapist working with complex trauma cannot assume that "what you see is what you get." When working explicitly and experientially with attachment in AEDP—that is, activating and restructuring attachment templates live in the therapeutic dyad—it may be more prudent and nuanced to track attachment *strategies* or neural network *pockets* than to assume fixed attachment styles. This allows therapists to fluidly shift intervention strategies when, for example, a patient who first appears to exhibit avoidant tendencies touches into long-banished dependency longings, or, when working with a client with disorganized attachment, the therapist can flow with interwoven shades of avoidance and dependency, and even glimmers of secure attachment, that alternately surface and sink.

To concretize this constellation of attachment strategies in clinical dynamics, consider, for example, a highly dissociative client with discrete parts of the self that might present in session one moment as very young, helpless, and wounded, eliciting strong caregiving urges in the therapist. However, once an intervention of support, care, or recognition is offered by the therapist, another child part might arise (or, even worse, get activated silently in the background), ostensibly exhibiting fears that a connection will lead to sexual abuse or abandonment. This may trigger yet another part: adolescent, surly, rebuffing, protective. Depending on the client's (and therapist's!) awareness of these separate parts, the relational sequence may manifest as fleeting, disorganized impulses or feelings, swinging back and forth between extremes, or as parts that after the session enact backlash behaviors, such as self-harm, compulsive seeking of contact with the therapist, or missed sessions. When the deeper logic of these sequences is revealed we can appreciate that the elements of secure, healthy attachment are present, even though they are segregated, unbalanced, and enacted to the extreme.

The clinical solution is not to downplay, ignore, or avoid relational interventions for fear of inflaming other parts or contradictory needs. To the contrary, it is precisely the experiential activation of these relational dilemmas that draws them to the surface, exposes them, and makes them available for transformation (Fosha, 2000, 2003, 2009). Such attachment dilemmas in fragmented and disorganized systems give rise to the need to transcend shifting either–or relational enactments and move to a both–and stance (Pando-Mars, 2016). Welcoming the opposite set of impulse/emotion/relational configurations to whatever is occurring *in the moment* begins to knit together experientially the fragments of attachment needs that will become the integrated tapestry of earned secure attachment. I explore this dynamic balance of AEDP interventions more fully in the following sections.

## INTRA-RELATIONAL INTERVENTIONS: BRIDGING THE DISSOCIATIVE GAPS AND FORGING INTERNAL ATTACHMENT BONDS

AEDP offers many interventions that are well suited to navigate the relational and emotional complexity of treating survivors of chronic trauma who present with dissociative fragmentation of the self (Fosha et al., 2009; Gleiser et al., 2008; Lamagna, 2011; Lamagna & Gleiser, 2007). These interventions include microtracking and working explicitly with present-moment relational dynamics to create the felt sense of safety, ongoing dyadic regulation of distress, full emotional processing of avoided traumatic memories and affects, and transformation of old reservoirs of shame and aloneness (Fosha, 2000, 2003, 2009, 2017; see Tunnell & Osiason, Chapter 3; Russell, Chapter 9; and Piliero, Chapter 10, this volume). In addition, experiential, fantasized scenes and dialogues with dissociated parts of the self, known in AEDP as "portrayals" (see Medley, Chapter 8, this volume), allow for gradual rapprochement with lost parts of the self and the building of mastery by reintegrating what was previously disowned and isolated.

*Transformance*, a central philosophical underpinning of AEDP, posits that survivors have within them all they need to heal: Latent capacities, resources, and strivings are awaiting conditions of safety to come to the fore (Fosha, 2017a). The conundrum created by complex trauma and neglect is that the mind learns (and the brain gets hard wired) to anticipate constant relational danger. When these patterns are recognized and a felt sense of safety is cocreated in the therapeutic dyad, the mind's natural interest in engagement, curiosity, and integration can emerge (Fosha, 2013b). As more and more of these flickers of transformance appear and are "caught" (gently, like fireflies) by the therapist, the light accumulates and grows within the patient's internal system. This life is guided by intention, resources, and integrated function as opposed to flight from danger and distrust of the tender and most precious aspects of the self.

One branch of AEDP, *intra-relational theory and interventions* (Lamagna, 2011; Lamagna & Gleiser, 2007), extends AEDP's relational, experiential, and transformational interventions to work within the complex, fragmented intrapsychic systems of traumatized individuals.[2] Put more specifically, intra-relational theory and interventions highlight multiple avenues of connectivity, attachment, and relational dynamics that bridge survivors' internal (self-to-self or

---

[2]This chapter focuses on the clinical implementation of intra-relational AEDP in treating cases of complex trauma and dissociation. For a fuller discussion of the theoretical underpinning of intra-relational AEDP, see Lamagna (2011) and Lamagna and Gleiser (2007).

self-to-parts) and external (self-to-others) relationships. Instead of conceptualizing an attachment relationship as a linear phenomenon between two people (e.g., a mother–child dyad, or therapist–client dyad), the attachment relationship can be seen as having three interconnected axes: (a) the relational, intersubjective field between the therapist and client; (b) the relational, intersubjective field between the therapist and dissociated affects, memories, and parts of self of the client; and (c) the intra-relational, intra-subjective field between the client and their dissociated fragments of self. All three axes of this *Intra-Relational Triangle* (see Figure 12.1) are simultaneously present at any given relational moment in therapy. The simplified diagram in Figure 12.1 illustrates one dissociated node, but there are multiple nodes (in patient and therapist alike); hence the image of a relational prism. In a therapy milieu with a trauma survivor the therapist and patient are working within an attachment and relational matrix, with each axis manifesting its own unique attachment schemas and relational dynamics (Lamagna & Gleiser, 2007).

This conceptualization of attachment dynamics goes beyond the linear relational phenomenon between two people to include intrapsychic phenomena between a patient and their dissociated self states and a set of multidimensional phenomena between therapist and a patient's parts, which allows for a more nuanced map for working with dissociative patients. The goal of therapy is to transform internalized negative relational dynamics and cocreate secure attachment on each of the three axes of the Intra-Relational Triangle (Lamagna, 2011; Lamagna & Gleiser, 2007).

**FIGURE 12.1. The Intra-Relational Triangle: Three Axes of Connectivity**

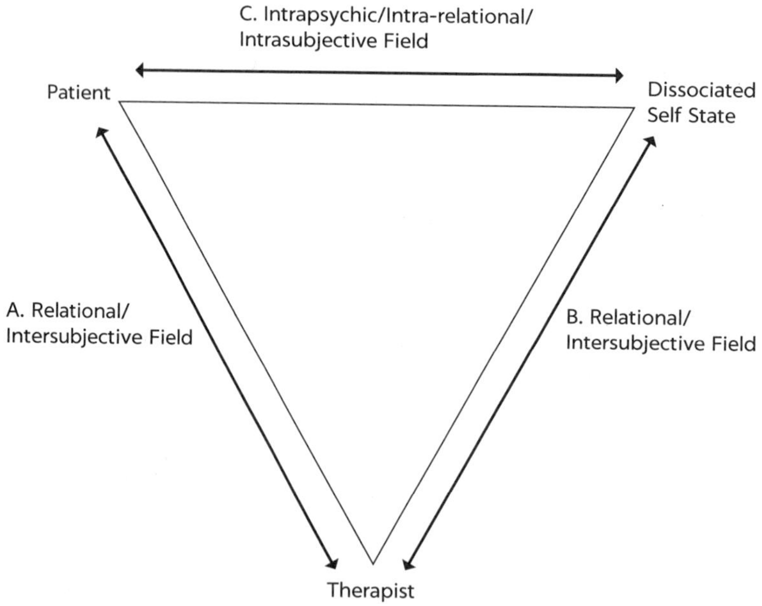

*Note.* Copyright 2020 by K. A. Gleiser.

Figure 12.2 illustrates the mechanism of internalization (Blizard & Bluhm, 1994; Kohut, 1977, 1984) by which children and, later, adults, internally perpetuate relational patterns learned from caregivers. If a child's sadness and vulnerability was met by a parent's chronic scorn and withdrawal, that child learned to split off and banish sadness, dissociating it into a "not-me" (Chefetz & Bromberg, 2004) part of the self. The child, and later adult, learns to habitually distance from the part of the self that experiences sadness to preserve attachment to the caregiver, leaving the dissociated part feeling not only sadness but also shame and unbearable aloneness (Fosha, 2000, 2013a, 2013b). These deleterious relational patterns generated in the parent–child

**FIGURE 12.2. The Genesis of Internalized, Disorganized Attachment Patterns**

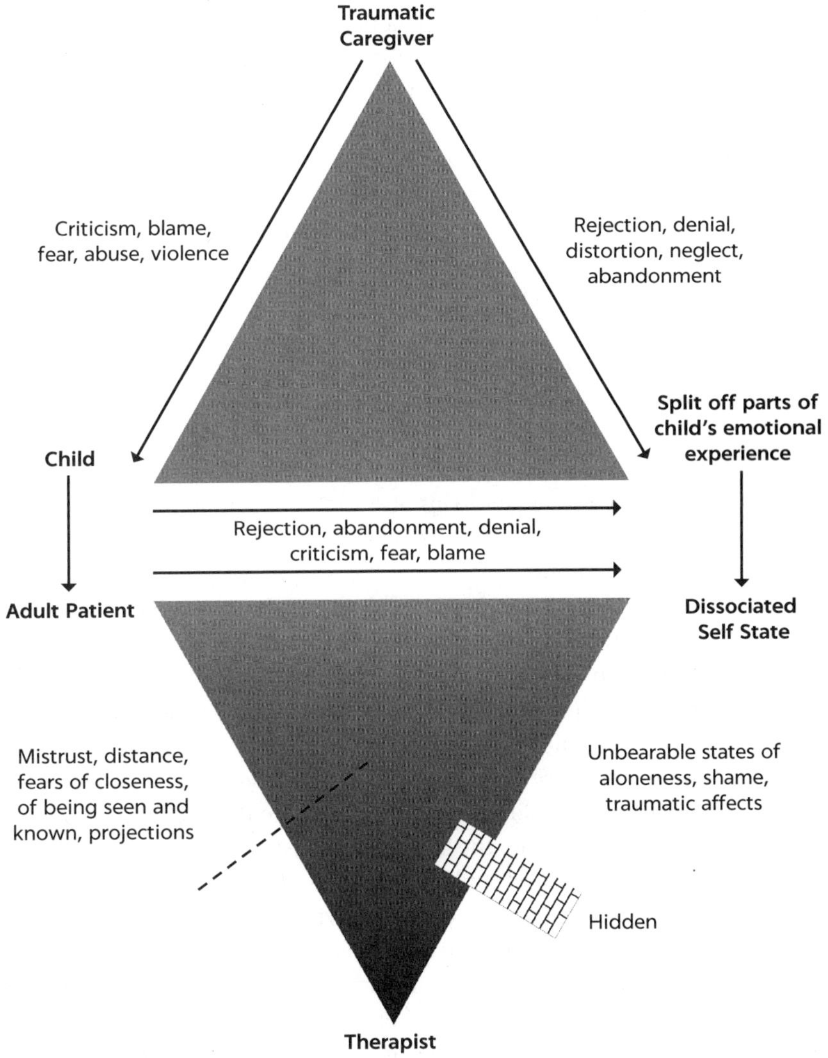

*Note.* Copyright 2020 by K. A. Gleiser.

dyad (transmitted by the parent on the two descending arms of the triangle) are endlessly repeated within the adult patient in an internal drama of abandonment and rejection of dissociated parts, which languish in the pathogenic affects of fear, shame, and unbearable aloneness (Fosha, 2000). Patients come to therapy harboring these negative internal structures and corresponding relational dynamics.

The situation is further confounded by profound mistrust that early caregiving experiences created; trauma survivors may display entrenched and compromised internal patterns of relating as well as strong fears and projections of how they will be treated and judged by the therapist, which can impede receptivity to present-moment experience. For example, a therapist may extend compassion, which the patient perceives as pity, scorn, or a confirmation of weakness, or the patient may simply doubt the therapist's emotional authenticity. In this example the patient's projected internalized toxic schemas defining the self and other do not fit the relational content offered by the therapist, and these rigid schemas can block or distort the present-moment relational offering. Furthermore, dissociated parts of the self that hold toxic emotion, traumatic memories, and feared or forbidden impulses are often invisible. They are shielded behind dissociative barriers and burst through only when triggered or when floods of dysregulated emotion rise above the threshold of consciousness. Breaching these protective barriers can create even more secondary reactions of self-criticism, self-loathing, and inner turmoil.

Figure 12.2, therefore, represents the Intra-Relational Triangle's conceptualization of the pathogenesis of disorganized attachment in external self–other relationships and internal self–self relationships. The fragmented system of untreated trauma survivors is often disjointed, conflictual, unpredictable, and shaming and is largely cut off from new experiences in the present; in other words, preserving and paralleling attributes from the very situations the patient has survived and tried to escape. This also can be a source of shame, until a light is shone on how these dynamics were created, transmitted, and deeply imprinted by past experience.

Seeing the invisible (Gleiser, 2013) is a key transformative force in AEDP's intra-relational approach. The invisible waiting to be illuminated by the recognition first of the therapist and, eventually, the patient includes how maladaptive relational and intra-relational dynamics were created and managed by the patient as well as how hidden parts of the self were sequestered behind dissociative walls. Often, the very act of being seen, understood, and witnessed begins to undo shame and aloneness. Connecting the dots between relational/emotional lessons learned in the context of past attachment trauma can bring meaning, cohesion, and understanding to current patterns of negative self–self and self–other relating. Seeing the invisible is a powerful experience of recognition that is profoundly transformative. Fosha (2009, 2013a) has rendered an elegant model of recognition as a key relational moment that occurs between self and self or self and other, heralding an emotional "click" of rightness, deep truth, or goodness of fit. Such moments are inherently integrative because they are deeply felt in the body and represent glimmers of the neurobiological core self (Damasio, 2010; Panksepp & Northoff, 2009), untouched by trauma. Ample internal resources and positive affective markers of vitality, energy, coherence, and wisdom await only an act of being seen, and thus awakened, by an other or the self (Fosha, 2013a). AEDP's explicit relational, attachment-focused interventions are powerful tools that introduce new relational experiences to restructure attachment templates (Fosha, 2000, 2017b) on each side of the Intra-Relational Triangle.

AEDP's relational interventions originate with the therapist (i.e., bottom of the triangle) and flow upward into the relational and intersubjective fields with both the patient and dissociated parts of the patient (see Figure 12.3). The therapist is the source of new relational dynamics in the relational matrix. The hallmarks of AEDP's explicitly affirming, embodied therapeutic stance include attunement to and authentic engagement with all parts of the patient; therapist emotional vulnerability and self-disclosure; empathy, recognition, and affirmation of the adaptiveness of even the most ostensibly maladaptive coping strategies; transformance detection; and the creation of alliances and relational bonds with every part of the self (Fosha, 2000; Lipton & Fosha, 2011). These characteristics, when cocreated in the matrix of therapist and patient and the patient's parts, become emotionally charged relational experiences to be explored.

When the therapist recognizes, engages, and values an "invisible" part of the self, such as a hidden, vulnerable child part that is holding traumatic memories, that experience becomes yet another dimension to explore: the patient's reaction to having that part witnessed and addressed as well as that part's reaction to being seen, understood, and included. Through the same

**FIGURE 12.3. Progression of Relational and Intra-Relational Transformation**

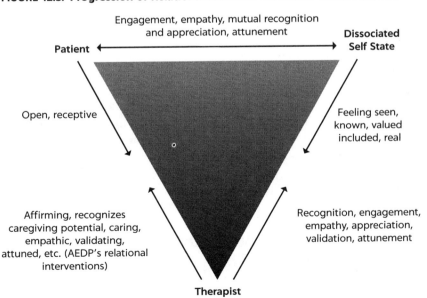

*Note.* AEDP = accelerated experiential dynamic psychotherapy. Copyright 2020 by K. A. Gleiser.

process by which negative interactions with early caregivers was internalized, the new relational dynamics eventually spread to the intra-relational domain. Fantasized scenes (i.e., portrayals) give rise to emotionally charged interactions between the patient and formerly invisible parts to incorporate new elements of empathy, attunement, recognition, care, dyadic regulation of distress, witnessing, play, and comfort (see the top of the Intra-Relational Triangle of Figure 12.3). As these new experiences accrue and become the focus of exploration with meta-processing interventions (e.g., "What is it like for that lonely teenage part to feel that you're on her side?"), the filaments of the integrative relational bond thicken within the patient, essentially undoing dissociation. Internal abandonment is replaced by the elements of secure attachment: Defensive exclusion is replaced by witnessing, and hiding is replaced by active protection, engagement, and regulation.

This process helps the patient simultaneously strengthen responsive and trustworthy internal self-to-self and external self-to-other relational bonds, creating an equilibrium of safety and trust across the whole system of parts. Over time, the tension of unmet needs, the chaos of swinging between conflicting impulses, motivated by fear and confusion, begins to transform into a more predictable cadence of listening, adjusting, responding, and tolerating the conflicting feelings and points of view held by various parts of the self.

This therapeutic process rarely unfolds smoothly in the treatment of complex trauma and dissociation. For example, different parts of the self may hold different ideas of what constitutes "safety" or regulation of emotion. For parts that hold and enact the remnants of maladaptive coping strategies, such as self-harm, substance abuse, or eating disorders, their inclusion in the treatment and recovery process is essential from the get-go. Early treatment interventions often focus on brokering repairs to long-standing internal ruptures and resentments between parts of the self. Just as therapeutic ruptures, if left unrepaired, erode the therapeutic alliance (Safran & Muran, 1996), internal ruptures maintain ongoing conflict, tension, and estrangement (Lamagna & Gleiser, 2007). Internal repair and reconciliation, and the moment-to-moment tracking and deepening of the emotional experiences that accompany this process, are crucial elements for building inner harmony and collaboration.

In the next section I explore how each side of the Intra-Relational Triangle offers opportunities for igniting recognition and transformation processes. I demonstrate how to craft experiential interventions with the goal of achieving a dynamic equilibrium of strength, resilience, and positive relating across the matrix of internal and external relationships.

## BALANCE AND DYNAMIC EQUILIBRIUM AROUND THE INTRA-RELATIONAL TRIANGLE

Many of the relational dilemmas and conflicts posed by disorganized attachment—which are marked by violent swings between segregated extremes of desperate need and terrified avoidance, crushing dependency needs and lonely isolation—are responsible for the gridlock that can arise in trauma therapy. The more segregated and disavowed the conflicting needs (e.g., to feel strong and connected to oneself vs. to feel supported and connected to a strong other), the less likely they are to arise simultaneously, casting therapeutic dyads into alternating tsunamis of conflicting attachment needs.

AEDP therapists strive for a dynamic equilibrium of explicit, experiential relational interventions, balancing the focus of interventions across the three axes of the Intra-Relational Triangle (see Figure 12.1). Deadlocks, ruptures, reenactments, and crises in therapy with survivors of complex trauma often arise from an overemphasis of any one of these axes at the expense of the others.

In the intra-relational conceptualization, earned secure attachment is an integrated achievement that hinges on the coconstruction of relational safety and secure attachment on all three sides of the Intra-Relational Triangle. Neglecting or underemphasizing any one side can create a weakness or vulnerability in the system and topple the delicate balance of resources that support a patient's resilience. Interventions are selected with moment-to-moment tracking on the basis of emergent attachment patterns and strategies. Creating safety for a patient with a complex trauma history or dissociative disorder often entails a deliberate oscillation of interventions that address, restructure, and build resources on the outside, involving other people, including the therapist, and on the inside, involving the patient and dissociated parts of the self.

In the following sections I explore the implementation of AEDP's relational and emotional interventions for three clients with complex trauma histories on each of the three relational axes of the Intra-Relational Triangle, and I describe the pitfalls and risks that can arise when these interventions become unbalanced.

## Patient–Therapist Connection: Side A of the Intra-Relational Triangle

Bowlby (1969/1982) famously quipped that attachment is a phenomenon that operates "from the cradle to the grave," meaning that even adults have attachment needs and impulses. Showing up for therapy in distress, unable to face unbearable emotions, patients' attachment systems are already activated when they walk through the door. Knowing this allows the AEDP therapist to access the biological attachment system in vivo. The AEDP therapist seeks to foster a safe, affirming, authentic, and emotionally intimate relationship with each patient (Lipton & Fosha, 2011). This is not only an intention on the part of the therapist but also a deliberate, carefully tracked, explored, discussed, and meta-processed experience between therapist and patient (Fosha, 2000; Lipton & Fosha, 2011). If a therapist comments on appreciating the courage a patient exhibits, the intervention should be followed up by tracking the degree to which the patient is able to receive the sentiment and what their reaction is (i.e., tracking the patient's "receptive affective capacity" [Fosha, 2017b] to the affirmation). The therapeutic relationship becomes an active experiential tool for the transformation of attachment templates. When working on this side of the Intra-Relational Triangle the therapist is cognizant that their attunement, empathy, recognition and prizing of the patient model ways of relating that the patient can "try on," imitate, and eventually own. I often have observed a relational "echoing" effect, in which a relational action I have engaged in with the patient (e.g., "Can you feel me here with you? Can you feel my support in this moment?") is almost identically repeated in a portrayal with a dissociated part (in the same session), when the patient says of her relationship with a part, "That sad little girl can feel me here with her, supporting her."

The therapist also seeks transformance glimmers that evidence the patient's caregiving capacity, whether in the context of children, pets, plants, or friends, in order to deepen that capacity and eventually harness it in the service of the self. When these glimmers arise, the AEDP therapist names them, affirms them, and gauges the patient's receptivity to this recognition. These qualities, first highlighted by the therapist, are tucked away as resources on which to call in intra-relational work between patients and their dissociated parts.

### Benefits of Side A Work
Among the benefits of relational interventions on this side of the Intra-Relational Triangle are creating felt safety, undoing toxic projections from the past, accessing existing attachment templates in the service of restructuring them, and building secure attachment between therapist and patient. For patients presenting—whether typically, in the moment, or both—with pronounced avoidant attachment strategies (i.e., overly self-reliant, dismissive of attachment needs, cut off from feelings), this is a key side of the triangle to explore: The lived experience with the therapist is bound to both trigger, and contain the healing ingredients for, what is most feared and avoided.

### Risks of Side A Work
Risks of overfocusing on this side of the triangle include therapists' falling into the "rescuer" role (Karpman, 2007), believing they can meet all the patient's unmet attachment needs or can undo a traumatic attachment history. A balance tipped too far to this side of the triangle can overstimulate a patient's dependency needs, risking the patient's collapse, helplessness, and overreliance on the therapist. Conversely, it can aggravate dependency fears, leading to flight from therapy or a redoubling of relational defenses. It can also evoke an experience of excruciating relational vulnerability, triggering past attachment trauma. Too much attention or intervention on this axis can also collude with the fantasies of preoccupied or child parts of the patient, who might yearn to undo past abandonment by finding a parental figure in the therapist. Finally, overemphasizing this side of the triangle runs the risk of deflecting the spotlight of shared attention from the patient's inner emotional world, where the truly transformational emotional processing happens. These risks emphasize the need to simultaneously build and interweave external and internal relational resources.

Underemphasizing the therapist–patient side of the triangle also has risks. Doing so can collude with a patient's avoidant belief system ("I don't need anyone"; "I can do this by myself and for myself"). Insufficient attention to the moment-to-moment relational experience can sacrifice experiential moments of accessing and transforming attachment templates as they surface in session. A paucity of explicit relational qualities such as nurturance, responsivity, and caring in the therapist can feel, to the patient, like a repetition of parental neglect or emotional unavailability. Finally, ignoring this rich font of relational–experiential data can blind the therapist to the large-scale ruptures and micro-ruptures and reenactments that are inevitable in trauma work, which benefit from being recognized and repaired expeditiously.

### Case Study: Relational and Attachment Interventions Between Therapist and Patient (Side A of the Intra-Relational Triangle)

Josie is a 52-year-old woman with a horrific history of cult abuse.[3] She has been diagnosed with dissociative identity disorder and has been in therapy for most of her adult life. Side by side with coping with terrifying flashbacks, polyfragmentation of the self, and periodic dark episodes of suicidality and self-harm, she is also resilient, emotionally intelligent, articulate, and deeply relational. Over many years of treatment, Josie and I have navigated together the ups and downs of disorganized attachment within her highly fragmented internal system, creating secure bonds between not only me and her but also with parts that were suspicious and standoffish, parts that were terrified I was another perpetrator, and parts that desperately wanted mothering. Therapy with Josie is a prime example of my shifting attachment stances moment to moment, depending on what part was activated in our relational field: at one moment encouraging contact and building trust with mistrustful parts, at another coaxing young parts that wanted me to mother them to feel both my authentic care and support in the present moment and turn back inside to Josie for care and attention and, of course, always nurturing the tenuous bonds between Josie and the many parts of herself, even as she felt bombarded by the copious stressors of her external life and the ever-present needs of an intricate inner system of parts.

In the following vignette, an emotional self-disclosure from me deeply touches Josie (Side A of the Intra-Relational Triangle), which in turn illuminates an inner light of recognition from self to self (Side C).

**THERAPIST (T):** (*Interrupting a flow of the patient's narrative about her handling of current family stressors, with tears in my eyes*) I'm having a private moment of deep admiration for you. **[Self-disclosure of emotional experience of seeing positive qualities in patient]**

---

[3]Aspects of the patient's identity and background have been disguised to protect confidentiality.

**PATIENT (P):**   (*Surprised, smiling, a little self-consciously*) Why?

T:   For the sensitivity and care and mindfulness that you bring to understanding your relationships. **[Transformance detection: naming and affirming positive qualities in the patient]**

P:   (*Eyes fill with tears, and she cries softly.*)

T:   What's it like to hear me say that? I can see that it touches something deep inside. **[Exploring receptive affective response to my recognition]**

P:   It's the way that I've always wanted to be seen in the world, the values I've always wanted to live by and what I've always longed for others to see in me. And you see them. And what's sad is that I've always longed for my parents to see that in me, but I'm not going to deny myself that experience just because they are not capable. Because you see it, and I see it in myself, and it feels amazing. **[My seeing her deeply and positively allows her to see herself deeply and positively, which is a prime example of internalization.]**

### Therapist–Dissociated Part Connection: Side B of the Intra-Relational Triangle

Work on this side of the triangle begins to undo the aloneness and invisibility of abandoned parts of the self. The therapist can make "first contact" with dissociated parts when the patient's internal aversion or fear feels insurmountable. The therapist's courage to first see, and then understand and befriend, dissociated parts can be an essential preliminary step for inner safety building, explicitly modeling for the patient that there are safe and connected ways of being with these estranged parts of the self. Soliciting "hidden" reactions from dissociated parts of the self can also stave off postsession floods of distress, fear, or backlash in response to emotional processing done in therapy. When reactive parts are invited to come forth to be recognized and dyadically regulated they are less likely to burst through when the patient is alone. Furthermore, the therapist's explicit recognition, compassion, care, and solicitousness toward dissociated parts of the self make up a *corrective emotional experience* (Fosha, 2013a) that neurologically alters the template and memories (Ecker et al., 2012) of the abusive caregiver's attachment wounding and banishing.

### Benefits of Side B Work

Benefits of working this side of the triangle abound. When a therapist approaches a feared or despised dissociated part, the patient may begin to desensitize to contact with this part through the act of witnessing. If, for example, a therapist has the opportunity to dyadically regulate a distressed child part when the patient is unable or unwilling to do so, then the AEDP therapist tracks not only the response in the child part to being calmed and comforted but also the reaction of the patient to witnessing this encounter. When patients can feel in their body the difference between the intense, sidelined distress of a dysregulated part versus that same part calmed and connected, transformation is unfolding in the relationship between patient and dissociated part. Thus, when the therapist models good attachment figure behaviors with dissociated parts (i.e., soothing, protection, succor, care, validation, appreciation, recognition), the patient is witnessing, learning, and building capacities through the mechanism of mirror neurons (Iacoboni, 2009) and entraining the resonance circuits of the brain (Siegel, 1999). Witnessing often builds courage, and the part can be "handed over" to the care of the patient, who is now more willing to try, with the support and encouragement of the therapist. Work on Side B of the Intra-Relational Triangle can be a back door of sorts to intra-relational work between the patient and a dissociated part.

### Risks of Side B work

The risk of inflaming dependency needs is present on this side of the triangle, too, so caution is necessary to not overemphasize this side at the expense of intra-relational resource building. Dissociated parts, especially young parts, may be all too happy to be cared for, and patients, especially in preoccupied attachment moments, may be happy to let the therapist do the work of regulating, calming, and caring. Nevertheless, when done with intention and some measure of caution, this can be a powerful avenue of healing and intervention.

Some trauma experts discourage direct therapist attachment work with parts because of the potential risks, but this foregoes a valuable category of interventions that can bridge into the intra-relational axis. In cases of neglect and deprivation, the patient may have no templates or neural pathways laid down (Schore, 2009) to recognize or know the experience of secure caregiving. If the therapist withholds the felt experience of a responsive attachment figure from a part in moments of crisis, a potential for reenactment of abandonment and withdrawal exists. To mistakenly push for intra-relational responsivity and care between parts of the self when that capacity is underdeveloped or absent can be akin to demanding that the patient make something out of nothing. Sometimes the foundation of secure attachment needs to be built from the ground up by the therapist, even though this can never be the last step.

Here it is worth a brief digression. Just as patients harbor an internal network of parts, so too do therapists. The extent of dissociation or integration of the therapist, especially therapists with their own trauma histories, depends in large part on where they are in their own healing journey. It is vital to include a conceptualization of the therapist's parts in this model because, left unchecked, they can add another dimension of complexity in an attachment-based psychotherapy such as AEDP. Imagine, for example, that a part of a patient gets activated that unleashes a flood of dependency needs and attachment behaviors toward the therapist. If this triggers in the therapist fears of intrusion, merger, and suffocation, and the therapist does not recognize their own triggered part, the resulting intervention may be reactive as opposed to constructive. In fact, these entanglements of therapist's and patient's parts drive subtle and not-so-subtle ruptures and repetitions.

If the therapist retreats behind protective relational defenses, the patient may feel abandoned. Self-reflection and consultation that allow the therapist to engage in his or her own parts work is vital.

### Case Study: Relational and Attachment Interventions Between the Therapist and the Disowned Part of the Patient (Side B of the Intra-Relational Triangle)

Max, a 54-year-old man who never married and has no children, struggles with chronic loneliness, ruminative depression, and anxiety. He often exhibits a preoccupied attachment style, including intense unmet relational needs. He has shared shame-invoking regressive fantasies that he will fall ill with a terminal disease so that he will finally be taken care of. He struggles with withdrawal and isolation to cope with his social anxiety, and he fears the judgment of others. Max grew up in a high-conflict household; parental tensions and infidelities frequently erupted in fights, yelling, and emotional and physical violence. He describes being chronically afraid and insecure as a child. In therapy, we began to recognize that he suffered profound emotional neglect and role reversals in his family of origin.

In this session, Max described being flooded by worries, doubts, and fears while his new girlfriend was away. Although he could rationally acknowledge that these were old fears of abandonment and worthlessness activated by the current separation, he had trouble turning toward and soothing these fears.

T:   How are you feeling these fears right now, just as we are talking about them? **[Tracking the fears experientially and somatically]**

P:   (*Brow furrowed, puts hand on upper left belly*) It feels like a churning right here, an unsettledness. **[Patient can connect with the sensations of the fear and instinctually brings his hand to them for contact.]**

T:   Yeah, just feel into your hand right on that unsettledness. Notice what that contact feels like to the fear. **[Making the contact explicit, between his comforting hand and fearful belly; amplifies the gesture]**

P:   I know it's my little guy, but I just don't know how to help him feel less scared. **[Patient can identify the dissociated part but feels helpless to help; this is an inner recapitulation of the neglect he experienced from his parents.]**

(*Patient embarks on a long digression, marking defensive disengagement.*)

T:   Can we come back to these fears that need soothing? I don't want to forget about them. **[Bringing the patient back to the fears, seeing and responding as a responsive attachment figure where the patient cannot yet embody this role]**

P:   But I don't know what to do about them. **[Another admission of confusion and a lack of capacity, marking the need to be scaffolded by therapist]**

T: What if you put your hand back on them, and just notice what it feels like to give some comfort and recognition to that fear? **[Attempting to provide the scaffolding with a direct suggestion of internal dyadic regulation]**

P: (*Puts hand back on belly*) I don't feel anything. I lost connection to the fear. **[Dissociation and distancing from anxious young part; the fear and the part become "invisible"]**

T: Can we try something different? What if I put my hand right where you feel that fear, just to give it some comfort and soothing from me? (N.B.: I had previously obtained permission and used touch therapeutically in session, so this was not a new concept.) **[Asking permission to step in and do dyadic regulation with the dissociated part—Side B of the Intra-Relational Triangle]**

P: We can try that. **[Green signal affects—a willingness to accept comfort from an attachment figure. This is a moment of corrective emotional experience and gratifying the intense wish to be taken care of. Therapist is aware that it can't stop here if the experience is to be truly transformative.]**

T: (*Moves over and puts hand on patient's upper belly*) How's that? **[Tracking receptivity and response]**

P: (*Tears up*) That feels good. **[The care has been received and the anxiety regulated, releasing a wave of State 2 emotion.]**

T: Yeah, just let those feeling come. (*Pause while patient cries quietly*) It feels good how?

P: Like . . . soothing. Quiet. Like that little boy knows that someone cares about him. **[The State 2 emotion of the younger part is a relational affect—the experience of being cared for by an older, stronger, wiser other]**

T: Yeah, so just let him feel my caring. **[Staying with and deepening the experience]** (*Long pause and quiet*) Now, let's try something else. What if you add your hand on mine? (*Patient puts his hand on top of mine. I put my other hand on top of his, and he puts his other hand on top of mine, so that there is an interlocked stack of hands on top of his belly.*) What's *that* like? **[Adding work on Side C of the Intra-Relational Triangle to the experience, knowing that this is the side that is the hardest for the patient; in essence, using the relationship with the patient and the dissociated part to build a bridge internally]**

P: (*Long exhale*) I can really feel the power of both of us caring for that little boy. (*Pause*) I just realized something . . . I think I resist taking care of him because it feels too lonely . . . like if I do it for myself, I'll lose the chance of getting taken care of by someone else. **[In a moment of spontaneous**

**insight following the relational moments of caregiving by both therapist and patient, patient recognizes his own defensive pattern and the emotional motivation underlying it.]**

Immediately after this intervention, Max spontaneously connected with memories of an uncle who had cherished him and spent quality time with him as a little boy. Max cried deeply as he remembered this uncle as the only adult who truly saw and valued him. This experience was deeply calming for Max and led to his feeling "less young, more mature and solid." This thera-peutic moment illustrates how a therapist can cocreate a corrective emotional experience with a dissociated part of the self, not as a bypass but as a bridge to building internal capacities within the patient and fortifying the bond between the patient and the dissociated part. In this instance it is easy to see how a therapist might shy away from working directly with dissociated parts in a "needy" patient, but in doing so they would forfeit a precious pathway from relationship between therapist and young part to the emergent relation-ship between the patient and his dissociated child part.

### The Patient–Dissociated Part Connection: Side C of the Intra-Relational Triangle

This axis of experiential–relational work forges secure attachment bonds between the patient and formerly abandoned and neglected parts of the self. *Portrayals*—imagined yet deeply felt interactions between parts of the self, either at the scene of past trauma or at key developmental moments—vivify and fortify internal resources of self-soothing, self-regulating, self-compassion (see also Frederick, Chapter 7, this volume; Medley, Chapter 8, this volume).

#### Benefits of Side C Work

In Side C work the patient, guided and encouraged by the therapist, lives through new moments of responding to formerly dissociated parts of the self with healthy attachment behaviors and open-heartedness, thereby healing both historical attachment trauma and the ongoing internal patterns of neglect, abandonment, and rejection that have been perpetuated in the internal system. Work on this front is the culminating experience of recovery and integration for complex trauma survivors because, as secure attachment bonds between parts of the self strengthen, internal safety is more accessible and consistent and the fear and disconnection that maintain dissociation dissipate.

#### Risks of Side C Work

For patients who have strong avoidant tendencies, too much work on the intra-relational pathway can further embed the belief that "I can do this all alone." If interventions are overloaded on this axis, the opportunity to experi-ence safe relational vulnerability and new healing relational encounters with the therapist may be lost. Earned secure attachment in adulthood features two separate but equal capacities: the ability to (a) access internal resources of regulation, soothing, protection, and compassion and (b) rely on support-ive others when one's own capacities are breached. Too much emphasis on intra-relational interventions can overdevelop the former, while leaving the latter diminished.

Risks of underfocusing on this axis of the Intra-Relational Triangle include feeding a myth that the locus of healing is "out there" or located in the thera-pist as opposed to being a latent capacity that is waiting to be awakened within the patient. Neglecting to nurture and transform the relationship between the patient and dissociated parts allows for chronic strife and reenact-ment of abusive dynamics internally between parts to continue, colluding with a fantasy that healing is a matter of making behavioral changes alone, as opposed to transforming inner relationships. As long as self-abandonment, self-neglect, and self-hate reign in the patient's inner landscape, harmony, integration, and peace will remain elusive.

### Case Study: Intra-Relational Interventions Between Patient and a Dissociated Part of the Self (Side C of the Intra-Relational Triangle)

Laurel is a 50-year-old woman on disability for posttraumatic stress disorder, dissociative identify disorder, and a severe autoimmune malady that keeps her in chronic pain. As a child, she suffered a tragic history of physical, emo-tional, and sexual abuse and neglect at the hands of her caregivers: mother, father, and stepmother. She is highly resilient and is raising two challenging teenagers as a single mother. She is intelligent, sensitive, and attuned to her children. However, Laurel also struggles considerably; she has little visual or emotional connection to her parts, loses time under stress, can "switch" into terrified child alters when triggered, and is often flooded with extreme anxiety and sadness. Given how challenging it is for Laurel to connect to her parts, I remain alert to any opportunity for rapprochement between Laurel and dissociated parts of herself.

T: But I feel like you're fearing something different . . . and correct me if I'm wrong. I'm feeling that deep-seated fear is not afraid of the kind of day-to-day pains and disappointments that our kids are gonna have to get over because we're imperfect parents . . .

P: (*Nods*) Yeah . . .

T: I feel like that fear is coming from a place of how hurt and wounded you were growing up and the terror that these little beings that you love (*patient's face crumples, and she begins to cry*) could have any inkling of that. **[A moment of deep recognition when I name a buried, back-ground fear and link it to her trauma history]** (*Patient nods, facial expresses sadness.*) Yeah . . . I do see your face change and get little when I say that. Yeah. . . . (*Therapist's voice becomes soft and soothing.*) **[Noticing the shift to a younger self state in her facial expression and the way the patient is crying; this is the cue that a traumatized part we are referring to is present]**

P: (*Whispers, exhales*) Yeah.

T: How does it feel to have that named?

P: It's just . . . that is the kind of fear that I have been approaching and try to hold.

T: Yeah.

P: I recognize that there's no measure of comparison between my life and my children except for the good stuff. (*Smiles, face brightens*) **[Patient is disentangling past from present to regulate her own fears.]**

T: Yeah, so just (*hand on heart*) say that again inside. **[Transforms this cognitive realization into an experiential, intra-relational intervention, by inviting her to say it to the scared part of her]**

P: (*Reaches for tissue*) I mean, divorce of parents isn't great stuff (*presses tissue against eyes*), but the comparison of what my children are experiencing to what I did is closest on the good stuff. **[Resisting the relational connection and just repeating the cognitive insight]**

T: Yeah, so can you say that again inside—right to that little girl who holds all those pains and all those woundedness, all those fears that your kids will feel what she feels. (*Patient exhales, nods, gives slight smile.*) In whatever way feels right to reassure her. **[Insistent, wanting to work Side C of the Intra-Relational Triangle, which is hard for this patient]**

P: How do you reassure that? **[Confusion, lack of practice, lack of faith in self, lead to self-doubt.]**

T: I know that your heart will find a way. (*Patient nods, looks down at hands, cheeks glisten with tears.*) Mmm. What are you feeling to tell her? **[Expressing faith in patient's abilities to connect with this part]**

P: That I wish I could've been her mom . . . **[Strong statement of care and love and nascent attachment bond]**

T: Yeah . . .

P: (*Chuckles*) But that I get to be, I guess, in a weird way. **[Beginning to claim that role of attachment]**

T: Yes, yes! You get to be now and you are being it now. (*Patient wipes face with tissue.*) **[Giving credit for the bond that is already forming]**

P: I don't know there's any validity to this other metaphor but I'm sure that I have some sense of my autoimmunity—my overactive immune system attacking my own body, not recognizing it—being a physical manifestation of dissociation. **[Patient's spontaneous insight and wisdom about the relationship of her chronic pain to her trauma history: State 4]**

T: Mm-hmmm.

P: And (*sighs*) that there's something about like, to say well, yeah, I actually do get to kinda parent myself—[it's] a recognition that like it's something we all get to do. Like that's hopefully following the path of enlightenment. And just because maybe what I need is what a 6-year-old needs, you know: I don't necessarily need quite so much ego release work as I do just like basic, "It's OK for you to be here. You're worth it" work. **[More wisdom about the unmet development needs of this child part]**

T: Yeah, right. The soothing . . . nurturing . . . but really from the heart. (*Patient nods.*)

T: See how that little part is feeling (*hand on heart*) about you saying "I wish I could've been your mother. And now I get to be." **[Encouraging patient to attune to and track the receptive capacity of the traumatized child part]**

P: (*Smiles, nods*) "Please get your act together, Mom" (*both giggle, facial brightening*). Which has to do with actually wanting to do more things that just please me. . . . That the day-to-day chores of life, and my kids' needs are just overwhelming, and then become like a kind of block that reinforces a sense of deprivation. It's just because maybe I have my priorities wrong. You know like, who says the dishes actually have to be done in order to sit down and read a novel for awhile. **[Challenging own internal working model of deprivation]**

T: Amen to that.

P: I've actually been practicing that and that's a part of like . . .

T: Good for you. But that sounds like it's part of your grown-up analysis, which I think is super-important but I want to make sure we give a little bit to . . . **[Mini-rupture, where I am trying to track the little girl's reaction and the patient is still in her attuned insights about what this little part needs]**

P: But no, but I mean it's like saying to that little . . . (*fingers point toward gut, indicating the little part of her*) It's actually saying to that young part of me, when I'm making that analysis that, the need to feel soothed, to escape into a book or two, go for a walk or call my friends—that's actually important to be paying attention to. It helps get that part what it needs to feel OK, you know, some control, some recognition. **[Describing her new realization of the need to stay attuned to self-soothing this little girl]**

T: And how does that feel to her? If it's OK to drop into her reaction just for a minute. If it's not OK, 'cause I recognize we only have like 5 more minutes, so you tell me if it's not OK to touch into that again. If it feels too tender or too something. **[Giving permission to say no, to titrate amount of emotional processing]** But I do really kind of want to check her reactions to this budding connection here and to having both of you express so much pain. And touching the hurt a little. **[Acknowledging the patient's attunement and budding connection to this dissociated part of her, and gently insisting on tracking the reaction of that part]**

P:   It's interesting, the word just, it keeps coming up, is trust. **[Names a hallmark characteristic of secure attachment]**

T:   Mmm . . .

P:   I kind of, suspending disbelief that, just going back to that construct of what's real and what's not real, in the present, is such an immensely powerful tool to hold. Even huge past pain . . . so instead of feeling like I have a cauldron that's always overflowing and just focusing on it makes it boil over, it's more just like actually having a really large pot to use— just to be able to hold a little, and let it (*hands moving about*), you know . . . maybe it's alchemy as opposed to you know, cooking a stew, where you fill it all up and everything's in it. Where alchemy, you know, one little reaction at a time to build something. **[Using rich, right brain imagery to describe emotional regulation—disentangling past from present and titrating emotion]**

T:   I think that's a huge piece of it. And I also just (*hand on heart*) . . . it feels like a really important part of that trust is that little part of you feeling your heart, you know, not just the fear. **[Again emphasizing the emotional/affective component to the bond, since this is what is more frequently avoided]** (*Patient touches heart, nods.*) But really when you said, "I wish I could have been your mother." (*Patient's face brightens, smiles.*) And I want her to now, just feeling the bigness of your heart, and all the love in your heart, and that that's circling in to you. (*Patient cries softly.*) And really for the first time, directly . . . yeah . . . **[Stopping to inquire about emerging tears]** What are you feeling in here as you say that or as I say that?

P:   Just a lot of kind of moving around inside (*one hand makes big circles, other continues touching heart space in circular motion*). I know I'm crying but it's not a bad thing. **[The "good tears" of being moved—State 3]**

T:   In my book, it's never a bad thing unless it feels too . . .

P:   It doesn't feel painful. **[Patient is clear that this is a positive emotional experience.]**

T:   Feels like different tears. (*Patient nods, wipes eyes with tissue.*) Mmm-hmm. What's the movement? (*repeats patient's gesture of heart space circles*). I'm so curious to hear what your sensation is there, what you're feeling right now. **[Bringing attention to the movement of patient's hand]**

P:   (*Continues heart space circling*) It's just actively moving the heart energy around.

**T:**   And that little part of you feeling it too? (*Patient nods.*) Yeah, I'm so glad for that. **[Shared somatic experience between parts—a sign of integration]**

## CONCLUSION

In this chapter I have explored how, in the wake of complex, developmental trauma, dissociation disrupts and segregates biological attachment impulses in trauma survivors, organizing conflicting and apparently irreconcilable needs in disparate parts of the self. This fragmentation poses unique challenges to creating a safe connection and processing emotion in therapy. Intra-relational interventions import AEDP's relational–experiential strategies into the fragmented system of a patient's parts, guiding interventions between the therapist and patient, the therapist and dissociated parts, and the patient and dissociated parts, to restructure relational dynamics and create secure attachment on each of these axes. Guided by moment-to-moment tracking of emergent relational and attachment strategies and patterns, the AEDP therapist crafts experiential interventions on all three axes to achieve a dynamic equilibrium of attention, resources, and transformation across the entire matrix of multiple selves.

## REFERENCES

Blizard, R. A., & Bluhm, A. M. (1994). Attachment to the abuser: Integrating object-relations and trauma theories in treatment of abuse survivors. *Psychotherapy: Theory, Practice, Training, 31*(3), 383–390. https://doi.org/10.1037/0033-3204.31.3.383

Bowlby, J. (1982). *Attachment and loss: Vol. 1. Attachment.* Basic Books. (Original work published 1969)

Bowlby, J. (1988). *A secure base.* Basic Books.

Bromberg, P. M. (1998). *Standing in the spaces: Essays on clinical process, trauma and dissociation.* Analytic Press.

Chefetz, R. A., & Bromberg, P. M. (2004). Talking with "Me" and "Not-Me": A dialogue. *Contemporary Psychoanalysis, 40*(3), 409–464. https://doi.org/10.1080/00107530.2004.10745840

Damasio, A. R. (2010). *Self comes to mind: Constructing the conscious brain.* Pantheon Books.

Ecker, B., Ticic, R., & Hulley, L. (2012). *Unlocking the emotional brain: Eliminating symptoms at their roots using memory reconsolidation.* Routledge. https://doi.org/10.4324/9780203804377

Fisher, J. (2017). *Healing the fragmented selves of trauma survivors: Overcoming internal self-alienation.* Routledge. https://doi.org/10.4324/9781315886169

Fonagy, P., & Target, M. (1997). Attachment and reflective function: Their role in self-organization. *Development and Psychopathology, 9*(4), 679–700. https://doi.org/10.1017/S0954579497001399

Fosha, D. (2000). *The transforming power of affect: A model of accelerated change.* Basic Books.

Fosha, D. (2003). Dyadic regulation and experiential work with emotion and relatedness in trauma and disordered attachment. In M. F. Solomon & D. J. Siegel (Eds.), *Healing trauma: Attachment, mind, body, and brain* (pp. 221–281). W. W. Norton.

Fosha, D. (2009). Emotion and recognition at work: Energy, vitality, pleasure, truth, desire and the emergent phenomenology of transformational experience. In D. Fosha, D. J. Siegel, & M. F. Solomon (Eds.), *The healing power of emotion: Affective neuroscience, development, and clinical practice* (pp. 172–203). W. W. Norton.

Fosha, D. (2013a). A heaven in a wild flower: Self, dissociation, and treatment in the context of the neurobiological core self. *Psychoanalytic Inquiry, 33*(5), 496–523. https://doi.org/10.1080/07351690.2013.815067

Fosha, D. (2013b). Turbocharging the affects of healing and redressing the evolutionary tilt. In D. J. Siegel & Marion F. Solomon (Eds.), *Healing moments in psychotherapy* (pp. 129–168). W. W. Norton.

Fosha, D. (2017a). How to be a transformational therapist: AEDP harnesses innate healing affects to re-wire experience and accelerate transformation. In J. Loizzo, M. Neale, & E. Wolf (Eds.), *Advances in contemplative psychotherapy: Accelerating transformation* (pp. 204–219). Norton.

Fosha, D. (2017b). Something more than "something more than interpretation": AEDP works the experiential edge of transformational experience to transform the internal working model. In S. Lord (Ed.), *Moments of meeting in psychoanalysis: Interaction and change in the therapeutic encounter* (pp. 267–292). Routledge.

Fosha, D., Paivio, S. C., Gleiser, K., & Ford, J. (2009). Experiential and emotion-focused therapy. In C. Courtois & J. D. Ford (Eds.), *Complex traumatic stress disorders: An evidence-based clinician's guide* (pp. 286–311). Guilford Press.

Gleiser, K. (2013). Seeing the invisible: The role of recognition in healing from neglect and deprivation. *Transformance: The AEDP Journal, 3*(1).

Gleiser, K., Ford, J. D., & Fosha, D. (2008). Contrasting exposure and experiential therapies for complex posttraumatic stress disorder. *Psychotherapy: Theory, Research, Practice, Training, 45*(3), 340–360. https://doi.org/10.1037/a0013323

Iacoboni, M. (2009). *Mirroring people: The science of empathy and how we connect with others.* Picador.

Karpman, S. B. (2007, August 8–12). *The new drama triangles* [Lecture]. USA Transactional Analysis Association/International Transactional Analysis Association conference, San Francisco, CA.

Kohut, H. (1977). *The restoration of the self.* International Universities Press.

Kohut, H. (1984). *How does analysis cure?* University of Chicago Press.

Lamagna, J. (2011). Of the self, by the self, and for the self: An intra-relational perspective on intra-psychic attunement and psychological change. *Journal of Psychotherapy Integration, 21*(3), 280–307. https://doi.org/10.1037/a0025493

Lamagna, J., & Gleiser, K. A. (2007). Building a secure internal attachment: An intra-relational approach to ego strengthening and emotional processing with chronically traumatized clients. *Journal of Trauma & Dissociation, 8*(1), 25–52. https://doi.org/10.1300/J229v08n01_03

Lipton, B., & Fosha, D. (2011). Attachment as a transformative process in AEDP: Operationalizing the intersection of attachment theory and affective neuroscience. *Journal of Psychotherapy Integration, 21*(3), 253–279. https://doi.org/10.1037/a0025421

Main, M. (2000). The organized categories of infant, child, and adult attachment: Flexible vs. inflexible attention under attachment-related stress. *Journal of the American Psychoanalytic Association, 48*(4), 1055–1096. https://doi.org/10.1177/00030651000480041801

Main, M., & Solomon, J. (1990). Procedures for identifying infants as disorganized/disoriented during the Ainsworth strange situation. In M. T. Greenberg, D. Cicchetti, & M. Cummings (Eds.), *Attachment in the preschool years: Theory, research, and intervention* (pp. 121–160). University of Chicago Press.

Pando-Mars, K. (2016). Tailoring AEDP interventions to attachment style. *Transformance: The AEDP Journal, 6*(2).

Panksepp, J., & Northoff, G. (2009). The trans-species core SELF: The emergence of active cultural and neuro-ecological agents through self-related processing within subcortical-cortical midline networks. *Consciousness and Cognition, 18*(1), 193–215. https://doi.org/10.1016/j.concog.2008.03.002

Safran, J. D., & Muran, J. C. (1996). The resolution of ruptures in the therapeutic alliance. *Journal of Consulting and Clinical Psychology, 64*(3), 447–458. https://doi.org/10.1037/0022-006X.64.3.447

Schore, A. N. (2009). Right-brain affect regulation: An essential mechanism of development, trauma, dissociation, and psychotherapy. In D. Fosha, D. J. Siegel, & M. F. Solomon (Eds.), *The healing power of emotion: Affective neuroscience, development and clinical practice* (pp. 112–144). W. W. Norton.

Siegel, D. J. (1999). *The developing mind: How relationships and the brain interact to shape who we are.* Guilford Press.

Steele, K., Boon, S., & van der Hart, O. (2016). *Treating trauma-related dissociation: A practical integrative approach.* W. W. Norton.

van der Hart, O., Nijenhuis, E. R. T., & Steele, K. (2006). *The haunted self: Structural dissociation and the treatment of chronic traumatization.* W. W. Norton.

van der Kolk, B. A. (2015). *The body keeps the score: Brain, mind and body in the healing of trauma.* Penguin Books.

# V

# INTEGRATION, FLOURISHING, CORE STATE, AND THE CORE SELF

# 13

# What Went Right?

## What Happens in the Brain During AEDP's Metatherapeutic Processing

Danny Yeung

Metatherapeutic processing (or "metaprocessing"; both terms are used in this chapter) is a major contribution of accelerated experiential dynamic psychotherapy (AEDP; Fosha, 2000a, 2003; Fosha & Yeung, 2006; Yeung, 2010; Yeung & Cheung, 2009; Yeung & Fosha, 2015). This technique exemplifies a paradigm shift from psychotherapy's preoccupation with psychopathology and negative affects to a more expansive focus on flourishing and positive experiences. The purpose of metatherapeutic processing is to clinically address and further harness the power of what was transformative in treatment. The core questions I hope to address in this chapter are "What just went right in therapy?" and "How do we work with it to make the most of it?" AEDP works to both repair "what went wrong" while simultaneously working to make sure that "what went right" in treatment is systematically worked with and can be savored and integrated into the self.

Insights from neuroscience inform the overarching modes of this chapter and are interwoven throughout the text. Research on the orbitofrontal cortex (OFC), smart vagus, and the insula and its Von Economo neurons (VENs) provides compelling correlative neurobiological and objective empirical evidence supporting what is subjectively observed phenomenologically and clinically in metatherapeutic processes and a highly integrative state, called "core state" by practitioners of AEDP. Core state is a deeply integrated and integrative state characterized by calm, openness, compassion for both others and self, the sense of things feeling "right," and more.

https://doi.org/10.1037/0000232-014
*Undoing Aloneness and the Transformation of Suffering Into Flourishing: AEDP 2.0*, D. Fosha (Editor)

Metatherapeutic processing alternates between experience and reflection. This experiential–reflective cycle promotes horizontal left brain–right brain integration and vertical bottom-up–top-down mind–body integration. In this chapter, I propose that this core state reflects a socially engaged, smart-vagus–mediated autonomic nervous system as well as mediation by the OFC and insula. Given that functioning mediated by the smart vagus and the OFC is associated with improved immune function, optimal health, a sense of well-being, and flourishing (Porges, 2011; Schore, 2012; Siegel, 2007), these hypotheses about what goes on the brain and nervous system can help shed greater light on what is really taking place in core state. They also allow us to speculate further about the mechanisms of change operating in this remarkable state, which yields some phenomena that are remarkably similar to ones that characterize spiritual experiences (e.g., ego dissolution and the dyadic experience of two souls meeting).[1] Thus, the neurobiological hypotheses explored here might shed light not only on core state phenomena but also on phenomena of spiritual practice.

Given that metatherapeutic processing is the method by which core state is reached in AEDP, in this chapter I explore the phenomenology of the transformational process, describe the six metatherapeutic processes with their corresponding transformational affects, and then describe core state.[2] I then discuss the neuroscience of positivity and explore its relationship with AEDP in general and with core state in particular. The chapter ends with vignettes from two clinical cases that illustrate these concepts.

## WHAT TRANSFORMS IN THE TRANSFORMATIONAL PROCESS?

The state-specific description of the phenomenology of the transformational process is a cornerstone of the theory and practice of AEDP. Figure 1 in the Appendix depicts the phases of the client's intrapsychic journey through the process of transformation and identifies the phenomena that characterize each state.[3] Organized around the centrality of moment-to-moment affective experience in treatment, this map helps AEDP therapists understand where the client is and helps them choose their next intervention.

The transformational process begins by accessing the painful, overwhelming emotional experiences associated with emotional suffering. A big part of AEDP's understanding of psychopathology—that is, what went wrong—

---

[1]The use of the word "soul" is inspired by the preeminent neurobiologist of our time, Jaak Panksepp (see Panksepp & Biven, 2012, p. 390), who used the same word as a referent to the neurobiological core self.

[2]Moran (2000) defined phenomena "in the broadest sense as whatever appears in the manner in which it appears, that is as it manifests itself to consciousness, to the experiencer" (p. 4).

[3]This figure, and diagrams for all of the representational schemas in AEDP 2.0, may be downloaded for free (http://pubs.apa.org/books/supp/fosha/).

is that the emotions evoked by traumatizing events are too overwhelming for the person to feel and process, exceeding their resources and requiring the institution of defenses to survive. Because of aloneness in the face of overwhelming emotions, people thus affected lose access to the adaptive advantages that emotions processed to completion confer. The work of AEDP States 1 and 2 is to take what went wrong and make it right. Phrased more specifically, unwilled and unwanted aloneness, defenses that have long outlived their usefulness, as well as unprocessed emotions, need to be transformed: A client's aloneness must be undone so as to be able to help them gain embodied access to the emotions and, with the therapist's help, process those emotions to completion and reap their adaptive benefits. Doing so ushers in State 3.

The metatherapeutic processing of transformational experience then follows, illuminating what just went right and experientially processing the positive emotions associated with what just went right. Spiraling rounds that alternate between processing the experience of transformation and reflecting on that new emergent experience as it is emerging gives rise to a new experience, which in turn is also processed and reflected on, and so on. The grand finale of the transformational process is core state, in which a person is most experientially connected to one's *neurobiological core self* (Fosha, 2013a, reflecting on Panksepp & Northoff's [2008] term; see also Damasio, 2010, and Chapter 12 in Panksepp & Biven, 2012). When clients first enter treatment, they feel deadened psychically because of their traumatic experiences. Once they go through the transformational process and reach core state, they often spontaneously declare, "This is who I am,"[4] or they might claim something like "I can wholly be me." It is not hyperbole to say that the transformational processing takes clients from suffering to flourishing, from compromised self to resilient self, and from false self to true self.

The emergence of the *felt core self* (Fosha, 2013a) is akin to the postrestorative appearance of Michelangelo's paintings in the Sistine Chapel, in which the true self's original colors, beauty, and aesthetic splendor are revealed. When the true self comes online experientially, it is experienced as the innermost self, sometimes with transpersonal unitive qualities.[5]

## THE METATHERAPEUTIC PROCESSING OF WHAT WENT RIGHT

*Metatherapeutic processing* (also called, as mentioned earlier, metaprocessing) refers to the work that begins after experiences that feel therapeutic to the client have occurred. In other words, in metatherapeutic processing we are processing the experience of what is therapeutic about therapy when therapy works. After the emotional experience has been processed to correct what

---

[4]This is illustrated in the "Monica, Vignette 2" section.
[5]This is illustrated in the "Steffan, Vignette 2" section.

went wrong with the client's life, which often was marred by trauma and suffering (States 1 and 2), metatherapeutic processing explores what just went right. Expressed differently, metatherapeutic processing focuses attention on the transformational experiences achieved through the emotional processing work (State 2), which are then broadened and built on through the metaprocessing work itself, bringing online the transformational affects (State 3) and core state (State 4).

## Therapeutic Stance in Metatherapeutic Processing

Metatherapeutic processing uses AEDP's therapeutic stance of *dyadic mindfulness* (Fosha, 2011, 2013b), which allows for the seamless integration of mindfulness, attachment, and intersubjectivity. *Mindfulness* implies attending to the present moment, specifically, awareness of the mind and body, without judgment (Kabat-Zinn, 2005). It includes attitudes of openness, acceptance, equanimity, compassion, and "loving-kindness," a term coined by Kabat-Zinn (2005). *Attachment* evokes the mindset of protection as an aspect of love (Golding & Hughes, 2012; Marks-Tarlow & Schore, 2017). *Intersubjectivity* emphasizes dyadic relatedness and moment-to-moment interactions. These three aspects of the therapeutic stance interweave each therapeutic dyad like the blending of three primary colors in varying hues.

Further unpacking dyadic mindfulness reveals the element of *felt sensing*, whereby the therapist accepts the mindful awareness of "what is coming up" not only inside the client but also between the members of the therapeutic dyad. Put another way, the therapist is informed by what is becoming conscious and possibly takes actions because of the emerging images, thoughts, sensations, and emotions. Dyadic mindfulness emphasizes the mutuality and reciprocity of the dyad, simultaneously operating in both client and therapist (see also Hanakawa, Lipton, Chapters 4 and 5, respectively, this volume). Unlike contemplative practices, however, the dyadic mindfulness used in AEDP has an intention: It is the therapist who leads the process and tracks it so as to facilitate its move toward transformation.

## Therapeutic Skills in Metatherapeutic Processing

Metatherapeutic processing involves another round of experiential work with transformational experiences. It includes seizing, naming, affirming, and experientially working with the celebration of change for the better. It privileges the emergent positive and new experiences, thoughts, feelings, and action tendencies and behaviors.

Therapeutic skills required for metatherapeutic processing involve facilitating the experiential exploration of the emergent transformational affects, followed by encouraging the client to engage in embodied reflection on the experience (Fosha, 2000b, 2009; Russell & Fosha, 2008). The basic AEDP goals of making the implicit explicit (Fosha, 2000a), the explicit experiential (Fosha, 2010), and the experiential relational (Pando-Mars, 2011) definitely apply to the metatherapeutic processing of anything new and positive that happens in the session and beyond (Prenn, 2009, 2011).

Mencius (372–289 BCE) is the second-most-venerated Confucian philosopher in classical pre-Qin China, and an adaptation of Mencian technique can be applied to metaprocessing. The Mencian technique (Mencius, 1999) applied to metaprocessing involves a series of four microsteps developed to "hold" the client and expand the processing work.[6] These steps apply to the experiential part of the process have affect the reflections that follow. The following are four examples of how an AEDP therapist cultivates, nurtures, and enhances the processing of an experience of transformation for the client when using this microstep process:

- Micro-Step 1/*Staying*: Where are you noticing the (positive experience) in your body? Notice what you feel, especially around your throat, your heart, your belly area. Stay with what you sense. Stay with the energy. (Inspired by the work of Hansen & Mendius, 2009, showing that holding the positive experience in awareness strengthens the memory trace, I urge my clients to hold the experience silently for about 30 seconds.)

- Micro-Step 2/*Savoring*: Welcome the experience. Savor it. Taste it. Sense it. Embrace it. Hold the experience silently for about 30 seconds.

- Micro-Step 3/*Spreading*: Allow the experience to spread through your body. Allow the energy to radiate, percolate, permeate. Hold the experience silently for about 30 seconds.

- Micro-Step 4/*Saturating*: Allow the sensation or the energy to fill your whole body. Allow it to go even beyond the boundaries of your body. Hold the experience silently about 30 seconds.

As the therapist works with the client's experiences, metatherapeutic processes and their corresponding transformational affects emerge. Witnessing these affects—and helping the client name, experience, and reflect on them—provides assurance that the client will register what went on in the therapy hour that was effective and positive, thus consolidating therapeutic experiences and further rooting them in the body. Although the emotions processed in State 2 may indeed be quite painful for the client, what feels "right" about them is vital, and processing them to completion feels good. Metaprocessing and the transformational affects to which it gives rise signify a change for the better and broadens and builds "what felt good" as a result of the State 2 work.

---

[6]Mencius (1999) proposed that we could "cultivate great valor" (p. 46) and "nurture" the four seeds of humanity, duty, ritual, and wisdom (p. 56). This Chinese version of experiential processing is my creative adaptation to contextualize and indigenize this therapeutic skill for my Chinese colleagues in Shanghai and Hong Kong.

## Metatherapeutic Processes and Their Transformational Affects

Six metatherapeutic processes, along with their corresponding transformational affects, have been identified (Fosha, 2000a, 2017, 2018) and constitute State 3 work. All of the transformational affects are positive emotions, with one exception. The emotional pain associated with the process of mourning the self is not necessarily positive in affective valence, but the experience it evokes is positive, that is, an experience of change for the better in the here and now. These transformational affects are essential to the mining, broadening, and building of positive resources that otherwise might lie dormant within the client, restricting that client's opportunities for flourishing (Fosha et al., 2019; Fredrickson, 2009; Fredrickson et al., 2008; Russell, 2015):

- *Mastery.* Overcoming past limitations, undoing the self's sense of imprisonment, of being alienated by shame and fear, evokes the *mastery affects* of joy, pride, confidence, and the somatic sense of strength and positive energy.

- *Mourning the self.* The current here-and-now good experience evokes the emotional acknowledgment of losses of precious time, opportunities, or relationships associated with the previous splitting off or exiling of parts of the self; it is this comparison that evokes the transformational affect of *emotional pain.*

- *Traversing the crisis of healing change.* Processing the newness of the new positive experiences and the suddenness and the discontinuous quality of the emergent transformation evokes the *tremulous affects* of surprise and a positive tremulousness (i.e., a normative anxiety in the face of the new, though positive, unfamiliar experience and some discomfort with the unexpectedness of freedom).

- *Affirming recognition of the self and its transformation.* Recognition and affirmation of the transformation of the self and, very importantly, of the other who helped the self do so, evokes the *healing affects,* which include feeling moved, touched, or emotional within oneself and/or feelings of tenderness, love, or gratitude toward the other, in this case, the therapist.

- *Delighting in the surprise of the emerging transformation.* This involves the client delighting in the change that is taking place in light of the self's previous belief that such a change was not possible. The actuality of the surprising and very welcome transformation yields the *enlivening affects: exuberance, delight, and pleasure,* and the sense of exploratory zest is associated with emerging transformation about future possibilities.

- *Taking in the new understanding.* Awareness of the enormity of the transformation evokes the eureka-like *realization affects* of "Yes!" and "Wow!"

Metatherapeutic processing involves repeated rounds of working with one or more of these processes and their corresponding transformational affects, that is, repeated rounds of experience followed by embodied reflecting on the experience and then repeating the process with the new experience. This leads to upward spirals of vitality and energy (also described by Fredrickson, 2009; Fredrickson et al., 2008; and Fredrickson & Joiner, 2002, outside of the clinical situation), which in turn culminate in the emergence of State 4.

### The Culmination of Metatherapeutic Processing: Core State

Core state experiencing includes openness, flow, ease, kindness, generosity, compassion for self and others, and an I–Thou sense and stance (Fosha, 2000a; Fosha & Yeung, 2006; Russell & Fosha, 2008). Core state resonates with contemplative experiences (Fosha, 2017) and could have transpersonal unitive qualities.[7] It is a deeply integrated and integrative state. One's autobiographical narrative becomes adaptively reconstructed with a profound sense of purpose and meaning. What used to be experienced as weaker parts of the self are now experienced in core state as strength and a sense of treasure. The affective marker for core state is the *truth sense* (Fosha, 2005). The term "truth sense" does not refer to the objective correspondence to factual reality; instead, it is a subjective experience of personal emotional truth in the experiential moment, an unveiling of what is at the core of one's innermost self at a given moment of embodied experience.

In the next section, I discuss some emotion research and neuroscientific findings that shed further light on what is happening in the brain that results in these integrative phenomena that manifest in core state. I then present two clinical examples that illustrate core state phenomenology coming to life.

## THE NEUROSCIENCE OF POSITIVITY AND TRANSFORMATION IN AEDP

The past 20 years have seen an explosive rise in our understanding of the evolutionary function of positive emotion as well as in how the brain and nervous system process our experiences. These insights shed further light on what is at work in core state. I begin this section with a discussion of the broaden-and-build theory of positive emotion and continue with an exploration of the neurobiology of positive affects that pays special attention to OFC activation. I finish with a hypothesis about the relationship between core state and smart vagus activation.

### Positive Affects and the Broaden-and-Build Theory of Positive Emotion

Metatherapeutic processing yields the transformational affects and core state, which constitute a veritable treasure trove of positive affects ready to be mined and harnessed. Fredrickson's (2001, 2004, 2009) broaden-and-build theory helps us appreciate the profound value of these positive emotional states that

---

[7]This is illustrated in the "Steffan, Vignette 2" section.

AEDP's metatherapeutic processing both works with and systematically yields. Hypothesizing that these positive emotions occur when the autonomic nervous system's social engagement system is online (Kok & Fredrickson, 2010; Porges, 2011), Fredrickson's broaden-and-build theory highlights the evolutionary value of positive emotions.

In contrast with the narrowing mindset that characterizes the negative emotions, the positive emotions bring forth a broadened state of mind that is associated with increased "thought–action repertoire"; in this broadened state characteristic of the positive emotions it becomes possible to play, explore, savor, and integrate them. The broadened mindsets associated with positive affects promote the discovery of new and creative ideas as well as the exploration of new actions leading to the development and building of personal and interpersonal resources conducive not only to surviving but also to thriving.

Furthermore, compelling evidence of the effects of positive affects on health and wellness has been provided by Tugade et al. (2004) and Tugade and Fredrickson (2004). Benefits include enhanced immune functioning, better recovery after coronary bypass, fewer physical complaints, more hours of sleep and better sleep quality, longevity, reduced stress and depression, undoing of the after-effects of negative emotional reactivity, and psychological resilience. On the basis of these findings I hypothesize that the fundamentally positive transformational affects and core state experiences that metatherapeutic processing yields will be shown to be associated with enhanced thriving, resilience, physical health, and even longevity.

Having seen the evolutionary importance of positive emotions and their beneficial effects, I next investigate the OFC of the brain (see Figure 13.1), which has been shown to play a role in both positive affects and in integration, to see what further light it sheds on the positive affects that metatherapeutic processing yields.

## Positive Affects and the Orbitofrontal Cortex

The OFC is the prefrontal cortical region of the brain's frontal lobes and is located immediately above the eye sockets. Supporting neurobiological integration, the OFC is associated with nine functions: bodily regulation, attuned communication, emotional balance, response flexibility, empathy, insight, fear modulation, intuition, and morality (Siegel, 2007). The OFC also serves as a convergence zone for multisensory and emotional information (Cozolino, 2014). It acts as the "senior executive of the emotional brain" and "the brain's most complex affect and stress regulatory system" (Schore, 2012). Moreover, looking at it through the lens of attachment, the OFC, with its subcortical connections, serves as the biological control system that regulates emotionally driven behavior; specifically, attachment can be understood as the "interactive regulation of biological synchronicity" between parent and child or therapist and client (Schore, 2000). In plain English, the attachment-seeker's OFC is being emotionally calibrated by the attachment-giver's OFC.

**FIGURE 13.1. Location of the Orbitofrontal Cortex and Insular Cortex in the Brain**

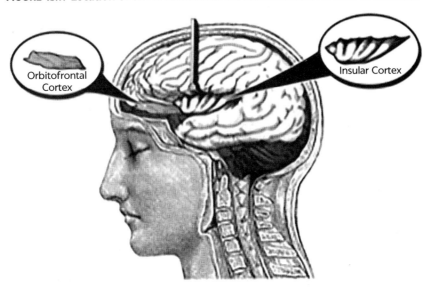

*Note.* Courtesy of Virginia Law. Reprinted with permission.

In the neuroscience research on positive affects and their relationship with the OFC, functional magnetic resonance imaging studies (Burgdorf & Panksepp, 2006) have suggested that positive affects appear to activate the OFC; therefore, it seems reasonable to hypothesize that the mechanism of metatherapeutic processing is mediated by the OFC. Its activation is reflected in the transformational affects, those gold mines of positive affects and core state.

## Positive Affects, Attachment, and the Orbitofrontal Cortex

I now turn my attention to the research on positive affects associated with attachment relationships. AEDP is fundamentally an attachment-based model in which the therapist–client dyad simulates and embodies the optimal security engendering the mother–infant relationship. This optimal attachment security-engendering dyadic relationship is an ever-present intersubjective field that envelops all four states of the transformational process, including core state. It is in the relational context that all emotion processing occurs in AEDP, whether it is the processing of the painful emotions of trauma or the metaprocessing of the positive emotions accompanying transformation. Furthermore, when the client experiences an emotional state, *a fortiori* core state, it is common for the therapist to experience this too (Schoettle, 2009; see also Lipton, Chapter 5, this volume). Core state experiencing is a parallel and synchronous state for both client and therapist.

Two studies have examined the possible neurobiological mechanism underlying this clinical phenomenon of relationality, and the OFC figures prominently. First, in a functional magnetic resonancing imaging study, Nitschke et al. (2004) discovered that mothers showed bilateral OFC activation when viewing pictures of their babies. The positive affects associated with maternal attachment—warmth, joy, fulfillment, and contentment—have been described as postgoal attainment positive affects (Davidson et al., 2003). These positive affects are similar to those experienced by therapists when clients reach core state, which signals the therapeutic goal of completing the transformational process. They also are similar to the affects clients experience in core state, which possibly is a reflection of intra-relational attachment dynamics as contributing to the integration characteristic of core state (see Lamagna, Chapter 11, this volume; and Lamagna & Gleiser, 2007). Second, Minagawa-Kawai et al. (2009), using near-infrared spectroscopy, replicated and further refined Nitschke et al.'s (2004) results, demonstrating that mothers viewing photos of their own infants triggered activation of the anterior parts of the OFC as well. These researchers also discovered reciprocal activation of the infants' anterior OFC in response to their own mother's smile.

In applying the results of these neuroimaging studies, I suggest that core state phenomenology, with its corresponding positive affects in both members of the dyad, reflects the activation of the OFC in both therapist and client. The richly positive transformational affects and core state might reflect mediation by the OFC with its deeply integrative capacity. Thus, experiencing core state is a parallel and synchronous condition for both client and therapist that reflects a shared experience of positivity and deep neurological integration.

## The Smart Vagus and Core State

Porges's (2011) work on the autonomic nervous system helps us further understand what might be happening in core state. In essence, core state is a phenomenological and dynamic equivalent of the neurophysiological state mediated by the evolutionarily new myelinated branch of the vagal nerve, or "smart vagus" (Porges, 2011). I hypothesize that the processing of core affective experience and the processing of transformational experience, followed by the processing of core state experience, parallels the shift from the high-arousal states mediated by the sympathetic nervous system to the low-arousal states mediated by the ventral vagal parasympathetic system (Fosha, 2017; Russell & Fosha, 2008). If I may take a bit of poetic license, the wind, earthquake, and fire associated with the high-arousal roar of processing negative emotional experience (State 2) and transformational experience (State 3) have passed, and the low-arousal gentleness of core state emerges, whispering peace, serenity, and wholeness.

Why is the myelinated branch of vagus nerve "smart"? According to Porges (2011), researcher and developer of the polyvagal theory of the autonomic nervous system, the unmyelinated, or vegetative, vagus, which originates in the dorsal motor nucleus, with efferents to the trachea, lungs, stomach, intestines, pancreas, and colon, is involved with the involuntary vegetative functions of respiration and digestion, whereas the myelinated vagus, which originates in the nucleus ambiguus, with efferents to the heart, soft palate, pharynx, larynx, esophagus, and bronchi and muscles of the face and ear, is involved in the voluntary social functions of motion, emotion, and, most important, differentiated expression and social communication and hence is a smart vagus.

From a neurophysiological perspective, why is it adaptive to have the social engagement system online, that is, to have the smart vagus engaged? Alternatively, from AEDP's phenomenological perspective, why is it adaptive for the individual to reach core state? There are three reasons:

1. The positive affects of vibrant well-being, calm, flow, and ease are associated with the low arousal state mediated by the smart vagus. The smart vagus functions as a vagal brake of sorts, with the ability to regulate cardiac output in a way that reduces the cardiac costs of sympathetic activation. Core state and engaging the smart vagus or the vagal brake reduces immediately the cardiac output; enhances oxygenation of the brain; and promotes self-soothing, calm, and conservation of energy.

2. Core state, indicating an increased smart vagal tone and inhibition of the sympathetic nervous system, may have a direct efferent neural influence on the thymus gland, thus evoking a state that promotes enhanced immune function.

3. I must note that there is interneuronal wiring between the source nuclei of the special visceral efferent pathways (controlling gaze, facial expression, focus on human voice, prosody and intonations, head gestures) and the source nucleus of the smart vagus. The increased smart vagal tone associated with core state switches on the social engagement system by means of facial expressivity and vocal modulation. The operation of the social engagement system is associated with promoting prosocial behaviors to support health, growth and restoration, and heightened adaptation. This happens through social communication and coordination, rather than the fight-or-flight of sympathetic arousal or the immobility and shut down mediated by the old vagus, that is, the dorsal vagal branch of the parasympathetic nervous system.

To summarize and translate all of the above neuroscience lingo into plain language: "Underneath the hood" of what we observe phenomenologically as core state is the smart vagus firing full throttle. When it is, the brain is more energized. The body is more calm. Stress is low or absent. Immune function is better. We are more effectively socially engaged. All of these support better cardiac health, are optimal for personal well-being, and allow flourishing and thriving.

At this juncture I would like to spotlight the felt core self, a special phenomenon within core state experiencing, and explore its neurobiological correlates.

### The Insula, the Neurobiological Core Self, and Core State: The Felt Core Self

In a clinical context, the felt core self manifests phenomenologically when clients in AEDP's core state declare, "This is me," "This is who I am, the real me." The felt core self, a distinctive feature of core state, is the closest "instantiation of the neurobiological core self in actual experience" (Fosha, 2013a). Panksepp and colleagues (Panksepp & Biven, 2012; Panksepp & Northoff, 2008) and Damasio (2010) have independently noted the genetically based wired-in connection of a series of subcortical structures that are coordinated from birth. In other words, their being wired together and firing together is the result not of experience but of genetic programming. The coordinated activation of the *subcortical midline structures* (SCMSs) underlies what can be psychologically described as agency, ownership of experience, and identity. The SCMSs, with the *periaqueductal gray* as a converging processing structure, is what neurobiologically constitutes the neurobiological core self (Panksepp & Biven, 2012).

Self-related processes such as identity, agency, initiative, and so on, mediated by the SCMSs, with development also entrain cortical midline structures, such as the insular cortex, medial frontal cortex, and OFC. The neurobiological substrate for the felt core self requires connectivity between the SCMSs, the cortical midline structures, and the insula. When activated, this is experienced as our innermost core and fundamental self (Craig, 2015; Fosha, 2013a, 2013b; Panksepp & Biven, 2012).

### The Insula, Van Economo Neurons, Intuition, and Resonance Circuits

Neurobiology helps us speculate about the processes that might be involved in AEDP's transformational phenomena and the neurophysiological underpinnings of these phenomena. Felt experience invariably involves the insula, which is always involved in the mediation of embodied experience. I am also interested in exploring the possible role that the VENs, which exist in the insula and are crucial to felt experience, might play in the transformational affects and core state.

Two structures associated with the insula are particularly relevant: (a) the anterior insular cortex (AIC) and (b) the anterior cingulate cortex (ACC). The AIC, activated synergistically with its highly interdependent neighbor the ACC, is implicated in the integration of top-down cognitive and bottom-up somatic–affective processing, awareness of self experience (self-with-self), simulation of the inner experience of others (self-with-others), and selection of appropriate responses to the world (self-with-the world; Cozolino, 2014; Craig, 2015).

These phenomena are likely mediated by VENs, which have been of great interest lately, along with mirror neurons, because they allow us to better understand phenomena of human resonance and intersubjective communication. VENs, restricted to the AIC and ACC in human brains, are implicated in social empathy and emotional self-awareness (Craig, 2015). Other important neurobiological structures, such as mirror neurons, are involved in resonance, attunement, and empathy (Siegel, 2010).

Furthermore, VENs are implicated in intuition. Allman et al. (2005, 2011) have suggested that VENs may be involved in the "fast intuitive assessment of complex situations." They proposed that the VENs relay an output to the parts to brain associated with "theory of mind, where fast intuitions are melded with slower deliberative judgements" (Allman et al., 2005, p. 367). VENs may well be regarded as neurons of intuition, intricately involved in the circuitry for "mind reading." Allman et al. (2005) further contended that "intuition is based on experience-based probabilistic models. We experience the intuitive process at a visceral level. Intuitive decision-making enables us to react quickly in situations that involve a high degree of uncertainty which involve social interactions" (pp. 369–370). The point? I am hypothesizing that the true self, core state experiencing, operating simultaneously in both members of the therapeutic dyad, activates our intuitive capacity and includes empathy and appropriate action tendencies for self, others, and the world. In short, true self experiencing not only makes us gentler, kinder, and wiser but also allows these experiences to become dyadically amplified through resonance, empathy, and intuition, mediated by means of their neurobiological substrates: mirror neurons and the VENs. By adding intuition, and *mutual dyadic intuition,* to our understanding of what happens in core state, we can further understand its power.

## BRINGING IT ALL TOGETHER

Weaving together the research on the OFC, smart vagus, and the insula and its VENs provides compelling correlative neurobiological evidence supporting what is observed phenomenologically in metatherapeutic processes and core state. These neurobiological insights are a powerful substantive validation of why we do what we do, that is, AEDP's revolutionary emphasis on metatherapeutic processing.

In addition, these correlative neurological insights become guideposts into what AEDP may explore next phenomenologically. For example, if OFC activation is associated with a sense of right and moral action (Siegel, 2007), then core state, where OFC activation is a possible neurobiological substrate, would be consistent with the emergence of moral virtues (Peterson & Seligman, 2004) as an action tendency in clinical phenomenology. These virtues include confidence, humility, and a sense of that which is sacred (Fosha & Thoma, 2020). Traditionally cultivated as a rigorous practice, and the object of arduous teaching, these virtues are an emergent bottom-up phenomenon in AEDP, rather than the result of top-down efforts.

Also, what we observe as positive transformational processes in the psychosocial domain are correlated with health in the biological domain: improved cardiac function as well as improved immune function, growth and restoration.

The health implications of AEDP's transformational work with trauma are an exciting avenue for future research.

Finally, as I have shown, AEDP's transformational phenomenology is hypothesized to be rooted in neurobiology. However, AEDP's epistemological orientation goes beyond reductionist physicalism to also embrace what our civilization cherishes as sacred, awe inspiring, and transpersonal.

Let me end this section with a self-disclosure. I first met book editor Diana Fosha face to face in February 2003, at a 1-day AEDP workshop organized and hosted by the Washington School of Psychiatry in Washington, DC.[8] In the Q&A segment, near the end of her presentation, I asked Diana, "Why is it that in core state, the phenomenology looked so much like a spiritual experience?" Diana's response was at once precise, wise, enlightening, and fascinating: "It is in core state that I now know why people would believe in God!" Fourteen years later, we have come full circle; Diana contends that in AEDP we "pay attention to facts of the sort dear to mystics" (James, 1890) while reflecting on them in "*neuro*scientific *and phenomenological* ways" (Fosha, 2017, p. 204).

## CLINICAL ILLUSTRATIONS

Shifting from theory to practice, I offer the following annotated vignettes, from two clients, which illustrate how the phenomenology of metatherapeutic processing and the hypothesized neurobiological insights operate together underneath the clinical conversation in AEDP.[9]

### Monica, Vignette 1: "It Feels Right"

Monica, a Caucasian woman in her late 20s—who incidentally is a neuroscience researcher—returned to psychotherapy to deal with emotions regarding both her cancer treatment and her recent divorce (Yeung, 2010). The transcript that follows comes from Session 3, with Monica emotionally recalling a recent experience with her oncologist when he mistook her for another client. In this transcript I point out examples of tremulous affect and the "click" of new understanding, mindful awakening, and spirals of transformation. As I slow the pace down, I speculate, on the basis of the hypotheses outlined earlier, that mutual smart vagus activation is taking place. (N.B.: All the neurobiological descriptions in the clinical vignettes are to be considered speculation and hypothesizing. For the sake of brevity, please assume those qualifiers.)

The first part of the session involved work to decrease Monica's anxiety (State 1 work); I helped her slow down the pace of her affect, which in turn helped her access the emotions of anger, which ushered in State 2 processing.

---

[8]A note on usage: With the genre of self disclosure, I have decided to address Dr. Diana Fosha by her first name; otherwise, I have adopted the standard academic address by last name throughout the chapter.
[9]Aspects of the clients' identities and backgrounds have been disguised to protect confidentiality.

The State 2 work involved a portrayal (see Medley, Chapter 8, this volume, for a description of State 2 emotion processing work and the use of portrayals to achieve it): What unfolded was a fantasized interaction between Monica and her oncologist. She imagined "shaking" the oncologist and asserting strongly, on her own behalf, "Just do your job! It's not that hard!" In this vignette, which follows that portrayal, I as the therapist am working in State 3 to help the client metaprocess the consequences of her being able to experience and express her anger.

**THERAPIST (T):** (*Slowly, tenderly, being mindful*) What is it like for you to hear me? **[Checking client's receptiveness to my acceptance of her assertive expression]** What is it like for you inside? **[Metaprocessing query, Micro-Step 1]**

**CLIENT (C):** (*Tentatively*) I think maybe it feels right. (*More confidently*) Even when I feel this way based on the situation, it feels right. **[Core state: feels right]**

**T:** (*Tender, playful*) It feels right. **[Mirroring client's assertion]**

**C:** (*With emphasis*) Yeah! **[Amplification of assertion, as a result of dyadic mirroring]**

**T:** Could we make room for that feeling, right feeling? **[Privileging positive emotion]**

**C:** (*Assertively*) Like it feels right to be angry in a justified way.

**T:** Absolutely.

**C:** . . . Like it feels like an expression of something I would normally not express. **[Transformational experience for client]**

**T:** That's right.

**C:** So it's weird, but it's good. . . . **[Tremulous affect]**

**T:** We'll go with that.

**C:** Like it's new, but it feels like this is how it's supposed to be, or you know . . . **[Simultaneous tremulousness and core state, new and right, both transformational experiences, awaiting further metaprocessing]**

**T:** We'll go with both . . . well, it's up to you. We could go to the new feeling, the newness of it. Or we could go to the "it feels right," and we could go with that. They are all connected. **[New and right: notice and seize]**

**C:** (*Gazes down in self-reflection*)

**T:** My gut reaction tells me, why don't we make room for the right feeling first. **[VEN-mediated awareness, empathy, intuitive timing and focus]**

C:   I think you're right, that's what I was thinking too . . . **[Confirming therapist's intuitive timing and focus]** The way it feels is sort of like I'm treating myself like I treat someone else. If that happened to someone else, I'd be very upset on their behalf. **[Emerging self compassion]**

T:   Precisely.

C:   You know what I mean? But for myself, I don't usually afford myself the same. **[Reflection contrasting self-denial of before with the self-compassion of now before the transformation of now]**

T:   That's right. So we'll stay with that feeling now. OK? **[Empathic attunement, mirroring]**

C:   Yeah . . .

T:   We'll slow down a little more. **[Deepening mutual smart vagus activation]**

C:   OK . . . we'll have time to put it into words but now we will pay attention to that experience. **[Dyadic mindfulness]** That feeling inside. **[Focus on affect]** (*Eyes closed, attention inward, mindful*)

T:   (*Very slow pace, tenderly*) **[Deepening smart vagus activation]** Where that right feeling is **[Somatic focus]**. . . . Just staying with it, by that I mean, just being attentive to it. No need to analyze it. **[Avoiding defensive intellectualization]** Staying with the whole thing . . . (*Client nods.*) . . . And allow the images to gradually form . . . from that place. And we'll notice what comes up. Maybe in the form of pictures, words, or impulses, we'll welcome them.

C:   (*Eyes closed, mindful*) I just saw like, more of an image, that's sort of vegetative kind of growth **[Image that captures the emerging transformation]**. Jungle kind of context I guess.

T:   Jungle kind of context . . .

C:   (*Waving hands*) Yeah, like life and growth. **[Deepening emerging transformation]** Green. Like just that vegetative, you're surrounded by nature, that kind of thing. **[Right brain–dreamlike imagery, a correlate of flourishing, emerging spirals of transformation]** And as for word, it was just *love*. **[The integration of experience and reflection yields love.]**

T:   Stay with that. **[Privileging positive shift]**

C:   I think for myself, it has to do with settling in, and it's something like that. It's sort of, allowing myself. **[Self-compassion; therapist allowing this]** And treating myself. Something like that . . .

T:   Absolutely . . .

C: (*Declarative tone*) I love myself. **[Deepening self-compassion, core state]** I do a lot to try to take care of myself, but this is like another piece of the puzzle.

T: It's absolutely another piece of the puzzle. It is a deeper experience. **[Further mirroring]**

C: (*Gently, mindful assertiveness*) And it's just like it's subtle, a really subtle kind of love like not gushing by any means, it's just trickling or filtering kind of . . .

T: (*Slowly, mindful*) Sure. Could we make room for that as well? (*Client nods in resonance.*) . . . Go inside, staying with that image. (*Pace slows.*) Savoring and welcoming that love for yourself, that green. **[Privileging positive shift and affect]** Staying with that. (*Client nods in resonance . . . 10-second pause*) **[Deepening mutual smart vagus activation]** And noticing what else comes up.

C: The sense of, like, a tipping point or a breaking point or something. **[Experience of quantum change: deepening transformation]** I feel closer to some kind of growth, but I'm not really sure what it is . . .

T: Stay with that.

C: I feel like something's changing . . . **[Deepening spirals of transformation]**

T: Stay with the tipping point. The breaking point. The changing . . . emerging stuff. **[Privileging positive transformative emergent experience]** Simply noticing, no need to hurry. **[Inviting mindful attention: Micro-Steps 1 and 2]**

C: I don't know, it also kind of, as much as it is a tipping point, I also see foundational things too. **[Rich imagery, deepening spirals of transformation]** Or maybe I don't know, things are being laid down or solidified . . . **[Core state]**

T: Sure.

C: . . . It's difficult to probe it, like I'm really trying. **[Minimal anxious striving]**

T: (*Tenderly, firmly*) Again, we will put a gentle, curious, compassionate, observing. **[Inviting nonstriving]** What it is like inside. Gradually welcoming it to the fore.

C: I just thought of . . . sort of like an awakening. **[Mindful awakening]**

T: An awakening . . .

C: And it's almost like there's another facet or aspect of me that's starting to come out that I'm really not that comfortable with yet. **[More**

**tremulous affect combined with core state: more true self emergence]** But it feels right. **["Click" of recognition]** You know what I mean?

T:    Absolutely.

The deepening spirals of transformation continue for Monica for the next 5 minutes. Core state phenomenology emerges as she expresses compassion for both herself and others.

### Monica, Vignette 2: "Yeah, That's Who I Am!"

The following vignette is the immediate continuation of the previous discussion; in it, Monica demonstrates openness to the reconstruction of her own autobiographical narrative as she imagines the assertion of her own needs in the future. The session demonstrates the openness and centeredness of core state, reconstruction of autobiographical narrative in light of the transformational experience and, finally, integration and OFC activation.

C:    I always considered that the weaker parts of myself, but as these things come out, I'm feeling like maybe this is a strength. **[Shift in perspective]** It's adding like a strength to strength almost. **[Emerging reconstruction of parts of self-narrative]**

T:    Stay with that. Especially where you are noticing that in the body now. **[Inviting somatic focus]**

C:    Mostly in my chest.

T:    Stay with that.

C:    Even like anchoring down into my gut or the core of my being, you know? **[Emergence of core state]**

T:    Stay with that. **[Privileging positive transformation, savoring: Micro-Step 2]** Again, welcoming it. **[Affirmation]**

C:    Mmmm.

T:    Cherishing it. And then let it lead us, guide us. **[Deepening savoring]**

C:    The sense of . . . you hide these things away, you do it to protect yourself or protect others from the intensity of your feelings or whatever the reason is. **[Reflection of old self narrative]** But it's almost like that's your greatest treasure in a way, that's how I'm starting to feel now. **[Deepening new self narrative]** You've been keeping this stuff, but maybe this is your best gift too. **[Further deepening of new self narrative]** Or it's somehow . . .

T:    Stay with this stuff!

C:    It doesn't have to be like poisonous kind of "Oh, nobody can be here." Maybe it can be . . . (*Big smile of contentment*) I don't know. It's what it feels like . . .

T: That's right . . . now let it guide us. Staying with this stuff. This best gift that you have to offer. The strength on strength. Which is experienced in your core right now. **[Mirroring experience near language]** Staying with that. **[Encouraging focus on experience]**

C: It's new. You don't know how people are going to respond. It's mostly like that, it's closer to your real self **[True self, experience near language]**, so if people respond badly or reject that, then it's that much more difficult to put out there because of those reasons. **[Potential relational rejection needing correction]**

T: (*Smiling, tender*) What do you see in my face? **[Relational invitation to client to be mindful and aware of therapist's affective expression]**

C: (*Chuckling*) Like, acceptance **[Corrective relational experience]**

T: Especially when you say it's closer to your real self! What do you see in my face? **[More relational invitation to client to be mindful and aware of therapist's affective expression]**

C: Joy, even?

T: And what's that like for you to see my joy on my face?

C: It challenges the fear, it challenges the hesitance and it encourages expression and taking risks to be authentic and feel things. **[Deepening corrective emotional and relational experience; resonates with Fredrickson's (2009) finding that accessing positive emotional states helps downregulate negative emotional states]**

T: May I invite you to stay with that?

C: (*Nodding*) **[Receptiveness]**

T: Taking in the joy at the degree that you're comfortable with, and then let's approach that real self. **[Savoring and privileging positive transformational experience]**

C: (*Nodding, chuckling*) Yeah. 'Cause I guess it's my mind more that makes this duality, but it's really just one person. **[Emerging integration of parts of self, up dialing OFC activation]**

T: Yes.

C: It's not really like there's two "me"s inside my body. There are just parts of me that are more dominant and, I don't know, like I really want to get there . . .

T: (*Tenderly, slowly, firmly*) We will try. **["We" language]** In this present moment, and the way to do it, simply to slow down **[Deepening smart vagus activation]** continuing to slow down. That's right, breathing into that place. (*Client nods, gazes down, meditative*) . . . Breathing out of that place. Bring with it a curiosity.

C:  Yeah . . .

T:  Simply seeing that place, noticing that place. And then notice what comes up. **[Inviting dyadic mindful awareness]**

C:  (*Declarative*) It's kind of like a sense of, "Oh! Who are you?" (*Speaking to herself*) Maybe not so much that, but "Nice to meet you," or like there's some sort of "Yeah, that's who I am!" **[True self declaration]** . . . a little bit of, as much as it's unfamiliar, uncomfortable, it's also incredibly familiar at the same time.

T:  Stay with that . . .

C:  . . . Like it feels like I guess, it would be like reconnecting . . . Yeah! Reconnecting **[Integration, OFC activation]** . . . or like meeting a sibling you didn't know you had, but you somehow always knew. It's that kind of feeling, you know? **[The paradox of core state: discovering something one has always known]**

T:  Looking back at that moment of meeting . . . like with . . . your . . . self? **[Affirming integration]** What's that like for you? **[Metaprocessing query]**

C:  (*Gazing up*) **[Sign of integration, and OFC activation]** It fills me with some longing or desire to figure this out, or to be more authentic and not hold back so much **[Activation of motivation for true self living]** . . . I feel much more centered here. . . . This feels better! How do I do this more? Can I have homework or something? To practice this? **[Motivation for more change; exploratory zest]**

T:  Yes, you can! Promise you we'll get to the homework, promise. (*Client laughs in amusement*) . . . But first now, looking back at what we just did. I'm curious, what it's like for you having done this work here, in the last while? **[Another spiral of metaprocessing]**

C:  (*Animated, excited*) It just accelerates (actual client word) so many of the processes to making progress in some ways, just because I really feel an acceptance or openness or you know, it's OK. . . . It's sort of like every cell in my body is acutely aware of that. **[Enlivening affect]** It's just that my brain doesn't know what's happening exactly. But my body is like "Oh! Something's happening! Things are changing!" **[Tremulous affects: The mind has not yet caught up with what the body knows; enlivening affect crescendoing]** and things I've wanted to work on, and been struggling through not such a struggle anymore, it's the groundwork or foundation is there . . .

T:  I was just going to ask you, how does it look like to you, from this perspective, looking into the future?

C:  I feel almost, pregnant with potential or like you know? **[Enlivening affect; pregnant with new self, new possibilities]**

T: Mmm . . .

C: I just feel like I'm learning a lot and growing a lot in various aspects . . . I feel willful, and purposeful, determined, toward the life that I'm living and the steps that I'm taking. **[Autobiographical narrative reconstructing with deep sense of meaning and agency]**

In this vignette we witness the emergence of State 3 phenomenology: the "click" of recognition, tremulous affect, and enlivening affect, together with State 4 phenomenology. These positive affects were noticed and seized by the therapist, privileged, and affirmed with an invitation the to client to savor the positive experience. Spirals of metatherapeutic processing climaxed in core state with a true self declaration and meaningful reconstruction of the self narrative.

## Steffan, Vignette 1: Unfamiliar and Sad

Steffan, a Caucasian man in his mid-60s and an avid meditator in the Hindu Vedanta tradition, came to the first session of treatment. He wanted to work through issues of "aloneness" and "fear of being overwhelmed by emotions." State 1 work in that first session began with me leading the client–therapist dyad to cocreate an intersubjective field of security to undo Steffan's aloneness; he was receptive to my presence. The unfolding of State 2 was reflected in working with coordinated relational experience and involving continued deepening connection between therapist and client, manifesting as periods of silent, mutual gazing and delight in being in each other's presence. This vignette demonstrates tremulous affect and the mourning of self. Relational synchronicity and VENs awareness, empathy, and intuitive timing are at work here in State 3. Therapist and client emerge from the silence and begin to metaprocess the relational experience they have been coconstructing as the client reflects on his experience.

C: It's so . . . familiar with being, that there's something unfamiliar. **[Shift toward positive yet unfamiliar closeness; tremulous affect]**

T: Absolutely! **[Affirmation: privileging emergence of new and positive]** I also want to check in with that part . . . that felt alone. How's that part now? **[Metaprocessing inquiry: confirming positive shift]**

C: (*With declarative emphasis*) It doesn't feel *so* alone **[Unbearable aloneness partially undone]** But it feels . . . actually, when you said it . . . you know, I felt . . . less alone? . . . Sad. **[Metatherapeutic process with mourning the self]**

T: Yes! Let's make room for the sadness. **[Staying with mourning the self]**

C: It feels overwhelming. **[Original anxiety of emotional dysregulation]**

T: (*Very tender, firm*) That's right . . . I'm here with you. You will not be alone with that feeling. **[Further undoing of aloneness, dyadic regulation** of affect, corrective emotional and relational experience] I sense the sadness. **[VENs awareness and empathy]**

C: (*Tearful, tremulous*) Yeah . . . I feel like . . . I spent a long time covering it up. **[Chronic cover-up, metatherapeutic reflection on the why of mourning]**

T: Yes. Thank you for . . . being here **[Deepening affirmation of transformation: wholly being present, no cover-up]** . . . the sadness . . . let's welcome **[Privileging and savoring positive shift]** . . . the sadness . . . (*Silent mutual gaze for 60 seconds*) . . . **[Client–therapist VENs awareness, empathy, and intuitive timing]** . . . And we'll give the tears some words! Give it a voice. **[Inviting metatherapeutic reflection]**

C: . Yeah . . . you know . . . (*Clears throat*) . . . I don't think that tears are for sadness. **[Sudden shift in the meaning of client's tears]**

T: OK. Say more. **[Openness to the shift. Staying out of the way]**

C: I'm not sure . . . but it seemed like . . . it was . . . there was initially like tears of sadness **[Confirming earlier mourning of self]** and then quickly it turned into this . . . relief . . . release. . . . And maybe just have that sadness *seen* . . . about . . . I think . . . but the tears became something different. **[VENs nuanced awareness: sadness shifting into relief, maybe healing affects associated with feeling seen]**

## Steffan, Vignette 2: Expansiveness, Openness, Aliveness

The next discussion immediately followed the previous dialogue, both of which occurred in the first session of psychotherapy. In it you will see intimate tenderness, truth sense, and a transpersonal unitive state, indicating perhaps that the smart vagus and OFC are dialing up. Relational synchronicity is illustrated in VENs awareness; empathy and intuitive timing are in full throttle. This vignette demonstrates a client shifting into State 4: core state experiencing.

T: Right, indeed, indeed. And what's that like, for the tears, to be seen? **[Metaprocessing inquiry, VENs' intuitive grasp of client's sadness seen as critical]**

C: It feels . . . the feeling of it . . . it expand . . . expansiveness. **[Rounds of metaprocessing culminating in emergence of core state phenomenology, somatic expansiveness as smart vagus activation]**

T: Wow! Stay with the expansiveness. Savor it . . . **[Affirmation: privileging positive emergent experience, staying out of the way]** (*Silent mutual gazing for 35 seconds; Micro-Steps 2 and 3*) **[VENs awareness, empathy, and intuitive timing]** . . . What's coming up? **[Deepening core state exploration]**

C: Ummm. There's this huh . . . just . . . huh . . . in light of being here . . . umm . . . just . . . this . . . this has been really great, I feel, so, happy that, to have met you. **[Core state: metaprocessing with tenderness towards therapist]**

T: Wow! (*Gazes away briefly*) I'm trying to find a right word to . . . happiness doesn't quite describe what I feel inside. Joy is more like it. To know you . . . very deep inside. Think you know what I mean? **[Self-disclosure of joy associated with an emergent soul-to-soul meeting; core state]**

C: (*Nods vigorously*) I do, I do. **[Confirming deepening intimacy; dyadic core state]**

T: Say more about what you're noticing inside. Yourself. Or your state of mind, or your body. **[Further exploration of core state]**

C: Ummm . . . I can still feel this openness (*Both hands gesturing an expansive open space*) . . . you know. **[Somatic openness as smart vagus activation]**

T: Mm-hmm.

C: . . . And the . . . tightness, is sort of hovering on the peripheral. **[Minimal anxiety, amygdala dialing down, further dialing up of OFC]**

T: Right.

C: So it's not, uh . . . (*Hand gesturing to indicate minimal anxiety that is not interfering with him*)

T: Sure. Honor that. **[Honoring his new experience]** . . . (*Silent mutual gaze for 10 seconds*) . . . **[VENs awareness, empathy, and intuitive timing]** . . . Any feelings you have toward yourself? Your witness, your-self, even as we speak, right now, in this state of mind and body—how would you describe that . . . sense you may have for yourself. **[Deepening exploration of intra-relational aspects of core state]**

C: One word that comes up . . . and that, uuh, that is "aliveness." **[Vitality affect associated with both the enlivening affects and core state: smart vagus activation]**

T: (*Nods in resonance*) Stay with the aliveness. **[Core state work, simply following the client, staying out of the way]**

C: And, not a thought. It's a feeling. **[VENs self-awareness]**

T: Yes. (*Nods in resonance, tender smile*) Stay with that feeling. That experi-ence. The expansiveness, the aliveness. The openness. **[Platforming the next intervention]** If I may be allowed to share some experience with mine, here are some of these moments where . . . you and I, I feel . . . no boundaries. If you know what I mean, not in the sense of professional boundaries, but ego boundaries. Do you sense that? **[Self-disclosure of nondual unitive transpersonal experience]**

C: Yes! . . . **[Tonal emphasis indicative of experiential recognition of the dyadic aspects of the transpersonal unitive state]**

T: What's that like for you? **[Metaprocessing inquiry]** To . . . or at least some form of the dissolution of the ego boundaries. What's that like for you? . . . **[Deepening exploration of transpersonal experience]**

C: Ummm . . . it's new . . . **[This newness is associated with the client's experience of non-duality in a relationship]**

T: To experience that . . .

C: It's new and it's nonthreatening. **[Absence of anxiety]**

T: Right. Exactly! **[Nonthreatening experience as transcending the ego, not fragmentation]** . . . (*3-second pause*) Wow! **[Left brain catching up: recognition of the awe-inspiring immensity of the transpersonal unitive experience]**

C: (*Staying in mutual gaze with therapist, mutual tender smile*) It feels like there's a rush of . . . you know . . . a child . . . that feels safe enough to be seen. **[Encounter of a vulnerable "soul" part]**

T: Stay with that child. Thank you for allowing me to see . . . that child. To see, to witness. (*Mutual tender, delightful gaze for 20 seconds*) **[Therapist–client VENs awareness, empathy, and intuitive timing; shared dyadic core state]**

C: (*In declarative tone*) I never thought of this before but . . . just want this child . . . all the child really wanted was to feel, to know it's loved. **[Truth sense, new understanding]**

T: (*With emphasis*) Indeed, indeed. And what do you sense from me? **[Fearless openness to taboo-breaking acknowledgment of therapist–client "love" in therapeutic relationship]**

C: (*Delighted*) I sense that love. **[Making the implicit explicit; deep corrective relational experience]**

T: (*Smiles tenderly*) Yup. Very much so. Very much so. **[Affirmation and recognition]** Deep . . . cherishing **[Nuanced terminology]** . . . And deep . . . lovingkindnness **[Nuanced terminology]** . . . toward you. **[Explicit use of cherishing and loving-kindness as therapeutic love]**

C: (*Nods in resonance*) Thank you. **[Receptiveness of therapist's cherishing and loving-kindness]**

T: You're most welcome. Thank you. For receiving it. (*Mutual delightful, tender gaze in silence for 20 seconds*) **[Therapist–client VENs awareness, empathy, and intuitive timing]**

In this vignette we bear witness to the transpersonal dissolution of ego boundaries between therapist and client, a profound mutual soul-to-soul encounter in this dyadic coshared core state. This nondual experience emerged as a deep authentic connection, in state of dyadic mindfulness, and immersed in a cocreated intersubjective field of loving-kindness in a coordinated core state experience of each member of the therapeutic dyad.

## CONCLUSION

I hypothesized that the positive transformational affects and core state yielded by metatherapeutic processing in AEDP activate the OFC and its highly integrative capacity. The fundamental importance of metatherapeutic processing is further supported by Fredrickson's (2001) broaden-and-build theory of positive emotions and the compelling evidence that access to positive emotions downregulates states of fear and other negative emotions and leads to enhanced mental capacity and the building of personal resources, thus promoting flourishing, resilience, and overall health. The neurobiological substrate of core state at the physiological level is associated with activation of the smart vagus that maximizes subjective and intersubjective adaptability by promoting self-soothing, cardiac energy conservation, immune function, and prosocial behaviors that facilitate health, growth, and restoration. The insula, frequently coactivated with the ACC, also plays a significant role: It mediates the integrated embodiment of experience and, given that it is rich with VENs, implicates it in experiences such as subjective awareness of self, compassion, and intuition. I explored all these phenomena in the preceding clinical examples both intrapsychically, as they operate for the individual undergoing the transformative process, and relationally or dyadically, as they operate for both members of the therapeutic dyad. Given resonance circuits, the dyadic nature of these phenomena only amplifies them, thus potentiating their effectiveness.

Finally, it is in core state that we experience our innermost authentic self-in-the-world, our own felt sense of sacredness or transcendence (Yeung, 2010; Yeung & Cheung, 2009; Yeung et al., 2019). This sense of sacredness and transcendence is shared with the major contemplative traditions of our civilization, which function to undo our sense of existential aloneness. It is in core state that we discover that we share the plight of the suffering around the globe, that AEDP can be our way of being-in-the world. We can accomplish this by cultivating the spirit of African *ubuntu*, which holds that all humans are bonded universally. Or of the ancient Greeks, including Socrates, who lived a therapeutic way of life. Or of the Hebrew prophets, who subverted the prevailing establishment and cried with the oppressed people. Or of the ancient Chinese sages, who urged us to see each other as fellow brothers and sisters. Or by living a bodhisattva's way of life, seeking to share enlightenment with others. In this way we will always be on the path of becoming—or realizing ourselves! Never alone, together with one another.

## REFERENCES

Allman, J. M., Tetreault, N. A., Hakeem, A. Y., Manaye, K. F., Semendeferi, K., Erwin, J. M., Park, S., Goubert, V., & Hof, P. R. (2011). The von Economo neurons in the frontoinsular and anterior cingulate cortex. In J. I. Johnson, H. P. Zeigler, & P. R. Hof (Eds.), *Annals of the New York Academy of Sciences: Vol. 1225. New perspectives on neurobehavioral evolution* (pp. 59–71). New York Academy of Sciences. https://doi.org/10.1111/j.1749-6632.2011.06011.x

Allman, J. M., Watson, K. K., Tetreault, N. A., & Hakeem, A. Y. (2005). Intuition and autism: A possible role for Von Economo neurons. *Trends in Cognitive Sciences, 9*(8), 367–373. https://doi.org/10.1016/j.tics.2005.06.008

Burgdorf, J., & Panksepp, J. (2006). The neurobiology of positive emotions. *Neuroscience & Biobehavioral Reviews, 30*(2), 173–187. https://doi.org/10.1016/j.neubiorev.2005.06.001

Cozolino, L. (2014). *The neuroscience of human relationships: Attachment and the developing social brain.* W. W. Norton.

Craig, A. D. (2015). *How do you feel? An interoceptive moment with your neurobiological self.* Princeton University Press.

Damasio, A. (2010). *Self comes to mind: Constructing the conscious brain.* Pantheon Books.

Davidson, R. J., Pizzagalli, D., Nitschke, J. B., & Kalin, N. H. (2003). Parsing the subcomponents of emotion and disorders of emotion: Perspectives from affective neuroscience. In R. J. Davidson, K. R. Scherer, & H. H. Goldsmith (Eds.), *Handbook of affective sciences* (pp. 8–24). Oxford University Press.

Fosha, D. (2000a). Meta-therapeutic processes and the affects of transformation: Affirmation and the healing affects. *Journal of Psychotherapy Integration, 10*(1), 71–97. https://doi.org/10.1023/A:1009422511959

Fosha, D. (2000b). *Transforming power of affect: A model for accelerated change.* Basic Books.

Fosha, D. (2003). Dyadic regulation and experiential work with emotion and relatedness in trauma and disordered attachment. In M. F. Solomon & D. J. Siegel (Eds.), *Healing trauma: Attachment, mind, body, and brain* (pp. 221–281). W. W. Norton.

Fosha, D. (2005). Emotion, true self, true other, core state: Toward a clinical theory of affective change process. *Psychoanalytic Review, 92*(4), 513–551. https://doi.org/10.1521/prev.2005.92.4.513

Fosha, D. (2009). Emotion and recognition at work: Energy, vitality, pleasure, truth, desire and the emergent phenomenology of transformational experience. In D. Fosha, D. J. Siegel, & M. F. Solomon (Eds.), *The healing power of emotion: Affective neuroscience, development, clinical practice* (pp. 172–203). W. W. Norton.

Fosha, D. (2010). Wired for healing: Thirteen ways of looking at AEDP. *Transformance: The AEDP Journal, 1*(1).

Fosha, D. (2011, March 11). *Using dyadic mindfulness to enhance receptive affective capacity in both patient and therapist* [Paper]. Healing Moments in Trauma Treatment conference, Los Angeles, CA.

Fosha, D. (2013a). A heaven in a wild flower: Self, dissociation, and treatment in the context of the neurobiological core self. *Psychoanalytic Inquiry, 33*(5), 496–523. https://doi.org/10.1080/07351690.2013.815067

Fosha, D. (2013b). Turbocharging the affects of healing and redressing the evolutionary tilt. In D. J. Siegel & Marion F. Solomon (Eds.), *Healing moments in psychotherapy* (pp. 129–168). W. W. Norton.

Fosha, D. (2017). How to be a transformational therapist: AEDP harnesses innate healing affects to re-wire experience and accelerate transformation. In J. Loizzo, M. Neale, & E. J. Wolf (Eds.), *Advances in contemplative psychotherapy: Accelerating healing and transformation* (pp. 204–219). Routledge/Taylor & Francis Group. https://doi.org/10.4324/9781315630045-18

Fosha, D. (2018). Moment-to-moment guidance of clinical interventions by AEDP's healing-oriented transformational phenomenology. *Pragmatic Case Studies in Psychotherapy, 14*(2), 87–114. https://doi.org/10.14713/pcsp.v14i2.2038

Fosha, D., & Thoma, N. (2020). Metatherapeutic processing supports the emergence of flourishing in psychotherapy. *Psychotherapy.* Advance online publication. https://doi.org/10.1037/pst0000289

Fosha, D., Thoma, N., & Yeung, D. (2019). Transforming emotional suffering into flourishing: Metatherapeutic processing of positive affect as a trans-theoretical vehicle for change. *Counseling Psychology Quarterly, 32*(3–4), 563–572. https://doi.org/10.1080/09515070.2019.1642852

Fosha, D., & Yeung, D. (2006). Accelerated Experiential-Dynamic Psychotherapy: The seamless integration of emotional transformation and dyadic relatedness at work. In G. Stricker & J. Gold (Eds.), *A casebook of psychotherapy integration* (pp. 165–184). American Psychological Association. https://doi.org/10.1037/11436-013

Fredrickson, B. L. (2001). The role of positive emotions in positive psychology. The broaden-and-build theory of positive emotions. *American Psychologist, 56*(3), 218–226. https://doi.org/10.1037/0003-066X.56.3.218

Fredrickson, B. L. (2004). The broaden-and-build theory of positive emotions. *Philosophical Transactions of the Royal Society of London: Series B. Biological Sciences, 359*(1449), 1367–1378. https://doi.org/10.1098/rstb.2004.1512

Fredrickson, B. L. (2009). *Positivity: Groundbreaking research reveals how to embrace the hidden strength of positive emotions, overcome negativity, and thrive.* Random House.

Fredrickson, B. L., Cohn, M. A., Coffey, K. A., Pek, J., & Finkel, S. M. (2008). Open hearts build lives: Positive emotions, induced through loving-kindness meditation, build consequential personal resources. *Journal of Personality and Social Psychology, 95*(5), 1045–1062. https://doi.org/10.1037/a0013262

Fredrickson, B. L., & Joiner, T. (2002). Positive emotions trigger upward spirals toward emotional well-being. *Psychological Science, 13*(2), 172–175. https://doi.org/10.1111/1467-9280.00431

Golding, K., & Hughes, D. (2012). *Creating loving attachments: Parenting with PACE to nurture confidence and security in the troubled child.* Jessica Kingsley.

Hansen, R., & Mendius, R. (2009). *Buddha's brain: The practical neuroscience of happiness, love and wisdom.* New Harbinger.

James, W. (1890, March). The hidden self. *Scribner's,* pp. 361–373.

Kabat-Zinn, J. (2005). *Full catastrophe living: Using the wisdom of your body and mind to face stress, pain and illness.* Bantam Dell.

Kok, B. E., & Fredrickson, B. L. (2010). Upward spirals of the heart: Autonomic flexibility, as indexed by vagal tone, reciprocally and prospectively predicts positive emotions and social connectedness. *Biological Psychology, 85*(3), 432–436. https://doi.org/10.1016/j.biopsycho.2010.09.005

Lamagna, J., & Gleiser, K. A. (2007). Building a secure internal attachment: An intra-relational approach to ego strengthening and emotional processing with chronically traumatized clients. *Journal of Trauma & Dissociation, 8*(1), 25–52. https://doi.org/10.1300/J229v08n01_03

Marks-Tarlow, T., & Schore, A. N. (2017). How love opens creativity, play and the arts through early right brain development. In T. Marks-Tarlow, M. Solomon, & D. J. Siegel (Eds.), *Play and creativity in psychotherapy* (pp. 64–91). W. W. Norton.

Mencius. (1999). *Mencius* (D. Hinton, Trans.). Counterpoint.

Minagawa-Kawai, Y., Matsuoka, S., Dan, I., Naoi, N., Nakamura, K., & Kojima, S. (2009). Prefrontal activation associated with social attachment: Facial-emotion recognition in mothers and infants. *Cerebral Cortex, 19*(2), 284–292. https://doi.org/10.1093/cercor/bhn081

Moran, D. (2000). *Introduction to phenomenology.* New York: Routledge.

Nitschke, J. B., Nelson, E. E., Rusch, B. D., Fox, A. S., Oakes, T. R., & Davidson, R. J. (2004). Orbitofrontal cortex tracks positive mood in mothers viewing pictures of their newborn infants. *NeuroImage, 21*(2), 583–592. https://doi.org/10.1016/j.neuroimage.2003.10.005

Pando-Mars, K. (2011). Building attachment bonds in AEDP in the wake of neglect and abandonment: Through the lens and practice of AEDP, attachment, and polyvagal theory. *Transformance: The AEDP Journal, 1*(2).

Panksepp, J., & Biven, L. (2012). *The archeology of mind: Neuroevolutionary origins of human emotions.* W. W. Norton.

Panksepp, J., & Northoff, G. (2008). The trans-species core SELF: The emergence of active cultural and neuro-ecological agents through self-related processing within subcortical–cortical midline networks. *Consciousness and Cognition, 18*(1), 193–215. https://doi.org/10.1016/j.concog.2008.03.002

Peterson, C., & Seligman, M. E. P. (2004). *Character strengths and virtues: A handbook and classification.* American Psychological Association.

Porges, S. W. (2011). *The polyvagal theory: Neurophysiological foundations of emotions, attachment, communication, and self regulation.* W. W. Norton.

Prenn, N. (2009). I second that emotion! On self-disclosure and its metaprocessing. In A. Bloomgarden & R. B. Mennuti (Eds.), *Psychotherapist revealed: Therapists speak about self-disclosure in psychotherapy* (pp. 85–99). Routledge.

Prenn, N. (2011). Mind the gap: AEDP interventions translating attachment theory into clinical practice. *Journal of Psychotherapy Integration, 21*(3), 308–329. https://doi.org/10.1037/a0025491

Russell, E. (2015). *Restoring resilience: Discovering your clients' capacity for healing.* W. W. Norton.

Russell, E., & Fosha, D. (2008). Transformational affects and core state in AEDP: The emergence and consolidation of joy, hope, gratitude and confidence in the (solid goodness of the) self. *Journal of Psychotherapy Integration, 18*(2), 167–190. https://doi.org/10.1037/1053-0479.18.2.167

Schoettle, E. (2009). *A qualitative study of the therapist's experience practicing Accelerated Experiential Dynamic Psychotherapy (AEDP): An exploration of the dyadic process from the clinician's perspective* [Unpublished doctoral dissertation]. Wright Institute.

Schore, A. N. (2000). Attachment and the regulation of the right brain. *Attachment & Human Development, 2*(1), 23–47. https://doi.org/10.1080/146167300361309

Schore, A. N. (2012). *The science of the art of psychotherapy.* W. W. Norton.

Siegel, D. J. (2007). *The mindful brain: Reflection and attunement in the cultivation of well-being.* W. W. Norton.

Siegel, D. J. (2010). *Mindsight: The new science of personal transformation.* Random House.

Tugade, M. M., & Fredrickson, B. L. (2004). Resilient individuals use positive emotions to bounce back from negative emotional experiences. *Journal of Personality and Social Psychology, 86*(2), 320–333. https://doi.org/10.1037/0022-3514.86.2.320

Tugade, M. M., Fredrickson, B. L., & Barrett, L. F. (2004). Psychological resilience and positive emotional granularity: Examining the benefits of positive emotions on coping and health. *Journal of Personality, 72*(6), 1161–1190. https://doi.org/10.1111/j.1467-6494.2004.00294.x

Yeung, D. (2010). Transformance and the phenomenology of transformation: Self transcendence as an aspect of core state. *Transformance: The AEDP Journal, 2*(1).

Yeung, D., & Cheung, V. (2009). *The rainbow after: Psychological trauma and Accelerated Experiential Dynamic Psychotherapy.* Ming Fung Press.

Yeung, D., & Fosha, D. (2015). Accelerated Experiential Dynamic Psychotherapy. In E. S. Neukrug (Ed.), *The Sage encyclopedia of theory in counseling and psychotherapy* (Vol. 1, pp. 1–5). Sage. https://doi.org/10.4135/9781483346502.n10

Yeung, D., Fosha, D., Ye Perman, J., & Xu, Y. (2019). After Freud meets Zhuangzi: Stance and the dance of the self-in-transformation with the other-in-contemplative presence. *Psychological Communications, 2*(3), 179–185.

# 14

# "We Are Organized to Be Better Than Fine"

## Building the Transformational Theory of AEDP 2.0

Diana Fosha

ollowing the thread of energy and vitality, with its intimate linking to positive neuroplasticity, in this chapter I attempt to expand the conceptual framework that supports accelerated experiential dynamic psychotherapy (AEDP) 2.0. I seek to do so through dialogue with certain developments in emotion science and neurobiology that allow speculations on neurobiological and emotion-based processes that underlie AEDP's mechanisms of transformational change. If Chapter 1 of this volume is the *what*—that is, the fundamentals—of AEDP, and Chapters 2 through 13 are the *how*—how those fundamentals are translated into clinical practice and applied to different clinical concerns—then this 14th chapter is about the *why* of it all. Seeking to integrate the preceding work, it will be the last and latest iteration of the evolving theory of healing and transformation of what we have come to call AEDP 2.0.

This chapter consists of five main sections. In the first, I articulate a taxonomy of positive affects that arise in the context of experiential work with healing and transformation. In the sections that follow, I discuss various bodies of work in neurobiology and emotion science related to how transformation takes place and is integrated: positive neuroplasticity, the energy management function of emotion, the broaden-and-build theory of positive emotion, the evolutionary mandate to flourish, and the neurobiological core-self.[1] Each of

---

[1] I follow the late Jaak Panksepp's usage and hyphenate "core-self" (cf. Panksepp & Northoff, 2009).

https://doi.org/10.1037/0000232-015
*Undoing Aloneness and the Transformation of Suffering Into Flourishing: AEDP 2.0*, D. Fosha (Editor)

these aspects of basic science corresponds to, and has implications for, central aspects of AEDP, both supporting and further illuminating them. After that discussion, I offer a reverie on how a neurobiologically informed conceptualization of the core-self can shed light on transformance glimmers and their detection in State 1, and "this is me" core state phenomena in State 4, as well as the intrinsic connection between them.

The chapter concludes with a brief articulation of the transformational theory of AEDP 2.0 that synthesizes the insights of the five bodies of science presented and speculates on their translation into AEDP 2.0 and its hypothesized mechanisms of change. As a result, the transformational theory of AEDP 2.0 emerges enlarged, with a fresh coherence. I conclude with a discussion of one of the finer points of AEDP 2.0 terminology: the meaning of "core" redefined.

## A BRIEF TAXONOMY OF ENERGY-ENRICHING POSITIVE AFFECTS

*Positive affects* are the phenomenological expression of processes that underlie optimal adaptation, resilience, plasticity, and subjective well-being. Energy-enriching, positive affects are the result of change for the better (e.g., processing a negative emotion to completion leads to a positive emotion). The result of change for the better, positive affects can also function as a marker of change for the better, for both therapist and patient. Furthermore, positive affects can themselves generate further positive affects, as in the more-begets-more upward spiral of the broaden-and-build feedback loop. In short, positive affects are the raw materials of transformational work.

Positive affects themselves have been shown to play a vital role in enhancing health and longevity; immune system and cardiac function, as well as recovery from surgery; secure attachment and resilience-building caregiver–child relationships and practices in early development; relational health throughout the life cycle; and creative and cultural processes that deepen intersubjective connection. They are also key components of the cascading processes that characterize flourishing.

Inspired by Darwin (1872/1965), and with a debt of gratitude to William James (1902/1985), I have sought to describe the varieties of positive affective experiences that emerge in therapy in moments of healing, connection, and transformation. The clinical practice of AEDP has allowed us the opportunity to observe many. We have gone on to name and codify varieties of distinct positive emotions associated with different types of transformational experiences.

My AEDP colleagues and I believe that the specificity and distinctness of the different transformational affects, and other transformational phenomena described in this book, are very much in line with the call of Shiota et al. (2017) for studies with an emphasis on the "differentiation among 'discrete' positive emotions" (p. 618). We also hope to contribute to Lomas's (2017) efforts to catalogue positive emotions in the cultures of the world, by enriching the lexicon with nondenominational words that capture the quality of positive and transformational affective experiences.

Phenomena lie at the nexus of therapy and science. Detailed descriptions of the different affective states associated with safety, connection, ameliorated emotional suffering, and healing can provide a way for therapists of different orientations to speak to each other about clinical phenomena that denote the presence of change. Well-described phenomena also have the potential to enhance communication between psychotherapy researchers and neuroscientists.

The important thing about the taxonomy of positive affects is that it is not just a list. Each positive affect discussed below has been described with some phenomenological granularity on the basis of the observations of AEDP clinicians; moreover, examples of each can be viewed on many psychotherapy videotapes of AEDP practitioners worldwide. We know the situations that evoke each categorical emotion and hence understand their function; the same is true of the positive affects I identify shortly. They are known to occur in specific emotional–relational–transformational situations, at precisely articulated points of the transformational process. Much like we know that danger reliably gives rise to fear and that loss gives rise to grief, we have learned through AEDP that feeling helped when we thought help was not possible reliably gives rise to the *healing affects* (see Item 7 in the list below) and does so, as best as we can tell from our clinical observations, in all of the cultures of the world where AEDP is practiced. Likewise, we know that the healing affects are marked by "good tears" that accompany the experience of feeling moved within oneself, and feeling gratitude to the helping other, and that they arise with regularity in the context of metatherapeutic processing (Iwakabe & Conceição, 2016). Space limitations prevent me from doing such an analysis for each affect listed below; however, the preceding chapters of this volume offer ample and precise examples of each positive affect, clearly linked to particular therapeutic events and to an identifiable point in the transformational process of the session and of the therapy.

The first group of the 10-component taxonomy of positive affect based on AEDP clinical work follows:

1. The *safety feeling*, that is, the felt sense associated with feeling safe

2. The *vitality affects*, the positive somatic and affective markers of transformance and of transformational processes that are on track, for example, a fleeting smile, an exhale, a brightening of the eyes, a sideways tilt of the head

3. The *receptive affective experiences*, that is, affective experiences of feeling felt, feeling seen, feeling loved, feeling cared for, and feeling delighted in, that are the result of "taking in" that which the secure-attachment engendering figure is offering

4. The *relational "we" affects* of relational resonance and of being in sync

5. The *delight* of the intersubjective knowing of the other

6. The *postbreakthrough affects*, for example, relief, release, feeling better, clearer, and lighter, that follow the processing to completion of a core affective experience

7. The affects associated with the release of *adaptive action tendencies*: determination to act, competence, confidence, initiative, agency, as well as experiences of agency, will, and desire arising as expressions of the self (see Chapter 9, this volume)

8. The *"click" of recognition* evoked by a match between something inside the person and something outside the self that is deemed salient to the self

Two more classes of positive affects each deserve their own paragraphs because each contains multiple discrete positive affects within each class and each is associated with a particular aspect of the transformational process. They are the *transformational affects* that emerge during metatherapeutic processing (i.e., State 3 work), and the affective phenomena of core-state, associated with the fundamentally integrative State 4. Whereas all State 3 transformational affects have contrast as intrinsic to them (i.e., the contrast of the good of now compared with the painful of before, which makes them congruent with Ecker et al.'s, 2012, work on memory reconsolidation), the State 4 affective phenomena of core state are fundamentally unitive, and this makes them congruent with the spiritual and contemplative traditions of the world, East and West, northern hemisphere and southern hemisphere (see Chapter 13, this volume). Below is a non-finite list of the affects associated with each of these two classes of positive affect:

9. *The transformational affects,* what William James (1902/1985) called the "melting emotions and the tumultuous affections connected with the crisis of healing change" (p. 238), include the *healing affects* of gratitude and love toward the other and feeling moved, emotional, or touched within oneself; the *tremulous affects* of positive trepidation, responding to novelty by being poised between fear and excitement, and with support, being able to lean into the latter; the *realization affects,* the "Wow," and "Yes!" associated with grasping the magnitude of the positive change taking place; the *enlivening affects* of exuberance, liveliness, and enthusiasm associated with delight at the surprising unbrokenness of the self; and the *mastery affects* of pride and confidence associated with the undoing of shame and fear

10. The deeply integrative unitive positive affective phenomena of *core state,* a state similar to what William James (1902/1985) called the "state of assurance," are marked by the *truth sense* (Fosha, 2005), a deeply held sense of truth.[2] [N.B.: Although it is true that there is no such thing as "the truth,"

---

[2]Although it is true that there is no such thing as "the truth," there most definitely *is* such a thing as *the experience of truth* in a given moment.

there most definitely is such a thing as *the experience of truth* in a given moment.] The more commonly observed core state phenomena, organized in clusters that share a similar quality, include

- calm;
- clarity, feeling centered;
- simplicity;
- compassion for self and others;
- feeling relaxed or energetic, or both;
- ease, flow, naturalness;
- feeling vital, vibrant, alive;
- *photisms* (James, 1902/1985, p. 223, i.e., phenomena associated with light, such as everything seeming brighter);
- "This is me" phenomena;
- congruence, authenticity, and deep self knowledge;
- openness;
- connection;
- authentic I/Thou–True Self/True Other relating;
- love;
- wisdom, acceptance, and equanimity;
- kindness;
- well-being;
- savoring;
- meaning making;
- a sense of knowing;
- feeling free and unencumbered;
- creativity, spontaneity, and playfulness;
- generativity;
- generosity;
- faith;
- hope; and, last but not least,
- a sense of the sacred and profound.

This is an impressive lexicon of positive, phenomenologically distinct affects associated with distinct transformational situations that are ripe for being put to therapeutic use. Descriptive phenomenology can help transcend local differences and explore global effects. It is possible that different clusters of emergent positive affective phenomena are related to different areas of enhanced therapeutic outcome. Although it is beyond the scope of this chapter to explore those topics or engage in informed speculation, ideas such as these can be addressed more rigorously once there is further empirical work providing differentiation among discrete positive emotions.

What *is* possible, and very definitely *within* the scope of this chapter, however, is to enter into dialogue with constructs and theories coming from emotion science and neurobiology to help us understand both how positive affects function to achieve their beneficial results and how we can make better use of them. I now go on to explore some possible mechanisms that may shed further light on how AEDP achieves its results.

## AEDP IN DIALOGUE WITH RECENT DEVELOPMENTS IN NEUROBIOLOGY AND EMOTION SCIENCE

In this section, I present four developments in the fields of neurobiology and emotion science: (a) work on positive neuroplasticity by Norman Doidge, Rick Hanson, Richard Davidson, and others; (b) Bud Craig's work on the differential energy management function of negative and positive emotions; (c) Barbara Fredrickson's broaden-and-build theory of positive emotion; and (d) Antonio Damasio's recent reconceiving of the evolutionary mandate of living things as being to flourish, and not just survive. Each of these aspects of science and emotion science corresponds to, and has implications for, central aspects of AEDP. Energy and neuroplasticity will be our two through lines.

### Positive Neuroplasticity

As AEDP's healing orientation was acquiring an increasingly cogent theory, and its transformational theory started to grow in elaboration and sophistication (Fosha, 2002, 2005, 2006, 2008; Fosha & Yeung, 2006; Russell & Fosha, 2008), research on neuroplasticity came to upend previously held assumptions about the brain's ability to undergo structural change (e.g., Davidson et al., 2000, 2003; Doidge, 2007; Lazar et al., 2005). Prior to this work, it was assumed that after some critical periods in development, connections in the brain were no longer plastic, or able to be rewired. However, notions of the limitations of neuroplasticity to earlier parts of the life cycle became rapidly obsolete as the field awoke to the fact that neuroplasticity—to appropriate Bowlby's (1982) phrase regarding attachment—operates from the cradle to the grave.

The notion of *lifelong, experience-dependent neuroplasticity* refers to the brain's capacity to change, adapt, and reorganize itself by continually forming new neural connections throughout a person's life. The connections among brain cells reorganize in response to changing needs and new experiences. Neuroplasticity is "an intrinsic property of the human brain and represents evolution's invention to enable the nervous system to escape the restrictions of its own genome and thus adapt to environmental pressures, physiological changes, and experiences" (Pascual-Leone et al., 2005, p. 377).

However, writers on neuroplasticity warn that this astonishing capacity gets entrained for both better and worse: Although positive neuroplasticity does indeed manifest in healing and flourishing, negative neuroplasticity underlies trauma, languishing, and deterioration. As Pascual-Leone et al. further wrote in 2005, "The challenge we face is to learn enough about the mechanisms of plasticity to modulate them to achieve the best behavioral outcomes for a given subject" (p. 377).

As a result of work completed in the past 10 years (Bushell et al., 2009; Davidson & Schuyler, 2015; Doidge, 2007, 2016; Hanson & Hanson, 2018; Siegel, 2010), we now know a lot more about the conditions that promote *positive neuroplasticity* (see also Chapter 7, this volume). They include fundamental safety (i.e., the social engagement system needs to be online), focused attention, novelty (which also stimulates the growth of new neurons), emotional arousal that is within the window of tolerance, repetition and the practice of the new skills, positive motivation, and, finally, pleasure and reward (Doidge, 2007; Hanson, 2017; Hanson & Hanson, 2018).

All those conditions obtain in AEDP as it is practiced: *Fundamental safety* (i.e., the fact that the social engagement system needs to be online) is engaged through AEDP's attachment-informed therapeutic stance and relational work. *Focused attention* is engaged through AEDP's practice of maintaining an experiential focus, staying with and returning attention to felt experience, and moment-to-moment tracking of fluctuations in experience (see Chapter 4, this volume). *Novelty* is activated through AEDP's focus on privileging the new and good and is reflected in the tremulous affects, with relational support to contain the (normative) anxiety associated with the new. *Emotional arousal that is within the window of tolerance* is part and parcel of AEDP by means of our affective focus and use of dyadic affect regulation to keep experiences within the window of tolerance while processing both the wrenching negative emotions of emotional suffering and the enriching positive emotions associated with change for the better and flourishing (Fosha et al., 2019). *Repetition and the practice of the new skills* is manifested in AEDP's repeated rounds of metaprocessing. *Positive motivation* and its importance are reflected in the elevation of transformance as a central construct and transformance detection as a central therapeutic activity. Finally, *pleasure and reward* are entrained through AEDP's relentless and systematic focus on experientially processing positive experiences, be they relational, emotional, or transformational (Fosha, 2013b).

Although the claim that AEDP therapeutic work activates positive neuroplasticity is one that can be definitively answered only through empirical methods, it is possible to state with confidence that, as elaborated above, AEDP therapy practice as usual meets all the conditions conducive to promoting positive neuroplasticity.

In a report on worldwide well-being published by the United Nations, Davidson and Schuyler (2015) identified the four constituents of well-being: (a) savoring (the capacity to be able to sustain positive emotion and enjoy it); (b) resilience (the capacity to experience negative emotion and recover from it in a timely fashion); (c) mindfulness (the capacity to focus attention); and (d) empathy, altruism, and prosocial behavior. They concluded that "the circuits we identify as underlying these four constituents of well-being all exhibit plasticity and thus can be transformed through experience and training" (p. 101). The clinical practice of AEDP therapy actively and specifically engages all four of those constituents: savoring through metatherapeutic processing and relational work with receptive affective experience; resilience through the processing of negative emotion to completion; mindfulness through the experiential method; and empathy, altruism, and prosocial behavior through AEDP's deliberately affirmative stance and undoing-aloneness practices as well as the blossoming of patients' compassion and self compassion that we witness in core state.

Davidson and Schuyler (2015) also state, "how these four constituents may synergistically work together has not been studied" (p. 101). Throughout this volume, the chapter authors and I have sought to show clinically how these four constituents may synergistically work together: We look forward to the possibility of process research that will demonstrate empirically AEDP's entrainment of these four constituents (and we most certainly invite collaboration from any researchers who would be interested in further pursuing this kind of work).

## The Broaden-and-Build Theory of Positive Emotion

If negative emotions help us survive by narrowing our focus so that we can attend to and directly address the dangers and challenges facing us, what then is the evolutionary function of positive emotions? That is the question that Barbara Fredrickson asked, and the broaden-and-build theory of positive emotion is her answer. Fredrickson (2001, 2013; Fredrickson & Joiner, 2002, 2018) has proposed that the evolutionary function of positive emotions is to broaden our attentional scope, enlarging our perspective of possibilities for growth and exploration; in turn, this broadening, and the expanded exploration it supports, allows us to then build more resources, which in turn enhance our adaptation and resilience. Also, "the further building of resources gives rise to further positive emotions which then lead to more broadening, and then more building, in ever growing upward spirals of positive affect" (Fredrickson & Joiner, 2002, p. 172).

In an example of convergent evolution, AEDP clinicians came up with a similar upwardly spiraling process, not in the psychology laboratory but in the psychotherapy office. At the same time that Fredrickson (2001) was articulating her ideas, I (Fosha, 2000a, 2000b) was developing mine: Metatherapeutic processing as a clinical method for the systematic processing of transformational experiences and the positive affects associated with them was being offered as a central aspect of AEDP's quest for transformational methods. As has been amply shown in countless clinical examples in the preceding chapters, upward spirals of vitality and energy are also a commonly observed clinical phenomenon during AEDP State 3 metaprocessing work. Although AEDP's metatherapeutic processing was initially developed independently of Frederickson's work, the authors of three recent articles (Fosha et al., 2019; Fosha & Thoma, 2020; Harrison, 2020) have proposed that AEDP effects in the clinical realm the broaden-and-build process that Fredrickson outlined and tested in the laboratory. We now view AEDP's metatherapeutic processing as a clinical methodology for systematically broadening and building the inner resources released by successfully processing trauma and bringing flourishing to bear in psychotherapy sessions.

In the course of working with trauma and emotional suffering and the negative emotions associated with them, through harnessing processes marked by and leading to positive affective phenomena, with their subsequent cascading benefits, AEDP recruits new capacities that open new horizons. As trauma clinicians, it is our mission to work to make those capacities and cascading upward spiral lift phenomena also the province of those whose mental suffering has had them in the grip of downward spirals.

## Energy-Consuming Versus Energy-Enriching Emotions

From an evolutionarily informed perspective on emotion theory, both the negative emotions associated emotional suffering and the positive emotions associated with good connection, change for the better, integration, and well-being are adaptive. However, although both negative and positive emotion are essential to adaptation, they serve distinct evolutionary functions, present different therapeutic opportunities, and signal the need for different therapeutic interventions. Negative emotions signal that something is wrong and that corrective action needs to be taken; positive emotions signal that something is right for the organism and that actions should maximize those opportunities.

Bud Craig's (2005, 2015) work on a region of the cerebral cortex known as the *insula* adds another dimension to this functional differentiation, and it has to do with energy management: He stated that negative and positive emotions are also "neurobiologically differentiated by their roles in the enrichment or expenditure of physical and mental energy," adding that "energization is a key dimension" of "core affect" (Craig, 2005, p. 569). Although indeed both negative and positive emotions are adaptive and serve the organism's survival, negative emotions do so at a cost, whereas positive emotions enhance the organism's energy balance. Craig wrote of negative emotions as *energy-consuming* (in terms of the toll their impact takes on the organism) and of positive emotions as *energy-enriching*.

The negative emotions of "arousal, danger, negative affect, withdrawal (aversive) behavior, and individual-oriented (survival) emotions" (Craig, 2005, p. 566) involving sympathetic activity and mediated by the right forebrain require energy expenditure and, as such, take a physiological toll on the system: thus Craig's (2005) characterization of them as energy-consuming. On the other hand, the positive emotions involving nourishment, safety, positive affect, approach (appetitive) behavior, and group-oriented (affiliative) emotions, mediated by the left forebrain, are associated predominantly with ventral vagal-mediated parasympathetic activity. They are physiologically restorative, thus the characterization of them as energy-enriching. Craig saw the conversion of energy-consuming negative emotions to energy-enriching positive emotions as a highly desirable goal for humanity. This, of course, is precisely what is achieved in AEDP by means of the emotion processing of State 2 work.

As I discussed earlier, energy is central in understanding the spiraling, recursive affective processes, which—at opposite ends of the mental health spectrum—result either in psychopathology and languishing, or in resilience and flourishing (Fosha, 2009b; Fosha & Thoma, 2020; Keyes et al., 2012; Loizzo, 2009; McEwen & Seeman, 1999). Psychopathology and the downward spiraling negative affects associated with stress and trauma progressively drain energy and vitality from the person, leading to more and more emotional withdrawal, which in turn leads to lowered functioning, social isolation, languishing, demoralization, and despair. This is the downward spiral of negative neuroplasticity in action. In contradistinction, when we are healing trauma through processing the associated negative emotions to completion, yielding positive emotions that are further amplified through metatherapeutic processing, we can bring about positive upward spiraling. Upward spiraling positive affects, associated with vibrant mental health, fuel the system with energy and vitality and culminate in health, resilience, flourishing, and well-being (Fosha, 2009a, 2009b; Fredrickson, 2009; Ryan & Frederick, 1997). This, of course, is positive neuroplasticity in exemplary action.

## The Evolutionary Imperative to Flourish

"We are organized to be better than fine," proclaimed Antonio Damasio (2018), one of the premier affective neuroscientists of our time. According to Damasio, we are evolutionarily programmed not only to survive but also to flourish: Flourishing is in our DNA. Damasio proposed that all living creatures—not just humans, or even mammals, mind you—share the imperative of regulating life processes such that life can not only persist but also flourish and project itself into the future. The goal of homeostasis (i.e., life-regulating processes) "is not just to yield the required amount of energy for life to continue, but rather to yield an energy surplus, resulting in a positive energy balance" (Damasio, 2018, p. 45). This surplus of energy is necessary not only to promote survival but also to grow, develop, thrive, and progress; the surplus of energy is necessary to live and adapt optimally, to improve one's own lot in life as well as that of one's own offspring. This, of course, leads to enhanced adaptation. We do not want to live paycheck to paycheck; we want to have money in the bank to be able to invest in what makes life worth living and thus ensure the future of subsequent generations.

Similar arguments have also been made by another premier affective neuroscientist of our time, Jaak Panksepp. He also asserted the importance of going beyond survival. In seeking to articulate an evolutionarily based understanding of the neurobiology of human functioning, he spoke of the importance of *neural energy* to fuel the organism's maximally optimal adaptation (Panksepp & Biven, 2012). A defining characteristic of the dopaminergic SEEKING[3] system, neural energy supports the organism's optimal engagement in what Panksepp called the "mind–body–world connection" (Panksepp & Northoff, 2009, p. 203).

With this in mind, another goal of therapy can be defined as having the therapeutic process itself result in that positive energy balance. The transformational process that AEDP seeks to set in motion meets the evolutionary

---

[3]In using capital letters to refer to any of the seven primary emotional systems Panksepp (1998) described, here "SEEKING," I am honoring both the convention Panksepp used and his request that others follow that convention as well.

imperative Damasio (2018) articulated. *State 2 emotion processing* is a method for achieving what Bud Craig (2005) called for, that is, the transformation of the energy-consuming negative emotions into energy-enriching positive emotions. *State 3 metatherapeutic processing* broadens and builds the energy residing in the positive emotions, with the resulting positive energy balance being able to support enhanced resilience, flourishing, and positive neuroplasticity. The value of going beyond survival to fulfill the evolutionarily based organismic goals of flourishing, thriving, and achieving a positive energy balance is 100% congruent with AEDP's goals of going beyond the amelioration of emotional suffering first by processing the negative emotions associated with it to completion and then by aiming to further promote flourishing through the metatherapeutic processing of the positive affects associated with change for the better.

There is one more neurobiological development whose potential to contribute to an understanding of the mechanisms that make AEDP psychotherapy effective is simultaneously immense and yet barely tapped. Something about it allows us to better understand both how healing from the get-go and transformance detection can operate and what neurobiological mechanisms might be responsible for some of the integrative phenomena of core state.

## THE NEUROBIOLOGY OF THE CORE-SELF

Current neurobiology tells us the *neurobiological core-self*—the very term used by Panksepp to refer to the collection of subcortical midline structures of the brain, dynamically working together in coordinated fashion—is innately wired in: Neither a construction nor an achievement, it is there from the get-go (Damasio, 2010; Northoff & Panksepp, 2008; Panksepp & Northoff, 2009). Affective and somatic, its constituent subcortical structures connected by means of a dopaminergic circuits, deeply supported by and rooted in "the neural correlates that represent organisms as living creatures" (Panksepp & Northoff, 2009, p. 193), the neurobiological core-self is "a dynamic collection of integrated *neural* processes that finds expression in a dynamic collection of integrated *mental* processes [emphasis added]" (Damasio, 2010, p. 9). Located deep in the center of the brain, on either side of the midline, literally at the core of the brain, the neurobiological core-self is automatic and action based. It has coherence, drive, and direction. Operating as an organizer of function and experience, the core-self is intrinsically integrative.

Within a region of the midbrain known as the *periaqueductal gray*, massive interconnections link upper brain stem regions to higher medial regions of the frontal and prefrontal cortices, and vice versa. What results from this bidirectional—that is, both bottom-up and top-down coordination of subcortical and cortical midline structures—is manifested in integrated affective–cognitive processes that give rise to identity, agency, ownership of experience, and behavioral coherence. Reserving the term *neurobiological core-self* for operations mediated solely by subcortical midline structures, the coordination of both subcortical and cortical midline structures constitutes the core-self.

Whereas the neurobiological core-self (mediated solely by subcortical structure) is wired in, the more broadly named core-self, or "self" for short, is not static. Dynamic and emergent, the self develops uniquely as it epigenetically unfolds over the course of a lifetime:

> The core-self is a process through which we gain knowledge about ourselves and our environments. It is this emergent coordination of internality and externality, of a mind–body–world connection . . . which [enables us] . . . to become intentional and . . . empathic agents in the world. (Panksepp & Northoff, 2009, p. 11)

Our uniqueness is not an illusion reflecting human hubris: Guided by recognition processes (see below) that view everything through the valuative lens of salience to self, a path of emergent coordination of internality and externality is forged through each individual self's unique—to it—interactions with the mind–body–world.

### Self-Related Processes and Recognition

Damasio (2018) and Panksepp (Panksepp & Northoff, 2009) both have made the point that the self's activities—that is, the *self-related processes,* a mode of interaction between the self and the environment—are guided by *self-related values,* that is, the values selectively accorded to environmental stimuli with respect to their salience to self, values both unique and emergent. Recognition at this level is the automatic process that registers a "match" between something inside and something out there deemed salient to the self (Edelman, 1992).[4] When that match occurs, it is expressed in a "click of recognition," a vitalizing, energizing experience (Fosha, 2009a, 2013a).

### The Dopamine-Mediated SEEKING System: Drive, Direction, Reward

A dopamine-mediated circuit connects the various subcortical structures that constitute the neurobiological core-self. This dopamine-mediated circuit is part of what Panksepp (1998) called the SEEKING system, which is "the active 'explorer' inside the brain," an "appetitive motivational system [that] energizes the many engagements with the world as individuals seek goods from the environment as well as meaning from everyday occurrences of life and it is also a system that energizes our intentions in actions" (Panksepp, 2009, p. 9).

---

[4]Edelman (1992) regarded the match between self and the world brokered by recognition processes as essential. He defined recognition as "the continual adaptive matching or fitting of elements in one physical domain to novelty occurring in elements of another, more or less independent physical domain, a matching that occurs without prior instruction" (p. 74). He felt that "neurobiology is a science of recognition" (p. 79).

Thus, drive and energy for the self's interactions with the mind–body–world come from the SEEKING system, the motivational aspect of the core-self. Pursuits with the qualities of coherence, initiative, salience to self, and drive that are rewarding and pleasurable, marked by vitality and energy, also the affective–somatic markers of transformance, become recursive appetitive processes, whereby more begets more, thus leading the plastic brain to change (Fosha, 2009a, 2009b; Fredrickson, 2009; Ghent, 2002; McEwen & Seeman, 1999).

"I have the intuition that one's feeling of a normal self as well as all the energetic–euphoric vitalities of our life are closely affiliated with the health of the SEEKING system" (J. Panksepp, personal communication, April 1, 2012). Like oxytocin, dopamine flows in conditions of low stress and low threat (K. MacDonald, personal communication, December 9, 2012). In affectively thwarting environments where stress and threat are high, are not regulated, and thus cannot be rapidly metabolized (Schore, 2009), the combination of oxytocin and dopamine is supplanted by cortisol and the other neurotransmitters of stress management.[5] However, in facilitating environments—that is, in conditions conducive to transformance—the SEEKING system can come to the fore.

To summarize, the following are some of the referents of the *neurobiological core-self*: organization, integration, behavioral coherence, and viewing the world of stimuli (internal, external, and proprioceptive) through the lens of the self (i.e., self-related processing fueled by dopamine, reflecting the operation of the SEEKING motivational drive and its qualities of vitality, pleasure, and neural energy). At the higher levels of the more language-rooted, less automatic core-self, where there is a bidirectional coordination of subcortical and cortical mediation, we find identity, ownership of experience, agency, desire, initiative, and idiosyncratic and uniquely personal aspects of the self and self experience that experientially culminate in the felt sense of "I" and "this is me." It does not seem like a stretch to conclude that the core-self's SEEKING system and its dopamine-mediated pursuits, which are dependent on safety to operate and are energy enriching, are a pathway to positive neuroplasticity. *In the process of the self manifesting itself, the self is simultaneously growing and evolving.*

## A NEUROBIOLOGICALLY INFORMED REVERIE: WITH A LITTLE HELP FROM T. S. ELIOT

Knowing about the neurobiological core-self allows us to speculate about the change mechanisms underlying phenomena and processes at either end of the transformational process, how *healing from the get-go* and *transformance*

---

[5]Although dopamine and cortisol (the hypothalamic–pituitary–adrenal axis) are inversely related, oxytocin and dopamine are congruent and positively correlated (K. MacDonald, personal communication, December 9, 2012).

*detection* can operate from the very first minutes of the very first session (see Chapter 2, this volume), and what might be at work to account for some of the extraordinary integrative phenomena of core state (see Chapter 13) that are the culmination of the transformational process.

In light of the neurobiology of the core-self, one could say of transformance, healing from the get-go, and the positive vitality affects, "The end is where we start from," in the words of T. S. Eliot in his poem *Little Gidding* (1943). If core state is where we end, the first glimmers of transformance are where we start from. And the core-self is there in the transformance glimmers we begin with, little fireflies[6] in the darkness of psychopathology that, when detected, affirmed, and reflected to the patient, lead to energizing and vitalizing "clicks" of recognition that can lead to moments of change and even state shifts. Transformance and the positive somatic–affective vitality affects that mark it have a direct link to core-self: They emanate from it. I am suggesting that that is precisely what happens when the therapist reflects back the little glimmer to the patient, drawing a big conclusion about the essence of the patient's self from a little moment, and patients, feeling seen, respond with a "click" of recognition, a big Duchenne smile lighting their countenance.

This is why the following happens. It is early in the first session with Sam, the patient depicted in Chapter 2. Much as he wants to avoid it, Sam is very concerned with all that is "wrong" with him. Karen Kranz, his therapist, and the author of the chapter, says to him, "We don't want to change Sam . . . we actually want to kind of bring Sam to life. . . . In the fullness, the sense of him and so it's not like a new improved Sam, but it's the Sam that's already there." Sam relaxes. He nods with relief. He *knows* what his therapist is talking about, and so he says: "That makes a lot of sense . . . yeah." Ten minutes into the first session, there is a quantum leap in his trust of both his therapist and the therapeutic process. Later in that session, after some trauma processing work, and after metaprocessing the resulting transformational experiences clear the way for core state and some kind of "this is me" experience to come forth, we will understand more about just why reflecting those transformance glimmers of OK-ness was so powerful and effective for Sam.

Another passage from the Eliot poem *Little Gidding* reads, "And the end of all our exploring / Will be to arrive where we started / And know the place for the first time" (Eliot, 1943, p. 145). We get to experience this exploration and return to where we started in another context.

Because my AEDP colleagues and I offer our teaching presentations from audiovisual recordings of therapy sessions, the following is a common occurrence. I am preparing a presentation focused on some mid-therapy or late-in-therapy work. To give the participants a sense of the process that has been traversed, once the presentation tape is edited I go back to the first session ever to look for a few minutes of tape that will give the participants a sense of how we started. Almost always, looking at the first session from the vantage

---

[6]I thank Kari Gleiser (Chapter 12, this volume) for that felicitous image.

point of a finished treatment, I am astonished: Everything is all there, in the first session. After the treatment is done, as we review the tape we notice and understand those early moments so much better. As we reflect on and amplify those early transformance glimmers, we realize we were much more on target than we could have ever guessed at the time.

How did we know? How could we know? What guided us? Recognition—the "matching" between something inside the self and something out there deemed salient to the self—is what allows the detection of transformance glimmers to be so transformative. The core-self is the template that informs the recognition. The mechanism of recognition, fundamentally connected with the core-self, explains the emergence of positive vitality affects that guide the process and the therapist and help therapists know they are on track. (Or not! In which case negative somatic–affective markers guide us to do something different, quickly, to put us back on track.) These positive vitality affects, from the opening moments of the therapy and throughout its duration, mark or represent a match: a moment of goodness-of-fit, a being seen that feels right, a state of being known that engenders self-knowing. Phenomenologically speaking, this match, experienced as a "click" of recognition, is akin to the Goldilocks phenomenon, whereby something that is just right:

> And every phrase
> And sentence that is right (where every word is at home),
> Taking its place to support the others . . .
> Every phrase and every sentence is an end and a beginning.
> (Eliot, 1943, p. 144)

It is not the intrinsic rightness of the intervention that makes it effective; instead, it is the rightness of the intervention for *this* person at *this* time—which, by the way, we know it to be so only after it has happened. In AEDP, the unit of intervention is *not* the therapist's comment: The unit of intervention is the therapist's comment *and* the patient's response.

We know an intervention is right if what unfolds subsequent to the intervention, often after a little pause, is greater access to bodily based emotion, greater closeness, or more access to material (Malan, 1979). We also know an intervention is right if the positive vitality affects indicate it, through their positive affective dynamics (e.g., leaning forward, becoming more animated). Those glimmers of vitality and moments of positive affect give the therapist a thumbs up, and so we pay attention to them. It is the equivalent of a music program such as Pandora, which after every song asks us to make a choice: "more of this" (and "less of that"). Eventually, through successive approximations of likes and dislikes, our bursts of positive affect and negative affect, the program figures out who we are, that is, what we like. And when it delivers songs we have never heard yet we really like, we feel weirdly and uncannily understood. Something outside (in this case, the therapist) got something about something inside (the self of the patient). When that happens (i.e., something outside meets and matches something inside that is important to self), it is good, and it feels good. The patient feels "gotten," seen, understood.

And that sense of being gotten, that "click" of recognition, is also accompanied by aliveness, vitality, and energy.

From the first moment of the first contact, and throughout treatment thereafter, the patient needs to have an experience, a *new* experience. And that experience needs to be good. The aim and method of AEDP are the provision and facilitation of such experiences. "Good" here relates to the receptive affective experience of being gotten: subliminal in the positive vitality affects, i.e., the somatic-affective markers of transformational experiences, liminal and overt in the positive receptive affects. As we know not just from experience but also from Craig (2005)'s work on energy-enriching emotions and Fredrickson's (2013) work on positive emotion processes, positive affects are the tools for, the markers of and also the result of broadening and building and of energy enrichment.

On core state and the felt core-self, one could reiterate these words from Eliot's (1943) poem:

We shall not cease from exploration
And the end of all our exploring
Will be to arrive where we started
And know the place for the first time. (p. 145)

There is one more thing: In Chapter 1 of this volume, I wrote, "Healing, safety, attachment, relatedness, and transformation are not only processes to be activated and engaged; in AEDP, they are also *experiences* to be explored" (p. 31). This is also true of the core-self and its self-related processing. As a rule, the core-self is a process inferred from integrative experiences of coherence, initiative, and identity (Fosha, 2013a). However, in AEDP, much like healing or attachment, the core-self is not only a process to be inferred; it is also an experience to be explored. Core state presents us with a rare opportunity: direct contact with the deeply *felt sense* of "I" and "this is me."

Deeply felt moments of personal truth, vitality, energy, agency, and coherence are a characteristic feature of core state, the state of calm and integration that is the culmination of the transformational process (Fosha, 2013a). Deeply pleasurable—again, pleasurable not in the sense of necessarily happy but in the sense of feeling deeply right and true—at these moments, the individual has a sense that "this is me." This is the *felt core-self*: It is as close as we get to a concrete pure expression of core-self in actual experience. However, it is also important to remember that the felt core-self is not an entity, like a geographical landmark: It is an emergent property and a felt sense. Although invariably accompanied by the truth sense, its content is not static. In one moment, "this is me" is associated with feeling strong and clear; in another moment it can be associated with innocence and wonder, or with deep acceptance. Like Damasio (2018) said, the core-self is dynamic, and, like Edelman (1992) said about recognition, you know it only after the fact, like my friend who realized that he had always wanted a statue of the prosperity Buddha only after I gave one to him, or like a patient of mine who said, "Thank you for giving me back the self I never had."

Metaprocessing the experience of such moments leads to further unfolding: The felt core-self of "this is me" deepens, consolidates, and becomes more textured. Such moments allow us to directly witness, experience, and thus grasp the essence of the core-self through its experiential manifestations. The *truth sense* that accompanies the experience of felt core-self is a crucial aspect of such experiences.

There is something in such moments that is simultaneously orienting and organizing, integrative and transformational. A paradigm shift (Kuhn, 1970) takes place within the individual: There is a reorganization of one's self based on *felt core-self experiencing*. This affects the sense of self in both feed-forward and feed-back mechanisms. There is a reinterpretation of everything in light of the new experience: It is this new self, so to speak, that will now define the lens through which self-related processing will proceed from this point forward, including how the past is viewed (Nadel & Moscovitch, 1997). In the end there is seamless integration, what Craig (2005) called a "unitive state." In the end is the beginning. Having arrived here, the self is broadened and built, with new experiences integrated and assimilated into the self.

> Many tastes we think "natural" are acquired through learning and become "second nature" to us. We are unable to distinguish our "second nature" from our "original nature" because our neuroplastic brains, once rewired, develop a new nature, every bit as biological as our original. (Doidge, 2007, p. 102)

This is the new platform, the new felt core-self, "more like myself" than ever. When the next challenge comes, as it invariably does, we start all over again, but from a stronger and more resilient place where the self we have always known ourselves to be will be easier to find again next time.

## THE TRANSFORMATIONAL THEORY OF AEDP 2.0

*Which end is nearer to God, if I may use religious metaphor, beauty and hope, or the fundamental laws? I think that the right way of course, is to say that what we have to look at is the whole structural interconnection of the thing [emphasis added]; and that all the sciences, and not just the sciences but all the efforts of intellectual kinds, are an endeavor to see the connections of the hierarchies, to connect beauty to history, to connect [humans'] history to [humans'] psychology, [humans'] psychology to the working of the brain, the brain to the neural impulse, the neural impulse to the chemistry, and so forth, up and down, both ways [emphasis added]. . . . And I do not think either end is nearer to God.*

—RICHARD FEYNMAN, AS QUOTED IN EDELMAN, 1992

The beauty of the four-state transformational process in AEDP (see Appendix Figure 1)[7] is that it connects everything: suffering with flourishing, trauma with transcendence, our animal biology (i.e., our emotions) with our highest

---

[7]This figure, and diagrams for all of the representational schemas in AEDP 2.0, may be downloaded for free (http://pubs.apa.org/books/supp/fosha).

human strivings (i.e., truth, beauty, compassion, wisdom, generosity, knowing), thus showing the whole structural interconnection of the thing and how it is connected up and down, brain stem and limbic to the prefrontal cortex, both ways.

The transformational process takes us between the *transformance glimmers* at one end (State 1) and *the felt core-self* at the other end (State 4). In the course of so doing (i.e., getting from State 1 to State 4), the transformational process proceeds through a dialectical alternation between recognition and emotion (Fosha, 2009a, 2013a). The vitality affects allow us to track the emotion moment by moment and, through experiential processing, have it move toward completion.

## Negative Emotion and the Self: The Work of State 2

Negative emotion is a perturbation (Damasio, 1999). It marks the self's differentiation from anything aversive to it, that is, "anything which is degrading, abusive, neglectful, enmeshed, sabotaging, hateful, annihilating, or oppressive" (Russell, 2015, p. 30). We can say that, just as positive emotion signals that the core-self is on its path, the path that is right for it, negative emotion signals that the core-self is off its path and furthermore is experiencing something aversive to the self. This is the essence of emotional suffering: Where we are is not where we are meant to be, and it is not right, and thus we suffer the negative emotion. In therapy, once aloneness is undone, the negative emotion, with dyadic support, is worked through; the completion of the processing of the negative emotion releases an adaptive action tendency associated with that emotion. Having the wired-in adaptive action tendency now online means that action will now be taken on behalf of the self. Adaptive action tendencies activate the resources in us that we need in order to intervene in the environment so as to restore equilibrium after the disturbance caused by the perturbation. When that is done, positive emotion emerges to accompany the completion and its aftermath; the negative emotion is no longer in our system. Through the State 2 work of processing a negative emotion through to its adaptive action tendency, we demonstrate AEDP's answer to Craig's (2005) query as to how to change energy-consuming emotions into energy-enriching emotions.

However, in AEDP there is even more.

## Positive Emotion and the Self

Positive emotion is the self's embrace of anything good for it, true to it. It also is conducive to energy enrichment (Craig, 2005). Fredrickson's (2001) broaden-and-build theory of positive emotion helps us understand the evolutionary mechanism underlying what we already know well from experience: AEDP's metatherapeutic processing expands, deepens, and consolidates positive affective states that come on the heels of change for the better. Moreover, the AEDP therapist stance supports this expansion, this broadening and building.

When an AEDP therapist actively engages emotionally and shares, through judicious self-disclosure (Prenn, 2009), how they are affected, moved, or delighted by our patient's change process, this enhances the relational resonance between the two, which is itself a positively valenced affective experience. This resonance typically further amplifies and deepens the patient's already-positive experience. As Rick Hanson (Hanson & Hanson, 2018) has helped us understand, staying with the felt sense of positive emotional experience contributes to positive neuroplasticity. Thus, when we work with positive emotion metatherapeutically in State 3 we not only facilitate the broaden-and-build process; we also cocreate a relational, experiential, affective mind–body–world environment that fulfills Damasio's (2018) mandate to move beyond survival and achieve a homeostasis of positive energy balance and flourishing.

Everything that changes for the better is associated with positive affect and, as result of that, with energy and vitality. Positive affect and energy are keys to AEDP's transformational theory and its mechanisms of therapeutic action. It is what allows the potential for positive neuroplasticity in all four states. And it is what allows us as AEDP therapists practicing our craft to fulfill Damasio's (2018) articulation of our evolutionary mandate: that we want our therapeutic activities to result in a surplus of energy to have it available for living life fully, having that extra energy for meeting life's challenges, so as to have energy to fuel our lived lives, growth-producing, self-expanding explorations that broaden and build the self.

## CONCLUSION: HEALTHY AT THE CORE

In Damasio's (2018) and Panksepp's (e.g., Panksepp & Northoff, 2009) work, "the neurobiological core-self" refers to a set of subcortical midline brain structures, located literally at the core of the brain, on either side of the midline.[8] The neurobiological core-self is hypothesized to be innate and intrinsically integrative from the get-go. Identity, coherence, ownership of experience, and the vitalizing drive that fuels our engagements with the mind–body–world as its correlates.

As I have been discussing in this chapter, a deeply integrative phenomenon frequently encountered in core state is the patient's deeply felt and explicitly articulated experience of "this is me": an immensely powerful, in-the-moment felt sense experience of the essence of self (see Chapter 13, this volume) that I have called the "*felt* core-self" (italics in original; Fosha, 2013a).

Much as transformance is the instantiation of positive neuroplasticity in action, the experience of the felt core-self, that is, core state experiences of "this is me," appears to be an instantiation of the neurobiological core-self. The construct of the neurobiological core-self and its manifestations in the

---

[8]By the time we humans become adults, the neurobiological self is constituted of the bidirectional communication of subcortical and cortical midline structures.

phenomena of core state links back to transformance and its glimmers. When those vitality-marked glimmers of core-self are recognized and affirmed even in the midst of psychopathology, the effect can be profound. We can hypothesize that the innate, organizing integrative aspects of the neurobiological core-self, there from the get-go, is why *healing from the get-go* can operate from the very first moments of the first session of the first therapeutic encounter as well as why feeling seen is such a powerful mechanism. This brings us full circle, from core-self to transformance glimmers, back to core self again. And so on.

I close with a last note about AEDP 2.0 terminology: The word "core" has been a "core" part of AEDP. Never precisely defined, it has had the powerful resonant meaning of "central," and "essential," as in "core affect," which, in the context of an affect-facilitating therapeutic relationship, was seen as the central agent of change in AEDP 1.0 (see Introduction, this volume). As AEDP 2.0 has been developed over these past 20 years, and as both its neurobiological foundations and transpersonal resonances are being explored (Fosha, 2013a; Russell, 2015; Yeung et al., 2019; see also Chapter 13, this volume), a dawning realization has been that the very meaning of "core" has subtly transformed over the years and has de facto come to have a more precise and specific meaning: "Core" has come to mean fundamentally intact, good, innate, whole, healthy, vital, and life affirming.

This meaning of "core" is, as we have been exploring this chapter, easily resonant with positive neuroplasticity, healing from the get-go, transformance, and the neurobiology of the core-self; however, it is also deeply congruent with Winnicott's (1954, 1965) profound understanding of the fundamental intactness of the true self and with wisdom traditions East and West, North and South that believe in the intactness and fundamental goodness of the self prior to experience (e.g., the Zen Buddhist kōan "What did your face look like before your parents were born?"; see https://en.wikipedia.org/wiki/Original_face).

We can now say that by "core" we mean something specific: an intact core, fundamentally healthy, where the core self and fundamental healing reside. Making use of and extending Eileen Russell's (2015) definition of "resilience" as "the self's differentiation from anything aversive to it," we can aver: The impact of those aversive experiences on the individual, including when internalized in the individual's psyche soma, however important and central to the individual and their therapy they may be, nevertheless are not "core," nor are they in the "core." The term "core" is reserved for intactness, core-self, fundamental health, and uncompromised transformance, that is, healing potential.

Health, healing, and the drive toward integration emanate from the intact core of the self.

## REFERENCES

Bowlby, J. (1982). *Attachment and loss: Vol. 1. Attachment.* New York: Basic Books.

Bushell, W. C., Olivo, E. L., & Theise, N. D. (Eds.). (2009). *Annals of the New York Academy of Sciences: Vol. 1172. Longevity, regeneration, and optimal health: Integrating Eastern and Western perspectives.* New York Academy of Sciences. https://doi.org/10.1111/j.1749-6632.2009.04501.x

Craig, A. D. (2005). Forebrain emotional asymmetry: A neuroanatomical basis? *Trends in Cognitive Sciences, 9*(12), 566–571. https://doi.org/10.1016/j.tics.2005.10.005

Craig, A. D. (2015). *How do you feel? An interoceptive moment with your neurobiological self.* Princeton University Press. https://doi.org/10.1515/9781400852727

Damasio, A. (1999). *The feeling of what happens: Body and emotion in the making of consciousness.* Harcourt Brace.

Damasio, A. (2010). *Self comes to mind: Constructing the conscious brain.* Pantheon Books.

Damasio, A. (2018). *The strange order of things: Life, feeling, and the making of cultures.* Pantheon Books.

Darwin, C. (1965). *The expression of emotion in man and animals.* University of Chicago Press. (Original work published 1872) https://doi.org/10.7208/chicago/9780226220802.001.0001

Davidson, R. J., Jackson, D. C., & Kalin, N. H. (2000). Emotion, plasticity, context, and regulation: Perspectives from affective neuroscience. *Psychological Bulletin, 126*(6), 890–909. https://doi.org/10.1037/0033-2909.126.6.890

Davidson, R. J., Kabat-Zinn, J., Schumacher, J., Rosenkranz, M., Muller, D., Santorelli, S. F., Urbanowski, F., Harrington, A., Bonus, K., & Sheridan, J. F. (2003). Alterations in brain and immune function produced by mindfulness meditation. *Psychosomatic Medicine, 65*(4), 564–570. https://doi.org/10.1097/01.PSY.0000077505.67574.E3

Davidson, R. J., & Schuyler, B. S. (2015). The neuroscience of happiness. In J. F. Helliwell, R. Laryard, & Sachs, J. (Eds.), *World happiness report 2015* (pp. 82–105). United Nations Sustainable Development Solutions Network.

Doidge, N. (2007). *The brain that changes itself: Stories of personal triumph from the frontiers of brain science.* Penguin Books.

Doidge, N. (2016). *The brain's way of healing: Remarkable discoveries and recoveries from the frontiers of neuroplasticity.* Penguin.

Ecker, B., Ticic, R., & Hulley, L. (2012). *Unlocking the emotional brain: Eliminating symptoms at their roots using memory reconsolidation.* Routledge. https://doi.org/10.4324/9780203804377

Edelman, G. M. (1992). *Bright air, brilliant fire: On the matter of the mind.* Basic Books.

Eliot, T. S. (1943). *Quartets: Little Gidding.* In *T. S. Eliot: The complete poems and plays, 1909–1950* (pp. 138–145). Harcourt Brace.

Fosha, D. (2000a). Meta-therapeutic processes and the affects of transformation: Affirmation and the healing affects. *Journal of Psychotherapy Integration, 10*(1), 71–97. https://doi.org/10.1023/A:1009422511959

Fosha, D. (2000b). *The transforming power of affect: A model for accelerated change.* Basic Books.

Fosha, D. (2002). The activation of affective change processes in AEDP. In J. J. Magnavita (Ed.), *Comprehensive handbook of psychotherapy: Vol. 1. Psychodynamic and object relations psychotherapies* (pp. 309–344). Wiley.

Fosha, D. (2005). Emotion, true self, true other, core state: Toward a clinical theory of affective change process. *Psychoanalytic Review, 92*(4), 513–551. https://doi.org/10.1521/prev.2005.92.4.513

Fosha, D. (2006). Quantum transformation in trauma and treatment: Traversing the crisis of healing change. *Journal of Clinical Psychology, 62*(5), 569–583. https://doi.org/10.1002/jclp.20249

Fosha, D. (2008). Transformance, recognition of self by self, and effective action. In K. J. Schneider (Ed.), *Existential–integrative psychotherapy: Guideposts to the core of practice* (pp. 290–320). Routledge.

Fosha, D. (2009a). Emotion and recognition at work: Energy, vitality, pleasure, truth, desire and the emergent phenomenology of transformational experience. In D. Fosha, D. J. Siegel, & M. F. Solomon (Eds.), *The healing power of emotion: Affective neuroscience, development, and clinical practice* (pp. 172–201). W. W. Norton.

Fosha, D. (2009b). Positive affects and the transformation of suffering into flourishing. In W. C. Bushell, E. L. Olivo, & N. D. Theise (Eds.), *Annals of the New York Academy of Sciences: Vol. 1172. Longevity, regeneration, and optimal health: Integrating Eastern and Western perspectives* (pp. 252–261). New York Academy of Sciences. https://doi.org/10.1111/j.1749-6632.2009.04501.x

Fosha, D. (2013a). A heaven in a wildflower: Self, dissociation, and treatment in the context of the neurobiological core self. *Psychoanalytic Inquiry, 33*(5), 496–523. https://doi.org/10.1080/07351690.2013.815067

Fosha, D. (2013b). Turbocharging the affects of healing and redressing the evolutionary tilt. In D. Siegel & M. Solomon (Eds.), *Healing moments in psychotherapy* (pp. 129–168). W. W. Norton.

Fosha, D., & Thoma, N. (2020). Metatherapeutic processing supports the emergence of flourishing in psychotherapy. *Psychotherapy.* Advance online publication. https://doi.org/10.1037/pst0000289

Fosha, D., Thoma, N., & Yeung, D. (2019). Transforming emotional suffering into flourishing: Metatherapeutic processing of positive affect as a trans-theoretical vehicle for change. *Counselling Psychology Quarterly, 32*(3–4), 563–593. https://doi.org/10.1080/09515070.2019.1642852

Fosha, D., & Yeung, D. (2006). AEDP exemplifies the seamless integration of emotional transformation and dyadic relatedness at work. In G. Stricker & J. Gold (Eds.), *A casebook of integrative psychotherapy* (pp. 165–184). American Psychological Association. https://doi.org/10.1037/11436-013

Fredrickson, B. L. (2001). The role of positive emotions in positive psychology: The broaden-and-build theory of positive emotions. *American Psychologist, 56*(3), 218–226. https://doi.org/10.1037/0003-066X.56.3.218

Fredrickson, B. L. (2009). *Positivity: Groundbreaking research reveals how to embrace the hidden strength of positive emotions, overcome negativity, and thrive.* Crown.

Fredrickson, B. L. (2013). Positive emotions broaden and build. *Advances in Experimental Social Psychology, 47*, 1–53. https://doi.org/10.1016/B978-0-12-407236-7.00001-2

Fredrickson, B. L., & Joiner, T. (2002). Positive emotions trigger upward spirals toward emotional well-being. *Psychological Science, 13*(2), 172–175. https://doi.org/10.1111/1467-9280.00431

Fredrickson, B. L., & Joiner, T. (2018). Reflections on positive emotions and upward spirals. *Perspectives on Psychological Science, 13*(2), 194–199. https://doi.org/10.1177/1745691617692106

Ghent, E. (2002). Wish, need, drive: Motive in light of dynamic systems theory and Edelman's selectionist theory. *Psychoanalytic Dialogues, 12*(5), 763–808. https://doi.org/10.1080/10481881209348705

Hanson, R. (2017). Positive neuroplasticity: The neuroscience of mindfulness. In J. Loizzo, M. Neale, & E. Wolf (Eds.), *Advances in contemplative psychotherapy: Accelerating transformation* (pp. 48–60). W. W. Norton. https://doi.org/10.4324/9781315630045-5

Hanson, R., & Hanson, F. (2018). *Resilient: How to grow an unshakeable core of calm, strength, and happiness.* Harmony.

Harrison, R. L. (2020). Termination in 16-session accelerated experiential dynamic psychotherapy (AEDP): Together in how we say goodbye. *Psychotherapy, 57*(4), 531–547. https://doi.org/10.1037/pst000343

Iwakabe, S., & Conceição, N. (2016). Metatherapeutic processing as a change-based therapeutic immediacy task: Building an initial process model using a task-analytic research strategy. *Journal of Psychotherapy Integration, 26*(3), 230–247. https://doi.org/10.1037/int0000016

James, W. (1985). *The varieties of religious experience: A study in human nature.* Penguin Books. (Original work published 1902)

Keyes, L. M., Frederickson, B. L., & Park, N. (2012). Positive psychology and the quality of life. In K. Land (Ed.), *Handbook of social indicators and quality of life research* (pp. 99–112). Springer.

Kuhn, T. (1970). *The structure of scientific revolutions* (2nd ed.). University of Chicago Press.

Lazar, S. W., Kerr, C. E., Wasserman, R. H., Gray, J. R., Greve, D. N., Treadway, M. T., McGarvey, M., Quinn, B. T., Dusek, J. A., Benson, H., Rauch, S. L., Moore, C. I., & Fischl, B. (2005). Meditation experience is associated with increased cortical thickness. *NeuroReport, 16*(17), 1893–1897. https://doi.org/10.1097/01.wnr.0000186598. 66243.19

Loizzo, J. (2009). Optimizing learning and quality of life throughout the lifespan: A global framework for research and application. In W. C. Bushell, E. L. Olivo, & N. D. Theise (Eds.), *Annals of the New York Academy of Sciences: Vol. 1172. Longevity, regeneration, and optimal health: Integrating Eastern and Western perspectives* (pp. 186–198). New York Academy of Sciences. https://doi.org/10.1196/annals.1393.006

Lomas, T. (2017). The spectrum of positive affect: A cross-cultural lexical analysis. *International Journal of Wellbeing, 7*(3), 1–18. https://doi.org/10.5502/ijw.v7i3.608

Malan, D. H. (1979). *Individual psychotherapy and the science of psychodynamics*. CRC Press.

McEwen, B., & Seeman, T. (1999). Protective and damaging effects of mediators of stress: Elaborating and testing the concepts of allostasis and allostatic load. In N. E. Adler, M. Marmot, B. S. McEwen, & J. Stewart (Eds.), *Annals of the New York Academy of Sciences: Vol. 896. Socioeconomic status and health in industrial nations: Social, psychological, and biological pathways* (pp. 30–47). New York Academy of Sciences.

Nadel, L., & Moscovitch, M. (1997). Memory consolidation, retrograde amnesia and the hippocampal complex. *Current Opinion in Neurobiology, 7*(2), 217–227. https://doi.org/10.1016/S0959-4388(97)80010-4

Northoff, G., & Panksepp, J. (2008). The trans-species concept of self and the subcortical–cortical midline system. *Trends in Cognitive Sciences, 12*(7), 259–264. https://doi.org/10.1016/j.tics.2008.04.007

Panksepp, J. (1998). *Affective neuroscience: The foundations of human and animal emotions*. Oxford University Press.

Panksepp, J. (2009). Brain emotional systems and qualities of mental life: From animal models of affect to implications for psychotherapeutics. In D. Fosha, D. J. Siegel, & M. F. Solomon (Eds.), *The healing power of emotion: Affective neuroscience, development, clinical practice* (pp. 1–26). W. W. Norton.

Panksepp, J., & Biven, L. (2012). *The archaeology of mind: Neuroevolutionary origins of human emotions*. W. W. Norton.

Panksepp, J., & Northoff, G. (2009). The trans-species core SELF: The emergence of active cultural and neuro-ecological agents through self-related processing within subcortical–cortical midline networks. *Consciousness and Cognition, 18*(1), 193–215. https://doi.org/10.1016/j.concog.2008.03.002

Pascual-Leone, A., Amedi, A., Fregni, F., & Merabet, L. B. (2005). The plastic human brain cortex. *Annual Review of Neuroscience, 28*, 377–401. https://doi.org/10.1146/annurev.neuro.27.070203.144216

Prenn, N. (2009). I second that emotion! On self-disclosure and its metaprocessing. In A. Bloomgarden & R. B. Mennuti (Eds.), *Psychotherapist revealed: Therapists speak about self-disclosure in psychotherapy* (pp. 85–99). Routledge.

Russell, E. (2015). *Restoring resilience: Discovering your clients' capacity for healing*. W. W. Norton.

Russell, E., & Fosha, D. (2008). Transformational affects and core state in AEDP: The emergence and consolidation of joy, hope, gratitude and confidence in the (solid goodness of the) self. *Journal of Psychotherapy Integration, 18*(2), 167–190. https://doi.org/10.1037/1053-0479.18.2.167

Ryan, R. M., & Frederick, C. (1997). On energy, personality, and health: Subjective vitality as a dynamic reflection of well-being. *Journal of Personality, 65*(3), 529–565. https://doi.org/10.1111/j.1467-6494.1997.tb00326.x

Schore, A. N. (2009). Right-brain affect regulation: An essential mechanism of development, trauma, dissociation, and psychotherapy. In D. Fosha, D. J. Siegel, & M. F. Solomon (Eds.), *The healing power of emotion: Affective neuroscience, development, and clinical practice* (pp. 112–144). W. W. Norton.

Shiota, M. N., Campos, B., Oveis, C., Hertenstein, M. J., Simon-Thomas, E., & Keltner, D. (2017). Beyond happiness: Building a science of discrete positive emotions. *American Psychologist, 72*(7), 617–643. https://doi.org/10.1037/a0040456

Siegel, D. (2010). *Mindsight: The new science of personal transformation.* Bantam Books.

Winnicott, D. W. (1954). Mind and its relation to the psyche-soma. *British Journal of Medical Psychology, 27*(4), 201–209. https://doi.org/10.1111/j.2044-8341.1954.tb00864.x.

Winnicott, D. W. (1965). Ego distortion in terms of true and false self. In *The maturational processes and the facilitating environment* (pp. 140–152). International Universities Press.

Yeung, D., Fosha, D., Ye Perman, J., & Xu, Y. (2019). After Freud meets Zhuangzi: Stance and the dance of the self-in-transformation with the other-in-contemplative presence. *Psychological Communications, 2*(3), 179–185.

# 15

# Future Directions

Diana Fosha

And now, we envision future directions. With accelerated experiential dynamic psychotherapy (AEDP) as a dynamic, ever-emergent model, and with AEDP 2.0 as its current platform, we look beyond the horizon to AEDP 3.0 and beyond. I wish to identify four areas of emergent exploration: (a) developments in the application of AEDP in the treatment of social groups suffering from systemic racism and injustice, with explorations of how AEDP theory and practice might grow as a result; (b) reimagining the "D" ("dynamic") in AEDP; (c) the expansion of empirical research on AEDP; and (d) imagining collaborative investigations into the neurobiology of AEDP change processes.

## AEDP AND RECOGNITION OF THE IMPACT OF SYSTEMIC RACISM AND INJUSTICE[1]

As AEDP therapists, we recognize the importance of understanding and acknowledging how societal, institutional, interrelational, and intrarelational oppression (Medley, 2020) affects our patients, people of color in particular, and/or members of other social groups who suffer discrimination based on race, class, socioeconomic status, gender, sexual orientation, religious belief or lack

---

[1]I thank my colleagues Joy McQuery, Ben Medley, Ben Lipton, Connie Rhodes, Karen Pando-Mars, Andrew Joseph, and Monica Hodges, and my daughters, Molly and Zoe Lubin-Fosha, for thoughtful reading of and constructive feedback on this section of the chapter. I am grateful for all I have learned in the process.

https://doi.org/10.1037/0000232-016
*Undoing Aloneness and the Transformation of Suffering Into Flourishing: AEDP 2.0*, D. Fosha (Editor)

thereof, ethnicity, disability, age, and so on. These forces, of course, affect therapists as well. Recognition of the traumatic impact of systemic racism and other forms of injustice needs to inform our work as AEDP therapists and our actions as a unique group within the profession.

The first step must involve naming and acknowledging the problem. We are becoming increasingly aware of the intersectionality of privilege and lack thereof in both patient and therapist and the need to be attuned to the intersectional identities that exist in each member of the therapeutic dyad. Daily we seek to grow in our own racial and multicultural awareness and competence and to work to decenter from privilege, especially Whiteness. We are committed to expanding our exploration of how privilege, especially Whiteness, in either member of the therapeutic dyad affects the therapy and thus how to work with it in an AEDP therapy session.

As elaborated in the preceding chapters, AEDP is an inherently bottom-up approach, which begins with undoing aloneness and cocreating safety and then works with bodily based emotions and sensations to reveal profound bodily based truths for patient and therapist. This somatic foundation for therapeutic work is crucial to what Resmaa Menakem (2017) advocated in his highly acclaimed and influential book, *My Grandmother's Hands*.

Menakem's (2017) work makes clear that cocreating safety in therapeutic work with "bodies of culture" (his term for people of color), must first recognize, acknowledge, and validate the fundamental unsafety that is likely to exist at baseline, given the intergenerational transmission of trauma resulting from centuries of White supremacy, anti-Black racism, and other forms of racism and oppression. We as therapists must endeavor to find AEDP-specific ways to name, acknowledge, and work with that bodily rooted unsafety while also, in AEDP-specific ways, continue to look for glimmers of transformance and unexpected moments of hope, faith, healing, and/or trust. Only by recognizing unsafety—and, when it applies, privilege in the therapist—can we hope to maximize the possibility of cocreating therapeutic environments in which people who live with injustice and oppression might heal.

Rigorous education and personal work for therapists to unlearn racism and forms of systemic injustice is essential. Given AEDP's focus on recognition and receptive affective experiences, these sociocultural and economic realities must be sensitively yet explicitly named in treatment. In doing so, we aspire to further elevate our patients' felt sense of being seen. AEDP's *make the implicit explicit* and *make the explicit experiential* definitely apply here. Psychotherapy can be an opportunity to acknowledge and experientially process the complex interaction of race, gender, class, ethnicity, and other forms of intersectionality and to understand how it can affect a person's susceptibility to ongoing suffering, and to healing. Given AEDP's championing of the transformative power of the dyad, psychotherapy can be even more powerful when these interactions can be explored in both members of the dyad. Furthermore, this work can also contribute to broadening and deepening AEDP's fundamental stance: In addition to empathy, affirmation, and patient advocacy, we can add *courage,* buttressed by attunement and moment-to-moment tracking, to the qualities that define AEDP's therapeutic stance.

Our work with ourselves as therapists is equally important. Awareness, ownership, and accountability are required to change the skewed conditions and power dynamics we are seeking to rectify:

> Not only do we want to assist our patients in addressing the oppression they face in the world at large but we want to interrogate our own potential to unwittingly participate in oppressive dynamics. In order to create a safe space for our patients we must begin to identify our own privileged positions of power which, almost by definition, are often opaque to us but, like anything that is not fully brought into awareness, can become enacted. Without this awareness, we can replicate societal power dynamics within the very therapy itself (Quinones-Rosado, 2020). (J. McQuery, personal communication, November 17, 2020)

The more the issues of systemic racism are exposed, the more we as AEDP therapists can come to recognize subtle and not-so-subtle forms of micro- and macroaggressions, beginning with our own. Mindful of the potential of such aggressions to cause harm, retraumatize our patients, and unwittingly perpetuate racial trauma and oppression, we can notice them, name them, own them, and, together with our patients, track their impact. By doing this, we enhance the likelihood that they can make use of what AEDP has to offer that is nurturing, patient, and collaborative. The belief in healing that lies at the core of AEDP can help foster healing for patients experiencing racial trauma and oppression.

The AEDP Institute has had an active diversity scholarship program, as well as a committee for diversity, equity, and inclusion. In 2020, during the COVID-19 pandemic, our commitment to active antiracism work took a quantum leap. In the wake of the murder of George Floyd on May 25, 2020 by Derek Chauvin, who at the time was a police officer in the Minneapolis Police Department ("Killing of George Floyd," 2021), we, as an institute dedicated to the healing of trauma, our hearts hurting, opened our eyes to the need to stand in solidarity with the Black community.

We are making our courses, trainings, and supervision more easily accessible to Black therapists and other people of color, aiming to facilitate and accelerate their path to AEDP certification and leadership. We are actively working to increase the diversity of therapists, supervisors, and teachers of AEDP, especially in terms of race: People can then have the choice to be in treatment with, learn from, and be supervised by people of color.

The AEDP faculty are engaging in various trainings to better understand, analyze, and create new initiatives to mitigate inadvertent yet inevitable manifestations of White advantage[2] and institutionalized racism in our clinical work and in our teaching of the AEDP model. We have partnered with Della Mosely's online antiracism and accountability program (https://www. academics4blacklives.com/) and facilitated access to that collective's antiracism

---

[2]See Racial Equity Institute (2020) for why I use the term "White advantage" rather than "White privilege."

training for all White and non-Black members of our AEDP community wishing to pursue it.

We are only in the early stages of making these important changes and recognize that much more is needed; nevertheless, we have started to incorporate considerations of systemic racism and other forms of oppression into our presentations (Hanakawa, 2019; Lipton & Medley, 2019; Medley, 2020). Writings on this topic are on the horizon.

Several published articles have already addressed work with multicultural issues in the context of AEDP treatment (Fosha, 2018; Medley, 2018; Simpson, 2016; Urquiza Mendoza, 2018; Vigoda Gonzales, 2018; Ye-Perman, 2018), including published cases of AEDP therapy with members with members of populations suffering systemic injustice and discrimination (Medley, 2018; Simpson, 2016; Vigoda Gonzales, 2018). These are interesting, though very preliminary, developments.

Simpson (2016) focused her discussion on the *invisibility syndrome*. The invisibility syndrome references how racial indignities and lived experiences of systemic racism can engender a subjective sense of invisibility in which people feel the dominant culture fails to recognize their worth. According to Simpson, this is especially pronounced in Black men, who paradoxically are simultaneously both highly visible and invisible in a White-dominant society. Black men in the United States receive heightened negatively valenced attention that is in fact scrutiny or surveillance. They are often maligned as posing a threat, while their intrinsic humanity, abilities, and qualities of character go unseen. Simpson published a case in which she successfully treated with AEDP a Black man who presented with trauma and other issues. Because AEDP's methodology emphasizes recognition and focuses on working with the patient's perception of therapist empathy and recognition, Simpson's experience using AEDP led her to suggest that AEDP can be a powerful antidote to the pernicious effects of the invisibility syndrome. Similarly, Medley (2018) suggested that AEDP is a model of therapy that is easily integrated with gay-affirmative therapy in helping to heal the traumatic experiences and internalized heterosexism gay men carry in a heterosexist society.

AEDP's stance and interventions are congruent with embodying fundamental elements of the multicultural orientation paradigm described by Owen and colleagues (Davis et al., 2018; Owen, 2013; Owen et al., 2016), that is, cultural humility, benefiting from opportunities, and developing cultural comfort. AEDP's affirmative, nonhierarchical stance, with its emphasis on cocreation, its practice of undoing aloneness, its focus on recognition, and its explicit exploration of receptive affective experiences of recognition are well suited to addressing some of the core issues: the shame, isolation, and dehumanization that often wounds oppressed populations. Nevertheless, we as AEDP therapists need to continuously optimize our interventions in order to meet the challenges of the multicultural orientation framework in the context of systemic racism and other forms of injustice and oppression in U.S. society and elsewhere in the world.

It is imperative that we, current and future practitioners of AEDP, continue to engage these increasingly pressing concerns knowing that the work developed to address them will influence AEDP's framework as a whole. The dream of AEDP 2.0 is to have an AEDP 3.0 enriched by theoretical and clinical developments emerging from these initiatives.

## REIMAGINING THE "D" IN AEDP

Innovations and scientific revolutions (Kuhn, 1970) are spurred by bumping against the limitations of a model. Attempts to address those limitations often lead not only to some changes but also to a whole reconception. Given its psychodynamic antecedents (see the Appendix of Fosha's 2000 book for AEDP's origin story), when AEDP 1.0 was born, the "E" (for "experiential") in AEDP was the leading edge; the "D" (for "dynamic," as in "psychodynamic") was assumed and foundational.

Twenty years later, what does the "D" mean in the context of AEDP's healing-oriented ethos and trauma-informed understanding of psychopathology; its affirmative, collaborative, deliberatively positive, decidedly not neutral therapeutic stance; and its well-articulated transformational phenomenology? A future direction would be to reimagine the "D" in AEDP in a way that encompasses these developments. Next, I outline some specific questions guiding that reimagination.

### What Does an AEDP, Healing-Forward Psychodynamic Formulation Look Like?

What is the role of the psychodynamic formulation in AEDP? What does an AEDP, healing-forward psychodynamic formulation look like, and how does it work in the context of a treatment that proceeds from the bottom up and uses moment-to-moment tracking? What does it look like in the early phases of a treatment rooted in transformation and healing from the get-go? What does it look like in the middle of treatment? The Triangle of Experience, the Self–Other–Emotion Triangle (see Chapters 6, 7 and 11, this volume, for more details on both), and the Triangle of Relational Comparisons (see Chapter 6), as well as Gleiser's *relational prism* (Chapter 12), could anchor a psychodynamic formulation that would address the dynamics of healing (and self-at-best) and psychopathology (and self-at-worst) respectively (R. Harrison, personal communication, April 1, 2020). Existing work relevant to the quest of developing psychodynamic formulations that stay true to AEDP's ethos includes Karen Pando-Mars's (2016) work on the four attachment styles from an AEDP perspective and her AEDP 2.0 updating of AEDP's representational schemas (Chapter 6); Ron Frederick's (2019; see also Chapter 7, this volume) work on the internal working model and its rewiring; and Hilary Hendel's (2018) work on the Triangle of Experience (which she calls the "Triangle of Change") to decode repetitive, nonproductive patterns and support corrective healing patterns.

## Expanding Theory, Stance, and Technique

Although repetition compulsion is not inevitable and not all, or even most, forms of psychopathology are motivated by the punitiveness of the superego toward the self, nevertheless those dynamics do exist and, for some people, predominate. If we stay rigorous and do not assume they operate across the board but instead honor them and work with them when they do in fact operate, what might that work look like? What does AEDP have to contribute to the theory of repetition compulsion?

Another question is this: When affirming transformance, and using moment-to-moment tracking, dyadic affect regulation, and experiential facilitation do not lead to the natural emergence of adaptive affective phenomena, how do we work to bring them onboard? The operative phrase here is *when the phenomena do not emerge naturally* from our affect-facilitating, healing-forward work. When defenses do not melt, when adaptive action tendencies do not spontaneously come forth, then what?

Developments to expand AEDP theory, stance, and technique abound. Ben Lipton (Chapter 5, this volume), in his work on *therapeutic presence as an affective change process* in its own right, emphasizes the importance of attending to therapist experiences that may complement, not only parallel, those of the patient. Delving into therapist complementary experiences might be a way into dissociated and defensively excluded areas of the patient's experience that would extend both AEDP's theory and practice with respect to those challenging areas of clinical work. SueAnne Piliero (Chapter 10, this volume) is developing *Fierce Love*, a stance and a series of interventions aimed at working with entrenched self-punitive defenses, with "fierce" being as important a term as "love." In this volume, Eileen Russell (Chapter 9) introduced the term *attuned disruption*: It refers to a stance and a series of attuned though intentionally disruptive interventions designed to bring online undeveloped agency, will, desire, and so on. Russell advocates going beyond the early aspects of mother–infant communication and exploring the potential of different developmental periods to inform aspects of the therapeutic stance that might be used to foster autonomy, initiative, industry, and other capacities (Erikson, 1968).

## Work to Foster the Assumption of Personal Responsibility

A related area has to do with fostering patients' assumption of personal responsibility for their actions and their impact on others. Step 4 in 12-step work involves "taking a fearless moral inventory." It presents a challenge to AEDP: How do we maintain our deliberately positive affirmative stance and our affirmative advocacy on behalf of the patient and at the same time encourage an examination of accountability and personal responsibility? How do we promote the equivalent of taking of a fearless moral inventory when the patient is not naturally oriented that way and when a given therapy's emergent processes do not naturally go in that direction?

For instance, when a patient is mourning the costs and consequences of their defenses and how they have hurt the self, how might we as therapists extend the work to also encourage exploring, and mourning how those same mechanisms and the resulting errors of either omission or commission might have hurt, or even harmed, others? And how do we do that in an affirmative, actively non-shaming fashion? These issues might also be explored in areas that focus on taking responsibility with respect not only to personal issues involving significant others but also to larger issues, such as the fate of the environment and the corrosive prevalence of racism.[3]

Given AEDP's attachment orientation, a promising area of exploration is making use of, and experientially working with, the biologically rooted caregiver system (Bowlby, 1982). The caregiving behavioral system, which is the wired-in tendency to respond to the distress of those perceived as more vulnerable with care and caregiving, has been explored in terms of its engagement to inform the AEDP therapist's stance (Fosha, 2000). However, as Joy McQuery pointed out, we have yet to investigate how the caregiving behavioral system might be entrained in patients to enhance their altruism and caregiving toward others perceived as more in need than themselves, be those others family members or members of oppressed groups:

> Does AEDP have something to contribute, not just to suffering individuals, but to a suffering world? In order to speak to the needs of the culture at large, we need to find a way to move beyond the dyad. AEDP, and therapy as a whole, is fashioned from the vantage point of the patient as care-receiver. Staying within the attachment (care receiving) framework, there is a more limited maneuverability in making the needs of others a primary focus of the therapy, because the patient is cast in the role of 'the one in need of care'. But, in fact, our patients do not only have an attachment system, but also a biologically mediated caregiving system (Bowlby, 1982). . . . The neural systems regulating caregiving "appear to serve as a core for all empathic, compassionate reactions to another person's need" (Mikulincer & Shaver, 2012, p. 40) which can then lead to deep senses of meaning, purpose, fulfillment, satisfaction, personal growth and wisdom for the caregiver. The caregiving system can also motivate profound and at times startlingly rapid personal transformation.
>
> While the attachment system is inward facing, helping the patient get their own needs met, the caregiving system is outward facing, helping the patient meet the needs of others (Shaver et al., 2010). When we bring the caregiving system into the foreground, suddenly within clinical reach are altruism, moral behavior (Krebs, 2012), the common good and social justice (Brown, Brown, & Penner, 2012), a host of phenomena that appeared nearly clinically inaccessible from a viewpoint based solely on the attachment system. AEDP might benefit from a deeper exploration into this other half of the human experience to help our patients create a fuller, more well rounded human expression.
>
> Many of the gifts of AEDP have come from attending to areas that have been discouraged or downplayed in traditional psychological practice such as bringing in the therapist as a real person or privileging the positive. Perhaps, this shift to engaging our patients" caregiving system to move "beyond self interests" will open a new frontier in AEDP (Brown, Brown, & Penner, 2012). (McQuery, personal communication, December 3, 2020)

---

[3] I thank Joy McQuery for our conversations and her raising these important issues with me.

Launching explorations from the platform of AEDP 2.0, and engaging questions from a loving and nonshaming perspective, would constitute a reimagining of the "D" in AEDP.

## EMPIRICAL RESEARCH INTO AEDP

After 20 years of theory building, phenomenological discoveries, and clinical innovations, the next decade promises to also bring new insights into AEDP's mechanisms of change, based on and informed by empirical research. An AEDP research program (Edlin et al., 2020) that started 5 years before this book went into production is starting to yield results, and our first published outcome article documenting the effectiveness of AEDP has been published (Iwakabe, Edlin, Fosha, Gretton, Joseph, et al., 2020), with our next paper documenting the maintenance of gains at 6- and 12-month follow-ups (Iwakabe, Edlin, Fosha, Gretton, Thoma, et al., 2020). We have three research endeavors: (a) an ambitious process/outcome project conducted in the context of an AEDP Practice Research Network (PRN; Edlin et al., 2020), (b) the development of the experience-based Moments of Flourishing Experience Scale (MFES; Fosha, Coleman, et al., 2021), and (c) the use of AEDP with patients being treated in a residential setting for treatment-resistant depression (Iwakabe, Edlin, Fosha, et al., 2018).

### Process/Outcome Research

AEDP practitioners have heeded the calls to bridge the clinician–researcher gap with the development of collaborative PRNs (Castonguay et al., 2013; Koerner & Castonguay, 2015). We are conducting our process/outcome research program within the context of an already well-established, vibrant AEDP PRN. We have developed a 16-session model of AEDP treatment (Edlin & Fosha, 2016; Harrison, 2020). Moreover, at the time of this writing, we have a community of more than 50 private practice therapists on four continents involved in the project. We believe our process/outcome research, being conducted within an AEDP PRN, is of a magnitude that is unprecedented in terms of (a) its being carried out with no funding, on the basis of 'clinicians' commitment, dedication, and enthusiasm; and (b) the extensive committed participation, including the regular video recording of every session, by practitioners in private practice. AEDP treatment is being hosted in private practice settings so researchers can investigate the effectiveness of AEDP as it is offered in everyday clinical practice. Our goal is not only to evaluate the effectiveness of AEDP in this naturalistic, ecologically valid context, but also to have outcome monitoring embedded into everyday AEDP practice so that the involvement in research is sustainable and can eventually become a part of the daily practice of AEDP clinicians at large.

For our research, we have a multitude of measures administered before and after therapy, as well as at 6 months and 12 months after the end of treatment.

These are both (a) traditional measures of psychopathology that allow us to compare the effectiveness of AEDP with other clinical models and (b) newer measures of positive affect and positive functioning, which will allow us to study both the transformation of suffering and the emergence of flourishing. Patients complete both outcome and process measures. Therapists complete postsession measures after every session. An article on the first 62 dyads who finished the therapy (Iwakabe, Edlin, Fosha, Gretton, Joseph, et al., 2020) documents the effectiveness of AEDP. The results indicate that the 62 patients improved significantly on a number of outcome measures, with large effect sizes at posttreatment. The largest effects were seen in regard to patients' main target problems, including depression, experiential avoidance, emotion regulation, and general symptom distress. There was also a significant decrease in negative automatic thoughts, despite the fact that automatic thoughts specifically, and cognitions in general, are not targeted for restructuring in AEDP. There were also significant changes and improvement in nonpathological measures that centered on positive capacities, such as self-compassion and self-esteem. These findings show initial support for the AEDP aim of facilitating not only therapeutic changes from the negative range to the normal range (i.e., the reduction of emotional suffering) but also improvement from normal range to stronger functioning (i.e., the promotion of flourishing). A follow-up paper reporting results for those first 62 dyads at 6 and 12 months (Iwakabe, Edlin, Fosha, Gretton, Thoma, et al., 2020) is in the works. Other studies are also in progress.

Phase 2 of our process/outcome research reflects a concerted commitment to continue to thoroughly measure many aspects of psychopathology as well as expand our measurement of the positive aspects of mental function. We thus have added the MFES (Fosha, Coleman, et al., 2021), both as an outcome measure and as a postsession measure. We have also added several other measures of both positive affect and in-session relational closeness and genuineness for a thorough empirical exploration of those aspects that are particularly crucial to, and singularly characteristic of, AEDP work.

Finally, in preparation for investigating process as well as outcome, we have developed some measures specific to AEDP: the Transformational Affects and Core State Scale and the Undoing Aloneness Scale for patients to fill out after every session, and the Magnificent Nine + One AEDP Change Processes Scale (Fosha, Edlin, & Iwakabe, 2020) for therapists to fill out after every session. Work on a scale to categorize moment-to-moment session material according to AEDP's four-state transformational model is currently in development (Iwakabe & Thoma, 2020).

## A Scale to Measure In-Session and Out-of-Session Flourishing

In collaboration with Jesse Owen and his colleagues, we have been developing the MFES and have established both nonclinical and clinical population norms and validation studies (Fosha, Coleman, et al., 2021). The scale is a multipurpose instrument that can be used to study flourishing experience in everyday contexts, as well as, of course, in psychotherapy to study in-session flourishing. It is a transtheoretical scale that can help examine flourishing phenomena, including their evolution, in a variety of psychotherapeutic models.

Until now, flourishing has been studied primarily as either a trait or an outcome of therapy. The MFES will also allow the study of flourishing as an experience and a process, as well as an outcome. We believe the MFES can lead to a greater understanding of positive mental health and its coexistence with trauma and other forms of emotional suffering, even at the start of treatment (Iwakabe, Edlin, Fosha, & Nakamura, 2018). Furthermore, unlike any other currently available scale, it will allow the study of the facilitation and emergence of in-session flourishing in psychotherapy given that the scale is focused on moments of experience, rather than well-established aspects of functioning.

### Effectiveness Study on Treatment-Recalcitrant Depression

In collaboration with Bruce Wampold, we are investigating the effectiveness of AEDP in the treatment of treatment-resistant depression in a residential program at the Modum Bad Psychiatric Center in Vikersund, Norway. In addition to extensive measures of both symptoms and functioning, we are measuring flourishing in patients using the MFES, both as a pre–post outcome assessment and as a postsession evaluation after every psychotherapy session. We hope to be able to assess at a more granular level the process by which patients change from admission to discharge and, we hope, also from severe emotional suffering to flourishing. We also hope to be able to investigate, as has been theoretically proposed, that mental illness and flourishing occur on two independent, though possibly interrelated, continua (Keyes, 2002). Another Norway study (Fosha, Iwakabe, et al., 2021) includes an investigation of the effect of AEDP supervision on both therapist development and patient improvement and outcome.

Effectiveness looks promising in all of these studies, and it has begun to be empirically demonstrated in our first outcome study (Iwakabe, Edlin, Fosha, Gretton, Joseph, et al., 2020). Once the effectiveness of AEDP therapy has been empirically established, our treasure trove of more than 1,200 (and growing) video recordings of AEDP therapy sessions awaits our deep dive into process research. From the platform of AEDP 2.0, the dream is of an AEDP 3.0 enriched by an empirically supported articulation of key affective change mechanisms.

## NEUROBIOLOGICAL STUDIES OF AEDP CHANGE PROCESSES

Descriptive phenomenology can help transcend local differences and explore global effects. It can also provide a common language for clinicians and neurobiologists. It is likely that different clusters of emergent positive affective phenomena are manifestations of different neuro-psycho-bio-chemical processes, which in turn play a role in different aspects not only of emotional and relational well-being but also of physiologically based measures of health and well-being; for example, the regulation of the inflammation response, recovery rates from cancer, enhanced immune responses, or stress regulation might each be more affected by different clusters of positive affect. It is possible that different clusters of emergent positive affective phenomena are related to different areas of enhanced therapeutic outcome. For instance, do experiences of hope and faith have different underlying neurotransmitter circuitries than experiences of playfulness, spontaneity, exuberance, and creativity? Do energizing positive affective states reflect bidirectional communication between aspects of the autonomic nervous system and the central nervous system, whereas states in which kindness and compassion are at the forefront are more likely to reflect the coming online of the (ventral vagal) parasympathetic system (see also Chapter 13, this volume)? Might one or the other have a differential effect on positive neuroplasticity? If so, will they be reflected in different aspects of long-term therapeutic outcome? These and so many other questions could be investigated by exploring change processes at both the neurobiological and the psychological levels.

In Chapter 14, I proposed that AEDP might be able to answer certain questions raised by neuroscientists, that is, that AEDP treatment engages mechanisms of change that correspond to neurobiological change mechanisms articulated by contemporary neuroscience (including positive neuroplasticity). For example, Davidson and Schuyler (2015) identified savoring, resilience, mindfulness, and a prosocial altruistic orientation as key constituents of well-being worldwide and asserted the importance of studies that would explore "how these four constituents . . . synergistically work together" (p. 101). To this I suggested that indeed these four constituents do "synergistically work together" in AEDP. Similarly, insula specialist neurophysiologist Craig (2005) asked, "How can 'positive' (energy enrichment) emotions be induced (or perhaps enabled) that activate the left [anterior insula]? This seems very important, because modalities that activate 'parasympathetic' energy enrichment could directly augment mental and physical health" (p. 570). On the face of it, it seems that the answer to Craig's question can be found in AEDP's technique of metatherapeutic processing. However, further empirical research is needed to elucidate whether and the extent to which AEDP's metatherapeutic processing provides an avenue to this desired end.

As I have mentioned, the dream of AEDP 2.0 is to have an AEDP 3.0 also enriched by an understanding of the neurobiological mechanisms that underlie transformational phenomena. The fact that AEDP has articulated both core affective mechanisms of change (Fosha, Edlin, & Iwakabe, 2020) and an extensive, precise, and granular transformational phenomenology of the affects associated with the different phases of the change process, including a phenomenology of positive emotions and affective states, holds promise as to the feasibility of this endeavor.

We hope that what clinical experience reveals about the mind, as instantiated in a highly specific transformational phenomenology of the affects associated with the different phases of the change process, can contribute to the further unlocking of the secrets of the brain by which it is molded; such scientific advances can, in turn, only further enhance the effectiveness of therapeutic intervention.

## REFERENCES

Bowlby, J. (1982). Attachment and loss: Retrospect and prospect. *American Journal of Orthopsychiatry, 52*(4), 664–678. https://doi.org/10.1111/j.1939-0025.1982.tb01456.x

Brown, S., Brown, M., & Penner, L. A. (2012). Acknowledgments. In S. L. Brown, M. R. Brown, & L. A. Penner (Eds.), *Moving beyond self interest: Perspectives from evolutionary biology, neuroscience, and the social sciences* (pp. xvii–xviii). Oxford University Press.

Castonguay, L. G., Barkham, M., Lutz, W., & McAleavy, A. (2013). Practice-oriented research: Approaches and applications. In M. J. Lambert (Ed.), *Bergin & Garfield's handbook of psychotherapy and behavior change* (6th ed., pp. 85–133). Wiley.

Craig, A. D. (2005). Forebrain emotional asymmetry: A neuroanatomical basis? *Trends in Cognitive Sciences, 9*(12), 566–571. https://doi.org/10.1016/j.tics.2005.10.005

Davidson, R. J., & Schuyler, B. S. (2015). Neuroscience of happiness. In J. F. Helliwell, R. Laryard, & J. Sachs (Eds.), *World happiness report 2015* (pp. 82–105). United Nations Sustainable Development Solutions Network.

Davis, D. E., DeBlaere, C., Owen, J., Hook, J. N., Rivera, D. P., Choe, E., Van Tongeren, D. R., Worthington, E. L., & Placeres, V. (2018). The multicultural orientation framework: A narrative review. *Psychotherapy, 55*(1), 89–100. https://doi.org/10.1037/pst0000160

Edlin, J., & Fosha, D. (2016). *16 points on how to conduct 16-session AEDP* [Video]. YouTube. https://youtu.be/PBRlkQbDwZU

Edlin, J., Iwakabe, S., & Fosha, D. (2020). *The AEDP process/outcome research initiative: A description of the program and its scope* [Unpublished manuscript]. Ochanomizu University, Tokyo, Japan.

Erikson, E. H. (1968). *Identity, youth and crisis.* W. W. Norton.

Fosha, D. (2000). *The transforming power of affect: A model for accelerated change.* Basic Books.

Fosha, D. (2018). Introduction to commentaries on sociocultural identity, trauma treatment, and AEDP through the lens of bilingualism in the case of "Rosa." *Pragmatic Case Studies in Psychotherapy, 14*(2), 115–130. https://pcsp.libraries.rutgers.edu/index.php/pcsp/article/view/2039

Fosha, D., Coleman, J. J., Iwakabe, S., Nunnink, S., Joseph, A., Quirk, K., & Owen, J. (2021). *The development of the Moments of Flourishing Experience Scale (MFES): Initial scale development* [Manuscript in preparation]. AEDP Institute; Department of Psychology, University of Denver.

Fosha, D., Edlin, J., & Iwakabe, S. (2020). *The Magnificent 9 + 1 AEDP Change Processes Scale* [Unpublished manuscript]. AEDP Institute.

Fosha, D., Iwakabe, S., Wampold, B., Owen, J., & Edlin, J. (2021). *The effect of AEDP supervision on patient improvement and outcome in a residential setting* [Manuscript in preparation]. AEDP Institute.

Frederick, R. (2019). *Loving like you mean it: Use the power of emotional mindfulness to transform your relationships.* Central Recovery Press.

Hanakawa, Y. (2019, August 8). *The light never goes out: Working with severe trauma and serious mental illness in AEDP* [Presentation]. AEDP Immersion Course, New York, NY. https://drive.google.com/file/d/15ggluqTrK1sbL4sVHvXt3KI3futNsLZ-/view

Harrison, R. L. (2020). Termination in 16-session accelerated experiential dynamic psychotherapy (AEDP): Together in how we say goodbye. *Psychotherapy, 57*(4), 531–547. https://doi.org/10.1037/pst0000343

Hendel, H. J. (2018). *It's not always depression: Working the change triangle to listen to the body, discover core emotions, and connect with your authentic self.* Penguin Random House.

Iwakabe, S., Edlin, J., Fosha, D., Gretton, H., Joseph, A. J., Nunnink, S. E., Nakamura, K., & Thoma, N. C. (2020). The effectiveness of accelerated experiential dynamic psychotherapy (AEDP) in private practice settings: A transdiagnostic study conducted within the context of a practice-research network. *Psychotherapy, 57*(4), 548–561. https://doi.org/10.1037/pst0000344

Iwakabe, S., Edlin, J., Fosha, D., Gretton, H., Thoma, N., Joseph, A. J., Nunnink, S., & Nakamura, K. (2020). *Maintenance of change following accelerated experiential dynamic psychotherapy: 6 and 12 month follow-ups* [Unpublished manuscript]. Ichanamizu University, Tokyo, Japan.

Iwakabe, S., Edlin, J., Fosha, D., & Nakamura, K. (2018, May 31–June 2). *Healing from the get-go: Patients' experience in the first three sessions of accelerated dynamic psychotherapy (AEDP)* [Paper presentation]. Society for the Exploration of Psychotherapy Integration 34th Annual Meeting, New York, NY, United States.

Iwakabe, S., Edlin, E., Fosha, D., Owen, J., & Wampold, B. (2018). *The effectiveness of accelerated experiential dynamic psychotherapy (AEDP) training and supervision to effect improved outcomes for depressed patients* [Manuscript submitted for publication]. Ichanamizu University, Tokyo, Japan.

Iwakabe, S., & Thoma, N. (2020). *Four-state Transformational Model Classification Scale* [Unpublished manuscript]. Ochanamizu University, Tokyo, Japan.

Keyes, C. L. (2002). The mental health continuum: From languishing to flourishing in life. *Journal of Health and Social Behavior, 43*(2), 207–222. https://doi.org/10.2307/3090197

Killing of George Floyd. (2021, January 12). In *Wikipedia*. https://en.wikipedia.org/wiki/Killing_of_George_Floyd

Koerner, K., & Castonguay, L. G. (2015). Practice-oriented research: What it takes to do collaborative research in private practice. *Psychotherapy Research, 25*(1), 67–83. https://doi.org/10.1080/10503307.2014.939119

Krebs, D. (2012). How altruistic, by nature? In S. L. Brown, M. R. Brown, & L. A. Penner (Eds.), *Moving beyond self-interest: Perspectives from evolutionary biology, neuroscience, and the social sciences* (pp. 25–38). Oxford University Press. https://doi.org/10.1093/acprof:oso/9780195388107.003.0016

Kuhn, T. (1970). *The structure of scientific revolutions* (2nd ed.). University of Chicago Press.

Lipton, B., & Medley, M. (2019). *Feeling like a man: Using AEDP to overcome shame and heal attachment trauma with gay and straight men* [AEDP Tri-State Seminar]. AEDP Institute. https://aedpinstitute.org/events/feeling-like-a-man-using-aedp-to-overcome-shame-and-heal-attachment-trauma-with-gay-and-straight-men/

Medley, B. (2018). Recovering the true self: Affirmative therapy, attachment, and AEDP in psychotherapy with gay men. *Journal of Psychotherapy Integration*. Advance online publication. https://doi.org/10.1037/int0000132

Medley, B. (2020, February 28). *Clinically oppressed: Addressing the trauma of marginalization with AEDP* [Workshop]. AEDP Institute.

Menakem, R. (2017). *My grandmother's hands: Racialized trauma and the pathway to mending our hearts and bodies.* Central Recovery Press.

Mikulincer, M., & Shaver, P. (2012). Adult attachment and caregiving: Individual differences in providing a safe haven and secure base to others. In S. L. Brown, M. R. Brown, & L. A. Penner (Eds.), *Moving beyond self interest: Perspectives from evolutionary biology, neuroscience, and the social sciences* (pp. 39–52). Oxford University Press.

Owen, J. (2013). Early career perspectives on psychotherapy research and practice: Psychotherapist effects, multicultural orientation, and couple interventions. *Psychotherapy, 50*(4), 496–502. https://doi.org/10.1037/a0034617

Owen, J., Tao, K. W., Drinane, J. M., Hook, J., Davis, D. E., & Foo Kune, N. F. (2016). Client perceptions of therapists' multicultural orientation: Cultural (missed) opportunities and cultural humility. *Professional Psychology: Research and Practice, 47*(1), 30–37. https://doi.org/10.1037/pro0000046

Pando-Mars, K. (2016). Tailoring AEDP interventions to attachment style. *Transformance: The AEDP Journal, 4*(2), 1–91.

Racial Equity Institute. (2020, April 20). *The groundwater approach.* https://www.racialequityinstitute.com/groundwaterapproach

Shaver, P. R., Mikulincer, M., & Shemesh-Iron, M. (2010). A behavioral systems perspective on prosocial behavior. In M. Mikulincer & P. R. Shaver (Eds.), *Prosocial motives, emotions, and behavior: The better angels of our nature* (pp. 73–91). American Psychological Association.

Simpson, M. L. (2016). Feeling seen: A pathway to transformation. *International Journal of Transpersonal Studies, 35*(1), 78–91. https://doi.org/10.24972/ijts.2016.35.1.78

Urquiza Mendoza, Y. (2018). The case of "Rosa": The importance of specificity in our quest to integrate cultural competence in practice. *Pragmatic Case Studies in Psychotherapy, 14*(2), 138–146. https://doi.org/10.14713/pcsp.v14i2.2041

Vigoda Gonzales, N. V. (2018). The merits of integrating accelerated experiential dynamic psychotherapy and cultural competence strategies in the treatment of relational trauma: The case of "Rosa." *Pragmatic Case Studies in Psychotherapy, 14*(1), 1–57. https://doi.org/10.14713/pcsp.v14i1.2032

Ye-Perman, H. J. (2018). The case of "Rosa": AEDP in the realm of cultural diversity— One's new language as a vehicle for exploring new aspects of identity. *Pragmatic Case Studies in Psychotherapy, 14*(2), 147–157. https://doi.org/10.14713/pcsp.v14i2.2042

# Appendix

**FIGURE 1. The Phenomenology of the Four-State Transformational Process in AEDP**

**STATE 1: Stress, Distress, & Symptoms**
Defenses; inhibiting affects (e.g., anxiety, shame, guilt); stress; demoralization; entrenched defenses and pathogenic self states

**STATE 1: Transformance**
Glimmers of resilience, health, strength; manifestations of the drive to heal

**1st STATE TRANSFORMATION**
Cocreating safety; detecting transformance; promoting bodily-based affective experience

**Transitional Affects:** Intrapsychic crisis; heralding affects, i.e., glimmers of core affective experience
**GREEN Signal Affects:** Announcing openness to experience, signaling safety, readiness to shift

**STATE 2: Adaptive Core Affective Experiences**
**"The Wave"**
Categorical emotions; relational experiences, asymmetric (attachment) or symmetric (intersubjective); coordinated relational experiences; receptive affective experiences; somatic "drop-down" states; intrarelational experiences; authentic self-experiences; experiences of agency, will and desire; attachment strivings; the expression of core needs

**2nd STATE TRANSFORMATION**
The emergence of resilience

**Post-Breakthrough Affects:** Relief, hope, feeling stronger, lighter, etc.
**Adaptive Action Tendencies**

**STATE 3: Transformational Experiences**
**"The Spiral"**
*The mastery affects* (e.g., pride, joy); *the mourning-the-self affects* (emotional pain); *the healing affects* associated with recognition and affirmation of the transformation of the self (gratitude, tenderness, feeling moved); *the tremulous affects* associated with the intense, new experiences; *the enlivening affects* (exuberance, enthusiasm, exploratory zest) associated with delighting in the surprise at the unbrokenness of the self; *the realization affects* (e.g., the "yes!" and "wow" affects, the "click" of recognition) associated with new understanding

**3rd STATE TRANSFORMATION**
The coengendering of secure attachment and the positive valuation of the self

**Energy, Vitality, Openness, Aliveness**

**STATE 4: CORE STATE and The Truth Sense**
**"The Broad Path"**
Calm, flow, ease; I/Thou relating; openness; compassion and self-compassion; sense of clarity; wisdom, generosity, kindness; the sense of things feeling "right;" the experience of "this is me;" new truth, new meaning; the emergence of a coherent and cohesive autobiographical narrative

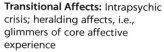

**FIGURE 2. The Phenomenology of the Four-State Transformational Process in AEDP, Including the Maladaptive Affective Experiences (i.e., the Pathogenic Affects and the Unbearable States of Traumatic Aloneness)**

**STATE 1: Stress, Distress, & Symptoms**
Defenses; inhibiting affects (e.g., anxiety, shame, guilt); stress; demoralization; entrenched defenses and pathogenic self states

**STATE 1: Transformance**
Glimmers of resilience, health, strength; manifestations of the drive to heal; glimmers of access to embodied affective experience

**Transitional Affects:** Intrapsychic crisis; heralding affects, i.e., glimmers of maladaptive affective experience; **RED Signal Affects:** Announcing danger of overwhelm, toxic shame etc.

**Transitional Affects:** Intrapsychic crisis; heralding affects, i.e., glimmers of core affective experience
**GREEN Signal Affects:** Announcing openness to experience, signaling safety, readiness to shift

**1ˢᵗ STATE TRANSFORMATION**
Cocreating safety

**STATE 2: Maladaptive Affective Experiences (need transforming)**
"The Abyss"
The pathogenic affects (e.g., overwhelm, toxic shame, fear without solution); unbearable states of traumatic aloneness (e.g., helplessness, fragmentation, brokenness; despair, "the black hole of trauma")

**STATE 2: Adaptive Core Affective Experiences (are transforming)**
"The Wave"
Categorical emotions; relational experiences, asymmetric (attachment) or symmetric (intersubjective); coordinated relational experiences; receptive affective experiences; somatic "drop-down" states; intra-relational experiences; authentic self-experiences; experiences of agency, will and desire; attachment strivings; the expression of core needs

**2ⁿᵈ STATE TRANSFORMATION**
The emergence of resilience

**Post-Breakthrough Affects:** Relief, hope, feeling stronger, lighter, etc.
**Adaptive Action Tendencies**

**STATE 3: Transformational Experiences**
"The Spiral"
*The mastery affects* (e.g., pride, joy); *the mourning-the-self affects* (emotional pain); *the healing affects* associated with recognition and affirmation of the transformation of the self (gratitude, tenderness, feeling moved); *the tremulous affects* associated with the intense, new experiences; *the enlivening affects* (exuberance, enthusiasm, exploratory zest) associated with delighting in the surprise at the unbrokenness of the self; *the realization affects* (e.g., the "yes!" and "wow" affects, the "click" of recognition) associated with new understanding

**3ʳᵈ STATE TRANSFORMATION**
The coengendering of secure attachment and the positive valuation of the self

**Energy, Vitality, Openness, Aliveness**

**STATE 4: CORE STATE and The Truth Sense**
"The Broad Path"
Calm, flow, ease; I/Thou relating; openness; compassion and self-compassion; sense of clarity; wisdom, generosity, kindness; the sense of things feeling "right;" the experience of "this is me;" new truth, new meaning; the emergence of a coherent and cohesive autobiographical narrative

*Note.* Copyright 2020 by Diana Fosha. Reprinted with permission.

**FIGURE 3. The Triangle of Experience**

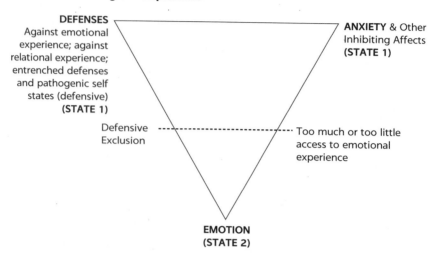

**DEFENSES**
Against emotional
experience; against
relational experience;
entrenched defenses
and pathogenic self
states (defensive)
**(STATE 1)**

**ANXIETY** & Other
Inhibiting Affects
**(STATE 1)**

Defensive
Exclusion

Too much or too little
access to emotional
experience

**EMOTION
(STATE 2)**

**MALADAPTIVE AFFECTIVE
EXPERIENCES
(need transforming)**

**ADAPTIVE CORE AFFECTIVE
EXPERIENCES
(are transforming)**

> **Legend: Affective Experiences**
>
> **Maladaptive Affective Experiences**
> The Pathogenic Affects (e.g., Overwhelm, Toxic Shame, Fear
> Without Solution); Unbearable States of Traumatic Aloneness
> (e.g., Helplessness, Fragmentation, Brokenness; Despair, "The
> Black Hole Of Trauma")
>
> **Adaptive Core Affective Experiences**
> Categorical Emotions; Relational Experiences, Asymmetric
> (Attachment) or Symmetric (Intersubjective); Coordinated
> Relational Experiences; Receptive Affective Experiences; Somatic
> "Drop-Down" States; Intrarelational Experiences; Authentic
> Self-Experiences; Experiences of Agency, Will Desire; Attachment
> Strivings; The Expression of Core Needs

*Note.* Copyright © 2020 by Diana Fosha. Reprinted with permission.

**FIGURE 4. The Triangle of Experience: Two Versions of the Triangle of Experience—The Self-at-Worst and the Self-at-Best**

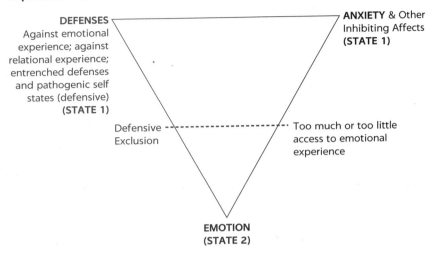

MALADAPTIVE AFFECTIVE
EXPERIENCES
(need transforming)

ADAPTIVE CORE AFFECTIVE
EXPERIENCES
(are transforming)

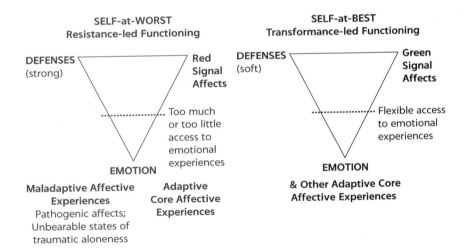

*Note.* Copyright © 2020 by Diana Fosha. Reprinted with permission.

**FIGURE 5.  The Self–Other–Emotion Triangle: Two Versions of the Self–Other–Emotion Triangle—The Self-at-Worst and the Self-at-Best**

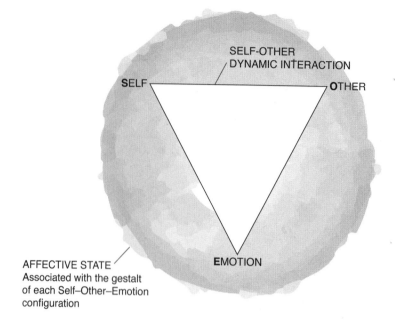

AFFECTIVE STATE
Associated with the gestalt
of each Self–Other–Emotion
configuration

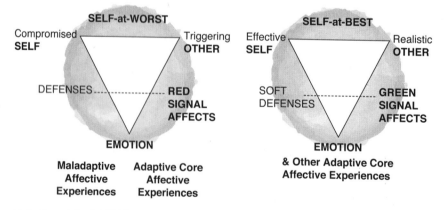

*Note.* Copyright © 2020 by Diana Fosha. Reprinted with permission.

**FIGURE 6. The Triangle of Relational Comparisons**

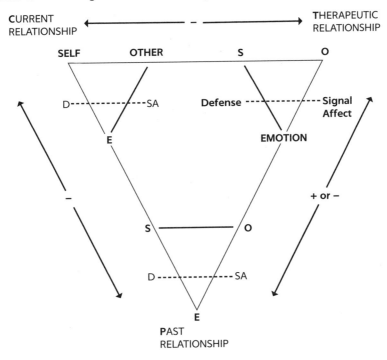

**Legend:**
**– (Minus) = Repetition** (Old, Same, Same Old Same Old)
**+ (Plus) = Corrective Experience** (New, Different)

**Triangle of Relational Comparisons**

C   Current Relationship
T   Therapeutic Relationship
P   Past Relationship

**Self-Other Emotion Triangle (Self-at-Worst or Self-at-Best)**

S   Self
O   Other
E   Emotion

**Triangle of Experience (Self-at-Worst or Self-at-Best)**

D   Defense
SA   Signal Affects (Red or Green)
E   Emotion

*Note.* Copyright © 2020 by Diana Fosha. Reprinted with permission.

# INDEX

# ABOUT THE EDITOR

**Diana Fosha, PhD,** is the developer of AEDP (accelerated experiential dynamic psychotherapy), a healing-oriented psychotherapy to treat attachment trauma and help people connect to their vitality, and director of the AEDP Institute. With an interest in the phenomenology of experience, she is on the cutting edge of transformational theory and practice. AEDP's transformational theory is similarly receiving increasing recognition. For the last 20 years, Diana has been active in promoting a scientific basis for a healing-oriented, attachment- and emotion-focused trauma treatment model. Her work focuses on integrating neuroplasticity, recognition science, and developmental dyadic research into clinical work with patients. Her most recent work focuses on in-session flourishing as an integral part of trauma-processing. Fosha has been on the faculties of the Departments of Psychiatry and Psychology of NYU and Mount Sinai Medical Centers, and of the PhD programs in clinical psychology at Adelphi and The City University of New York. She is the author of *The Transforming Power of Affect* (Basic Books, 2000) and of numerous articles and chapters; coauthor, with Natasha Prenn, of *Supervision Essentials for Accelerated Experiential Dynamic Psychotherapy* (American Psychological Association, 2017); and first editor, with Dan Siegel and Marion Solomon, of *The Healing Power of Emotion: Affective Neuroscience, Development and Clinical Practice* (Norton, 2009). Described by psychoanalyst James Grotstein as a "prizefighter of intimacy," and by David Malan as "the Winnicott of [accelerated dynamic] psychotherapy," Diana Fosha's powerful, precise yet poetic writing style captures the ethos of AEDP. She lives and practices in New York City, presents at international conferences, and leads workshops and trainings worldwide. Many of her papers are available through the AEDP website (https://www.aedpinstitute.org).